HARVARD HISTORICAL STUDIES, 136

Published under the auspices
of the Department of History
from the income of the
Paul Revere Frothingham Bequest
Robert Louis Stroock Fund
Henry Warren Torrey Fund

Gabriel Tortella

The Development of Modern Spain

An Economic History of the
Nineteenth and Twentieth Centuries

Translated by Valerie J. Herr

HARVARD UNIVERSITY PRESS

Cambridge, Massachusetts, and London, England
2000

Originally published as *El desarrollo de la España contemporánea: Historia económica de los siglos xix y xx,* © Gabriel Tortella, © Alianza Editorial, S.A.; Madrid, 1994, 1995, 1997, 1998.

Translated with the assistance of a subsidy from the Dirección General del Libro, Archivos y Bibliotecas, of Spain's Ministry of Education and Culture.

Published with the assistance of the Program for Cultural Cooperation between Spain's Ministry of Education and Culture and United States Universities.

Library of Congress Cataloging-in-Publication Data

Tortella Casares, Gabriel
    [Desarrollo de la España contemporánea. English]
    The development of modern Spain : an economic history of the nineteenth and
  twentieth centuries / Gabriel Tortella ; translated by Valerie J. Herr.
      p. cm. — (Harvard historical studies ; 136)
    Translation of: El desarrollo de la España contemporánea.
    Includes bibliographical references (p.) and index.
    ISBN 0-674-00094-3 (alk. paper)
    1. Spain—Economic conditions—19th century.   2. Spain—Economic conditions—
  20th century. I. Title. II. Series.
HC385.T64313   2000
330.946'07—dc21   99-056711

Contents

Preface *xi*

Abbreviations *xv*

1 Introduction: An Overview *1*

2 The Nineteenth Century: Politics, Population,
   and Human Capital *22*

3 Agriculture: Persistent Underdevelopment *50*

4 Industry: A Long Infancy *73*

5 Transportation and Commerce *115*

6 Money and Banking *156*

7 The Role of the State *173*

8 The Entrepreneurial Factor *206*

9 The Twentieth Century *228*

10 Demographic Modernization *241*

11 Agricultural Transformation:
    From Underdevelopment to Backwardness *267*

12 Industrial Takeoff *298*

13 The Foreign Sector *359*

14 The Evolution of Money and Banking *377*

15 The Changing Role of the State *408*

16 Conclusions *440*

Chronology *465*   Notes *473*

Works Cited *485*   Index *511*

Tables

Table 1.1. Indices of income per capita and industrial production in Spain, 1800–1980   *2*

Table 1.2. Income per capita in six European countries, 1800–1980   *3*

Table 1.3. Illiteracy rates in six European countries, 1850–1910   *13*

Table 1.4. Students attending primary school in seven European countries, 1850–1930   *18*

Table 2.1. Population of Spain, 1787–1900   *32*

Table 2.2. Growth and other demographic variables in various European countries, 1800–1900   *33*

Table 2.3. Emigration and demographic growth in seven European countries, 1830–1900   *34*

Table 2.4. Population of Spain by regions, 1787–1900   *42*

Table 3.1. Value of properties disentailed during the nineteenth century   *55*

Table 3.2 Production and yields of Spanish agriculture in 1857   *60*

Table 3.3. Estimated agricultural production, averages for decades, 1800–1899   *62*

Table 3.4. Indices of agricultural production, 1800–1899   *63*

Table 3.5. Agricultural production, area under cultivation, and productivity, 1893 and 1900 compared   *64*

Table 3.6. Agricultural yields in various European countries, 1890–1910   *66*

Table 4.1. Imports of raw baled cotton through the port of Barcelona, 1814–1913   *77*

Table 4.2. Growth rates of cotton imports   *78*

Table 4.3. Spanish production of iron and steel, 1860–1904   *88*

Table 4.4. Production of pig iron and steel in various European countries in 1900   *89*

Table 4.5. Spanish industry by sector, 1856, 1900, and 1922   *91*

Table 4.6. Spanish mining output, 1830–1904   *99*

Table 4.7. Spanish exports of ores and metals, 1850–1904   *100*

Table 4.8. Spanish exports of ores and metals as a percentage of production, 1850–1904   *101*

Table 4.9. Production and export of iron ore in various European countries in 1900 *102*

Table 4.10. Industrialization per capita in various European countries, 1800–1900 *114*

Table 5.1. The movement of goods in Spain, 1860–1910 *118*

Table 5.2. Extension of the Spanish railroad network, 1850–1935 *122*

Table 5.3. Composition of Spain's foreign trade, 1827 through 1910/1913 *137*

Table 5.4. Flows of foreign capital to Spain by country of origin, 1851–1913 *150*

Table 5.5. Spain's national debt: amounts paid up, 1768–1891 *151*

Table 5.6. Foreign investment and international trade *152*

Table 6.1. Approximate composition of the money supply around 1865 *161*

Table 6.2. Money stock and money supply in 1900 *161*

Table 7.1. Budget revenues, expenditures, and balances, 1850–1854 through 1899–1906 *177*

Table 7.2. Accumulated budget revenues by source, 1850–1890 *179*

Table 7.3. Accumulated budget expenditures, 1850–1890 *184*

Table 8.1. Attitudes of Spanish businessmen toward tariff reductions and the renewal of commercial treaties, 1889 *221*

Table 10.1. Population of Spain in the twentieth century *242*

Table 10.2. Population growth and other demographic variables in various European countries, 1900–1985 *243*

Table 10.3. Distribution of Spain's population by regions, 1787–1980 *257*

Table 10.4. Regional population densities, 1787 and 1980 *259*

Table 10.5. Indices of urbanization in Spain, 1900–1990 *260*

Table 10.6. Primary school attendance and literacy in Spain, 1910–1990 *263*

Table 10.7. Working population by economic sectors, 1900–1980 *266*

Table 11.1. Areas under specific crops, 1891/95 through 1985 *270*

Table 11.2. Agricultural output, productivity, and yields, 1900–1980 *282*

Table 11.3. Rates of growth of agricultural production, 1901–1983 *283*

Table 11.4. Indicators of capitalization in Spanish agriculture, 1907/8 through 1984 *285*

Table 11.5. Livestock censuses, 1891–1984 *289*

Table 11.6. Main products of the livestock industry, 1923–1984 *290*

Table 11.7. The share of agriculture in the GNP and its productivity among members of the European Economic Community, 1980 *295*

Table 12.1. Spanish industry by sectors, 1900–1980   *302*

Table 12.2. Steel production in various countries in 1930   *307*

Table 12.3. Aspects of the construction industry in Spain, 1860–1935   *309*

Table 12.4. Cement production in various countries, ca. 1933   *310*

Table 12.5. Imports of capital goods and the terms of trade between
  agriculture and industry, 1931–1959   *322*

Table 12.6. Main industrial sectors and their growth rates, 1958–1972   *329*

Table 12.7. Industrial production and productivity, 1964–1985   *330*

Table 12.8. Consumption of primary energy in Spain, 1860–1980   *347*

Table 12.9. Industrial production in four key sectors, 1900–1985   *356*

Table 13.1. The components of Spain's foreign trade, 1922–1985   *370*

Table 13.2. Exports of fresh fruit and olive oil as percentages of the total
  value of all exports, 1905–1950   *371*

Table 13.3. Geographic distribution of Spain's exports, 1915/1918 through
  1980/1984   *374*

Table 14.1. Number of banks in Spain, 1900–1983   *387*

Table 15.1. The share of public expenditure in national income in various
  countries, 1900–1902 through 1970–1972   *410*

Table 15.2. Comparison of the central government budgets of Spain,
  1850–90, 1971, and 1980   *417*

Table 15.3. The national debt as a percentage of national income,
  1880–1885 through 1985   *422*

Table 15.4. Disparities in income per capita in the Spanish regions,
  1800–1983   *437*

Table 16.1. Public expenditure as a percentage of GNP for various countries,
  1975 and 1986   *456*

Figures

1.1. Index of national income per capita in Spain, 1800–1980   4

1.2. Income per capita in six European countries, as a percentage of the combined average for Great Britain and France, 1800–1980   5

1.3. Index of industrial production in Spain, 1800–1980   6

1.4. The evolution of literacy rates in Europe, 1850–ca. 1970   13

1.5 Illiteracy rates in five European countries, 1850–1910   14

1.6 Students attending primary school in six European countries, 1860–1930   18

2.1. Indices of general and cereal prices in New Castile, 1700–1800   24

2.2. Indices of agrarian prices in New Castile, 1700–1800   24

2.3. Diagrammatic representation of the cereal market in Spain in the eighteenth century   25

4.1. Imports of raw baled cotton through the port of Barcelona, 1816–1911   78

4.2. Two indices of industrial production, 1800–1910   113

5.1. Indices of transport activities, 1860–1913   117

5.2. Wheat prices in three Spanish provinces, 1858–1904   132

5.3. Olive oil prices in three Spanish provinces, 1863–1905   133

5.4. Components of international trade, 1821–1913   139

7.1. Budget revenues, expenditures, and balances, 1850–1902   177

7.2. National debt in circulation and redemption payments, 1850–1902   185

7.3. Customs revenues, 1850–1902   201

7.4. Average discount rates, Bank of Barcelona, 1850–1904   203

9.1. Income per capita in Spain, Italy, and France, 1860–1990   229

9.2. Income per capita in Spain and Italy, 1900–1990   230

10.1. Crude birth and death rates and natural population growth in Spain, 1858–1983   244

10.2. The evolution of natural population growth in four European countries, 1800–1981   245

10.3. Excess male mortality in Spain by age, in 1900, 1950, and 1980   250

10.4. The decline in excess male mortality by age, 1900, 1950, and 1980   251

10.5. The crude birth rate and the percentage of marriages where the bride was under 20 years of age, 1913–1988   255

10.6. Literacy rates in Spain, France, Italy, and Portugal, 1890–1990   *262*

10.7. Students in primary and secondary schools as a percentage of total population, 1924–1989   *264*

10.8. Students enrolled in institutions of higher education as a percentage of total population, 1914–1989   *265*

11.1. Gross agricultural output in Spain, 1900–1985   *283*

11.2. Indices of key agricultural outputs, 1939–1985   *288*

11.3. Wheat production in kilograms per capita, 1901–1984   *288*

12.1. Indices of key industrial outputs, 1900 to 1984   *301*

12.2. Indices of industrial production, total and per capita, 1920–1960   *314*

12.3. Indices of industrial production in Spain and Italy, 1925–1960   *320*

12.4. Indices of key industrial outputs, 1955–1985   *332*

13.1. Three measures of the degree of commercial openness of the Spanish economy, 1930–1985   *360*

13.2. The degree of commercial openness of the Spanish economy: foreign trade as a percentage of national income, 1901–1984   *362*

13.3. The balance of payments: main sources of international earnings, 1930–1990   *363*

13.4. The balance of payments: main international outlays, 1930–1990   *364*

13.5. Net monetary movements in the Spanish balance of payments, 1940–1990   *368*

13.6. Net terms of trade between Spain and the rest of the world, 1900–1985.   *375*

14.1. Monetary aggregates, 1900–1980   *380*

14.2. Components of the money supply, 1900–1980   *382*

14.3. Velocity of circulation of money, on two measures, 1900–1980   *383*

14.4. Banknotes as a percentage of the money supply and as a percentage of high-powered money, 1900–1980   *384*

14.5 Ratios of bank assets to national income, 1915–1980   *392*

14.6. The market share of savings banks, 1900–1990   *400*

15.1. Expenditure of the economic ministries (*Fomento*) as a percentage of total government expenditure, 1900–1980   *420*

15.2. The Spanish price index, 1900–1985   *427*

Maps

2.1. Regional demographic growth, nineteenth century   *43*

5.1. Railroad network, ca. 1895   *126*

5.2. The main railroad lines and their owners   *127*

Preface

The principal aim of this book is to delineate the basic problems of modern Spanish economic history for the general reader. At the same time, for the specialized readers and scholars, I seek to document the interpretation of the historical reality which I present here, particularly to alert them to the value of the economist's point of view in illuminating diverse areas of history—without losing sight, of course, of the seemingly incurable circularity of the social sciences.

Modern Spain is a country that is poorly understood, even by Spaniards themselves. Not generally studious by nature, they distrust the official versions of history (and they are right to do so), but this distrust has often led them to approach all history with an attitude of repudiation (and they are wrong to do so). And Spain is also poorly understood by foreigners, who are little interested in a country that is far from the center of international attention. When they do show an interest, they tend to limit their focus to imperial Spain, which indeed was in its day the center of world attention. Those who are interested in modern Spain are usually attracted by the romanticism of the Civil War, with scarcely a thought for its socioeconomic background. Spain has recently attracted a certain amount of international interest because of its successful transition from dictatorship to democracy, and from a controlled economy to something more liberal. But a complete understanding of such a transformation demands a long-term view. One cannot understand the present without recent history, just as recent history cannot be understood without the medieval and early modern periods. But the historical perspective alone is not sufficient to understand the present. One needs analytical tools, and among these the economy is a *sine qua non*. The perspective and tools of economics can contribute to a better understanding of our recent past, as I intend to demonstrate. The reader must judge if the claim is justified.

The structure of the book is very simple, and a glance at the table of contents will show that I have combined the chronological method with the thematic. As I argue in the first chapter, the two centuries which this text covers are patently different, so the centuries are studied in sequence, but within each century the focus is thematic. As Chapter 9 indicates, this is a relatively new perspective for the twentieth century, which historians and economists alike have tended to approach in terms that are chronologically fragmentary.

The economist's task often reminds me of the croquet game in *Alice in Wonderland.* The reader will recall that this game was played using curled up hedgehogs as the croquet balls, flamingoes as the mallets (held by the body, using the head to strike with), and the personal assistants of the Queen of Hearts were the croquet wickets. The game proved complicated because the flamingoes kept turning their heads to see who it was that brandished them thus; the hedgehogs abandoned their spherical posture and began to walk away; and the wickets got impatient, straightened up, and moved off in all directions. The same thing happens to the economist. His task involves setting out the rules of the game and determining models; to do this he adopts the famous dictum of *ceteris paribus,* in a world that in fact is never still but constantly changing. Just when the economist has his model defined, some disturbance (war, drought, changes in tastes or customs, or some other calamity) overturns the assumptions and invalidates the model. Writing a book such as this one brings out similar problems, not only because the craft of the economic historian so much resembles that of the economist, but also because the book is a model of the economist's state-of-the art theory at a given time. But the scientific community is never at rest, and it can happen that some just completed chapters are rendered obsolete by newly published texts. One can go on putting a patch here and there, but in the end one has to put an end to the venture and deliver one's manuscript, knowing full well that the hedgehogs will go one way and the flamingoes another, and that the croquet game cannot be completed. This, however unnerving for the author, is a very good indicator of the health of the discipline. And I trust this long digression will serve as an apology for the many defects and shortcomings of the pages which follow!

Yet the basic underlying model has deep roots. Of course we are talking of an interpretive verbal model, not an econometric one. The book's major intellectual debt is owed to Antonio Ramos Oliveira, whose *History of Spain* I read even before beginning my career as an economic historian. His work has influenced my research and formed a connecting thread almost without my being aware of it. The other intellectual debts are owed to Raymond Carr and to Jaime Vicens Vives. These three authors have most influenced my own interpretation of modern Spain.

The greatest overall debt, however, which book and author both owe, is to Clara Eugenia Núñez, who has read the text in various versions, discussed and improved it, made suggestions and offered ideas, interpretations, additional and alternative information; she has given the author computer lessons, and made her expertise available in the manipulation of various programs and computers to resolve problems that without her would have made the completion of this book even slower and more difficult. Readers who know her will recognize her influence in many more passages than those where her work is directly cited.

Several friends and colleagues have contributed a great deal to this book. Many of them are included in the bibliography, but those who have not written on topics directly related to the economic history of modern Spain are omitted. Among the people with whom I have discussed themes and exchanged ideas and bibliographic information I want to mention Carlos Barciela, Mercedes Cabrera, Rondo Cameron, Albert Carreras, and John Coatsworth (whose invitation to spend a term in Chicago permitted me to begin this work in earnest, in the fall of 1988), Sebastián Coll, Paco Comín, Roberto Cortés Conde, Carlos Marichal, Stefano Fenoaltea, Pedro Fraile, Pablo Martín Aceña, Leandro Prados de la Escosura (who deserves special credit for having assumed the editorship of the *Revista de Historia Económica*, allowing me to devote more time to the book), Jordi Palafox, Jaime Reis, Felipe Ruíz Martín, James Simpson, Carles Sudrià, Pedro Tedde, Antonio Tena, Gianni Toniolo, Eugene White, and Vera Zamagni—by no means an exhaustive list. The many omissions may be remedied by a glance at the bibliography. I also want to acknowledge the support of my parents, Gabriel Tortella Oteo and María Teresa Casares, and Gregorio Núñez Noguerol. In addition to permitting me generous access to their private libraries, they also made presents of books which helped me a great deal in this study.

The institutional debts are also numerous. In first place is the Bank of Spain, whose "European Project" financed years of research on the modern Spanish economy with a group of economic historians whose work I coordinated. Some of these works have been published under separate authorship, and many of them (published or not), have provided the bases for several chapters of this book. The library of the Bank of Spain deserves special mention. Managed by a group of competent and amiable librarians, it is without doubt the best in the world to facilitate writing a book such as this one. The Ministry of Education and Science has also contributed, both through the University of Alcalá where I work (and whose sabbatical program I was the first to enjoy, with visits to Chicago and Princeton) and through the General Research Division and the C. I. C. Y. T., both of which have supported projects that have contributed to this study. The same must be said of the European Union, one of whose projects on education and human capital (the S. P. E. S.) has funded part of the research that this book is based upon. The universities of Chicago and Princeton (and their splendid libraries), and the Institute for Advanced Study at Princeton, where I was a visiting fellow in the first semester in 1989 (its library is smaller but very useful for research), also figure prominently in my list of debts. A more personal acknowledgment goes to John Elliott, who helped negotiate my stay at the Institute and was an impeccable host while I was there. The Juan March Foundation financed the initial stages of this work when it was no more than a sketchy plan. Some of these agencies may have felt, and with some reason, that the money was badly spent, but I hope they will decide otherwise when they read the book.

Likewise, I am grateful for the patience and care of friends at the Spanish publisher's, Alianza, particularly María Cifuentes and Rafael Martínez Alés, without whose faith this book would still be an ongoing project; for the warm kindness of María Eugenia Caumel, at the Ministry of Education, and her help with the illustrations; also for the illustrative materials provided by the Bank of Spain.

It was certainly gratifying to the author that the first Spanish edition was sold out almost immediately. For the second edition, students and friends have kindly contributed various emendations. Apart from correcting many errors, that edition included substantial changes in Chapter 5 and additions to the bibliography. I particularly want to thank Albert Carreras, José Luis García Ruíz, Jordi Palafox, and Carlos Rodríguez Braun for their comments. And finally I want to express my great sadness that my father, for whom this book was such a source of joy, did not live to see the second edition.

But all these expressions of gratitude are due to my creditors, so to speak; they certainly bear no responsibility. What flaws remain are exclusively mine. If the book turns out to resemble a chaotic croquet game, it will be the fault of the author, or of the Cheshire cat, but in no case the fault of those who tried to help him.

Abbreviations

ACB	Anuario de la Ciudad de Barcelona
AE	Anuario Estadístico de España
AEBP	Anuario Estadístico de la Banca Privada
AEG	Allgemeine Elektrizitaets Gesellschaft
AFYDSADE	Anuario Financiero y de las Sociedades Anónimas de España
AISA	American Iron and Steel Association
BCI	Banco de Crédito Industrial
BCL	Banco de Crédito Local
BHE	Banco Hipotecario de España
CAMPSA	Compañía Arrendetaria del Monopolio de Petróleos S. A.
CE	Comunidad Europea (later UE)
CEE	Comunidad Económica Europea (later CE)
CESPA	Compañía Española de Petróleos S. A.
CSB	Consejo Superior Bancario
CSIC	Consejo Superior de Investigaciones Científicas
ECE	Estadísticas del Comercio Exterior
EH	Estadísticas Históricas [see Carreras (1989) in bibliography]
EHPAE	Estadísticas Históricas de la Producción Agraria Española (see GEHR, 1991, in bibliography)
EM	Estadística Minera
ENSIDESA	Empresa Nacional de Siderúrgica S. A.
EP	Estadística de los Presupuestos Generales del Estado
FEOGA	Fondo Europeo de Orientación y Garantía Agricola
FGD	Fondo de Garantía de Depósitos
FMI	Fondo Monetario Internacional
FORPPA	Fondo para la Ordenación y Regulación de los Precios y Productos Agrarios
GEHR	Grupo de Estudios de Historia Rural
HUNOSA	Hulleras del Norte S. A.
ICCA	Instituto de Crédito de las Cajas de Ahorro
ICGI	Impuestos Compensadores de Gravámenes Interiores
ICMLP	Instituto de Crédito a Largo y Medio Plazo

ICO	Instituto de Crédito Oficial
ICONA	Instituto para la Conservación de la Naturaleza
IEME	Instituto Español de Moneda Extranjera
INE	Instituto Nacional de Estadística
INI	Instituto Nacional de Industria
INH	Instituto Nacional de Hidrocarburos
IRPF	Impuesto sobre la Renta de las Personas Físicas
IVA	Impuesto sobre el Valor Añadido
MATESA	Maquinaria Textil S. A.
MZA	Ferrocarril Madrid-Zaragoza-Alicante
OCDE	Organización de Cooperación y Desarrollo Económico
OECE	Organización Europea de Cooperación Económica (later OCDE)
PAC	Política Agraria Comunitaria
PIB	Producto Interior Bruto
PNB	Producto Nacional Bruto
RENFE	Red Nacional de Ferrocarriles Españoles
REPESA	Refinería de Petróleo de Escombreras S. A.
SEAT	Sociedad Española de Automóviles de Tourismo
SED	Sociedad Española de la Dinamita
SEMI	Sociedad Española Mercantil e Industrial
SENPA	Servicio Nacional de Productos Agrarios
SME	Sistema Monetario Europeo
SNT	Servicio Nacional de Trigo
UCD	Unión de Centro Democrático
UE	Unión Europea

CHAPTER 1

Introduction: An Overview[1]

The Nineteenth and Twentieth Centuries Compared

The economic history of modern Spain reveals a sharp contrast between a nineteenth century of slow growth and backwardness, measured in terms of the European norm, and a twentieth century of rapid growth that recovers much of the ground lost in the earlier period. A quick glance at Tables 1.1 and 1.2 and Figures 1.1, 1.2, and 1.3 allows us to verify that this assertion is correct. (To my mind the evolution of Italy and Portugal can, in outline, be considered comparable and parallel to the Spanish case.)

In similar fashion, the nineteenth century also comprises two clearly defined sub-periods. During the first half, the economy remained virtually stagnant, without growth, but this period can again be divided into two divergent phases: an economic contraction from 1800 to 1840 (the end of the first Carlist War), and a gradual economic recovery in the next twenty years, 1840 to 1860. In the second half of the century, connecting to the turnabout that started in 1840, a growth process was set in motion. Very gradual in the early years, it gained momentum as the century progressed and accelerated rapidly in the twentieth century.

Considered on its own, the twentieth century presents characteristics that are superficially similar to those of the previous hundred years: relative stagnation in the first half, and rapid growth in the second. The apparent stagnation of the first half of the century in fact represents a period of substantial growth from 1900 to 1930 and a long ensuing decline, the combined effects of the Great Depression, the Civil War, and a postwar depression that was exceptionally persistent. But around 1950 Spain experienced a spurt of economic growth that was rapid not only in terms of its own history but also in international terms.

Even though at first glance one might attribute some basic continuity to the process described above—namely, that except for the sole, striking interruption from 1930 to 1950, the country had experienced uniformly accelerating economic growth—the reality is that in economic history quantitative changes engender qualitative changes. Although we cannot deny that there was a certain amount of growth in the nineteenth century, the total change was small, and the country as a whole remained traditional, agrarian, and backward in comparison with Europe. It was in the twentieth century that Spain experienced the profound structural change that we call economic development—the transition to industrialization and modernity. This can be clearly seen from the index of industrial production shown in Figure 1.3. From the broad panoramic perspective of a hundred and fifty years, I be-

Table 1.1. Indices of income per capita and industrial production in Spain, 1800–1980 (1900 = 100)

Year	Income per capita[b]	Industrial production[a]	Industrial production[b]
1800	62	—	24
1810	62	—	25
1820	62	—	24
1830	61	11	24
1840	63	17	32
1850	65	26	40
1860	67	39	48
1870	75	49	60
1880	83	67	72
1890	91	80	85
1900	100	100	100
1910	109	122	115
1920	126	145	—
1930	143	193	—
1940	134	184	—
1950	124	234	—
1960	187	479	—
1970	342	1,135	—
1980	455	1,658	—

Sources: a. according to Carreras (1984); b. according to Prados (1988)

Table 1.2. Income per capita in six European countries, 1800–1980, as a percentage of the combined average for France and Great Britain (in $U.S. 1970 to indicate purchasing power)

Year	Spain	Italy	Great Britain	France	Germany	Portugal
1800	94	—	120	92	—	—
1810	89	—	121	91	—	—
1820	85	—	121	90	—	—
1830	80	89	121	89	84	54
1840	70	81	122	88	79	47
1850	63	75	123	87	74	42
1860	57	71	123	86	71	38
1870	56	64	123	83	70	35
1880	55	58	123	82	70	33
1890	55	54	123	80	70	30
1900	54	58	117	83	75	30
1910	53	61	114	86	79	29
1920	55	61	108	91	78	28
1930	57	61	104	95	78	27
1940	47	58	107	91	77	26
1950	39	55	110	88	76	26
1960	44	70	104	95	111	29
1970	58	81	93	107	114	43
1980	62	83	88	112	118	46

Source: see note 3

lieve the claim continues to be valid that "the principal economic events of Spain's nineteenth century can be reduced to the removal of certain obstacles, to clearing the way for twentieth century industrialization, by means of a series of changes in the social and institutional structure."[2]

Comparison with other European countries can lend a broader geographic perspective to this analysis. Table 1.2 and Figure 1.2 compare the performance of six European nations with an abstract measure, the average income per capita for Great Britain and France combined (and that explains why the measures for those two countries display a mirror image). In relation to the Anglo-French norm, the Spanish economy declined strikingly during the first half of the nineteenth century, remained almost stationary during the second half of the century, began to rise at the beginning of the twentieth, fell precipitously from 1930 to 1950, and picked up vigorously after that date. In contrast to the continual loss of ground in the nineteenth century, the trend reverses itself and the economy enjoys a partial recovery.

How can we explain this course of events? The next few pages will be dedicated to this question. To begin with, a second glance at Figure 1.2 shows us that the curves for Italy and Portugal follow trajectories very similar to that for Spain.[3] This leads me to wonder whether the explanation that might be given for this brief sketch of the Spanish experience, the country's relative backwardness in the nineteenth century and partial recovery in the twentieth, ought to be examined in conjunction with the Italian and Portuguese cases. Sidney Pollard (1973, 1982) maintains that the patterns of European industrialization are better understood from a regional rather than a national standpoint. That being so—and the evidence in support of this point seems beyond doubt to me—when we examine the Spanish case, which has such strong similarities with its neighbors in Southern Europe, should we not look for regional patterns of growth and backwardness—regional both in the supranational and intranational sense?

If we accept that there is a certain specific southwestern European or EuroLatin pattern of modernization, in which backwardness in the nineteenth century gives way to some recovery in the twentieth, our immediate

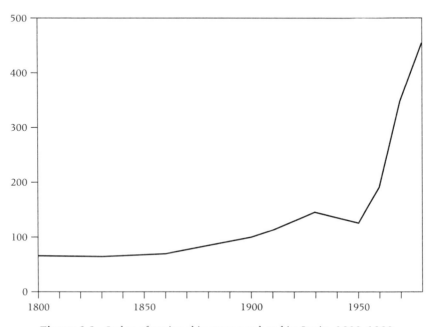

Figure 1.1. Index of national income per head in Spain, 1800–1980

task will be to look for possible explanations which might be applicable to all three countries in the region. The comparative regional framework has the advantage of forcing us to leave aside the anecdotal and exclusive details of each country's particular history, making us concentrate on those common characteristics from which generalizations can be drawn. For example, attributing backwardness in the Italian case to free trade,[4] in the Spanish case to the way that *desamortización*[5] (the sale of formerly entailed properties) was carried out, or in the Portuguese case to British imperialism[6] is not very satisfactory or even very elegant, from the comparative point of view. I find it difficult to believe that three different causes produced the same effects in three countries with similar characteristics, located in the same geographic region, during the same time period. It would be more satisfying to find one unique cause that produced the same effect: perhaps fiscal disarray, a feature which all three countries had in common during these years, would provide a more convincing explanation. And if this were so, one would want to investigate the common causes for such budgetary mismanagement.

Even if we accept that these societies were guilty of the "sin" of financial disorder, we still ought to explore every dimension of the geographic and

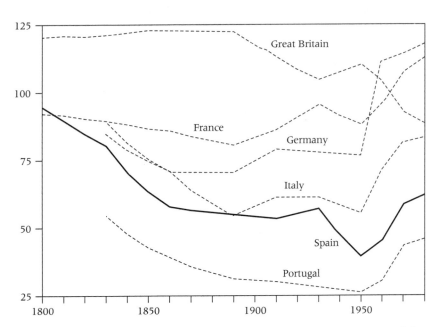

Figure 1.2. Income per capita in six European countries, as a percentage of the combined average for Great Britain and France, 1800–1980

cultural environments in the fullest sense. The culture of southwestern Europe can be conveniently referred to as EuroLatin, for it dates back to a common heritage under imperial Rome, a heritage which molded so many of its institutional features, so much of its behavior, from language and religion to the legal system. As far as the physical environment is concerned, the European sector of the Mediterranean basin is fairly homogeneous, and that geographic component has determined the choice of crops, the cultivation methods, even the shape of land plots, and of course the diet in these countries for many centuries. These two elements, which in turn are interrelated, can help to explain the broad contours of economic history in southwestern Europe in the nineteenth and twentieth centuries.

Perhaps this is the best moment to comment upon an article by Molinas and Prados, in which the existence of a "[Euro]Latin pattern of development" is explicitly denied. Although the argument is very imaginative and illuminating, the evidence is not sufficient to support the authors' assertion. On the contrary, their material rather confirms the premise of a parallelism in the growth patterns of Italy and Spain (the article does not consider Portugal), although their conclusion is that "the idea of two different pathways towards economic growth is more convincing than the [Euro]Latin pat-

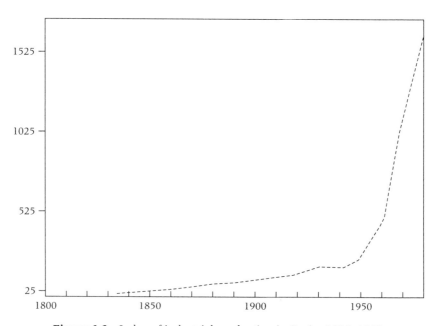

Figure 1.3. Index of industrial production in Spain, 1800–1980

tern."⁷ This is not the place to go into a detailed analysis of the evidence and the ingenious way the authors use it to support their argument. I simply wish to indicate a discrepancy in interpretation.

Causes of Economic Backwardness: Agriculture

The economic development of any human society is the result of the interplay of two broad sets of factors: the physical resource endowment of the area, and the technology available to its inhabitants. Between these two elements, however, a crucial mediating factor is the institutional structure of the society. If this proposition is accepted, then the retardation of southwestern Europe in the nineteenth century is a phenomenon whose origins date back to several centuries earlier. In fact, during the Middle Ages and the early modern period most technological innovations in agriculture were specifically adapted to the soils and climatic conditions of northern Europe: this is the case with every single agricultural innovation mentioned in the textbooks, from the heavy plow to the many varieties of "new husbandry," meaning intensive agriculture combined with raising livestock. While the agricultural revolution was taking place in northern Europe, southern Europe's agriculture, with only minor exceptions, continued to use the two-year rotation of cereal cultivation and fallow, plowing with the light plow in much the same way as had been done at the time of the Roman Empire, when this technique was, of course, the best available, the "state of the art" in ancient agriculture at a time when nomads predominated in northern Europe. This accumulation of agricultural innovations adapted to the moist, heavy, rich soils of northern Europe, culminating in the agricultural revolution of the modern period, first in the Netherlands and then in England, is the principal explanation for the growing gap in incomes and living standards between northern and southern Europe, which became increasingly apparent during the nineteenth century.⁸

It is hardly necessary to mention here the importance of agriculture in the first stages of the modernization of an economy. Those countries that had been able to import and adapt features of the agricultural revolution that suited their own conditions could then, in the nineteenth century, transform themselves into industrial powers and achieve success in the second wave of economic modernization that took place at the end of the nineteenth century and the beginning of the twentieth (as in the cases of Germany, Denmark, and Sweden, for instance). Conversely, countries which, for one reason or another, were unable to "revolutionize" their agriculture remained backward, and this is what happened to the EuroLatin countries. In the specific case of Spain, the physical obstacles to modernization were very strong, probably more so than in Italy or in Portugal. The sheer size and compact shape of the country, as well as the altitude and aridity of the central plateau (*Meseta Central*), make for costly transportation, isolate a large part of the country from trade in goods and ideas, and discourage the transfer of human resources to more productive activities. In Spain, geography and culture reinforced each other as obstacles to modernization from the seventeenth to the mid-twentieth century.

The primary sector, whose main component has been agriculture, occupied a high and almost constant share of the Spanish labor force, approximately two thirds, from the beginning to the end of the nineteenth century. The situation appears to have been quite similar in Italy and Portugal, although the Italian share of manpower in agriculture was lower and started to decline earlier.

It is clear that the existence of such a large agricultural sector was holding back the Spanish economy in many ways.[9] In the first place, low agricultural productivity kept the diet of the average Spaniard at about the subsistence level, with little improvement until well into the twentieth century; the gradual substitution of wheat for rye and other inferior cereals, and the introduction of the potato and maize seem to have been the most outstanding improvements; on the other hand, there are reasons to believe that meat consumption per capita decreased.[10] Comparative figures for several European countries by the end of the nineteenth century show that agricultural yields in Spain and Portugal, and to a lesser extent Italy, were well below those in France, Britain, or Germany in basic products such as wheat, rye, barley, and potatoes.[11] In Italy, however, the diet clearly improved and relative prices of basic foodstuffs declined late in the century.[12]

The stagnating agricultural sector also failed dismally as a market for industrial products and as a source of capital for modernization. This is very clear in the Spanish case.[13] In Portugal too agriculture remained technologically backward and constituted a poor market for consumer goods.[14] Only Italy is a partial exception to this rule. In the north agriculture started to modernize and mechanize at the turn of the century, and by the early twentieth century an imbalance between north and south was evident. In 1910 the Po valley, with 13% of arable land, produced 31% of Italian agricultural output, with a productivity three times that of the rest of the country.[15]

Nor did the demographic regime provide conditions that were likely to favor change. High death rates and relatively low birth rates in Spain and Portugal alike produced only moderate population growth, and consequently the land could export only a small percentage of its manpower. The level of urbanization in Spain and Portugal remained low throughout the nineteenth century, and even in Italy only 16% of the population lived in cities of more than 50,000 inhabitants by 1911.[16] It is hard to know to what extent it was the conservative temperament of the peasants that kept them attached to their villages, or how far it was the sluggish dynamic of the industrial sector that caused this inertia in the population.[17] In the end it was the external shock of competition from foreign cereals that pushed the Spanish, Portuguese, and Italian peasants and farmers into the cities and overseas: the well known agricultural depression of the last quarter of the century set in motion a mechanism that had failed to emerge spontaneously.[18] This incapacity, the failure of agriculture to generate a surplus population which would flock to the cities and work in the new factories, is obviously a common feature of the Latin countries of southwestern Europe, including France, in clear contrast to Great Britain from the mid-eighteenth century and Germany from the mid-nineteenth.

Furthermore, agriculture ought to generate an abundant flow of exports in the early stages of growth, and in this aspect both Spanish and Portuguese rural sectors failed almost totally. The word "almost" is used advisedly here, because it cannot be denied that the greater part of Spanish and Portuguese exports in the nineteenth century were agricultural, and most of the rest were mineral ores. In spite of this undeniable and inescapable fact—what else can a backward country export but primary products?—and in spite of the fact that Spanish exports grew absolutely and in relation to income, the share of foreign trade within the whole economy was very low, and thus the contribution of agriculture remained very small.[19] Only in Italy did foreign trade play a dynamic role at the end of the nineteenth century, and strong growth and modernization occurred in the agricultural sector at the beginning of the twentieth.[20]

The lack of progress in Spanish agriculture was therefore one of the chief obstacles to general economic modernization, and this lack of progress was caused, in turn, by a mixture of physical and cultural factors which are hard to separate. In my view, however, the importance of those climatic and soil conditions was very significant, and probably more so in Spain than in Portugal or Italy. In the words of N. G. Pounds's classic text:

Large areas, particularly on the Meseta, are almost bare of soil, and elsewhere the rainfall is so low that the land is barren steppe. The agrarian
problem turns on the rainfall and the fertility of the soil. In the North,
where rainfall is adequate—and often more than adequate—the land is
hilly and the soil thin and leached . . . On the Mediterranean coast the bare
mountains come down to the sea, but here there are small, fertile and irrigable patches, which form the intensively cultivated *huertas* and *vegas*. . . .
On the Meseta [. .the] country is naturally dry, poor, and unproductive.

Spain is commonly contrasted with Italy. They have large areas of waste
and unproductive land, and the climate of both has much in common. But
Italy, with rather more than half the area, supports almost twice the population of Spain.[21]

But neither in Italy nor in Portugal do the poor and rocky soils also have to
contend with a dearth of rainfall; it is this combination that renders so much
of Spain's land unsuitable for cultivation. Geographers have drawn an imag-
inary line, a climatic frontier that separates humid northern Europe from
dry Mediterranean Europe. North of this line the yearly average rainfall is
above 750 millimeters (30 inches), and average temperature and evaporation are such that minimum levels of soil moisture are maintained all
year round. South of this line yearly rainfall is below 750 millimeters, and
temperature and evaporation make the soils excessively dry. Now this line
would divide Portugal and Italy approximately in half: dry Portugal would
comprise the area south of the Tagus, dry Italy the land south of a line running from Elba to the Gargano peninsula, including Sardinia and Sicily.
In Spain, however, 90% of the territory would be classified as dry. Only
Galicia, the northern coastal strip, and a narrow fringe along the Pyrenees
lie north of the divide, and much of this land is mountainous. No other
western European country compares to Spain in terms of aridity; Greece
would possibly be the only nation in Europe which could qualify as drier
than Spain.[22] And to this one must add the altitude factor. As is frequently
remarked, only Switzerland in Europe has an average altitude higher than
Spain, and the consequent extremity of temperatures produces conditions
that are generally deleterious to agricultural productivity. As the second
highest and driest country in Europe, Spain is a very unsuitable country for
growing cereal crops.

One might think at first that a country so poorly suited to agriculture
might have a comparative advantage in industry, because the opportunity

cost for its population to abandon agricultural work and turn to industry would be low. This idea may be considered simplistic, but it is not altogether erroneous. The early and successful industrialization of Switzerland, where human (as contrasted to physical or geographical) factors appear to have played a key role, seems to lend support to this hypothesis. In that case, why didn't Spain achieve successful industrialization, thanks to its comparative advantage, as did Switzerland?

There are several answers to this question, but the basic one is that the comparative disadvantage of Switzerland in agriculture was much greater even than Spain's; according to Bergier,[23] from the Middle Ages to this day Switzerland has imported nearly 50% of its food. Because of the basic poverty of Swiss subsistence agriculture, and the location of Switzerland at the heart of Europe, its peasants and farmers from very early on diversified their efforts and worked part-time in cottage industries. By the same token, Switzerland never sought self-sufficiency. The transition to industry, therefore, was facilitated by a strong comparative advantage, application of free-trade economic policies, and a greater investment in human capital. Most of these factors were absent in Spain, Italy, and Portugal. Until the end of the nineteenth century, foreign trade hardly touched the lives of inhabitants of the central Spanish plateau; its inhabitants were practically self-sufficient at a low subsistence level. Education and literacy in the EuroLatin countries remained, as we shall presently see, among the lowest in Western Europe, while Switzerland was a pioneer in popular education.[24] In addition, tariff barriers in all three countries acted as buffers against trade-induced change, which could have promoted a more rapid transfer of resources from agriculture to industry and services.[25]

Institutional Factors: Education and Literacy

Cultural factors are not easily measured and therefore it is difficult to subject them to international comparisons. There are some facts, however, that suggest surprising affinities between our three EuroLatin countries. The most obvious, perhaps, is that Italy, Portugal, and Spain were all victims of dictatorial regimes during long and overlapping periods in the first half of the twentieth century (in Portugal and Spain through the 1970s), and this suggests a remarkable similarity in sociopolitical reactions to the problems and tensions introduced by incipient industrialization in all three countries.

Many other institutional parallels could be established between the three

EuroLatin countries. Earlier I mentioned the chronic budget deficits which plagued all three economies and produced similar effects. They impacted monetary policy and destabilized currencies; they drove up interest rates, causing serious problems for management of the public debt; they brought down the credit rating of the state and private borrowers alike in international financial markets, crowding out private borrowers from access to world capital markets; and in the end they forced the governments to nationalize and auction off Church and municipal properties. The structure of land tenure is another institutional feature that our EuroLatin countries have in common and share with other Latin or Catholic countries in Europe and America. This type of land tenure in turn is the result of a complex network of physical and historical factors: the characteristics of Mediterranean soils; extensive Church land ownership dating from the Middle Ages; and the effect of land reforms in the nineteenth century (the *Risorgimento* reform in Italy, the *desamortización* and *desamortizaçao* in Spain and Portugal). The combination of these factors resulted in the twin problems of latifundia and minifundia, plus absentee ownership and various forms of sharecropping (*mezzadria, parçaria, aparcería*). It is hazardous, however, to offer even the most general of suggestions about the exact causes and the consequences of this land tenure system. To what extent it has been caused by geographical factors and to what extent it can be explained in purely historical terms, and what effects latifundium, minifundium, sharecropping, and owner management have on agricultural productivity are problems one reads a great deal about, without being able to find any degree of unanimity, or even partial or provisional agreement.[26]

Fortunately, other social parameters are more amenable to measurement and can thus be compared. Figure 1.4 for example, gives an impressionistic overview of the historical evolution of literacy rates in Europe, and Table 1.3 and Figure 1.5 show in finer detail the literacy rates for six countries.[27] Both sources tell the same story; our EuroLatin countries had literacy rates well below those of most other European nations. Around 1900, for instance, nearly 50% of the adult population in Italy and Spain could not read (and, *a fortiori,* could not write). The Portuguese literacy rate was even lower. In Belgium, however, one of the least literate among the developed northern European countries, the proportion of those unable to read was less than one fifth (19%) of the adult population, and in France and England it was considerably lower, of course.

In the light of these disparities, it seems impossible not to establish a rela-

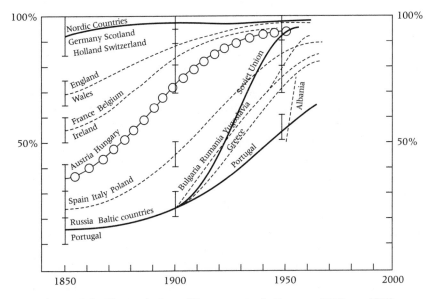

Figure 1.4.   The evolution of literacy rates in Europe, 1850–ca. 1970

Table 1.3.   Illiteracy rates in six European countries, 1850–1910 (percentages)

Year	(1) Spain	(2) Belgium	(3) France	(4) England	(5) Italy	(6) Russia
1850	75	47	42	38	75	90
1860	73	42	37	31	72	88
1870	71	36	32	24	69	86
1880	69	31	27	17	62	85
1890	61	26	22	8	55	83
1900	56	19	17	3	48	81
1910	50	15	13	0	38	79

Source: Cipolla (1969)

tionship between literacy and economic development in Europe. Several years ago Lars Sandberg made it explicit: ranking 21 European countries by their literacy rates in 1850, he showed that this gradation almost exactly matched the list of the same countries ordered by per capita income in 1970, though not in 1850. He concluded that the literacy rates, as "indicators of the stock of human capital per head. . . . are an amazingly good predictor of income per head" in the very long run.[28] This general principle seems to apply very well to the EuroLatin countries included in Sandberg's sample.

Let us briefly examine the causes and the consequences of illiteracy, considering first the consequences. At present a lively discussion is taking place about the economic effects of literacy. It would seem at first sight that a literate population, perforce an educated one, should be more productive than a population that is not able to read. The productivity problems intrinsically connected with functional illiteracy are being denounced almost daily in many developed countries, especially in the United States, and one might imagine it quite unnecessary and even inopportune to insist further on the point. However, since a series of literacy campaigns in Third World countries in the 1960s and 1970s apparently failed to produce immediate economic results, many scholars have criticized as unsustainable the premise of illiter-

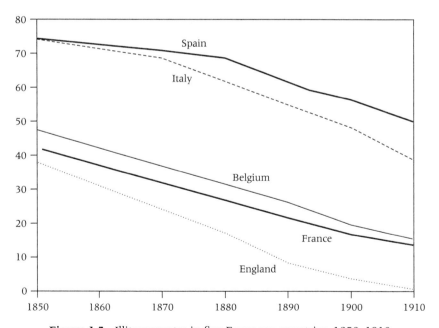

Figure 1.5. Illiteracy rates in five European countries, 1850–1910

acy as an obstacle to economic growth. The debate has been long and involved, and we cannot go into it here.[29] Suffice it to say that the discussion
has clarified and added depth to the arguments of both the pro-literacy ad-
vocates and those who are more skeptical. Summarized briefly, the economic contributions of literacy are as follows:

1. The most obvious contribution would be to provide workers with
   better communication skills, for example, the ability to read
   instruction manuals on how to operate a piece of machinery or
   simply to read company rules, etc. This was the first argument cited
   in support of literacy's role in economic growth advanced by the pro-
   literacy scholars, although the skeptics refuted this, claiming that
   most basic professional skills can be learned orally and by direct
   observation. It continues to be the most keenly debated question.
2. Literacy also provides workers with greater ability to expand their
   knowledge, to learn a new trade or new techniques within the same
   trade, thus adapting better and more rapidly to the vagaries of the
   market through retooling and mobility; and most importantly, it gives
   them a chance to reach higher educational levels.
3. There is growing acceptance among linguists and psychologists that
   literacy and the learning of grammar constitute a learning process of
   its own that brings about overall improvement in reasoning and
   learning abilities.

These statements seem, *a priori*, to be supported by empirical investigations
carried out recently in Spain, Italy, and Portugal. The work of Clara Eugenia
Núñez shows that Sandberg's hypothesis for European countries is statisti-
cally confirmed for Spain's 49 provinces, although with a shorter time lag
than what Sandberg found. Using cross-sectional historical provincial data
and allowing for a time lag of about 20 to 30 years, roughly a generation,
Núñez has found a high correlation between literacy and per capita income
in nineteenth- and early twentieth-century Spain.

The correlation improves considerably when a second variable is included, the so-called gender gap. This means that, other things being equal,
the narrower the gap between male and female literacy rates, the stronger
the positive impact of literacy on economic growth. Núñez's work has introduced a new variable into the analysis of the economic effects of literacy and
opened new vistas which we cannot examine here. Suffice it to say that the
discovery of the importance of the sex differential and of female literacy in

Table 1.4. Students attending primary school in seven European countries, 1850–1930 (per 1,000 population)

Year	(1) Italy	(2) Portugal	(3) Spain	(4) France	(5) Germany	(6) Sweden	(7) Great Britain
1850	—	11.0	—	92.8	—	—	18.0
1860	40.3	19.8	80.0	108.7	—	—	39.8
1870	53.1	28.6	92.1	120.8	—	133.4	58.8
1880	69.4	50.4	104.1	142.8	—	138.8	116.1
1890	80.5	46.5	98.0	145.7	—	144.2	133.5
1900	84.2	42.6	92.0	144.3	159.1	144.4	151.3
1910	96.7	49.7	85.9	145.0	158.8	144.0	148.8
1920	112.4	56.8	90.5	118.9	—	119.4	136.7
1930	115.6	63.9	95.1	119.2	—	108.1	125.3

Source: Mitchell (1976), with interpolation

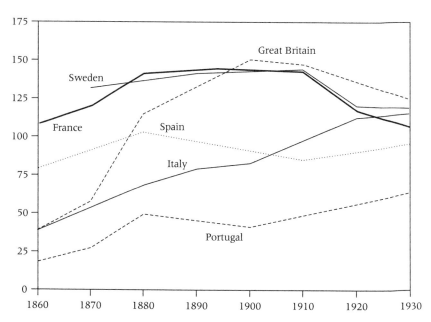

Figure 1.6. Students attending primary school in six European countries, 1860–1930 (per 1,000 population)

of the religious factor, which for various reasons was diminishing during the industrial era; gradually the Church was ceding its quasi-monopoly of education to the state; furthermore, the attitude of the Church itself was changing, even in those areas that were most solidly Catholic. However, the weight of the historical past certainly placed the EuroLatin countries in a position of initial disadvantage.

Given the growing role that the state has played in education in the contemporary period, it is the state that is held responsible for the low educational levels in the EuroLatin countries; indeed, there must have been serious shortages on the supply side of the education equation.[37] For various reasons, the state administrative systems at the central, regional, and local levels did not make enough of an effort to remedy educational deficiencies.[38] The explanation for neglect includes historical inertia, lack of political pressures, and perhaps insufficient economic resources. Here we find ourselves trapped in various vicious circles. On the one hand, poverty limits the potential for investment in education, and in turn the lack of education makes economic growth difficult, thereby perpetuating poverty. On the other hand, there is also a circular problem of educational demand. A population that is poor and ill-informed in a country that is technologically backward has difficulty appreciating the importance of education, beginning with the ability to read. Hence even if education were widely available, the offer might be underutilized among the very people for whom the services are intended.[39]

Demand and supply factors combined to keep the economically and educationally backward countries in a state of stagnation. Education is a very long-term investment[40] item, and politicians have very limited horizons. If there is no strong demand or social pressure, and if resources are scarce, they will be devoted to tasks that are more politically profitable, which is to say, profitable in terms of short-run returns. In consequence, the countries that most urgently need better education are exactly those that invest the least, and the income differential between rich and poor nations continues to increase. It is clear that this is what happened in Italy, Spain, and Portugal in the nineteenth century.

Factors That Weighed in Favor of Recovery

Despite the dead weight of these powerful physical and institutional factors, the EuroLatin countries in Europe have managed to turn the trend around, to stem the tide, or at least have fought energetically against the downward trend in relative income that was so evident in the nineteenth century. How did they do it? Here we can only sketch some key explanations.

It seems patently clear that to overcome the vicious circle that kept the majority of the population working the land at very low subsistence levels, some kind of jolt was necessary, whether negative or positive. In other words, the peasant population had to be induced to leave agriculture, either drawn by the attractions of industry and urban commerce or else forced off the land by deteriorating living conditions. In this case the peasants were being forced to leave the land, principally because of the massive shipments of Russian and North American cereals that entered Europe, shipments that depressed agricultural prices and left farmers and peasants unemployed.[41]

Competition from foreign agriculture undoubtedly accelerated the inevitable trends that were leading to the modernization of the EuroLatin economies. One of them was the transfer of population and resources from low-productivity agricultural activities such as cultivation of cereals and legumes to high-productivity crops such as grape vines, olives, fruits, and vegetables. These crops are much better suited to Mediterranean soil conditions, and they were finding better markets in a northern Europe that was growing ever more wealthy. If the technology of nineteenth-century agriculture had favored cereal cultivation to the detriment of the Mediterranean countries, twentieth-century technology developed favorably for the producers and exporters of fruits and vegetables, which benefited the EuroLatins.

Although the southern countries, like most of Europe, erected trade barriers in an attempt to lessen the shock of external competition,[42] the impact was nonetheless powerful and set in motion a mechanism of exceptional duration, given that the trend in outmigration from the Mediterranean countries has continued until today. This transfer of resources, principally human resources, although artificially curbed by agricultural protectionism until the second half of the twentieth century, made a powerful contribution to economic modernization and especially to industrialization, for it offered an abundant supply of cheap labor for urban activities and also permitted the import of capital and technology, thanks to the payments that migrants sent back to their homelands. The marketplace of a prosperous Europe, as I earlier suggested, was eager for primary products and semi-finished goods manufactured by the EuroLatins, who were thus able to benefit from the double advantage of low wages and a Ricardian rent situation, in being closer to the market than were their overseas competitors.

The institutional barriers too were yielding, although slowly and only partially. Parallel to urbanization, illiteracy declined gradually, and today it is nothing more than a residual item in the official statistics, although in reality a considerable amount of functional illiteracy remains. Secondary and higher education, to which I have not referred in this chapter, still leaves much to be desired in our three countries, although the turn to educational methods that sometimes resemble mass production may have managed to make up in quantity what it lacks in quality. Fiscal incompetence has certainly diminished in comparison with its pervasiveness a century earlier, but as any man in the street in each of the three countries would certainly attest, it has far from disappeared. The result of these improvements has been a degree of economic growth in the EuroLatin countries that on average—and let us not fall prey here to too many illusions—has done no more than reinstate them by 1980 to a position they had already occupied in 1830.

CHAPTER 2

The Nineteenth Century: Politics, Population, and Human Capital

The Legacy of the Old Regime

The scant half century between the American Revolution and the defeat of the Spanish colonial army at Ayacucho in Peru, 1776–1824, was a turbulent and decisive period on both sides of the Atlantic. Those years witnessed revolution on a continental scale both in Europe and in the Americas, and while there is no doubt that, as Tocqueville famously remarked, there was considerable continuity between the pre- and postrevolutionary situations, discontinuities were also glaringly evident. Although this caesura was most obvious in political terms in the Americas, where the old colonial status was exchanged for new independent nationhood, the parallel effects of the French Revolution and the English Industrial Revolution had more immediate impact in the Old World than did colonial emancipation in the New. In general, one might view the long and relatively peaceful nineteenth century in Europe, from 1815 to 1914, as a long assimilation of the consequences of these two revolutions, whose effects spread gradually from north to south and from west to east.

This period of change was particularly traumatic for Spain, which lost an empire without gaining the prerequisites of economic and political progress. Its decision to join France in supporting the American colonies' revolt against England brought very serious consequences in its wake. Taking part in that war entailed military expenses and consequent commercial losses, seriously destabilized government finances, and initiated a pattern of internal and external government debt which was endemic for most of the nineteenth century and seriously hindered the potential for economic development. From the 1770s onwards this growing indebtedness forced Spain to introduce a series of financial innovations,[1] most notably the creation of the

Bank of San Carlos in 1782 and the issue of the *vales reales,* a special form of government debt. In spite of their unquestionable originality, these measures unfortunately proved inadequate to resolve the situation. The burden of debt kept growing as military conflicts succeeded one after another: the War of the French Convention, against the French revolutionary forces in 1793–1795, the wars Spain fought in alliance with the French from 1796 onwards, the invasion of Portugal in 1801, the Battle of Trafalgar in 1805, then the War of Spanish Independence (against the French), 1808–1813, to which must be added the wars of Spanish American independence, 1808–1824. This financial burden was one of the principal determinants of the economic policies adopted throughout the nineteenth century. The insolvency was dearly bought. Chronic indebtedness weakened successive governments both militarily and politically, and continually forced them into desperate measures in their search of resources, such as selling national assets (land and mines), granting concessions in return for credit (typically monopolies and banking privileges, whose principal beneficiaries were the famous Rothschilds, although they were by no means the only ones), and increasing taxes as well; the high tariffs, for example, were designed to raise revenue. The high-handed and ill-conceived methods Spain adopted as it tried to solve its debt problems at the expense of the colonies undoubtedly contributed to their quest for independence, at least in the case of Mexico.[2]

To a large extent, the economic reforms adopted in the nineteenth century were prompted by the fiscal crisis that had been inherited from the past and aggravated by negligence since the reign of Carlos IV. The main effect of these reforms was to ease some of the worst institutional rigidities bequeathed by the old regime. The gradual improvement permitted a moderate expansion of the economy, but it was not enough to generate real sustained growth.

Nowhere were the rigidities of the old regime more obvious than in agriculture, nor their effects more widespread and injurious. Figure 2.1 shows the eighteenth-century evolution of general commodity prices and cereals in New Castile according to Hamilton,[3] and Figure 2.2 shows the evolution of an aggregate agricultural price index there, with a further index relating agricultural to nonagricultural prices, calculated from the same source. This relative price index, the broken line in Figure 2.2, can be interpreted as a crude measure of agriculture's terms of trade *vis-à-vis* the rest of the economy.

Both the index of agricultural prices and the aggregate price index (Figure

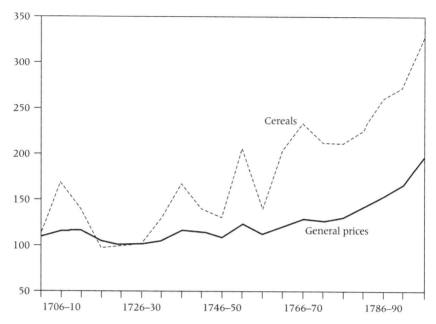

Figure 2.1. Indices of general and cereal prices in New Castile, 1700–1800

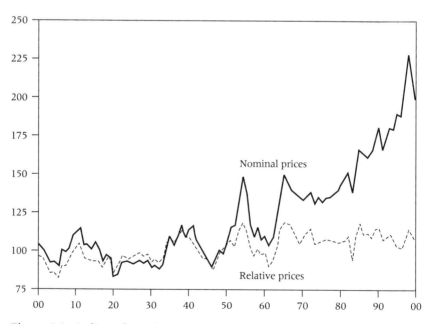

Figure 2.2. Indices of agrarian prices in New Castile, 1700–1800, nominal and relative

2.2) show a degree of long-term stability for the first half of the century, and a steady increase in the second half. Other things being equal, and taking into account that the Spanish population increased steadily during the eighteenth century, this rise in prices can be interpreted as the consequence of what is termed a kinky supply curve for agricultural products, a curve with two distinct sections, an elastic segment for volumes of output below the levels reached around 1750, and an inelastic segment for higher volumes of output; see Figure 2.3. According to this interpretation, during the first half of the eighteenth century increases in demand derived from population growth (D_1) were met with increases in agricultural output, with no effect on price (P_1), which thus remained stable over that period. During the second half, due to supply rigidities, the increases in demand (D_2, D_3) could not be met by increases in output, and price increases thus ensued (P_2, P_3).

Hamilton's figures show that nonagricultural prices also increased during the second half of the eighteenth century. This could mean that rigidities also existed in the nonagricultural sector and also that other factors, monetary factors for example, could have contributed to the inflation. We do not know enough about the evolution of the money supply in eighteenth-century Spain to be able to rule out this hypothesis completely, but it should be made clear that attributing some part of inflation to monetary causes does

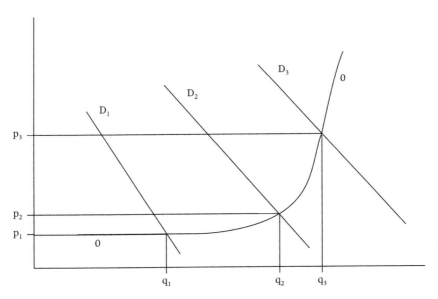

Figure 2.3. Diagrammatic representation of the cereal market in Spain in the eighteenth century

not contradict or exclude the hypothesis that agricultural rigidities were a serious limiting factor to economic growth.

And what was happening to nonagricultural prices? If they increased at about the same rate as agricultural prices, as Hamilton's figures seem to suggest,[4] is it not possible that inflation was induced by the nonagricultural sector? The overwhelming importance of agricultural prices in the mechanism of inflation seems to be clearly established, however, by the evolution of the agricultural terms of trade, since Figure 2.2 shows that the terms of trade of agriculture relative to the nonagricultural sector increased steadily during the eighteenth century. This seems to suggest, among other things, that agricultural prices were the first to rise, and nonagricultural prices followed suit.

Within the agricultural sector, it was grain prices that first increased and pushed the general agricultural price index higher throughout the whole century. Cereals were, of course, the basic staple of the diet, and the curve of the price series seems to imply that both supply and demand for them were inelastic.

Several explanations may account for these rigidities in the agricultural supply function. The two most important ones would be a lack of technological progress, on the one hand, and limited availability of cultivable land on the other. Both obstacles, which we shall examine in more detail in the next chapter, occupied the minds of thinkers and reformers during this period, precisely because such agricultural rigidities posed serious social and political problems. Some of the consequences of agricultural price increases during the second half of the eighteenth century are well known, particularly the riots and turmoil which occurred with relative frequency, the most famous without doubt being the Esquilache Riots in 1766, and these disturbances prompted serious plans for reform, especially under Carlos III (1759–1788). Although some elements of reform were achieved, the gains were obviously insufficient.[5] The most important reforms advocated by the enlightened thinkers of this period, Jovellanos, Floridablanca, and Campomanes, were directed towards solving the problem of inelasticity in the agricultural supply function: land reform, *desamortización*, and abolition of privileges of the powerful association of sheep growers, the Honorable Council of the Mesta. The effect of these reforms would have been to expand the cultivable area and perhaps also to stimulate technical improvements. The abolition of the Mesta privileges would have freed many areas that were restricted to pasture and sheep walks, making them available for food production. The *desamortización* would have expropriated entailed estates and lands belonging to institutional owners—the Church, villages and municipalities—and would have sold them to private owners, thus permitting more intense and rational cultivation (see Chapter 3). These reforms, however, although timidly broached under Carlos III and Carlos IV (1788–1808), were not fully and legally applied until well into the nineteenth century, although in reality they were spontaneously implemented in many places during and after the Napoleonic War (Llopis, 1983).

It was, in fact, the breaking apart of these institutional constraints from the Old Regime that permitted a modest agricultural expansion in the nineteenth century and thereby engendered a limited growth in population and in the economy at large.

Economic Backwardness and Political Frustration

For the reader interested in the political history of Spain in the 1800s, the general view is one of constant frustration. Although it was one of the cradles of liberalism (the word itself is of Spanish origin), Spain in the nineteenth century presents us with a scenario of repeated failures to install a liberal system, a struggle which achieved only a nominal success by the time of the Restoration (1876), because it was thwarted by the corrupt and abusive practices of *caciquismo* (bossism) and *pucherazo* (election-rigging)—both of them also good Spanish words which sadly tarnish and diminish the liberal ideal. During most of this period the country existed in a state of latent turmoil (with frequent eruptions of civil war), and *de facto* power was in the hands of military groups. In the end, the fragility of nineteenth-century Spanish liberalism was proved without any possible room for doubt by its collapse in the twentieth century, when the dictatorship of Primo de Rivera, the Civil War, and Franco's long dictatorship destroyed whatever illusions might have remained about the robustness of liberalism and democracy on Spanish soil (even though universal manhood suffrage had been adopted by law in the old Spanish homeland as early as 1890).

The nineteenth century both opened and closed with unrealistic hopes and important failures; the experience of the earliest years corroborated how worthless were the expectations of enlightened reform. Spanish society under the Old Regime, like all of continental Europe, showed itself incapable of internal reform; but the critical difference is that for Spain the liberal alternative also collapsed resoundingly. The hopes conceived under Carlos III gave way to the deceptions and scandals of the reign of Carlos IV, and the palace reformism of Manuel Godoy led in the end to the miserable populist uprising at Aranjuez. The war against the French invader exposed not only the collapse of the Old Regime but also territorial disintegration and the resurgence of factional bossism; it also revealed the grandeur and yet the impotence of the young liberal movement struggling to be born. In Marx's brilliant phrase, while in the rest of Spain action prevailed without ideas, in the Parliament in Cádiz ideas triumphed without action. The failure of the enlightened project envisioned by the Cortes of Cádiz was complete. Its two key programs were to make Fernando VII the first constitutional monarch within Spain, and to form a transatlantic federation out of the Spanish empire, but both key actors not only refused obstinately to fulfill their designated roles but took up arms against the well-meaning legislators. After the collapse of the Liberal Triennium (1820–1823), Fernando's second betrayal, and the complete destruction of the colonial army at Ayacucho, it seemed that Spanish liberalism was dead and buried in 1824.

But it was not so. Although throughout the nineteenth century liberalism was incapable of establishing itself firmly within Spain, it did nonetheless demonstrate a tenacious ability to survive. Reborn and returned to power after the death in 1833 of its implacable enemy, Fernando VII, the Liberal party, inheritor of the ideals of Cádiz, divided into two groups, the Progressives and the Moderates, and went on to govern Spain without interruption until 1923. But the Liberals did not manage to create a stable political system. Under the regency of María Cristina of Naples and later of her daughter, Queen Isabel II, the differences between the two factions became more entrenched, and two distinct, virtually irreconcilable parties were formed. Systematic election-rigging was facilitated by a census-based suffrage system which enabled local elites in rural areas to manipulate the right to vote and to bring many pressures to bear upon election results. The rural areas were numerically overwhelming, hence (thanks to the *caciques)* the party favored by the Crown remained in power, legally but illegitimately. That was invariably the Moderate party, the Moderados. Yet on the other hand, liberalism's military victory in 1839 over its out-and-out enemy, the Carlist party, bestowed disproportionate political luster upon a handful of generals (Espartero, Serrano, Narváez, O'Donnell, Prim) whose support was disputed between the two Liberal parties. Falsification of electoral results meant that the party in opposition could only make headway by means of force; insurrection, *pronunciamiento* (another universal word of Spanish coinage), or the military coup became an almost normal means of changing parties, and transformed the generals into major protagonists on the political scene.

The first military coup was carried out in 1814 by Fernando VII, with the support of General Elío, against the liberal Cortes of Cádiz; the second, under Commander Rafael del Riego, was against Fernando's absolutist regime. And thus was inaugurated a long series of insurrections, not all of them successful, which terminated with that of General Martínez Campos in Sagunto, in 1874. This last coup led to the apparent political stability of the Restoration. In this way, between 1833 and 1874, Moderates and Progressives or their successors were constantly fighting for power, more by the sword than by means of the ballot-box. The Liberal political system we associate with the regency and the reign of Isabel II was founded upon disgraceful fraud, as repeated recourse to military intervention indicates in the clearest possible manner. Within this system, elections were nothing more than the ritual confirmation of what had been resolved through military conflict. In view of the Crown's unconditional support for the Moderados, the Progressives governed only during brief periods initiated and terminated by coups of opposing political direction. Thus there were the Progressive Mendizábal years, 1835–1837, the Espartero Regency, in 1840–1843, and in the midst of the long Moderado decade, a two-year Progressive spell from 1854 to 1856. All these brief Progressive interludes, bustling with reform and legalistic dissension yet at the same time politically fragile, have much in common with the years of the Liberal Triennium, 1820 to 1823. The history of Spain's nineteenth century repeats itself lamentably.

The Glorious Revolution of 1868 was the apotheosis of the Progressive insurrection, and, like all its predecessors, it led to a period of feverish reformist activity marred by continuous disagreements between the government and the opposition conspirators. In reality, most of the nineteenth century's social improvements, from the *desamortización* to educational reforms, took root in the short periods of Progressive control and were consolidated thanks to the relative tolerance of the Moderates. With the revolutionary 1860s the era of insurrection closed, and the Restoration began.

The secret of the relative success of the Restoration is well known: its craftsman, Antonio Cánovas del Castillo, established a system of civilian government, enforcing a peaceful system of alternating control (the *turno pacífico*), and the parties, after various metamorphoses, became known as the Liberals and the Conservatives. This was not the result of honest elections; the cynical Cánovas never attempted to hold them, and in any case the relative backwardness of the country would probably have precluded their successful completion. His system worked because of scrupulous neutrality on the part of the Crown, in the persons of Alfonso XII (who had been Cánovas's pupil) and the Regent María Cristina of Hapsburg-Lorena, Alfonso's prudent and thoughtful widow. Renouncing the former intolerance which had produced such adverse results in the Isabeline period, both parties, through what became known as the Pardo Pact (the Pardo being a royal palace near Madrid), agreed to renounce all attempts to permanently exclude the other from power. Relatively reconciled, these two parties consolidated a monopoly of the old liberalism, keeping up political appearances by means of the *turno pacífico*. The military establishment, for the moment, returned to the barracks, but as the political system staggered towards breakdown during the first third of the twentieth century, they were to return to the scene with increasing violence.

The nineteenth century ended very much as it had begun, with political reforms frustrated (though in terms very different from those of a century earlier, of course), and with the colonial defeat of 1898 (loss of Cuba and Puerto Rico). For the time being the Cánovas system had resolved the question of military insurrections, but by consolidating power in the hands of the two old parties he had effectively installed a Liberal monopoly. Although it is certainly true that the two parties jointly represented a broad spectrum of political opinion, economic and social improvements fostered the growth of new groups that did not feel represented by the alternating parties: republicans, socialists, anarchists, and regionalists represented the new interests and constituted new groups of increasing strength. The Carlists, integrated within the Restoration system, also represented a distinct point of view, not in the ascendance but by no means negligible. The struggle of these new political protagonists to wrest power from the older parties was at the heart of the great political drama of the first years of the twentieth century, and it was the most important structural cause of political frustration as the old century closed. The inflexibility and lack of understanding that the older parties displayed towards the colonial question, which lead them blindly into the disaster of 1898, sharply underlined the total exhaustion of the old policies, indicated the distance between the old parties and society at large, and exacerbated the bitterness of the military. All this marked the beginning of the end of the Restoration equilibrium, which also coincided with the death of the old leaders of the system; Cánovas was assassinated in 1897, and the Liberal Sagasta died of natural causes in 1903.

Political stagnation, historical repetition, revisiting of the same old problems in circumstances hardly different from before—all these constitute an exact parallel to what was happening in the economy. Since the economic structure had changed very little, there was little change to be observed in the social structure. Thus, for example, agriculture employed the same proportion of the working population throughout the century, about two-thirds, according to Pérez Moreda. This population, mostly rural and preponderantly uneducated and illiterate, constituted only the most flimsy basis of support for any stable, responsible, progressive political life. This great mass of humanity, indifferent and at times hostile to the subtleties of modern politics, was manipulated by local elites when electoral circumstances so required, or by violent groups at times of political uprising or civil war. Day-to-day politics, thus deprived of any substantial common ground, was reduced to a constant round of struggles between elites and different urban strata: between upper, middle, and working classes, among whom certain institutions carried particular weight: the Crown, the Church, the army, and the political parties. The agreements and quarrels between these minority groups determined the political dynamic of the age. For Raymond Carr (1966), the decisive factor is the strategic role of three actors: the Crown, the Church, and the party elites. Ordinary people remained alienated, and on various occasions and regions they were openly and violently opposed to the Liberal political system. Only when economic change set in on a noticeable scale during the Restoration did the political panorama begin to change and to present new problems, whose solution was rendered difficult by the weight of tradition and the extreme rigidity of the institutional framework. In these conditions the only social change that took place stemmed from a combination of political interests and demographic change, resulting in disentailment, fiscal and administrative reorganization, liberalization of the economy, and educational reform. That change, although undeniable, was scarcely perceptible, especially compared with what was happening in other European countries.

All this does not imply that the Spanish case was exceptional and unusual. The liberal system was encountering difficulties in establishing itself all over Europe throughout the nineteenth century. The modalities of bossism *(caciquismo)* were abundantly evident in many countries, for instance the English "rotten boroughs" (although those were reformed in 1832, ninety-nine years before Spain). Similarities have also been pointed out between the French Vendée and Carlism; but this reactionary French movement wasted away in the nineteenth century, while Carlism remained a force until very recently. Clearly, the liberal system, with all its inherent difficulties, was consolidated in the nineteenth century in France, in England, and in almost all the more economically developed countries of northern Europe. In the peripheral countries of Europe which have more in common with Spain, especially Italy and Portugal, liberalism was more tentatively established during the nineteenth century and displayed more fragility in the twentieth, with the dictatorships of Mussolini and Salazar. The affinities and parallels that can be seen in the economic and political histories of Italy, Portugal, and Spain reinforce this interpretation of the interconnection between the two spheres, the economic and the political, for the Spanish case, and for Europe in general.

Population: The Causes of Stagnation

In comparison with the demographics of other European countries, Spanish population grew slowly in the nineteenth century: from some 10.5 million people in 1800, it reached a figure of 18.6 million one hundred years later (Table 2.1). Tables 2.2 and 2.3 permit a detailed comparison with other countries.

The third table reveals an interesting correlation between population growth and economic modernization; in general, those countries whose population more than doubled are those whose economy became industrialized. There are some possible borderline exceptions here, such as Austria-Hungary, a typical case of a dual economy, and France, whose proverbially sluggish population growth concealed a rate of economic progress that was far from slow, but in general the correspondence between economic and demographic growth can be seen clearly.

In the Spanish case, slow demographic growth was mainly due to high mortality which, although declining slightly over time, remained clearly above the Western European rates. Given this high death rate, the average

Table 2.1.   Population of Spain, 1787–1900 (in thousands)

Year	Population	Year	Population
1787	10,393	1860	15,645
1797	10,536	1877	16,622
1821	11,662	1887	17,550
1833	12,287	1897	18,109
1857	15,455	1900	18,594

Source: Pérez Moreda (1985, table 2.1)

Table 2.2. Growth and other demographic variables in various European countries, 1800–1900

Country	Population (in millions)		Percentage growth		Crude death rate in 1900 (per 1,000)	Crude birth rate in 1900 (per 1,000)
	1800	1900	Increase	Annual rate		
Great Britain	10.9	37.0	239.4	1.230	18	29
Holland	2.2	5.1	131.8	0.844	18	32
Belgium	3.0	6.7	123.3	0.807	19	29
Sweden	2.3	5.1	121.7	0.800	17	27
Germany	24.5	50.6	106.5	0.728	22	36
Austria/Hungary	23.3	47.0	101.7	0.704	25[a]	35[a]
Italy	17.2	32.5	88.4	0.635	24	33
Portugal	3.1	5.4	74.2	0.557	20	30
SPAIN	10.7	18.6	73.8	0.554	29	34
France	26.9	38.5	40.6	0.341	22	21
Ireland	5.0	4.5	−10.0	−0.105	20	23

a. Austria only

Sources: calculated from Armengaud (1973) and Mitchell (1976). For Spain, the figures are calculated from Table 2.1.

life expectancy was short at the start of the period and increased little. Life expectancy was under thirty years by the middle of the century, and it had not quite reached thirty-five years by 1900. In the Scandinavian countries that figure had been reached one and a half centuries earlier.

Among the factors which explain this excessive mortality are those which can be grouped under the heading of "economic backwardness": poor sanitation, low agricultural productivity, chronic housing shortages, an expensive and inadequate transportation network, widespread ignorance, especially about the causes and mechanisms of the transmission of illness, and so on. The combined action of these general factors periodically triggered the well-known Malthusian checks to population: famines due to subsistence crises, recurrent epidemics, and endemic maladies.

The Spanish subsistence crises in the nineteenth century have been studied and are well known to us, especially those of 1847, 1857, and 1867–68. In addition, Sánchez-Albornoz has found serious food shortages in the years 1804, 1812, 1817, 1823–1825, 1837, 1879, 1882, 1887, and 1898; all in all twelve major food crises in a century. In every case there was a correlation between food scarcity and mortality, both chronologically and geographically. In 1856–57 and 1867–68 the provinces which suffered the largest price increases had the smallest population growth (Sánchez-Albornoz, 1963, 1964, 1977).

The relationship between famines and deaths is well established, but what caused the famines? We must make a distinction between immediate or conjunctural causes and more permanent or structural ones. The immediate fundamental cause of food scarcities was climatic fluctuation: a year of excessive rain, or of late frosts, or, more frequently, of drought usually brought about a shortfall in the harvest, with famine and death as consequences. More profound causes, however, were related to social organization and economic development: if crop size was so dependent upon the weather, it was because agriculture was technically backward and yields were low, close to the subsistence level; and because the transportation system was slow and primitive, it failed in its role as redistributor of food products from surplus regions or ports of entry to the areas of scarcity. All this made the system more vulnerable to climatic fluctuations than a more technologically

Table 2.3. Emigration and demographic growth in seven European countries, 1830–1900 (in thousands)

	(1) Spain[a]	(2) Great Britain	(3) Portugal	(4) Sweden	(5) Italy	(6) Germany[e]	(7) France
A. Pop. in 1900[b]	18,594	37,000	5,423	5,137	32,475	56,367	38,451
B. Pop. in 1830[c]	12,131	16,261	3,051	2,347	20,655	27,176	32,561
C. Difference: A − B	6,463	20,739	2,372	2,790	11,080	29,191	5,890
D. Emigration[d]	1,386	8,501	706	774	2,772	4,296	299
E. Growth: C + D	7,849	29,240	3,078	3,564	14,592	33,487	6,189
F. Coeff. of emigration: D/E%	17.7	29.1	22.9	21.7	10.9	12.8	4.8
G. Demographic growth: E/B%	64.7	179.8	100.9	151.9	70.6	132.2	19.0

a. Spanish population interpolated from Table 2.1
b. For Great Britain, Italy and France the figures for 1900 are actually from 1901
c. For Great Britain and France the figures for 1830 are actually from 1831
d. Emigration from Great Britain may include Irish nationals before 1850
e. The territorial boundaries for Germany and France varied between 1830 and 1900
Sources: Calculated from Mitchell (1976) and Woodruff (1966)

advanced, better irrigated, higher-yield, more commercialized agriculture would have been.

Epidemics were the second major cause of the high mortality rate and its periodic catastrophic increases, and they were obviously related to subsistence crises in several ways. For one thing the food shortages, rather than directly killing great numbers of people, weakened the population and increased its susceptibility to infection. At the same time, Spain suffered the endemic traditional epidemics closely related to poor hygiene, poverty, and ignorance that are characteristic of backward societies. High infant mortality was due to the same factors, but specifically to primitive childbirth practices, lack of vaccines, and the devastating effect of childhood illnesses, frequently carried and transmitted by adults, such as whooping cough, smallpox, measles, typhus, dysentery, tuberculosis, and malaria.

One of the main traditional epidemics, the "black death" or "bubonic plague," had disappeared from Europe after the mid-eighteenth century, for reasons which are still not perfectly understood. The most lethal epidemics in nineteenth century Europe were smallpox, cholera, typhus, and yellow fever. In Spain, the two most widespread epidemic diseases were yellow fever, a semitropical malady which chiefly struck in Andalusia during the first three decades of the century, and cholera, of which there were four major outbreaks: in 1833–1835, in 1854–1855, in 1865–66, and in 1885. The provinces most affected by these outbreaks were the eastern interior provinces, especially those adjacent to the Cordillera Ibérica, between the Ebro valley and the central meseta. The cholera epidemics seem to have been related to political crises or military operations such as the outbreak of the Carlist War in 1833, the scarcities due to the Crimean War and the O'Donnell *pronunciamiento* (known to Spanish historians as the *Vicalvarada*) in 1854; the economic crisis of 1866–68, which was the prelude to the Glorious Revolution of September 1868, and the onset around 1884 of the long end-of-century agrarian depression, which in Spain was aggravated by the spread of phylloxera, a vine-destroying pest.

The reader may be surprised by this correlation between a gastrointestinal illness, caused by the consumption of contaminated food or drink, and political-economic events. But this can be easily explained: it appears, for instance, that troop movements during the Carlist War and the *Vicalvarada* helped the spread of a type of cholera which had been ravaging Europe for years. In addition, in times of famine it was all the more difficult to maintain emergency quarantine and hygienic measures ordered by the authorities, in part because there were more beggars and vagrants, and because people ate substandard food more often.

In addition to the deadly impact of epidemic diseases, one must also surmise that the incidence of endemic maladies also caused high mortality, and I write "surmise" advisedly, because their endemic nature made them more difficult to detect, diagnose, and record—all of this conducive to underestimation in the statistics. A typical example is tuberculosis, popularly termed "consumption" although other terms were also used, an infectious disease which attacks with particular virulence people who are undernourished, weak, and live in crowded conditions. We still know little about the incidence of this and other infectious diseases, such as smallpox, measles, scarlet fever, or typhus, in Spain in the nineteenth century, but there is no doubt that they were among the main causes of high mortality. Nor can there be any doubt that the ultimate explanation of their impact lies in economic underdevelopment and its concomitants, scarce and poor medical services. Among the consequences of an inadequate health policy we find undue laxity in carrying out vaccination campaigns throughout the whole of the nineteenth century. As Pérez Moreda points out, "smallpox vaccination, which had been embarked upon with a certain enthusiasm in the early years of the century, fell into disuse immediately after the Peninsular War and its general application during the rest of the century was to leave much to be desired" (Pérez Moreda, 1980). Following a series of failed or incomplete attempts to combat the disease (a sanitation code had been planned during the Liberal Triennium, and the National Vaccination Institute had been founded in 1871), smallpox vaccination was made general and compulsory only in 1902. After that date there was a sharp decline in infant mortality.

The consequence of this combination of famines, periodic epidemics, and endemic illnesses was, of course, the persistence of scandalously high mortality until very late in the nineteenth century.[6] Census figures show that a clear and sustained decline did not set in until after the great cholera epidemic of 1885, so that by century's end the transition towards modern mortality had barely started. In 1900 Spain's mortality rate was still 29 per 1,000, with life expectancy at birth of 34.8 years, well below the rates for most Western European countries. Bear in mind that, at about this date, mortality rates in countries of similar characteristics, such as Portugal, Italy, or Serbia (not in table for lack of 1900 data), were 20, 24, and 24 per 1,000 respectively; see Table 2.2. In the whole of Europe, only Russia surpassed Spain with a mortality rate of 31 per 1,000.

If mortality within the Spanish population was high compared with that of most other European nations, the birth rate, in comparative terms, was quite moderate. At first glance Table 2.2 may seem to indicate the opposite, since Spain's birth rate was among the highest in 1900 (34 per 1,000). Yet with mortality at 29 per 1,000, the differential between births and deaths was among the lowest, in fact the lowest for the countries shown, with the exception of only France and Ireland, where the difference was even smaller. This indicates that even Spain's relatively high birth rate was part and parcel of a delayed demographic transition. Thus, for example, when Germany (Prussia), a country of relatively late transition, had a death rate of 28 per 1,000 in 1866, its birth rate was about 40 per 1,000. The same was true for Italy at about the same time; likewise Romania, with a mortality similar to Spain's in 1900, had a birth rate of 42 per 1,000. England, around 1840, had a birth rate of 32 and mortality at only 22 per 1,000. Spain's birth rate then, apparently high in 1900, was actually low in relation to the mortality level and also low in relation to birth rates in other European countries in the early stages of their transition to demographic modernity.

This relatively moderate birth rate at the end of the nineteenth century appears to have been the product of a secular decline dating from the middle of the previous century, and its proximate cause was a gradual fall in marital fertility. In other words, from the middle of the eighteenth century something was happening in Spain that reduced the average number of children born within each marriage. In spite of the problems that the interpretation of these data present (the first official census was not carried out until 1857), it seems clear, according to Livi-Bacci (1972, p. 181) that "the transition the Spanish population experienced between the eighteenth and nineteenth centuries could support a theory that marital fertility declined because of an extension of birth control." From a period before Malthus, therefore, it seems that a process of voluntary and artificial birth control was taking hold in Spain and in other European countries. The same author points out that "voluntary control of fertility was practiced in pre-Malthusian societies," and the Spanish case seems to Livi-Bacci a good example to support this assertion.

We can now ask ourselves about the possible reasons for these Malthusian practices *avant la lettre*. The answer must be highly hypothetical, but it would seem natural to formulate it in Malthusian terms, that is, taking the standard of living as the explanatory variable. The poverty of the Spanish countryside and the low standard of living of the peasants, who at the end of the century continued to make up two-thirds of the population (the economic overpopulation, in short)—these factors seem to me to offer the best explanation of this voluntary limitation of the number of births.

Marriage and Seasonality

The work of John Hajnal has shown that Western Europe's marriage patterns, and to a lesser extent those of Eastern Europe, are unique in the modern world. Europeans had a very high rate of celibacy, and those who married did so later in life than people living in other continents. The main consequence of this pattern was a moderate rate of population growth, which in turn depended upon economic conditions. In terms of marriage patterns Spain was clearly a European country, though it was closer to the fringe than to the mainstream.

At the end of the eighteenth century, the celibacy rate in Spain was high, and so was the average age at first marriage, for men and women alike. From then on, however, the trends for both variables diverged. During the nineteenth century the percentage of single people declined while the marriage age increased, especially for men. By 1900 the celibacy rate was lower than it had been before, closer to rates in the east than in the west of Europe. The reasons for this decline in celibacy are not difficult to find: they are related to the breakdown of the Old Regime, particularly the decline in the number of lay and monastic clergy, as well as to the abolition of primogeniture *(mayorazgo),* an inheritance system of noble origin that was very widespread in Spain. Until then, *mayorazgo* had been a powerful reason for the celibacy of second-born children, who inherited little or nothing. Reform of inheritance was introduced at the beginning of the nineteenth century: the continued decline in celibacy during the second half of the century seems to have been related to the slow pace of urbanization, for celibacy rates were generally higher in the cities than in rural areas. Faster urban growth in the first decades of the twentieth century turned the trend around, making the celibacy rate rise again.

A rise in the average age at marriage was related in a complex way to economic and legal conditions. On the one hand, increasing prosperity usually brought about earlier marriages. On the other, access to land ownership usually produced the opposite effect, as sons customarily postponed marriage until they themselves became owners. Thus poor journeymen frequently married earlier than well-to-do landowners. A partial democratization of land ownership through the *desamortización* (see Chapter 3) may have contributed to raise the marriage age, and increasing urbanization had the same effect (Reher, 1986). But while the decline in the number of individuals remaining single may have pushed up the birth rate, the postponement of marriage is likely to have acted in the opposite direction. These increases in celibacy and declining nuptiality did not manifest themselves clearly until the twentieth century—another indication of Spain's scant modernization in the nineteenth.

Nicolás Sánchez-Albornoz (1975) finds an interesting indicator of modernization in the seasonality of vital events. Traditional peasant populations adjusted their yearly life cycle to a fairly rigid seasonal calendar: they married in the spring, gave birth in late winter, died of digestive diseases in the summer and of pulmonary diseases in the winter. This type of annual cycle went on unchanged in Spain until well into the second half of the nineteenth century. After that, things started to change gradually: summer deaths began to decline and births became more evenly distributed throughout the year. All these are signs of relative modernization: summer death rates, for instance, were caused by unhygienic conditions and affected mostly infants, so a decline in such deaths is a sign of progress. In turn, winter births were not only the product of amorous "spring fever" but also the result of deliberate calculation to avoid childbirth in the dangerous hot months. As that danger declined, because of improvements in hygiene brought about by development, there was less reason to seek that particular seasonal pattern of births. Industrialization and urbanization, for their part, were also largely independent of the notion of seasonality. Overall, the seasonal pattern of the life cycle in Spain was not completely overcome until well into the twentieth century, and this fluctuation corresponded closely to the rhythm of economic growth.

Migration, Regions, and Cities

In spite of relatively slow population growth, Spain had a considerable outflow of migrants in the second half of the nineteenth century. During the first half, remnants of old mercantilist ideas and the "populationist" mentality of enlightened despotism still presented legal barriers to an exodus which, in any event, would probably not have been substantial. Ideas changed gradually, and the laws relaxed with them. Legislators were doubtless influenced by evidence showing that, on a regional basis, the correlation between population density and prosperity in Spain was more clearly negative than positive. Moreover, it was becoming evident that prosperous countries like England and Prussia were already by mid-century producing an abundant outflow of migrants. One should also add that the increasingly favorable treatment given to immigrants by some Latin American countries, particularly Argentina, also contributed to this change in attitude.

It is difficult to know with any precision the volume of Spanish emigration throughout the nineteenth century, because the first comprehensive statistics were compiled and published only after 1882, when the predecessor of the Instituto Nacional de Emigración was created. Thanks to the work of this office and the corrections made by Sánchez Alonso (1993), we know that the total number of Spanish emigrants between 1882 and 1899 was around one million, an average annual rate of 61,000, while the total outmigration in the first thirteen years of the new century, not counting return migrants, amounted to some two million, at an annual average of 149,000. With the Great War the migratory flow diminished a little, but on average the annual flow in the first thirty years of this century amounts to 141,000, much more than twice the level at the end of the previous century. These figures clearly indicate that the major emigration from Spain took place in the twentieth century, to which the nineteenth century migration seems to have been merely a prologue.

From 1830 to 1880 there was a considerable migratory flow to Argentina, but this cannot be quantified for lack of even the most elementary data; the same can be said about emigration to other foreign parts, again without firm statistical information. Now if we accept the Woodruff figures, that total emigration from Spain amounted to approximately 1.4 million between 1830 and 1900, which would give an annual figure of 20,000 (a credible estimate given that in the decades prior to 1880 the volume of movement must have been much smaller), we can compare the importance of emigration in seven European countries in relation to their total population growth. In Table 2.3 I have determined the impact of emigration in modifying the growth of their respective populations. The relative emigration coefficient for Spain, at 17.7%, figures in the lower range, below Italy and Germany, and we should also keep in mind that Spain's natural increase was the smallest of all the countries except for France, whose demographic and migratory stagnation in the nineteenth century are proverbial.

In conclusion then, Spanish emigration began its expansive phase exactly at the end of the nineteenth century and reached its zenith in the first fifteen years of the twentieth century. Thus, judging by these comparative figures, for a considerable portion of the nineteenth century Spain appears to have been a country with a relatively low migratory pulse, which is to a large extent explained by the slow pace of demographic growth.

There remains, however, one final important factor to take into account when explaining the rhythm of Spanish emigration as we move from one century to the next; that factor is agricultural protectionism. In effect, one of the major causes of emigration at the century's end was the agricultural crisis that ruined landowners and threw out of work many who tilled the land throughout the whole of Europe. The protection of agricultural products against imports, a common reaction in the European countries at that time, reduced this impact, and it is likely that the reduction was greater where protection was strongest. In the Spanish case this argument has been confirmed by the research and analysis of Sánchez Alonso (1993, chap. 5). In effect, the figures on Spanish emigration show that the growing current of emigration in the years 1885 to 1889 was interrupted in the following decade, which coincides with the introduction of the Cánovas tariff in 1891, a measure that was powerfully protective of agriculture. If the migratory flow expanded again after the turn of the century (specifically starting in 1903), this was not due to a change in tariff policy (there was none), but rather to an appreciation of the peseta on the world market that was brought about by the Villaverde stabilization. The depreciation of the peseta in the 1890s, the result of the fiduciary character of Spain's currency (see Chapter 6) and of the inflation caused by the Cuban War of 1898 (also called the Spanish American War), had been operating to reinforce tariff protection by making the cost of imported items ever higher. It seems that this reinforcement had a greater effect on emigration than the tariff itself because, as Sánchez Alonso shows, the period 1891 to 1913 reveals a very high correlation between the world value of the peseta and the migratory outflow.

The combined effect of internal and external migrations, together with the differences in the birth and death rates, produced much faster increases in some regions than in others. Consequently, the geographical distribution of the Spanish population was considerably modified during the nineteenth century. Table 2.4 and Map 2.1 illustrate these movements. Essentially, a trend which had started as long ago as the late Middle Ages continued to operate, namely the movement of population from north to south and the tendency to concentrate on the Mediterranean and the southern Atlantic coasts, including the Canary Islands, while moving out of the central pla-

Table 2.4. Population of Spain by regions, 1787–1900 (in thousands)

Region	(1) 1787	(2) %	(3) 1857	(4) %	(5) 1900	(6) %	(7) % Growth 1787– 1900	(8) Annual growth rate
Andalucía	1,803.6	17.6	2,927.4	18.9	3,549.3	19.1	96.8	0.60
Catalonia	801.6	7.8	1,652.3	10.7	1,966.4	10.6	145.3	0.80
Valencia	771.9	7.5	1,246.5	8.1	1,587.5	8.5	105.7	0.64
Baleares	176.2	1.7	262.9	1.7	311.6	1.7	76.8	0.51
Canarias	167.2	1.6	234.0	1.5	358.6	1.9	114.5	0.68
Murcia	332.5	3.2	381.0	2.5	578.0	3.1	73.8	0.49
SOUTH	4,053.0	39.5	6,704.1	43.4	8,351.4	44.9	106.1	0.64
Asturias	345.8	3.4	524.5	3.4	627.1	3.4	81.3	0.53
Cantabria	128.3	1.3	214.4	1.4	276.0	1.5	115.1	0.68
Galicia	1,340.2	13.1	1,776.9	11.5	1,980.5	10.7	47.8	0.35
Basque Country	304.7	3.0	413.5	2.7	603.6	3.2	98.1	0.61
NORTH	2,119.0	20.7	2,929.3	19.0	3,487.2	18.8	64.6	0.44
Extremadura	412.0	4.0	707.1	4.6	882.4	4.7	114.2	0.68
Aragón	614.1	6.0	880.6	5.7	912.7	4.9	48.6	0.35
Madrid	205.8	2.0	475.8	3.1	775.0	4.2	276.6	1.18
Castile-Mancha	918.2	9.0	1,203.3	7.8	1,386.2	7.5	51.0	0.37
Castile-León	1,704.6	16.6 ⎱	2,083.1	13.5	2,302.4	12.4	35.1	0.27
Rioja	—	— ⎰	173.8	1.1	189.4	1.0	9.0	0.20
Navarra	224.5	2.2	297.4	1.9	307.7	1.7	37.1	0.28
CENTER	4,079.2	39.8	5,821.1	37.7	6,755.8	36.3	65.6	0.45
TOTAL	10,251.2	100.0	15,454.5	100.0	18,594.4	100.0	81.4	0.53

Sources: Estadísticas Históricas de España, siglos XIX-XX, (ed.) Carreras (1989), and my own calculations

teau. Indeed, the attraction of the southern and eastern coasts is perfectly rational from an economic point of view, as the land was more fertile and communications easier in the coastal regions than in the mountainous interior. There are indications that this was the pattern of Hispanic population settlement in antiquity, but this colonization had been interrupted by the Reconquest in the eleventh to the thirteenth centuries and the Black Death in the fourteenth. During the modern and contemporary periods a gradual process had been set in motion that was restoring the ancient equilibrium.

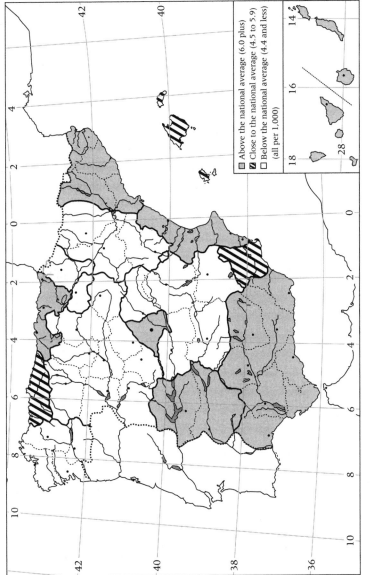

Map 2.1.   Regional demographic growth, nineteenth century

Above the national average (6.0 plus)

Close to the national average (4.5 to 5.9)

Below the national average (4.4 and less)
(all per 1,000)

Table 2.4 shows that the proportion of population in the Mediterranean and south Atlantic areas increased from 39.5% to 45% during the nineteenth century, while that of the north Atlantic zone fell somewhat, by 2%. It was the central zone that clearly lost relative weight within the national total, despite notable increases in Extremadura and the province of Madrid. Columns 7 and 8 in the table show growth rates in the period 1787 to 1900, by regions. Column 7 shows absolute percentage increases, and column 8 reduces those figures to annual averages. The average growth rate for the whole of Spain over this whole period was 5.3 per 1,000; in general, rates for the southern and Mediterranean regions were higher, those for the central areas were lower (except for Madrid) and the north Atlantic regions (except for Galicia) were about average. The map confirms these calculations.

Parallel to these changes in vital rates and population distribution, which amount to a real though very gradual modernization, another transformation was taking place, migration from the countryside to the towns. But as with all the major demographic and economic trends that begin in the nineteenth century, the full force of urbanization in Spain was to be experienced in the twentieth. At the end of the nineteenth century only two cities in Spain (Barcelona and Madrid) had as many as half a million people, while Europe at large contained 25 such cities, of which seven had more than a million inhabitants. Although some Spanish cities grew spectacularly at the end of the nineteenth century, Barcelona, Bilbao, and Gijón for example, most of their starting populations were very small. Even so, "this rhythm remains outdistanced with respect to other countries" (Reher, 1986) such as England, Germany, and even France and Italy. In general terms, the demographic behavior of city dwellers differed from that of rural dwellers. As in other countries, the city dwellers exhibited lower mortality, lower nuptiality, and lower fertility, all indications of modernization. But the relative weight of the urban population in Spain remained so small that the demographic transition, except in Catalonia, was postponed until the twentieth century.

In 1900 the majority of the Spanish population continued to be rural, both occupationally and demographically. Fifty-one percent of people lived in settlements of fewer than 5,000 persons and 91% in settlements under 100,000 persons. Only 9% of persons could really consider themselves to be urban residents. Except for Madrid, almost all the towns of any importance were on the periphery: Barcelona, Valencia, Seville, Cádiz, Málaga, Vigo, La Coruña, Oviedo, Gijón, Santander, and Bilbao.

The one exception to the general situation within the Spanish setting is Catalonia, as much in matters demographic as in others. While Spain as a whole continued throughout the nineteenth century to approximate a demographic model that was very close to that of the Old Regime, the Catalán population was developing its own demographic cycle that resembled the position in the advanced countries. The Catalán population grew very substantially from the beginning of the eighteenth century, increasing from 7% to 11% of the Spanish total between 1717 and 1857. But the rate of growth began to fall already in the second half of the nineteenth century, and from then on Catalonia's share of Spain's total population remained static until quite recently, and it was only in the second half of the twentieth century that it began to increase again significantly within the Spanish total.

As Nicolau indicates, "the demographic growth of Catalonia was probably as intense as that of England and Wales during the seventeen hundreds and the first half of the eighteen hundreds,"[7] but the determinants were not exactly the same. Catalán mortality was much higher, and thus the remarkable growth during this period is explained almost entirely by an increase in births, which in turn was due to an increase in marital fertility. And that, in its turn, occurred because of a modification in the marriage model. According to Nicolau, all this was determined by economic changes; the growth of commerce and industry already by the second half of the eighteenth century had altered the situation in the countryside. One of the social consequences of the structural transformation of the Catalán rural world at the end of the old regime was the collapse of the traditional marriage norms. The opportunity of finding salaried work in commercial agriculture or in rural industry diminished the importance of owning property in order to be able to marry and facilitated a greater number of marriages and at earlier ages. Thus, although mortality and natality were somewhat higher, the Catalán case had much in common with the British experience: while in the rest of Spain economic stagnation perpetuated the traditional demographic pattern, in Catalonia economic change clearly stimulated the demographic transition.

And finally, the occupational structure of the Catalán population too shows the effect of progress. In Spain, as Pérez Moreda has shown (1985), the proportion of the population working in agriculture did not change in the nineteenth century. In Catalonia, however, it declined constantly from mid-century onwards. Employment increased most in industry and commerce. Perhaps to the surprise of some, the sector that grew fastest in relation to Spain as a whole was in fact commerce, and the Catalans represented almost one-quarter (23.6%) of all the Spaniards who listed that as their occupation in the 1910 census. It was about the same for industry, where the Catalans represented 22.5% of the whole industrial manpower of Spain. It would surprise no one to learn that in textiles this figure amounted to 71%. Other industries with high Catalán manpower concentrations were leather goods and woodworking, both 38%, and chemicals, 28%.

Human Capital

But population does not just grow quantitatively; it also grows qualitatively, in various aspects. Its age composition changes, as well as its geographical and occupational distribution. So also does the coefficient of educational endowment—a crucial factor of production whose importance has been pointed out by outstanding economists, Adam Smith in particular. The modern "human capital" school of thought views education strictly as a capital investment made by a nation, society, family, or individual to improve future production or earning capacity and thereby their well-being. Obviously, education has more facets and offers more values than the strictly economic, although they may all be closely interrelated.

Technology, or the appropriate set of production techniques, a field that is very closely related to that of education *per se,* is of fundamental importance to economic growth. One of the early scholars who discussed this, Robert Solow, called it "the residual factor" since it is neither land, labor, nor physical capital. Although it is difficult to measure, its importance is widely recognized today because, in one way or another, it affects all of the more easily measured physical factors. Two aspects of technology interest us here. One is technological innovation in the Schumpeterian sense, broadly defined as a change in the productive system which increases factor productivity. The other is the capacity of populations and societies to adopt technological innovation, what has been called "technological diffusion." Schumpeter assumed that the diffusion of technological innovations would happen almost automatically: competition would see to it that, in relatively short periods of time, businessmen would adopt the latest and best technology. Economic historians have proved, however, that the adoption of new techniques, a process that has been shown to be crucial for development, is far from automatic. There are serious obstacles that we can classify into two groups: those dependent upon resource endowment and those that relate to the institutional framework. Economists understand the first set far better than the second, but within the second set education certainly occupies pride of place. It seems very clear that general education, or investment in human capital, is a great stimulus to economic innovation, in the sense both of inventiveness itself and of the more subtle aspects that relate to a society's capacity to absorb and adopt appropriate technologies.

In the case of Spain it is obvious that the country reached the modern era grossly underequipped educationally, with a deficit in terms of human capital formation. For centuries Spanish science and philosophy had been far from the forefront. The educational system was in a shambles from the seventeenth century onwards and collapsed completely in the terrible crisis at the beginning of the nineteenth, despite the meritorious but largely ineffectual efforts of the private institutions collectively known as Sociedades Económicas de Amigos del País, private organizations created in the eighteenth century by the upper classes to promote the welfare of the country. Government officials and educators launched a serious effort aimed at cultural and scientific reconstruction in the middle of the nineteenth century. Backed by the educators, the legislators passed the Moyano Law imposing educational reform, while the educators founded the Institución Libre de Enseñanza, a private educational institution. The Moyano reform established the bases of the state educational system as we know it today, although it has been considerably modified, particularly in the twentieth century.

Instruction was provided at three levels: elementary or primary; secondary, *bachillerato* or high school; and tertiary or higher education, largely at the university level. The poet Manuel José Quintana presided over the commission that issued the Quintana Report in 1813. It was a compendium of the educational ideology of Spanish liberalism, imbued with the ideas of Jovellanos, the precepts of the 1812 Constitution, and the ideas of contemporary liberal French philosophers. The Quintana Report established the principle of general and free education, and the state's responsibility in this; it also drew up the plan for a university structure with a central university located in Madrid, which was to be "a center of enlightenment that people would be drawn to, an outstanding model [for the rest] to imitate" and the only institution dedicated to serious research, whereas the other universities would be more like professional schools. Their liberal ideology drove the reformers to seek to remove theology from the university proper, relegating it to the religious seminaries, and the Revolution of 1868 did just that. Although the principles were established early enough, the actual reform of education was carried out only with the greatest difficulty, generally in those periods when the Liberals held power. Primary education, the only sector that could be considered subject to the principles of "free and universal," and even here applied only partially, remained in the hands of the municipal governments, which took on the task in an irregular and uneven fashion (Núñez, 1992). As far as secondary education was concerned, the state admitted a *de facto* position of sharing responsibility for it with the Church, which assumed the greater part of this teaching since the religious colleges educated approximately two-thirds of all secondary students, although only one in ten primary students took that route.

University education was reorganized during the Liberal Triennium, 1820–1823; in the 1830s by the Progressive governments, and again in the 1840s by the Moderado governments. In this sphere the principle of exclusiveness in public education survived, the notion that there should be one exclusive provider. Centralism ruled: the Central University of Madrid was founded in 1822 and Alcalá University was annexed to it in 1838; today's incongruous title of the Universidad Complutense de Madrid derives from that event.[8] Nine other universities, the number proposed by Quintana in 1813, were founded during the nineteenth century. The Moyano Law, in reality, did little more than recast the miscellaneous pieces of legislation that had been gradually emerging within the original educational system that Quintana had proposed.

The Institución Libre de Enseñanza of 1876, known simply by its devotees as the Institución, was the crowning work of a group of intellectuals called Krausistas. They, since the 1840s, had constituted the most creative and original current of Spanish intellectual endeavor, one could almost say the only one during this period. The Institución, which in principle was not only a private entity but also a refuge for professors who wished to repudiate the doctrinal authoritarianism of Cánovas and his Minister, Orovio, came to wield considerable influence over state educational policy: from 1881 until the Civil War its influence over scientific and intellectual life was much greater than anyone could have hoped for, given its modest origins and its scant resources; its impact, out of all proportion to its size and means, constitutes a classical example of the power of human capital.

But all this arrived so very late. Too much time was wasted in getting from the principles to an effective administrative system, and even then the system was applied at a desperately slow pace and with serious defects. The class basis of society was clearly reflected in the structure of education. The work of the Institución could scarcely reach out beyond the urban elites. Public expenditure on education remained at a standstill during the greater part of the century, and of this expenditure the lion's share was reserved for higher education, almost exclusively for the benefit of the upper class. After that came the secondary system. Primary education, the basic, the most productive in a backward country, the only sector accessible to the majority of the population, was not truly universal until the twentieth century. Rates for school attendance, although growing in the long run, were below 50% during the whole of the nineteenth century.

As a consequence of these priorities, the literacy rate, a simple and reliable indicator of human capital formation in a country in the first stages of development, remained very low, although it crept up throughout the nineteenth century. In 1860 less than 30% of the adult population was literate, and even by 1900 not quite one adult Spaniard in two could read. How much of an obstacle this was to economic progress is easy to surmise. C. E. Núñez (1992) has shown that for Spain in this period there is a strong correlation at the provincial level between literacy rates and rising incomes. Vizcaya, Guipúzcoa, Barcelona, Alava, Valladolid, Oviedo, Santander, and to a lesser extent Zaragoza, Navarra, the Balearic Islands, and Valencia are the provinces where literacy and income rose most rapidly. And if the crude literacy rate is a good indicator of income per capita, it is even better when we add the gender differential, that is, the difference between male and female literacy rates. Thus we find that higher literacy meant higher income, but for a given level of overall literacy, income was lower where female literacy was lower. This is natural enough; progress has always been produced by change and thus through learning, through apprenticeship. Since the majority of the population was unable to read and write, and given that the written word is even today the most frequent vehicle of information transmission (regardless of the diffusion of electronic methods), the goal of universal education came up against almost insurmountable barriers. The skeptic might ask, if most of the working population was male, why would it matter that women did or did not know how to read? The answer is obvious: the influence of mothers and wives on the education of children and the general behavior of the family is so important that it is clearly reflected in national income levels. In the words of the Quintana Report, "in the dictionary of reason, [the words] ignorant and slave are synonymous"; in the dictionary of economics, the equation is between ignorance and poverty.

CHAPTER 3

Agriculture: Persistent Underdevelopment

During the nineteenth century, agriculture was the most important economic activity in Spain, at least from a purely quantitative standpoint. In 1900, two-thirds of the Spanish labor force worked in agriculture; without doubt more than half of the national income was generated in this sector. Furthermore, agriculture and livestock occupied a predominant place in commercial export, and this in spite of the crisis in wine production and the boom in mining in the last decades of the century. Hence whatever happened in agriculture had, perforce, to be of fundamental significance for the country and its economy.

Contemporary scholars tend to attach great importance to economic progress in the agricultural sector as a precursor of industrial development; that is, they tend to agree that, at least before the twentieth century, the agricultural revolution was an essential precursor of the industrial revolution. More specifically, the argument is that agricultural progress in the sense of a sustained increase in agricultural production and productivity contributes to industrialization in three distinct ways. First, it produces a surplus food supply to feed the cities whose growth is an inherent part of the industrialization process. Second, agricultural progress permits demographic growth and spurs an exodus of rural population to the cities, which, far from reducing food production, often tends to produce an increase in the available surplus, so that the countryside both creates the industrial proletariat and feeds it. And third, the countryside constitutes the most extensive market for the industrial production that originates in the cities. Beyond these three essential functions, agriculture contributes, at least in part, to the process of capital accumulation from profits created from commercialization of the home market and from exports. As we shall see, Spanish agriculture was in no way able to fulfill these functions in a satisfactory manner.

Agricultural stagnation explains, at least in part, the lateness of Spain's economic modernization.[1] And in turn this stagnation can be attributed to natural and geographic features, what Jovellanos called physical obstacles, and to social and cultural factors, which he called moral and political obstacles. Later on we shall say something about geographic factors. On social and cultural features, suffice it to indicate here the unequal distribution of land in Spain. This existed from time immemorial, but there was one particular consequence of the colonization that occurred under the Reconquest, whereby a small number of aristocratic families and ecclesiastical entities emerged as owners of exceedingly large properties in the south of the Iberian Peninsula. The consequence of this distribution of agricultural property was extreme poverty for most of the country people and extreme wealth and power among the aristocratic *latifundistas*. One should not forget, however, that although the Spanish case was perhaps extreme in Europe, in almost all the other continental countries preindustrial land ownership exhibited similar characteristics. Eventually, in almost all of Europe some kind of property reform occurred that permitted the introduction of technical improvements and expanded production. Thus in sixteenth-century England it was the dissolution of the monasteries, and in eighteenth-century France it was the land reform following the French Revolution, to cite the two best known cases. A similar kind of reform was implemented in Spain, called *desamortización* (an approximate English equivalent would be "disentailment" or "disentail").

Desamortización

The real importance of the sale of Church lands has been the subject of a great deal of controversy. For Simón Segura it is the great event of the nineteenth century. Not so for Miguel Artola, because the amount of money it brought to the state was less than had been estimated.[2] However, the money that changed hands is only one of the consequences; as we shall see, the land area that changed hands was very considerable, and that should also be taken into account.

Furthermore, the importance of *desamortización* is not limited to a question of money or acreage. It was a measure that touched almost every sphere of social and economic life: agriculture, the peasantry, the Treasury, investment, social classes, the law, and political structure. In this last respect, it has also been hotly debated whether the *desamortización* constituted, or was closely related to, the bourgeois revolution. The question is interesting, but a rigorous analysis shows it to be artificial or more strictly speaking, nominalist. Everything would depend upon the definition of "bourgeois revolution." Here, we are not interested in questions of definition or classification, but in issues which are conceptually simpler. How did the *desamortización* affect the distribution of wealth and income, how did it affect production and productivity in agriculture, and what were the repercussions for the Treasury?

In its broad outlines, the Spanish land reform followed the model of that of the French Revolution, although already in the eighteenth century some timid steps towards *desamortización* had been taken, and the advisability of taking land out of mortmain had been widely debated since the reign of Carlos III (Herr, 1958 and 1989). In essence this eighteenth-century "liberal agrarian reform" consisted of the expropriation, with compensation, of a large portion of the land and buildings belonging to the Church and the municipalities. These expropriated lands ("nationalized" in the French terminology) were later sold at public auction and the proceeds constituted a substantial fraction of the income in the state budget (see Chapter 7).

The problems that the *desamortización* tried to resolve were of very long standing. The fact that large real estate assets were held in mortmain had already been recognized by eighteenth-century thinkers (Olavide, Campomanes, Jovellanos, among others) as one of the major social problems that contributed to Spain's backwardness. In the terminology of the period, the term "mortmain," *manos muertas,* was applied to the owners of properties that were inalienable, that is, that could not be sold. The characteristic example was the *mayorazgo,* an indivisible property that went from oldest son to oldest son, but most Church properties were also inalienable and could not be sold. Since such goods could not be disposed of nor divided, they could never be made smaller; they could, however, be added to. Already at the time of Carlos III people had begun to think about curtailing the growth of mortmain and putting some of these properties into circulation. As Tomás y Valiente indicates (1971, p. 31), in the eighteenth century no one thought in terms of expropriating lands from the Church, only of limiting the Church's potential for further acquisitions. The enlightened thinkers of the eighteenth century could conceive of the sale of properties owned by the clergy only through negotiations with the Holy See. It was quite another matter when it came to properties belonging to municipalities, which were considered to be under royal jurisdiction. Already during the reign of Carlos III, decrees had been issued requiring municipalities in parts of Extremadura and Andalucía to make some of their common or uncultivated waste lands available for the use of poor local peasants. The measure, however timely and well-intentioned, did not provide the relief that proponents had hoped for, and in the end it was repealed, very probably because of opposition from powerful local residents.

At the end of the eighteenth century and the beginning of the nineteenth, under the powerful aegis of Godoy, the first expropriations of Church properties took place "by a unilateral decision on the part of the state" (Tomás y Valiente, 1971); these properties were put up for sale, and the income from them went to pay off national debt bonds. The years of Godoy's influence were indeed years of serious deficit for the Spanish Treasury, and that indebtedness was responsible for the continual recourse to the seizure of municipal and ecclesiastical properties to remedy the state's financial crises. According to Herr's calculations, between 1798 and 1808 sales amounted to 1,600 million *reales,* a very high figure that reveals the true magnitude of the operation set in motion in the reign of Carlos IV.[3]

There was a further wave of sales of mortmain properties during the reign of Joseph Bonaparte, above all of properties belonging to the clergy and the aristocrats who opposed French control. More than collect funds for the Treasury, the aim of this operation seems to have been to favor (though eventually it ended up by compromising) Bonaparte's supporters, the *afrancesados,* people like Javier de Burgos, Mariano Luis de Urquijo, or Juan Antonio Llorente, all of them buyers of disentailed properties. The amount of sales under the Bonaparte disentail is not known, but it seems probable that the greater part of the properties acquired this way eventually found their way back to the former owners.

From the time of the Civil War of Independence onwards, the *desamortización* became one of the great burning political questions of the period, dividing Progressives and Conservatives throughout the nineteenth century. I find it interesting that even today many historians approach the theme with a partisan attitude.

On September 13, 1813, the Cortes issued a general decree on *desamortización* that was based upon a report by José Canga Argüelles. The decree provided for the nationalization of a body of real estate properties which comprised items confiscated from traitors (read *afrancesados),* from the Jesuits, from religious militant orders (land granted by the Crown at the time of the Reconquest), and from monasteries and convents that had been disbanded or destroyed during the war; to this add part of the Crown's property and half of all wastelands and lands directly under royal jurisdiction. All these properties could now be bought, in part with cash and in part with government bonds. In fact the decree was never implemented, for it was blocked by Fernando VII's coup d'état in 1814 (it was reinstated later under the Triennium). However, it already contained the essential elements of the broad measures that were adopted during the nineteenth century: the auction of national properties and the recognition of national debt bonds as a form of payment. That is to say, disentailment was conceived as a fiscal measure, not as an element of agricultural reform; it was intended to restore balance to the national Treasury by paying off the national debt, rather than to redistribute land to poor rural peasants. As a fiscal measure, it favored the middle and upper classes and holders of the national debt, and it did not favor (in fact it often harmed) the poor, who had formerly been able to benefit, in a more or less clandestine manner, from using both Church and common lands.

After the death of Fernando VII, the legislation on disentailment is voluminous, as indicated by the compilation of heavy legal tomes called Disentail Manuals. However, the fundamental norms are contained in a number of laws which can be counted on the fingers of one hand, and most of the land reform took place in certain well defined historic periods.

The disentailment of Church properties was carried out in two consecutive stages. The properties of the religious orders were nationalized and their sale was ordered in 1836 by a decree of February 19 issued by Prime Minister Juan Alvarez Mendizábal, whom the Cortes had empowered several weeks earlier. This decree was preceded and followed by various others which prepared, complemented, or clarified issues. But the importance of this lies not so much in the legislation as in the policy that was giving rise to these changes. The 1836 disentail was the keystone, the principal element of Mendizábal's three-pronged program: to finance the war against the Carlist party, at that point at the height of its political and military power; to return the Treasury to good health; and to create, in Mendizábal's own words, "a copious family of property owners" materially interested in the triumph of the Liberal cause. This idea had already been behind the aborted disentail attempted by Joseph Bonaparte, and it had guided the first great land reform of the French Revolution. Moreover, the confiscation of Church property in Protestant countries in the sixteenth century can be seen as an antecedent of disentail in the Catholic countries. The sale of nationalized properties went ahead quite expeditiously, although political and military ups and downs during the war certainly influenced the rhythm of events. During the five years following the Mendizábal decree, sales amounted to approximately 1,700 millions *reales,* some 430 million pesetas; unfortunately another figure that would interest us here, that is, the number of hectares that were sold, is not known and cannot be calculated from the value of the sales.

In 1841, under the regency of General Baldomero Espartero, a new and fundamental law was issued that expanded the real estate legislation; the law of 2 September 1841 included nonmonastic Church properties among those subject to nationalization, that is, expropriation. By this law all estates of the Spanish Church were considered subject to disentailment, excluding the monasteries which had already been affected by the Mendizábal legislation. Sales proceeded apace, including properties that had belonged to the Church and the monasteries, but in 1844 the Moderado party returned to power, and sales were practically suspended until the Pascual Madoz reform. Total sales during the period 1836–1844 amounted to 3,447 million *reales,* 862 million pesetas (Simón Segura, 1973, p. 152), equivalent to roughly three-fifths of total Church wealth in 1836 (see Table 3.1).

The so-called Madoz Law was promulgated on May 1, 1855, and con-

Table 3.1. Value of properties disentailed during the nineteenth century (in million *reales*)

Period	(1) Church	(2) Charitable institutions	(3) Government	(4) Others	(5) Total
1798–1814		1.505	0	0	1,505
1836–1844	3,447	0	0	0	3,447
1855–1856	324	167	160	116	767
1858–1867	1,253	461	1,998	438	4,150
1868–1900	888[a]	327[a]	1,415[a]	309[a]	2,939
Total (1836–1900)	5,912	955	3,573	863	11,303
Grand Total[b]		8,372	3,573	863	12,808

a. The allocation of properties among Church, charitable institutions, government and others is estimated on the basis of percentages in the earlier period

b. This does not include sales during the Liberal Triennium, which according to Fontana amounted to some 100 million *reales*

Source: Herr (1974), with minor modifications. Fontana (1973), pp. 178–179, presents a similar picture

trolled the last and most important stage of this great liquidation of entailed lands. It was referred to as the "law of general disentail" because it redefined the properties that were subject to disentailment. The new definition covered all properties under mortmain, that is, state and municipal lands in addition to Church properties. In short, the main aim of the legislation was to sell all real estate which did not belong to private individuals. Although subjected to minor changes, interruptions, and occasional suspensions, the Madoz Law remained in force until the twentieth century, and under its aegis practically all of the formerly entailed property was sold. In fact, the greater part of what could be disposed of had been sold before the Restoration. Of the 11,300 million *reales* (roughly 2,835 million pesetas) worth of national properties that were sold between 1836 and the end of the century, 4,900 million were sold between 1855 and 1867, and we have seen that between 1836 and 1844 sales had amounted to 3,447 million. This means that by the end of 1867 three-quarters of the formerly entailed national lands has been sold, for 8,300 million *reales.* Of the 3,000 million remaining, more than 2,000 millions were sold before 1876. From that date onwards sales were, comparatively speaking, merely a trickle, and in no year did the total value exceed 75 million *reales.*

How did disentailment affect the structure of land ownership? The most widespread opinion among people who have studied the matter is that it promoted the formation of large land holdings, thereby aggravating the unequal distribution of agrarian property. This thesis, however, is quite difficult to test empirically, for we lack the data which would allow us to measure the relative importance of large land holdings before and after disentailment: at present, for instance, we cannot compare the concentration of land ownership around 1800 with the same variable at the end of the nineteenth century. We do not have the necessary information. In the absence of objective evidence, historians have based their opinions on the mechanism through which expropriation was carried out. Disentailed lands were clearly not redistributed in accordance with principles of equity, but rather with the purpose of maximizing Treasury revenues in the shortest possible time. Properties were sold at public auction to the highest bidder. This implies that the buyers had to be people of means, able to outbid their competitors, and that the disentail did nothing for the poor peasants who most needed the land. This claim seems unassailable, although it is difficult to support with figures because the data available to us are far from clear. However, it is a considerable step to conclude from this that ownership became more unevenly distributed than before. It is one thing to say that the people who bought the land were wealthy; it is quite another to argue that the buyers were so few in number as to equal the number of former proprietors. The thesis stated this way seems difficult to sustain.

The research done so far appears to support the statement that the buyers of disentailed land were well-to-do, or at least of comfortable means in economic terms: aristocrats, military officers, civil servants, clergymen, rural landowners (*labradores*), merchants, and businessmen. Even here, however, one must rely upon fragmentary sources, for the profession of the buyer was only occasionally cited in the documents. On the question of how disentail affected the distribution of property ownership, the most solid work has been done by Richard Herr. Given the fragmentary character of the sources, he has chosen to deal with local cases rather than with the whole country or even large regions. Herr's work on the provinces of Salamanca and Jaén[4] fully supports his thesis that disentailment did not introduce any fundamental modification in the structure of ownership; in other words, though land changed hands from the Church and the municipalities to lay private owners, this did not bring about either increased concentration or significant dispersion of holdings. In villages where large landowners and absentees predominated, disentailed estates largely ended up in the hands of similar kinds of owners; in villages where ownership was not so concentrated, the lands put on sale were distributed more uniformly. Of course the Herr thesis is based upon relatively small samples both in space and in time (villages in Salamanca and Jaén, 1798–1808), but his statistical results appear very convincing.

Herr's (1974) view is that the most important effect of disentail was neither political nor social but economic. In his opinion, the main significance of the reform was that it brought into cultivation large tracts of land which had formerly been poorly cultivated, underutilized, or idle. And this increase in the area under cultivation was needed to feed a population that had been growing slowly but continuously since the beginning of the eighteenth century. Population pressure had brought about steady increases in food prices, and thereby in the price of land itself, and this made the land an increasingly attractive proposition as a solution to the Treasury's overwhelming fiscal problems. Disentail was thus the single stone which could thus kill two rather threatening birds: food scarcity and famine on the one hand, and a state of chronic financial crisis on the other. To Herr the proof that disentail was more an economic solution than an ideological issue lies in the fact that it was implemented by conservatives and liberals alike, by Carlos IV in 1798 and Mendizábal in 1836, and then by Madoz and the Liberals in 1855. With the constant rise in the price of land, disentail undoubtedly was good business for the wealthy and also for the aristocracy, whose lands were taken out of mortmain but not expropriated. It was probably the land-owning nobility that benefited most: in exchange for some seigniorial rights which often were purely symbolic, they obtained full title to lands that, strictly speaking, did not previously belong to them. Furthermore, they were often able to round out their properties under favorable terms. Where this occurred, the land holdings were probably expanded, although where Church lands were dispossessed, the opposite may have been the case.

The victims of *desamortización* were the Church, the municipalities, poor peasants, and the agricultural proletariat. The first, for obvious reasons. And municipalities suffered too because many of them had been able to benefit from ecclesiastical or common properties, either as a kind of charity or else renting mountainous terrain for little money and using it for pasture. The clear losers were the poor farmers and peasants, who had long encroached upon Church and public lands and had a more difficult time after these lands became private. In their plight historians have seen the social origins of the rural rebellions under the banners of Carlism or anarchism that periodically erupted during the nineteenth century. It is a reasonable hypothesis.

Production and Productivity

How did this gigantic real estate operation affect agriculture? Undoubtedly the impact was huge. In the end, the extent of the land sold is estimated, very provisionally, at some 10 million hectares, 20% of the whole Spanish territory but 50% of the cultivated part (Simón Segura, 1973, p. 282). Herr puts the value of this land at between 25% and 33% of the total value of Spanish real estate. Even admitting that not all of the disentailed land was arable, a transfer of ownership from mortmain to private buyers of such a considerable proportion of the land must have led to a large expansion in cultivation and production.

The explanation that is most commonly given is that the institutional landowners—the Church, the state, and the townships—were not very efficient managers, for reasons that Jovellanos had already outlined in his famous *Informe sobre la Ley Agraria:* the private proprietor is more efficient. According to this view, large amounts of land in the hands of the Church or the Crown lay untilled for lack of capital or entrepreneurship. The private owner considers the land as an investment, a productive asset. In trying to obtain the maximum benefit from it, he would exploit it more rationally, and thus more efficiently.

This reasoning is only convincing in certain circumstances, however. If the private owner is a large landowner who bought additional land for reasons of prestige, he might simply leave the former cultivation regime as was. Or the new buyer's only interest might be speculative, based upon the hope of rising land prices. Finally, newly purchased lands might remain uncultivated or be poorly tended, if the new proprietor lacked the necessary capital or technical knowledge to bring about the necessary changes or improvements. On the other hand, public owners could (and in fact did) rent out their lands to farmers and tenants who, if the leases were long enough and stable enough, would normally behave much like private owners. However, in much of Spain, with the exception of Galicia, Asturias, Catalonia, and Valencia, the leases of mortmain and entailed lands were relatively short, less than 10 years (García Sanz and Garrabou, 1985, p. 22), so one might surmise that cultivation would be relatively inefficient.

In conclusion, although it seems logical to assume that disentailment brought about an expansion in the cultivated acreage and better agricultural practices, it should not be considered axiomatic. Other factors, such as the abolition of the tithe, the suppression of the Mesta, the slow but undeniable improvement in transportation and communications, the decidedly protectionist policies in favor of grain cultivation after 1820, and the slow sustained increase in total population may all have exercised equal or even more powerful pressures to extend cultivation and to intensify methods than did changes in the property structure.

In fact, we still know very little about what happened to Spanish agriculture throughout the nineteenth century. The tithe was definitively abolished in the 1830s; indeed, in many areas its collection had already been discontinued during the War of Independence, and without the tithe the historian is deprived of a very useful source to estimate the volume of the most important agricultural crops. Until the end of the century no official body was organized to assemble reliable statistical materials on agriculture, so that information on the amount of cultivated land and output prior to 1900 is partial and hypothetical. The government did attempt to estimate agricultural output and acreage for the year 1857 (Table 3.2), but its authors themselves dismissed these estimates as too low. In fact, they might have been closer to reality than the authors thought, given that 1857 was a year

Table 3.2. Production and yields of Spanish agriculture in 1857

Commodity	(1) Area in thousand hectares	(2) Yield in thousand hectoliters	(3) Yield in hectoliters per hectare	(4) Yield in quintals[a] per hectare	(5) Quintals per hectoliter	(6) Production in thousand tons	(7) Percent of average for the decade
Wheat	2,925	17,192	5.87	4.57	0.78	1,338	56
Barley	1,273	10,086	7.92	4.51	0.57	574	—
Rye	1,185	5,995	5.05	3.64	0.72	432	90
Corn	368	3,448	9.36	7.02	0.75	259	68
Chickpeas	218	520	2.38	—			
Rice	29	268	9.17	—			
Wine	1,143	5,405	4.72	—			
Olive Oil	800	998	1.24	—			
Potatoes (tons)	204	467	2.29	22.90			

a. 1 quintal = 46 kgs.

Sources: cols. 1–4: Junta General de Estadística, see Tortella (1985), pp. 76–8; cols. 5–6: calculated from the above; col. 7: calculated from col. 6 and from Table 3.3

of agricultural crisis. The yields per hectare, productivity, and consumption per capita that these estimates imply are certainly on the low side, but when we compare them with the figures we have for the late nineteenth and early twentieth centuries they reveal an order of magnitude that is not at all unlikely. Column 7 compares figures from the Statistical Committee with ten-year averages derived from Simpson's estimates.

To derive production series for the principal Spanish crops during the nineteenth century we have to rely, at least for the time being, on indirect methods. Some recent attempts have been made in this direction, concretely by James Simpson (1985 and 1989) and Leandro Prados de la Escosura (1988, chap. 3). Simpson's method seems to be the most reliable and also the simpler. Starting with figures from one of the first censuses of production, the *Censo de Frutos y Manufacturas* of 1799 and other sources, Simpson has estimated per capita food consumption at the beginning of the nineteenth century; by relating these estimates to those obtained from official statistical sources for the early twentieth century, and making some assumptions about the way food consumption evolved, Simpson has arrived at the estimates which are summarized in Table 3.3 and converted to index numbers in Table 3.4.

What these figures reveal is a modest growth in total agricultural output until the end of the century. In per capita terms there was virtual stagnation until the last quarter of the century, when competition from foreign cereals stimulated emigration, changes in production methods, and increased productivity. The pattern of change was not uniform for all products. Wheat production grew faster than total output until the 1870s, when foreign competition caused rearrangements in the output mix, so that other crops such as maize, oranges, and fruits in general increased at a faster rate. In contrast, rye and other inferior, less popular grains like millet and sorghum stagnated relatively and in some cases absolutely.

Although the output mix changed somewhat at the end of the century, one can say with some assurance that the basic structure of Spanish agriculture remained essentially stable throughout the nineteenth century. It was a typically Mediterranean structure, based on grains, especially wheat, olive trees, and grapevines. Around 1890, these three crops (plus legumes, of lesser importance) occupied 90% of the arable land and produced about 80% of the total value of agricultural output, excluding forests and livestock. Of grain and vegetables, which together accounted for close to 75% of the land and 55% of the output, the production of wheat represented about

Table 3.3. Estimated agricultural production, averages for decades, 1800–1899

Period	(1) Wheat (in thousand tons)	(2) Rye (in thousand tons)	(3) Corn (in thousand tons)	(4) Rice (in thousand tons)	(5) Production in million pesetas at 1900 value	(6) Population (in millions)
1800–9	1,643	376	208	25	2,400	11.14
1810–9	1,722	383	229	34	2,468	11.45
1820–9	1,801	390	252	43	2,562	11.84
1830–9	1,938	408	282	54	2,722	12.51
1840–9	2,165	444	328	71	2,993	13.72
1850–9	2,404	481	379	93	3,287	15.08
1860–9	2,584	504	421	111	3,450	15.92
1870–9	2,778	514	457	124	3,666	16.50
1880–9	2,712	533	502	139	3,931	17.32
1890–9	2,816	550	547	166	4,254	18.01
Per capita (in kilograms and pesetas)						
1800	147.49	33.75	18.67	2.24	215.44	
1810	150.39	33.45	20.00	2.97	215.55	
1820	152.11	32.94	21.28	3.63	216.39	
1830	154.92	32.61	22.54	4.32	217.59	
1840	157.80	32.36	23.91	5.17	218.15	
1850	159.42	31.90	25.13	6.17	217.97	
1860	162.31	31.66	26.44	6.97	216.71	
1870	168.36	31.15	27.70	7.52	222.18	
1880	156.58	30.77	28.98	8.03	226.96	
1890	156.36	30.54	30.37	9.22	236.20	

Sources: Simpson (1985a), (1989)

one half, so that as a rule of thumb one can assume that wheat output was between 25 and 30% of agricultural production and occupied between 35 and 40% of the total cultivated area. Table 3.5 shows this structure for the last years of the century, a period for which we have more reliable statistics.

Table 3.5 also reveals some of the effects of the great agricultural depression at the end of the nineteenth century, and some consequences of the protectionist tariff of 1891. In effect, while cereal production was decreasing and fruit and irrigated vegetable gardening was increasing, the acreage devoted to cereals had expanded considerably. At first sight this may seem surprising. The explanation may lie in the complexities of the definition of the term "fallow." Spanish agriculture at that time still made wide use of the

Table 3.4.   Indices of agricultural production, 1800–1899

Decade	(1) Wheat	(2) Rye	(3) Corn	(4) Rice	(5) Total production	(6) Population
1800	100.00	100.00	100.00	100.00	100.00	100.00
1810	104.81	101.86	110.10	136.00	102.83	102.78
1820	109.62	103.72	121.15	172.00	106.75	106.28
1830	117.95	108.51	135.58	216.00	113.42	112.30
1840	131.77	118.09	157.69	284.00	124.71	123.16
1850	146.32	127.93	182.21	372.00	136.96	135.37
1860	157.27	134.04	202.40	444.00	143.75	142.91
1870	169.08	136.70	219.71	496.00	152.75	148.11
1880	165.06	141.76	241.35	556.00	163.79	155.48
1890	171.39	146.28	262.98	664.00	177.25	161.67
			Per capita			
1800	100.00	100.00	100.00	100.00	100.00	
1810	101.97	99.11	107.12	132.56	100.05	
1820	103.13	97.60	114.00	162.13	100.44	
1830	105.03	96.63	120.74	192.70	101.00	
1840	106.99	95.89	128.05	231.02	101.26	
1850	108.09	94.51	134.62	275.32	101.17	
1860	110.05	93.80	141.64	311.27	100.59	
1870	114.15	92.30	148.35	335.50	103.13	
1880	106.16	91.18	155.24	358.28	105.35	
1890	106.01	90.48	162.68	411.48	109.64	

Source: Calculated from Table 3.3

two-field system, so that a high proportion of land lay fallow each year. It is very likely then that a great deal of the expanded cereal acreage may have been fallow land that was partly used for pasture, which would explain why livestock output increased while the land officially devoted to pasture (Table 3.5, row 6) was shrinking. Enlarging the acreage under cereals may also be an early consequence of protection, since cereal output expanded again in the early twentieth century as a consequence of the tariff.

The increase in livestock output signifies a clear upswing after a long downward trend. Because of geographic conditions in much of Spain, agri-

Table 3.5.   Agricultural production, area under cultivation, and productivity, 1893 and 1900 compared

	Production (in million pesetas)[a]		Areas (in thousand hectares)		Productivity[b]	
	1893	1900	1893	1900	1893	1900
1. Cereals and pulses	2,027	1,992	11,777	13,706	172	145
2. Vines	568	424	1,460	1,429	389	297
3. Olives	257	227	1,123	1,197	229	190
4. Other crops[c]	777	800	1,464	1,490	529	537
5. Subtotal (1 + 2 + 3 + 4)	3,629	3,443	15,829	17,822	229	193
6. Woodlands and pasture	423	422	28,046	27,367	15	15
7. Livestock	736	810	—	—	—	—
8. Total (5 + 6 + 7)	4,788	4,675	43,875	45,189	109	103
9. Land productivity, excluding livestock	—	—	—	—	92	96
10. Labor productivity	—	—	—	—	1.188	1.087
	Percentages					
11. Cereals and pulses	56	58	74	77	75	75
12. Vines	16	12	9	8	170	154
13. Olives	7	7	7	7	100	98
14. Other crops	21	23	9	8	231	238
15. Total	100	100	100	100	100	100

a. Pesetas at 1910 value

b. In pesetas at 1910 value per hectare

c. Mostly orchards and irrigated vegetable gardens

Sources: Grupo de Estudios de Historia Rural (1983) and Tortella (1987), p. 53.

culture and stock-raising were alternative rather than complementary activities. After centuries of conflict between farmers and shepherds, a struggle which reached its peak of intensity during the eighteenth century (Herr, 1958; Ringrose, 1970), the Liberal reforms of the nineteenth century, chiefly the abolition of the Mesta and the disentailment program, favored the extension of arable land at the expense of pasture. The available data show a clear decline in livestock during the second half of the century, although work animals, horses, and mules fared less badly. The first signs of recovery appear only in the 1890s (Garrabou and Sanz, 1985, pp. 229–278).

The growth in production revealed in Tables 3.3, 3.4, and 3.5 by no means constitutes an agricultural revolution, far from it. As Table 3.6 shows, Spanish cereal yields were extremely low at the beginning of the twentieth century, which implies that increased production had only been possible because of a parallel expansion in cultivated land. The similarity between Spanish, Italian, and Portuguese yields suggests that the factors we analyzed in Chapter 1 operated as we had predicted. Given the physical and institutional parallels between the three countries, there is no doubt that low yields and general agricultural backwardness were the consequence of a complex mixture of geographical and cultural factors which are hard to separate.

The influence of climatic and soil conditions was probably stronger in Spain than in Italy or Portugal. The predominance of cereal cultivation in countries where these conditions prevented high yields was turning out to be a powerful drag on economies which were still very largely agrarian. But even these traditional agricultural economies showed signs of a more rational distribution of resources. Thus in Spain, as compared to Italy and Portugal, more arable land was put to barley, a crop which produced higher yields. All in all, however, the outlook was very discouraging, inasmuch as much of the Spanish land area was devoted to products in which the country had both a comparative and an absolute disadvantage.

There was, however, a brighter agricultural sector that was much more promising. Even before the nineteenth century, the Mediterranean coast had witnessed the start of commercialized fruit and vegetable farming which today is among the most competitive in Europe. Products such as wines, raisins, figs, almonds, hazelnuts, olive oil, and above all citrus fruits appear on the export side of the Spanish trade balance already by the middle of the nineteenth century. There lay the future of Spanish agriculture, but this future did not develop fully until well into the twentieth century. In 1900, tra-

Table 3.6.   Agricultural yields in various European countries, 1890–1910 (in quintals per hectare)

	(1) Wheat	(2) Barley	(3) Rye	(4) Oats	(5) Potatoes
SPAIN					
1891–1900	7.6	9.2	6.9	7.9	n.d.
1901–1910	9.0	11.5	7.9	7.7	n.d.
ITALY					
1890–1896	7.9[a]	6.5[b]	7.8[b]	7.1[b]	61.1[b]
1901–1910	9.5	9.0[c]	14.1[c]	9.3[c]	95.0[c]
PORTUGAL					
1901–1910	5.9	n.d.	n.d.	n.d.	70
FRANCE					
1892	12.7	11.9	11.0	10.8	105.0
1902	13.6	13.7	8.7	12.8	76.7
GREAT BRITAIN					
1891–1900	25.3	20.9[d]	n.d.	17.4[d]	146.2[d]
1901–1910	22.1	21.1[e]	n.d.	19.0[e]	141.1[e]
GERMANY					
1892	17.1	17.0	14.2	14.4	111.7
1902	19.7	18.9	15.4	18.0	134.1
UPPER SILESIA					
1891–1900	15.5	16.6	13.3	15.0	110.0
1901–1910	17.6	18.7	15.3	17.6	125.5

a. 1890–1896; b. 1890–1895; c. 1909–1910; d. 1892; e. 1902
Sources: Tortella (1987) and Lains (1988)

ditional crops occupied three-quarters of arable land and produced about one half of the total value of agricultural production, while cultivation of fruits and vegetables using about 12% of arable land produced almost one quarter, 23%, of the total value.

Why was the transition to modern agriculture so slow? There is a simple answer: because of tariff protection. Spanish tariffs on wheat had been high at least since 1820 (Sánchez-Albornoz, 1963), with the exception of the period subject to the 1869 tariff, under which rates were moderate (although increasing). After 1892 the tariff was very high indeed, and this protection became more and more vital for wheat farmers as transportation methods improved and competition from more efficient agricultural systems became keener. At the same time, better transportation favored the exportation of those perishable products in which Spain had an advantage. If wheat had not been so heavily protected, increased imports of this cereal would have caused a reduction in the number of Spanish wheat farmers, with the elimination of the less efficient ones. This would have set in motion a redeployment of resources towards products and techniques that were more productive and competitive, not only fruits and green vegetables, but also potatoes, maize, livestock, the introduction of more fertilizers, better rotations, more irrigation. In addition, this process of resource reallocation would have had the crucial effect of stimulating a flow of outmigration from the dry central plateau to the cities and abroad. Of course, all these processes did in fact take place, but at a very slow pace, and consequently they yielded only a slow rise in incomes. In fact, by opting for tariff protection, the Spanish politicians, consciously or unconsciously, made a choice in favor of social stability and against economic and social change. Free trade and the social transformation it would have stimulated could have brought about fast economic growth by permitting a speedy reallocation of resources, but this would have been a high-risk operation: rapid outmigration, with the almost inevitable hardships that are both its cause and its consequence, might have provoked a political explosion. After the *desamortización*, social and political tensions were already palpable, especially in the southern countryside. The high tariffs, while slowing down growth, helped preserve social peace and the status quo.

Tariff protection also contributed to economic stagnation by impeding the development of Mediterranean products, where Spain's advantage lay. This was so not only because tariffs hindered the mobility of resources, but also because protection provoked reprisals by other countries against Spanish exports. France protected its markets against fruits and vegetables. Sherry wine faced tariffs in England; raisins, onions and other products met the same problem in the United States. Tariffs are two-edged weapons, and in the Spanish case both edges of the sword served to oppose agricultural modernization.

Agriculture and Economic Growth

Agricultural change is a fundamental part of economic development. In their early stages, all economies are largely agrarian, and without agrarian change they can experience social and economic improvement only with the greatest difficulty. Furthermore, the agricultural sector must perform a series of functions during the process of economic modernization, as follows. (1) Food surpluses must be produced to feed a growing and increasingly urban population. (2) Agriculture must provide a strong market for industrial goods, typically clothing and other consumer goods, tools and machinery, fertilizers and construction industry components. In fact, economic growth is to a large extent the result of a powerful increase in this exchange between the agricultural and industrial sectors. (3) Savings must be accumulated in the agrarian sector and transferred, through capital markets, a banking system, or taxation to the industrial and service sectors for capital formation. (4) Increasing agricultural productivity and a better diet should generate population growth, and with that a labor surplus. The resultant outmigration contributes to the growth of the labor force in other sectors, and emigrants to other countries produce a flow of currency remittances to help the balance of payments. (5) Agricultural exports typically should help by financing the imports of equipment and technology needed for development.

How did Spanish agriculture perform with regard to these requirements during the nineteenth century? Aside from the expansion of cultivated land, an initial review of the points outlined above suggests that agriculture underwent little change; this is underscored by Vicente Pérez Moreda (1983), who has pointed out that the proportion of labor in agriculture hardly changed from the beginning of the century to the end. In view of persistent low levels of productivity and consumption, and given the aggregate output by the end of the century, one must conclude that agricultural growth appears to have been extremely slow. And we can strengthen this argument by pointing out that if agricultural growth had been substantial, then productivity and consumption around 1800 would necessarily have been well below minimum subsistence levels.

In fact, where the production of agricultural surplus is concerned, we have already seen that the result was not very satisfactory. Yes, there was some increase in cereal output, but just enough to keep up with the population growth, at least until the very last decades of the century. The rate of urbanization remained low: only 9% of the population lived in towns of more than 100,000 in 1900, and the proportion of nonagricultural labor remained almost constant, at about 33% throughout the century. All these points corroborate the figures and analysis that describe an agricultural sector that was almost stagnant, with only faint intimations of improvement in the very last decades. Further confirmation can be drawn from what we know about diet. We have scattered evidence for different times and places, but it is very consistent. On the one hand, we know that periodic famines occurred throughout the century, at least as late as the mid-1860s, and numerous testimonies indicate very low average calorie and protein intakes in cities, especially large cities, at the end of the nineteenth and well into the twentieth century.[5] If the average diet at the beginning of the nineteenth century had been much below what it was at the beginning of the twentieth century (as it would have been if growth had occurred), much of the Spanish population at the time of Carlos IV (1788–1808) would have literally died of starvation.

Exports of grain during the mid-nineteenth century have been adduced to prove that cereal output expanded during the whole of the century (Anes, 1970), but the amounts exported were usually small. According to research based on official figures by Prados (1982), the average net yearly export of wheat and flour for the period 1826–1849 was about 20,000 metric tons, slightly below 1% of the average yearly harvest. In time, however, even these net exports diminished and disappeared; after 1875, in spite of increasing tariff protection, Spain became a net grain importer. These figures suggest not only long-term stagnation in output per capita but also technological stagnation, since the period of maximum exports coincided with a decisive phase in the disentailment movement. The increase in output corresponds to the extension of acreage and seems to owe nothing to better crop yields.

Perhaps the most outstanding failure of Spanish agriculture in the nineteenth century was that it did not provide a market for industrial products. The role of peasant consumption as an important factor in the growth of the Catalán textile industry has been mentioned frequently and with justification. Nonetheless it is clear that low levels of consumption created a constant threat of overproduction after mid-century,[6] and that the development of the textile industry during the years 1830 to 1855 was mostly due to the substitution of Catalán cotton textiles for English, thanks to tariff protection along with the suppression of piracy. Moreover, local artisans turned to more traditional fibers such as wool and linen, rather than industrially produced cotton. Prados (1983) has established that Spanish textile consumption was below that of England and France and increased at a slower rate. Since the majority of Spaniards at that time were peasants and farmers, this demonstrates very clearly the inadequacy of the agricultural sector as a market for consumer goods.

The situation was even worse with regard to purchases of capital goods. With few exceptions, the agrarian sector simply did not acquire modern implements and remained wedded to the ancestral Roman plow, made entirely of wood except for a small iron plowshare, and to the primitive wood-and-stone thresher, both drawn by a mule or a donkey. The testimony of innumerable contemporaries and evidence from modern scholars all confirm the technological stagnation of Spanish agriculture.[7] This means that a rural market for iron and steel, metal manufactures, and chemicals hardly existed until well into the twentieth century. In comparison, agriculture was a key market for these industries in Britain, Germany, and the United States in the nineteenth century, but it played no such role in Spain. As a concrete example, when the Spanish Nobel Dynamite Company erected a super-phosphate factory in 1890 to take advantage of the surplus sulfuric acid, a byproduct of producing nitroglycerin, sales were so low that the plant was closed after a few years (Tortella, 1983b). Something similar happened in the 1920s and 1930s, when the Spanish Explosives Union opened a potash mine in Cardona; almost all of its production was exported because Spanish agriculture used very little potash as a fertilizer in those years. As far as machinery was concerned, and this was the case in Portugal as well, only a few steam threshers were imported, and they were bought at the end of the nineteenth century for large-scale operations that enjoyed considerable economies of scale, in a market made safe by tariff protection (Reis, 1982).

It is difficult to establish with any degree of precision the role of agriculture in providing capital to the other business sectors; the most that can be said is that it transferred a certain amount of capital, although clearly insufficient and poorly allocated.[8] One of the channels for this kind of transfer was the fiscal system. Although tax evasion by large landowners was an undisputed fact, the agricultural sector as a whole shouldered more than its proportional share of the tax burden, based upon production figures.[9] And to make matters worse, the greater part of the taxes extracted from agriculture was not invested productively, since so much of state expenditure in the nineteenth century was squandered on military and other unproductive uses (Tortella, 1978).

The amount of private savings accumulated in agriculture and channeled elsewhere is more difficult to track down. Indirect evidence suggests, however, that only a very small fraction of agricultural savings was productively invested in other sectors. In the first place, if farmers hardly invested in their own operations, which they knew well, why should they invest in industrial or commercial activities which were foreign to them? We have several indications of farmers' mistrust not only of industry and trade, but also of the banks. The mistrust was not unjustified, at least at that time, and it prompted the peasants to hoard precious metals rather than depositing funds to earn interest or investing them in search of profits. In the second place, the history of banking shows that the number of landowners among bank founders in the mid-nineteenth century was disproportionately meager (Sánchez-Albornoz, 1968; Tortella, 1973). Furthermore, the principal banks and savings institutions were invariably located in industrial and commercial areas, not in cities or regions that were predominantly agrarian.

The transfer of manpower from agriculture to industry was extremely limited during the nineteenth century; in fact nil in relative terms since the proportion of manpower in agriculture remained stable. The comparatively slow growth of Spanish population prior to 1900 is obviously the main explanation of this phenomenon, with high death rates the main cause of slow growth. And in turn the causes of high mortality are attributable to illiteracy and general ignorance, together with poor diet, low standard of living, and government neglect. Agriculture, therefore, is only partly responsible for the limited population transfer. It must be added, furthermore, that when migration from the countryside started in earnest from the 1880s onward, the cities absorbed only a small part of this flow, while a large part of the emigration went abroad. The problem, then, was more one of low demand and scant industrial development, rather than a limited supply of rural emigrants.

As far as the role of agriculture in external trade is concerned, some reference has already been made to grain exports in the mid-nineteenth century. In that respect, traditional agriculture made a small contribution to economic development, but it took place at the wrong time. By the time of the first stirrings of industrial diversification in the 1880s, Spanish grains (and this was also the case for most of Europe) were no longer an export commodity but instead were suffering from strong competition from abroad.

However, this was also the moment when another subsector of Spanish agriculture started to show its export potential. In the second half of the nineteenth century export capacity began to develop among those products where Spain had absolute and comparative advantages, the products of Mediterranean agriculture, plus some livestock items and forestry products, particularly cork. In spite of the small proportion of land and resources that these products occupied, they came to represent about 35% of total exports, counting both agricultural and nonagricultural components. Although its territorial expansion proceeded slowly even after 1900, this was the segment of Spanish agriculture that performed its role as exporter, even though the phylloxera plague reduced wine production so that wine lost its position as a leading export item in the mid-1890s.

To conclude, agricultural stagnation was one of the causes of the relative backwardness of the Spanish economy during the nineteenth century. In turn, the stagnation was determined by physical and institutional features which Spain generally shared with its neighbors in the western Mediterranean.

CHAPTER 4

Industry: A Long Infancy

Economic historians are generally in agreement that the nineteenth century witnessed "the failure of the Industrial Revolution in Spain," to use Jordi Nadal's popular phrase. Two more recent works, by Albert Carreras and Leandro Prados, confirm the notion in more precise, quantitative terms. According to Carreras, the author of an important annual index of Spanish industrial production, "it is not possible to detect anything like a sudden setting in motion, a jumpstart of industrial activity in any sense of the word, whether the 'take-off' that Rostow was looking for, or a 'big spurt' in Gerschenkron's sense of that term" (1987, p. 284); even "the highest rates are no more than mediocre." Prados (1988, pp. 167–175) shows that in various ways Spanish industry at the beginning of the twentieth century was more backward than British or even French industry had been at the beginning of the nineteenth century. Its slow rate of growth would "justify the most drastic interpretation of the word failure, in relative terms."

In effect, this assertion of failure means more than simply losing ground with respect to one's neighbors. It means that a series of public and private attempts to lead the Spanish nation along the path of economic modernization, which in the nineteenth century inevitably entailed industrialization, essentially miscarried. The Spanish economy remained overwhelmingly agrarian, as occupational statistics and various other indicators unequivocally show. Within Europe, Spain joined Russia and Italy in the group of economic laggards (Bairoch, 1965; Prados, 1988).

Among those attempts at modernization several examples of note can be cited. In the private sphere, Catalán businessmen made repeated efforts to create and develop an industrial base in their region (Vicens, 1961). In the public sphere, the Progressive party carried out several projects designed to create the political and institutional bases of an industrial, technologically advanced society. The most notable of those were the legislative program of the Progressive Biennium (1854–1856), and the executive and legislative measures enacted during the Glorious Revolution (1868–1874).[1] These efforts were not wholly fruitless, and not all of nineteenth-century Spain stagnated: Catalonia, and especially Barcelona, underwent considerable industrialization; land reform was carried out; a railroad network was built; improvements were made in the educational system; monetary, banking, and fiscal reforms were implemented; yearly budgets were duly prepared and enacted into law; some manufacturing industries developed and some older industries were partially modernized. Yet the much sought-after industrial revolution did not happen. Economic historians are still looking for the explanation.

Cotton and iron were the leading sectors in the original Industrial Revolution in eighteenth-century England. These were also the sectors which underwent the most profound transformations in nineteenth-century Spain, although it cannot be said that they were the leading forces in a real revolution. This was due in part to lack of support from the secondary characters in the drama, who played such a crucial role in the English transformation: a prosperous and market-oriented agriculture; an efficient transportation network; a multitude of other manufacturing activities such as the metal and mechanical trades, construction, engineering, chemicals, pottery, and other consumer industries; an effective service sector in which the banking system and capital markets were particularly important; and an effective and unobtrusive bureaucracy at both state and local levels. By contrast, in Spain all of these elements were missing or weak; at the same time, the conservative and protectionist proclivities of the manufacturers themselves must shoulder some of the responsibility.

Likewise, the physical factors which so influenced agricultural stagnation must also have affected the nascent industrial sector. (Later on we shall examine the serious energy problems that Spanish industry had to face.) Water shortage was another important factor. In Spain, rivers with irregular or limited water supply deprived industry of the valuable energy source which countries with wetter climates enjoyed; water is also an important factor of production for many industries such as chemicals and paper manufacturing. In short, the importance of water as a basic resource for industry and energy could be an explanation (the matter has been little studied) of why Spanish industry came to be localized in relatively water-rich regions like Catalonia and the Basque country, with the general scarcity of water counting as a serious factor in the country's overall industrial backwardness.

Textiles

Cotton

As in England a century earlier, it was the cotton industry that in Spain opened the way to modernization and mass production. Neither country seems to have had an initial natural advantage in this industry, since all of the chief basic material, raw cotton, had to be imported (although cotton could be grown in southern Spain, it could not be done competitively). In fact both countries used to import large quantities of cotton textiles before their domestic industries started the process of import substitution. The market, therefore, long antedated the industry. Both countries had a woolen industry which was overtaken by the new sector, cotton. We cannot enter here into a thorough examination of why cotton acquired such importance in England; the fact is, however, that once the spinning and weaving machines had been invented, England had at least two clear advantages: first, coal in large quantities and of suitable quality for the steam engines which provided motive force; and second, a strong and growing demand, thanks to improving living standards, fast population growth, and foreign markets eager to buy cheap British cloth. To this one must add an intelligent, educated, and abundant labor force and all the other external economies which economic progress generates.

Spain could count on none of these advantages. The two key factors were especially conspicuous by their absence. Spanish coal is neither good nor abundant, and Catalonia (the center of the textile industry) is situated far from any coal producing areas, so transport costs were high. Nor were demand conditions favorable. In the eighteenth century the cotton industry had developed under state protection, counting in part on colonial demand. The loss of the Spanish empire deprived the industry of an important market. Domestic demand should certainly not be disregarded, as Spain was then one of the most populous countries in Europe, but poverty, demographic stagnation, and poor transportation represented serious obstacles. Even so, the cotton industry did develop in Spain—no mean feat!

The explanation for this apparently paradoxical emergence lies in the relative advancement of Catalonia and in tariff protection. Although almost completely devoid of coal deposits (except lignite), Catalonia had been developing economically since the mid-eighteenth century, and its active trade with the Americas, its prosperous agriculture, and its demographic vitality had favored capital accumulation, a flourishing entrepreneurial spirit, an abundant labor supply, and the market conditions necessary to establish modern industry. During the nineteenth century, despite the loss of most of the American market and an absence of coal, the cotton industry, protected behind a solid tariff barrier and focused almost exclusively on the domestic market (plus Cuba and Puerto Rico in the last years of the century) managed to develop quite remarkably.

As in other European countries, the Spanish (or rather the Catalán) cotton industry followed the English model, but its techniques always lagged a step behind, its factories were smaller, its prices were higher. For most of the nineteenth century Britain maintained an innovator's lead, benefiting from all its headstart advantages: trade networks, state-of-the-art technology, optimum scale of production, highly trained manpower and personnel. In view of the British superiority, the European continental industries had two alternatives: either to compete by specializing in a few products in which they had a comparative advantage, as did Belgium and Switzerland, or to resort to tariff protection, as did France and Spain.[2]

This does not mean, however, that the Spanish industry was technologically stagnant. The Catalans developed the *bergadana*, a local version of the spinning jenny, and early in the nineteenth century the industrialists imported the "mule," a machine which, unlike the jenny, could be powered by steam engines or water wheels. After a long interruption caused by the War of Independence, followed by the depression and political repression under Fernando VII, Barcelona again took up mechanized spinning in the 1830s. The city soon witnessed the first Luddite episode in Spain: a factory called El Vapor (The Steam), owned by the Bonaplata brothers and devoted both to spinning and to making spinning machinery, was sacked and burned by workers in 1835, in a revolt in which churches also were gutted (Nadal, 1983). Notwithstanding this outburst, mechanization proceeded apace, and in the following decade the *selfactinas* (so called after the English self-acting machines) were introduced. These machines again provoked the ire of the workers, whose protests in 1854 forced manufacturers to reconvert them and use them as jennies so as not to economize on labor and, in the expression of the day, "to create work" (Izard, 1973). Despite these setbacks mechanization proceeded steadily during the 1830–1855 period, although it never reached levels comparable to those in England.

This is the period when the Catalán cotton industry enjoyed its highest growth rates, as measured by the most commonly accepted indicator, imports of raw cotton (see Tables 4.1 and 4.2 and Figure 4.1). Table 4.2 shows that in the twenty years before 1856 the industry grew at an average yearly rate of 8%, a figure which is more than respectable though accounted for in part by the very low starting level in the mid-1830s. In the initial stages it is typical that an industry will exhibit high rates of growth; for example, in

Table 4.1. Imports of raw baled cotton through the port of Barcelona, 1814–1913 (in metric tons, five-year averages)

Period	Metric tons
1814–1818[a]	1,038
1819–1823[b]	2,005
1824–1828[c]	2,246
1829–1833[d]	3,902
1834–1838	3,906
1839–1843	5,636
1844–1848	9,517
1849–1853	14,663
1854–1858	18,114
1859–1863	17,861
1864–1868	16,102
1869–1873	23,832
1874–1878	32,116
1879–1883	40,732
1884–1888	42,735
1889–1893	54,446
1894–1898	64,315
1899–1903	75,548
1904–1908	81,149
1909–1913	79,721

a. average 1816–1818
b. average 1819–1820
c. no data for 1828
d. only 1831
Source: Nadal (1975), pp. 207–208 and App. 7

England during the years 1773–1799, raw cotton imports grew at an average yearly rate of 9.2%; in Japan between 1889 and 1914 the rate was 13.7 (Deane, 1965; Lockwood, 1968). Even though the Catalán cotton industry grew faster than the British one over the course of the nineteenth century, the size of the two industries remained vastly different, for the Catalán industry never imported more than one-tenth of the volume of British raw cotton imports.

In addition to its fuel problems, the Spanish industry faced difficulties that neither Britain nor Japan encountered. First, although the Spanish market was not inconsiderable, it had limited purchasing power and was not grow-

Table 4.2. Growth rates of cotton imports

Period	Annual average %
1814–1823/1904–1913	4.5
1834–1838/1854–1858	8.0
1869–1873/1904–1908	3.6

Source: calculated from Table 4.1.

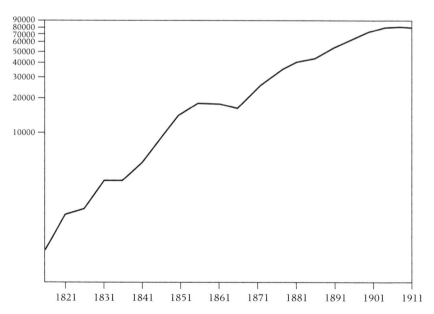

Figure 4.1. Imports of raw baled cotton through the port of Barcelona, 1816–1911 (five-year averages on semi-logarithmic scale)

ing; and second, the industry had little access to foreign markets as its prices were too high. This may appear to present something of a contradiction, given the industry's considerable growth rate of 4.5% per annum over the course of the century. The explanation lies in the processes of substitution which were taking place. In Spain, as in almost all other European countries at this time, cotton textiles were replacing woolens and linens, and in addition the Catalán cotton industry was gradually able to replace English goods in the home market, thanks to tariff protection and an increasingly effective suppression of contraband trade. In the first decades of the nineteenth century, cotton clothing items smuggled through the Pyrenees, the Portuguese frontier, and Gibraltar had supplied about 80% of the Spanish market. By the middle of the century illegal imports were reduced to 20% of domestic production and legal imports to less than 5 percent.[3] All in all, between the 1830s and the 1850s, the Catalán cotton industry went from supplying some 20% to about 75% of domestic demand. This explains the strong growth rates despite the market difficulties.

Development was interrupted around 1855 for various reasons In the first place, the economic policy of the Progressives in 1854–1856 opened up new investment opportunities in land, mining, banks, and railroads; secondly, the American Civil War caused a "cotton famine" from 1861 onwards; and thirdly, the end of that war caused a serious international depression, and cotton prices, which a few years earlier had been so high, fell precipitously. After 1868 the Catalán industry began to revive, contradicting the dire predictions of the manufacturers about the consequences of the relatively liberal Figuerola tariff (see Chapter 7).

The rate of growth was not as fast as it had been, however; it appears that part of the expansion of the 1870s was destined to meet the unfulfilled needs of the 1860s. Another crisis hit the industry in the 1880s, which was related to the international depression of those years. The Catalán banking industry was also affected, and a deep regional malaise that was as much political as economic permeated the whole region. The common feeling was that Catalonia ought to receive greater legislative protection, a sentiment expressed in the *Report in Defense of the Moral and Material Interests of Catalonia,* popularly know in Catalán as the *Memorial de Greuges* (grievances). Madrid obliged, and the Law of Commercial Relations with the Antilles was issued in 1882, which essentially reserved the markets of Cuba and Puerto Rico for Spanish (for which read Catalán) industry. Under this protective umbrella, the industry began to grow again, with the Cuban and Puerto Rican markets absorbing an expanding share of output (17% in the 1890s). The independence of Cuba and Puerto Rico in 1898 dealt yet another hard blow to the cotton industry, whose output stagnated during the first decades of the twentieth century (Sudrià, 1983).

The debate between free-traders and protectionists raged in nineteenth century Spain, as it did in other countries, and the cotton industry was in the eye of the storm. Many complained that it had grown at the expense of consumers, a fact which is hard to deny; thanks to protection, cotton manufacturers could sell their merchandise at prices higher than those of the international market, and this obviously hurt consumers. It also hurt the taxpayers (who were the same consumers), because these high, almost prohibitive tariffs promoted smuggling and yielded less revenue than could be obtained through a larger volume of legal imports. As various historians have pointed out, however (Sánchez-Albornoz, 1977, for example), the manufacturers made common cause with the landowners in the late nineteenth century and managed to form an invincible protectionist lobby, as in many other European countries at this time.

What did the cotton industry offer to the country in return for this protection? Undeniably, insofar as the industry replaced imports, it helped to alleviate the balance of trade deficit, but let us not forget that it imported raw cotton, coal, and machinery. At the same time, this sector was the backbone of industrialization in Catalonia, the only region which underwent a process of economic modernization in the nineteenth century. To what extent these contributions from the cotton industry benefited the rest of Spain and Catalonia itself is a question that is discussed with more passion than reason, and is still far from settled. Nevertheless it does not seem impossible to carry out a cost-benefit analysis of the effect of protecting the cotton industry, with assumptions based on partial equilibrium analysis or on a general equilibrium framework. In the first case we would compare the advantages of import substitution with the disadvantages of the more expensive product. And in the second we would include the complex but important question of the advantages and disadvantages of having a city and a region (Barcelona and Catalonia) which were far more advanced than the rest of the country. One must agree with Sánchez-Albornoz that the "leading-sector" effect of the cotton industry on the country as a whole was small, perhaps to a large extent because of the particular nature of the industry as a producer of consumer goods and an importer of raw materials. Yet it cannot be denied that its effect on the Barcelona region was positive, stimulating the growth of other industries, particularly chemicals and the mechanical trades. It also absorbed manpower from Catalonia and other regions such as Andalucía and Murcia. On the debit side, as a protected industry with very limited growth possibilities from mid-century onwards, it was probably responsible for eventually generating the long, drawn-out economic crisis of the Barcelonese economy in the last decades of the nineteenth century and the beginning of the twentieth. The resulting decline of the banking system, low profitability, low wages, and unemployment promoted a situation of endemic tension and social violence (Tedde, 1974; Nadal, 1975, pp. 215–217).

In any case, it was not a question of deciding whether the cotton industry should or should not exist, but rather whether it should be a protected industry or not. The industrialists' propagandists claimed that free trade would spell the disappearance of the industry, but this proposition was of very questionable validity. As one of the great economic historians of the nineteenth century wrote,

> Who is to give the assurance that the industry which is fostered [by means of a tariff] will be able after a time to dispense with the protection? Not the applicant, certainly. He never did and never will assure the country. On the contrary, he will tell those who have been rash enough to give him his head, "that the action of the Government has given him . . . 'a vested interest,' that the shock to the industry would be fatal, that workmen would be discharged and ruined, capital would be lost, and the latter end would be worse than the beginning. . . . It is base, cruel, dishonest, to induce us to start this industry and then to desert us. . . . We are the creation of the State in its wisdom, do not let us be the victims of its caprice."

With these words, Thorold Rogers (1891, p. 387) refuted the theory of "infant industry protection" expounded by J. Stuart Mill (yes, even in England you could find protectionists). Protected industries always feel themselves at the mercy of foreign competitors when the protection is lifted, but to a dispassionate observer these fears do not seem justified. In view of the internal and external economies of scale which had been achieved in Barcelona by the middle of the century and the degree of development of the various factors of production (physical capital, quality and quantity of the labor force, technical and entrepreneurial skills), the surest bet is that the cotton industry would have adapted to foreign competition, transforming itself into an industry that no doubt would have been very different from that which developed under the shelter of the tariff, certainly more efficient, perhaps less profitable, much better suited to the international division of labor: a natural organism rather than a hothouse plant.

Other Textile Industries

In addition to "king cotton," other textile fibers had traditionally been spun and woven in Spain: wool, silk, and flax or linen. Of these only wool retained some of its important past during the nineteenth century.

As in so many European countries, the woolen industry, based upon the use of locally produced raw material, was the most important textile manufacture in Spain under the Old Regime. Wool workshops and artisan factories were widely distributed throughout the country and chiefly served local markets; they were more abundant in sheep-shearing areas, notably Old Castile and León. But this situation changed drastically during the nineteenth century because of the competition from cotton. To face this competition the woolen industry had to become mechanized, which frequently meant the displacement of old artisan workshops by more modern factories. As the cotton industry would have done had it been forced to compete, the woolen industry set about specializing in a range of modern products such as ready-made clothing and overcoats, paying more attention to fashion and the tastes of the urban consumer, increasingly relying on the services of designers and specialized industrial engineers.

Modern industry became concentrated in two neighboring towns near Barcelona, Sabadell and Terrasa, which had clear locational advantages. Proximity to Barcelona facilitated the regular exchange of workers and engineers from the cotton mills; it further gave the industry all the commercial and credit advantages of the larger, older city and its port services for imports of coal and wool. These imports were growing, and by the end of the nineteenth century Spain, the grand old exporter of this basic raw material, had become a net importer. Coming from Argentina or Australia, the raw wool was usually imported by France, washed, and re-exported to Spain (Parejo, 1989, chap. 4). Although wool made more use of steam power than cotton, the streams that were relatively abundant in the vicinity offered an additional energy source, and proximity to the Zaragoza railroad connected the region, the Vallés district, to the rest of Spain, both for the domestic supply of raw wool and for access to the other regional markets for the finished products. By the end of the century the Vallés area was operating 40% of all wool-spinning machines in Spain, and 50% of all mechanical looms (Nadal,

1987). What Parejo calls the "Catalanization of the woolen industry" had been completed.

The old, traditional wool centers like Béjar, Segovia, Avila, Antequera, and Palencia, in Castile and Andalucía, which had been able to benefit from the exceptional quality of the legendary Merino wool, lost relative importance as the smaller artisan centers disappeared. The industry managed to keep going in Béjar, Palencia, Antequera, and Alcoy by specializing in particular items, military capes in Béjar, blankets in Palencia, baize[4] in Antequera, and flannel in Alcoy, but in the long run they were gradually disappearing under the combined competition of the Vallés district and English and French imports. On the whole, according to Parejo's estimates, the Spanish woolen industry grew in the central decades of the nineteenth century thanks to growing mechanization and concentration in the Vallés district, but stagnated in the last quarter of the century, an evolution that was not entirely different from that of the cotton industry, although colonial demand could not be the escape valve for wool as it was for cotton.

The silk industry also had a long tradition in Spain, particularly in the east (Valencia and Murcia) and in Andalucía (Granada), but during the nineteenth century it also tended to concentrate in Barcelona. The decline of the Valencian silk industry is well known thanks to the work of Martínez-Santos (1981), and more recently Fernando Díez (1992). Its causes are not altogether clear, however, since the mulberry tree on which the silkworm feeds grows very well on the Mediterranean coast. It is not clear whether the expansion of orange groves was a cause or a consequence of the decline of silk, although in my opinion the second hypothesis is the more probable. In Valencia there were serious labor problems, particularly in the first-stage operation of handling the silk cocoons, because of the field conditions where this work was carried out. It seems that the local peasants lacked the special dexterity required in the delicate operation of reeling the silk from the cocoon, and this has repercussions in successive production phases. Something similar must have happened with the silk industry in Granada, whose decline was already evident by the middle of the eighteenth century (Vincent, 1983, p. 400). These structural problems in the old silk regions were further aggravated in the nineteenth century, first because of the disruption of wars and later by the increase in international trade, which sharpened the competition from other, more efficient silk producers. In any case, the power that Catalonia exerted on the textile industries, pulling them away from their traditional locations close to sources of raw materials (the same was the case with wool), is a good example of the power of external economies and the importance of human capital. The advantages of a big industrial center, with its good harbor and other communication facilities, networks of services in credit and insurance, a developed labor market, and a higher quality and greater variety of skills and trades more than compensated for the relative distances from the mulberry plantations. Thus Valencian and Murcian workers migrated to Barcelona to spin and weave silk that originated in Valencia and Murcia.

The decline of the linen industry in Galicia parallels the problems of silk in the east. The rural location, the low level of manpower skills, the technical problems of mechanization, and competition from Catalán cotton all contributed to the demise of an artisan industry which had thrived as recently as the late eighteenth century, but which proved unable to adapt to the exigencies of modernization (Carmona, 1990). The cases of linen and silk illustrate very clearly the great obstacles to mechanization for an industry in a rural setting where the human capital is poorly equipped, proving that not all cases of "proto-industrialization" bloom into a successful, modern industry.

Iron and Steel

It is a well known fact of economic location theory that in the nineteenth century, when coal was relatively more expensive to transport than iron ore, the iron industry needed to be located near the source of coke rather than at the source of iron, because it took about four tons of coal to process one ton of ore. This was the key problem of the Spanish iron industry, since what Spain produced competitively was iron, not coal. In theory, therefore, the rational location of the Spanish iron industry would have been Cardiff, Newcastle, Essen, or Pittsburgh, rather than Bilbao, Avilés, Málaga, or Sagunto. And to a certain extent this is what happened, because Spain exported a very large part of its iron ore.

From a strictly economic standpoint, having good iron deposits was not the most important factor in becoming a leading iron manufacturer. The essentials were an abundant supply of good coking coal and a strong domestic market for the industry's products. As both were missing in Spain, it is not surprising that the development of the iron and steel industry encountered great difficulties. Rich iron deposits do not necessarily foster the growth of a powerful iron industry, as is illustrated by the other major European exporter of iron ore, Sweden, whose economic strengths were agriculture, forestry, light industries, and iron ore exports, not iron and steel production.

Let us go over, albeit in a very simple manner, some elements of the process for producing iron. Just as the textile industry has two basic processes, spinning and weaving, with the latter followed by a series of finishing steps, so the iron industry also has two basic processes, smelting and refining, the latter process producing the basic material for a complex industry that transforms metal into a host of finished goods. Smelting extracts the metal from the ore; this is a high-temperature, complex chemical process (iron fusion occurs at 1535° C) whereby coal and mineral ore are mixed and heated in a furnace. The coal fulfills a double function, as fuel and as a reducing agent. The result of this chemical process is pig iron, which is still impure because of its high carbon content and other impurities; at this stage it is hard but also relatively brittle.

The carbon and other impurities are reduced by the refining process, which involves reheating the pig iron and removing the foreign matter by various mechanical means until reaching the desired levels of purity. Reducing the carbon to below .2% produces a very pure iron called forged iron, relatively soft and malleable. Iron with a relatively high carbon content (between 1.5 and 4.5%) is called cast iron; this cheapest form of iron is hard but brittle, not very malleable or ductile. Steel is an intermediate variety of iron, with between .2 and 1.5% of carbon. It is superior because it is hard but also elastic. It is difficult, however, to keep the carbon content within precise bounds, which accounts for steel's traditionally higher price. The art of steel-making was rather similar to that of cooking rice or making good wine; it was a question of timing, and since both basic components could vary in their chemical content, a high degree of experience was called for. Because of this, high-quality steel was a quasi-precious metal before the Industrial Revolution. Until the end of the nineteenth century, the most common process for producing medium-quality steel involved a puddling furnace: hot air was pumped through the molten iron to hasten combustion and to eliminate impurities, and hammering and laminating completed the process. High-quality steel was produced by the crucible method. First the Bessemer process and then the Siemens-Martin and the Thomas-Gilchrist methods came to revolutionize steel-making because they permitted mass production of steel within the required quality limits.

Iron and steel thus consume huge amounts of fuel in both smelting and refining. But in refining, which is purely mechanical, coal is needed only as a source of energy, to get the furnace to the required high temperature, whereas in smelting coal functions as an agent in a complex chemical process, and it must therefore be nearly pure carbon so that the chemical process of reduction is not impaired. This was the reason why charcoal was used in continental Europe until well into the nineteenth century; most mineral coal contains too many impurities. In England, deforested since the seventeenth century, the coking process was discovered in the eighteenth century, whereby mineral coal was purified for metallurgical use by burning off the impurities. But not all coal produces good coke, and herein lies the superiority of the English, Belgian, and German coal deposits; in contrast, Spanish coal does not produce good coke.

The problem of location in the Spanish iron and steel industry is perfectly illustrated by the succession of establishments, at almost every point of the compass, which were eliminated one after the other because they could not compete. In almost all these locations, companies had to confront the problem of coal that was expensive and remote. The location that finally took hold, in Vizcaya, was also, paradoxically, the most rational. In Vizcaya, the abundant item was iron ore, not fuel, but that abundance drew the area into close economic proximity to sources of fuel. The massive export of raw mineral ore to Britain gave rise to very low transport costs for British coke, a cheap return cargo in the very ships that were crossing to Bilbao to take on Spanish iron ore.

Spain's modern iron industry originated in Andalucía: the first blast furnaces were built in Málaga, in a region that abounded in mineral wealth, particularly the iron deposits in the Ojén and Marbella districts. A company called La Constancia had been created in 1826 with the object of exploiting those deposits, but a series of technical difficulties delayed the production stage for its two factories, La Concepción and La Constancia. The decisions about what kind of furnaces to use and what techniques to adopt were taken after a long and costly investigation into the most appropriate smelting method for the region's magnetic ores. In the end they adopted the English processes, that is to say the most modern and doubtless the most expensive. Madoz tells us that "a colony of English workmen of all classes" was installed in Málaga for this purpose. The guiding spirit and financier of the company was Manuel Agustín de Heredia, an exporter of olive oil and wine, who had made his fortune from exporting graphite (Nadal, 1972 and 1975); he was a member of the Chamber of Commerce and a promoter of the Banco de Málaga. In Seville the iron ore deposits in Cazalla de la Sierra had been known for many years, and a company called El Pedroso, created to exploit them, also went into production during this period. Conditions were favorable because the first Carlist War was about to put the traditional Basque iron forges out of business for a while. In the excitement of these circumstances a second metallurgical company, El Angel, was founded in Málaga. The Andalusian disadvantage, however, was very serious. Given the cost of hard coal, most of the fuel consumed by these installations was wood; although this had some advantages, it was becoming increasingly expensive in a country as deforested as Spain. The hegemony of Andalucía began to decline starting in 1860.

Next came the stage we may identify as locationally rational, that is to say, the predominance of the Asturian iron industry in the vicinity of the coal mines in Mieres and Langreo. The Asturian component had two factories, one at Mieres and the other at La Felguera. The Mieres factory, established in 1848, was always in foreign hands. Created by an English company, it was purchased in 1852 by the Compagnie Minière des Asturies, with a capital of four million francs, but despite the injection of capital and optimistic plans, the company had to be dissolved in 1868. The plant was acquired in 1870 by another French banker, Numa Guilhou. The La Felguera factory belonged to a partnership, the Sociedad Pedro Duro y Compañía. These two factories were using Asturian hard coal, which promised considerable savings in comparison with the Andalusian companies that used either wood or coal from Asturias, from Córdoba, or from England, all with high transportation costs.

In the end, the district that became the symbol of the Spanish metallurgical industry was Vizcaya, whose initial business was exporting iron ore, and in a later phase, pig iron bars. The existence of abundant iron close to Bilbao had been known since Roman times (Pliny, *Natural History*, chap. 34). But problems with fuel, transportation, and entrepreneurial innovation kept the Basque iron industry underdeveloped until the middle of the nineteenth century. The first corporation organized to exploit the rich Vizcayan mineral deposits, the Santa Ana de Bolueta company, was created in Begoña through the initiative of a group of Bilbao financiers who together raised 200,000 pesetas. In 1848 this company constructed a blast furnace in Bolueta that was fired and went into production in the following year. The company prospered and in 1860 constructed two more blast furnaces.

Another Basque iron company that flourished in these years was that of the Ybarra family, which in 1827 had begun operating with a simple forge.

The company prospered and expanded by bringing in partners from outside the family, but it was still essentially a family company when in 1854 it inaugurated a new factory in Baracaldo. In 1860, still a family firm, it was restructured to form a limited liability partnership called the Compañía Ybarra, with capital of 1.5 million pesetas, of which the family held 60%.

Basque iron production multiplied five-fold between 1856 and 1871, although the total yields always remained modest. The industry did not achieve sustained growth until the Restoration, and that thanks to the production of a number of large firms, the first of which was the Fábrica de San Francisco located in El Desierto (Sestao), whose promoter was Francisco de las Rivas, later ennobled as the Marqués of Mudela. The Fábrica del Desierto, as it was commonly known, went into operation in 1879. In 1882 the Ybarra partnership was converted to a public company under the name Altos Hornos y Fábricas de Hierro y Acero, with a capital of 12.5 million pesetas. This company combined both capital and management from Catalonia and the Basque provinces, as its antecedent, the Ybarra partnership had also done. In this same year another public company was formed, the Vizcaya, also capitalized at 12.5 million pesetas. A great deal of the capital that contributed to the formation of these companies was generated by iron ore exports, which during these years reached tremendous proportions. In 1888

Table 4.3.   Spanish production of iron and steel, 1860–1904 (in thousand metric tons, five-year averages)

Period	(1) Pig iron	(2) Cast iron	(3) Steel
1860–64[a]	78.0	44.7	0
1865–69	82.0[b]	41.7	0
1870–74	—	49.0	0
1875–79	—	52.8	0
1880–84	129.4	116.9	0
1885–89	–	169.2	46.0
1890–94	271.6	174.1	89.0
1895–99	281.6	274.5	105.6
1900–04	299.2	341.0	167.2

a. No data for 1860

b. Only 1865 and 1866

Sources: calculated from the following: col. 1, Mitchell (1976); col. 2, Nadal (1975); col. 3, Svennilson (1954).

Table 4.4. Production of pig iron and steel in various European countries in 1900 (in thousand metric tons)

Country	Pig iron	Steel
United Kingdom	9,104	4,980
Germany	7,550	6,461
Russia	2,937	2,216
France	2,714	1,516
Austria/Hungary	1,456	1,170
Belgium	1,019	655
Sweden	526	300
Luxembourg	971	185
Spain	295	122
Italy	24	116

Source: Mitchell (1976)

another large iron and steel company was formed, the Sociedad Anónima Iberia. These three large companies, Altos Hornos, the Vizcaya, and the Iberia merged in 1902 to form Altos Hornos de Vizcaya.

During the last decades of the century Spain's iron and steel output increased rapidly, and Basque production in particular gained in importance as the industry grew and modernized in a remarkable fashion. In 1884 the first Bessemer converters were introduced, and soon thereafter the first Siemens-Martin furnaces were built. With these in operation, steel output, which had been insignificant up to this point, began to grow apace. Table 4.3 shows the evolution of the principal outputs in five-year averages. This rapid growth, a 5.2% yearly increase in the production of cast iron over the years 1860–1864 to 1900–1904 (or 7.8% measured from 1875–1879 to 1900–1904) was not enough, however, to make Spain's output significant within the European context, as can be seen in Table 4.4. By 1900 Spanish outputs of pig iron and steel were merely one thirtieth and one fortieth of the respective British outputs—but, in its turn, English steel production had been overtaken by Germany.

Several authors, among others Jordi Nadal (1975, pp. 158 ff.) and Tortella (1973, pp. 51, 237), have suggested that the backwardness of the Spanish iron and steel industry may have been due, at least in part, to the tariff exemption which was granted to railroad materials under the *Ley de Ferrocarriles* (Railroad Law) of 1855. Today I find the argument not particularly convincing. There is no doubt that had the builders of Spanish railroads been forced to use national iron during the years 1855 to 1864, when construction was fastest and the waiver was on the books, the stronger demand for Spanish iron would have stimulated production. But it is not clear that the Spanish iron masters could have met this increased demand and if so, at what price. An increase of this magnitude would have necessitated a large expansion in productive capacity and massive technical modernization, which would have required years of construction and very heavy investment. Furthermore, it is more than doubtful that the railroad construction companies would have accepted the terms of the concession without the exemption, because under such circumstances the prospects would have been very different and more uncertain. In other words, first, the whole construction plan would have had to be postponed, to gain time for new firms and factories to be established and the industry's capacity enlarged. Second, the whole cost structure would have had to be modified drastically, with costs revised upwards, and then surely some powerful foreign entrepreneurs would have shied away from the enterprise. Was alternative capital available within Spain? It seems very doubtful that such a mobilization would have been possible in the short run.[5] In this scenario, railroad construction would therefore have taken place at a much slower tempo than was actually achieved; this might have been better for the economy at large, but that is not the point at discussion here. At any rate, what would have happened to the metallurgical industry without the tariff exemption is a complex question which we cannot resolve at this moment.[6] Rather than blame the "lost opportunity" of railroad construction, backwardness in Spain's iron and steel industry ought to be attributed to the general, permanent, underlying features of technological and educational backwardness and insufficient demand: in other words, underequipment in agriculture and in industry alike (Bilbao, 1985, esp. pp. 220–223), plus the scarcity of coal. It was these factors, and not the tariff exemption, that explain the apparent paradox of an abundance of iron ore and a parlous state of underdevelopment in the iron industry.

Other Industries

Fascinated, perhaps to excess (because of the classical English model) with the textile and metallurgical industries, we historians of Spanish nineteenth-century economic history have until recently paid very little attention to other industries, which perhaps were more important than we realize (see Table 4.5). History is, however, the science of change, and these industries, traditional in character, attracted little attention because they exhibited little change. Among these other industries the most important one, speaking quantitatively, was the super-traditional industry of grain-milling, which underwent modernization and geographical relocation during the second half of the nineteenth century. In effect, the traditional system of grain-milling with rollers or millstones powered by wind or water, with the mills situated in the cereal producing regions, particularly Old Castile, was gradually being replaced by the introduction of the steam engine and a process involving cylindrical metal rollers, which was quicker and yielded a higher-quality product. The introduction of these new systems was not swift, however, and in 1906, when the flour-milling industry employed 85,000 workers, 60% of all mills still worked on water power, and only 25% were powered with steam or gas (Gómez Mendoza and Martín Aceña, 1983, p. 5). As the industry modernized, it also shifted location, first to Aragón and

Table 4.5. Spanish industry by sector, 1856, 1900, and 1922

	Panel A			Panel B		
	1856	1900	1922		1856	1900
Foodstuffs	56.20	41.40	28.76	Foodstuffs	55.78	40.33
				(Flour)	26.95	13.20
				(Olive oil)	14.73	4.96
				(Alcoholic beverages)	6.47	15.74
				(Canned food)	2.34	3.18
				(Others)	5.29	4.20
Textiles	23.04	26.48	27.71	Textiles	23.65	26.67
Metal manuf.	3.76	9.58	11.44	Metal manuf.	3.24	8.11
Mining	5.14	9.67	17.91			
Chemicals	5.46	4.17	3.61	Chemicals	3.50	5.57
Leather	3.78	2.95	4.82	Leather	3.82	2.93
Paper	2.62	5.75	5.75	Paper, etc.	2.33	5.03
TOTAL	100.00	100.00	100.00	Glass and ceramics	5.34	4.00
				Wood and cork	1.23	3.25
				Other	1.10	4.10
				TOTAL	99.99	99.99

Sources: Panel A, Prados (1988), p. 163; Panel B, Nadal (1987), App. 2.1 and App. 2.2

later to Catalonia. There it could take advantage of foreign grains imported through Barcelona, easier access to the whole Spanish interior market thanks to the railroad system, and other external economies. Catalonia came to play an important role in grain-milling, even though it was not self-sufficient in cereals.

The production of olive oil, traditionally an export item, was also being gradually modernized. At the beginning of the nineteenth century it was used for industrial purposes or for oil lamps, but its use for table consumption expanded as the century wore on. As this happened, production techniques were improved, for the palate is more demanding than machinery. The traditional oil press powered by animals or water was in time replaced by steam-powered machines, which improved quality because they worked faster and thus prevented fermentation, which produced a rancid taste. Chemical methods were also introduced to purify the product and control the desired degree of acidity (Simpson, 1992; Zambrana, 1987, pp. 136–160).

There is no doubt that the food industry, although still primitive in almost every sector except wine, compensated at least partially in Andalucía (mining also made a contribution) for the relative failure of the iron industry and various consumer industries like textiles.

The wine industry, in the nineteenth and twentieth centuries alike, was widely distributed over almost the whole of the Iberian Peninsula, although some zones, because of the nature of their products, specialized more in inter-regional and international trade. The major exporting areas were Andalucía, Catalonia, and Valencia. The traditional Catalán specialty had been the export of brandies and other hard spirits to America. During the nineteenth century (along with Valencia and other regions), it exported large amounts of ordinary wine, *vino de pasto,* to France for the *coupage,* a mixing and blending of foreign wines of higher alcohol content with the smoother French wines, a process used to achieve the required blend of body and aroma. The Andalusian wines, sherry and Málaga principally, were exported predominantly to Britain. As was to happen in so many other industries (see Chapter 8), foreign capitalists and businessmen established companies in Spain to organize exports to their home countries. The names are proof enough: Garvey, Terry, Osborne, Sandeman, Byass, Humbert, and Domecq (this last is French, but all the other names are British or Irish). The Domecq family, from Gascony, had exported French wines to England until they were forced to seek refuge in Spain during the French Revolution.

The phylloxera plague—the scourge of Europe during the last third of the nineteenth century—brought the most serious change to the wine industry. The plague affected France first, which produced a decade of prosperity for the Spanish winegrowers (1875–1885, approximately), but the following ten years saw its extension into Spain, where it affected most critically just those areas which had benefited from the preceding boom. More terrible than the phylloxera itself was the recovery of the French industry, which produced a sharp fall in Spanish demand as French competition returned. The coincidence of these two phenomena led to fierce demands for compensation from the Spanish producers, and in many cases they made no attempt to replant immune stock in vineyards laid waste by the disease, not even with public help.

Closely related to the wine industry was the cork and corkstopper industry, located chiefly in Gerona, which had already become important in the nineteenth century. Its raw material was the bark of the acorn oak, a tree that is abundant in the Mediterranean basin. Spanish exports of cork declined from 1875 to 1879, coinciding with the French phylloxera disaster, but the industry drew strength from growth in Spanish exports of higher-quality wine, which was exported in individual glass bottles that were corked. The industry, which met the needs of local markets and the export sector alike, became localized in San Felíu de Guíxols, Palamós, and Palafrugell, attracting not only Spanish business interests but also foreign capital and entrepreneurs.

During almost all of the nineteenth century the chemical industry played an auxiliary role, that is, it supplied other industries. It first became important in the textile industry, but also for pottery, soap, and perfumes, and finally in mining. In other countries by the nineteenth century agriculture was already a large consumer of chemicals, but not in Spain. During this period agriculture hardly consumed any industrial products at all, and this was a major problem, or seen from another perspective, perhaps this is the solution to the larger question of the failure of Spanish industry in the last century.

The production of sulfuric and nitric acids, potash, and soda was largely connected to the demand for colors and bleaches from the textile industry, and for this reason it became another industry located in Barcelona. The largest company with the longest tradition was the Sociedad Anónima Cros, but its volume of production was still very small in international terms.

With the expansion of mining a new branch of the chemical industry evolved: the manufacture of explosives, concretely dynamite and its derivative, blasting gelatins. La Sociedad Española de la Dinamita, holding the Nobel patent and funded by largely French, English, and Belgian capital, was established in Galdácano, near Bilbao, in 1882. Its output grew rapidly at an average rate of around 15% per annum as mining output increased. The company's principal customers were the major mining operators, the Río Tinto Company, Tharsis, Asturiana de Minas, and Orconera. The Dinamita company soon found it had competitors in Asturias, Vizcaya, and Catalonia, most of which were partially or totally financed from abroad. The bitter competition of the 1880s and 1890s produced in the end a cartel agreement, which was officially recognized when the Explosives Monopoly (the Unión Española de Explosivos) was formed in the summer of 1897 with monopoly rights for 20 years. In addition to serving as another example of the state's connivance with monopolies, the case of the Unión is of interest because it illustrates the chain of events and history of the progressive development of this auxiliary industry. Towards 1892 the Sociedad de la Dinamita began to produce the nitric and sulfuric acids which it used and had formerly imported; a little later it began to utilize its by-products by manufacturing superphosphates, a sideline that grew very slowly for lack of demand. During the first decades of the twentieth century, Spanish nationals began to replace foreign technical personnel as the various companies within the Unión Española de Explosivos cartel became more diversified (Tortella, 1983, 1987, and 1992).

Another branch of the chemical industry, the sector of the wine industry devoted to alcohol production, was quite important in the nineteenth century and very widespread. The technical advances that occurred were modest, and because the transition from artisan to industrial production introduced economies of scale, the industry became ever more concentrated in one place. Yet despite the abundance of raw materials and cheap labor, the Spanish alcohol industry was not very competitive, and because of this it sought and received state protection.[7]

Other industries also began to develop, if rather timidly, during the nineteenth century. The development of industrial engineering is more of token interest than substance, since the size of the companies and their outputs were minuscule. In Catalonia, in spite of the ill-fated episode of the El Vapor factory (an integrated plant that produced and repaired textile machinery in addition to actually spinning and weaving), new businesses continued to emerge, and already by the first half of the nineteenth century a number of metallurgical and mechanical workshops were producing textile machinery, machine tools, and even the first steamship constructed in Spain, the *Delfín,* made in the New Vulcan workshops in Barceloneta. The other two heavy engineering establishments of note were the Compañía de Fundición y Construcción de Máquinas and the Sociedad de Navegación e Industria. Behind these companies were names that were very familiar in the local economy during the century, including Bonaplata, Tous, Esparó, Güell, and Girona. The Girona family was involved in the Banco de Barcelona, the Banco de Castilla, the Banco Hispano Colonial, the Compañía Transatlántica and the Altos Hornos y Fábricas de Bilbao, among other enterprises.

Several mechanical and metallurgical businesses joined together to form the Maquinista Terrestre y Marítima in 1855, which from then onwards was the most important company in this sector. But in Barcelona there were others, such as Material para Ferrocarriles y Construcciones, which produced textile machinery, machine tools, transportation equipment, steam engines, turbines, and locomotives. The main problem the Barcelona metallurgical industry faced was its distance from the major centers of the iron and steel industry; its advantage lay in the external economies of this large industrial city. In contrast, the Basque heavy engineering companies that began to appear at the end of the century—the Vasco-Belge, the Sociedad Anónima Echeverría, and the Euskalduna company—had better access to iron and steel.

Many of these companies also produced materials for the shipping industry. Until about 1870, the Barcelona and Vizcaya shipyards had produced wooden sailing ships for fishing and for the commercial fleet. The revolutionary impact of the steamship on maritime navigation called for a complete reconversion of the naval construction industry, which began initially in Vizcaya, favored by the proximity of the new iron and steel industry. It also gave rise to a protectionist state policy introduced by the *Ley de Protección a la Escuadra* (Law of Protection of the Fleet), in 1887. Thus was born the ship builder Astilleros del Nervión in 1888 (on the Bilbao estuary), but this new industry too suffered from the limitations of the steel industry, both in Vizcaya and nationally. Only slowly and with difficulty did wood and sail give way to steel and steam; clearly, developments at the end of the nineteenth century were no more than a prelude to the growth that was to occur in the twentieth.

Mining

During the greater part of the nineteenth century Spain's tremendous hoard of mineral wealth lay largely undisturbed and contributed very little to the country's development. In the last quarter of the century, however, this underground wealth was tapped, and mining became the nation's most dynamic economic sector. The factors that permitted this dramatic upheaval were partly internal and partly external.

Although Spain has generally poor agricultural resources, the country is compensated with good mineral wealth. Moreover, the abundant deposits of mercury, iron, copper, lead, zinc, wolfram, etc. are conveniently located near coastal sites, which was very important in the nineteenth century in facilitating transportation, particularly for exports. This was the case with iron ore, especially in Vizcaya, Santander, and Málaga; the cost of transportation was decisive and explains why the coastal deposits were exploited, while inland resources, the deposits in León, Teruel, and Guadalajara, were hardly touched. The same can be said about copper and copper pyrites in Huelva, lead in Cartagena, and zinc in Asturias.

There are several reasons for the stagnation of Spanish mining until close to the end of the century. On the supply side, lack of capital and of technical know-how were obstacles to production on any adequate scale. On the demand side, general economic backwardness deprived this infant industry of market demand that would justify its development. One factor that was bound to discourage private initiative was legislation that blatantly favored the Crown. The Mining Law of 1825, for instance, while trying to stimulate private investment, clearly established the principle of "eminent domain" which placed private owners in a precarious position *vis à vis* the Crown with respect to property rights (Chastagnaret, 1972). As the century wore on, legislation softened the regalistic principle (the Mining Laws of 1849 and 1859), but in the end it was the legislation and the general policies of the Glorious Revolution of September 1868 that finally unleashed the feverish mining energy of the last quarter of the century.

On 29 December 1868 a new basic mining law was published, which simplified the adjudication of concessions and increased the security of ownership titles in relation to profits that might be generated. Ten months later (19 October 1869), a General Company Law facilitated incorporation in general, including mining companies. This legislation and other complementary measures, plus the general atmosphere created by the revolutionary government, clearly favored the mining boom. Nor can there be any doubt, as Vicens Vives, Sánchez-Albornoz, and Nadal have all pointed out, that urgent budgetary problems at that time also shaped the government's policy about concessions to private enterprise. But they were not the only factors. On the one hand, it is logical to suppose that a liberal free-trade government would have pursued this kind of policy even in the absence of budgetary problems. On the other hand, we must also look at the stimulus of demand. The mines were not developed simply because the government wanted it but chiefly because there was a growing international demand for mineral products, a demand that could not wait for the most favorable legislation, although it is to be supposed that pressure was brought to bear in favor of more liberal treatment. The Tharsis Sulphur Company, for example, had been founded in 1866 to replace another foreign concern, the Compagnie des Mines d'Huelva created eleven years earlier; demand for copper and later for sulfur had turned the attention of foreign entrepreneurs towards Spain before the liberal legislation was introduced. The exploitation of zinc and lead also shows that neither national initiative nor foreign capital waited for the 1868 legislation to start pushing the sector towards growth.

The real and deep causes of stagnation in the mining business were not so much legislative as they were economic; without human and physical capital and without markets to sell to, mining was unable to develop no matter how many laws were passed. And the reality is that the capital and the markets that the industry needed were not going to be available within Spain for many years: the metallurgical industry that could have used these resources was yet to be born. Nor were the capital and technical know-how for exploitation available at home. And in the early 1870s it did not look likely that they would be available for at least some time to come. The question thus was clear: either the mines would be exploited with substantial help from foreign capital, by companies interested in exports, or else they would remain idle for a long time. The gentlemen of the Glorious Revolution who set the mining legislation in motion were very aware of these alternatives, and they themselves considered, as Nadal pointed out more recently (1975, pp. 87–121), that this legislation represented an extension of the notion of *desamortización*, now applied to the subsoil.

The most remarkable story is that of iron ore. The slow development of the Spanish smelting industry was but scant stimulus to the large-scale development of Spain's abundant iron ore deposits. Instead, the stimulus was provided by the growth of the British (and to a lesser extent, German) steel industry. Concretely, it was the rapid expansion of steel technology begun by the introduction of the Bessemer converter (1856) which stimulated the demand for Spanish ore. The facts are well known. The converter invented by Henry Bessemer, a giant retort in which the liquid iron was subjected to a current of air to accelerate combustion, permitted the large-scale manufacture of high-quality steel from pig iron. But in order for the Bessemer steel to be of the desired quality, the pig iron that formed the raw material had to be free of phosphorus, which meant that the iron ore used to produce the pig iron should also be free of phosphorus. Now non-phosphoric ore is relatively rare in nature. Britain had some, but not in sufficient quantities to meet the growing demand for steel. In Europe, some other high-yield, non-phosphoric deposits were known, but the best located reserves were situated in the basin between Bilbao and Santander, and it was upon them that the British focused their attention. The deposits near Málaga, although close to the sea, were farther away from Britain, and those in the Kiruna-Gallivare region of Sweden, although closer to Britain, were farther away from the coast, and in an inhospitable climate (Flinn, 1955).

Even though Bessemer patented his converter in 1856, the problems of phosphorus-laden ore and other problems slowed down the adoption of the process until some fifteen years later. The interest of British iron smelters in Spanish mining was thus awakened when the legislation and the progressive politics were already in place, although there had already been a small amount of ore exported to Britain before the Revolution of September 1868. In the matter of a few years, starting in 1871, more than twenty British companies were founded to exploit Spanish iron ores, among the more important being the Orconera Iron Ore Company, the Luchana Mining Company, the Parcocha Iron Ore and Railway Company, the Salvador Spanish Iron Company, and the Marbella Iron Company. There were French firms too, such as the Schneider Company and the Franco-Belge des Mines de Somorrostro, this latter obviously with Belgian participation. Along with the foreign capitalists Spanish financiers also put the shoulder to the wheel of iron ore exploitation.[8] The Compañía Ybarra, for instance, owned a considerable part of the Orconera Company, and also extracted ore at its own mines, at Saltacaballo. Numerous other Spanish companies also appeared on the scene, to exploit ores in Vizcaya, Santander, and Andalucía.

Exploitation required a minimum scale of operation that was quite considerable, for, although the mining sites were close to the sea, the ore had to be extracted and transported in very large quantities. The task involved substantial infrastructure, such as railroads, loading wharves and piers, washing and concentrating sheds. The Orconera Company, for instance, built a railroad to transport ore from its workings to Baracaldo (Chilcote, 1968, p. 21). It is obvious that without the stimulus of foreign markets and foreign capital, the construction of this much infrastructure would have been unthinkable.

The Carlist War (1872–1876) interfered, to be sure, with the industry's forward march, particularly in Vizcaya. But at the same time, a certain disjuncture between the onset of preparations and the production stage was to be anticipated. Table 4.6 shows the growth in ore extraction during these years. Between the periods 1870–1874 and 1880–1884 output grew from less than .6 million tons per annum to more than four million tons, for an average annual growth of 21.1%, while growth between 1860–1864 and

Table 4.6. Spanish mining output, 1830–1904 (in thousand metric tons, five-year averages)

Period	(1) Coal	(2) Mercury	(3) Iron ore	(4) Lead ingots
1830–1834	—	.9484	—	—
1835–1839	—	.9751	—	—
1840–1844	—	.9195	—	—
1845–1849	—	.8868	—	—
1850–1854	—	.7006	—	—
1855–1859	—	.7597	—	—
1860–1864	370.1	.8359	198.4	65.5
1865–1869	489.1	1.0766	264.4	71.6
1870–1874	653.4	1.1429	595.8	96.9
1875–1879	671.4	1.3979	1,288.6	100.8
1880–1884	1,032.0	1.5927	4,045.4	88.3
1885–1889	1,000.0	1.7283	4,625.6	117.9
1890–1894	1,226.0	1.5397	5,422.8	163.5
1895–1899	2,116.5	1.4585	7,258.4	164.8
1900–1904	2,637.3	1.0288	8,155.4	173.8

		Rates of growth		
1860–1864 to 1900–1904	5.0	.5	9.7	2.5

Source: Tortella (1981), p. 52

1870–1874 had been 11.6% per annum. And in turn, output doubled again from 1880–1884 to the end of the century.

Most of this output (90% on average, see Table 4.8) was shipped out to other countries, and most of it went through the port of Bilbao, generally between 80% and 90% in the 1880s and the first years of the 1890s, according to figures of the American Iron and Steel Association. On the basis of Spanish mining statistics, Nadal has calculated (1975, p. 116) that the Basque percentage of the total output during these years was somewhat lower, about 75%, but given the inaccuracies in sources from this period, one can say nothing further about this relatively minor discrepancy. The greater part of the amount exported through Bilbao, about two-thirds, went to England, and an increasing share of the remainder was destined for Germany. France and Belgium took most of the rest. The share of Spanish mineral ore that went to the United States was very small, and it came mostly from Málaga. It is of note that from roughly 1885 onwards, after the first modern furnaces were built, Spain started to export pig iron, chiefly to Germany and Italy (data again from the AISA).

Table 4.7.   Spanish exports of ores and metals, 1850–1904 (in thousand metric tons, five-year averages)

Period	(1) Copper ore	(2) Mercury	(3) Iron ore	(4) Lead ingots
1850–1854	—	.5403	3.6	45.2
1855–1859	—	.3009	17.2	51.1
1860–1864	—	.8394	49.8	56.1
1865–1869	—	.3249	72.5	60.0
1870–1874	—	1.1888	578.2	76.9
1875–1879	443.1	1.6031	936.8	101.3
1880–1884	544.5	1.1775	3,632.6	114.6
1885–1889	762.4	1.1942	4,543.2	112.6
1890–1894	593.8	1.3896	4,922.6	150.1
1895–1899	764.2	1.9206	6,700.7	176.6
1900–1904	1,004.6	1.0623	7,452.1	164.4
		Rates of Growth		
1860–1864 to 1900–1904	3.3	1.4	16.5	2.6

Source: Tortella (1981), p. 53

Table 4.8.   Spanish exports of ores and metals as a percentage of production, 1850–1904 (five-year averages)

Period	(1) Mercury	(2) Iron ore	(3) Lead ingots
1850–54	77.1	—	—
1855–59	39.6	—	—
1860–64	100.4	25.1	85.6
1865–69	30.2	27.4	83.4
1870–74	104.0[a]	97.0	79.4
1875–79	114.7	72.7	100.5
1880–84	73.9	89.8	129.8
1885–89	69.1	98.2	95.5
1890–94	90.3	90.8	91.8
1895–99	131.7	92.3	101.7
1900–04	103.3	91.4	94.6
Averages	87.0	90.7	96.2

a. Percentages over 100 may be due to export of stocks or reexport
Source: calculated from Tables 4.6 and 4.7.

Rapid growth in exports during these decades made Spain the greatest exporter of iron ore in Europe at the end of the century, far ahead of Sweden, whose exports were about a fifth of Spain's (Table 4.9). This is far from saying that Spain was the major producer of iron ore, as can also be seen in Table 4.9. What draws attention in the Spanish case is the enormous imbalance between production and exports. A North American observer in 1882 put it this way:

> This country is interesting and well endowed, but backward, and makes no noticeable progress in developing its own metallurgical industry, although it shows energy enough in yearly exports of its precious iron ore, to the enrichment of others. Yet Spain does not benefit as much as you might think at first sight from this plundering of its treasures because the capital devoted to extracting and exporting the ore is principally English, French, German, and Belgian; the profits from this pillage hardly amount to anything for the Spaniards; they leave with the mineral ore.

This is how James M. Swank, the secretary of the American Iron and Steel Association, described the situation in the Association's annual report. The quotation, reproduced here for its interest and sincerity of expression, may

Table 4.9.   Production and export of iron ore in various European countries in 1900 (in thousand metric tons)

Country	Production	Export
Spain	8,676	7,823
Sweden	2,610	1,620
France	5,448	372
Norway[a]	18	27
United Kingdom	14,253	0
Germany	12,793	0
Luxembourg	6,171	0
Russia	6,001	0
Austria/Hungary	1,894	0

a. The anomalous case of Norway, with exports almost twice as high as production, may be due to exports from stocks, or perhaps a statistical error because some Swedish ore was shipped out of Norwegian ports

Source: Mitchell (1976)

profit from a comment. It represents a one-sided point of view of the secretary of a highly protectionist professional association in a country that was itself protectionist; a few years later the same observer would deliver impressive eulogies on the installation of the first Bessemer converters in Spain, thus contradicting the pessimistic analysis that we have just read. In the first place, an important part of the capital dedicated to extraction and export of the ore was Spanish. As Flinn (1955, p. 89) pointed out, "the Spaniards joined in the spoliation, rather than take more positive steps towards the development of a large-scale national industry." Secondly, although without a doubt a considerable fraction of the profits did "walk away with the ore," another portion, not to be dismissed, remained in the country. Prados (1988, pp. 192–194) has compiled and calculated figures to estimate the "value retained" from Spain's mineral exports, and demonstrates that, contrary to logical expectation and the undeniable returns on foreign investment in Spanish mining, the proportion of the value of the exported mineral that was retained in Spain oscillated around 65% for iron ore, with higher percentages for other metals. Moreover, as we have seen, the Spanish economy had no alternative; either the ore could be worked with foreign capital, or it would be left in the ground. And what the detractors of this export policy do not seem to point out is that the sale of Spanish ore took place at the best possible moment, insofar as the boom in Bessemer steel gave these exports their highest possible earning value. Later on, with the diffusion of other processes which did not demand non-phosphoric ore (Thomas-Gilchrist and Siemens-Martin), the discovery of new deposits, and falling transport costs, the price of Spanish iron ore fell. As Flinn points out, "In the early twentieth century, when the British steel industry gradually turned to the more general use of the Thomas basic process, its dependence on supplies of non-phosphoric ore declined. The importance of the Spanish source of ore waned."

On the whole question of the effect of foreign investment, the eventual destination of the profits generated is one of the aspects that should be kept in mind, something that we still have not studied in any depth. More important from the point of view of the exporting nation is the general dynamic effect that exports produced in the economy as a whole. The reinvestment of profits would obviously be important here, but there are many aspects to bear in mind: specifically the multiplier effects, the forward and backward linkages, technological and dynamic impacts, and so on.

In fact, the export of such a massive amount of iron ore certainly did affect the Spanish economy, and particularly the Basque region, by generating extraordinary dynamic changes. All scholars, including the most severe critics of foreign capital investment, recognize that the Basque iron and steel industry owed its development to "the capitalization that was generated by high profitability in the export of ore to England" (Tamames, 1990, p. 322). When Nicolás Sánchez-Albornoz tells us that "the mines ended up more or less resembling foreign enclaves, only attached to Spain by virtue of location, but without articulation with the rest of the economy," he expressly excepted the case of iron as "something later and of different significance." Now by the end of the century iron ore represented more than 60% of raw mineral exports, so that the "enclave," if it existed at all, would in any case be smaller than one might suppose at first. Even for products with only the most modest connections with the Spanish economy, like copper pyrites and lead, it still remains to be seen just how much they did constitute enclaves. That these exports generated a demand for labor; that they stimulated the development of a national mining technology, a capital goods industry, and the explosives industry; that they called forth considerable investment in infrastructure such as railroads and ports; that the earnings generated served to palliate the balance of payments deficit—all this is evident: the total impact still remains to be determined. It is worth adding, also, that the period of maximum mineral exports coincides with that of maximum imports of capital (that is to say from 1870 onwards), and also with the clearest impact upon the economy.

Returning to the question of iron ore, its stimulating effect on the Basque economy is beyond any doubt. It is sufficient to consider the increase in population in Bilbao and the whole region, the increase in employment in industry and commerce, the development of industrial activities, the creation of commercial businesses, the growth of the Basque banking industry and savings deposits,[9] to realize the extent of the change that was taking place in the wake of the massive ore exports. This impact of mining on the whole Basque region, and particularly in the area around Bilbao, is recognized by several authors. Some works have highlighted particular aspects: perhaps the most noteworthy is the study by Valerie Shaw (1977) calculating the multiplier impact of mining on total employment (three jobs close by for every job in mining, which the author considers a high figure), and also detailing the industrial and commercial growth in the Bilbao region during the last quarter of the nineteenth century. Of course, it is one thing to talk about the zone's economic modernization and quite another to make favorable judgments about its every aspect; many of the results were disastrous, from the increase in mortality rates to the exploitation of workers and the growing disparity in the distribution of incomes and wealth. Lamentably, we still lack serious studies about the impact of industrialization on the distribution of income and living standards, both in the Basque country and in the rest of Spain.

One must emphasize that the case of iron ore is the most striking one in almost every aspect: the most spectacular growth, the largest tonnage, and the largest earnings. If in the three-year period from 1899 to 1901 average annual export of minerals in bulk was valued at 162 million pesetas, the value for iron ore alone stood at 100.2 million pesetas, that is about 62%, and with little variation that proportion had been maintained since 1875.

Lead, which was not included in the above statistics, was ahead of iron, however, in terms of aggregated export value throughout the century; first because exploitation and export on a large scale dated from much earlier, and second because it was the metal, not the ore, that was exported, in bars or ingots that obviously had a higher value-added component. Quite distinct from iron, lead has a relatively low melting point, and refining was simple enough to carry out close to the mining sites.

Lead was abundant in southern Spain, mainly in Granada, Almería, Murcia, Jaén, and particularly in Córdoba, and relatively modern production methods have been in use since approximately the 1830s. The lead ore was first extracted in the Sierra de Gádor, and later on in other mountains close by in the Sierra Almagrera, near Cartagena, a mountain chain which runs parallel to the coast near the sea in the provinces of Granada, Almería, and Murcia. During the central decades of the nineteenth century the industry was run essentially by Spanish, largely local, enterprises. By mid-century foreign capitalists gradually began to express an interest. As Nadal explains, "the early Spanish developers had not been capable of making the heavy investment necessary to fully develop gallery mining, and this facilitated the foreign intrusion." The Spanish producers, who were still hauling water from the mine workings by hand, soon found that exploitation at this level was not profitable. The deposits in Jaén, abandoned by Gaspar Remisa as tumbledown and worthless, were acquired by a French and an English company, "and both of them, after installing steam engines to pump out water and after making other improvements, took up mining again with excellent yields."[10] During the second half of the nineteenth century British and French firms dominated lead mining in Córdoba and Jaén. This inflow of capital and foreign technology, combined with the extension of the railroad network and the exhaustion of the Gádor and Almagrera deposits, contributed to the gradual transfer of production from coastal to inland sites.

The case of lead extraction illustrates the problems of domestic operations. Nadal himself, so critical of what he calls foreign "intrusion," points out how scant the multiplier effect of lead mining becomes in the hands of small local operators, "speculators, not . . . true entrepreneurs." Something similar happened when local entrepreneurs leased the Arrayanes deposits from the state: they plundered the reserves, spending as little as they possibly could and rendering fraudulent accounting to boot.[11] Rapacity and plain lack of interest in the social effects of mining were not the monopoly of outsiders; foreigners and Spaniards alike all tried to maximize profits. The difference lay in the long-term planning, the technical knowledge, the capital brought to the task, and the knowledge of the market. And in this it was almost always the foreigners that held the advantage and could develop mine workings more rationally and on a larger scale.

A similar picture emerges from copper mining. The large copper deposits in the southwest of the Peninsula had been known since the dawn of history and the fabulous kingdom of Tharsis. The copper deposits extend like a fringe over a wide area, parallel to the coast north of Huelva, between the Guadiana and the Guadalquivir rivers. The most important deposits are located between two smaller rivers, the Río Tinto, tinted red by the ore it carries, and the Río Odiel. The best-known ones are the Río Tinto and Tharsis deposits; on the west bank of the Río Guadiana, in Portugal, lie the São Domingos deposits. During the greater part of the nineteenth century the Río Tinto mines were worked inefficiently (and on occasions fraudulently) by concessions, with little profit to the state. The mines of Tharsis lay idle during most of the nineteenth century, until the French Compagnie des Mines de Cuivre d'Huelva acquired a concession to extract copper from them in 1855. But the strong demand and the necessary capital lay in Britain. In addition to copper, the Huelva pyrites offered sulfur, the raw material for caustic soda and sulfuric acid, vital inputs for the British chemical industry. In 1866 a consortium of British chemical companies organized the Tharsis Sulphur and Copper Company, which replaced the Compagnie des Mines by means of an "amicable arrangement" (Checkland, 1967, p. 105). The British company immediately undertook the necessary work for large-scale exploitation: earth removal for "open-cast" mining, a narrow-gauge railroad to the Bay of Huelva, and a pier and loading facilities. The company refined part of the mineral *in situ* to obtain copper directly, and shipped the rest to Britain as raw pyrites, where it was sold to chemical companies. Production and exports remained at very high levels for the remainder of the century.

The case of the Río Tinto mines is similar, but at a later date. The mines, whose wealth was well known, had produced little or no profit for the state (their owner), nor had they realized their economic potential. Finally, in 1870, dogged by debts and deficits and bent upon getting some kind of tangible profit, the Spanish government decided to sell the concession to the highest bidder, but in spite of the quality of the deposits at first there were no takers; the asking price was high, and a substantial investment was needed to operate adequately. Finally, in 1873, an interested party appeared in the form of an international syndicate headed by a London banker (Hugh Matheson, a Scotsman) with the involvement of a German bank and some Spanish financing. The Río Tinto Company was capitalized at the then enormous sum of six million pounds sterling, 150 million in pesetas; the Bank of Spain's capital at the time was one third of this amount. The selling price had been fixed at 95 million pesetas, and almost two-thirds of the capital was allocated to pay it off in ten annual installments. The rest was largely for infrastructure investment, and a small but substantial amount went to pay off the original partners. Several years were spent in constructing the mining railroad from Río Tinto to Huelva, the wharves, and generally getting the facility ready. But when the preparations were completed and production began, the results were impressive. Output, exports, and profits surpassed even those of the Tharsis operation. These were the two largest firms mining Spanish copper pyrites,[12] but by no means the only ones.

If in iron, lead, and copper mining circumstances rendered the importation of foreign capital unavoidable, in the case of mercury this was not so. Obtaining mercury from its ore, cynabrium, is a simple process which involves neither complex techniques nor heavy capital investments. And of course it was not necessary to export the ore itself, which the far-inland location of the deposits would have made uneconomical. The extraction process was really quite simple, but even so, the commercialization of Spanish mercury was to end up in the hands of the Rothschilds during most of the nineteenth century.

The mercury mines in Almadén ("the mine" in Arabic), the richest in the world, had been known since time immemorial and had been exploited at least since Roman times. They had become the property of the Spanish state in the fifteenth century and had often been used by the state as its best collateral asset to guarantee its debts. This is how the Rothschilds were able to profit from their commercialization. As Carande says, "the impecunious princes, willy-nilly, provide the large merchants who could make credit available to them with numerous occasions to make handsome profits; profits above and beyond the growing interest payments . . . thanks to privileged situations which open up legal channels to commercial practices quite incompatible with the premise of the just price, and incubators of veritable monopolies" (1949, p. 42). Carande is referring here to the case of Almadén in the sixteenth century, when the Fuggers tried to take advantage of the indebtedness of the Hapsburgs to gain a monopoly of the world mercury market; but the same occurred again in the nineteenth century, when the Rothschilds tried a similar coup taking advantage of the impecunious state of the Spanish governments, both under Isabel II and under the Glorious Revolution government after 1868.

Mercury was used a great deal in metallurgy and in medicine, particularly starting in the sixteenth century, when the amalgam process for extracting silver was discovered, and when Paracelsus recommended mercury for its curative qualities (Kearney, 1971, p. 118). It was also employed in making mirrors. With the Industrial Revolution its uses multiplied, from electricity and photography to the manufacture of instruments and explosives; since that time its main market has been in London, where on average 88% of the Spanish output was exported.

During the periods when the Rothschilds, more or less with official connivance, manipulated the concessions they held to sell the Almadén mercury (which is most of the period that this chapter addresses), their role was to act as agents, whether buying Spanish mercury at auctions that were frequently rigged, or selling it in London on behalf of the Spanish state.[13] Either way, the Rothschilds took the lion's share of the profits, especially after 1868, when the government borrowed heavily from them and agreed in return to attach the sale of mercury to the loan repayment, giving the bankers exclusive selling rights. With this agreement the Rothschilds controlled, at least for several years, the greater part of the world supply of mercury, since they owned the Idria mine in Italy and could also influence the volume of North American production. At the beginning prices went up and so did profits, but in the long run the monopoly did not hold. If we analyze these sales operations independently, they do not seem to have been at all ruinous for the Spanish state, since it came to receive on average about 80% of the proceeds.[14] However, there are a couple of problems here. In the first place, the value of the sales might have been calculated in such a manner that the Rothschilds pocketed large sums as "costs" before arriving at the agreed share of profits, though this hypothesis does not seem to square with the facts published by the state. The second problem, much more real, was the almost incredible interest rate of 200% that was paid on the original loan; taking this factor into account, one can see that the operation was frankly not between equal partners. Yet the Spanish government renewed its contract with the Rothschilds in the first years of the twentieth century, improving the terms, so that the state received about 90% of the sales. In conclusion, in contrast to the other metals, where mercury is concerned, foreign capital played no essential role and the industry could have operated without it. The commercialization of mercury could have been made profitable for agents of the Spanish state. In this case it was the government's budgetary problems that allowed the Rothschilds to acquire large profits from the sale of mercury, with little risk or effort.

Zinc was also extracted during the nineteenth century. The best deposits of this metal were found in Reocín, near Santander, and they were exploited by the Belgian-owned Real Compañía Asturiana de Minas, which exported the greater part of the ore to be smelted in Belgium. Zinc was also mined and exported from the Cartagena region by the same companies that were mining lead, since both ores were frequently found together.

Let us now try to summarize in a few words the contribution that mining made to the Spanish economy in the nineteenth century. On the positive side, the sector contributed to the foreign trade balance, attracting capital and generating up to one-third of the value of exports. The mining industry has been reproached for being an enclave of foreigners with hardly any economic spin-off for the home economy. Certainly there is some truth to this charge, and this seems to be characteristic of mining in other underdeveloped countries. However, there are reasons to suppose that this restricting element was not so complete in the case of Spanish mining as it may have been in other areas. Even though a large part of the profits were exported, another part was reinvested, characteristically in the iron and steel sector; as we saw earlier, iron ore was the motive force behind the economic modernization of the Basque country. Although it is true that foreign companies, and even Spanish ones, initially employed foreign methods and foreign senior personnel, in the long run the trend was to employ an increasing proportion of nationals; mining engineering was probably one of the fields where Spanish science and technology rose to their greatest height in the nineteenth century. As far as backward linkages are concerned, the isolation of mining is not at all evident. An activity of such scope gave employment to many thousands of people and created demands for a wide range of goods and services, from banks and businesses to housing and food, including transportation, public works, and machinery.[15] Let us bring up here by way of example the already mentioned manufacture of dynamite in Bilbao, almost exclusively devoted to the mining industry. In a few decades, a series of foreign companies managed to construct the largest chemical company in Spain, with a majority of Spanish shareholders. But the important point here is not the nationality of the shareholders but the stimulus that demand from the mining industry created within the chemical industry. One has to suppose that something similar happened with other industries, particularly in iron and steel manufacture, construction, and transportation. The theme is open for further investigation.

On the negative side is the fundamental question of the price that the country received for the exploitation of its mineral resources. Such resources, of course, are nonrenewable; deposits in the long run become used up, often permanently, although frequently technological progress makes it cost-effective to work with low content ores and sometimes even to rework the spoil of earlier operations. For this reason it seems more justified to speak of pillage and plunder when referring to mineral exports, as did the secretary of the American Iron and Steel Association in 1882. But the real question is about the price received for the ore, and here the issue of the exchange rate comes in, as well as the more obvious question about the profits of the companies involved. Sánchez-Albornoz (1977, p. 140) has shown that the price of minerals fell on the international market during the last quarter of the nineteenth century; however, it is also true that general prices were falling during this period: what is interesting therefore is not the absolute price of minerals, but their relative price. Recent studies by Prados (1985, 1988, ch. 5) show that the relative prices of minerals did not fall and that Spain's terms of trade improved until well into the twentieth century, especially keeping in mind the improvements in mining productivity. Thus it seems that although the question is complex, our knowledge to date does not lend support to the assertion that Spain was exploited in the exportation of its mineral wealth. There is no doubt that the profits of the companies were very high and that much of the wealth was repatriated. It also seems clear that they paid little in taxation, but that is the price that Spain paid for its lack of human and physical capital, and for the mismanagement of its Treasury.

Energy

The substitution of hydraulic and especially of coal energy for the work of animals and men is the major distinctive characteristic of the first Industrial Revolution. In Spain this transition was set in motion during the nineteenth century, but it was not completed.

Spanish economic historians agree, at least since Jaime Vicens Vives, that the scarcity of energy resources has been a powerful obstacle to the economic development of the country. Catalán writers especially have bemoaned the paucity of coal reserves, attributing the region's failure to develop a powerful capital goods industry—given the success of its consumer goods industries—to what they termed a "betrayal of the subsoil." Their complaints may be justified to a certain extent, although the expansion of heavy industry in Japan and in Italy would seem to contradict this notion.

During the first half of the nineteenth century energy sources in Spain remained largely the traditional ones, human and animal, with a marginal contribution from hydraulic power, and of course wind power for windmills and sailing ships, and wood as the basic domestic fuel. The consumption of coal increased during the second half of the century, owing to the extension of the railroad network and the use of coal in navigation and for industry.

Coal consumption was supplied, in almost equal parts, by domestic production and imports.

Spain has coal deposits scattered around the country, the most important of which are located in the northern provinces of León and Asturias, and in the southern provinces of Ciudad Real and Córdoba. These provinces produce hard coal. Catalonia, in contrast, has abundant deposits of soft coal or lignite whose thermal capacity is too low for most branches of industry. But generally speaking coal supply is a serious problem in Spain, because in comparison with Europe's major coal basins its deposits are scanty, expensive to mine, and of low quality. The reserves are relatively scarce, the hard coal is full of impurities and friable, hence much inferior to English, German, Belgian, and much of French coal. Spain's coal seams are narrow and discontinuous, which makes the product doubly expensive because mining it requires high infrastructure costs, and mechanization cannot be easily adopted. Furthermore, the output is not suitable for coking. To put this picture into a comparative focus, we can look at prices. For similar qualities, the f.o.b. price of Asturian coal was nearly double that of English coal from Newcastle.[16]

The consequences for entrepreneurs attempting to establish modern industries are easy to imagine. According to the calculations of Catalán cotton millowners, in 1865 the cost of producing one unit of steam HP in Catalonia was about three times that in England (Ministerio de Industria y Energía, 1988, p. 42). The calculation was probably biased to exaggerate the Catalán disadvantage so as to better support the industrialists' continuous pleas for increased tariff protection, but there is no doubt that "the coal problem" was serious. More convincing than the self-interested calculations of cotton manufacturers was their behavior. In a brilliant paper, Albert Carreras (1983a) describes how the high cost of coal pushed millowners to search for alternative energy sources, which they found in water power, much of it from the slopes of the Pyrenees. According to Carreras's approximate estimates, in 1861 hydraulic power provided Catalán industry with the equivalent of 10% of its coal imports, and by 1901 that figure had risen to 25%. In a country as dry as Spain, these figures present an eloquent measure of the extent of the coal problem.

For all these reasons I would be inclined to say that Spain's coal has been a major obstacle to economic growth, since coal mining has been a classic case of a noncompetitive industry that survived thanks to protection, passing on the real costs to all energy consumers, and that amounts to nothing less than

everyone involved in the processes that are integral to industrialization. The protection of Spanish coal was becoming an increasingly weighty burden, on the one hand, because more coal was needed as the industrial structure of the country began to modernize, and on the other hand, because improved extraction and transportation technologies brought down the price of coal on the international market, which made Spanish coal increasingly expensive in relative terms. Inasmuch as Spanish coal was protected, the economy failed to take advantage of the opportunity that falling world prices offered. When we study industry in the twentieth century, we shall see the estimates that have been made of the cost of protecting coal.

In some cases the problems of supply were compounded by those of demand, as in the coal-gas industry. Gas, a coal by-product, was used during the greater part of the nineteenth century for public lighting and domestic consumption in cities. The first urban center to use it was Barcelona, in 1842, where it was introduced by a Frenchman, Charles Lebon, and the local banker Pedro Gil. Soon there were several companies and production sites in the town. In Valencia the Charles Lebon Company, in association with the local banker-politician José Campo, introduced gas in 1843. In Madrid it was brought in by an English company in 1846 (see Chapter 8). According to Sudrià (1983), in about 1861 Spain had 25 gas fabrication plants, of which 11 were in Catalonia, and in 1901 the number had increased to 81, with 33 in Catalonia, 15 in Andalucía, 8 in Valencia and smaller numbers in other regions. All in all, gas consumption in Spain remained low in comparison with other European countries, and thus production tended to stagnate. Now gas was used primarily for illumination, both public and private. Could this low level of gas consumption be related to low literacy rates and poor reading habits in the Spanish population? Here we have a clear case where the gas industry is trapped between a soft demand situation and high prices for its raw material, coal; hence both demand and supply militated against industrial development. In this case history left its imprint in present-day conditions; gas consumption levels continue to be low in Spain (Sudrià, 1983 and 1987).

The electrical industry also got its start in Barcelona, where in 1875 the Dalmau and Xifra Company installed the first electricity-generating plant, which distributed power to various industrial establishments; fifteen years later the Compañía Madrileña de Electricidad was founded, and shortly afterwards others appeared, like the Sevillana de Electricidad, the Eléctrica de San Sebastián and the Eléctrica del Nervión, in the Bilbao region, all private commercial undertakings. But this was just the beginning; the electrical industry in Spain, as in the world at large, is a twentieth-century phenomenon.

An Overview

Figure 4.2 compares two recent indices of industrial production, from Carreras (1983) and Prados (1988, chap. 4). Their trajectories seem parallel and convergent, largely because their sources are similar and because the end year is the same, but the Prados curve is smoother, because instead of building a year-by-year index, as Carreras did, its author has chosen a few benchmark dates (1800, 1830, 1860, 1890, and 1910) for his estimates. In order to facilitate comparison, I have linearly interpolated values for the missing years. In fact, the Prados index is an attempt to correct the only serious defect of the Carreras series, namely, that it exaggerates early rates of growth because it gives excessive weight to the cotton industry, which, as we saw, grew very rapidly in the years 1830 to 1855, beginning from very low initial levels of output.

The main upshot of these small discrepancies is that Carreras draws an op-

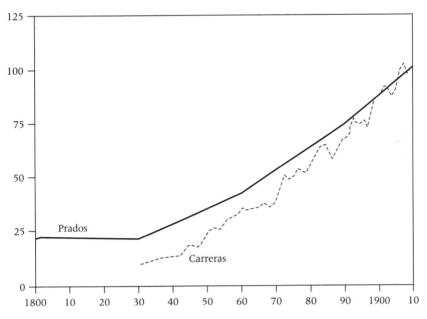

Figure 4.2. Two indices of industrial production, 1800–1910

Table 4.10. Industrialization per capita in various European countries, 1800–1910 (in $U.S. 1970, at parity purchasing power)

Country	1800	1830	1860	1890	1910
Great Britain	89	139	257	391	458
France	59	92	164	250	356
Germany	—	—	102	134	391
Sweden	—	—	46	97	198
Italy	—	—	35	63	145
Hungary	—	—	—	—	157
Spain	34	29	50	93	122

Source: Prados (1988), p. 169.

timistic vision of the performance of the Spanish economy in the mid-nineteenth century, a period which he describes as the "take-off of the industrial revolution in Spain," and a pessimistic one of the late nineteenth century, which he describes as "an early climacteric . . . following the pattern of Victorian England . . . before having consolidated her industrial progresses" (Carreras, 1983, pp. 141–142). In contrast, if one accepts the Prados corrections, the curve describes a more uniform pattern and, overall, slower rates of industrial growth. According to this version, Spain's industrialization in the nineteenth century did not altogether stagnate but proceeded at such a slow relative pace that at the end of the period, by 1910, Spain's level of industrialization was among the lowest in Europe (Table 4.10). In nineteenth-century Europe, as in Alice's country in *Through the Looking Glass,* you had to run as fast as you could to remain in the same place; Spanish industry, obviously, did not run fast enough.

CHAPTER 5

Transportation
and Commerce

Transportation Problems

Transportation costs are one of the major obstacles to economic modernization. In the famous dictum of Adam Smith, "the division of labour is limited by the extent of the market": effective division of labor, large-scale production, and technical progress require access to extensive markets, and this implies large urban agglomerations and transportation that is both rapid and inexpensive. History documents the crucial role that transportation has played in economic development: Mediterranean navigation and the Roman roads in the ancient and early medieval world; transatlantic and other oceanic navigation and major rivers in the modern period; the construction of roads and canals in England in the eighteenth century; the roads, canals, railroads, and steam navigation in the nineteenth-century industrial revolutions. And as far as the twentieth century is concerned, it seems almost superfluous to mention the economic importance of transport in our contemporary economy.

There is also general agreement that the lack of an adequate transportation network (and the difficulty of establishing it) proved to be a major obstacle to Spain's economic development. The Iberian Peninsula is large and rudely mountainous, with a high central plateau separated from the periphery by fault lines or mountain chains. The countryside is generally speaking arid; the rivers are either short, steep, and swift or else shallow, irregular, and sluggish for many months of the year. All this makes transportation difficult in the interior, whether by land or by water, and historically the peninsula has been fragmented into isolated markets. There cannot be the slightest doubt that these conditions have been a serious hindrance to economic growth. Because of this geographical configuration, the coastal fringes on the Atlantic and the Mediterranean, accessible to each other and to exterior commerce thanks to their maritime position, have been the zones of greater economic development since the seventeenth century, while the isolated interior stagnated both economically and demographically.

Contemporary thinkers were clearly aware of the transportation problem, as is proved by the repeated failed attempts to construct navigable waterways in the eighteenth and nineteenth centuries. In the 1800s the Bourbon kings also made efforts to improve the roads, but the Napoleonic wars were as destructively disastrous in this endeavor as they were in so many others. The same can be said about the Carlist wars. But during the nineteenth century, particularly after 1840, a substantial program of road construction was carried out. This probably served to reduce transport costs in terms of both money and time, although it did not suffice to put Spain on a par with other European countries that were richer and enjoyed better overall accessibility. At the end of the century Spain could count on some 36,000 kilometers of roadways, 16,000 of which were classified as first or second class. In about 1840 the total extent of the road network amounted to only 9,000 kilometers; by 1865 the figure had reached some 16,000, of which 12,000 were first or second class. These achievements were considerable. There was also a certain amount of progress in terms of the vehicles that were used. The carriage came to take the place of traveling on horseback, and carriage design also was continually improving. The amount of time it took to travel by Spanish roads in the nineteenth century was reduced quite impressively (Madrazo, 1991, esp. pp. 154–161).

Maritime transport too underwent a major transformation. Navigation by sail expanded, and, very late in the century, steamships began to operate. In spite of an extensive coastline and numerous ports, 90% of Spain's maritime trade was concentrated in Barcelona, Bilbao, Santander, Sevilla, Valencia, Málaga, and Cádiz. During the century the importance of Barcelona and Bilbao increased considerably. Port improvements—enlarging and dredging, building wharves and breakwaters—came largely in the second half of the century, but important as they were, in no way did they measure up to the changes that were to be realized by the introduction of railroads.

In contrast with other European countries, notably England and Holland, internal water transport was practically nonexistent in Spain; in contrast, the volume of maritime trade was very considerable. Within it we can distinguish between *cabotaje,* which is coastal trade, some of it only short-distance and all between national ports, and long-distance trade, *navegación de altura*, of longer distance and generally international. It is possible that coastal trade increased during the first half of the nineteenth century. The figures that we have for the second half, analyzed by Frax (1981), indicate stagnation during the central decades of the century, slow growth between 1870 and 1890, and considerable growth thereafter. Figure 5.1 shows, in index form, the growth of the principal transport components from 1860 to 1913. One can see that railroad transport increased considerably more than *cabotaje*. Between 1881 and 1904 the volume of goods transported by sea represented only 12% of what was transported by railroad. This by no means indicates that these two transport modes were in competition with each other. On the contrary: maritime coastal trade had slowed down even before the major railroad links were completed and grew rapidly after the 1890s, when the northern coastal narrow gauge lines began to enter into service, a development which in principle should have been in major competition with coastal shipping.[1] In fact coastal trade continued to expand in the twentieth century. What seems to be implied by Figure 5.1 is that the transportation systems were complementary rather than competitive, each of them being a function of the level of economic development.

Given the geographically compact configuration of the Iberian Peninsula,

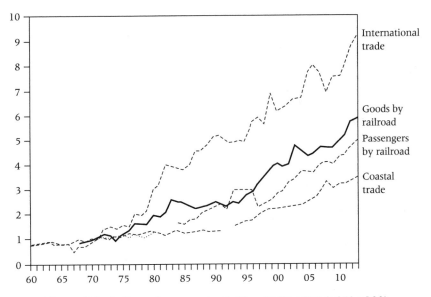

Figure 5.1. Indices of transport activities, 1860–1913 (1871=100)

it seems natural that railroad and coastal maritime transport did not compete with each other, because the large interior zone, even though less densely populated, included half or even more of the population, which maritime trade clearly could not serve. The growth of the railroads in the 1870s and 1880s indicates a demand for interior transportation that waterborne shipping could not reach; in that vast inland region the railroad was in fact competing with road transport. While Spanish coastal maritime trade grew very slowly, the expansion of such trade was even slower in Italy, with a geographical configuration that might be considered more favorable. Whereas Italian coastal trade was twice as large in terms of tonnage as the Spanish in 1880, by 1930 the levels were virtually the same (Frax, 1981, p. 39).

As can be seen from Figure 5.1, it was international shipping that achieved the fastest growth during the second half of the century. Table 5.1 shows the actual tonnage moved (in five-year averages) by the railroads, by national coastal shipping (cabotaje), and by international shipping. It also

Table 5.1. The movement of goods in Spain, 1860–1910 (in thousand tons, five-year averages)

Year	(1) Railroad (broad gauge)	(2) Coastal shipping (cabotaje)	(3) International shipping	(4) Shipping by Spanish merchant fleet	(5) Total shipping, international + cabotaje
1860	n.a.	709	1,576	(411)	2,285
1865	n.a.	681	1,799	(453)	2,480
1870	3,202	789	2,321	(638)	3,110
1875	4,014	1,009	3,513	(729)	4,522
1880	6,080	1,039	6,316	(973)	7,355
1885	8,438	1,147	8,975	(1,479)	10,122
1889	9,284	1,175	10,789	(1,968)	11,964
1895	12,227[a]	1,559	11,701	(2,198)	13,260
1900	15,336	2,038	13,963	(3,973)	16,001
1905	17,960	2,346	16,412	(5,013)	18,758
1910	20,976	2,965	17,237	(5,248)	20,202

a. By interpolation

Sources: calculated from the following: col. 1, Gómez Mendoza (1989); col. 2, Frax (1981); cols. 3 and 4, Valdaliso (1991), App. 3

shows the share of international shipping carried by Spanish vessels. The overall importance of shipping is indicated in the last column, which adds together international traffic and national coastal shipping. In absolute volume, the amount the railroads carried was remarkably close to the total maritime tonnage throughout the period. Around 1900 coastal shipping amounted to some 2 million tons, and the railroads carried 15 million tons; the Spanish international fleet carried almost 4 million tons of the 14 million tons of international trade. The total maritime trade, international plus national, amounted to 16 million tons, just a little more than what the railroads carried in those years.

Although the table does not really tell the whole story, because movement of goods by road is not included, it is clear that the orders of magnitude are not very different. Even in 1910 total maritime trade amounted to more than 96% of the tonnage moved by the railroad, and at that date, when the automobile was still of little importance, we may assume that the volume of goods transported by road would have been merely a fraction of that transported by rail. Until well into the twentieth century, therefore, maritime and railroad traffic were about equally important, which leads to the assumption that the modest investments made in ports had greater marginal utility than investments made in railroads, or at least they were equally valuable. Figure 5.1 allows us to establish one further fact: railroad traffic and shipping by sea seem to be complementary, since they fluctuate in a parallel manner, especially between 1870 and 1885, a period of very rapid growth for both transportation systems.

During the major part of the century, maritime trade was carried under sail: until 1860, Catalan vessels predominated and Barcelona had the largest ships' registry. From then on, however, a competitor began to emerge, one that in the long run became utterly invincible, steam navigation. However, as is well known, steam navigation signaled the beginning of a long swan song for the sailing vessel, which lasted almost to the end of the century: this was the era of the clippers, elegant in design, long in range, and amazingly speedy, which plowed the oceans competing with steamships. Barcelona was the headquarters of the major shipping company of the period, the Compañía Transatlántica, pioneered in 1881 by Antonio López López (who became the Marqués of Comillas). The company maintained, under official auspices, steam-shipping lines to Cuba, the Philippines, and other, largely American ports; other important steamship companies also operated out of Barcelona. Even so, the Catalan industry remained devoted to sail for far too long, and the proportion of registered vessels that operated under sail remained very high. As Vicens Vives conjectured (Vicens Vives, 1959, p. 619), "perhaps we have here a Catalan anachronism which explains the [successful] future of the Basque shipping industry." It is tempting to relate this "anachronism" to the problems of Catalan banking and industry during these years.

The Basque shipping industry, much smaller in scope at mid-century and thus with a lesser investment in sail, adapted rapidly to steam, spurred on by the profits to be realized in exporting iron ore, especially to England. Although the major part of this traffic was under the British flag, and the Spanish fraction was relatively small, it was in absolute terms sufficiently important to radically transform the structure of the Spanish merchant marine and the Basque sector of it, which changed over from sail to steam between 1870 and 1885, exactly the same period that saw tremendous growth in iron ore exports. This rapid transformation was made by acquiring British ships, many of them at second hand.[2] The correlation between the tonnage of steamships in the Spanish fleet and mineral ore exports during the last twenty-five years of the century is very strong proof of the importance of this traffic in the fleet's modernization. This is especially true for the Basque fleet, whose most important companies were the well-known Bilbaína de Navegación, Sota y Aznar, and Ibarra y Compañía, which operated from Bilbao but had its headquarters in Seville.

The Railroads

In land transportation the most critical innovation was the construction of the railroad network. With the exception of a few short lines, Barcelona to Mataró, Madrid to Aranjuez, and Langreo to Gijón, construction of the major network did not begin until the 1855 *Ley General de Ferrocarriles* (General Railroads Law). Before that, since the end of Fernando VII's reign (1833) a few plans for railroads had been effected, generally for short sections to link areas producing export items to the coast. Developers could count on very little help from the government; indeed it was sometimes openly hostile. Unfortunately, the bureaucratic apparatus set up during the 1840s produced the famous royal decree of 1844 mandating, among other things, that the width of the Spanish railroad system should be six Castilian feet; which is 1.67 meters. This is some 15 centimeters broader than the European gauge, and the Spanish economy, even today, continues to pay for the technical blunder that led to such a fateful decision.[3]

The short lines mentioned above were constructed under the shelter—or perhaps better said the lack of shelter—of the 1844 royal decree, and many more lines were planned in an orgy of speculation that produced many scandals and few tangible realities in terms of transportation capacity. But this speculation in the end produced serious political repercussions and seems to have been one of the causes of the O'Donnell uprising and the rise to power, in 1854, of the Progressive party that went on to introduce the 1855 legislation.

Why was railroad construction so slow to take root in a country where it was so patently needed? The answer lies in the combination of two major factors: the vicious circle of underdevelopment, and government ineptitude and inertia. Social and economic backwardness meant that capital, technical capacity, and entrepreneurial initiative were in short supply, and the lack of vision and competence, far from supplementing that shortfall, merely exacerbated the problem.

Things changed with the incoming Progressive government, a party that favored economic development and the import of capital from abroad. The Progressives considered railroads an essential part of Spain's modernization and pursued that goal explicitly. In order to get the railroad network constructed, they were prepared to seek the necessary resources wherever they could, whether the capital was Spanish or foreign. To this end the 1855 law facilitated the incorporation of railroad companies, envisaged the payment of subsidies, guaranteed investors against a series of risks, and decreed that imported railroad materials were free of customs tariffs. Furthermore, the Railroads Law was complemented with two additional laws, the *Ley de Bancos de Emisión* and the *Ley de Sociedades de Crédito* (one allowing certain banks to issue banknotes and the other facilitating the formation of business banks), which together permitted the rapid formation of a banking system able to finance the construction of the first phase of the railroad network, from 1856 to 1866. In the decade following these laws, some 4,500 kilometers of rail were put into service, an average annual construction of 450 kilometers, a rate that Spain never achieved again. In 1866 some 5,000 kilometers were in operation; in 1900 there were about 13,200 kilometers, of which 2,200 were narrow gauge (see Table 5.2). This means that the construction rate during the last third of the century, including the narrow

Table 5.2. Extension of the Spanish railroad network, 1850–1935

Year	(1) Kilometers in operation, broad gauge	(2) Five-year increase	(3) Average annual increase	(4) Average increase in the decade	(5) Kilometers in operation, narrow gauge
1850	28	—	—	—	—
1855	440	412	82.4	—	—
1860	1,880	1,440	288.0	185.2	—
1865	4,756	2,876	575.2	431.6	76
1870	5,316	560	112.0	343.6	138
1875	5,840	524	104.8	108.4	254
1880	7,086	1,246	249.2	177.0	405
1885	8,399	1,313	262.6	255.9	607
1890	9,083	684	136.8	199.7	1,080
1895	10,526	1,443	288.6	212.7	2,086
1900	11,040	514	102.8	195.7	2,166
1905	11,309	269	53.8	78.3	2,728
1910	11,362	53	10.6	32.2	3,332
1915	11,424	62	12.4	11.5	4,247
1920	11,445	21	4.2	8.3	4,644
1925	11,543	98	19.6	11.9	4,997
1930	12,030	487	97.4	58.5	5,248
1935	12,254	224	44.8	71.1	5,184

Sources: col. 1, Cordero and Menéndez (1978), App. II-2, pp. 324–325; col. 5:
Estadísticas Históricas, (ed.) Carreras (1989); cols. 2, 3, and 4, calculated

gauge, was only 240 kilometers per year, a little less than half of what had been achieved in the first heady years of euphoria.

Several factors are responsible for this rapid construction rate in the first ten years: first, the very resolute state support already mentioned; second, the massive influx of foreign capital, technology, and initiative, above all from France; third, the additional and considerable contribution of Spanish capital and initiative, particularly in Catalonia, the Basque provinces, and the Valencia region. A score of private railroad companies emerged, the most important of them predominantly French, like the Madrid-Zaragoza-Alicante Company (MZA), the Ferrocarril del Norte, and the Seville-Jerez-Cádiz Company. These were the largest, but others were predominantly Spanish and quite substantial, such as the Barcelona-Zaragoza-Pamplona, the Barcelona-Tarragona-Francia, the Tarragona-Valencia-Almansa, and the Tudela to Bilbao. The construction companies were spurred on by subsidies and state guarantees, the anticipation of high operating profits, and the total certainty of high profits from the construction itself, thanks to the same subsidies and guarantees. Much was sacrificed in the name of speedy construction, and when the major trunk lines began to approach completion, starting in 1864, it became clear that the expectations of profitable operation had been largely and fraudulently overstated; incomes were not enough even to cover costs, let alone repay the capital invested.

Thus began a dramatic decade for the railroads, for the economy, and for Spanish politics. As was to happen again in the 1930s, in the 1860s the repercussion of an international crisis coincided with an internal depression to generate a political and social upheaval of the first order. The financial failure of the railroads caused a complete collapse of the banking system; the cotton famine induced by the American Civil War caused prices to rise at the beginning of the decade, which paralyzed the cotton industry; the fall in cotton prices when the war ended provoked panic in banking and commerce in general throughout Europe, with serious repercussions in Spain; a succession of budget deficits further aggravated the situation; and bad harvests in 1867 and 1868 provided the final death blow to an economy already gravely wounded. The political consequences are well known: the Glorious Revolution of September 1868.

Railroad construction was virtually suspended in this critical decade; between 1866 and 1876 a mere 1,000 additional kilometers were laid. The industry attempted a new start during the last quarter of the century, this time aiming to achieve concentration and rationalization. Few companies survived the crisis. The two big ones, the Norte and the MZA, although they also went through serious difficulties, were clearly the strongest, and thanks to a tacit agreement not to engage in unreasonable competition, they were able to round out their systems by acquiring smaller companies and completing their networks with some new construction. Essentially the basic network had already been completed during the first construction phase; perhaps the most important additions during this end-of-century period are the connection of Galicia and Asturias to the national network, the coastal link from Bilbao to San Sebastián, the line from Madrid to Portugal through Cáceres, the line from Seville to Huelva, and the formation of a new company, Ferrocarriles Andaluces.[4] Noting that almost all of this new construction connected mining areas to the rest of the country, one can surmise with some confidence that the greater part of this activity was related to the mining boom.

By the end of the century the MZA and Norte companies each controlled a third of the total operating track: the MZA company included the line from France through Barcelona to Zaragoza and Madrid, and the lines from Madrid that radiated out to Alicante and Cartagena, to Córdoba, Seville, and Huelva, and to Portugal through Mérida and Badajoz, plus a few secondary branch lines. The Norte system comprised a major east-west axis from Vigo and La Coruña to Barcelona, passing through León, Palencia, Burgos, Zaragoza, and Lérida; in its eastern section this axis came to form a kind of railroad equivalent of the *Camino de Santiago* (the medieval route of pilgrimage through the Pyrenees), since it connected Galicia with France through Burgos, with a branch to Vitoria and Pamplona. This broad east-west axis crossed over and connected with a north-south axis from Madrid to Santander going through Avila, Segovia, and Valladolid. Again there was a series of collateral branches that connected to the coast, León-Gijón-Avilés and Miranda-Bilbao-Irun, or to the Pyrenees through Zaragoza and Jaca. The third large company, Ferrocarriles Andaluces, connected the principal Andalusian cities that fall south of the MZA line from Madrid to Huelva (Cordero y Menéndez, 1978; Tedde, 1978). These three companies, representing about 90% of the Spanish railroad holdings, were largely owned by foreigners, mostly the French. All in all the foreign (we can say the French) capital amounted to some 60% of the total by about 1894.[5]

To estimate the impact of the railroads on the Spanish economy we have to address a series of questions, the most important of which must be, "Was the railroad indispensable to Spanish economic modernization?" My answer is "yes," and given that, other questions come up: "Were the railroads built in the best possible manner?" "What alternatives were there?" And in considering these alternatives we should ask about the rate of construction of railroads, about how they were financed, and about the physical characteristics of the network, the length, the structure, and infrastructure, etc. The picture will be clearer after we explore these questions briefly, one by one.

First, the axiom of indispensability, brought into the limelight by the work of Robert Fogel. Until about thirty years ago it was taken for granted that a railroad network had been indispensable for the economic modernization in the advanced countries, notably the United States, England, and Germany. Drawing upon econometric techniques, Fogel's work attempted to demonstrate that the U.S. economy and standard of living would not have been enormously affected if the railroads had not been built. This thesis created a great stir, and initially it was thought that the case could be generalized to other countries, especially in the light of parallel studies on the English case which seemed to lead to similar conclusions (Hawke, 1970). More recent studies have shown, however, that in countries like Mexico or Germany the railroads were indeed indispensable, or at least they made a decisive contribution (Coatsworth, 1976; Fremdling, 1977). Of course, the conclusions of the two groups are not mutually contradictory; in the United States and England the opportunities for waterborne transport were so good that the railroad advantage might be considered rather small.[6] In Mexico and Germany physical and political conditions were very different; Germany was not yet politically unified, and Mexico was only sparsely and irregularly settled, and administratively chaotic. We can say then, that there is no hard-and-fast rule about the economic impact of railroads.

The Spanish case clearly aligns more closely with Mexico and Germany. The alternatives to the railroad, above all in interior transport, were few and inferior; applying Fogel's method, Gómez Mendoza (1982, 1989) has shown that the railroads made a considerable contribution to Spain's growth, in the region of 10% of national income in 1878, according to this author.[7] The economic repercussions of railroad building are usually considered in the light of backward linkages (the impact of the new sector on industries that supply components), and forward linkages (impacts which the new sector has upon the economy at large because people use the new product, in this case transport services). In the next section we shall see some of the most important forward linkages. The backward linkages associated with Spanish railroad construction were not particularly important. The stimulus to the demand for iron and steel products during the first phase of construction was insignificant, mainly because of the tariff exemptions on imported raw materials and components introduced by the Railroad Law of 1855, which was not definitively abolished until 1891. Later on, in the twentieth century, the railroad-related demand generated for Spanish metallurgical products was larger, but probably it was never more than 10% of that industry's total production. As for the engineering industry, particularly the production of rolling stock, the tariff exemption was again important, and by the beginning of the twentieth century railroads had little visible effect on this industry, although right at the end of the nineteenth century there were a few isolated sales of Spanish-manufactured rolling stock that have been much

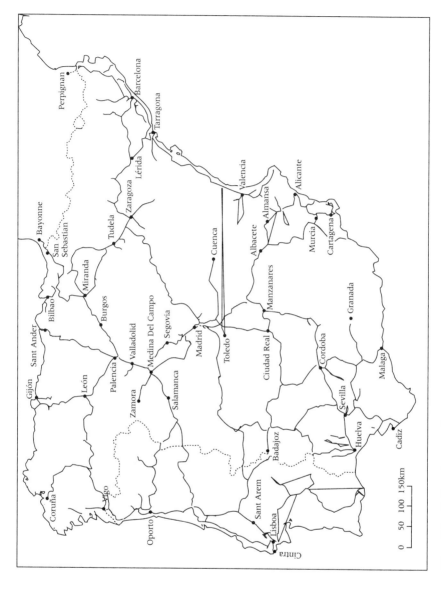

Map 5.1. Railroad network, ca. 1895

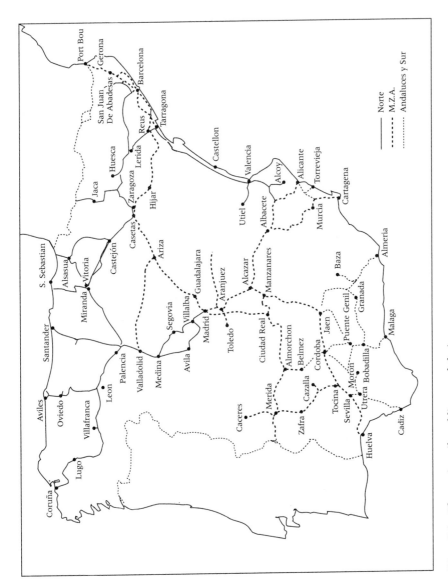

Map 5.2. The main railroad lines and their owners

cited. Of greater importance by far was the demand upon the coal industry, where 25% of all output went to the railroads. The impact on the timber industry must also have been considerable, especially for railroad sleepers. As far as the demand for labor is concerned, the railroad clearly played an important role. During the period of accelerated construction some 60,000 workers were employed, or more than 3% of all Spanish men aged between 16 and 40 years, and in 1935 there were 125,000 permanent employees, approximately one-third of the total transport sector at that date. To qualify these facts we should add that the productivity of these workers was very low, that the Spanish coal industry never amounted to very much, and that the use of timber for sleepers "accelerated the deforestation of the country."[8] As far as the forward linkages are concerned, there is no doubt that a country of Spain's particular physical characteristics would not have been able to modernize without a railroad network to modify its dreadfully restrictive natural transportation possibilities. Without railroads to supply the cities with food and raw materials, to transport industrial products from one urban center to another and from those centers to the rural communities, and to introduce fluidity to the labor market, it would have been impossible to achieve any progress, not even a modicum of growth in the agricultural sector, never mind industrialization and modernization.

But from establishing that the railroads were indispensable it does not follow that they had to be bought at any price, or constructed at any speed and manner. In fact the construction of the Spanish railroad network began too late and then proceeded at an excessive pace. The consequences of such haste were deficient planning, inadequate financing, and a geographic layout that was basically speculative. As a result, both physical infrastructure and the business structure itself were feeble at best. It is difficult to comprehend, otherwise, why a sector that was so urgently needed and so socially productive yielded such mediocre results. As Tedde points out, "the railroad, in general terms, amounted to [only] a mediocre business, that provided profits that were appreciably lower than those offered by other alternatives" (Tedde, 1978a, p. 233). In contrast, the English, French, and Germany railroads turned out to be wonderfully profitable in the nineteenth century. In the Spanish case, the profound difference between social profitability and private profit is to be explained by the factors already mentioned: trying to make up for lost time, the 1855–56 Progressive legislation created a mechanism whereby capital was drawn towards this new sector in a thoughtless and indiscriminate manner. Concessions for the lines were allocated through an auction system, favoring the contractor who would accept the lowest subsidy, and in the absence of any serious attempt at technical inspection, this clearly promoted shoddy construction. It is an important part of this story that the builders' secure profits became automatically converted into additional costs for the operators, and furthermore, in the speculative atmosphere of these years, companies financed their activity with bank loans and securities at very high financial costs that would later weigh heavy as a tombstone on the profit-and-loss accounts. These shortcomings in the financial structure and in the material infrastructure explain the paradox that the operating companies incurred losses both in periods of low demand, 1893 to 1895, and when demand was unusually high, during World War I—losses that were aggravated by fluctuations in the international value of the peseta, since to a large extent dividends had to be paid in francs. Under the weight of such financial burdens the companies sustained a loss when traffic was scarce and insufficient; yet when business was brisk, larger traffic volumes made excessive demands on fragile infrastructure so that rails, bridges, ballast, and rolling stock broke down and needed to be repaired or replaced at a cost that the highly indebted companies could not pay. It was yet again another case of a vicious circle or poverty and indebtedness. Hence excessive speed at the construction stage was counterproductive in the long run. It left Spain with railroad companies so encumbered with debt that any incentive for further investment had died out, and this was particularly important because the network was, in any case, too sparse, insufficiently dense. A slower and more regular speed of construction would doubtless have been more beneficial to all concerned.[9]

If the speed of construction and mode of financing left much to be desired, much the same can be said about the technical characteristics of the network. We have already mentioned the monumental error of the broad gauge, which contributed to Spain's isolation from Europe, erecting as it were a second Pyrenean barrier, and without a doubt contributing to the slow growth of railroad traffic in comparison with shipping. We have seen that the infrastructure was of poor quality and why that was so (in England errors have also been documented, poor routing, differences in gauge and poor construction, but there railroads were constructed with almost no government control!). In Spain the radial structure of the network has also been criticized. However, Figure 5.1 provides evidence that the structure adopted played a significant positive role. The absence of competition between railroads and coastal shipping and the rapid increase in railroad traffic after

1870 show that there was, indeed, a strong demand for interior transport, where rail was in competition only with road traffic, and was vastly superior to it right up to the middle of the twentieth century, when rapid diffusion of the internal combustion engine made road transport tremendously popular. The railroads that connected the interior regions with the coast and the coastal cities with each other necessarily had to rely upon various transshipment points, especially one that was centrally located. Madrid was thus strategically placed as the railroad hub, with the added advantage that its size made it the largest interior market for consumer goods, a factor that was to confer large economies of scale as a point of transshipment. So in the end, and for identical reasons, Madrid was to fulfill a role similar to that played by London, Berlin, and Paris, cities that were all less centrally located in a geographical sense within their respective networks.

To sum up, although railroads were very important, there are various reasons to believe that the role they played within the Spanish economy has been exaggerated, or that their potential contribution has been confused with the much smaller actual contribution they could provide given the multiple errors made during construction.

Internal Trade

At the beginning of the nineteenth century, both legal and geographic obstacles so divided Spain that the country was effectively a series of regional markets isolated from each other and from the exterior. Unfortunately, small and fragmented markets are a powerful obstacle to economic growth because they frustrate the development of economies of scale and with them the division of labor; furthermore, in limiting the sphere within which competition can operate, small markets favor the formation of monopolies. The progress in means of transportation which we have just reviewed served to palliate, although very slowly, this fragmentation of markets. Legal restrictions were also gradually eliminated. Little by little a unified national market began to emerge.

As Frax and Matilla indicate (1988, pp. 246–247), from the beginning of the nineteenth century and even earlier, the legal obstacles to a unified market were being removed. The Cortes of Cádiz and the *Código Comercial* drawn up in 1829 proclaimed the principle of freedom of trade, although to have any real validity, this abstract proclamation needed to be backed up by the abolition of a series of specific obstacles. The guilds were ultimately abolished in 1834 (in France this had been done during the French Revolution, and almost simultaneously in England). Fees such as the *portazgos,* duties that were paid when merchandise entered a city, the *pontazgos,* to cross a river, the *peajes,* road tolls, the *barcazgos,* for using boats, were either abolished or gradually reduced. Interior tariffs that separated some kingdoms and territories from others were also gradually abolished; those that separated the kingdom of Aragón from the rest of Spain had been removed in the eighteenth century, after the War of Succession. The last regional tariffs, between the Basque country and Castile, were removed after the first Carlist War in 1841, although the Basques managed to maintain, with some interruptions, a special fiscal regime. In this general expansion of measures that were essentially pro-trade, the unification and codification of the laws of commerce, in 1829 and 1885, were important. So was the unification of the monetary system (see Chapter 6) and weights and measures, as the metric system gradually took hold in the central decades of the century.

The test of whether a unified market exists or not is very simple; we look for a single price. In the nineteenth century Spain could not pass this test, not even for a product so basic and homogeneous as wheat. Figure 5.2 shows, for 1855 through 1905, five-year moving averages for the price of wheat in three important provinces, a producer, Valladolid, a consumer, Madrid, and a maritime consumer, Barcelona. At the beginning of the twentieth century considerable differences still existed between coastal and interior prices, but though the chart by no means indicates a completely integrated market, we can point to a substantial degree of convergence. The curves for Madrid and Valladolid, already close and parallel by the middle of the nineteenth century, are practically superimposed by the beginning of the twentieth; here at last we can see a unification of these two submarkets. As far as Barcelona is concerned, its fluctuations become attuned to the interior market pattern as the century evolves; also prices are tending to converge, particularly in the last decade. It is interesting to note that although, as a nonproducing area, Barcelona has prices that are regularly higher, as a port it is sheltered from the tremendous fluctuations of a poorly connected internal market; in the dreadful year of 1868 wheat was actually cheaper in Barcelona than in Madrid. This Figure gives us a good visual image of what is shown with greater accuracy in the studies carried out by Sánchez-Albornoz and the Grupo de Estudios de Historia Rural.[10] It is also interesting to corroborate that incomplete market integration in Spain corresponds to a similar situation in Italy at about the same date, in contrast to an almost completely integrated market in France, which certainly reveals their different degree of development in general, and of the railroad systems in particular (Sánchez-Albornoz, 1975b, pp. 134–143).

Market integration was far from complete in many sectors. Figure 5.3 charts a similar analysis for olive oil prices, in which the producing province is Jaén. In this graph we find no evidence of convergence at all, quite the contrary.[11] The cost of transport from Jaén to the centers of consumption does not appear to have diminished with the introduction of the railroad. Barcelona seems to have imported a considerable share of the olive oil it consumed until the 1890s, since from 1892–1894 prices began to increase, in a trend that was different from that for Jaén and Madrid. It is likely that a substantial tax increase for olive oil in the 1892 tariff reform brought about a reduction in imports and a consequent price increase. Olive oil appears to be only of secondary importance among the items carried by rail by the MZA and the Norte lines, although it should be pointed out that the volume did not increase much over time, so this traffic may have been more local than national.

The consumer items which the railroads carried in largest quantities were

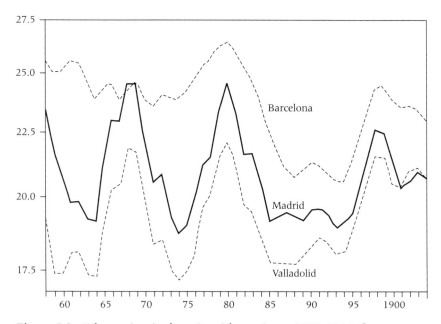

Figure 5.2. Wheat prices in three Spanish provinces, 1858–1904 (five-year moving averages, in pesetas per hectoliter)

wine, cereals, particularly wheat, and coal, and this has been interpreted as a measure of the primary character of the Spanish economy throughout the nineteenth century (Anes, 1978, pp. 385–391; Gómez Mendoza, 1989, pp. 145–153). However, is it certainly true that the railroads contributed to unifying one particularly important element, the labor market, as reflected in the increase in passengers carried (Sánchez Alonso, 1995). It would be absurd to doubt that the railroads served to unify the national market. But the effects were more perceptible in the twentieth century than the nineteenth.

Lastly, there is another kind of merchandise which, when transported or transferred, serves to unify and facilitate market exchanges, and that is information. The improvement in communications in Spain in the nineteenth century is very clear. The mail system (*correos*), already set in place in the eighteenth century, was modernized in the nineteenth by the introduction in 1850 of the postage stamp (England introduced it first in 1837) and by the railroad. The telegraph system, whose construction had begun in the United States and England in the 1840s, began to be developed in Spain in 1853, with the first lines going into operation two years later (Bahamonde, 1993).

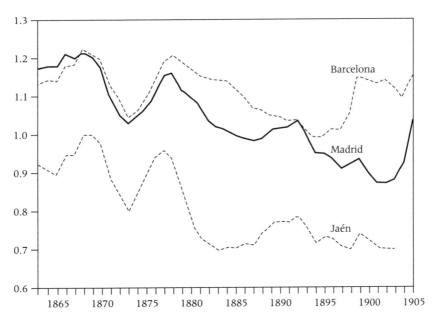

Figure 5.3. Olive oil prices in three Spanish provinces, 1863–1905 (five-year moving averages, in pesetas per liter)

The improvements in communications helped to increase productivity and unify markets. But the changes came slowly and late. Statistics from the postal service show an interesting correlation with income levels, as Crafts (1983) has shown, and in effect they place Spain among the laggards of Europe. This is hardly surprising; the process of urbanization, again undeniable, was slow, as indeed was the expansion of literacy. As Sánchez-Albornoz incisively points out (1975a, p. 97),

> it was not so much a question of contact between regions or sectors, but rather of insufficient development of the factors of production and markets. Putting producers and consumers together in the village store did not necessarily mean that there would be much to exchange. When people got together, it turned out that they did not have much to say to each other. Consequently, growth of the productive sectors and the formation of markets was less automatic and slower than what the appetites, the demonstration effect, and the rhetoric against inactivity had lead one to envision.

In the course of the nineteenth century communications made another important step toward modernization: the telephone. One very important move was the founding of the Compañía Telefónica Nacional de España in 1924. In a period that was intensely pro-monopoly (CAMPSA, the gasoline monopoly dates from 1927) the Telefónica was created in monopoly form, although in fact it was a subsidiary of ITT, and it included some Spanish capital from the big banks like the Banco Urquijo and the Banco Hispano. On the credit side the Telefónica managed to create a national network by joining together the small existing companies (Bahamonde, 1993, chap. IV); on the debit side it provided services clearly inferior to those available in the United States and elsewhere in Europe, at rates that were clearly more expensive; in short, what classical economic theory leads one to expect from a monopoly.

The Foreign Sector

For a country in process of development, external trade is an essential part of its economic system. Through exchanges with the rest of the world the country will obtain the goods that its own industry does not produce, especially capital goods and the technology it needs to renovate and improve its own productive structure. These imports are normally financed by loans, foreign capital investment, and the export of primary goods that the underdeveloped country produces competitively. The underdeveloped country will be competitive in primary goods because their production does not require complex production processes, or because the country's physical conditions are comparatively advantageous (it has mineral wealth or grows marketable agricultural products), or because in the underdeveloped country unskilled labor is abundant and cheap. Moreover, a foreign market will frequently serve to supplement insufficient market demand at home, acting thereby as a stimulant for an emergent industry. Given the low level of purchasing power of this country's population, the limited capacity of local markets to absorb output can be a powerful brake on its industrialization. The likelihood that the international market will absorb an important part of the output of a newly emerging industry can, in fact, be decisive in the modernization of that industry and can contribute to the modernization of the whole economy. These considerations underlie the interest that developing countries have in studying the role of the exterior sector.

Furthermore, the statistics of foreign trade are frequently the first that nations assemble, organize, and publish, and this accounting is usually done with considerable attention to minute detail, although not without some problems in the Spanish case. This source, then, permits us to follow the development of foreign trade with greater precision than other economic series of equal or even greater importance, such as consumption, investment, and national income, and reveals quite a lot about the evolution of the country's economy as a whole.

The Balance of Trade

The official statistics of Spanish external trade have been published annually since 1850, and fragmentary data exist for earlier periods. Their interpretation does, however, present some problems. At times the composition and continuity in some sections leave something to be desired: entries appear and disappear in certain years, evidently because they are added into, and sometimes excluded from, other categories, which complicates the analysis considerably. In other cases, certain headings, such as "machines and separate pieces," for example, leave one in doubt about what the exact composition might have been. This is particularly noticeable in the case of the section "equipment for railroads and public works," which, rumor has it, on occasions went as far as to include French champagne and lace underwear. The question also remains, of course, of contraband and dissimulation, which in some sections is significant. And above and beyond this, the question remains of how goods were valued, that is, the official prices that were assigned to goods within the statistics published. These official values were often biased so that they exaggerated the value of imports and understated the value of exports. All these uncertainties force us to handle the figures on Spanish external trade with a heightened sense of caution. There has been a long debate on this issue, which today seems to be happily resolved, thanks to the work of Prados,[12] who has completed a meticulous task in cleaning up, reconstructing, and analyzing the statistics of external trade for his long-range study, including a large part of the eighteenth century.

Table 5.3 and Figure 5.4 present a panorama of Spanish external trade during the nineteenth century based on the Prados figures. The first conclusion that jumps to view is that the second half of the period was much more active than the first, which agrees with what we know about the growth of national income; the Spanish economy displayed much greater dynamism after the middle of the last century. In total, the figures show that Spain's foreign trade grew during the nineteenth century at rates that are comparable with, or better than, France and England, especially where exports were concerned.

But foreign trade suffered a drastic restructuring after the loss of the imperial colonies. Until then, Spain, as the metropolis, had played the role of intermediary between Europe and the colonies, developing an extensive re-export trade. Thanks to its monopoly of trade with its New World colonies, Spain shipped a considerable amount of manufactured goods there, most of which had been previously imported from other European countries, while some had been produced domestically. In turn, Spain exported to Europe, above and beyond its domestic manufactures, a variety of primary products from the Indies. The end of the empire, therefore, imposed a radical change on this trade pattern. On losing its metropolis status, or almost losing it, Spain had to surrender its lucrative role of intermediary. Exports to Central and South America were spectacularly reduced, and to a large measure the re-exports too. In a matter of a few years the country lost its status as the capital of a great colonial empire and became instead merely an underdeveloped country on the European periphery. Trade had to be limited now, essentially to exporting raw materials and semi-finished goods and importing industrial products. Thus there was a significant decline in exports of manufactured goods like pig iron and wrought iron, cotton textiles, spun silk thread, paper, and brandy, which traditionally had found their markets in

Table 5.3. Composition of Spain's foreign trade, 1827 through 1910/1913

1827	(%)	1855/1859	(%)	1875/1879	(%)	1890/1894	(%)	1910/1913	(%)
				Main Exports					
Olive oil	17.0	Wine	26.0	Wine	26.6	Wine	23.1	Iron ore	8.6
Wine	16.6	Flour	9.3	Lead	10.9	Lead	7.0	Wine	8.0
Wool	9.6	Lead	8.1	Copper ore	7.0	Iron ore	5.9	Lead	6.7
Lead	7.4	Olive oil	6.5	Raisins	5.3	Cotton textiles	4.7	Oranges	5.5
Brandy	6.0	Raisins	5.4	Flour	3.8	Cork	3.0	Cotton textiles	4.5
Raisins	5.5	Wheat	5.1	Mercury	2.5	Copper ore	3.0	Cork	4.3
Flour	3.0	Wool	2.9	Livestock	2.4	Copper	2.7	Copper	4.2
Cork	2.9	Cork	2.6	Cork	2.4	Raisins	2.4	Canned foods	4.2
Silk fabric	2.8	Chickpeas	1.8	Olive oil	2.2	Oranges	2.1	Olive Oil	3.8
Oranges	2.7	Brandy	1.6	Iron Ore	2.1	Olive oil	2.0	Almonds	2.0
Silk thread	2.6	Livestock	1.3	Oranges	2.0	Footwear	1.7	Livestock	1.9
Barilla[a]	2.4	Salt	1.2	Footwear	1.8	Livestock	1.7	Skins and hides	1.8
Paper	1.6	Rice	1.1	Esparto grass	1.7	Wool	1.3	Grapes	1.7
Almonds	1.3	Hazelnuts	1.1	Wool	1.3	Grapes	1.2	Onions	1.6
Livestock	1.1	Oranges	1.0	Skins & hides	1.2	Almonds	1.1	Wool	1.6
	(82.5%)		(75.0%)		(73.2%)		(62.8%)		(60.4%)
				Main Imports					
Cotton textiles	21.3	Sugar	9.6	Raw baled cotton	12.3	Raw baled cotton	9.1	Raw baled cotton	10.6
Linen textiles	12.6	Raw baled cotton	8.8	Sugar	4.5	Coal	6.1	Coal	8.6

Table 5.3 *(continued)*

1827	(%)	1855/1859	(%)	1875/1879	(%)	1890/1894	(%)	1910/1913	(%)
Sugar	9.5	Wheat	7.1	Timber	4.3	Wheat	5.4	Machinery	7.7
Wool cloth	6.2	Iron/steel products	5.7	Linen & hemp thread	4.2	Timber	4.8	Chemicals	5.2
Raw baled cotton	5.6	Wool cloth	4.5	Coal	3.9	Tobacco	3.9	Timber	4.5
Silk fabrics	5.6	Cotton textiles	4.4	Railroad equipment	3.6	Machinery	3.8	Iron/steel products	3.5
Raw linen & hemp	3.7	Codfish	3.9	Wool cloth	3.4	Sugar	3.6	Codfish	3.3
Timber	3.6	Wheat flour	3.8	Cotton textiles	3.3	Codfish	3.0	Tobacco	3.1
Codfish	3.5	Cocoa	3.1	Skins and hides	3.2	Iron/steel products	2.8	Skins and hides	2.9
Cinnamon	3.3	Linen & hemp thread	2.9	Codfish	3.0	Chemicals	2.2	Livestock	2.7
Cocoa	3.1	Timber	2.7	Wheat	2.6	Wool cloth	2.1	Wheat	2.3
Skins and hides	2.8	Coal	2.6	Bitumen	2.4	Skins and hides	1.9	Boats	2.2
Dyestuffs	1.4	Silk textiles	2.5	Iron/steel products	2.4	Cocoa	1.6	Coffee	2.2
Iron/steel products	1.2	Machinery	2.3	Machinery	2.3	Coffee	1.6	Cotton fabrics	1.3
Rice	1.0	Skins and hides	2.1	Brandy	2.2	Linen & hemp thread	1.5	Raw wool	1.1
	(84.4%)		(66.0%)		(57.6%)		(53.4%)		(61.2%)

a. A plant source of sodium carbonate used in production of soap, glass, and bleach

Source: Prados (1988), p. 200

the Americas. In contrast, we find increases in exports of primary and semi-manufactured items such as cork, mercury, lead, raw silk, olive oil, and citrus fruits that found expanding markets in the neighboring European countries (Prados, 1982b).

The history of Spain's foreign trade in the nineteenth century is largely the story of how the economy adapted to this new role. Without the privileges, but also without the distortions which the metropolitan role had entailed, the Spanish economy had to assume its new and modest function as a backward participant in world commerce, above all with Europe. In the long run the adaptation was successful, the outcome positive. Foreign trade was one of the dynamic elements within Spain's economy, and everything indicates that the positive effects would have been more powerful if the economy had been more open.

As we have seen, foreign trade grew significantly throughout the nineteenth century: Figure 5.4 shows the joint repercussions of these various circumstances and of economic policy on the volume of trade, all of this featured in curves where the trend is approximately exponential. Until the middle of the 1830s trade remained practically stagnant. From then on some

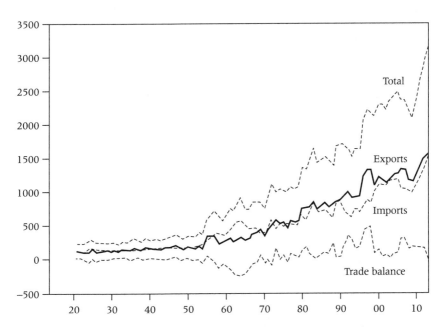

Figure 5.4. Components of international trade, 1821–1913 (in million pesetas at current values)

modest growth takes place, with a small dip in 1848 because of the crisis of that year, and a timid recovery thereafter.

After the middle of the century, growth occurs in stages, with strong surges and abrupt interruptions. Once into the 1850s rapid growth takes place in the years of the Crimean War, related no doubt to wheat exports stimulated by the war: but those years come to an end with the depression of 1857–1859, which translated into a fall in the volume of trade in the years 1858 and 1859 (in 1857 wheat exports keep the total figure high). In spite of this depression and a dip in 1862, related to the outbreak of the American Civil War and the suspension of cotton imports, the decade from 1855 to 1864 was one of forthright expansion, encouraged by intensive railroad construction and the imports directly stimulated by this development, such as railroad materials, and those fostered indirectly, through rising demand for other imports because of credit expansion and growing employment.

The years 1865–1870 were a period of deep depression, which is clearly reflected in the figures for foreign trade, with the only apparent interruption, a rise in cereal imports in 1868, caused by the bad harvest (as in 1857). The railroad and banking crises, combined with bad harvests in 1867 and 1868, produced effects that were the exact reverse of those resulting from the railroad euphoria of the earlier decade.

In contrast, the years that followed the new tariff of 1869 saw tremendous commercial expansion, which was soon to be interrupted by political events in Cuba, by a renewed outbreak of the Carlist War in the north, by the cantonal (anarchist) uprising in the south, and possibly by the moderately protectionist attitude of the first Restoration governments. But after 1878, thanks no doubt to the end of the civil wars in the mainland and in Cuba, and the increasing ravages of the phylloxera plague in France, trade experienced another major upturn, expanding more than 50% in the five years from 1878 to 1883.

The 1884 crisis reversed the trend again. The fall in worldwide agricultural prices could not fail to affect Spain, because most of its exports were agricultural. And a particular circumstance was aggravating an already difficult situation: the phylloxera had begun to lay waste to the Spanish vines during these years, consequently limiting exports of Spanish wine. Yet in spite of the phylloxera and French recovery from it, both of which affected Spanish wine exports well into the twentieth century, the years 1889 and 1890 saw a decided improvement in trade. This was followed in 1891 and 1892 by a violent fall, 17% in 1892 alone, which must be attributed to the

1891 protectionist tariff in force after April 1892, and the commercial wars of those years.

The war with Cuba, which began in 1895, gave a new stimulus to foreign trade. On the one hand, the expansion of internal credit caused by the hostilities was bound to stimulate imports. And on the other hand, exports were also powerfully stimulated by two primordial elements: the first, a rapid depreciation of the peseta (the consequence in turn of a complex bundle of factors that we shall analyze in Chapter 6), which made Spanish products cheap for foreigners; and second, the supplies for the Cuban expeditionary force, included in the statistics because those items were registered in the figures for foreign trade, since the Spanish tariff system treated the colonial territories as foreign countries.

The volume of international trade failed to grow between 1898 and 1909. The fall in 1898, the disaster year, should not surprise us, nor the halting and partial recovery in the years that followed. Monetary and budgetary contraction, and the revaluation of the peseta that resulted from the famous Villaverde stabilization plan and its successors in the years that followed the loss of the colonies, clearly explain this lack of energy. Starting in 1909, exports began to increase again. After a moderate rise in the first five years of the century, a decline occurred, due in part to yet another round of protectionist tariffs in 1906 and in part to the world depression of 1907; in the following years, however, trade showed a strong upwards surge until the beginning of the First World War.

Taken all together, the high rates of growth in foreign trade reveal greater advances in development and commercialization than we might have expected. One reason for this is the heightened protectionism that characterized Spanish economic policy during this period. It seems that the impact of the tariffs on the volume of trade, however unquestionable in theory, in practice produced short-term rather than long-term effects; as we have seen, Spanish foreign trade experienced growth that was superior to that of free-trade Great Britain. The second reason is the rather scanty commercialization of the Spanish production system and the fragmentation of her interior markets. This considerable growth in foreign trade is an indicator, perhaps not conclusive but at least powerfully suggestive, of important modernizing transformations in some sectors of Spain's economy during this period.

Let us now separate the total trade picture into its two major components. In the long run, exports grew at approximately the same speed as European exports, while imports grew more slowly than exports and also more slowly than European imports. The strong expansion in exports in the second half of the nineteenth century is largely due, according to the Prados analysis (1988, chap. V), to two factors: *the expansion of world demand,* caused by strong growth in Atlantic economies during what has become known as the second Industrial Revolution; and *the improved competitive position* of the Spanish economy, which became especially evident during the last decades of the century thanks to the export of products in which Spain had a large comparative and absolute advantage, that is, minerals and metals. According to Prados, of these two factors—world demand (dependent upon world income) and Spanish export prices—it was world demand that was the stronger determinant. This means that Spain's neighbors, the developed parts of Europe, contributed to the growth of its commerce and thus, as we shall see, to its economic modernization. In any case, the period of greatest expansion in Spanish exports coincides with its own "free trade" era, 1869–1891, the epoch of the "*librecambistas.*"

This gradual modernization can be seen in the changing structure of trade. Although for many years in the new century the distribution of exports continued to be typical of a semi-developed country (in 1920 foodstuffs and raw materials accounted for almost two-thirds of foreign sales), nonetheless various hopeful signs could be detected. One of these was that the percentage of manufactures, especially textiles and footwear, which had remained at very low levels throughout the nineteenth century, began to increase after 1880 (see Table 5.3). Another favorable sign was the relative flexibility of the production function, which is usually characteristic of an economy with a certain degree of maturity. Now one of the fundamental characteristics of the so-called backward countries is their incapacity to overcome the vagaries of market conditions or human or natural disasters. In an underdeveloped country, the fall of a certain price on the international market, a drought, or the devastation of a war can reduce a whole generation to misery or even to death, while the capacity of a developed country to overcome these circumstances is far greater. The example of Germany and Europe generally after the Second World War is classic.

In the Spanish case, even though mineral ores and wine together amounted to 64% of exports for the period 1880–1884, these years were clearly exceptional, when high volume exports of iron ore and copper to England (because of the growing importance of Bessemer steel and the chemical and metallurgical industries) coincided with extraordinary wine exports to France (because the phylloxera had not yet reached Spain). In contrast, on the eve of the First World War the proportion of these two staples had fallen to only 20% of total exports. The fall in these export components did not produce major upheavals, however, because it was compensated by substantial increases in other exports, such as cork, oranges, cotton textiles, livestock, and other fruits such as lemons, almonds, and grapes, while many of the traditional products maintained their positions, items such as raw wool, lead ingots, olive oil, rice, mercury, fortified and sparkling wines, and woolen textiles. In addition, some of the items mentioned were finished products, or at least high value-added products, such as textiles, footwear (although here exports began to decline at the beginning of the new century), fortified and sparkling wines, and lead ingots.

In summary, then, it is clear that by the end of the nineteenth century the Spanish economy was showing signs of a remarkable capacity to overcome the phylloxera crisis (roughly the years 1885 to 1905) and to diversify its exportable production. A similar conclusion may be drawn by noting the lag in more traditional exports such as raisins or raw wool, and their replacement by iron, copper, zinc, oranges, or cotton textiles. The impression, thus, is one of an economy by no means devoid of dynamism. Although some signs remained of a bias towards primary goods, Spanish exports in the second half of the nineteenth century reveal a degree of complexity and flexibility far superior to those of today's underdeveloped countries, many of which concentrate their exports on two or three primary products.

Imports show a rather similar pattern. First, they are somewhat less concentrated than exports, but it is natural that a middle-sized country should have a broader range of imports than exports. Yet we also find that imports of consumer goods seem to have remained relatively stationary, or even to have declined (notable stability in *bacalao* or dried cod fish, a decline almost to zero in sugar, and erratic fluctuations in wheat), while imports of industrial raw materials, raw cotton, coal, and capital goods (machinery, machines and spare parts, iron and steel goods) went up slightly. Combined imports of coal, iron and steel and machinery went from 10.6% in 1855–1859 to 19.8% in the four years prior to the Great War, which means that the relative weight of fuels and industrial equipment doubled. All these are indications of modernization, very much in agreement with what we have seen on the exports side of the trade balance.

With all its limitations, then, the data on foreign trade indicate that the Spanish economy certainly did not remain stationary during the nineteenth century. In relation to Europe's more advanced countries like Great Britain, Belgium, Switzerland, and Germany, Spain obviously did lose ground and in that sense was relatively more underdeveloped at the end of the century than at the beginning. However, the external trade data show that, albeit slowly, Spain had by 1850 entered into a process of modernization that was gradual but undeniable.

The geographic distribution of Spain's foreign trade is also illuminating. The two big customers during the nineteenth century were also the two main suppliers, Great Britain and France. As early as 1827 these two countries absorbed 56.2% of Spain's exports and sold to it 65.5% of its imports, and they later came to make up, to some extent, for the trade lost with the Spanish colonies, although it was of course a very different relationship. Spain would now acquire from those countries ready-made goods, and would sell them raw materials and foodstuffs. Other countries that were important in the trading pattern were Germany and the United States, with which similar relationships were also maintained. Although different in character, relations with Cuba and Argentina were important, and let us remember that Cuba retained the status of a colony until 1898. Throughout the century Spain's trading pattern diversified geographically. The dominant connection with France and England was reduced, and trade with Italy and Cuba also diminished. In contrast, relations with Germany, the United States, and Argentina intensified. In total, the weight of these six countries (Cuba excluded) in the foreign trade picture diminished; they absorbed 85% of Spain's exports in 1827 but the figure had fallen to 73% on the eve of World War I. The same period saw greater diversification in import sources, with their corresponding share of imports falling from 93% in 1827 to only 61% in 1914.

The contribution of foreign trade to economic growth is a very controversial subject. Until about 15 years ago the predominant opinion in Spain was that international trade was harmful to nonindustrialized countries and thus, since Spain was an underdeveloped country, it was appropriate to close off international commerce, as indeed was effectively done. The simple idea behind this move is the old doctrine about "infant industries," to the effect that the industries of a backward country can never develop in competition with those already established in the more advanced countries. But this idea is excessively simple. Already in the nineteenth century industrial complexity was such that in many cases the development of one industry stimulated that of a complementary one: Switzerland was using English yarn, Italy was using Spanish pig iron, for example; in fact many industries were complementary across national borders. By then Adam Smith had already established his most famous tenet, that the division of labor (and technical progress) is a function of the size of the market, and David Ricardo had demonstrated, with his theorem of "comparative advantage," later refined by John Stuart Mill, that the worse-off a country might be, the more it would benefit from foreign trade. The bases of the theory of international trade were well known by the middle of the nineteenth century, but neither the theory nor the practice could allay the fears of the Spanish protectionists.

Today we distinguish between the static and dynamic consequences of trade. With regard to the static advantages, no one with the least knowledge of economics could remain unconvinced. In contrast, the dynamic advantages are much more debatable, because by definition various unknown elements enter into the calculation. The effects which international trade, or its restriction, can have upon future production conditions (economies of scale or the diffusion of technical processes, for example) are, strictly speaking, incalculable, although some conjectures can and should be made about them. In general, the monopoly conditions created by restrictions on trade inhibit progress, but there have been important exceptions. In the Spanish case the static advantages of trade are today very clear: although in real terms the Spanish economy remained very closed, the degree of its openness (the proportion of external trade to the gross national income) grew throughout the nineteenth century, and a correlation exists between the periods of expanding trade and those of economic growth.[13] It is also the case that the exporting sectors in general were more advanced technically and more productive than those that supplied the home market, and that they grew faster than the rest of the economy. Likewise the exporting regions, the Basque country, Catalonia, and the Valencia region, grew more rapidly than the non-exporting regions. Even within Andalucía itself, which one might think constitutes an exception, the exporting areas, Huelva and Jerez, were clearly the most prosperous (Tedde, 1985).

This situation arose in part—and here we are already entering into the issue of dynamic advantages—through the stimulating effects of backward linkages which the growing sectors exerted on their surroundings. Thus export-oriented mining stimulated the explosives industry and development of the transportation network, particularly railroads and mining roadways, wharves, docks, port improvements, and navigation companies (notably in the Basque country). Wine exports stimulated the cork industry, glass, cooperage, and the alcohol industry; export activities in general stimulated banking and the commercial sector to affect a range of elements from urban development to insurance. Although it is difficult to measure exactly, exports influenced employment considerably. Other dynamic aspects, such as economies of scale and technological progress derived from export activities deserve study, but much of this still remains to be done.

One aspect that has been studied, and brilliantly so, is that of the changing terms of trade between Spain and the rest of the world.[14] Indices of the terms of trade measure the direct gains or losses from the trade carried out by a particular country, and it turns out that the terms of trade between Spain and England (and also France, the United States, and Germany) improved notably during the nineteenth century. There are various ways of measuring these relationships. The simplest, the so-called net barter terms of trade, is a simple quotient of two indices, an index of export prices divided by an index of import prices. This index improved for Spain during the nineteenth century until about 1880; from then onwards it declined gently, but was always well above the initial value. This means that every unit of value exported by Spain permitted the purchase of an increasingly greater quantity of imports, at least until 1880, and even afterwards exports bought more than they would have done early in the century. This contradicts the widely held belief that countries that export raw materials come out the losers in international trade. Other more complex estimates, which attempt to calculate how much was imported for each hour worked in the export sector, show a similar picture, one that is even more favorable to Spain. And thanks to improvements in productivity, the factorial terms of trade did not fall after 1880. Here we have yet another measure of the advantages that Spain obtained from international commerce.

The net balance of trade which emerges from official statistics is not worth taking very seriously, because the official valuations assigned to imports and exports introduce a bias, with exports valued too low and imports too high. One reason is that, insofar as the Valuation and Tariff Board was guided by interior prices, it would make sense for the board to assign lower than actual prices to export items and higher ones to import items: after all, that is precisely why goods were, and are, imported and exported. And the disparity is enhanced because the figures on imports include the cost of transportation and insurance, while for exports these charges were normally omitted. But probably the most important source of bias was the Valuation Board's deliberate effort, under pressure from protectionist interests, to magnify these differences in order to exaggerate the commercial deficit; this was done to justify the high tariffs, and also to increase the revenue from *ad valorem* tariffs, that is, those tariffs that were assessed as a percentage of the estimated value of imported items. For all these reasons the chronic commercial deficit that emerges from the Commercial Trade Statistics must be highly exaggerated. Leandro Prados has completed the long and worthy task of reconstructing the statistics of Spain's international trade using the sources of other countries, our major trading partners. His results turn the story upside down, showing the trade balance to be positive for the period beginning in 1870 (Prados, 1988, esp. p. 189). This result is only natural, given that the statistics of other countries must contain similar biases but in the opposite direction.

It seems strange, however, that the Prados figures should give such a clear indication of surplus. It is more probable that the long-run trend was in fact a commercial deficit, although neither in the amount nor the regularity that figures from the General Customs Office suggest. This would be natural in a country with the characteristics of Spain a century ago. The growth in total foreign trade and the relative compositions of imports and exports reveal a relatively backward country but one in the process of development; it is not unusual, in cases like this, that imports should regularly exceed exports. At the same time, it would be difficult to explain the persistent fall of the peseta during these years if there had been a strong commercial surplus at the time.

The Balance of Payments

The question is: if the trend in Spain's foreign trade was towards a deficit, how was this deficit financed? Obviously, at that time tourism, meaning the export value that tourist services represent, did not play the decisive role that it has performed since 1959. Other "invisibles," such as insurance or maritime transport, were not important either; in fact, any balance accruing from these items would probably have been negative. The one invisible item that might have carried some weight, although certainly not comparable with the importance it had in the 1960s, would be emigrant remittances. In the chapter on population we have seen that Spanish emigration, particularly after 1880, cannot be ignored. and it is well known that part of the money that emigrants earned was remitted to the home country. Not all the *Indianos*, the returnees from South America, came back as great tycoons, in the style of the musical theater of the period, and probably the wealthy people that did return were not responsible for the largest fraction of total remittances. But there can be no doubt that the export of labor and favorable opportunities that emigration presented did have its monetary counterpart.

Were these emigrant remittances sufficient to balance the commercial deficit? Without knowing how much it was, an answer might seem rather risky. But in fact it is obvious that the remittances could not have been sufficient.[15] It seems quite clear that the major part of the deficit was met with imported capital, and to arrive at a net balance it would be necessary to deduct dividends and interest payments to foreign countries and the repatriation of capital. On the other side of the balance sheet one would have to keep in mind the small amount of Spanish capital that was exported, almost exclusively to Cuba and Argentina, again to be offset by interest, dividends, and repatriations. These latter remittances were clearly important during the Cuban and Philippine wars of independence and the years immediately following.

The question of how the commercial deficit was settled leads us thus to another very important issue, that of capital importation. The subject of foreign investment is debated with passion and intensity, not only in connection with Spanish economic history, but also as a part of the theories that seek to explain imperialism, underdevelopment, and the international distribution of income. To try even to make the briefest of syntheses of the huge bibliography and the complex arguments would be impossible within the context of the present volume.

Suffice it to say here that international investment has many sides. In the earlier section we presented it as the flow of foreign credits which promotes a balance, redressing a deficit in trade and services. In theory, these payments can be in the form of short-term loans, nothing of great significance. This would be the case when deficits in the balance of goods and services exchanged would be not chronic but rather sporadic; the credits received in deficit years would be balanced out by the payments made in years of surplus. But if the account is chronically in deficit, these debts can not be balanced so easily; by one means or another the short-term credits have to be converted to long-term credits. Or else the country will have to dispose of some of its national assets to pay its debts, like any private individual in financial difficulty. And thus all kinds of items get into the hands of foreigners, like national debt bonds, company shares and debentures, factories, mines, landed properties, buildings, and concessions. Now whether the alienation of these properties is good or bad depends upon many circumstances, as is the case with any private loan, but it is easy to understand that it may provoke hostile reactions of an emotional nature. For example, if a person rents out to a stranger the house that he and his parents before him have lived in, it is easy to imagine that he and his family might suffer distress or even revulsion, and that has nothing to do with the fact that the rental itself may be very good business. It is with an economic point of view, not a nationalistic or emotional one, that we economic historians have to judge the role of foreign investment.

It is to be expected that a country in the process of development, in the transitional stage between an Old Regime economy and a modern one, might enter into considerable debt and seek loans from abroad. Low income levels, weak savings capacity, poor technological know-how, and an inadequate, poorly educated work force necessitate that all these elements be imported. In exceptional cases these imports can be bought in totality with a country's own exports (the case of today's oil-producing nations) but more frequently a backward country with limited production capacity can only finance part of its imports and goes into debt for the rest, hoping that its own productive capacity, once modernized, will generate a sufficient surplus to repay the creditor. Of course, these loans will not come free; the country will have to pay a price for them, namely the interest. And the interest for loans will depend on several circumstances, principal among them the condition of the international capital market and the negotiating capacity of the particular country. That in turn will depend on the overall standing of the borrower as debtor or creditor, elements like punctuality in meeting payments, and a general evaluation of that country's economic future.

Spain's negotiating position was not strong during the nineteenth century. The country had been carrying a debt on the international market since the end of the eighteenth century, and punctuality in meeting payments left much to be desired, in fact on occasions, not infrequently, the government simply failed to meet its obligations (see more later, Chapter 7). Both the international commercial account and Treasury were chronically in deficit, and the problem was exacerbated by an unstable political system and an outdated social structure. For all these reasons those who were investing in Spain, be they foreigners or nationals, demanded high interest rates and powerful guarantees in return for loaning their fortunes, and each time that Spain's negotiating position became weaker the lenders' demands became proportionately greater.

The extent of foreign loans and sales to foreign subjects is difficult to quantify, because the operations were heterogeneous and the sources are very scattered. Hence the estimates are vague and somewhat approximate, and they cannot be more than that. In the last analysis, the division between foreign and national investments contains a clear element of artificiality; often a simple repatriation of capital is accounted for as a foreign investment, or in the frequent case where a national frontier divides a natural region in two, an investment is counted as foreign though it originated from a nearby settlement. Conversely, an investment would be counted as domestic if it came from someone living in a distant region but still within the same nation.

At any rate, it is quite clear that during the nineteenth century Spain got into considerable debt with her close European neighbors, as can be seen in Table 5.4. As its title indicates, this table shows us the flow of private capital into Spain by decades, not the stock of foreign investment at any given moment. The first feature that springs to mind is the fluctuation in volumes of capital imported, high in the years 1861–1870, 1881–1891, and 1901–1913, and low in the other years. (Since the last period covers thirteen years the corresponding figure is not strictly comparable with the others, but a simple calculation allows us to estimate the decennial rate at 567.4 million pesetas, which is the third highest.) What this table cannot tell us is the amount of dividends paid and capital redemptions made in respect of these loans, nor

Table 5.4. Flows of foreign capital to Spain (excluding the national debt) by country of origin, 1851–1913 (percentage distribution of ten-year totals)

Period	Total in millions of Fr. francs, current value	France	Belgium	United Kingdom	Germany	Others
1851–1860	328.9	94.7	3.4	1.0	0.0	0.9
1861–1870	609.9	88.7	10.0	1.4	0.0	0.0
1871–1880	488.1	44.5	8.9	43.7	2.9	0.0
1881–1890	718.0	60.8	6.2	31.6	0.0	1.4
1891–1900	382.7	42.0	18.1	18.9	19.8	1.1
1901–1913	737.6	53.9	19.5	20.5	6.1	0.0
Grand Totals	3,265.2	63.2	11.4	20.7	4.1	0.5

Source: calculated from Broder (1976)

Table 5.5.   Spain's national debt: amounts paid up, 1768–1891

Period	Debt in million French francs
1768–1815	53.3
1820–1823	128.4
1823–1850	293.0
1851–1891	1,226.8
Accumulated Total	1,701.5

Source: Broder (1976)

can it help us put a simple figure on the accumulated amount of foreign capital invested in the country.

In principle, we can obtain the figure for gross accumulated capital from tables 5.4 and 5.5. Other researchers have calculated the figures for accumulated investment at specific times. Thus, Sardá estimates that in 1881 foreign investments in Spain amounted to 4,200 million pesetas, and of this 2,000 was private investment while 2,200 represented national debt bonds in the hands of foreigners. These figures, calculated in a very impressionistic manner, are not very close to those compiled by Broder, which are quoted in tables 5.4 and 5.5. Cumulating figures from Table 5.4 up to 1880 would yield about 1,400 millions of francs of private investment, practically equivalent to just as many millions of pesetas. The margins of error that would be necessary to render the Broder and the Sardá figures compatible are very wide, above 27%. Broder's figure seems to me to be more trustworthy, because it is based upon a direct calculation and is much more recent.

Table 5.5 gives Broder's estimates of foreign holdings of the national debt, estimated by periods. In comparison, Sardá's figure for 1881 is some 500 millions higher than Broder's figure for ten years later. The table also shows that the periodization of growth in the national debt was different from that for private foreign investment, something that Sardá had already pointed out.[16] The private debt appeared later, but starting in 1850 it outgrew the other. This should not surprise us, given what we already know about Spain's economic history in the nineteenth century; in reality it was during the second half of the century that the country moved into a phase of modest but sustained economic development, putting its natural resources to work, both above ground and below. It is not surprising therefore that the country turned to importing foreign capital and technology at that time, given the low levels of savings and the limitations of the domestic labor force.

And what of the connection between capital imports and foreign trade? We have already seen that *a priori* there must have been one, and a close one at that. Table 5.6 shows that the total amount of imported capital during the period 1850–1891 was some 3,371.7 million francs (until this date the peseta and the franc were practically equivalent). During this same period Spain's total foreign commercial trade (imports plus exports, official figures) amounted to some 39,548 millions of pesetas, which signifies that foreign investment was approximately 8.5% of Spain's international trade; calculating the same proportion simply in terms of aggregated imports, we get 15.8%. The accumulated deficit during this period is around 3,118.6 million pesetas, a figure that comes very close to the accumulated imported capital, in fact 92.5% of it. These relationships are very similar for the period 1891 to 1913, as Table 5.6 indicates.

Overall, Table 5.6 reveals an interesting parallelism between the foreign trade deficit calculated from the official Spanish figures and the flow of foreign investment, calculated by Broder from private French and Spanish sources. This is particularly interesting because the figures were obtained by very different procedures, yet they reveal similar orders of magnitude, so

Table 5.6. Foreign investment and international trade (in million pesetas)

		1850–1890	1891–1913
Foreign investment	Public indebtedness	1,226.8	0.0
(figures from Broder)	Private indebtedness	2,144.9	1,352.3[a]
	Total	**3,371.7**	**1,352.3**
International trade	Exports	18,214.7	21,445.6
(official figures)	Imports	21,333.3	22,619.7
	Balance	**−3,118.6**	**−1,174.1**
International trade	Exports	19,120.2	27,618.9
(figures from Prados)	Imports	19,915.9	23,199.8
	Balance	**−795.7**	**4,419.1**

[a] The original figure of 1,120.3 million French francs has been multiplied by an average depreciation factor of 1.20709 to convert the francs into pesetas. This depreciation factor is derived from Table III in Tortella et al. (1978)

Sources: calculated from Broder (1976), *Estadística del Comercio Exterior,* and Prados (1986)

that the one reinforces the other. For both periods the commercial deficit is about 90% of the capital imported, 92.5% in 1850–1890 and 86.8% from 1891 to 1913. Taking into account that a wide margin of error is to be expected in historical statistics (something around 10% would not be surprising), and that the margin could be even greater for the estimated commercial deficits—and knowing that the flow of capital calculated by Broder is, by his own testimony, approximate (because he excludes interest, dividends, and repatriations of capital)—the coincidences between the Broder figures and the official statistics are, to say the least, suggestive. In contrast, the figures that Prados has corrected do not square with what we know about imported capital, and that could suggest that the correction he applied is excessive, while the original figures are incomplete. This would not be surprising since his principal source, foreign statistics, have the same biases as the Spanish ones, and when applied to the Spanish figure, produce the inverse effect. And we know that the peseta depreciated notably during the 1890s; with a positive flow of both capital and emigrant remittances, it is difficult to explain this depreciation if the commercial balance was also in surplus. Taking into account that these were the most important items in the Spanish balance of payments, it would be paradoxical indeed if a country whose international trade balance was in surplus faced the problem of persistent currency depreciation.

Foreign capital was invested as follows: until 1850, investment was predominantly in public loans; from 1850 to 1890 private sector investment was already more important, but two-thirds of this represented railroad investment, and the rest was almost all in mining. And from 1891 to 1913 foreign investment in the national debt was zero, and investment in railroads declined a great deal, becoming only one-fifth of the total; mining investment declined as well, but in contrast there was increasing investment in banking, water supply, public works in general, and industry, above all chemicals. Clearly, as the country was developing, the sectoral distribution of foreign investment was changing, both adapting to the existing possibilities and stimulating them.

What can we say in general about the effects of foreign investment in Spain during the nineteenth century? In the first place, that it played quite an important role, in quantitative terms. From tables 5.4 and 5.6 one can estimate how large accumulated foreign investment had become by the end of the century: the total amounted to some 3,848.0 million pesetas,[17] a figure that exceeds by more than one-third the value of the national goods sold through the *desamortización* between 1836 and 1900 (see Chapter 3). To make the comparison easier, we can take this estimate of foreign accumulated investment, from 1850 to 1890, and compare it with various Treasury incomes similarly accumulated in Chapter 7, Table 7.2. We see that accumulated foreign investment amounted to almost 15% of the total accumulated budget receipts during the same period, a quantity equal to the tax collected by the tobacco monopoly and greater by 10% than that collected through customs.

These simple comparisons are the best and most trustworthy points we can make with the data available to us. Other more exciting questions will have to remain unanswered, at least for the moment. Was foreign investment good or bad? This most basic question is very difficult to answer. To begin to answer it one has to ask another question; what alternatives were there? The alternatives will lie between the extremes of attracting no foreign investment at all, and of receiving loans under optimum circumstances. Let us examine both extremes in the briefest possible manner. It takes only a moment's reflection to realize that in the absence of foreign investment the economic situation in Spain would have been worse than it was. Foreign investment financed both budgetary and commercial trade deficits, that is to say, the expenses of state and the high level of imports. Without it, capital formation would have been smaller; public works, railroads, industries, and mines would have been much less developed. Now then, compared to zero investment, it is obvious that foreign investment has had a positive impact on the Spanish economy, but what would have happened if the investment had been made in the best possible conditions, at lower costs, and above all in exchange for less power and privilege? There is no shadow of doubt that the foreign loans were bought dearly, both in terms of interest and dividends—a claim that is relatively easy to quantify—and in terms of influence and prerogatives, which is almost impossible to measure. Obviously it is true that if in place of loans Spain had received those 3,848 million pesetas as an unconditional donation to the Spanish economy, all other things being equal, it would have been more prosperous.

These comparisons reveal just how difficult it is to answer the simple question whether foreign investment was good or bad. At one extreme we arrive at the conclusion that is was bad; if we take the other assumption we find it was good. Clearly the comparison ought to be made in some less extreme form, posed as a realistic alternative which must be quantifiable, if we want a precise answer. The case of the railroads offers a simple example that is appropriate to illustrate these difficulties. Was foreign investment in the railroads prejudicial to the Spanish economy? In absolute terms, no; the Spanish railroads would have been less extensive and more expensive without that investment. But then, compared to a realistic alternative, that of getting them constructed at a pace that was more appropriate to the growth of demand for railroad services, one can say that yes, it was clearly prejudicial that the big French companies, with the consent of Spain's politicians, organized the construction in accordance with their own plans and convenience. When it comes to assigning blame and responsibility, however, we move on to a different plane, because it is not sensible to expect that French business leaders should have been more concerned with the Spanish economy than Spain's own political representatives showed themselves to be at that time. The conclusion regarding this particular enterprise and the question of foreign investment in general is thus difficult to establish: for lack of better information, each one of us is free to form an opinion. Certainly it was better to import capital than to be deprived of it. But it is also beyond question that better economic policy would have managed to achieve better conditions for those loans. And finally, let us not forget that we are stepping here into the quagmire of hypothetical argument.

CHAPTER 6

Money and Banking

Introduction

Consistent with the rest of the economy, the banking, monetary, and financial sectors also modernized during the nineteenth century. The question of state finance (to be examined more closely in the following chapter) is of interest here because of the bearing it has upon the money and capital markets. Government finances were the object of a very important program of reform and modernization during this period. The first efforts to organize state incomes and expenditures into a budget date from the reign of Fernando VII, and some budgets were also drawn up during the 1840s, but the practice of making budgets and publishing them annually was definitively established by the Mon-Santillán reform of 1845. This very important step in organizing the economic and financial affairs of state was not enough, however, to achieve a balance between government revenues and expenditures. Deficits were endemic, and in consequence of this disequilibrium, which continued into the twentieth century, Spain was constantly a debtor nation. Over the years, as the public debt accumulated, it was paid little serious attention; frequent negligence, impunctual payments, and even repudiations of course further prejudiced the financial standing of public credit. This growing indebtedness and Spain's aggravated credit position could not help but increase the price of money and capital in Spanish markets, and this indeed did happen. High interest rates and the chronic budgetary deficit, along with other anomalies in the monetary and financial markets, were bound to affect the economy in many different areas, from the balance of payments to industrial development, in a chain of events that touched upon the supply of money, the structure of the banking system, and capital formation.

Now during the second half of the nineteenth century, the Spanish economy had three principal and privileged consumers of capital: the state, the *desamortización* (costs of the disentailed lands), and the railroads. (The first and second sectors overlap to a considerable extent, the first and third only marginally.) The question that the historian has to pose, therefore, is the following: even taking into account that a considerable amount of foreign capital was imported (it could not be otherwise, given the circumstances) and realizing that the savings generated by the poor economy of Spain during this period were only meager, were not the remaining sectors, with less negotiating power in the capital markets, deprived of capital that was vital to them in their first stages of growth? Were areas such as manufacturing industry, small and middle-size agriculturalists, education, various branches of transport and commerce in fact shut out of the market by the strength of their privileged competitors? The indications that this was so are numerous, from Clara Núñez's work that shows there was not enough money to finance Spanish education in the nineteenth century (Núñez, 1992, chap. 8, and Núñez, 1991), through to Hoyo's work (1993), which demonstrates that the Madrid stockmarket was completely dominated by national debt bonds at mid-century, whereas private bonds were utterly marginal, representing less than 1% of traded volume. Some scholars, alleging that the total budget deficit was a small fraction of national income, have argued against the crowding-out effect in Spain's nineteenth century capital market (a term that describes a situation where the state's demand for capital absorbs a substantial proportion of the country's savings, making loans expensive and thus excluding private investment demand from the market). For my part, I do not find their argument against the crowding-out hypothesis very convincing, because savings were also a very small fraction of national income, so that relative to the size of the total capital market, the state's need for capital was very large indeed, large enough to crowd out competitors.

The Monetary System

The modernization of the monetary system was one of the principal visible components of the transition of the Spanish economy from the Old Regime into the modern world. The process was carried out on several levels. On one side there were a series of reforms that set up the decimalization of coinage and unified the system nationally. During the first third of the nineteenth century, various monetary systems were still coexisting, dating from distinct epochs and serving different regions, none of which was decimal, and in addition there was an abundance of foreign and colonial coinage in circulation; the hodgepodge of coins and the confusion of how the systems related to each other caused uncertainty and made transactions difficult (Sardá, 1948, pp. 5–33). The first attempts at reform were embodied in the legislation of 1848 and 1864, which made honest but insufficient attempts to reduce the confusion. The 1848 law set up a system based upon bimetallism with the *real* as the basic unit of currency, but it was unable to achieve its objectives. Among the various obstacles two were critical: first, the government did not manage to carry out the drastic program of minting new coins that the new system required; and second, the price of gold began to fall on the international markets starting in 1850, so that silver began to disappear from circulation and gold became *de facto* Spain's standard currency. In an attempt to resolve these problems, the 1864 reform introduced the *escudo* or half *duro,* divided into ten *reales,* as the monetary unit, and tried to adapt the official bimetallic ratio (the exchange rate between gold and silver) to market prices. The importance of these measures lies more in the attempt at standardization than in what was actually achieved. The authorities were trying to replace a currency system still tied to a heterogeneous and disjointed coinage (the inheritance of random decisions from Spain's pre-modern past) with a single, simple, and homogenous system which would facilitate transactions enormously. In fact this was achieved gradually through a second reform in 1868, whose two principal innovations were the installation of yet another unit, the *peseta,* which has survived until today, and the creation of a bimetallic system which survived less than fifteen years.

The name "peseta" is Catalán (it can be translated as "little piece"), probably dates from the seventeenth century, and was introduced by the Treasury Minister Laureano Figuerola, also a Catalán. That was not the reason for its success, however, but rather that among the coins in circulation nationally at that time, it was the one whose value most closely approximated the French franc, which was the basic unit of the Latin Monetary Union, and Figuerola along with his contemporaries in his Progressive ministry wished Spain to establish some kind of adherence to that international monetary agreement. The peseta, made up of four *reales* (25 *céntimos* each), was obviously not imposed overnight, but its use became gradually more widespread during the last decades of the century, thanks to the mintings which were carried out in accordance with the new law, and thanks to another important component of this monetary transition: the growing circulation of banknotes which, issued exclusively by the Bank of Spain after 1874, substantially advanced the diffusion of the peseta as the new unit of currency.

If the peseta turned out to be a sturdy monetary unit, the bimetallic system created by the same 1868 law was, by contrast, very short-lived. The principal argument in favor of bimetallism is that basing the monetary system on two metals, generally gold and silver, permits a greater expansion in the money supply. One tremendous inconvenience, however, is that for both metals to be equally and indistinguishably acceptable, there must be an official parity at which the state will convert one metal to the other. The problem arises when this parity does not coincide with market prices. Then private individuals will find it lucrative to buy the cheaper metal on the open market and sell it to the state at the official price, or, conversely, to take out of circulation the coinage struck in the costlier metal and sell it on the market, either melted down or not, at a higher price than the official value. This phenomenon is known in economics as Gresham's Law: the bad coinage replaces the good. This had happened in Europe after 1850, when new gold mines were discovered, the price of gold fell, and thereupon silver disappeared from circulation. The Latin Monetary Union was formed with the object of keeping silver in circulation, but it fell on hard times because the trend was reversed a few years later, around 1870, when new silver mines were discovered in the United States. Various countries (including Germany) then abandoned the silver standard or bimetallism. The result was that in the bimetallist countries it was now silver that came back into circulation and gold that tended to disappear. Faced with this situation the bimetallist countries could do three things; the first option was to do nothing and wait until silver displaced gold completely and the country found itself with a *de facto* single metal currency based on silver; the second option was to demonetize silver, that is, to adopt a single standard based upon gold; the third option was to try to maintain the bimetallic system, changing the gold-silver parity ratio frequently to keep it close to market prices. This system seems the most logical if one really wants to maintain bimetallism, but is has a tremendous drawback: the intense speculation related to successive changes in the parity gives rise to dangerous temptations for civil servants and members of the government. In fact, the countries in the Latin Monetary Union and the greater part of the other bimetallist countries ended up abandoning silver and adopting, *de jure* or *de facto,* a system based upon gold. But Spain adopted the first solution, the passive one, so that it was left in the 1880s with a monetary system that was *de facto* based upon a silver standard. In a country where in the mid-1860s the monetary system had been based upon gold, twenty years later the precious yellow metal had disappeared from circulation.

The importance of the disappearance of circulating gold in Spain goes far beyond the anecdotal. One problem is that Spain's abandonment of gold took place when most of the economically advanced countries, which were its principal trading partners, were in fact adopting the gold standard, and this contributed to her economic isolation. Second, the persistent fall in the value of silver in the open market meant that the real value of the money in circulation was much less than its face value (in 1886 the silver content of a peseta coin was in fact worth only 75 centimos) and that meant that silver was performing the role of a fiduciary money, essentially with the same characteristics as fractional coinage or banknotes. Consequently, since it was profitable to strike silver coins, there were no automatic limits on the quantity of money in circulation, since silver was abundant and therefore inexpensive. In comparison, starting in about 1870 gold was becoming scarce and therefore expensive, and this limited the possibility of indefinitely extending the money supply in countries which were on the gold standard. So Spain's silver standard was in fact a fiduciary standard, essentially identical to those which today operate throughout the world, where the supply of money is subject to no limits except those which the governments impose at their own discretion. This meant that in Spain monetary policy and the level of prices could diverge somewhat from the rest of Western Europe, even though the Spanish monetary authorities, as a matter of policy, made repeated efforts to maintain the kind of discipline which the gold standard enforced in a more automatic manner.

At the same time that silver was taking the place of gold, two new components of the supply of money came into the picture; from an insignificant position in 1830, and still of little importance in 1850, these new sources came to represent more than half of the supply of money by the end of the century. These new components, which today jointly account for almost the whole of this important macroeconomic variable, are banknotes and current account balances. The circulation of notes grew from a very small indeterminate quantity in 1830 to some 30 million pesetas in 1850 and about 1,600 million at the century's end. As far as current accounts are concerned, the totals are difficult, if not impossible, to establish, because the information from various banks is missing; but we can get a benchmark from the ac-

Table 6.1. Approximate composition of the money supply around 1865 (in million pesetas)

Banknotes	100
Current account deposits	60
Silver	250
Gold	1,100
Money supply (M_1)	1,510

Source: Banco de España (1970a)

Table 6.2. Money stock and money supply in 1900 (in million pesetas)

Banknotes	1,600
Current account deposits	960
Silver	1,300
Gold	395
Money stock	4,255
Gold reserves	(395)
Silver reserves and notes	(610)
Total reserves	−1,005
Money supply (M_1)	3,250

Source: Tortella (1974)

counts held in the Bank of Spain, which grew between 1850 and 1900 from 25 to 700 million approximately (see Tables 6.1 and 6.2).

Along with these modifications in the composition of the money supply, the total volume increased vastly, probably tripling between 1850 and 1900. The disappearance of gold was more than compensated by the growth of the other components.

The Banking System

Parallel to the monetary transition, the banking system also evolved, essentially from an embryonic stage of development to one that was relatively diversified, although certainly far from what we could call "mature." An enumeration of just the incorporated banks (the private banks are difficult to track down and count, although there has been much recent research into them, particularly by J. R. García López) would reveal an increase from only one in 1830, the Banco de San Fernando, some three or four banks at mid-century, and about 50 towards 1900, without counting the 58 branches of the Bank of Spain that were in existence by that date.

The Early Years

The first major Spanish bank, the Banco Nacional de San Carlos, was created in 1782. Among other missions this bank, which was an official bank (that is, sponsored by the state), was put in charge of administering the national debt, the sadly notorious *vales reales* which the government never repaid. Because of this burden and what can only be described as incompetent administration, the Banco de San Carlos, which Pedro Tedde (1988) has called "a giant with feet of clay," entered the nineteenth century virtually in a state of suspended payments and encountered a range of complex problems during the politically tortured first third of the century. Although a great deal has been written about the Bank of San Carlos, beginning with Count Mirabeau in 1785, the definitive work, already cited, is that by Tedde.

To bring closure to the long paralysis of the Bank of San Carlos, a new bank was founded in 1829, called the Banco Español de San Fernando. To a certain extent the establishment of this new bank represents a solution to the problem of the *vales reales,* since it was based upon an "agreement" between the state and the private shareholders of the San Carlos, through which the shareholders renounced their claims in return for shares in the new bank. The deal meant that the shareholders would receive one *real* for every eight that was owed to them; in a hopeless situation, at the end of no less than thirty years when they had collected no dividends, and with the *vales reales* worthless on the market, the shareholders really had no other option than to accept.

During its first fifteen years, the Bank of San Fernando issued banknotes in small amounts and discounted letters of credit, but above all it lent money to the government. With little variation this was going to be its role for the rest of its life. In 1844 two more banking companies were formed, the Banco de Isabel II in Madrid and the Banco de Barcelona. The Isabel II Bank, one of the first business ventures of José Salamanca, immediately became a rival of the San Fernando. The competition between the two banks increased the fiduciary circulation, making credit cheaper in Madrid, but in a very short time the crisis of 1847–48 and the temerity and inexperience of both, particularly the Isabel II, brought each of them to the verge of bankruptcy. By 1848 the government could find no other solution than to merge the two into the Nuevo Banco de San Fernando, but the new entity, overwhelmed by the debts of the Isabel II (which had extended large loans to companies that became insolvent) reached 1850 in a situation of virtual suspension of payments, although in the long run it managed to recover. The 1856 Law on Issuing Banks re-baptized the Banco de San Fernando; it was henceforth the Bank of Spain.[1]

The Banco de Barcelona, the flagship company of the banker Manuel Girona, with issuing rights in the city of Barcelona, rode out the storm of the crisis much better, thanks to a prudent and conservative policy, and it became the most important and prestigious private bank for the rest of the century. The third issuing bank founded before 1850 was in Cádiz. It began as a branch of the Isabel II and became independent at the time of the fusion with the San Fernando. During the euphoric decade of the 1840s many banking institutions were founded, almost all of them short-lived.[2]

The Years 1850–1874

This quarter-century was one of broad fluctuations. It began in economic depression, the result of the 1848 crisis; experienced expansion, 1854 to 1864, although not free from fluctuations; and then entered a phase of uncertainty resulting from several major events including the crisis of 1866, the Revolution of 1868, the war in Cuba, the proclamation and abdication of Amadeo I, the cantonal uprising, and the Carlist War. The period's economic and political turbulence can be traced in banking history. In effect, in the short space of these twenty-five years, the banking system experienced strong expansion, 1855–1864, followed by a severe crisis and contraction, 1864–1870, and then conversion to a new structure that abolished the provincial issuing banks and conceded monopoly issuing rights to the Bank of Spain.

Let us examine briefly the most important stages of these restless years. The crisis of 1848 had interrupted the first period of banking expansion in contemporary Spain. The legislation and the anti-expansionist policy of the depression kept the banking industry in an embryonic state until 1855, although a degree of postcyclical recovery and intense mercantile activity brought about by the Crimean War generated pressure among the financial power brokers in favor of a more expansive policy. This came with the Progressive legislation, 1855–1856, which helped railroad and banking companies, whose numbers increased considerably, but did nothing for industrial or mercantile activities. Under the Banking Laws of 1856, two types of banks emerged. One group comprised note-issuing banks, just one per city, which were authorized to issue banknotes in accordance with fairly strict norms about gold and silver holdings that served as guarantees; they were also authorized to make loans and to discount bills, but little else. The other banks permitted by the 1856 law were called credit societies; these were really business banks whose structure was modeled on the French Crédit Mobilier, without right to issue banknotes but with broad powers to participate in all kinds of business activities. It was practically inevitable that this improvised banking system, instead of contributing to the development of industry or agriculture, should turn its newly minted credit capacity toward the railroads, whose company structure, intense activity, and above all official support made them, apparently, very attractive for investment.

The growth of the banking system during these years is quite remarkable; the number of issuing banks increased from three to twenty and the credit societies from zero to 35 during the ten years that followed the Progressive legislation. If we include some other banking societies that do not exactly fit into either of these two categories along with the already existing branches of the Bank of Spain, we find that a system that scarcely amounted to five or six banking societies in 1855 (the issuing banks in Madrid, Barcelona, and Cádiz, plus one or two more in Barcelona, Zaragoza, and Valencia) had reached 60 establishments ten years later. But this tremendous growth hid some profound structural defects, the most important of which was a lack of diversification in asset investment; banks concentrated on loans to railroad companies and almost all the rest had been invested in the national debt. When, towards 1864, it turned out that the railroad traffic would not even cover the variable costs of the companies and that they would have to suspend interest payments, the consequences for the banking industry were clearly foreseeable: many of them also suspended payments, and not a few closed their doors for ever, leaving many millions in debts unpaid. A financial and stockmarket panic immediately ensued, and a few years later gave rise to the Revolution of 1868.

In the ten years following 1865, the number of banks was reduced drastically. At the beginning of 1874 the number was not much above 15, of which the majority were issuing banks. The credit societies which had most compromised their position with loans to the railroad companies, disappeared as rapidly as they had arrived on the scene. Almost the only one that survived this transformation, although much reduced in terms of capital and activity, was the Crédito Mobiliario Español, the Spanish branch of the Crédit Mobilier of the Pereire brothers, the first and largest of those founded under the 1856 legislation. Between 1870 and 1874 a few new banks did emerge, with more modest aims; they dedicated themselves principally to mortgage credit, an area almost totally ignored in previous years.[3]

The supply of money during these years remained strictly within the full content norm: gold and silver constituted approximately 90% of the money in circulation. In spite of impressive growth in the banking sector, the money created by the banks (banknotes plus deposits) continued to be only a small proportion of the whole, although it may have grown faster than full-bodied money. The approximate composition of the money supply in 1865 is presented in Table 6.1.

This estimate, based principally on work by Rafael Anes and myself, includes bank reserves (the specie held by the banks) which, strictly speaking, ought to be deducted if one wants to speak accurately about the amount of money in circulation. Bank reserves amounted to some 60 million pesetas in 1865. The figures are considered approximate principally because the information we have to hand about monetary activities by the credit societies is uncertain. The issuing banks were legally obliged to publish clear balance sheets; the credit societies had more freedom and made use of it by publishing accounts that were few, far between, and confused. Thus we cannot be sure about their current account deposits; and although we know that some of them did issue paper money regardless of the prohibition, we do not know with any certainty how many did so, nor in what quantity.

The Years 1874–1900

The last quarter-century, although not exempt from fluctuations, does not present such severe ups and downs as the period we have just described. During this new phase the monetary and banking systems acquired some of their more permanent characteristics. Perhaps the most far-reaching event of this period happened right at the outset: in 1874 the Bank of Spain obtained the monopoly of note issue for the whole of the country.[4] This decision had very little to do with policy, although probably, given the peculiarities of the Spanish monetary system, the measure was inevitable in the long run; a system based on fiduciary issue needs a certain minimum degree of centralization in the creation of money. Adam Smith says that the concession of royal privileges by the English Crown was rarely done in the public interest, but rather "for extorting money from the subject" (1937 ed., ch. X): this maxim applies perfectly to the Provisional Republican Government, which at the beginning of 1874, desperately short of funds, conceded the monopoly of banknote issue to the Bank of Spain in order to obtain from it an indefinite loan, of the then fabulous and unheard of amount of 125 million pesetas. In addition to the monopoly, the bank was authorized to issue notes in twice the amount that had formerly been permitted, a level that until that point had not been even closely approached. Henceforth the bank used the issuing privilege extensively, at the same time that it was making generous loans to the national Treasury. Through this mechanism the bank was essentially "monetizing the national debt," to use a common expression. The Bank of Spain lent money to the Treasury, and the public, by accepting the banknotes, was loaning to the bank.

Thus it turned out that the volume of banknotes in circulation—increasingly the more important part of the supply of money—came to depend more upon the budgetary problems of the state than on the guidelines of any particular monetary policy. This volume increased very rapidly in the last quarter of the century, at a rate of 11% annually, which implies that the volume would double every six and a half years. At this speed any formerly established maximum was soon reached, but the government kept making upward adjustments as was necessary.

At the time the Bank of Spain was granted the monopoly to issue banknotes, some fifteen issuing banks operated in the country, although some were in business in a very nominal way. Most of these voluntarily annexed themselves to the Bank of Spain, which converted them to branches and opened additional ones. (Other institutions like the Banks of Barcelona and Bilbao were openly opposed to the monopoly, which they considered, not without justification, an illegal limitation on their rights, since their issuing privileges had not expired.) Thus the Bank of Spain, which had never had more than two branches in the earlier period (in Alicante and Valencia), was operating seventeen by the end of 1874, and it further continued to expand; at the end of the century there were 58 branches. This expansionist policy could not but cause problems of competition and rivalry in various cities, particularly where there had been an earlier tradition of successful banking, as in Barcelona and Bilbao. But the Bank of Spain could count on the firm support of whatever government was in power, and these problems never affected it very seriously.

In December 1872 the Banco Hipotecario (a mortgage bank) was founded under official auspices, and for motives that were very similar to those which led to the authorization of the Bank of Spain's monopoly of issuing rights. The Banco Hipotecario soon enjoyed its own monopoly of issue, not of banknotes but of mortgage bonds. There are many reasons to suppose that the Banco Hipotecario, at least during its first quarter-century, paid more attention to its origins than to its name, that is to say, it loaned more to the state than to private individuals, so that it served to complement the Bank of Spain in its role of banker to the state. This latter made short-term loans to the state preferentially, with funds raised through the issue of banknotes; the Banco Hipotecario loaned at longer term, using funds it obtained from the issue of mortgage bonds. The Hipotecario was the first member of a group that during the twentieth century would become numerous: the institutions of official credit.[5]

The 1866 crisis and its consequences brought about a general downsizing in private banking, a significant reduction that was completed when the Bank of Spain absorbed most of the issuing banks. The private banking industry was reduced to a handful of institutions whose lineage and broadly based holdings had allowed them to resist the impact of so many blows and to maintain sufficient optimism to reject the offers of the new monopolists; the most important of these survivors were the Banks of Barcelona, Bilbao, and Santander, plus the already mentioned Crédito Mobiliario. Thus this last quarter-century was a reconstruction period for the banking system, with growth far more gradual than the years 1855 to 1864. In addition to the relatively slow rate of development, the distinguishing features of this period were the predominance of mixed banking with much less emphasis on railroad activities; the eclipse of the Andalusian banking industry; the specialization of Madrid in official credit; the onset of decline in Catalán banking; and the powerful emergence of the industry in the Basque country and Navarra.

The legal separation between issuing banks and business banks or credit societies has a clear doctrinal justification. The issuing banks obtain the greater part of their holdings of other people's money in the form of short-term liabilities (notes and current accounts), and thus they specialize in short-term credit (loans and discounts). In contrast, the credit societies obtain their resources at long term (capital and securities) and can commit a substantial part of their assets to long-term projects (promoting companies, shared subscriptions, underwriting, revolving loans). But in practice the division was not so successful, largely because the credit societies misused their privileges and made poor use of their prerogatives, issuing undue amounts of notes and making speculative investments. Meanwhile, some issuing banks, like the Bilbao and Santander, began to expand operations by obtaining long-run funds and using them in the promotion and financing of companies. This modality continued to be practiced during the last quarter of the century, particularly in the Basque provinces, with growing success for the Banco de Bilbao and later for the Banco del Comercio. There is no doubt that the boom in the Bilbao region, due in great part but not exclusively to the export of iron ore and to iron manufacturing, created a demand for this new type of banking, which during the same years was so unequivocally successful in Germany, where rapid and profound industrialization was also under way.

In Catalonia, on the other hand, mixed banking did not prosper, perhaps because a long-standing tradition in banking and commerce obstructed the bankers' innovative impulses, perhaps for sociological or structural reasons within the dominant and long-standing textile industry, which inhibited the demand for these kinds of bank services. Nor did the specialized banks prosper. From about 1884 most Catalán banking establishments, the business banks and commercial banks too, entered a long period of contraction, and eventually almost all of them disappeared. The trend culminated thirty years later with the sensational bankruptcy of the eighty-year old Bank of Barcelona.

Alongside the joint-stock banks, large public companies regulated by the Commercial Code and special laws, there was of course a network of private banks and bankers that predated the modern banks, whose era, as we saw, began in 1782. In many cases this network was of only limited importance, comprising small lenders issuing loans that more often than not were related to consumption rather than production, and often pejoratively referred to as usurers. Yet in many big cities this credit network performed an authentically productive role, contributing to the financing of industry and commerce. Particularly in Barcelona and Madrid the list of private banks includes some outstanding names and numbers. This has been documented by several authors: Castañeda's work (1983) on the networks for bill discounting in Barcelona; Tedde (1983) on Madrid's private bankers; Otazu (1987) on the Rothschilds in Madrid; Rosés (1993) on the savings and loan system in Barcelona; and García López (1987) on private banking in Asturias. There is also evidence of complementarity between both systems, similar to that between the issuing banks and the credit societies. There were cases where an issuing bank and a credit society worked in association with each other, as did the joint-stock banks and the private banking houses.[6]

The savings banks must also be mentioned as part of the credit system. These had different origins; some of them were created as appendages to already existing *Montes de Piedad* (municipal, charitable pawnshops) (Titos, 1989). Such was the case of the oldest one, the Madrid Savings Bank, founded in 1838. In general the savings banks in their original objectives leaned more toward humane assistance than finance, trying to develop the savings habit in people of modest means, as Manuel Titos (1991) has shown, an idea that was very widespread (Tedde, 1991); but in some cases it was the bankers who formed their own savings banks, to gain access to these small savings. The growth of these long-term deposits was very strong in the last quarter of the nineteenth century, and, especially in the north, by 1900 the savings banks had transcended their social-benefit function. In the words of Titos (1991), "[they] began to develop a noticeable economic role,"[7] although the real economic importance of the savings banks did not emerge until the twentieth century. Another integral part of the nineteenth-century financial system was the *Caja de Depósitos,* a French-inspired, rather short-lived official savings bank, founded in 1852 with the mission of receiving escrow funds and other public deposits, which soon became the custodian of a considerable volume of private savings; the government's improper appropriation of the *Caja's* deposits, however, brought it to a virtual suspension of payments during the 1866 crisis, and the institution had to be liquidated in later years (Titos, 1979).

To summarize, the most outstanding events within the monetary system of this period are the considerable expansion of the money supply (even though the advanced countries saw much faster growth in this area), and radical change in its composition, with the disappearance of gold and the absolute predominance of fiduciary money, silver, and notes, with a growing importance of bank deposits.

Table 6.2, which draws inspiration from the same authors as the earlier table, with the addition of Pedro Tedde in this case, offers an estimate of the money supply at the end of the nineteenth century[8] (for an explanation of the expression M_1 see Chapter 14). A comparison with Table 6.1 gives numerical form to Spain's monetary evolution in the second half of the nineteenth century.

One of the phenomena of this period that has been hotly debated recently is the demise of the Catalán banking industry. The causes, which are undoubtedly complex, can be summarized in a simple phrase: the disadvantages of being early in the field. On the supply side, the admirable success of the Bank of Barcelona over a long period undoubtedly stimulated in the Catalán bankers (which is almost to say the Barcelona bankers) a certain fondness for their established practices which prevented them from realizing that the moment of change had arrived. (And when they did change, not until the twentieth century, they demonstrated a lamentable lack of skill in the new practices.) On the demand side, the industry that was most firmly rooted in Catalonia, textiles, was traditionally the sector that resorted very little to outside finance; this was true for English and French textile industries as well. In Catalonia the textile industry set the prevailing tone, and it instilled a certain aversion to any close dependency between industry and banking throughout the region (Rosés, 1993). Tallada (1946) describes expressively that special point of view of the Catalán industrialist, for whom asking for a loan amounted to a humiliating loss of face. When the demand for mixed banking emerged, it was the banking sector from outside of Catalonia which had the requisite experience and competed successfully with the Catalán banking sector in its own backyard.

In the Basque country, in contrast, banking was born with an inclination towards mixed financial activities, viewing favorably both help from the large companies and direct involvement with them. Supported by the rapid economic development of the region and the formidable savings capacity of the citizenry, the Basque banking industry established itself very firmly during the last quarter of the nineteenth century, and began to extend its sphere of influence further afield.

Conclusion

To conclude, the most important assertions contained in the section can be recapitulated as follows:

1. From the point of view of money and banking, the nineteenth century is a period of incomplete transition. One measure of the relative backwardness of the banking system at the end of the century is indicated by the continued overwhelming importance of the Bank of Spain. It says enough that this bank alone held 75% of the current account deposits in the whole banking sector. In more evolved systems the central bank would be relatively less important. Martín Aceña (1985a) offers us further indicators of this same

backwardness. In 1900 bank deposits amounted to no more than 3.3% of the national income, a very low proportion, which 30 years later was to climb to 21.4%. In comparison with Europe, the financial system was only partially evolved. A commonly used indicator, the coefficient of total financial assets as a proportion of national income, was 39 for Spain in 1900 compared with a European average of 104, and 61 for Italy, the most comparable country. To be sure, the banking sector was about to experience some changes, above all some important additions which would modify completely the situation that had existed at the end of the nineteenth century (see Chapter 14).

2. In this period the fiduciary standard was established in Spain, years ahead of most other countries. Gold coinage, abandoned between 1873 and 1993, was never reestablished in spite of repeated attempts to do so. This factor, along with the chronic commercial deficit, meant that the peseta was subject to periodic devaluation whenever a crisis of confidence (political, military, or other) cut off the flow of foreign capital needed for balancing the payments deficit; classic examples were the depreciations during the Cuban War and the last years of Primo de Rivera's dictatorship. The implementation of the fiduciary system was not a deliberate political decision but rather, as the French say, a *pis aller*, a bad arrangement, a worse-case solution: a view certainly confirmed by the continuous efforts that were made to return to the gold standard. In consequence, monetary policy was never really used as a stimulus to development. Instead of devaluing to stimulate exports, the devaluation crises were inevitably followed by drastic austerity policies, whose effects were clearly to depress the economy. But that is the story of the twentieth century. In any case, this precocious fiduciary system, however reluctantly accepted, imparts a remarkably original flavor to Spain's monetary history within Western Europe.

3. The evolution of the banking sector reveals the search for a structure that could be adequate to finance growth—to use banking as an instrument of development, in accordance with the theories of Schumpeter, Gerschenkron, or Cameron. In the first stage the banks made a conscious imitation of French practice in respect of credit societies, which failed for reasons similar to those which also caused the French Crédit Mobilier to fail: recklessness, inexperience, and a dangerous failure to maintain a judicious relationship between investments and liquid funds. In the second stage, along with the exclusive monopoly of note-issuing conceded to the Bank of

Spain, private banking was organized with greater discretionary powers, and profound changes occurred in that structure, both organizationally and geographically.

In concluding, let me point out that the Spanish case in the nineteenth century and during the present century too seems to conform quite well to the Gerschenkron hypothesis about the role of banks in relatively backward countries, where they fulfill the role of market mechanisms in the generation of loanable funds and the promotion of industrial companies. In this Spain clearly fits into the same group as Germany or Japan, where the banks played such a crucial role in the process of industrialization and modernization.

CHAPTER 7

The Role of the State

The Evolution of Public Finance

Public finance was one of the key problems of Spanish economy in the nineteenth century. This was true for all countries, of course, but more so for those like Spain, where a constant imbalance between incomes and expenditures created serious problems for other sectors of the economy, from the mechanisms that control savings and investment right through to international relations.

That the Spanish Treasury was the source of serious problems that called for immediate resolution was quite evident to the politicians of the period, particularly the Liberal party, which did what it could to find solutions. Indeed, one of the most basic characteristics of the transition from the Old Regime to the modern state system is the transformation of the Office of the Treasury. In general, old regime treasuries, not just in Spain but elsewhere too, were archaic institutions inherited from feudalism, and although modified a little by the absolute monarchs, they lacked the most elemental principles of equity, flexibility, and even judicial coherence. In spite of these defects, the pre-Liberal Treasury kept going for centuries without actually going bankrupt until the demands of modernization brought its limitations patently to light. These limitations became increasingly evident in a mounting deficit, which eventually produced political problems that were quite beyond resolution within the old framework. All the major revolutions that mark the passage from the early to the modern period have some kind of fiscal origin, including the English Revolution in the seventeenth century and the North American and French revolutions in the eighteenth, and the solution is found in the birth of a modern state with a more or less representative Parliament, one of whose fundamental missions is to approve the state budget for incomes and expenditures and to supervise its operations.

The requisites of modern taxation that the Old Regime systems were lacking are the following: (1) *equity,* a principle according to which the load of taxation is distributed between the contributors in proportion to their capacity to pay; (2) *legality,* according to which there is only an obligation to pay those taxes approved by the Parliament (which implies juridically that citizens only pay those taxes which their representatives have approved in their name); (3) *generality,* which is the fiscal correlative of equity before the law, a principle that seeks to ensure that all people pay, with no personal or territorial exemptions, the only differences being those agreed under the equity principle; (4) *sufficiency,* so that the state's income ought to be enough to cover the expenditures (in other words, there should be no deficit); (5) *simplicity,* according to which taxes should be few and double taxation excluded, so that on every taxable base or resource only one tax should be imposed; (6) *neutrality,* a requirement that the taxation system should not greatly distort the pattern of relative prices; and (7) *flexibility,* through which the total volume of taxation collected ought to maintain a certain relationship to national income, growing as it grows and decreasing whenever national income declines. In reality, it was the lack of this last attribute that brought down the treasuries of the old regimes, because when the economies grew expenditures increased as well, but when rigidities prevented a parallel rise in treasury incomes, the deficits became excessive. It is worth observing that this lack of flexibility stemmed largely from a lack of equity; since in general the poor paid more than the rich, revenues hardly grew at all when income was growing. And here was the crux of the problem; to remedy the situation and make the taxation system more flexible, one had to make the rich pay too, but these people were not disposed to do so without greater control over expenditures, which implied more political power. The only solution lay in a representative political system, and hence revolution.

As in almost all the other countries, in Spain too the Treasury's transition towards modernity was made very slowly. As Comín shows (1990b, p. 86) there were only two genuine taxation reforms in Spain, one in 1845, and the other in 1977 (see Chapter 15). Attempts to modernize public finance go back as far as the eighteenth century, with the plan for a single tax (*única contribución*) of the Marqués de la Ensenada. But a century later things were even worse. Until 1845 the Spanish taxation system was a disorganized and unsystematic mosaic which violated all the principles enunciated above: not only were the privileged classes virtually exempt from taxation, but the

Church and the nobility often had quasi-fiscal prerogatives, since they collected in their own names rents which looked very much like taxes. The tax burden varied from region to region and there were even specific taxes for particular cities or districts, the *Servicio de Navarra* and the *seda de Granada*, for example. The total taxation picture was a hodgepodge of incomplete and variable components, some with such picturesque names as "straw and tools," "the seven little revenues," and "the codfish tax," with the added anomaly that the state would appropriate a part of the taxes collected by the Church, the *diezmos* (tithes). As a consequence of this lack of equity, generality, legality, and simplicity, there was neither sufficiency nor flexibility, and probably no neutrality either (Comín, 1990).

To a great extent, as Fontana in particular has indicated (1971, 1973, and 1977), the tensions and struggles between Liberals and absolutists (later the Carlists) during the first half of the nineteenth century revolve around the question of public finance reform. The Liberals tried to carry out reforms more or less in accordance with the principles described above, and the absolutists tried to keep things the way they had been before; for Fernando VII, for example, a budget was a subversive and criminal document that aimed to divest him of royal power. Because of this basic difference of perspective characteristic of the period, several attempts at Liberal reform (concretely in the Cortes of Cádiz and later in the Cortes of the Triennium), and also efforts at absolutist reform (by Martín de Garay and Luis López Ballesteros), all tried to augment revenues without changing the basic system. All these attempts failed, for reasons that were as much political as technical.

The Carlists struggled passionately against Liberalism, largely against the principles of fiscal equity, legality, and generality, and only when the Carlist War was over and the power of the Moderados was established could the so long-awaited taxation reform be embarked upon. The reform plan came from Ramón Santillán, a military and taxation expert who, among other distinctions, held the honor of becoming the first governor of the Bank of Spain. Treasury Minister Alejandro Mon shepherded the plan through the Cortes and managed to get it approved into law in 1845. Among those who should harbor gratitude for this reform are the historians, because from then onwards not only were the accounts of the Treasury published annually, but so were many other related statistics, such as figures on international trade. In spite of some grave defects which we shall now examine, the 1845 Mon-Santillán Reform represents a fundamental milestone in the modernization of the Spanish Treasury. Santillán knew how to combine the thrust towards modernization with a prudent respect for what was possible, incorporating many innovations from France and combining features of the taxation system extant in the kingdoms of Castile and Aragón, conserving traditional forms and changing only the parts that lent themselves to improvement. The tax system was simplified and rationalized, with a clear distinction between direct and indirect taxes. Probably the most important of its shortcomings was that it failed to meet the problem of insufficiency: the deficit that had long been dragging down the old system continued to plague the new one.

Later on various partial modifications to the Mon-Santillán scheme were introduced; it was not surprising that the construct should require a certain amount of touching up. Among the most important changes Comín singles out Laureano Figuerola's attempt in 1869 to replace consumer taxes with a more advanced direct tax, a personal tax assessment which failed roundly, perhaps because in the full flood of the "revolutionary period" experiments were too risky. Apart from the Camacho arrangement (*arreglo*), which as we shall see later was little more than a debt settlement, the only other serious change was that introduced by Fernández Villaverde on the threshold of the new century, which we shall review in Chapter 15.

Fiscal Policy: The Budget

The first feature of the Spanish national budgets in the nineteenth century that catches the eye is a chronic deficit, which means that expenses were ordinarily greater than revenues. Figure 7.1 and Table 7.1 show in a very palpable manner the meaning of a chronic deficit. A summary inspection of the figures of the annual budgets[1] would reveal that during the second half of the nineteenth century there were only four years when the budget was in surplus, 1876, 1882, 1893 and 1899.[2]

The principal consequence of this persistent budget deficit was an accumulation of public debt, whose interest payments weighed heavily on the budget expenses. On average, the debt service payment amounted to more than a quarter of the budget expenses in the period 1850–1890, actually 27%. If we factor in pension payments, the total contractual responsibilities that the state owed for loans or past services rendered came to more than a third of total expenditures. The state was trapped in a vicious circle; the dead weight of debt was causing the deficit, and the deficit was being financed by new debts. The old debts, or part of them as we shall see, were being paid

Table 7.1. Budget revenues, expenditures, and balances, 1850–1854 through 1899–1906 (in million pesetas, five-year averages at current values)

	Revenues	Expenditures	Balances
1850–1854	337	353	−16
1855–1859	422	467	−45
1860–1864	521	663	−142
1865–1869	536	748	−170
1870–1874	541	748	−108
1874–1880	737	784	−48
1881–1886	818	863	−45
1887–1892	760	825	−65
1893–1898	820	842	−22
1899–1906	1,022	970	53

Source: Comín (1988), *passim,* and my own calculations

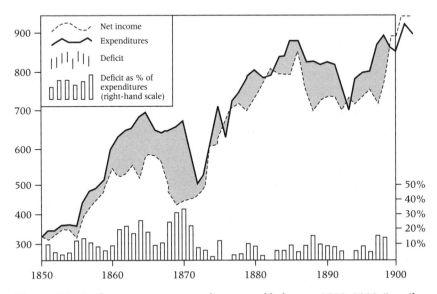

Figure 7.1. Budget revenues, expenditures, and balances, 1850–1902 (in million pesetas)

by newly borrowed money. In real terms this amounted to a substantial sacrifice on the part of the taxpayers, because although part of the debt was being deferred, the other part, plus the interest, was coming out of the pockets of Spaniards, and not the most prosperous ones, to be sure. To aggravate matters even further, the state's difficulty in maintaining solvency, and the partial bankruptcies and repudiations it resorted to from time to time, were well known to lenders. They were thus able to demand high interest rates for their loans, to make stringent conditions, and to demand strong guarantees in order to indemnify themselves for the risks inherent in lending to a client of such doubtful solvency; effectively, they were thus able to feather their own nests by taking advantage of the scant negotiating capacity of a government in constant difficulties. Beyond its direct impact on taxation, the deficit was also extremely damaging to agriculture and industry, which had difficulty raising funds in a market where the state made such massive demands upon the available capital. In comparison with a client of such clout, the needs of industry and agriculture seemed small to the lenders of the day. Bankers and financiers negotiated the national debt with scant attention to the seemingly insignificant demands of the productive sectors. In a word, the deficit aggravated the shortage of capital that so distressed agriculture and industry alike.

We shall return to examine the other causes of chronic deficit. But for now let us look at problems on the other side of the balance sheet, to investigate the chronic shortfall of income. For that, it is sufficient to look at Table 7.2, which shows the contribution of the various taxes and other sources to aggregate Treasury income from 1850 to 1890. The first surprise is that the *contribución territorial* (land tax) levied on property, cultivation, and livestock—the main tax on agriculture (it also included some urban real estate)—should yield little more than a fifth of income; this is surprising because in the second half of the nineteenth century, agriculture clearly represented more than half of Spain's national income and perhaps even more than three-quarters. (In 1962, after a long period of industrialization, agriculture represented not 21% of the national income, but in fact 26%.) It is evident therefore that the tax system was particularly benevolent towards landowners who held the major part of the country's wealth. This, of course, is nothing new; it was well known at the time.

The land tax (on property, cultivation, and livestock) was created as part of the 1845 reform by combining a series of earlier taxes on agriculture. Its fundamental obstacle was a dearth of good data on the extent of taxable

Table 7.2. Accumulated budget revenues by source, 1850–1890 (in million pesetas)

		Pesetas	%
1	Land tax	4,915	21.3
2	Taxes on industry and commerce	930	4.0
3	Poll taxes	110	0.5
4	Taxes on salaries and appointments	604	2.6
5	Taxes on property transfers	601	2.6
6	Stamp tax	1,149	5.0
7	Income from customs	3,064	13.3
8	Consumer taxes on spirits and alcohol	1,965	8.5
9	Railroad taxes on travelers and merchandise	170	0.7
10	Tobacco taxes	3,339	14.5
11	Salt tax	560	2.4
12	Lotteries	1,921	8.3
13	Sale of national properties	1,292	5.6
14	Income from state properties and rights	331	1.4
15	Income from state mines	199	0.9
16	Exemptions from military service	299	1.3
17	Seigniorage (income from the mint)	119	0.5
18	Taxes on mining activities	52	0.2
19	Other taxes	1,439	5.9
20	Total	23,059	100.0

Source: Calculated from *Estadística de los Presupuestos Generales del Estado, 1891*

assets. In the absence of such basic data, the reformers introduced a system of allocation; they figured out a total budget income and then parceled out the requisite amounts between the provinces and cities. In July 1846 the Dirección General de Estadística de la Riqueza was created (General Office of Statistics on National Resources), whose aim was to assess the agricultural resource base by means of a fiscal register which would then serve as the appropriate framework for tax collection. But the task was no easy one; in the preface to the first tome the editor of the *Estadística de los Presupuestos* (Budget Statistics) branded the task "difficult" and "thorny." There were technical problems, of course, but beyond that the task met with bitter resistance on the part of landowners who wanted to conceal their wealth in order to avoid taxes. Very shortly after the office had been created, its planners decided that the formation of a full and exact register was too expensive and time-consuming; a cheaper, easier system was preferred, a casual system based upon "information presented by the contributors [about their holdings]" (Tomás y Valiente, 1971, p. 225). One can imagine the accuracy of the register of holdings created in this manner. The system produced the so-called *cartillas de evaluación* (valuation books) which defined the tax to be collected per hectare as a function of the quality of the land and the type of crop. Of course, fraud was rampant. According to Martín Niño (1972), "the central administration could not confront tax evaders because they were almost universally aided and abetted by local municipal authorities." This is one of the economic faces of *caciquismo*.

Let us point out in passing that the cadastre or register was considered too long and expensive a task because it was estimated to take 20 years in the making, at a cost of 4.3 million pesetas per year. Taking into account that the lowest yield from this tax, in 1852, brought in 74 million pesetas, and that in addition it was estimated (moderately, as we shall see) that 50% of the true property value was fraudulently concealed, one can safely say that if the cadastre had been properly compiled and the resulting tax system properly managed, it would have yielded at least an additional 37 million pesetas yearly, which is 50% of the lowest annual yield achieved. Judge for yourself if it would have been worthwhile to undertake the work speedily, paying the estimated cost. And as far as the estimated twenty years is concerned, we can point out that a definitive cadastre was finally initiated in 1906, sixty years after it was rejected as too slow and too expensive, taking not twenty years but more than fifty to reach completion, and that not for technical reasons, but for political ones (Malefakis, 1971, pp. 457–469). Furthermore, from twentieth-century cadastral information we now know that the full extent of assets in land turned out to be more than twice what had been formerly estimated.

During the whole period under discussion there is continuous tension between property owners who brought all their political influence into play to conceal the extent of their land holdings, and the Ministry of Finance whose repeated legal dispositions stated what was obvious to the most casual observer, "that the Land Tax, in the form it had been established, yielded far less than the old taxes did" *(Estadística de los Presupuestos del Estado, 1891,* p. 225). Proof of concealment, in those provinces where an accurate comparison can be made, is that the territorial wealth in 1879 (according to the *registro de fincas,* or estates' register) was estimated to be much the same as that compiled in the Cadastre of the Marqués de la Ensenada one hundred and twenty years earlier. If that were true, the implication would be that there had been no improvement in agricultural methods, that there had been no increase in production, and that therefore labor productivity had fallen radically, all of which is patently not so.

One law after another made recommendations and took measures which aimed at a better assessment of the taxable base, but to no avail. The preamble to an 1885 law stated that "The *cartillas de evaluación* have not been adjusted since 1860, with serious damage to those branches of agriculture that have suffered a decline during the last quarter of a century, and perhaps with unintended benefit to those sectors that have increased in value," referring with exquisite delicacy to those who benefited from the administrative gridlock.

The Geographic and Statistical Yearbook (*Reseña Geográfica y Estadística)* for 1888 (pp. 489–493) commented that the data on property values was "necessarily incomplete." According to the *Yearbook,* the seven provinces the Geographic Institute had studied had concealed, on average, 46% of their assessable property, a figure they considered extremely high, but if we recognize also partial concealment, that is to say the systematic undervaluation of lands that were actually declared, then clearly the 46% must have fallen short of the mark. In Alcalá de los Gazules, Cádiz province, concealment reached 78%. There were also curious cases of errors in the other direction, as in Jerez de la Frontera, where fields and wastelands were declared at almost twice the true amount. To understand this anomaly it helps to realize that this was common practice in the sherry vineyards, and the reason obvious. Vineyard proprietors passed off their land as wasteland or uncultivated common land in order to pay tax at a lower rate, or to pay none at all. The Valencian journal *La Agricultura Española* showed that in October 1899 in Andalucía, the best catalogued zone, the degree of concealing land subject to taxes varied between 28% in Cádiz to more than 100% in Córdoba, so that in Córdoba province the owners concealed more territorial wealth than they declared.

The consequences of this deception and other forms of opposition by the taxpayers were as we have seen: a low yield from the land tax to the benefit of landowners and to the detriment of all others. Furthermore, the tax was very inflexible. Between 1850 and 1890 the sum generated by the land tax increased by only 12%, while general tax revenue rose by 34%. In other words, in spite of the huge increase in cultivated land that resulted from the sale of Church and public lands, revenue from the land tax grew very little, the only slower revenue growth being from the tax on mines at 5%, another present to the owners.

Yet this systematic evasion did not benefit all landowners equally; quite the contrary. It was the important people with political clout both in Madrid and in the city councils, with large holdings that were difficult to survey and to measure, who were most able to perpetrate this kind of fraud and to secure the greater benefit from it. Through the quota system (*cupos, repartimientos,* or *encabezamientos),* global tax payments were assigned to a given region or city and apportioned among taxpayers by local officials. The small landowners, with less influence and less opportunity to cheat, often found themselves overwhelmed; small payers were responsible for larger and larger shares as the large would-be payers became more and more conspicuous by their absence. Although the total land tax collected was well below the capacity of the agricultural sector as a whole, the clamor that was heard from many proprietors about excessive taxation was certainly not without justification.

Much the same can be said about the *contribución industrial y de comercio* (tax on industry and commerce), which ought to have raised at least twice as much as it did. This tax was also levied by a quota system imposed on localities, with a quota for each guild and individual allocations set for guild members. Again, we need hardly mention that the system favored the strong and influential, and the problems of unequal tax assessment were similar to those for the land tax. If it was difficult to estimate the taxable wealth of land and buildings, just imagine the difficulty of knowing the true taxable basis of commercial and industrial activities, particularly since so many enterprises were small and informal.

These two direct taxes together raised 25% of the total tax revenue. Practically all the rest came from indirect taxes, and in fact the Treasury wrongly included many indirect taxes under direct tax categories. If the direct taxes were regressive, the indirect ones, by their very nature, were even more so. For example, the *cédula personal* was in fact a poll tax levied on rich and poor alike, and the tax on *sueldos y asignaciones* (salaries and allowances) was also regressive, in that salaried officers and civil servants by no means represented the most prosperous sectors of the population; by contrast, rents, dividends, and interests escaped this tax. These two taxes together raised only about 3% of total revenue. Rather more came from the tax on *derechos reales* (real estate taxes) and the stamp tax, which are also indirect taxes, although the first of these can be seen as progressive, since it falls upon real estate transactions and inheritances. But the mainstay of the system was the revenue derived from taxes on consumer items, which raised about 40% of total income. We include here customs revenues (13%), the much-hated excise taxes *(consumos)*, the liquor taxes that were assessed separately from 1888 onwards, taxes on transport, and the monopoly taxes on tobacco (14.5%) and salt.

Of the remaining revenue sources, the state lottery was the most important, and it is interesting to note that according to the *Estadística de los Presupuestos,* incomes derived from the disentail during these forty years were less than those generated by the lotteries. There are various explanations for this apparently surprising phenomenon. In the first place, not all the lands sold were included in the statistics; the greater part of municipal sales were excluded (although these were a small fraction of the whole operation). In the second place, we already know that income from the land sales began to fall rapidly after 1875, whereas lottery incomes increased during these years. And thirdly, there was much defaulting on the payment for disentailed lands. All in all, it is remarkable how little income was generated; the figures confirm the frequent claim that, as a fiscal expedient, Church land sales were not the panacea that had been anticipated. The value of disentailed properties sold between 1855 and 1895 (from this one would have to deduct the unpaid balances to obtain the actual sum collected) amounted to some 1,964 million pesetas, a figure very close to the income from the lotteries between 1850 and 1890. Other incomes worth mentioning came from state properties and franchises, from fees in lieu of military service, and from the mint *seigniorage.*

In short, it is obvious that the taxation system rested much more heavily on the poor than on the rich and that it lacked the necessary flexibility to actually cover public expenditures. And this was after the Mon-Santillán reform!

How were the expenditures distributed? We have already seen that one-third of the budget went to meet debt payments and pensions. Another third paid for the military, the police, and the clergy. It is interesting to observe that the cost of maintaining the Church during these forty years when income from disentailed properties was at a maximum was actually larger than the amount earned by those sales. It seems, therefore, that the alleged "plunder" implied by the sale of Church lands was somewhat relative. The Finance and Public Works ministries received 27% of the budget. Three-quarters of the public works budget was devoted directly to public works and 14% went on education.

More than half of the finance budget was spent on managing the lotteries

Table 7.3.   Accumulated budget expenditures, 1850–1890 (in million pesetas)

		Pesetas	% of total
1.	National debt	7,034	27.3
2.	Pensions	1,697	6.6
3.	Ministry of Justice: ordinary expenditures	491	1.9
4.	Ministry of Justice: ecclesiastical subsidies	1,471	5.7
5.	Ministry of War	5,228	20.3
6.	Navy	1,283	5.0
7.	Ministry of the Interior	788	3.1
8.	Development (*Fomento*)	2,308	9.0
9.	Treasury	4,622	18.0
10.	Other	426	1.7
11.	TOTAL	25,730	100.0

Source: as for Table 7.2

and tobacco manufacture, and to reduce these high costs the tobacco monopoly was leased out in 1887. Among the remaining expenditures, the 1.5% that went to support the royal household should be noted. One might think that this was a small enough item. Yet during the years of Alfonso XII and María Cristina (1875–1902), the royal household cost less than it did during the reign of Isabel II, and today we note that the combined expenditures of the Ministry of State and Foreign Affairs, plus those for the Ministry of Justice, the President of Council, and the Cortes are actually well below this figure.

Perhaps the single most serious problem of budget administration during these years was structural. Almost invariably revenues came in well below projections, while expenditures were higher than budgeted. According to my calculations, with these inflexibilities the accumulated deficit during the second half of the century rose to some 3,185 million pesetas, which implies an average deficit of some 65 million pesetas annually, although, as Figure 7.1 shows, fluctuations around the average were quite considerable.

Fiscal Policy: The National Debt

Practically every year, in a regular and almost habitual manner, the state would spend around 65 million pesetas more than it collected in revenue, and the national debt—the volume of public indebtedness—continued to rise, as can be seen in Figure 7.2. We have already seen the effect of this massive volume of debt: the need to expend a high fraction of the budget to service that debt, an amount large enough to impose an enormous sacrifice on the country but still not large enough to cover the government's obligations, so that the value of government bonds continued to fall and the rates of interest continued to rise. In the words of one Treasury Minister Constantino Ardanaz, "the constant fall in the value of state bonds depreciates every kind of real estate; the high price for hard cash makes it impossible to develop industry" (Martín Niño, 1972, p. 52); the capital that industry needed became excessively expensive. The fall in the value of public bonds depreciated real estate values because state properties could be purchased with state bonds at their nominal price, their face value rather than their actual value. The price paid for a regressive and badly administered fiscal system was high indeed: on the one hand a sale of Church and state lands under the *desamortización* that was ill-planned and socially unjust; on the other hand a rising price for capital in a country where it was in notoriously short supply.

The immediate origin of the massive national debt that encumbered the Spanish economy during the whole of the nineteenth century is plain

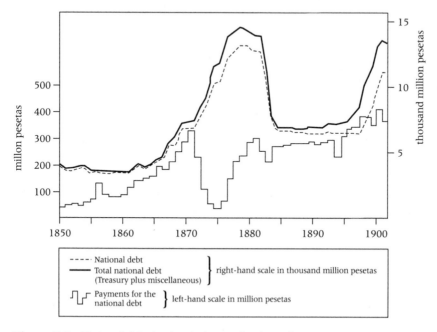

Figure 7.2. National debt in circulation and redemption payments, 1850–1902

enough; it goes back to the reign of Carlos IV and the War of Independence. The innumerable military campaigns of that period caused enormous indebtedness which later governments, beginning with Godoy, were simply unable to pay, in spite of the disentailment policy that he resorted to. The real cause of the growing national debt is to be found in the breakdown of the equilibrium established in the eighteenth century whereby the excess of expenditures over domestic incomes was offset by "American remittances," which is to say that there was a colonial surplus, and taxes paid by the colonies were greater than expenditures incurred there. The abnormal military expenditures of the period 1793 to 1815 came up against incomes that were reduced because of the impoverishment caused by the war, the administrative chaos that made collecting taxes more difficult, and—perhaps the most important reason of all—the loss of American remittances, the last hope for their restoration disappearing in the final defeat at Ayacucho (1824).

The budget problems and the national debt form the backdrop, the *mise en scene,* for the fierce political struggles of Fernando VII's reign. At his death the national debt had grown enormously and weighed like a tombstone upon the regency governments, on top of which came the costs of the Carlist wars that further reduced the country's output and consequently its capacity to raise taxes at a time when costs were increasing and the reputation of government debt was being called into question by both national and international lenders. This was one of the legacies of Fernando VII. It was natural, in this situation, that the Mendizábal government should turn to the same kind of solution that Godoy had attempted to resolve the problem of the debt and the annual deficits, which was the sale of Church lands. There was a difference, however: the Mendizábal plan was on a much larger scale.

During the rest of the century the issue of the debt and its possible solution was handled more or less as it had been during the reign of Fernando VII: constant deficits, enormous accumulation of debt, and periodic "conversions" or "arrangements" *(arreglos),* essentially partial repudiations, more or less with the consent of the creditors, who were largely resigned to their plight and were frequently taken advantage of. In general, and this had already been the case under Fernando VII, one can make a distinction between the political position of Liberals and Conservatives towards the debt: the latter were much more ready to resort to repudiation. The Liberals, or Progressives were much more oriented towards development policies and laissez-faire economics, could see the necessity of importing capital, and thus favored fiscal responsibility. Their great panacea was the state disentail, a policy which aimed at wresting power from the aristocrats and landowners (which it did not accomplish) while increasing the area of cultivated land. The resulting increase in production and reduction in the price of food was supposed to fill the void that declining American remittances had created in the budget.

Although on various occasions disentailment was to resolve burning political problems, in the end it was far from providing the solution to the budget's structural deficiencies. The national debt continued to climb, even though the growth was interrupted by various "agreements" during the century. If in 1850 the total debt was about 3,900 million pesetas, at the beginning of the twentieth century it was more than 12,300 million; in the first years of the Restoration it has reached even higher levels. As Luis María Pastor, one of the first historians of the modern Spanish Treasury, would say, the history of the debt agreements makes one blush. Cameron[3] has a memorable paragraph on the subject:

> Old debts were consolidated, deferred, reformed, and reactivated, but rarely repaid. The securities ceased to be investments, even speculative ones, and became mere gamblers' tokens. In the 1840s the Paris Bourse carried six different Spanish securities; quotations on them ranged from a high of 40 percent of their nominal value to a low of two and one-half percent. In 1850 a disgruntled investor wrote: "Spanish loan history is really one sad, long-continued and disgraceful 'history of a HOAX'. . . . Men when buying what are called 'Government Bonds' or 'National Securities' . . . of a great and powerful state, neither expect nor prepare themselves for a fleecing such as occasionally comes off at deep play in a gaming house, or at the hazard table, race-course, or roulette. . . . During the last thirty years, the credit of Spain has fallen so low, that the very expression 'Spanish stock' has become almost synonymous with epithets of the most opprobrious nature, which we refrain from specifying."

Apart from the labyrinthine and fraudulent manipulations prior to 1830, conscientiously studied and clearly set out by Fontana (1971, 1973a), the three most important conversions of the nineteenth century are those under Bravo Murillo (1851), Camacho (1882), and Fernández Villaverde (1899–1900). Of course they were not the only ones, far from it, but the mechanism was essentially the same each time. It consisted of creating and issuing of a new type of debt, generally with an interesting, appealing name, "consolidated" or "redeemable" or "mortgage," which was launched with a public relations fanfare giving the impression that from then on the government was going to meet all contracted obligations punctually. Holders of old bonds were offered an exchange or "conversion" of those titles for new ones, a maneuver which of course implied losses of capital or interest or both but offered the inducement of assets that were more secure than the earlier ones. Terms were negotiated with debtors in such a way that the government would substantially lighten the load of the debt, under conditions that were acceptable to the majority of the holders. In these negotiations the government always held the trump card in the promise that the new title holders would be better treated than the old ones, a promise that had also been made on the previous conversion. These maneuvers and shrewd, often one-sided, negotiations were the obsession of politicians and men of affairs in the period we are studying; Torquemada, the usurer-turned-banker in the novels of Galdós, speaks on his deathbed of "conversion" without the reader being sure whether he is speaking of the debt or of his soul!

The famous Bravo Murillo settlement, which came after the Treasury reform of Mon and Santillán, and after the suspension of interest payments because of the 1848 crisis, was just an ill-camouflaged bankruptcy. The government consolidated into one *deuda del personal* the unpaid salaries of public officials, and into another *deuda del material* what it owed its suppliers. In addition it unilaterally lowered both interest and principal on foreign and domestic debts, without in any way speeding up interest payments or capital redemptions. The indignation of English creditors was such that they managed to exclude Spanish securities from the London Stock Exchange.

The national debt was reduced slightly after 1854, thanks to Progressive policies which used the disentail revenues to pay off stockholders, but this policy was abandoned by later governments, Moderates and Unionists alike, which seem to have preferred military adventures to meeting financial obligations. In protest, the stock market in Paris imitated London and prohibited Spanish stock trading in 1861. From then on the accumulated debt increased almost exponentially, and so did the payments. I have explored the relationship between the growing debt and political instability in the period 1864–1876 elsewhere (Tortella, 1977, chaps. VII and VIII). It is sufficient to point out here the literally catastrophic situation delineated in Figure 7.2, which shows that from 1871 to 1874 debt interest payments fell precipitously because the Treasury was completely unable to meet them. These outlays had risen to more than half of the total budget in the year 1870–71, at a time when income was plummeting (see Figure 7.1). To pay the debt it was necessary to create more debt, but not even that was a solution. Because quotation prices were so low, the government had to incur a debt of 100 pesetas for every 15 pesetas raised, not counting interest. Under these circumstances, the suspension of payments was utterly inevitable. In the fiscal year 1870–71 the budget called for 432 million pesetas to pay debt interest, but only 327 million was actually paid. And more of this lay ahead: in 1871–72 the government allocated 331 million but only 228 million were paid; in the following year they allocated 308 and paid 109. One year later the allocation was 238, but they paid only 55 million. The allocations were reduced, but the payments went down much faster; in 1874–75 only 40 million of an allocation of 89 million pesetas was paid out. In the face of such disaster the panaceas, the quick fixes, the remedies, the agreements, and the conversions came tumbling one after another. In 1870 Spain signed a lease contract for the Almadén mercury mines with the Rothschilds in return for a loan of 42 million pesetas. In 1872 the official Mortgage Bank (Banco Hipotecario) was created in exchange for a series of loans, and the rate of interest paid on the debt was, once more, unilaterally reduced. In 1873 the Río Tinto Mines were leased out for 94 million pesetas. In 1874 the monopoly right to banknote issue was given to the Bank of Spain in return for a donation of 125 million pesetas. In 1876, the Salaverría agreement once more reduced the interest rate; in 1881–82, under the Camacho conversion, the interest and principal to be paid were again drastically reduced, through the creation of a "redeemable debt" at 4%. This last and famous conversion should perhaps be viewed with some sense of long-term perspective. Camacho, who had been Minister of the Treasury under Sagasta during the Revolution, had surely reflected long and hard since then about how to resolve the overwhelming problem of the national debt.

The Camacho reform, or conversion, was followed by a period of relative calm so far as the debt is concerned, thanks mainly to the transformation of the monetary system, concretely the demonetization of gold (see Chapter 6). One of its outstanding features was a guarantee to pay foreign bondholders in Paris or London in francs or pounds. In the 1880s the peseta began to depreciate, a process that reached its peak at the end of the century; under these circumstances guaranteed payments in foreign money made the debt very attractive, and many Spaniards purchased it precisely to protect themselves from depreciation. The conversion was a success, but payments in foreign money involved a considerable export of gold, which, together with the commercial deficit and speculative exports, eventually liquidated Spain's gold reserves by about 1890. From then onwards, punctuality in meeting debt payments once again became problematical. If Spain had had a surplus, either from trade or services like insurance, gold would have been coming in to compensate the losses, but as this was probably not so (see Chapter 5), the country had to keep going deeper into debt, importing private or public capital to keep up with the payments. Without doubt, this situation contributed to the proclamation, in 1891, of a new series of radically protectionist import duties, in an attempt to reduce the trade deficit.

The situation was very seriously aggravated by the beginning of the War of Cuban Independence in 1895, because financing the war produced new growth of the national debt, a steep rise in prices, and a major decline in the peseta on the international market. As the peseta fell, it became more and more expensive to buy the French francs and British pounds necessary to service the external debt, and the increased purchases of these foreign currencies further contributed to the fall of the peseta; growing inflation was adding more problems. The disastrous outcome of the war necessitated yet another reform of the fiscal system, the famous Villaverde stabilization. Among its measures were a new conversion of the debt and another settlement, plus a further trimming of interest rates and the rights of bondholders. The so-called López Puigcerver "affidavit" eliminated payments in foreign currencies to debt holders who were either Spanish or domiciled in Spain. The Villaverde conversion effectively trimmed the domestic debt, both interest and principal.

Given this concise history of the conversions of the national debt, it is now appropriate to explore the real significance of this series of lamentable episodes. Concretely, there are four questions that the reader ought to have posed. In the first place, why did this complete disorder, this serious irresponsibility, occur? Secondly, why did people who had money lend to such a patently fraudulent debtor? Thirdly, who suffered from the system and who benefited? And fourthly, was Spain the only country where this was happening?

The causes of the disorder we have already seen: persistent deficit, insufficient taxes, and excessive expenditures. But clearly, in theory at least, this could have been remedied: taxes could have been raised, especially at the expense of landowners and business men, and costs could have been reduced, at the expense of the military, the Church, and civil servants, even including the royal family. If this was not done it was because the political system had no interest in doing so: the cost of restoring public credit was simply too high. To attempt to bring order to the problem in a manner detrimental to the captains of commerce and industry would have been political suicide for any government. Perhaps the Spanish ruling class, accustomed from the early modern period on to a government that spent more than it raised in revenues and restored the equilibrium by exploiting the American colonies, had decided to continue as though the colonies had not been lost, confident that by some means or other someone would finance the deficit. And nothing less than the definitive liquidation of the colonial empire could produce a shock strong enough for the politicians to see the need to renounce that fiscal irresponsibility: the Villaverde stabilization produced the first series of budgetary surpluses in the history of Spain.

The shareholders of the Spanish National Debt can be divided into two groups: the experts and the unwary. The unwary were those people who bought Spanish securities knowing nothing of the particulars of how the debt was managed. The experts knew what they had in their hands, which gave them no guarantee that they would turn a profit, but at least they more or less knew the rules of the game. The unwary were small investors who acquired the securities through agents or banks, and frequently they were foreigners. The experts were bankers or professional financiers, often with good contacts or political influence, who hoped to make money on rising prices or from the conversions. Frequently they loaned directly to the government and this way obtained certain concessions that interested them. Indeed, these concessions were often the principal objective, and losing or gaining on the debt was of secondary importance. This was characteristically true for the Rothschilds, for the Pereire brothers, for Prost, for Guilhou, and for many of those who, in 1855, sought favorable concessions in the fields of banking and railroad development. Thus the Rothschild family repeatedly extended loans to the Spanish government to obtain the lease for the Almadén mercury mines and subsidies for its Spanish railroad company, the MZA; in return for loans the Banque de Paris et des Pays Bas obtained the concession for the Banco Hipotecario; the Bank of Spain obtained the monopoly of banknote issue, and many others acquired lands at laughable prices through the purchase of a depreciated debt that was then accepted at its face value when buying state lands at auction. In order to maintain this strangest of all systems of budgetary finance and keep it working for so long, the *quid pro quo* was the gradual dismemberment of the national heritage, including the stock of gold.

Personal comparisons are sometimes misleading when applied to social or community issues, but in this case the image of the individual whose debts and expenses oblige him to pawn his property is very appropriate. As Adam

Smith wrote, "Nations, like private men, have generally begun to borrow upon what may be called personal credit, without assigning or mortgaging any particular fund for the payment of the debt; and when this resource has failed them, they have gone on to borrow upon assignments or mortgages of particular funds."[4] The utter exhaustion of Spanish credit forced the state to hand over real resources, concessions, and privileges, or to pay exorbitant prices for the credit it received. For many years the Bank of Spain controlled the collection of taxes, and the Banco Hipotecario collected the income from customs duties to repay loans it had made to the state. Thus many expert lenders, Spaniards and foreigners alike, knew how to benefit from this fragile credit situation, at the cost, in the last resort, of the Spanish taxpayers, both the living and the generations to follow. The expert lender might also benefit at the expense of the unwary in another way: by selling, under normal circumstances and at regular prices, high-risk bonds that had been acquired under exceptional circumstances and for a low price; the unwary buyer would then be left shouldering a risk of which he had not been properly advised.

And now we have almost answered the question about who benefited from the system and who suffered. The expert lenders were not the only beneficiaries, because thanks to this method of financing the deficit, some people could pay very low taxes in relation to their wealth, or could collect salaries or incomes far above what their work could justify, at the expense of the national budget. The group that suffered, in addition to the unwary lenders, was the Spanish people as a whole, and in particular the poorer taxpayers as well as the peasants who were impacted by the *desamortización*.

In closing, let us indicate that Spain was not the only country that experienced serious problems with the budget or the national debt. During the nineteenth century such problems were endemic in the Mediterranean basin. Egypt, Turkey, Greece, Italy, and Portugal, with particular variations in each case, found themselves tied up in similar situations, if not worse ones. The same happened in Latin America, and there were instances where delays, suspensions, and repudiations of debt served as a pretext for foreign intervention, which was the case of Mexico in 1862, and Egypt after 1876.

Commercial Policies

The customs tariff is one of the taxes we have already considered in exploring the budget and the deficit. Why look at this subject again? For a very simple reason: customs tariffs encumber a very important activity, namely foreign trade; by making items more expensive, tariffs modify the patterns of exchange between countries. In other words, the tariff, in addition to being a tax, is also an instrument of commercial policy. In economics textbooks a distinction is drawn between fiscal or revenue tariffs and protective tariffs, and this is exactly the distinction that interests us here.

The fiscal tariff is a tax whose aim is principally to raise revenue, and this was indeed how the tariffs were originally conceived: just one more tax that was easy to collect, similar to the tolls imposed for highways or bridges. With the development of the nation states, however, it was soon realized that the tariff could also serve to inhibit trade. Like any other tax, it can obstruct and constrain the activity upon which it is levied: fix the tax sufficiently high, and the fiscal tariff turns into a protective tariff. Now a tariff set so high that it cuts off the activity in question can be seen as prohibitive: a tax of a million dollars levied upon every imported packet of cigarettes would certainly do away with the import of tobacco, at least within the legal orbit. But it would not, of course, collect a single dime in revenue. For this reason, when it is a question of protecting a national industry from foreign competition at all costs, or of preventing the export of a certain product, the government simply prohibits it instead of placing a prohibitive tariff on the product. Conversely, a tariff is used to kill two birds with one stone; not only to protect but also to raise revenue. One should observe, however, that although it can achieve both ends, the gain of one is at the expense of the other: when it most protects, it raises the least in revenue, and vice versa.[5]

All this has to be taken into account in assessing the tariff as an instrument of commercial policy. During the nineteenth century Spanish governments argued continually about the two alternatives. On the one hand, extreme budgetary difficulties made the revenue tariff look very attractive; if it were relatively low, it might not affect the volume of trade too much, and a high volume of trade would generate high revenues. On the other hand, Spain's emerging industries and some agricultural sectors noisily sought protection against foreign competition, calling for protective tariffs that would raise little revenue.

Throughout the nineteenth century the economic polemic between free traders and protectionists certainly attracted the most public attention, as much in Spain as in most parts of Europe and the Americas. To a large extent the argument between free traders and protectionists was an economic version of the political argument between Liberals and Conservatives, a question of progress or standing still, but not altogether. Industrialists and businessmen often sided with the Liberals in everything except the question of tariffs, and the landowners too were often free traders in spite of their reactionary positions on internal questions. In general, the tariff affected each sector of the economy in a specific way, and each sector tended to support the commercial policy which suited it best, independently of ideology. Furthermore, the same individual could advocate free trade for one product and protection for another; characteristically, the cotton producer wanted protection for his finished goods but free importation of machinery, coal, and raw cotton. The agriculturalist wanted protection for grain, but free imports of fertilizers and agricultural machinery; iron and steel producers wanted protection for machinery and free import of coal, foodstuffs, and other goods.

Now the protectionist position is difficult to defend theoretically; the only convincing protectionist argument is one that justifies protection as a provisional instrument, to be used for emergencies. The famous argument about infant industries was made by Friedrich List, who felt that newly emerging industries should be protected up to the point where they could compete. Protectionism as a permanent system has two serious defects: it is unjust, and it is inefficient. As Antonio Flores de Lemus pointed out, it is unjust because it is not possible to protect any one industry without damaging another or the consumer or both. And it is inefficient because the activity needing protection must be inefficient; if it were not, it would be able to compete and not need protection. Thus, to the extent that it is unjust and inefficient, the protectionist system is an obstacle to real economic growth. These arguments have been well known, at least since Adam Smith, and comment would be quite unnecessary here, were it not that in Spain (and in many other countries too) protectionist postures enjoy a popularity among economists and economic historians which has no justification, not in theory, nor in practice.

Spain has a long history of protectionism which dates from at least the fifteenth century. It goes far beyond tariffs; is prohibitionist and monopolist in nature, it has been known since the time of Adam Smith as mercantilism. From the middle of the eighteenth century, however, a slow evolution set in, not so much towards free trade as towards tariff protectionism; the political tendency was to abandon prohibition and monopoly in favor of high tariffs. This is the essence of the celebrated commercial measures adopted by Carlos III most signally in 1778. Contrary to what Vicens Vives asserts, these were not free trade measures but merely protectionist tariffs set in place of the earlier prohibitions. Metaphorically speaking, these measures broadened the channels and reduced the dikes and sea walls that the government had put in the way of colonial trade, but they did not, by any means, remove all trade barriers. However, these relatively liberating measures were followed by a remarkable increase in colonial trade and unquestionable prosperity on both sides of the Atlantic,[6] benefits that were interrupted by a long period of war starting in the 1790s and concluding only in 1824 with the independence of Spanish America.

During the nineteenth century Spain's tariff policies were not too different from those of the rest of Western Europe, although somewhat more protectionist. Faced with England's patently superior industrial capacity, all the other nations generated some form of protectionist response, trying to protect infant industries from their far more evolved British competitors. It is not clear that this political response was successful. The decidedly protectionist countries, like France and Spain, evolved much more slowly than the smaller countries which abandoned all attempt at self-sufficiency and opted for free trade, specializing in those industries where they had a comparative advantage: Belgium with iron and steel and Switzerland with watches. For Prussia the relatively liberal tariff policy adopted until the end of the century proved to be an effective instrument of political unification and economic growth. Even in England itself, the Free Traders did not triumph entirely until 1846, when the laws protecting cereals, the famous Corn Laws, were repealed, and the country finally accepted the implications of free trade, an international division of labor completely devoid of any pretension of agricultural self-sufficiency. It is worth noting that the upturn in the standard of living of the British working class coincides chronologically with the demise of protection and the resulting lowering of the price of food.

When England turned away from agricultural protection, powerful shock waves were felt throughout Europe that helped launch a free trade movement which reached even countries as protectionist as France and Spain. In Spain this impulse produced only a very gradual reduction in duties. During the reign of Fernando VII, both the absolute governments and the Cortes of the Triennium had established strongly protectionist tariffs, including a high duty on goods delivered in foreign vessels, the *derecho diferencial de bandera* (flag tax). This preferential system, which favored goods carried under the Spanish flag and substantially penalized all others, was an ancient mercantilist device that had been the keystone of the English Navigation Acts from the eighteenth century. The progressive Cortes of 1841 approved a duty regime which, although clearly protectionist, was perhaps less stringent than the earlier ones. However, it still retained clear vestiges of mercantilism, since it continued a prohibition on the import of 83 products, among them some very basic items like cotton cloth, metal manufactures, wool, wheat, and all other cereals.

In 1849, right in the middle of the Moderado decade and the depression following the 1847–48 crisis, a new tariff was announced which toned down the earlier legislation. The number of outright prohibitions was reduced substantially, to 14, although practically all the items that were newly admitted remained heavily taxed. Prohibitions remained in place on imported spun and woven cottons of the types that were produced and consumed domestically, and the differential flag duties were retained, though slightly lowered. There is no doubt that the Free Trade movement in England influenced the introduction of these relatively moderate changes, just three years after the repeal of the British Corn Laws.

In Spain at mid-century arguments between those who favored free trade and those who favored protectionism were intense, and they lasted until the beginning of the new century. We shall not enter here into details of the debate, which are the delight of some historians but have very little intellectual interest: with the exception of a few peculiar colorful nuances, the debate was but a pallid reflection of what was happening in England, France, and Prussia. The free traders had little or nothing to say that had not already been said by Smith, Ricardo, or Say, while the protectionists invoked List's arguments adapted to the Spanish case. If the special pleadings of the free traders were hardly original, those of the protectionists were clearly unsustainable. To pretend that the tariff was a temporary measure until Spain could compete with England was faulty reasoning: for the industries that grow under tariff protection, their very existence is the most formidable argument against the reduction of that tariff. This was particularly the case for the cotton industry, cited time and time again by the protectionists as a "source of wealth and employment" which would be "destroyed" if it were forced to compete with foreign industries.

The sociological background of the opposing sides holds more interest for us than their arguments. The protectionists were united around the Barcelona association of cotton producers, a group with origins going back to the eighteenth century whose structure changed frequently during the nineteenth. The association has survived through to today, under the name of Fomento del Trabajo Nacional (Promotion of National Work), as it was known during the period of its most powerful influence. The Fomento group tried to broaden its area of influence geographically, economically, and socially. On the geographic and economic fronts it attempted to achieve national status by becoming active outside of the Barcelona province, looking for agreements of mutual benefit with Castilian cereal producers and other sectors that were not economic competitors. On the labor front it tried to gain the support of the workers, particular cotton workers, by warning of the risk of unemployment if the tariffs were reduced. Among the most eloquent defenders of protectionism were Eudaldo Jaumandreu, Benaventura Carlos Aribau, Juan Güell y Ferrer, Andrés Borrego, and Pedro Bosch y Labrús.

The free traders were a less tightly knit group, socially more diffuse and generally more invested in theory and ideology. People with clearly economic interests carried less weight than in the protectionist group, although the free traders had the support of the Andalusian wine exporters and also of the railroad companies (which expected that lower tariffs would increase the amount of freight traffic). More amorphous and diverse support came from merchants, small traders, and the urban masses, for whom free trade meant cheap bread. The principal free trade organization was called the Association for Tariff Reform, with head offices in Madrid and branches and parallel organizations in other cities. Among the free traders were "figures of the first order of magnitude on the national political scene" (Vicens Vives, 1961, p. 685) such as José Echegaray, Segismundo Moret, Emilio Castelar, Laureano Figuerola, Gumersindo Azcárate, Luis María Pastor, Gabriel Rodríguez, and Manuel Colmeiro.

The controversy continued during the twenty years that the 1849 Trade Act was operative, and became even more heated when, in 1869, the Cortes debated and approved the Figuerola tariff. This tariff has repeatedly been represented as a free trade measure, but such a qualification is only correct from a relative point of view. Certainly it is the most liberal trade act that Spain had known, but from the perspective of ideology it is, after all, a compromise between two camps. The Figuerola tariff, although lower than its predecessors or successors, was still relatively high. Most tariffs were set at between 20% and 35%. In the words of a contemporary observer, "it was not a step from protectionism to free trade, but a substitution of moderately protective tariffs and powerful provisions for a system of prohibitions and obstructions to trade" (Gwinner, 1973, p. 279). What infuriated the protectionists was the complete absence of prohibitions, and above all, the famous *base quinta,* the fifth clause. Item number five of the *Ley de Bases Arancelarias*

(Law of Tariff Bases), issued a little before the tariff schedule, anticipated that tariffs should decline gradually from 1875 onwards, so that by 1881 no tariff should exceed 15%, which was an attempt to reduce tariffs to a purely fiscal role. Furthermore, the elimination of the famous differential duty on trade from foreign ships scandalized the protectionists. The important thing to bear in mind here is that the tariff liberalization, real but only relative at this point, was ultimately dependent upon the eventual application of the fifth clause, which never actually occurred. As events transpired, King Alfonso XII was reinstated just six months before the fifth clause was to have come into force, and one of the first tasks of the Treasury Minister under the newly reinstated monarchy was to suspend its application.

Many harsh things have been said about the Figuerola tariff, not only by his contemporaries but also by present-day historians and economists. Thus Tamames (1990, p. 520) asserts that "The 1869 tariff, had it been maintained and observed in the following decades, would have impeded the development of Spanish industry and would have caused the disappearance of a good part of the industries that were already established. As dangerous as total protectionism was this extremist Free Tradism, that every country in Europe, except England, had already turned away from by 1869."

Of course, one can no more speak here of "extreme Free Tradism" than one can say that the European countries "had already turned away" from it in 1869, nor does it seem that complete protectionism is as "dangerous" as Tamames suggests in the same text two pages later. Another author who makes counterfactual assertions is Vicens Vives (1961, p. 108). "Today one does not even argue about what would have happened if the governments in Madrid had imposed Free Trade; the absolute disaster."

Naturally, these hypothetical assertions are offered to the reader without any empirical support. Moreover, it is curious that two pages earlier Vicens Vives had just said that despite the complaints of the protectionists, "the person who was right was Figuerola . . . his work was greatly to the benefit of Catalonia. . . . A new and powerful force stormed through the arteries of the Catalán economy, as all the relevant measures of activity indicate."

Regardless of the protests of the protectionists, the evidence seems to indicate that the Figuerola tariff was followed by a modest economic recovery. Just how far this can be attributed to the changes in the tariff is another question, but it does seem difficult to maintain that it would have impeded Spain's industrial development or caused "the absolute catastrophe."

Once the application of the fifth clause of the *Ley de Bases Arancelarias* had been suspended, the free trade potential of the Figuerola tariff was also put on hold, and a little later it was actually replaced by the 1877 tariff which, although it appeared to be a simple modification of the 1869 act, in fact introduced some "short-term extraordinary supplements" which were the equivalent of tariff increases. These surcharges, however, were intended more to raise revenue than to protect.

When the Liberals returned to power in 1881, the trade policy was again relaxed. In 1882 the fifth clause was restored and most of the tariffs were reduced. The mechanism of the *base quinta* was to become operational in 1887, and ought to have reduced all tariffs to a maximum of 15% by 1892, but once again this famous concept was not to be enacted, as we shall see. Another tenet of the Liberal position was the policy of adopting commercial treaties, of which the most important ones were signed with France in 1882 and with England in 1886; there were similar treaties with Switzerland, Sweden, Norway, Portugal, and Germany, but the French and British were the most important, simply because trade with those two countries at that time was about two-thirds of Spanish exports and more than half of imports. These treaties, which included a "most favored nation" clause, irritated the protectionists. But the decisive factor that turned opinion firmly against free trade was the so-called "agricultural crisis," the persistent fall in the price of food that so powerfully affected the whole of Europe during the last quarter of the century. The return to protectionism is a major European phenomenon of the period, to which Spain was no stranger (the only exceptions were England, Holland, Denmark, and Finland); as elsewhere, the protectionist camp had been actively supported by the agriculturalists. Thus on December 31, 1891, the government approved a tariff which one contemporary writer characterized as "the Wall of China" (Gwinner, 1973, p 333), and another called the "hunger tax" for the increase it caused in the food prices. The preamble to the law claimed that the new tariffs contained "simultaneously, elements of protection that were needed for the development of a rich agriculture and the industry that our country needs," in other words, it offered what at that time was called *protección integral*, complete protection, as much for industry as for agriculture. (On the contradictory nature of this concept Flores de Lemus wrote eloquently.) Meanwhile, the 1869 *Ley de Bases Arancelarias* had been repealed, and with it our much abused fifth clause, and most of the trade treaties had also been repudiated. Spain entered yet another period of intense protectionism which was confirmed in the 1906 Law on Tariff Bases, a law which persisted through to very recent times.[7]

"The Spanish economy remained sheltered by complete protectionism, which made possible the development of industry and the expansion of agriculture and livestock production," writes Tamames. Is this true? Perhaps, but it remains to be proved. The *prima facie* evidence does not seem to support this position very well. We have already seen that Europe's most protectionist countries in the nineteenth century are not those which grew the most rapidly, and Spain is an example of this. An elemental rationalization confirms this impression: an industry that needs protection is inefficient; to protect it implies a squandering of resources. In the long run, save for exceptional cases of activities of unusually great promise which in growing gain in efficiency, the protection of noncompetitive activities has to be recognized as a deterrent to growth. For example, without the tariff the cotton industry would probably have been able to compete with the British in certain types of cloth, as did Belgium and Switzerland, by cutting costs and profits and increasing productivity through specialization and mechanization. This would have implied risks and sacrifices for the manufacturers, and better prices and quality of goods for the consumers, but the manufacturers engaged instead in political agitation and succeeded in getting Madrid to concede a high tariff that would help them to get rich without great effort or risk. A business life sheltered from international competition (though foregoing international markets) was more comfortable and profitable than investing and risking capital in machinery and innovations (Harrison, 1974, p. 432). The same happened with agriculture; the new proprietors of disentailed properties preferred to harvest and sell expensive grain cultivated by primitive methods within the domestic market, rather than risk their capital in increasing productivity or looking for new crops more suitable to the dictates of Castilian geography. The "complete protection" in fact created a vicious circle: the high cost of protected wheat made industrial manpower expensive, which raised the price of fabrics; Spain's impoverished agricultural sector was but a poor market for Catalán cotton, which thus had no incentive to mechanize or to increase productivity. The consequences were a low standard of living, a lack of competitiveness, and general stagnation within the Spanish economy.

The evidence assembled from the data we possess fails to show that periods of tariff protection were prosperous and those of relatively free trade were depressed. One thing that does appear clear is that the moderate duties produced far greater revenues; see Figure 7.3. The income from customs duties was determined in part by the general economic situation, as is shown by revenue declines in the periods 1862 to 1868, 1883 to 1888, and 1894 to 1898. But the rapid rise in tariff revenue, which is particularly clear after the introduction of the Figuerola tariff, speaks eloquently. There was also a marked increase in revenue in the 1850s, after the 1849 tariff, although this was interrupted by a decline in imports because of the Crimean War. Insofar as it contributed to budgetary stability, free trade clearly favored economic growth. As for its direct effects—the development of a rational distribution of resources and the elimination of uneconomic activities—we do not yet have sufficient details to make a secure case. But it is true beyond any doubt that the strident assertions on the pernicious effects of free trade, as we have just seen in the pages above, are lacking in foundation.

I would like to conclude with one observation that confirms the need for caution in interpreting these materials. As we have already indicated, Spain was one of the countries of highest tariff protection in nineteenth-century Europe, yet when we look at international trade after 1850, we see that it grew more rapidly in Spain than in any of the other countries we have considered. How is this apparent contradiction to be interpreted? The question requires detailed study, but a quick first impression is that the impact of the tariff on international trade was not so radical as its most rancorous detrac-

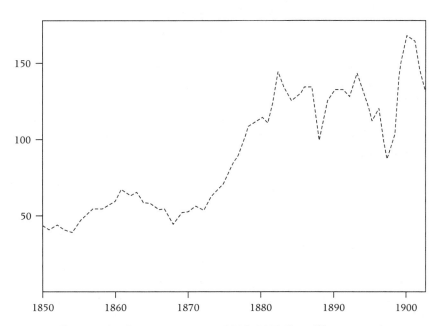

Figure 7.3. Customs revenues, 1850–1902 (in million pesetas)

tors or its most ardent defenders believed. On this point it is important to realize that the customs tariffs represent a very complex system of duties applied to thousands of articles, so that measuring the degree of protectionism under a particular tariff regime is a difficult task: the result will always be an approximate figure, never exact. It would be interesting to try to apply modern estimation techniques to gauge the true degree of protection involved in the nineteenth-century duties. One might find that the effective protection was not so high as so many people thought.

Monetary Policy

Finally, it remains for us to discuss monetary policy, or perhaps it is better to say its absence, because during the nineteenth century one cannot speak of a real policy on money management but rather a series of measures with little connection between them, more related to what was happening in other spheres, especially at the Treasury.[8]

From the point of view of monetary policy, our period can be divided in two stages, before and after 1874. The divide corresponds to the concession of monopoly rights of banknote issue to the Bank of Spain, and like all dividing lines this one contains some elements that are arbitrary. Essentially the aim is to separate the period when money was fully backed by gold reserves from the later period when fiduciary money dominated.

It is true that the emergence of fiduciary money was gradual, for the Banks of San Carlos and San Fernando had already issued banknotes. However, as we saw in Chapter 6, even in 1865 (see Figure 6.1) the fiduciary circulation did not amount to more than 10% of the total money supply, even though the 1856 Law on Issuing Banks and the greater number of banks in existence gave room for considerable expansion in banknote issue. It is likely therefore that during the first half of the century practically all of the money supply was fully backed by reserves of gold and silver.

The importance of the distinction between money fully backed by proper reserves and fiduciary money is very important, for the simple reason that fully backed money is difficult to control as far as the volume in circulation is concerned. Gold and silver are scarce, and the only two ways that a country can obtain them is either through mineral extraction or importing. The first requires the existence of such resources, and the mines in Spain were almost worked out by the nineteenth century; the second source depends either upon a favorable balance of payments (payments for goods and services), or a surplus of capital that can be used to buy the precious metals abroad.

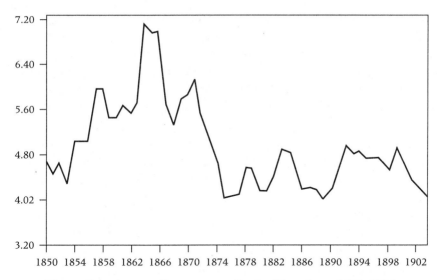

Figure 7.4. Average discount rates, Bank of Barcelona, 1850–1904

Now the Spanish balance of trade and services, as we already know, was generally in deficit, so that in the absence of imported capital the result was the export of precious metals to other countries. In a fully backed monetary system the net export of gold and silver implies deflation. A reduction of the amount of money in circulation tends to reduce prices, which customarily depresses the level of economic activity,[9] in part because credit is restricted when money is scarce, and this may be as important as the actual fall in prices. In brief, this was Spain's major monetary problem during the first half of the nineteenth century. The fully backed system, along with a tendency towards commercial deficit, impeded the expansion of the economy.

From 1855 onwards, the situation changed. First, the new Law on Issuing Banks fostered an expansion in fiduciary circulation, limited but not to be underestimated. And second, the economy received an injection of capital during the period of accelerated railroad building (Cameron, 1961; Tortella, 1973, pp. 104–106; Broder, 1976, 1981). These two phenomena expanded the money supply, so prices rose and there was an increase in economic activity for several years. However, it is interesting to note (Figure 7.4) that short-term interest rates also rose during this period, which indicates that the expansion in the money supply did not expand credit sufficiently to satisfy that demand.

The monetary situation between 1864 and 1874 was rather chaotic because of a series of crises in the economy, in banking, in politics, and in the military. The banknote monopoly granted to the Bank of Spain could not in the short run save the country from financial chaos, but it did permit a drastic modification in the composition of the money supply. For one thing, the rapid expansion of banknotes and current account deposits popularized what we might call "bank money" at a rate that more than compensated for the disappearing gold coinage. And for another, a passive policy towards rising gold prices during the 1870s, culminating in 1883 with the suspension of gold convertibility of Bank of Spain notes, encouraged the disappearance of circulating gold, and silver became the only metallic currency. In this way, within about 20 years the Spanish monetary system changed from being fully bimetallic to becoming one of the few silver systems within Europe (see Chapter 6 passim, esp. Figure 6.2), just when the gold standard was being established throughout the world.

Despite the adoption of a *de facto* fiduciary system (since the steady fall in the price of silver put the intrinsic value of coins far below their face value), and despite substantial growth in the money supply during the last quarter of the century, prices remained relatively stable except for the last five years, the years of the Cuban War. There are various reasons for this relative stability. International prices were falling, and they exerted a powerful influence on national prices, since Spain's role in the world economy was intensifying. Moreover, these were years of slow but steady growth for the Spanish economy, a growth that increased the demand for money and credit, for which an approximately equal supply of credit became available, as is indicated by relative stability in interest rates. And in spite of the *de facto* fiduciary system, successive governments made great efforts to maintain monetary discipline (except during the difficult years of the Cuban War). This achievement, although not exactly equivalent to a gold standard, was not much different from it in the results. In other words, they restricted as much as they could the expansion of the volume of paper money in circulation. If they did not restrict it even more, it was probably because there were close ties between the Bank of Spain and the Treasury whereby money was created to finance necessary public expenditure, in a situation where the utter petrification of the tax system left this as the only means of getting public works under way (R. Anes, 1974, p. 211). Here is a clear example of how monetary policy became determined by fiscal imperatives.

Regardless of the embarrassment of the Spanish government about abandoning gold convertibility, this was the best possible alternative, or anyway the lesser evil. As we have seen, the survival of a rigid, full-content system, either under bimetallism or a gold standard, was an obstacle to growth. The Spanish money supply grew slowly during the last quarter of the century compared with other countries like the United States, England, or France (Tortella, 1974, pp. 465–469), but growth would have been even smaller if the discipline of the gold standard had been maintained. In an underdeveloped country like Spain, the gold standard was a very expensive luxury. It was more logical to devote the gold to the purchase of food, equipment, and technology than to use it for currency circulation. It makes more sense to create a cheap circulating medium, paper money, depreciated silver, or bank balances, and to invest the gold in other necessities. Yet the fiduciary standard also had a negative impact, since it reinforced the effect of tariffs, increasing the isolation of the Spanish economy.

In conclusion, of the various state interventions in the economy—its fiscal, commercial, and monetary policies—it was probably in this last area that the state took the most correct measures during the years of the Restoration. I find this paradoxical, because this sector received the least attention, was considered of low priority, and it yielded by far the least satisfaction to the politicians of the day.

CHAPTER 8

The Entrepreneurial Factor

In the opinion of one nineteenth-century observer, "Spaniards are not enterprising in business, and few care to venture on a new industry or undertaking. But no sooner has one done so with success, than his example is certain to be copied by many others, and over-supply rapidly ensues."[1] Nearly a century later, a modern economist comments:

> Where is the Spanish comparative advantage going to lie? In the world of the future the principal source of advantage will be brain power. You are going to need a competitive strategy to play that game. Korea, with a population similar to yours, is a good example. Its strategy is to build up three or four companies that are competitive in the world market through research and development. Which are those Spanish companies? You don't have them. I don't see your strategic industrial capacity with which to confront the 21st century.[2]

The second quote exposes one of the major problems of the Spanish economy today: not only is it very uncompetitive in the international market, but the state does not even have a plan to address the issue. Spanish industry has a long tradition of being backward, congenitally unable and unwilling to compete abroad. It is difficult today to find a Spanish industrial company of prestigious international standing comparable to the Korean Hyundai or the Italian Fiat, to give two examples of countries that Spain can compare with on many fronts. Today perhaps one can blame the state, but the problem is one of long standing.

It is difficult to know just how far one can hold business leaders responsible for Spain's backwardness. In the first place, Spain is not an isolated case but rather belongs to a group of European laggards, mostly Mediterranean and Eastern European countries. If the scarcity of entrepreneurial spirit were one of the factors responsible for Spanish backwardness, it ought to apply to Italy and Portugal as well. The theme has been very little studied and is difficult to resolve; even in the case of Great Britain, which has received the keenest attention, with discussion both intense and profound, there is still no general agreement about the responsibility of businessmen for its slowdown since the end of the last century. I cannot hope (nor do I wish) to present the last word on this theme as it relates to Spain, but I do hope to stimulate a debate about a matter which until now has been little considered; it deserves attention.

The weakness of the Spanish entrepreneurial spirit is underlined by two factors: one is the major importance of foreign businessmen within the economic history of Spain, from at least the end of the Middle Ages; the other is the keen propensity of Spanish companies to seek state protection in order to increase profits and shelter themselves from competition.

The shortage of entrepreneurial spirit in Spain during the Golden Century (the early modern or Hapsburg period) comes as no surprise. As early as the Catholic kings, the Spanish government, wittingly or unwittingly, eliminated those social groups most likely to generate entrepreneurial talent. In effect, the expulsion and repression of the Jews in 1492 deprived the country of managers and financiers just at the dawn of the commercial adventure of the Spanish Indies. It is hardly surprising, then, that the merchants who controlled the trade between Spain and the Indies were from Genoa, especially because the value system of contemporary Spanish society glorified nobility and purity of blood, with consequent stigma for trade and enterprise. Thus Ruth Pike remarks that the Genoese colony in Seville endeavored not to become absorbed into the local culture, because assimilation into Spanish society implied shunning mercantile activities and embracing instead careers in the military, the Church, or the bureaucracy. The famous Francisco Pinelo (Pinelli), for example, who financed the Columbus voyages and was one of the leading figures in the Casa de Contratación de las Indias,[3] married into the Spanish aristocracy only to find that his two sons were totally disinterested in commerce, the father's lucrative profession, and chose instead to take religious orders (Pike, 1966, chap. 1).

The defeat of the local middle classes by the Crown and the upper nobility in Castile and Valencia in the early 1520s (wars of the *comuneros* and the *germanías)* could only produce similar effects, since the *comuneros* were mostly urban middle-class citizens and the *germanías* mostly farmers and craftsmen, although in both cases they were initially led by members of the lower nobility. The predominance of foreign businessmen in Hapsburg Spain has been well documented by historians of the stature of Carande, Ruiz Martín, and more recently, Sanz Ayán.

Banking and Railroads

In the most recent past foreigners have played an especially prominent role in Spanish banking. To begin with, the Bank of San Carlos was founded by a Frenchman, François Cabarrus, who not only created it but also ran the operation in its early years. Although he made his home in Spain, Cabarrus always retained his French nationality and maintained such close contacts in France that his famous daughter, Madame Tallien, who was an outstanding figure in revolutionary Paris, was able to bring French diplomatic pressure to bear in the defense of her father when he had problems with the Spanish judiciary system.[4]

An article by Tedde de Lorca (1983) calls attention to the abundance of foreign names among Madrid bankers at the end of the eighteenth century and the beginning of the nineteenth. According to some sources, such as the *Almanac Mercantil,* the number of foreign bankers in Madrid at the beginning of the nineteenth century was between 30% and 40% of the total.

The great tidal wave of French influence crested at mid-century, when Spanish banking was tremendously stimulated by the secondary effects of railroad construction. As a major economic historian has written, without exaggeration, "what little economic development Spain achieved in the nineteenth century was to a large part the result of these credit companies of French inspiration"; with this in mind, he quotes the French ambassador who in 1856 wrote that "Spanish imaginations have been vividly impressed by the generous help that French capital and know-how has extended towards national industry." And Cameron adds: "But however much impressed, the Spanish did little about it, as evidenced by the fact that at the end of the century Frenchmen still controlled the greater part of Spanish heavy industry, and still took the initiative in creating new enterprises."[5]

The French brought not only capital and technical know-how but also legislative initiative. Various French firms like Kervegen, Millaud, Pereire, Weisweiller (representing James de Rothschild), and Prost took an active part in drawing up the banking legislation of 1856. As a result of that law three large French banks were founded, the Crédit Mobilier Español (Pereire), the Sociedad Española Mercantil e Industrial (Rothschild), and the

Compañía General de Crédito Español (Prost and Guilhou). Their example and the legislative framework encouraged the growth of Spanish banking (as we have seen in Chapter 6), confirming the opinion of the British assistant commercial attaché, Cockerell, that the Spanish were more followers than leaders. Although the crisis which in 1866 destroyed this short-lived banking system also hit the French banks, so that only the Crédit Mobilier Español remained in operation, the French presence certainly did not evaporate. Not only did the Pereires and their companies stay intact; the house of Rothschild, after liquidating the Sociedad Española Mercantil e Industrial in 1868, continued to operate through its representatives, Weisweiller and Bauer, who established one of the principal banking houses in Madrid during the Restoration. The Compañía General de Crédito went bankrupt and sold its domestic gas companies, but the Guilhou brothers, who had been managing the operations, took up other business activities in Spain.

The second official bank, second in importance as well as chronologically, was the Banco Hipotecario. Founded in 1872, it was also largely a French creation (concretely of the Banque de Paris et Pays Bas, familiarly known as Paribas) and clearly drew its inspiration from the Crédit Foncier. Although in the long run the capital and management of the Banco Hipotecario fell into Spanish hands, during its first thirty years or more the majority of shares were French and it was co-directed, if not entirely managed, by a steering committee, the Committee of Paris.[6] In 1902 the Paribas was involved in the creation of the Banco Español de Crédito, successor to the outdated Crédito Mobiliario Español, which needed an injection of capital and some structural reform in order to attract Spanish investors. Both these ends were achieved. Although at the beginning the bank was very strongly connected to the Paribas and most of the capital was French, a large share of the capital was acquired by Spaniards during World War I; from that time onwards the Paris Committee was little more than a symbol and it was dissolved in 1927.[7]

Without a shadow of doubt, the French were the major foreign contingent within Spanish banking. There were other French ventures of less stature in the same field: the Banco General de Madrid, the Banco Popular de España (not to be confused with the present day Banco Popular), the Banco Franco-Español, the Crédit Foncier et Agricole du Sud d'Espagne. The Crédit Lyonnais opened various branches, notably in Barcelona, Madrid, and Valencia. But businessmen from other countries also launched ventures of greater or lesser importance and permanence. Although German banking did not achieve in Spain the importance that it did in Italy, the Deutsche Bank, for example, maintained a bridgehead which took various forms over the years (the Banco Hispano-Alemán, Guillermo Vogel y Compañía, the Banco Alemán Transatlántico) but always specialized in extending credit to the electrical industry. The Banco Español Comercial in Valencia was organized by German, Belgian, and French capital. The Banco di Roma always had a branch in Barcelona. The Union Bank of Spain and England was the only British joint-stock bank in Spain, but apart from the highly influential Weisweiller y Bauer, the London house of Baring, with its Irish representative Henry O'Shea, was the most important private banking operation in Madrid in the middle of the nineteenth century.

And as for the railroads, we already know that they were constructed for the most part with French capital, initiative, and know-how. These facts are well established, especially after the publication of Cameron's book on the contribution of France to the economic development of Europe (1961). Since then a lot of research has been done which has enriched our understanding of this subject, but the crucial French role has not been called into question. It is true that there were also Belgian companies, and of course Spanish ones. The only debatable item of discussion is the precise extent of effective foreign investment in the railroad companies, since we know that in many cases Spanish capitalists bought shares on the Paris stock exchange. Christopher Platt was of the opinion that the greater part of the capital was local, while Tedde thinks that the greater part was French.[8] The difference is not so great as it might seem, because both of them are quoting figures not very far from 50%, and the proportions varied over time. In any case, no one disputes that the initiative was French and that the Spaniards, once again, became followers. It is also true, however, that the Spanish case is hardly an exception since, as Cameron shows, the French built almost all the railroads in southern Europe.

Agricultural Industries

Like any other agricultural country, nineteenth-century Spain exported mostly agrarian products, foodstuffs, animals, and raw materials. Of course the majority of the agricultural producers were native, and it is also true that they were generally conservative and backward.[9] How far this extreme form of conservatism was rational is something that historians will continue to discuss at very great length; the fact is that Spanish agriculturalists were extremely resistant to innovation. That, however, was quite frequent throughout Mediterranean Europe, although there was no shortage of exceptions to this rule among Spain's own farmers, particularly in the export sector, where innovations were not unusual. Specialization in certain orchard crops and garden vegetables constituted one such innovation, particularly the development of citrus crops. The growth of orange cultivation, in the Valencia region especially, shows that not all Spanish agriculturists were completely resistant to innovation (Palafox, 1987).

Oranges were not particularly important until the twentieth century, and the same can be said of the fruit and vegetable canning industry which was slow to develop in Spain, probably because of limited purchasing power at home. And here again it seems that foreigners were influential: thus Martínez Carrión (1989) mentions "the influence of North Americans, who had arrived by way of Cuba, in Logroño, and of the French in the Island of Mallorca." According to this author, when Murcia province took over the leadership in this branch of industry, "one also has to point to the presence of foreign capital" such as "the Swiss group of preserve and canned food manufacturers, Lenzbourg, which joined with Spanish capital to form the Hero-Alcantarilla corporation."

The export of olive oil was also important (Zambrana, 1987, chap. VI), but here we again detect a lack of vision among the Spanish companies. Once more it was French companies that first introduced modern machinery to produce high-quality oils about 1880, in Tarragona. In addition, French and Italian companies imported large amounts of Spanish olive oil in bulk and re-exported the product in bottles with their own trademarks. The Spanish entrepreneurs, both growers and exporters, seemed incapable of popularizing Spanish brand names in the international market and thus failed to capitalize on what could have been an important source of added value (Simpson, 1992). Another example, but in reverse, was the import of wool at the end of the nineteenth century: instead of bringing raw wool directly from Australia or Argentina, Spanish manufacturers bought wool that had been washed in France (Parejo, 1989, pp. 136–138).

Another agricultural sector where exports expanded in the second half of the nineteenth century was, of course, the wine industry. It is indeed an ill wind that blows no one good, and the phylloxera that wrecked the vineyards in France caused Spanish wine exports to reach unprecedented levels in the 1870s and 1880s. Many regions, among them again Valencia, benefited from the bonanza which required little in the way of entrepreneurial innovation. But there was a sector of the wine export business where production and commercialization certainly did require innovation and entrepreneurial skills: I refer of course to the fortified wines, and particularly to sherry. The peak in sherry exports occurred earlier, in the 1850s and 1860s, spurred on by a change in British taste away from sweet wines to the drier varieties. The district of Jerez had been exporting the dark and sweeter fragrant wines, *olorosos,* at least since the end of the eighteenth century, and in the middle of the nineteenth was changing over to *finos,* the light and dryer wines, a change which required new techniques and considerable investment (Simpson, 1985). The production and export of these wines, seen as so typically Spanish, was largely in the hands of foreign companies, French, British, and Irish. The Domecq family was French, of provincial nobility from Gascony. They were traditional exporters of wines from Bordeaux to England, who escaped to Spain during the French Revolution and established themselves in Jerez de la Frontera in the same trade, probably reconnecting with the same commercial interests in Britain, simply changing the origin and the nature of the product (Delgado and Orellana, 1966). The names of the most famous wine cellars in Jerez—González-Byass, Osborne, Garvey, Terry, Sandeman, Williams & Humbert, Duff-Gordon—clearly point to the English and Irish origins of the major companies in this trade. All of which should not be taken to imply the absence of notable Spanish businessmen such as Manuel González Angel, the principal partner in the González-Byass partnership.

Mining and Metallurgical Industries

In spite of their tremendous wealth, many Spanish mines were not seriously exploited until the last decades of the nineteenth century. During those years, however, they became the most dynamic sector of the Spanish economy. This renewed attention to Spanish subsoil deposits can be attributed to both internal and external factors. The internal factors largely explain why those resources at that point still remained available underground. On the supply side, a shortage of capital and skilled personnel kept the production function inelastic and the industry underdeveloped. On the demand side, limited purchasing power deprived the sector of an effective market. Moreover, the existing legislation gave overwhelming powers to the Crown; one example is the Mining Law of 1825, whose principle of "eminent domain" gave the Crown confiscatory powers over the mines (Chastagnaret, 1972).

Obviously, insecurity in an industry that required such costly investment would discourage the potential entrepreneur. Later on, according to this interpretation, the progressive softening of successive mining laws, culminating in the resolute liberalism of the Glorious Revolution, unleashed a feverish rush of mining activity in the last quarter of the century.

In my opinion, however, economic factors were, and indeed continue to be, more powerful than legal ones. It is economic factors that shape events, rather than the reverse. The mines were developed because there was strong international demand for minerals and because both capital and the necessary technology were available to put the mines into effective production. Neither the demand nor the entrepreneurial initiative waited for the laws to be changed, although they probably played a role in shaping those legislative changes. The decisive developments were being forged abroad. The overwhelming majority of demand was there, in countries like England, Belgium, France, and Germany, where there were also capitalists, entrepreneurs, and engineers able to bring the mines into effective and economic production. The revolutionaries of 1868 saw it clearly: either the mines would be opened up to international capitalism, or else the mineral wealth would remain underground. And they decided in favor of development.

Iron ore represents the most important component, the clearest example. The slow growth of Spain's metallurgical industries could not provide sufficient stimulus for the ore mining industry. The big push forward came principally from the British steel industry, whose commitment to the Bessemer process made phosphorus-free ore a necessity. Although the British did not become involved with Spanish iron ore production to any great extent until the 1870s, within a few years large British companies were flourishing (the Orconera, the Luchana, the Parcocha, the Salvador, the Marbella), and so were such French companies as Schneider and the Mines de Somorrostro. It is true that there was also Spanish capital: the Ybarra family participated in the Orconera and the Somorrostro ventures and had its own mines, Saltacaballo for example; and there were many other, smaller Spanish companies. But it is evident that the initiative and the largest mining companies were foreign. For the manufacture of iron and derivatives the story is different. Its entrepreneurs exhibited arch-conservatism, and their "business strategy . . . was focused very closely upon . . . seeking tariff protections, which in maintaining the rates of profitability and neutralizing their lack of competitiveness certainly did nothing to foster technological innovation" (Bilbao, 1983, p. 84). Along with serious political problems this orientation contributed to technological backwardness and a stagnation in productivity during almost the whole century, in spite of the country's immense mineral wealth.

In contrast, lead, which is simple to produce, was manufactured in large quantities throughout the nineteenth century, almost exclusively in Spanish hands until about 1850. But Spanish operators limited themselves to working where the lead could be found close to the surface and often sold out to foreigners when the surface veins became exhausted (Nadal, 1975, pp. 102–103; Núñez Romero-Balmas, 1985). During the second half of the nineteenth century, lead mining in Córdoba and Jaén came to be dominated by the French and the English. This influx of capital and foreign entrepreneurs, along with railroad construction and the depletion of deposits in Almería and Murcia, shifted the center of gravity of lead mining towards the interior. Nadal and Estevan Senís have criticized the Spanish operators for being short-sighted: "speculators and not . . . real entrepreneurs," Nadal calls them (1975, p 100; Estevan Senís, 1966). Of course neither nationals nor foreigners were motivated by anything higher than the keen desire for profit; the difference lay in the degree of farsightedness, in the professional training, in the volume of resources, and in knowledge of the market. In every aspect, the foreigners were at the forefront.

Something similar can be said of copper mining. The famous Tharsis mines remained dormant during the greater part of the nineteenth century, until the Compagnie des Mines de Cuivre d'Huelva acquired the concession in 1855. The major demand and the majority of capital, however, were British. The copper pyrites of the great basin of the rivers Tinto and Odiel also contained sulfur, which was of equal or even greater importance than the copper because it was a basic constituent of sulfuric acid and caustic soda, both vital to the British chemical industry. Eventually a consortium of British chemical companies organized the Tharsis Sulfur and Copper Company, which replaced the former French concession through an amicable agreement in 1866. The British company immediately set about the groundwork necessary to exploit the deposits on a large scale by opening up the terrain for strip mining and building a narrow-gauge railroad to the coast and a loading wharf near Huelva. At Tharsis some of the pyrites were treated at the site to obtain copper, and the remaining output was sent to England, where it was sold as raw material to the chemical industry for sulfur and other byproducts [Checkland (1967)]. The profits were substantial. In the meantime, exploitation of the Río Tinto mines was in the hands of local companies, inefficient in operation and occasionally fraudulent, thus rendering little financial benefit to the owner, the Spanish state. When the government, overwhelmed by debt, decided to auction off the concession in 1870, it found no takers; the asking price was high, and political conditions in Spain and Europe were unfavorable. In the end, in 1873 an international consortium under the leadership of Hugh Matheson took charge of the mines, and a decade of substantial investment, similar to that at the Tharsis mines but on a larger scale, eventually produced a highly successful venture.

These large foreign copper companies had been notoriously unpopular in Spain. With respect to the most hated Río Tinto Company, Nadal has asserted that the amount of money that the company paid to lease the deposits was "insufficient," in light of the "fabulous" profits that the operation produced (1975, pp. 107–108). Apart from questioning whether the Río Tinto yield ought to be classified as "fabulous," if the price of the lease was "insufficient," one can ask why Spaniards did not assume the lease themselves, since the auction was a public affair and Spanish entrepreneurs would have been in the best position to know the conditions of the contract. In fact, it was some local people who told Matheson about this opportunity and later on bought shares in the new company, but those "local elements" were two Germans, Heinrich Doetsch and Wilhelm Sundheim, who had settled in Huelva. The entrepreneurial vision of the Spaniards was, once more, conspicuous by its absence (Coll, 1983).

In the case of mercury, where the relative simplicity of the extraction process precluded any need for foreign entrepreneurs, it was the weakness and disorganization of the Spanish state which attracted the Rothschilds, whose international network for selling the product would have been essential in any case. As for zinc, the major production company, the Real Compañía Asturiana de Minas, was Belgian. At mid-century the bulk of the capital had been in Spanish hands, but the Spanish partners withdrew when reorganization and amplification became necessary, so that on the very eve of its unprecedented prosperity the company became predominantly foreign (Chastagnaret, 1973).

In summary, mineral extraction and processing constitute a classic example of the failure of Spanish entrepreneurs to confront the problems of developing an industrial sector with complex technology, intensive use of capital, a fast-expanding horizon, and important international ramifications.

The space they left vacant was occupied by foreign entrepreneurs, by and large natives of those countries which constituted the great international markets of the period.

Capital Goods and Energy

Almost all the machinery and other equipment necessary for mining and mineral extraction was imported. Only the explosives, which constitute an important factor of production in mining and public works, were produced domestically, especially after 1872, when the Sociedad Española de la Dinamita was installed in Bilbao. Needless to say all but one of the managers, the engineers, the technology, even the greater part of the raw materials for this company were initially imported, particularly from France, and the capital was largely German, British, and Belgian. Manufacture, not surprisingly, followed the techniques invented by Alfred Nobel, who was a member of the Board of Directors. Years later other competitors and Spanish entrepreneurs entered the field, confirming once more what the British consul Cockerell had said. The demand for sulfuric acid, nitric acid, and other products was growing, and national production increased. Some of the industry's byproducts were used to make fertilizers (superphosphates). In the long run all the Spanish explosives manufacturers merged, and by the beginning of the twentieth century the resulting consortium, created to a large extent by foreign capitalists, had become largely Spanish (Tortella, 1983, 1987, 1992). Several years earlier a small chemicals industry had evolved in Spain to supply the textile industry with sulfuric acid, caustic soda, and hydrochloric acid. The first Spanish chemical company was created in Barcelona at the beginning of the nineteenth century by a Frenchman, François Cros, a student of Jean-Antoine Chaptal who became a refugee in Catalonia after the Napoleonic wars (Nadal, 1986).

Other modern industries—gas, electricity, and urban transport, for instance—were also introduced into Spain by foreign entrepreneurs and capitalists. Gas was introduced by three separate companies. In Barcelona, Charles Lebon, whose French father (Philippe) was one of the original inventors of coal gas, founded the Catalana de Gas in 1842 in association with the banker Pedro Gil, and later went on to extend his activities in other cities and other countries (Sudrià, 1983; Broder, 1981, pp. 1663 ff. gives the son's first name as Pierre). In Madrid gas was first introduced by the British company Manby and Partington in 1846, although experiments had been carried out as early as 1826. The company decided to withdraw from the field during the 1847–48 crisis, and the enterprise came into the hands of the banker Gregorio López de Mollinedo, who finally bought the company in 1856 and immediately sold it to the Crédito Mobiliario Español, a French bank (Madoz, 1848, p. 185; Tortella, 1971, pp. 71–72). The third venture was that of the Compañía General de Crédito en España, also French, which created a network of six gas companies in as many Spanish provincial capitals starting in Valladolid, where production began in 1859 (Tortella, 1973, p. 143). The only clearly local initiative in the gas industry was that of José Campo in Valencia, who launched the enterprise in cooperation with Lebon but later got rid of him.

It will surprise no one that the introduction of electricity in Spain was predominantly in the hands of German companies such as AEG, Siemens, and Schuckert, and as happened in other European countries, the Deutsche Bank was one of their major financial supporters. What is remarkable, and less well known, is that Spanish businessmen, no doubt with state aid, played a larger part in this field than in other sectors of modern industry. Indeed, the first electrical generator in Spain was installed in Barcelona by a local company whose partners were both Catalán, Tomás Dalmau and Narcís Xifra. The Dalmau-Xifra Company was small, however; it generated power with gas engines and supplied electrical current for public lighting and the motive force for some factories. It tried to expand to the rest of Spain, but could not compete with the multinational giants which at that time were absorbing small companies all over southern Europe (Broder, 1985). AEG first entered Spanish business through Madrid, joining up with the Madrid Gas Company and the Pereire brothers to form the Compañía Madrileña de Electricidad in 1890. Schuckert Company entered the Madrid market in 1898, with an electrical plant called the Central Norte. AEG also created the Sevillana de Electricidad, similar companies in Barcelona and Vizcaya, and various others in different provinces. In 1897 Schuckert also founded the first electrochemical company in Spain, the Electroquímica de Flix, in Catalonia. Meanwhile, as Sudrià tells us, "Spanish capital at the beginning seemed uninterested in investing in the electrical undertakings." Broder (1981, p. 1745) also mentions that a few years later the Catalán banks displayed a negative attitude towards investing in hydroelectricity schemes, in sharp contrast with their Basque and Madrid counterparts.

Things changed in this area, however, at least in part because of legislation that reserved to Spaniards the right to own waterfalls and river power in general. This proved no obstacle, however, to the consolidation of the electricity and tramway systems in Barcelona under the control of a complex multinational, the Barcelona Traction, Light, and Power Company. This outfit, through a series of operations that are not yet completely clear, managed to acquire two companies, Barcelona de Electricidad and Energía Eléctrica de Cataluña. The first had belonged to the AEG; the second to Indelec, the bank of the Siemens Company, and it had been founded in 1910 under pressure from the journalist and businessman Emilio Riu, who went to the Siemens Company after having been rejected by various Catalán banks in his efforts to exploit his water power concessions (Broder, 1981, pp. 1745 ff.).

The history of the streetcar companies is similar, since frequently the same companies that distributed electrical power also ran the tramway networks. The first streetcar companies in Barcelona were English and French, but the Belgian companies soon became dominant. At the beginning of the twentieth century Belgian companies operated the systems in Madrid, Barcelona, Valencia, Valladolid, Málaga, Santander, Granada, Zaragoza, Mallorca, and several other cities. AEG, for its part, controlled the systems in Bilbao and Seville (Broder, 1981, pp. 1724 ff.; G. Núñez, 1991).

The problems of Spanish entrepreneurship continued in the twentieth century. In recent works comparing Spanish companies with U.S., British, and German firms for a number of benchmark years, Carreras and Tafunell (1994, 1996) show the "lack of dynamism of Spanish business" in this century.

> [Although] in 1917 Spain's largest firms had respectable sizes in international terms . . ., Spain's big business lost ground and was definitively left behind between 1930 and 1948, [and] although we lack comparable data for later years, our impression is that this declining trend continued for a long time, probably beyond 1960. If we move to the present (1990) and credit the data published by *Fortune* magazine about the world's 500 largest corporations, we can infer that, within an international context, Spain's big business is not in a better situation than in 1939. . . . So it does not seem that [Spain] may have recovered from her retardation in the development of big business. (Carreras and Tafunell, 1994, pp. 441-43)

The authors attribute the failure of Spain's big business to excessive interference by Franco's governments, since "the Spanish experience was quite normal until the Civil War." This is corroborated by their analysis, which shows that after the Civil War Spain's big firms were mostly public (big private firms were either banks or electric utilities) and, generally speaking, neither dynamic nor very profitable. But these analysts overlook an important qualification regarding the "normal" years preceding the Civil War, and this is that foreign firms predominated among the twenty largest in Spain in 1917 and 1930 (and even in 1948). The fact is that of the twenty largest firms in 1917 and 1930, fifteen either had been founded by foreign citizens or had a strong component of foreign capital. Even in 1948, despite the undisguised xenophobia of Francoist policies, the second, third, and fourth largest Spanish firms were originally foreign, and there were five more foreign firms among the top twenty. The largest firm at the time, RENFE (the railroad state monopoly), was the product of a series of mergers and nationalization of large railroad companies, nearly all of them also created by foreigners. Even in 1960 six foreign firms were among Spain's top twenty; such has been the sway of foreign capital and entrepreneurship until very recently.

Patent statistics also reflect the paramount role played by foreign entrepreneurs in Spanish economic development. The work of Ortiz-Villajos (1997, chap. 8, esp. table 8.1) reveals that in 1882, 69% of patents registered in Spain had been submitted by citizens or companies of foreign origin. As the Spanish economy became more modern and its educational and scientific systems progressed, the proportion of foreign patents declined gradually: in 1935 they were no more than 46% of those registered that year. International comparison shows that the number of per capita patents registered in Spain between the mid-nineteenth century and the Spanish Civil War was way below similar statistics for developed countries such as Belgium, United States, Great Britain, France, and even Italy, but clearly above those for less developed countries such as Portugal, Brazil, or Serbia (Ortiz-Villajos, 1994). Somewhat ominously, however, the weight of foreign firms among those registering patents in Spain has increased recently, reaching an average proportion of 82% for the years 1967–1986 (Buesa, 1992), which appears to show that the shortage of entrepreneurs is still a problem in Spain today, or at least until very recently.

Entrepreneurial Attitudes

We have surveyed, extensively but not exhaustively, the role foreign business entrepreneurs played in various important sectors of the Spanish economy during the nineteenth century and the beginning of the twentieth. In my judgment, this survey constitutes clear evidence of the weakness of the

Spanish entrepreneurial spirit in this period. At the same time it is also true that in other important industrial sectors, which grew in different circumstances and at different rhythms during these years—the various branches of metal production, textiles, cement, and the food industry, for example— the role of foreign businessmen was much smaller and that of Spaniards correspondingly much larger. However, these were sectors where competition was restricted in one way or another and high profit levels were almost guaranteed. The textile entrepreneurs, although operating in a seemingly atomized market, managed to establish a powerful pressure group that was effective in attaining tariff protection (Tortella, 1981). The metallurgical business leaders, and especially those in the iron and steel industry, constructed an oligopoly which was also highly successful in pushing for high tariffs (in both the nineteenth and twentieth centuries), thus protecting them from foreign competition (Bilbao, 1983; Fraile, 1991). Cement producers also formed an oligopoly which, at the beginning of the twentieth century, repeatedly pressured the government to undertake public works programs, almost always successfully. They even managed to get government help in enforcing the agreements and norms that had been privately established by the cartel itself (Gómez Mendoza, 1987). Similar developments occurred in the food industry: Martín Rodríguez (1987) has shown that the sugar industry responded to the problems of chronic overproduction by organizing a cartel and getting various forms of government protection from tariffs, again with official recognition of the cartel. And the same can be said about the explosives manufacturers (Tortella, 1983, 1987).

It would be pointless to deny that some of the notable businessmen of this period were Spanish. In banking we should mention Manuel Girona, the founder and almost perpetual president of the Bank of Barcelona, the first Spanish private commercial bank; José Campo, the creator of the first business bank, the Sociedad Valenciana de Crédito y Fomento, and thus the precursor of the credit societies, ahead of the Pereire Brothers' Crédit Mobilier by six years (and it was Campo who introduced railroads and gas street lighting to Valencia) (Tortella, 1973); Antonio López, the Marqués de Comillas, an associate of Girona's, a banker and shipping magnate (Tortella, 1974); Estanislao de Urquijo, a Basque of humble origin who migrated to Madrid, established himself in the Rothschild agency with Daniel Weisweiller, and was very successful, becoming the grand old man of Spanish business bankers in the second half of the nineteenth century (Otazu, 1987); Antonio Basagoiti, who emigrated to Mexico where he made a fortune and later founded, in Madrid, the Banco Hispano Americano, the largest Spanish bank by the middle of the twentieth century (García Ruiz and Tortella, 1993); and there were many other eminent businessmen in the banking sector and other diverse spheres. But except for Basagoiti, they were purely local figures whose work rarely had much impact outside of Spain, or in many cases even outside of the cities where they operated. Essentially they are better characterized as capable administrators rather than daring innovators, and that, I believe, is the keynote feature of the best Spanish businessmen of the period.

The truth is that the Spaniards who decided to turn their energies to business generally tended rather to look to secure or improve their positions through noncompetitive structures: cartels, tariffs, legal monopolies or *de facto* monopolistic arrangements, and state protection in whatever form possible. Table 8.1 presents the results of an analysis of business attitudes based on an 1889 official questionnaire about tariff reform.

The inquiry included 26 questions about economic conditions and per-

Table 8.1. Attitudes of Spanish businessmen toward tariff reductions and the renewal of commercial treaties, 1889

	Industry	Agriculture	Commerce	Trade associations	Others	Total
Tariff reform						
Favorable	4	0	7	14	11	36
Opposed	37	13	0	66	11	127
Totals	41	13	7	80	22	163
Treaty renewal						
Favorable	3	0	7	23	9	42
Opposed	13	6	0	43	8	70
Totals	16	6	7	66	17	102
			Percentages			
Tariff reform						
Favorable	9.8	0.0	100.0	17.5	50.0	22.1
Opposed	90.2	100.0	0.0	82.5	50.0	77.9
Treaty renewal						
Favorable	18.8	0.0	100.0	34.8	52.9	37.5
Opposed	81.2	100.0	0.0	65.2	47.1	62.5

Source: calculated from *La Reforma Arancelaria;* see text

spectives in different industrial sectors, and reported the opinions of those surveyed on issues of economic policy, among them possible modifications of tariff rates and commercial treaties. I have selected the answers relative to these two themes and classified them according to attitudes, favorable or unfavorable, and according the profession or origin of the respondent, for example industrialist, agriculturalist, merchant, professional (almost always a member of a chamber of commerce) and other (almost always civil servants). Although there were 240 respondents in total, not all the answers could be tabulated because they failed to present definitive opinions. Two-thirds of the respondents, for example, had clear opinions about the tariffs, while less than half expressed views about the trade treaties. Almost half of the responses came from members of professional organizations, which in my opinion, makes them adequately representative.

The hostility against free trade was overwhelming. Almost four out of five respondents, 78%, were against tariff reduction, and often very emphatically so. Although this cannot be reflected in the table, in reality the dominant opinion was not just against tariff reduction but in favor of an increase, which indeed was soon to take place. Among the professionals the proportion opposed to a tariff reduction was even higher at 83%, and this is probably a very representative figure since the sample is large and we are looking here at groups rather than individuals. In some cases they were strictly professional bodies, but more frequently the responses came from chambers of commerce which included a wide range of commercial activities. The sample of industrialists is also large, one-quarter of all respondents, and again the respondents were almost unanimously against tariff reduction. Agriculturalists were completely unanimous against a tariff reduction; in contrast, the merchants were uniformly in favor. Although these examples are based on rather small numbers, surely they are representative. It is interesting to note that civil servants were divided equally on this topic.

On the question of trade treaties the panorama is similar although opinions were less well defined. There are fewer clear answers and also less unanimity, although hostility against free trade continued to dominate, as here indicated by attitudes towards the treaties themselves. Among the professional organizations 65% were against the treaties, as were 81% of industrialists. Agriculturalists and merchants continued in unanimity in their respective postures, but less than half of the agriculturalists who were against tariff reduction expressed an opinion. The civil servants again remained almost equally divided. In total 63% of all respondents were against renewing the trade treaties.

It would be interesting to compare these results with similar studies carried out in other countries, but shortage of time and space precludes my doing it here. In any case, the results confirm attitudes we have been deducing from other kinds of evidence: even in the climate of free trade that was flourishing in the nineteenth century, Spanish entrepreneurs predominantly opted against free trade and against free, open competition. It is true that in the final decades of the nineteenth century business opinion in many countries began to mistrust free trade, but the near-unanimity among Spain's agriculturalists and industrialists is impressive. It seems to confirm this proclivity for state protection, the inclination towards monopoly, and the aversion to risk-taking that we have detected in analyzing the predominance of foreign entrepreneurs in sectors of Spain's economy which were competitive, which were subject to powerful innovations, and which demanded large investments of capital. According to Pedro Fraile (1991, p. 202):

> What truly distinguished Spain from the majority of her neighbors was the proclivity of the institutional framework to generate and maintain, over a long period of time, supply structures of a markedly restrictive and monopolistic character, which tended to distance Spanish industry from international competition by means of tariff protection. With an appropriate institutional framework, Spanish industrialists chose a maximization strategy based upon relative factor prices and expected profit rates . . . the ease with which they could obtain rents from the state made it comparatively disadvantageous to engage in competition in the open market and in the processes of production, and in contrast made it more attractive to expend their resources and energy in search of [monopoly] rents.[10]

Some Hypotheses

There is space here to offer only some brief conjectures about the causes of such attitudes. The relationship between social values and Spanish underdevelopment has been grist to the mill of a venerable and long-standing argument. The social characteristics most cited as responsible for this backwardness are the following:

1. The old aristocratic prejudice against work, particularly manual work.
2. The traditional Catholic distrust of capitalism (laws against usury, the eulogy of poverty, mistrust of competition, materialism, and rational attitudes).

3. Intellectual passivity and the respect for orthodoxy imposed by the Inquisition.
4. Low educational levels.
5. The long mercantilist tradition supporting state intervention in the economy and the regulation, with the help of guild control, of work and business activities.
6. The well-recognized vicious circle; backwardness itself is an obstacle to economic development and a barrier to business initiative.

Let us briefly examine these factors, keeping in mind that they are not alternatives but more likely to operate jointly and cumulatively.

Returning to (1): among the causes of Spanish backwardness in the seventeenth century, Hamilton (1938) found "contempt for manual labor and arts." An economist of the nineteenth century, Manuel Colmeiro (1965, p. 807), wrote: "One of the first necessities of the Spanish people in the eighteenth century was to honor and ennoble the mechanical arts, in general little valued and some of them even considered infamous, the remains of that ancient silly and vulgar preoccupation that the lily-white hands of a noble or a gentleman should not become stained nor made coarse with common labor." And a more recent author (G. Anes, 1975, p. 131), writing about the eighteenth century, confirmed that "The ideal of the noble life pervaded the mentality of every level of Spanish society under the Old Regime and was solidly rooted among those at the lowest levels, with the result that work in particular trades was socially discredited. And the most serious was that . . . this discredit was even reflected in certain provisions embodied in the legal codes of the kingdom."

It is true that the enlightened governments of the eighteenth century opposed such attitudes and that the laws that defined certain activities as pariah trades were withdrawn by Carlos III (Colmeiro, 1965). But the attitudes were very pervasive: "the reformist legislation was much more generous in this respect than popular opinion" (Palacio Atard quoted by Anes, 1975, p. 131). According to Jean Sarrailh (1957, p. 890), at the end of the eighteenth century "the practice of working in industry or commerce continued to seem incompatible with the condition of being noble." To what point this mentality persisted into the nineteenth century is difficult to establish firmly, but given that it had existed during centuries and that the social prestige of the nobility continued to be high, it seems very unlikely that these attitudes would have disappeared completely.

With regard to (2), it seems unnecessary here to enlarge upon the subject of anticapitalist prejudice in the Catholic church. The topic has been widely discussed, at least since Max Weber, but I do not believe that economic historians are going to deny a certain validity to the Weber thesis, that Catholic doctrine looked with less sympathy than did the Protestant upon the basic premises of the market economy. It is worth quoting one of Hamilton's (1938) pithy phrases: "During the century of decline the Church seems to have been the only institution that grew."

With regard to (3): Karl Vossler used to say that the Spaniards were disciplined in their thought and undisciplined in their conduct, quite the reverse of the Germans in both respects. The Spaniards became reduced to this state of mental submission after centuries of imposed orthodoxy. "In every European country during the seventeenth century censorship of the press and speech undoubtedly stifled the intellectual progress upon which economic advancement has always largely depended; but owing to the heavy hand of the Inquisition, the interference of the Church with learning was at its worst in Spain" (Hamilton, 1938, p. 223).

With regard to (4), Richard Kagan has shown how the universities fell into decline after the sixteenth century, and how interest in philosophical questions diminished in favor of more practical and immediate disciplines like law and medicine. He argues that this change dates from a decline in the influence of Erasmus, concretely from the symbolic date of 1559, when an important *auto de fe* was celebrated in Valladolid (Kagan, 1974, chap. 9, esp. p. 217). The decline of the Spanish universities (which, according to Kagan, had placed Castile among the most highly educated regions of Europe at the end of the sixteenth century) was abysmal in the following century, and they never recovered until the reforms of the nineteenth century that amounted to a virtual reconstruction. In the eighteenth century, according to Sarrailh (1957, p. 98): "University professors, for the most part, demonstrated an obstinate adherence to the past, and they refused, in so far as it was possible, to adopt the reforms that could have introduced to these rigidly unhealthy institutions, a little youth and daring, a little curiosity of spirit, perhaps a little freedom of opinion."

In 1772, for example, there was a great argument between the government and the University of Salamanca because that august body refused to teach the works of Newton, Gassendi, Hobbes, Locke, and Descartes (whom they rejected because his principles "do not symbolize [sic] enough with the revealed truths such as those of Aristotle)." In this same year the Theology

Faculty of the University of Santiago insisted on teaching St. Thomas Aquinas to the complete exclusion of any other theologian, even the most orthodox, such as Saint Isidore, Saint Anselm, and Duns Scotus. In this connection Sarrailh observed (1957, pp. 98–103) that the politicians were more liberal than the professors. C. E. Núñez (1992) has studied certain quantitative aspects of the relationship between economic and educational backwardness in nineteenth-century Spain, and it seems beyond question that there is a very close connection. Educational backwardness in Spain has very deep roots.

Finally, with regard to (5), Angel García Sanz, in attempting to explain economic backwardness in nineteenth-century Castile (1991), declares a skepticism towards those "sociological and psychological arguments which propose explanations such as 'lack of entrepreneurial spirit or initiative or appetite for risk,' while at the same time [they emphasize] the transcendent power of conservatism and traditionalism in economic behaviors." He maintains that the entrepreneurial spirit was in fact present in Castile; what was lacking, he argues, were the physical conditions for growth, what he terms the natural environment, the *medio natural* for development (p. 38); this was the reason why "the road to rational capitalism [would lead] into a cul-de-sac." However, this author also admits that "one of the most critical features in the rise of agricultural capitalism in Castile and León in the nineteenth century was the continued political protection of cereal prices" (pp. 36–37). It seems, therefore, that the position of García Sanz is not substantially different from my own. The Castilian grain producers had anchored themselves to protectionism, just as their cotton and metallurgical counterparts had done in order, paraphrasing Bilbao, to maintain profit rates, to neutralize their lack of competitiveness, and to avoid the risks of technological innovation. The point is, there is not one single form of logical capitalism but many. That businessman who is prepared to compete in the open market is just as much a capitalist as the one who devotes his energies instead to obtaining government protection, or he who strives to arrive at agreements with his competitors. My argument here is that for Spanish businessmen, for historical reasons which molded both the conduct and attitudes of society at large, the second and third options were more attractive than the first. Table 8.1 demonstrates this; in the Spain of the nineteenth century there was no shortage of businessmen so long as their profits were guaranteed by the state, above all the tariff. The missing element was a business sector with a vision of the long term, prepared to take risks and to invest in new technologies, to achieve economies of scale, to seek comparative advantage, to reduce prices by reducing costs—in short, entrepreneurs with contempt for state protection and for the immorality of oligopolistic conspiracies. Such true and authentic capitalists were conspicuous by their absence. But the capitalists who preferred to manipulate the market in search of profits that were extremely high and economically unjustified, of those there were plenty, in fact too many.

It would be naive to attribute the economic backwardness of Spain solely to the mediocre caliber of its business entrepreneurs. The causes are more complex and have deep roots, as my interpretation in Chapter 1 attempts to show. But neither can one deny that social attitudes, difficult as they are to grasp, were very pervasive. My principal hypothesis throughout this chapter has been that a society which from the sixteenth century onwards was, intellectually speaking, frozen solid into an orthodoxy that systematically repressed original thought and freedom of action in the search for earthly happiness, finished up three centuries later without a competitive, dynamic entrepreneurial class. The social attitudes, the accepted norms, I repeat, have been very persistent; some indications still suggest that the problem has not yet been resolved.

CHAPTER 9

The Twentieth Century

Macroeconomic Dimensions

The twentieth century, as we have already seen, is the century of Spain's fast economic growth. This is also true for most European countries, and indeed for many countries in the world. The twentieth century, in effect, represents that moment in time when mankind gathers in the gains harvested from the Industrial Revolution. In terms of numbers of people, in terms of life expectancy, in terms of income per head (which we economists generally consider to be closely related to utility, and that to earthly happiness), this harvest is without historical precedent. Of course, not all of the harvest is wheat; there is chaff as well. The astronomical increase in population along with increasing consumption levels and tremendous geographical and historical disparities contribute dangerously to two phenomena that are enormously threatening; on the one hand, ecological destruction of parts of the planet, from the ozone layer to the rain forests, and on the other hand, increasing differences in income levels, from one country to another.

A glance at Figure 9.1 confirms that, in broad measure, growth of income per capita in Spain, France, and Italy from the middle of the nineteenth century to the end of the twentieth century has followed a parallel course, and the same is true of many other European countries. All three seem to achieve a fairly constant rate of growth from the nineteenth century until well into the twentieth; they experience a sudden halt in the 1930s and 1940s (doubtless because of the Great Depression and World War II), and return to strong, rapid growth in the 1950s. From this century-long perspective, therefore, the Spanish case does not look particularly unusual. We have to take a closer look, to pay attention to certain details and periods to appreciate the differences. To capture some of them, let us return for a moment to Chapter 1, Table 1.2 and Figure 1.2, where I introduced the concept of the average income of France and Britain as a benchmark for the long-run evolution of various European economies, a procedure that led us to recognize a Mediterranean (or EuroLatin) pattern of modern economic growth.[1]

For the features that interest us here, it is sufficient to compare the Spanish data with that for our neighbors, and especially Italy, to clarify what is unusual about the Spanish case. One immediately salient feature of Figure 9.1 is that Spanish income per capita has been consistently lower than that for France (except for the World War II years; the other odd moments when Spanish income seems to be higher are likely to be statistical aberrations). Yet the relationship with Italy is different, changing to the detriment of Spain as the years go by. One can see that Spain lost ground to Italy in three phases. In the first phase, the years prior to World War I, it seems that of the three countries represented, Spain suffered most from the depression of the 1880s, probably because of rigidity in the agricultural sector. Furthermore, we see no evidence in Spain for the early twentieth century burst of industrialization that Gerschenkron noted for Italy (1965). In comparison, Spain's recovery from the end-of-century depression is slower. The second phase

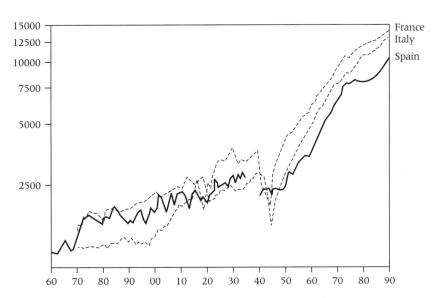

Figure 9.1. Income per capita in Spain, Italy, and France, 1860–1990 (in $U.S. 1985, at purchasing power parity, semi-logarithmic scale)

during which Spain also loses ground corresponds to the 1940s, the years following the Civil War for Spain and World War II for Italy, and this can be seen more readily in Figure 9.2, which shows the Spanish and Italian series from 1900 onwards.

These are the years when Spain definitely falls behind Italy—the price exacted for the political autarky and interventionism of the early Franco years. Figure 9.2 indicates Spain's desperately slow recovery during this time, in sad contrast with the speedy upturn that the Italian economy enjoyed after the abyss of the world war. The third sluggish phase corresponds to Spain's late return to democracy. This is the second invoice to be billed to Francoism: just as Spain had paid with economic backwardness in the early years of the dictatorship, so also was there an account to pay after Franco's death. The costly transition to an economy and a society that would be more aligned with the rest of Western Europe can be seen in the clear inflection point, beginning already in 1974, with stagnation and even a small decline in real purchasing power at the beginning of the 1980s.

If the three legs of the race with Italy were lost, it is nonetheless true that Italy also paid a high price for fascism. After World War I the postwar crisis affected Italy severely, a situation that doubtless favored Mussolini and his

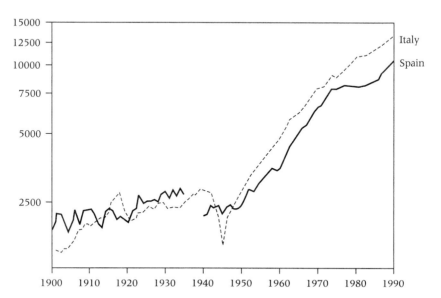

Figure 9.2. Income per capita in Spain and Italy, 1900–1990 (in $U.S. 1985, at purchasing power parity, semi-logarithmic scale)

party. But as was to happen in Spain twenty years later, triumphant fascism, far from being an economic panacea, became instead a brake on growth and change. Recovery from World War I was faster for Spain, and the country surged ahead of Italy, whose newly industrializing, more open economy had been seriously hurt by the Great Depression of the 1930s.

The singular feature of twentieth-century Spain, therefore, is that while it has followed the Mediterranean pattern, it has also been losing ground to the leader of the squad. Certain political factors and critically important deficiencies in human capital formation explain that loss of ground; let us remember here the growing disparity between Spain and Italy in literacy and school attendance.

Advantages and Disadvantages of Historical Periodization

Spanish economic historians who are specialists in the modern period have traditionally focused on the nineteenth century, leaving the twentieth century to economists or people interested simply in specialized monographic studies. Thus studies of this or that period of the twentieth century abound. Economists have been more interested in the recent decades, whereas historians (economic historians and others) have concentrated more on the troubled years between the two world wars. Given that recent Spanish (and European) history comprises a number of short subperiods, each giving rise to numerous, sometimes passionate monographic studies: on World War I, the postwar crisis, the dictatorship of Primo de Rivera, the Republic, the Depression and its effects on Spain, the Civil War, Francoism in its various phases, the transition to democracy, all of which are topics of great interest in themselves. Because of this ardent interest in detail, however, there has been a dearth of studies that approach the question of Spain's twentieth century economic history in its totality. This relative disinterest in the twentieth century can be explained but not condoned; the consequences are regrettable, because this absence has deprived us of a genuine historical view of a crucial period of Spain's industrialization and modernization.

This historical view, the long-run perspective, is utterly essential to our complete understanding of an important social phenomenon. The proverbial cliché of not being able to see the wood for the trees can be applied yet one more time to many studies of this century. The debates about the Civil War, about the dictators' economic policies, about the crises in the 1970s and 1980s have confused us and obscured the powerful, normal, and predictable long-run trends, which, if carefully examined, can illuminate each of the particular features that have been so intensely, so blindly debated.

The long-run view reveals facts that are scarcely recognized, even among specialists. In the first place, the long perspective lets us see very clearly that the twentieth century is, for the Spanish economy, the time when "more things are happening." Its study really deserves a unified historical perspective. In the second place, change is not concentrated, as the Franco propaganda machine would have had us believe, in the second half of the century. Notwithstanding the tremendous social and political instabilities of this period—world wars, the Depression, the Civil War, a succession of governments and changes of regime—economic evolution displays a clear degree of continuity, with only one major interruption, from 1935 to 1950. On both sides of this great divide the general trend is in the direction of growth. In the third place, in spite of the proclivity of Spanish governments for isolation and self-sufficiency, the rhythms of the Spanish economy have indeed responded to those of its surrounding European neighbors. High growth rates in the 1950s and 1960s do not so much reflect the much vaunted "Spanish miracle" as the "European miracle." And fourthly, a careful look at the twentieth century long-run picture gives perspective to an important, basic continuity, a unity that embraces the whole of contemporary history within our gaze. In plain words, the Spanish economy has not stopped growing since 1800, not only in absolute terms but also in terms of income per head. The rates of growth, modest in the nineteenth century, continued accelerating progressively throughout these two hundred years. As a result, in comparison with the average for Western Europe Spain lost ground in the nineteenth century and recouped at least part of that loss in the twentieth.

The long run, then, allows us a contextual view of some economic changes which until now, without any frame of reference, have been floating around dangerously, occasionally giving rise to some very strange assertions. At this point we might ask why the economic historians had renounced such a fruitful perspective. To begin with, the economic historiography of modern Spain is relatively recent. With notable exceptions (Juan Sardá's book of 1948 stands out), the field substantially dates from the work of Jaime Vicens Vives, published about 1960. Vicens, a medievalist by training, became interested in modern themes at the end of his life, concentrating on the nineteenth century, particularly on the origins of industry in Catalonia. A series of secondary historians, without much sense of proportion, had been interpreting the remarkable growth of the Catalán textile in-dustry at the end of the eighteenth century and the beginning of the nine-teenth as a fully fledged industrial revolution, almost comparable with the English development. Vicens and his disciples (Jordi Nadal and his school particularly stand out) have studied this phenomenon and situated their re-sults within the whole Spanish context, which led them to concentrate their investigations on the nineteenth century. The work culminated in Nadal's important book (1975), whose expressive title synthesizes his conclusion: *The Failure of the Industrial Revolution in Spain.* In contrast, historians outside Catalonia paid less attention to Catalán industry and more to the Spanish economy as a whole, and they soon realized that the most remarkable phe-nomenon of nineteenth-century Spain was not so much industrialization *per se,* but the degree to which Spain lagged behind Europe. Indeed, this fo-cus on the causes of backwardness, concentrated in the nineteenth century, has come to dominate economic historiography until the present. And to the above one must add the aversion of traditional historians for the recent past, the contentious point of view that the present is not history. All this has conspired to deprive us until now of the study of one of the most interesting periods of our recent past, history indeed, however close it may seem to us today.

In view of the above, how much discontinuity do we really find in the growth of modern Spain? Or put in other words, are the disparities between the nineteenth and twentieth centuries really to be believed, do they really exist? Might they not be simply a consequence of the properties of exponen-tial curves, which in their first sections seem almost flat, although in reality the growth rates may be quite high? Unfortunately, we are not yet in a posi-tion to give a totally satisfactory answer. There are indications of continuity, as evidenced by the Carreras series on industrial production (1984), and also indications of discontinuity, like the demographic variables. Quantitative monetary measures and data from banking and external trade also reveal distinct discontinuities around the year 1900. But apart from the demo-graphic measures, the other interruptions do not seem really important and can be attributed to external factors (the loss of Cuba and the Philippines) and economic policy, such as the drastic fiscal measures adopted by Villa-verde in 1899 and the twists and turns of protectionist policy in 1891 and 1906. The demographic discontinuity is more interesting and puzzling. Arango (1987, p. 201) wittily suggests that demography sustains itself with two of the principal ingredients of the best detective novels, sex and death, but goes on to say that unfortunately "on occasions a third indispensable ingredient is lacking in such stories, which is mystery." On the contrary, I would argue strongly that the demographic transitions are sufficiently full of mysterious elements to satisfy Conan Doyle himself. Why, after a century of disquietingly archaic demographic rates, does modernization take off speedily just at the turn of the century? The unknown remains to be resolved, but the facts are these: natality and mortality began to decline in parallel fashion at about that date, setting in motion a process that started out from very backward demographic rates in 1900, but today situates Spain very close to the European demographic norm (see Chapter 10).

Another persistent question, which recent studies help us to unravel, is asked almost daily in the street: is Spain economically different? (from Europe, one understands). The answer again is ambiguous; as we have seen earlier, Spain's history does present peculiarities, but as a whole it fits well enough into the pattern for southwestern Europe. One undeniable Spanish peculiarity is, of course, its economic isolationism, although this again is surely a question of degree. Under Franco this isolation reached dizzy heights, but the unattractive face of autarky, a political preference for self-sufficiency, is endemic in Spanish history. To a certain point it is this tendency that traditional economists have identified in attaching blame to tariff protection and the many and varied commercial restrictions that hobbled the pace of industrialization. Some of us have long questioned this diagnosis. The works of Leandro Prados on nineteenth-century international trade shatter the argument for the earlier period. Carreras and Fraile in their studies of twentieth-century industry also leave the old thesis in a decidedly shaky state. This issue is of immediate importance because it affects the attitudes of the political parties, the politicians themselves, and the contemporary Spanish voters. We have witnessed a turning point, a parallel change of direction in both policy and the interpretation of history. The protectionist thesis seems to have been put quietly to rest.

Economic Evolution and Political Regression

Spain's twentieth-century history might be used to support the interpretation that democracy and economic growth are incompatible. In effect, while the country was growing economically, the day-to-day problems of living together peaceably were becoming more acute, leading eventually to open civil warfare and a dictatorship of extraordinary length. Does all this mean, as many have argued, that "Spain is different"?, that its history evolves differently from Western Europe, where democracy and economic growth seem to have developed side by side? This might be a possible interpretation, although to me it does not seem the most convincing one.

The turbulent political evolution of twentieth-century Spain can be interpreted as a series of attempts to find political and institutional channels through which the processes of economic growth could most easily flow. These attempts, of course, were themselves affected not only by the internal problems that economic and social change created, but also by the repercussions of external events, disturbances from the outside world, particularly from the closest international neighbors of the Atlantic community (Western Europe and North America), countries which were themselves also struggling at their own level to create appropriate political channels for strong economic growth. Only thus can one understand Spain's terrible changes of direction, from monarchy to dictatorship, from the republic to a new and longer dictatorship by way of a bloody Civil War, all this opening out, towards the end of the century, into a monarchy again, this time authentically democratic and constitutional and with expectations of stability.

For Spain, the opening years of the twentieth century were full of politically dramatic events fraught with economic consequences—the humiliating military defeat and loss of Cuba, Puerto Rico, and the Philippines—humiliating in that it revealed an almost universal lack of direction among ordinary people and the political elites as well. The short-run economic consequences of the colonial trauma can be separated into negative and positive components. Among the former we count the loss of markets for industry and agriculture, the loss of human life, of physical and military resources and income to the Treasury, the disappearance of various transportation and communications networks, and perhaps the most important, a widespread sense of revulsion and demoralization. The "disaster" (as it is known in Spanish historiography) was enormously important, though impossible to quantify; yet it had a positive side to it, for it also produced a determined response that acknowledged the need for renovation and reform. This took various and sometimes surprising forms of expression in diverse fields of human endeavor; in literature, the Generation of '98; among politicians and the cultured elite, the movement known as "regenerationism," from which political parties and schools of thought evolved. In the economic arena the most notable outcome was the legislative program known as the Villaverde stabilization. This program was particularly remarkable because it managed to do what in Spain had appeared to be historically impossible, to balance the budget and produce a series of surpluses, not for a single year, not even five years, but for a whole decade. Moreover, this very dramatic stabilization was not incompatible with maintaining a favorable balance of trade (Prados, 1988, table 5.1A) and coincided with considerable industrial growth, assisted by the repatriation of capital from the lost colonies, a fact that is often mentioned but is difficult to quantify and substantiate (Maluquer de Motes, 1987, pp. 77 ff.).

Unfortunately, this stability did not last very long. The social tensions—some economic in origin, like worker unrest in the cities and above all the growth of anarchism, and others more political in nature, such as problems with Morocco and right-wing radicalism in the military after the defeat at the hands of the United States—in the end destroyed this stabilization policy and shattered the relative equilibrium of the first ten years of the century. After the "tragic week" (1909), the country was caught in a spiral of violence and social polarization that led to the first dictatorship (the short one of Primo de Rivera), to the Civil War, and to the second long dictatorship under Franco. Undoubtedly the immediate cause of the explosion was the problem of military recruitment for the Moroccan war, because military obligations did not fall equally on the various social strata. But the deep causes lay in tensions that industrialization was creating in the cities, especially Barcelona, where the major conflicts occurred. From data in the *Anuario de la Ciudad de Barcelona* one can calculate the number of worker days lost in strikes, which increased in that city from 8,342 in 1905 to no less than 1,784,000 in 1913. Even if we exclude two large strikes in 1913, one which was not industrial but agricultural (33,000 days) and the other simply by virtue of its size (1.3 million days were lost by textile workers, mostly women), that still leaves 451,000 days lost through conflicts in 1913, more than 50 times more than only eight years earlier. The number of strikes had gone from 23 to 41, excluding the two large ones, and the medium length of strike from 6.5 days to 21 days. It seems patently clear that social unrest was on the upswing in Spain's most industrial city.

With incipient industrialization, an exodus from countryside to town was set in motion. It created tensions similar to those that England had suffered a hundred years earlier, caused by the difficult adjustments that a population of rural origin had to make to a different life style: to an urban culture that was hostile and indifferent to personal problems, to the pressure and rhythm of a crowded urban lifestyle, to insecurity in the labor market, in a word, to the conditions that Karl Marx termed "alienation." Politically, the result was the creation of revolutionary groups, which in Barcelona took on markedly anarchist views and exhibited a propensity towards violence. Conservative business groups and government authorities (which in general took the side of the employers) also adopted confrontational attitudes. The violence that erupted in Barcelona in the first third of the century made a powerful impression on the whole of Spain's political life, because it created a climate of irreconcilable hatred and struggle with no holds barred between the social groups which defined themselves simply as either "bourgeois" or "proletarian." This climate of division and hatred spread to other Spanish cities and regions, and in the end contributed substantially to setting the country on the path to the Civil War.

Summarizing then, the first third of the twentieth century was a period of economic growth in Spain. This growth brought with it serious social tensions, as had already happened in England, France, and Germany (to quote the best known cases), and these tensions endangered the fragile political stability of the times. The fear of revolution, no doubt heightened by the Bolshevik triumph in Russia, by the truculent polemics of the Spanish left wing, and by the growing climate of violence, convinced the conservative classes to put their faith in a dictatorial solution. The tensions that growth induced and the fear of revolution polarized a society whose middle class was not numerous enough to successfully moderate the increasing political swings from left to right, which in the early twentieth century were first clearly recognized during the "tragic week." For the right wing, the temptation that dictatorship presented had already been made patently clear in the dictatorship of Miguel Primo de Rivera (1923–1929). After General Rivera's fall, the democratic solution represented by the Second Republic also succumbed, unraveling under the combined assault of the tensions of economic growth, the world crisis of the 1930s, and a further sharpening of political confrontations. The Civil War (1936–1939) became the testing ground, the tournament to determine which institutional framework would rule society during the next stage of growth and transition to modernity. The triumph of the extreme right was pregnant with consequences about the form in which the next stage would evolve. But that next stage was anyway practically inevitable, however much the Civil War and the economic ineptitude of the Franco regime may have imposed delays.

From the economic point of view, the Franco dictatorship comprised two clearly different periods. The first fifteen years saw economic stagnation and only a slow recovery, while the following twenty years saw rapid economic growth, intense industrialization, and profound social change. The first period was one of radical economic interventionism and autarky; the second contemplated a degree of lukewarm liberalization. Assessment of economic management under the Franco regime is extremely controversial. While political repudiation of the dictatorship has been almost unanimous, in the economic field the successes of the second period have led some people to forget the failures of the first and to attribute economic growth, as Franco himself did, to the wisdom of his government. Chapter 16 will discuss in greater detail the economic significance of the Franco dictatorship. Here we shall simply try to give a balanced response to the question posed at the beginning of this section.

To attempt an evaluation of the economic contribution of Francoism, one has to turn to counterfactual history. Would things have gone better or worse with some of the alternative regimes that were possible? Of all the imaginable situations, a democratic regime seems the only likely alternative for the long run, and more concretely a constitutional monarchy. In 1946 this was at the point of being installed, with the help of a group of monarchist generals and U.S. and British governments, effectively duplicating a situation similar to that in Italy at this time, but with a monarchy rather than a republic. A left-wing regime, something like a popular democracy, might have been the consequence of a hypothetical Republican victory in the Civil War, but it would not have been a permanent situation. Invaded by the Axis powers as Spain certainly would have been if a Communist or leftist regime had been in power in 1939, Spain would have been reconquered by the allies, as were Italy and France in the final stages of World War II, and without a shadow of doubt would have followed a political path similar to theirs. In stark contrast to what Franco repeated in tiresome tones for so many years, a democratic regime was in fact the reasonable alternative to his own, not a Communist one. Two sturdy facts support this argument: first, the scant electoral success of the Communist party in Spain both before and after Franco, and second, the case of Italy, where in historical, geographic, and social conditions very similar to Spain, a completely viable democratic regime took root after 1946.

Comparison with the Italian case gives us the true measure of Franco's many claims to economic success. Italy's democracy was compatible with the transition to economic modernity that took place there in the postwar period, and it fulfilled that assignment in a manner that was both less bloody and more efficient than the Francoist regime in Spain. As we have seen, economic growth rates in Italy were constantly above those for Spain during the thirty years that followed World War II, so that by 1975 Italy was surpassing Spain in practically every indicator of socioeconomic well-being, beginning with the most basic and well known, which is income per capita. There is no reason to suppose that a democratic Spain would not have managed to achieve the same gains as did Italy in the same period, by avoiding the monumental economic errors of the early Franco years.

The democratic alternative would have been superior to the dictatorial one in Spain after World War II for at least two reasons. First, because a democratic Spain would have benefited from Marshall Plan aid and from economic cooperation with the rest of Europe, including entry into the European Economic Community, benefits that were prohibited to it because of the Francoist government. Second, a democratic government would have freed the country from extremely costly obstacles resulting from economic policies that were autarkic in nature, interventionist, and xenophobic, policies that were right at the heart of the Franco ideology. These policies cost the country more than ten years of economic stagnation. In Italy and France, after the Second World War, economic reorganization was achieved in some three years. Spain after the Civil War took much longer, between eleven and fourteen years, depending on the measures one adopts.

Hence it seems incorrect to credit Franco with the economic growth that Spain achieved under his domination; rather, his political system was more like an obstruction, a brake upon enterprise in the first period, with only the narrowest of alleys open in the later years. As we shall see, once the driving force of the market system had been grudgingly accepted, all the economic forces of the Franco regime went ahead in their highly restricted way along the rough-hewn pathways defined by the casuistry of interventionism. That the economy did actually grow at all depended upon three important factors. In the first place, despite apparent inertia, the development process was imbued with a latent vitality, the accumulated impetus of decades. In the second place, it is clear that tightly controlled economies have certain advantages if they are prepared to allow market mechanisms some room to operate. These advantages include the certainties, to investors and managers alike, of a labor market that is both stable and tightly suppressed, of an indulgent taxation system, and of a captive domestic market, thanks to protectionism and autarky. But finally we have to recognize the significance of an expanding international economy whose powerful momentum neither the keenest protectionists nor the most retrogressive autarkists were able to contain.

As for the sociopolitical evolution of twentieth century Spain, there is no doubt that the country pursued a different path from that of Western Europe in general, although very similar to that of Portugal and with parallels in Eastern Europe and Germany. Yet the course of events in the Iberian Peninsula, and recently in Eastern Europe, seems to confirm that in the long run, democracy and economic growth follow paths that converge.

CHAPTER 10

Demographic Modernization

Births and Deaths

The trajectory of demographic events in the twentieth century bears a close resemblance to aspects of the course of national income. In contrast to the years before 1900, within the context of Europe Spain showed remarkable demographic vitality in the twentieth century. Table 10.1 presents the principal parameters of Spain's twentieth-century demographic evolution, and Table 10.2 shows overall demographic parameters from 1900 to 1985 for a number of European countries, including Spain.

A simple comparison of the two tables points out a twentieth-century transition to modernity on the demographic front that parallels industrial and economic modernization. To begin with, Spain's population more than doubled from 1900 to 1985, whereas an increase this large had not been achieved in the whole of the previous one hundred years. With close to 40 million inhabitants at the end of the twentieth century, Spain is one of the most populous countries in Europe, though naturally behind Russia, Germany, Italy, the United Kingdom, France, and the Ukraine, with Poland a close follower. With a population density of 77 persons per square kilometer, similar to that of Greece, Spain is among the least densely settled countries in Europe; density is only lower in Russia, Sweden, Norway, Finland, and Ireland. Given the scant average rainfall and corresponding dryness of terrain, this relatively low density can be considered an advantage.

It is well known that the most conspicuous elements of demographic modernization are strong declines in the rates of mortality and fertility, and we shall look at them in more detail a little later. There is, however, a further important conclusion to be drawn from comparing the two tables; in the European context, the lateness of Spain's demographic transition produced certain unusual features. The most notable element is that the birth and death rates, whose decline set in firmly about 1890, declined in parallel fashion, with both falling simultaneously over the same period of years (see Figure 10.1). It is here that the Spanish transition is different, because in Western Europe the onset of demographic modernization in the nineteenth century had been achieved through falling mortality rates that were accompanied by rising birth rates. As a consequence, many European countries experienced very high rates of population growth, with rates sometimes as high as 1% yearly, in many cases over several decades. This happened in England during the first half of the nineteenth century, in Germany during approximately the same period (although for historical reasons the data are of lesser quality), and in Denmark in the second half of the century. The same growth would have been observed in Sweden except for its high rate of emigration. In Spain, on the contrary, birth and death rates began to fall in parallel fashion at the end of the century; the trends of both curves are very similar and show little divergence. In those decades that exhibit

Table 10.1.   Population of Spain in the twentieth century

	(1) Population (in thousands)[a]	(2) Birth rate[b] per 1,000	(3) Death rate[b] per 1,000	(4) Natural increase per 1,000[c]	(5) % Annual intercensal growth rate
1900	18,594	34.3	27.9	6.4	0.44[d]
1910	19,927	33.5	22.9	9.6	0.69
1920	21,303	29.4	24.2	5.2	0.67
1930	23,564	28.2	17.2	11.0	1.01
1940	25,874	20.1	17.5	2.6	0.94
1950	27,977	21.1	10.8	10.3	0.78
1960	30,431	21.4	8.7	12.7	0.84
1970	33,824	19.7	8.5	11.2	1.06
1981	37,617	14.4	7.7	6.7	0.97
1991	39,434	12.0	8.0	4.0	0.47

Average growth rate 1900–1970 = 0.86%
Average growth rate 1900–1990 = 0.84%
a. Excluding Ceuta, Melilla and smaller places
b. Five-year averages
c. Col. 2 minus col. 3
d. Measured from the 1878 census
Sources: censuses and World Bank

Table 10.2. Population growth and other demographic variables in various European countries, 1900–1985

Country	(1) Population (in thousands) 1900	(2) Population (in thousands) 1985	(3) Percentage growth Increase	(4) Percentage growth Annual rate	(5) Crude birth rate in 1985[a]	(6) Crude death rate in 1985[a]
Holland	5,104[b]	14,482	183.8	1.22	12	8
Spain	18,594	38,730	108.3	0.87	13	7
Portugal	5,423	10,198	88.1	0.75	14	9
Italy	32,475[c]	56,945	75.4	0.67	10	9
Sweden	5,137	8,330	62.2	0.57	11	11
United Kingdom[d]	38,338[c]	56,539	47.5	0.46	13	12
Belgium	6,694	9,853	47.2	0.46	12	11
France	38,451[c]	55,133	43.3	0.43	14	10
Germany	56,367	77,781	38.0	0.38	14[e]	13[e]
Ireland	4,459[c]	3,560	−20.2	−0.27	19	9

a. per 1,000 population

b. 1899

c. 1901

d. Great Britain and Northern Ireland

e. German Federal Republic (for Eastern Germany, 10 and 11 respectively)

Sources: Mitchell (1976) and World Bank

the highest rates of population growth, 1920–30, 1960–70, and 1970–80, growth occurred only because mortality was falling faster than fertility. For this reason, within the common European context, population growth in Spain was moderate; in the words of Joaquín Arango, "there was nothing comparable to a demographic explosion," in contrast to what has happened in many countries of America, Asia, or Africa.

Nevertheless, the average population growth rate in Spain, 1900 to 1985, at .87 per 100 annually, was among the highest in Western Europe in this century, and comparable to the highest in the nineteenth century. It is also important to point out that growth accelerated as the century advanced because mortality fell faster than fertility, although in this overall pattern there were some major fluctuations. Thus in addition to the fast-growth decades already mentioned we also find a high growth rate for the period 1930–40, and this in spite of the world Depression and the Spanish Civil War (see Table 10.1, col. 5).

From this perspective then, it is clear that the period from 1940 to 1960 constituted an interruption, a break in the earlier pattern, with causes that are probably sociopolitical in nature. It is worth noting here that although the Civil War was over in 1939, its principal impact came in the 1940s, when average population growth in Spain was close to its lowest since the 1920s. The immediate explanation lies in the extremely high mortality levels and low fertility levels, particularly in the first half of the 1940s. At a deeper level, we must assume that the anomalous rates are a direct reflection of the anomalous social situation (Díez Nicolás, 1985). The dramatic circumstances and the aberrant characteristics of the first years of Franco regime included brutal political repression and shortages of food and other basic necessities resulting from the serious economic errors committed by an autarchic political system, and this alongside of the economic repercussions of World War

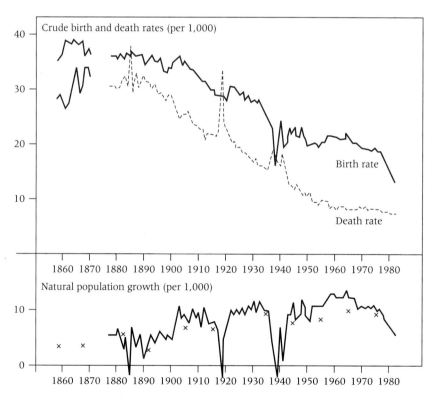

Figure 10.1. Crude birth and death rates and natural population growth in Spain, 1858–1983

II. All these conditions became less harsh in later years, but the recovery, evidently, was very slow.

Another peculiarity of the Spanish demographic transition is that the period of falling mortality and stable fertility did not happen, as in the majority of European cases, at the beginning of the transition, but rather at the end. This is clear from Figures 10.1 and 10.2 and column 4 of Table 10.1, showing that the highest rates of population growth took place in the 1960s and

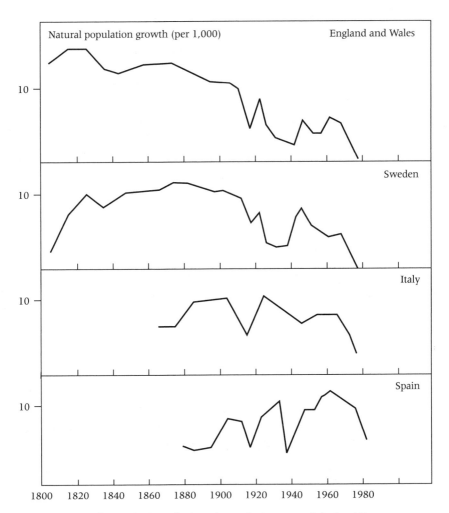

Figure 10.2. The evolution of natural population growth in four European countries, 1800–1981 (per thousand)

1970s. And this presents an interesting parallel with a feature already recognized in other countries in nineteenth-century Europe, the coincidence of periods of strong economic growth and strong demographic growth. It is only the very recent arrival at a relatively mature economic stage that brings Spain to what is generally considered a clear indication of demographic maturity, namely a precipitous fall in fertility (since 1975), and it is worth underlining that this coincides with a third modernization, the political modernization. The birth rate had been falling gradually from its maximum in 1965, but this gentle decline turned into a massive collapse after the death of Franco, a turn of events which continues to bear a certain symbolic message. Today we find fertility almost matched at very low levels with mortality rates, as is characteristic of the mature economies of Western Europe.

Fewer Deaths

The key factor in Spain's demographic modernization in the twentieth century has been falling mortality rates. As in the world at large, this reduction has been achieved *pari passu* with economic and social modernization, processes that are interconnected in intimate and complex ways. The first stages of economic growth usually bring improvements in the availability of the three basic necessities of life, food, clothing and shelter, and these three jointly bear the fruit of better health and thus lower death rates. To these factors, which we might call the private component, we have to add a public contribution, state-engendered improvements in the quantity and quality of public health services such as hospitals, vaccinations, instruction and diffusion of information on medicine and matters of hygiene, public works, and the provision of running water and sewage systems. Most of these improvements were introduced gradually throughout the century, but they were particularly conspicuous early on, because of their novelty. For instance, mortality conditions that were more appropriate for a country under the Old Regime than for a modern nation were cut almost in half by the eve of the Civil War—the crude death rate declined from 2.9 per 1,000 in 1900 to 1.6 in 1935, a striking improvement that is somewhat masked in Table 10.1, which presents five-year averages. The budget devoted to public health measures, very small indeed at the beginning of the century, took three giant steps forward during the early decades, under the "long government" of Maura (1907–1909), during Primo de Rivera's dictatorship, and again during the Second Republic. There can be no doubt about the relationship between this large increase in public health expenditures and the fall in mortality.

The important overall linkage between economic development and improved mortality rates (a feature easily recognized on the international scene) can be proved in the Spanish case from data for particular provinces. Catalonia and the Basque provinces, followed by the community of Valencia, had lower mortality at the beginning of the century, while Extremadura, Andalucía, Murcia, and the two Castiles had the highest mortality indices.

In the second half of the century, in addition to the continuation and extension of public health improvements, the public benefited from the diffusion of new medical techniques, concretely the sulfonamides and antibiotics, along with increasingly important government medical services. In Spain the Social Security system included a large medical component, and the delivery of these new services was facilitated by that important and complex social phenomenon, increasing urbanization. Economic modernization brought growth in the secondary and tertiary sectors of the economy, and these new activities were overridingly urban, with the consequent relocation of workers towards the cities and depopulation of the countryside. In preindustrial economies the cities had much higher death rates than the countryside, but in this period of urban growth, with the benefit of public works policies, sewage systems, paved roads, running water, and health services, the situation was reversed. This phenomenon occurred in Spain at the beginning of the twentieth century, and induced a marked decline in infant mortality—a major component of the death rate—so this was a key element in attenuating mortality in general. And here we have a further example of the close connection between demographic and economic modernization.

All the factors cited above contributed to a major reduction in the incidence and spread of infectious diseases such as small pox, typhus, tuberculosis, influenza, and cholera, which today have virtually disappeared in Spain or appear more as items of curiosity rather than a threat, but at the beginning of the century they caused serious endemic and epidemic mortality. Nowadays the noninfectious causes of death, characteristically cancer and the cardiovascular diseases, have become more important, along with new types of infection like AIDS, and also deaths by violence, characteristically in the workplace or on the highway. It is worth observing here that the prevention of these newly important causes of morbidity and mortality will call for modifications in social behavior rather than additional measures that are strictly medical in nature. I refer to changes in dietary habits and sexual practices, the treatment of drug addiction, and attention to personal security in the workplace and on the roads. In many cases present-day infirmities and risks of illnesses are, in the broadest sense, contracted voluntarily.

Another way of measuring the modernization and well-being of a society is by studying life expectancy at birth, in other words, average longevity. The longevity of Spaniards is another measure that points to spectacular progress, since it doubled in the first 60 years of the century, from 35 to 70 years in round numbers. It has continued to increase to a figure of 76 years today, a figure that puts Spain's average life expectancy among the highest in the world, only exceeded by Japan (the highest at 78 years), Canada, Italy, France, Sweden, Ireland, Norway, Holland, and Switzerland.

Let us examine for a moment fluctuations in the life expectancy at birth. The decade 1910 to 1920 is well known as a period of generally falling life expectancy, as a result of the penuries Spain suffered, albeit a nonparticipating country, during and after World War I. This decline in life expectancy, affecting women as well as men, was fundamentally caused by rising world mortality in 1918 and 1919 from the influenza pandemic, which was followed by a striking improvement in the 1920s, a period of recovery. We find something similar again in the decades of the 1930s and 1940s. Life expectancy stagnated between 1930 and 1940, again for reasons of war, although this time unfortunately the war was Spain's own. The endogenous nature of this feature is clearly reflected in the disparities that emerged between male and female life expectancy. Whereas in World War I the hardships were felt by the Spanish population as a whole (and the effect on life expectancy was similar for males and females), the Civil War reduced the life expectancy for males but not for females, for whom mortality rates continued to improve, although at a more modest rate. We can assume that the strong rebound in the 1940s includes a significant make-up element because, excluding the first decade of the century, this was the only intercensal period when life expectancy increased more for males than for females.

During the second half of the twentieth century economic growth, the general application of public health measures, and the introduction of anti-infection medicines together produced a steadier increase in life expectancy, so that by the beginning of the 1960s the average expectation of life at birth in Spain was comparable to that of the most advanced countries. This progressive trend continued in the following decades, so that Spain today holds joint tenth place in the world classification of nations by life expectancy at birth. At the same time that mortality conditions were improving, an increasing disparity was developing between the sexes, and women (who from the beginning of the modern period at least always held the advantage) increased their life expectancy much more than men. In 1900, when overall life expectancy was 35 years, that for a man was barely 34 years, and for a woman close to 36 years, so that the average Spanish woman lived two years longer than the male, the absolute levels of both mortality regimes betrayed a truly lamentable situation. Half a century later things were much improved and average life expectancy was above 62 years; male life expectancy had taken a great step forward, but measured at a little short of 60 years it was still well below female life expectancy, which was above 64 years. Comparative figures for today show that Spaniards can boast of even greater longevity, and the discrepancy is even greater, 72 years for males and 79 years for females. This growth in excess mortality among males is even more remarkable because it is progressing in relative terms as well. In 1900 the two-year advantage that the woman held over the man represented 5% of the hypothetical average life span, while the 4.5 years difference in 1950 represented 7.3% of the average life span, with a difference of 8% in 1980. In other words, the spectacular increase in longevity that the Spanish population has experienced has benefited women considerably more than men and gives the impression, on the basis of the Spanish case, that increasing life expectancy seems to involve an increase in the differential impact of mortality.

One of the principal causes of this phenomenon, and perhaps the principal one, is not difficult to find. Traditionally, the stronger physical constitution of the female had been offset by the dangers of childbirth. There are clear indications that in the premodern period life expectancy for women was shorter than that for men, specifically for this reason. Progress in modern medicine and hygiene has made this cause of differential mortality disappear, and maternity in advanced countries is today much less dangerous than many other illnesses and surgical interventions. Observe Figures 10.3 and 10.4, which show the evolution of male excess mortality by age. Figure 10.3 shows data for 1900, 1950, and 1980, covering most of the century. Of course excess male mortality diminishes gradually over the life span and almost disappears at age 95. This can be seen in all three curves, but apart from the tremendous change in vertical displacement, which has taken place over the century and represents the growing differential, we can see other interesting variations in the curves that are not always easy to explain. While the curve for 1980 descends smoothly through the whole age range, the pattern for 1900 presents ups and downs which in more moderate form are also present in 1950. The peak at age 20 in 1900 is particularly interesting, and we shall comment upon it a little later. The figures to the left indicate extra years lived by the hypothetical female in comparison with the same-aged male. Thus, the expectancy of life at birth was 6 years higher for females than males in 1980, and four and a half years higher in 1950. Also we can see that by age 50 the female advantage was only one year in 1900, but it had risen to more than four and a half years by 1980.

The degree of excess male mortality tends to decline over the whole life cycle, as we have seen. Figure 10.4 shows data derived from the earlier figure with a different focus; in mathematical terms the curves in Figure 10.4 show rates of change, the derivatives of the three basic curves in Figure 10.3. Thus the rise in excess mortality for males aged 1 to 20 in 1900 is reflected in Figure 10.4 as a decline (an increase is a negative decrement). Basically, Figure 10.4 restates Figure 10.3 in a manner that draws attention to the fluctuations.

The disparities between life expectation for males and females are spectacular and the ups and downs impressive, if somewhat mysterious. Little has

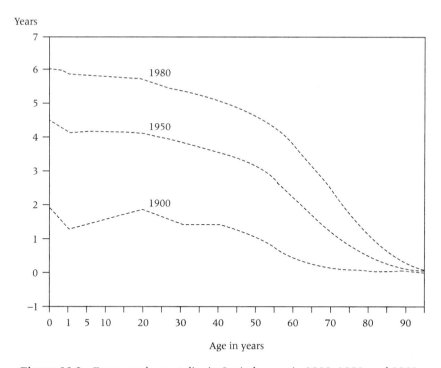

Figure 10.3. Excess male mortality in Spain by age, in 1900, 1950, and 1980

been written about this to date, so we can only offer some suggestions. Evidently, the causes of these differences can be divided into two major categories: natural causes and social causes. It seems beyond dispute that, setting aside the problems of childbirth, nature has made females more resistant and longer-living than males. In Spain, as most modern societies, infant mortality strikes the neonatal male harder than the female, and at that age and in these societies, one can all but totally discard any concern about social causes. In Figures 10.3 and 10.4 the discrepancy diminishes considerably after the first year of life, precisely because of high male infant mortality. In other words, after the first year of life there is not so much difference in the chance of later survival for boy and girl babies. Let us also observe, and this is much clearer in Figure 10.4, that as overall infant mortality declined over time, the tendency for male and female life expectancies to approximate each other has been reduced.

The most remarkable element of the 1900 curve is the increase in excess

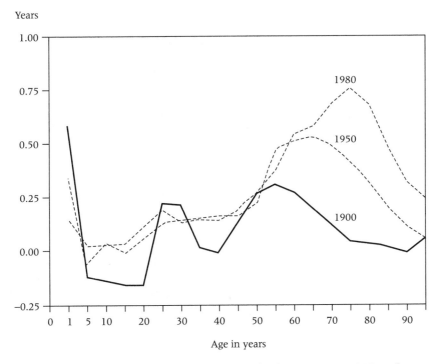

Figure 10.4. The decline in excess male mortality by age, 1900, 1950, and 1980

male mortality in the adolescent period, which makes the risk as high at twenty years of age as it had been at birth. Given that this surprising increase had almost disappeared by 1950, I believe we must assume that the causes were largely social in nature, rather than physical. Without doubt men are more prone to serious and life threatening accidents than women, but I think we also have to consider workplace accidents; child labor must have fallen more seriously upon young boys, in addition, of course, to military service. Very probably the full range of consequences of the war with Cuba in the late nineteenth century must include an impact on male mortality rates in 1900. These factors, which in the early years differentially affected male mortality rates, seem to disappear as the century progressed. Over the years another set of conditions, medical, hygienic, and social, helped to extend female life expectancy by reducing the risks of childbirth (birth rates were falling as well), whereas the slow incorporation of women into the labor force and the "greater work-related risks in jobs that are normally done by men" conspired in great measure to produce this notable increase in excess male mortality. In the words of an important sociological report (Fundación Foessa, 1976, pp. 22 and 24), "excess male mortality stems from the different roles that are assigned to males within Spanish society." Other important socially contributing factors may be the greater tendency for men to use dangerous drugs, tobacco, and alcohol, and their greater proclivity for high-risk, dangerous pastimes, driving automobiles, and playing certain sports, along with the greater participation of males in the more dangerous work activities, including military service.

Fewer Births

Natality has been declining gradually in Spain since the end of the last century, see Table 10.1. Today Spain's birth rate corresponds to its socioeconomic status: a country that is modern and advanced within the world context and in tune with the Western European mode. This is another way of saying that Spain now has a very moderate birth rate indeed, achieved through a very rapid decline in the last twenty years.

What are the factors that explain this decline? Amando de Miguel, with his characteristic sharp wit, ponders how, "being a country that is relatively scantily populated (in European terms) and almost universally Catholic (at least theoretically), [Spain] has arrived at one of the lowest birth rates . . .

without any serious ideological upheaval. These facts have to be explained"
(Miguel, 1977, p. 13).

Our author is right; the fall in the birth rate does need to be explained, but
not in the terms that he sets out, because neither is the case of Spain exceptional among the Catholic countries in Europe (see Portugal, France, Italy,
and Belgium in Table 10.2), nor are high birth rates in the least peculiar to
Catholic countries (the lowest rates in 1900 corresponded to Catholic France
and Ireland, while Holland and Germany, predominantly Protestant, were
producing the highest rates), nor is Spain's low population density out of
line within the European Mediterranean context, bearing in mind the poverty of its agricultural resources. On the contrary, Table 10.2 shows that the
fall in natality in the twentieth century has been a general phenomenon of
both Catholic and non-Catholic countries, although in France and Ireland,
where the rates were low to begin with, the declines have been smaller.

The conclusions that seem to emerge from this summary analysis are,
first, that the introduction of the religious factor does not serve to illuminate
why fertility declined in Spain, but rather adds to the confusion. The second
point is that since the Spanish case is rather similar to that of the other European countries, the factors that have been in operation ought to be rather
closely similar to those operating throughout Western Europe.

Of course there is a correlation between modernization and industrialization and falling fertility rates, but through what mechanism? Perhaps one
should turn first to the Livi-Bacci hypothesis about Spain's rather moderate
fertility rates in the eighteenth century: as in the greater part of Western Europe, the Spanish population knew and utilized primitive methods of birth
control from preindustrial times. Here we include the postponement of marriage or even lifelong celibacy, elementary contraceptive methods during in-
tercourse, and the interruptions of fertility caused by pregnancy and lacta-
tion. It is to be supposed that these practices, traceable in the statistical
record from long ago, surely became more generalized in use during the socioeconomic transition, and above all, during the process of urbanization.

The stimulus that urbanization provides to limit the number of offspring is
well known among sociologists and anthropologists. A child in the countryside represents little charge upon the adults and soon comes to constitute a
useful additional source of labor. In the city, and above all in the modern
city, the child does not usually become productive in the labor force until
puberty or later, and this normally implies a considerable investment in

terms of space, time, education costs, and clothing. In an agricultural community a child can be viewed as an investment; in the urban community a child may be considered, as some North American economists have suggested (Willis, 1974), more as an expensive consumer good. This analysis stands confirmed by the distinct difference in fertility rates, which are generally higher in the countryside than in the town.

The modernization and urbanization processes also brought into play other factors that acted to discourage procreation. Perhaps the most important of these was the tendency for women to move into nondomestic work, which thus reduced the opportunities for procreation as much as the incentive. The spread of education and diffusion of information were also very important. Modernization brought about a massive rupture, a disengagement from the sources of rural cultures and from traditional authorities, a change that favored a rational attitude towards childbirth and towards planning and limiting the number of births.

All the factors cited above refer to the decision to limit the number of births. As for access to the means of effectively carrying out such decisions, the city again provided the better information. But although a great deal has been written and argued about the role of chemical contraceptives in permitting and facilitating birth control, it is patently obvious that the declining birth rate, both definite and widespread as can be seen in Table 10.1 and Figure 10.1, occurred well before the market appearance of the birth control pill. This is interesting because it reveals, at least in respect of these kinds of questions, the primacy of the individual decision over accessibility to the various means available.

This impression is corroborated by the lack of correlation, in recent decades, between the average age at marriage and the birth rate. Logically, in the absence of other factors, early marriage leads to an increase in fertility, and postponement produces a decline. This happens for the simple reason that since the number of fecund years is limited, an earlier onset of sexual relations normally increases the probability of a higher number of offspring. Naturally, in this context, it is the age at marriage of the woman that is important; that of the man is almost irrelevant. Now Figure 10.5 presents data on the age at marriage, 1913 to 1988, for Spanish women, using as a surrogate measure the percentage of all brides who were under 20 years of age, and this is contrasted with the fertility rate. The graph show how age at marriage for Spanish women has evolved in three stages. If we exclude the obvious impact of the Civil War in causing a sudden, short-term rise in the number of young marriages, the general trend from 1913 through to 1957 over the half-century seems to suggest a fall in the percentage of young marriages, from about 10% of brides under 20 years at the beginning of the period to only 6% in 1957. In contrast, the later years show much larger changes, with the young marriages increasing from 6% to about 21% in the short period of 21 years, from 1957 to 1978, and then falling back to 12%, more than a 40% change in 11 years. It appears that a wide range of factors, social, economic, cultural and generational, have affected the age at marriage with different intensity. Excluding the years of the Civil War, both variables, age at marriage and the birth rate, seem to evolve in parallel fashion between 1913 and 1957, and again between 1979 and 1988, but a reverse correlation occurs between 1958 and 1978. One can say, however, that in the long run of the whole twentieth century Spanish women have tended to marry earlier and to have fewer children, further evidence of the supremacy of willpower over other factors.

In total, as Table 10.2 shows, Spanish natality during the twentieth century exhibits a very similar trend to that of other European countries, that is, a century-long decline. The only country that escapes this law is Ireland, for very particular historical reasons. In addition to this general decline, the Eu-

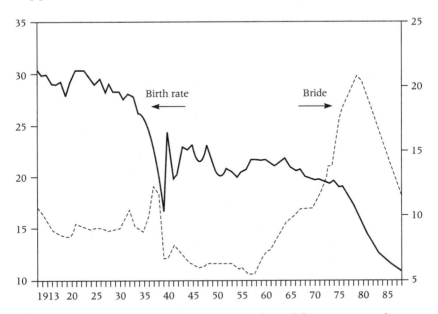

Figure 10.5. The crude birth rate (per thousand), and the percentage of marriages where the bride was under 20 years of age, 1913–1988

ropean rates show another characteristic, that of convergence. Although it is perhaps asymptotical, there seems to be some minimum birth rate, close to 1 per 100, against which all the falling birth curves seem to come to rest; this convergence is due, no doubt, to the homogenization of living standards in Europe.

Looking at Spanish fertility in a little more detail (Figure 10.5), we can identify four stages. The first stage, 1913 to 1940, is a period of sustained decline, moving in this period from about 35 per 1,000 in round figures to about 20 per 1,000, with the fall engendered by the Civil War. The second stage, from 1940 to 1964, displays a steady rate at about 20 per 1,000. From 1965 to 1974 we again see a steady decline, though it is relatively moderate, a fall of less than one decimal point in the decade. In the last stage (1975–1989) we find a steep decline, one which suggests a rate of about 10 per 1,000 by the end of the decade of the 1980s. It seems beyond doubt that even if in the short run improved living standards can bring about an increase in fertility, in the longer haul social and economic modernization has limited the fertility of Spanish women powerfully and permanently, and this has had very little to do with the age at marriage; in other words, the matter goes beyond the purely biological.

Regions and Migrations

The Spanish population has exhibited a century-long tendency to redistribute itself geographically in a centrifugal manner, as we have already seen in Chapter 2. Table 2.4 shows this tendency, which perhaps began as early as the Middle Ages, when the population began to drift from the central Meseta to the coast. The movement has not diminished; in fact it has accelerated, as Table 10.3 indicates. As is generally the case, economic development produced a disproportionate growth in urban centers. But these centers, with the very important exception of Madrid, were located in the coastal regions, and this accentuated the contrast between an interior that was every year more deserted and a periphery that was every year more populated. If at the end of the eighteenth century the central Meseta contained 40% of Spain's total population, the Mediterranean coast and islands a further 40%, and the northern fringe the remaining 20%, the percentages had been modified a century later to the detriment of the center and the north. By 1980 the change has become greatly accentuated because the process has speeded up. The Mediterranean coast and islands now contain more

Table 10.3. Distribution of Spain's population by regions, 1787–1980 (in percentages)

	1787	1857	1900	1930	1950	1980
Andalucía	17.6	18.9	19.1	19.6	20.0	17.1
Catalonia	7.8	10.7	10.6	11.8	11.6	15.8
Valencia	7.5	8.1	8.5	8.0	8.2	9.7
Baleares	1.7	1.7	1.7	1.6	1.5	1.8
Canarias	1.6	1.5	1.9	2.4	2.8	3.8
Murcia	3.2	2.5	3.1	2.7	2.7	2.5
Mediterranean & South Atlantic Total	39.54	43.4	44.9	46.1	46.9	50.9
Asturias	3.4	3.4	3.4	3.4	3.2	3.0
Cantabria	1.3	1.4	1.5	1.5	1.4	1.4
Galicia	13.1	11.5	10.7	9.5	9.3	7.3
País Vasco	3.0	2.7	3.2	3.8	3.8	5.7
North Coast Total	20.7	19.0	18.8	18.2	17.7	17.4
Extremadura	4.0	4.6	4.7	4.9	4.9	2.8
Aragón	6.0	5.7	4.9	4.4	3.9	3.2
Madrid	2.0	3.1	4.2	5.9	6.9	12.6
Castilla-La Mancha	9.0	7.8	7.5	7.8	7.3	4.3
Castilla-León	16.6	13.5	12.4	10.5	10.2	6.9
Rioja		1.1	1.0	0.9	0.8	0.7
Navarra	2.2	1.9	1.7	1.5	1.4	1.3
Center Total	39.8	37.7	36.3	35.7	35.4	31.8
Spain, in millions	10.3	15.5	18.6	23.6	28.0	37.6

Source: censuses

than half of the Spanish population, the central Meseta less than one third, and the north much less than a fifth (Table 10.3).

In clear exception to the centrifugal principle, the most dynamic region has been Madrid. In 1900 there were eight regions with populations greater than Madrid, but by 1980 this was the third largest region, and it had tripled its share of the national total population. Catalonia is the second largest community in terms of total population, and continues to exhibit remarkable demographic dynamism, regardless of the somber predictions of Vandellós (1985). Yet some mild justification for his view lies in the fact that from the mid-nineteenth century and for the next hundred years Cata-

behavior, especially in the demographic variables (birth and death rates), but also in political and cultural attitudes.

Table 10.5 shows the process of urbanization in Spain in the twentieth century, the century in which Spain's population became urban. If we consider as city every agglomeration of 100,000 persons or more, a definition which is certainly not too exacting, then less than 10% of Spaniards were urban dwellers at the beginning of the century. If we were to extend our urban definition to places of 50,000 or more inhabitants, the proportion would obviously exceed 10%, though it would not reach 15%. In other words, we are talking about a very low degree of urbanization in the first years of the twentieth century.

In 1930 the degree of urbanization (at the 100,000 population level) continued to be very low, less than 15%, although it had grown from 9% in 1900, an increase of almost two-thirds. In the next thirty years, however, that rate almost doubled, and the thirty years between 1960 and 1990 saw a further increase of more than 50%. In fact the degree of urbanization seems to have reached a plateau, with very little change in the rates between 1980 and 1990. This may be due to a saturation of the urbanization process itself, or it may stem from the phenomenon of satellite or dormitory cities, places

Table 10.5. Indices of urbanization in Spain: numbers and percentages of inhabitants of towns over 50,000 and over 100,000, 1900–1990

Year	Inhabitants (in thousands) in cities of		Percent of total population in cities of		
	50,000 and under 100,000	100,000 and over	50,000 and under 100,000	100,000 and over	50,000 and over
1900	857	1,677	4.6	9.0	13.6
1910	935	2,054	4.7	10.3	15.0
1920	1,264	2,567	5.9	12.0	17.9
1930	1,276	3,513	5.4	14.8	20.2
1940	1,512	4,972	5.8	19.1	24.9
1950	1,884	6,741	6.7	24.0	30.7
1960	2,442	8,483	8.0	27.7	35.7
1970	2,470	12,489	7.3	36.8	44.1
1980	3,521	15,864	9.3	42.0	51.4
1990	3,774	16,917	9.6	42.9	52.5

Source: calculated from *Anuarios Estadísticos de España*

not included in the great conurbations to which they rightly belong, but which do not separately reach the required size category to be counted as urban. Today we can say that slightly more than 50% of all Spaniards live in cities, two out of every five in a large city, one in every ten in a medium-sized city.

Urbanization is an essential part of modernization, but it is a source of major problems. The cities have to expand physically to make room for newcomers; the process is expensive and often the required investments in infrastructure are not made at the necessary pace. In addition, urban development can bring into conflict people with many diverse interests, creating powerful tensions. In broad strokes, we can characterize the period before the Civil War as a phase of slow and relatively harmonious urban growth. This was so simply because growth was slow, and also because of a political or cultural attitude that was both rationalist and in favor of some kind of planning. Already by the end of the nineteenth century the notion of the Urban Expansion Plan had been generally recognized, a good example being the famous Plan Cerdá for Barcelona, the work of the urbanist Ildefonso Cerdá. Madrid also adopted a planned expansion, although less spectacular and less appreciated. For instance, the Salamanca district was an upper-class residential development promoted by the financier José Salamanca as part of that expansion plan. In the twentieth century the plans characteristically involve new, broad avenues through the old districts of the larger cities, connecting the older districts to the newer ones in an attempt to unify the whole city. This was the aim of the Gran Vía in Madrid and the Vía Layetana in Barcelona, part of an incomplete downtown plan. In the first third of the twentieth century European and American influences began to make themselves felt in Spanish city planning. The influence of public transport and the automobile are fundamental to the plan for Arturo Soria's Linear City, which was built on the outskirts of Madrid in the 1930s.

After the Civil War, Spanish city planning entered a chaotic phase, and it is difficult to know at present whether we have now emerged from it or whether the current slackening of momentum in city growth is simply giving the Spanish urban public a moment to breathe. Unsystematic and speculative construction of horrendous buildings that are badly built, dangerous, and not very serviceable, packed together in zones of particularly fast growth (what happened on the Mediterranean coast is a good example of the worst of this), all this has been one of the very worst legacies of the Franco regime's pro-development stance. This lamentable situation was, of course, aggravated by the rapid city growth of those years, and it is today a very serious problem that such a high proportion of Spain's urban housing stock was constructed under such unfavorable conditions.

Work and Human Capital

The importance of human capital in economic development has been recognized more or less explicitly by economists at least since Adam Smith wrote (1937 ed., bk. l, chap. 10) that "A man educated at the expense of much labour and time to any of those employments which require extraordinary dexterity and skill may be compared to [an] expensive machine." Among contemporary economists, Robert Solow and Theodore Schultz have made perhaps the largest contributions to our understanding of the notion of human capital and how to measure it. By different methods and from different points of view they have made us aware that the greater part of economic growth in North America and Europe in the twentieth century cannot be explained merely in terms of physical capital, and this has led them to emphasize what Schultz defined as human capital (Solow, 1957; Schultz, 1971).

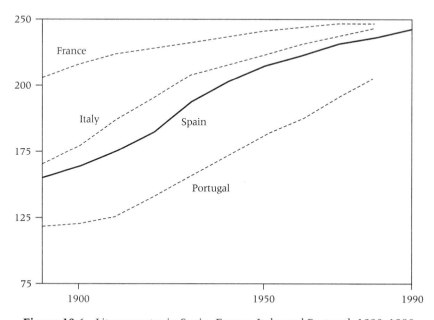

Figure 10.6. Literacy rates in Spain, France, Italy, and Portugal, 1890–1990

Table 10.6. Primary school attendance and literacy in Spain, 1910–1990

Year	(1) Students (in thousands)	(2) Pop. 5–14 years (in thousands)	(3) Percentage enrolled	(4) Literacy rate
1910	1,600	4,419	36.2	49.69
1920	1,950	4,639	42.0	57.12
1930	2,598	4,876	53.3	68.87
1940	3,012	5,501	54.7	76.83
1950	2,791	4,762	58.6	82.66
1960	3,387	5,378	63.0	86.36
1970	4,763	6,250	76.2	91.20
1980	6,788	6,610	102.7[a]	93.64
1990	6,181	5,518	112.0	96.72

Source: calculated from *Anuarios Estadísticos de España*
a. Over 100% includes children older (or younger) than the legal age group

The historical evidence seems to support the conclusions of Solow and Schultz, as we saw already in Chapter 1. Figure 10.6 shows literacy rates in Spain and three close neighbors, France, Italy, and Portugal, indicating what progress has been made and also what differences remain among the four countries. It is interesting to compare this graph with Figure 9.1, a comparison that confirms Sandberg's assertion that literacy rates are good predictors of per capita income in the long run. Although at the end of the nineteenth century Spain was very close to France and ahead of Italy in per capita income, the story was different for literacy, an area in which Spain was clearly less advanced. And in the middle of the next century that is precisely the order for income per capita, with Spain behind both Italy and France. It is also worth observing that the fastest increase in this measure occurred between 1920 and 1930, when Spain achieved its greatest relative advance in literacy (see Table 10.6).

In the decades prior to the Civil War, and particularly in the years of the Second Republic, the government made a serious effort to improve attendance rates for elementary school children, but they were still very low. Typically, in the 1930s, one child out of every two of school age went to school in Spain, while in France the comparable figure was eight out of ten, and in Italy, six (Flora, 1983, chap. 10). But that was not the worst of it; after all, a continuation of the initial effort under the Republic would have raised literacy rates to acceptable levels in a period of ten years. The worst of the story told by Table 10.6 and Figure 10.7 is this; from the time of the Civil War, the level of primary and secondary school attendance remained virtually stagnant for a whole generation. The Franco regime abdicated all responsibility towards the educational effort during more than twenty five years, and that represents an obstacle which even today continues to hold back the nation.

Figure 10.7 shows the number of students in primary and secondary education, from 1925 onwards, as a percentage of the total population; the reason for putting these two categories together is that at various times legislative changes assigned certain age groups to one or the other type of education, so that separate groupings somewhat falsify the story. In particular the reform of Villar Palasí in 1970, which lengthened the primary sector and reduced the secondary, produced the impression that there was a steep decline in secondary education and a correlated increase in primary, but this in no way corresponds to reality. (Because these two groups are combined, the graph does not indicate these complementary changes.) The graph shows a strong educational push in the years of the Republic and a desolat-

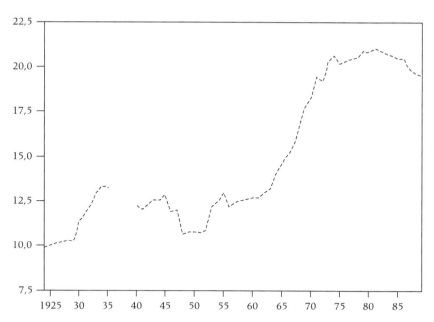

Figure 10.7. Students in primary and secondary schools as a percentage of total population, 1924–1989

ing, complete shutdown under Franco; it is indeed justifiable to call it a lost generation in terms of instruction. Note that the 1935 crude levels of school attendance were not reached again until 1964, almost 30 years later. The consequences of this under-education, I repeat, are still being paid for today. The dramatic decline around 1950 cannot be put down to any major educational change but rather reflects the void left by the Civil War; from 1945 to 1953 we can see the effect of falling birth rates because of it.

The Spanish educational system has tended to be elitist, that is, it has overinvested in higher-level studies to the detriment of the primary sector. Traditionally, although the overall number of students who went to school was low, a large section of those who completed secondary school also went on to university (Núñez, 1992, pp. 291–301). This tendency has prevailed into the second half of the twentieth century, so that while levels of primary school attendance and literacy are lower than those for France and Italy, Spain had, and continues to have, a very similar proportion of university students. As Núñez says "Spain has an educational pyramid with a relatively narrow base and broad shoulders."

Figure 10.8 shows the number of university students as a proportion of

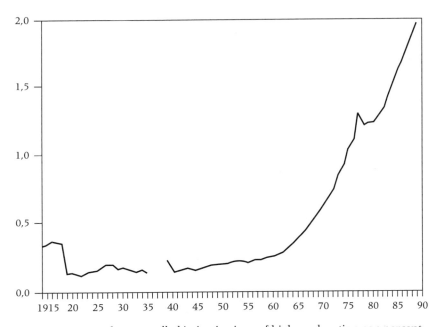

Figure 10.8. Students enrolled in institutions of higher education as a percentage of total population, 1914–1989

Table 10.7.   Working population by economic sectors, 1900–1980 (in percentages)

Year	Agriculture and fishing	Industry	Construction	Transport & communications	Commerce	Other
1900	66.3	11.9	4.1	2.1	4.5	11.1
1910	66.0	11.8	4.0	2.2	4.7	11.3
1920	57.2	17.9	4.1	2.9	5.9	12.0
1930	45.5	21.3	5.2	4.6	7.6	15.8
1940	50.5	17.0	5.2	3.9	7.3	16.1
1950	47.6	19.9	6.6	4.1	9.3	12.5
1960	36.6	23.5	6.7	4.7	8.4	20.1
1970	22.8	27.9	10.5	5.7	15.6	17.5
1980	14.4	26.1	9.8	11.9	22.2	16.6

*Sources: Estadísticas Históricas de España, (*ed.) Carreras (1989), and *Anuarios Estadísticos de España*

the total population; after a long period of slow growth from 1920 onwards, during which the proportion was never far from .25 per 100 (or one in 400), the university explosion began in the 1960s, approximately ten years behind neighboring France and Italy. The proportion today is about 2%, very much as it is in those countries. The relatively high levels the graph indicates at the time of World War I and the rapid fall thereafter are difficult to explain at this time. The slight fall in the years of the Republic seems to me to indicate the healthy political attitude of the era, which was to concentrate educational efforts at the base of the educational pyramid, which produced a relative slimming down in the ranks of the upper reaches. The very high figure for 1939 arises from an influx of war veterans. And the decline in the 1970s and first years of the 1980s indicates the economic crisis that forced a larger proportion of young people to go directly into the labor force.

Finally, Table 10.7 shows the distribution of the workforce among major economic activities. (We will need to look at it again while studying the different economic sectors in the following chapters.) It is worth mentioning here the major about-face that was a consequence of the Civil War and the first period of the Franco regime; deindustralization and the reorganization of agriculture during the 1940s and beginning 1950s are patently obvious. From 1960 onwards the tables are turned: the agricultural population declines rapidly, and the industrial sector grows, only to stagnate later as the process of tertiary growth sets in, a characteristic of mature economies.

CHAPTER 11

Agricultural Transformation:
From Underdevelopment
to Backwardness

As one early observer (1921) noted, Spanish agriculture suffered the ravages of climate and policy alike:

> The geographic factor, then, that Spain is dry, in general terms always favors woody vegetation and is hostile to green growth. . . . To proceed in the opposite direction from what nature calls for, destroying trees and insisting on making Spain only a granary, has resulted in the desertification of such large areas that, if the process were continued, it would convert arid Spain into a true desert of clay, limestone, sand or granite according to the region, but in whichever case eroded beyond repair, shorn and useless for life.[1]

Old and New Policies

In Spain agriculture has traditionally been the object of preferential political treatment because of the quantitative and qualitative importance of the sector. Although its importance declined radically as economic development surged ahead, agriculture continued to receive considerable attention in the twentieth century, and this is not only out of inertia but also because the agricultural sector has retained a political influence disproportionate to its size.

Tariff Protection

As we saw in Chapter 3, the customs tariff was traditionally the principal instrument of agricultural policy, characterized by resolute protection for wheat and other cereals. Above all, wheat was the primary raw material for bread, the staple, the most popular food *par excellence*. In consequence, what we might call "wheat politics" was dominated by two ideas that are basically

267

contradictory: on the one hand, to guarantee a supply of affordable bread, and on the other, to secure suitably rewarding incomes to the wheat growers, the most numerous group in the agricultural sector. Given that this protectionist policy permitted virtual self-sufficiency in wheat, and given that Spain's physical geography was essentially disadvantageous to wheat production, both in comparison with the Americas and even with the countries of northern Europe, the incompatibility of these two major aims is patently obvious. Compared with that of its European neighbors, Spain's bread has been dearly bought, as has been demonstrated by the Grupo de Estudios de Historia Rural (1980, pp. 81–111) and Jordi Palafox (1991, pp. 322–348), among other authors.

The traditional policy of protecting wheat was exacerbated by the crisis at the end of the nineteenth century, which stimulated an increase in tariff rates in a reaction similar to that of many other countries. The 1891 legislation raised the tariff on wheat to eight *céntimos* per kilo, and since the price at that time was about 20 *céntimos* per kilo, the resulting tariff was close to 40% of the price. This degree of protection was maintained in later legislation and augmented further as the peseta gradually depreciated. In 1922, the Cambó tariff increased protection yet again, but when it seemed that rising prices were weakening the protective capacity of even this enormous tariff increase, quantitative restrictions on imports were also introduced. This policy of reserving the national market for national producers, followed continuously (with some variations) throughout the whole of the contemporary period, has been responsible for the survival of some crops and cultivation methods that the free run of a market economy would have reduced or eliminated many years ago. "The agriculturalist in Spain has lost all notion of the market price, and only considers just that price which is determined by the cost of agricultural production imposed by the state" (Perpiñá, 1972, p. 93).

With this inefficient sector graced by such political protection, the inevitable changes that needed to be made (and had been timidly initiated at the beginning of the twentieth century) were essentially held back for forty years. Thus in the period between 1891 and 1935, when enormous increases in agricultural productivity caused the world price of wheat to fall and thereby reduced the amount of land under wheat cultivation throughout Europe, the price of wheat was maintained in Spain, the area under cultivation increased by 40% (see Table 11.1), and productivity increases were only modest. In the words of a group of specialists (GEHR, 1980, pp. 121–122):

> Protection at no matter what cost kept the interior market reserved for some of the most cautious operators, who were not concerned that their production methods were not competitive so long as they had a share in the profits, nor could they see anything wrong with this impossible policy of self-sufficiency. And we use the word impossible because the same prevailing ideas that were intended to isolate the Spanish economy from the rest of the world were creating our backwardness and hence our dependency.

To be sure, this policy was complemented by other components: subsidies for agricultural credit provided by the National Agricultural Credit Service established in 1925; the plans of the Agricultural Reform Act of 1932; water policy; plans for new agricultural settlements; and above all the various policies developed by the National Wheat Service after 1937.

Agricultural Reform under the Republic

When the Second Republic was proclaimed in April 1931, one of most urgent questions to be confronted was that of agricultural reform. The *desamortización*, as we have seen, certainly extended the amount of land under cultivation, thus resolving in a rather elemental manner the pressing problem of food supply in the nineteenth century, but it did nothing to resolve the problem of unequal land distribution. In a country that was largely agricultural and poor, as Spain was at that time, the theme of land ownership seemed to be of the highest priority. The question presented itself with particular urgency in the zones of large landholdings (*latifundia*), broadly speaking the southeast quadrant of Spain including Extremadura, western Andalucía, and La Mancha, areas where some people owned huge properties of thousands of hectares while many peasant families were landless. The heightened expectation that came with political change made it utterly inevitable that some law should be introduced that would begin to resolve the major socioeconomic problem of the day.

There is a tradition of agricultural reform in Spain that goes back to the middle of the eighteenth century; its important figures are Jovellanos and Flórez Estrada; its ideal is that of egalitarian land distribution, with the family farm as the basic unit of production. During the twentieth century, be-

Table 11.1.   Areas under specific crops, 1891/95 through 1985 (in million hectares)

	1891/ 1895	1900	1922	1931/ 1935	1939/ 1941	1949	1960	1971	1985
Wheat	3.2	3.8	4.2	4.6	3.6	3.9	4.2	3.7	2.0
Other cereals	2.6	3.1	3.6	3.8	3.2	3.2	3.0	4.2	5.5
Legumes	0.7	0.7	1.2	1.1	1.2	1.2	1.0	0.8	0.4
Fallow	5.3	6.1	6.5	5.1	4.6	5.1	5.7	5.1	4.1
Vines	1.5	1.4	1.3	1.6	1.5	1.6	1.6	1.5	1.6
Olive	1.1	1.2	1.6	2.1	2.1	2.2	2.1	2.0	2.1
Orchards	0.3	0.3	0.4	0.5	0.6	0.6	1.0	1.4	1.2
Potatoes & onions	0.4	0.4	0.5	0.6	0.6	0.4	0.4	0.4	0.4
Industrial crops	0.5	0.6	0.6	0.7	0.7	0.8	0.5	0.7	1.2
Vegetables	0.1	0.1	0.1	0.2	0.2	0.2	0.2	0.4	0.3
Fodder	0.1	0.1	0.3	0.4	0.4	0.5	0.8	1.1	1.4
Total	15.8	17.8	20.3	20.6	18.8	19.5	20.5	21.2	20.4

Percentages

	1891/ 1895	1900	1922	1931/ 1935	1939/ 1941	1949	1960	1971	1985
Wheat	19.9	21.3	20.6	22.1	19.3	20.0	20.6	17.3	10.0
Other cereals	16.7	18.0	17.9	18.6	17.3	16.2	14.7	19.8	27.2
Legumes	4.4	4.2	5.8	5.5	6.6	6.3	4.8	3.8	2.0
Fallow	33.4	34.2	32.1	24.5	24.5	25.9	27.7	24.0	20.2
Vines	9.2	8.0	6.6	7.6	8.1	8.0	7.8	7.0	7.6
Olives	7.1	6.7	8.0	10.1	11.3	11.3	10.5	9.3	10.0
Orchards	1.9	1.7	2.1	2.4	3.0	2.9	4.8	6.6	6.1
Potatoes & onions	2.4	2.1	2.3	2.9	3.3	2.0	2.1	2.1	2.0
Industrial crops	3.5	3.2	2.7	3.6	3.6	3.9	2.4	3.1	6.3
Vegetables	0.6	0.6	0.4	0.8	1.0	0.8	0.8	1.9	1.7
Fodder	0.9	0.8	1.3	1.8	1.9	2.7	3.9	5.1	6.9
Total	100	100	100	100	100	100	100	100	100

Sources: through 1931/5, *Estadísticas Históricas,* (ed.) Carreras (1989); afterwards *Anuarios Estadísticos de España*

cause of the influence of anarchism and communism, a somewhat confused collectivist agrarian mentality came to dominate the parties of the left. As these two groups became vocal at the advent of the Republic, each was to press elements of its own program that further complicated the task facing the legislators in 1932. And as if this were not enough, we have to add the factor of Spain's heterogeneity; while in the south the problems were those of *latifundia,* in the north the holdings were exceptionally small; Catalonia, meanwhile, was still struggling with the effects of phylloxera. There were also legal disparities, since rental contracts varied a great deal from region to region. In general, social problems were less acute in those regions where tenancies were of longer duration, such as under the emphyteutic contracts in Catalonia or the *foro* in Galicia, and also where small and medium-sized properties predominated, as in Old Castile and the north in general, and in the old Kingdom of Aragón. However, overpopulation in Galicia had seriously aggravated the problem of *minifundia,* while in Catalonia the phylloxera plague had created a serious social problem.

The land problem in Catalonia can be summarized as follows. The emphyteutic leasing agreement (*rabassa morta),* of Roman origin, was an instrument of long historical usage that was very common in the wine-producing areas. It was based upon the concept of a lease that endured for the life of the vines themselves. The renter would enjoy *dominio útil,* use of the farm whilst the vines he had planted survived. By working the land he effectively became owner, but he did not hold title, *dominio directo,* nor could he sell the land. He was obligated to pay the title holder a rent throughout the life of the vines. The lease could, however, be transferred to his inheritors, especially thanks to the disputed practice of grafting new shoots to the old vines (*colgats*) and transplanting. As we already know, the area under vines expanded a great deal at the end of the nineteenth century, stimulated by the destruction of the French wine industry by the phylloxera. From 1890 onward, however, the tables were turned. France recovered while the plague extended its grasp over Catalonia and most of Spain.

The fall in domestic wine prices after the rapid and glorious recovery of the French vineyards naturally motivated the Catalán landowners to look for other, more profitable crops. To this end they were able to benefit substantially from the death of the vines that were damaged by the phylloxera, which permitted them to rescind contracts with renters. In consequence, numerous *rabassaires,* renters under the *rabassa morta* regime, saw themselves dispossessed of lands which they had formerly considered their own.

The hopes of resolving these many and disparate conflicts were centered upon the Agricultural Reform Law (Malefakis, 1971). Given its enormous importance, the Azaña government decided to transact the measure as a Law of the Parliament instead of legislating it by government decree, which several experts had advocated. The parliamentary process complicated even further a measure that was complex enough in itself. The final objective of the law was to settle as many landless peasants as possible on lands that were either public or confiscated or expropriated. But to reconcile the competing interests of the collectivists and those who believed in private ownership, and to resolve the diverse problems of different regions, the legislation had to arbitrate some very complicated procedures which in the end slowed down the process or even obstructed it, eroded the law's popularity, and frustrated the hopes that so many had put in it. To obtain the lands that were to be resettled the law anticipated some confiscations, particularly of large landholdings of noble families, and the expropriation of large holdings above a certain size; the limit was about 250 hectares but varied according to the kind of crop under cultivation. Other sorts of expropriations were also envisaged: lands deemed to be poorly cultivated; lands that had been habitually rented; and even some lands that enjoyed situational rents, for instance parcels located near cities. The law anticipated only the expropriation of arable land; grazing and mountainous terrain was excluded. The particulars and the amounts of indemnification were left in the hands of provincial committees, with final control in the courts, but the first task was to compile a Register of Lands for Expropriation. As a consequence of this casuistic complexity many modest proprietors found themselves subject to expropriation while other large landowners escaped because their lands did not qualify as cultivable terrain.

On the settlement of peasants (based on a Census of Beneficiaries), the reform also permitted a great deal of latitude to the local committees in choosing collectivism or private management. Often a settlement simply consisted of a change of status for the former cultivator, but some of these new settlements needed a good deal of capital investment, especially where the new set-up involved a different kind of undertaking. As a consequence of all these problems, the pace of settling people on the land was much slower than had been hoped. Moreover, the law was only in effect for a short time, since its application was suspended after the elections of 1933. One of the first tasks of the Franco regime, even during the Civil War itself, was to dismantle the Republican agrarian reform and return lands to their previous owners, throwing out peasants and residents of the newly settled agricultural villages (*colonias*), and doing it illegally more often than not (Barciela, 1986b, p. 401–406). Thus we find that although the Agrarian Reform Law confronted fundamental problems and tried to resolve them with impartiality and technical competence, in fact it achieved virtually nothing because of the complexity of its solutions and because it was in operation for such a short time.

Credits, Subsidies, and Pricing Policies

The dire shortage of agricultural credit has been a constant theme of lamentation among politicians and essayists since the time of the Old Regime. The aged and revered institution of the *pósito* (public granary) had shown itself to be insufficient to the task. The creation of the Banco Hipotecario also proved to be disappointing, insofar it focused more on urban properties than on agricultural enterprises. The voices that had been calling for an authentic agricultural bank were still doing so in the twentieth century. The proposals were many, the achievements few. In 1925 the National Agricultural Credit Service was established for the purpose of making loans on favorable terms to modest farm operators. It was not strictly speaking a bank (and thus its name) but rather an office dependent upon the Ministry of Development *(Fomento)*, which at that time included the Ministry of Agriculture. Although complicated procedures and scarce resources limited the efficiency of the enterprise, it continued in operation until it was converted into the Banco de Crédito Agrícola in 1962. During the twentieth century various other groups came to specialize in agricultural credit: savings banks, rural banks, and credit cooperatives, in addition to private banks whose branches have, little by little, reached into agricultural areas. These institutions have been able to count on the support of the Agricultural Credit Bank, most of whose loans have been channeled through these various collaborating units, in particular the rural savings banks.

True, the question of agricultural credit does pose some difficult problems, which explains but does not justify the traditional disadvantage in terms of credit accessibility that Spanish agriculture has suffered until very recently. These difficulties consist of high transaction costs and high risk factors. High transaction costs are rooted in the wide geographic range of operations, which makes it difficult to gather the information that is indispensable when credit is to be granted. Branch banks are generally established in urban areas because they can reach more people this way; low rural population density is a serious hindrance to the creation of banking services in the villages, yet from a town it is very often difficult to be well informed about the issues of a particular rural economy. Moreover, however much information may be available nowadays, and despite progress in meteorology, it is still impossible to predict natural catastrophes and calamities, which invariably have localized impacts, so it is very difficult to achieve an adequate diversification of risk in agriculture. To minimize these problems we need a scheme with two essential features: a national plan capable of withstanding the inherent risk factors, plus a private network of agricultural credit able to overcome the information problems. These requisites—a nation state that is rich enough to withstand the possibility of catastrophic losses, and an agrarian private sector capable of generating a financial network—presuppose a certain degree of economic development. Thus we find ourselves in one of those frequent economic vicious circles, whereby to achieve further development it is necessary to have already achieved a certain amount of development.

And this is exactly how things have turned out for Spain; the problem of agricultural credit has been gradually resolved at the same time that economic development has been moving ahead. After centuries of scarce agricultural credit, in the central decades of the twentieth century the official organs of credit, including the Bank of Spain, made financial resources available for the growing capital necessities of an agricultural sector that was every day becoming more technically advanced. In the last third of the century, private banks along with savings banks and rural banks have been increasingly fulfilling the role formerly played by "official credit." As agriculture has modernized, savings rates have increased, encouraging the creation of cooperative and rural savings banks as well as rural branches of private institutions and savings banks. And if initially these financial networks began by drawing capital away from agricultural areas towards other sectors, the modernization and capitalization of the countryside starting in the 1960s turned the agricultural sector into a net importer of capital.

But the chief protagonist in the area of agricultural politics in the central decades of the twentieth century, if not exactly the hero of the piece, has been the National Wheat Service (Servicio Nacional de Trigo, SNT) created by the Franco regime right in the middle of the Civil War, August 1937, at the critical moment of the first symbolic harvest of National Spain.[2] The purpose of the SNT was to intervene in the wheat market, but it soon extended its orbit of operation to include cereals and vegetables, thus decisively controlling much of Spain's agricultural sector. The SNT indeed represents the culmination of a growing interventionist trend within the Spanish state, both in the wheat market and in so many other markets, a trend that reached its zenith in the Franco regime of the 1940s with disastrous consequences. Already in the 1920s the wheat tariff policy had been considered insufficient, and the government resorted to more energetic expedients such as price fixing and state control of foreign trade in cereals. This policy had produced successive maladjustments. The reason is clear: state intervention, subject to all kinds of pressures, aggravates rather than remedies market inefficiencies. Obviously, there are cases where some state intervention, administratively neutral and scientifically applied, may be justified, as when inelasticities of supply and demand provoke tremendous price oscillations and on occasion even revolutions and riots.[3] To avoid these oscillations the state can play a stabilizing role by fixing maximum and minimum prices, buying when the market reaches the bottom, and selling when it goes over the top. The problem lies in deciding what those prices should be. If they are fixed too high, one runs the risk of chronic oversupply; if they are too low, there will be a deficit. The behavior of the SNT illustrates these simple arguments perfectly.

The SNT came into being under the assumption that Spain was self-sufficient in wheat, and that there was a danger of excess supply. For more than a decade, the wheat market had suffered serious maladjustments because of a series of erroneous interventions during the Primo de Rivera dictatorship and even during the Republic itself. After the wheat shortage of 1931, two good harvests followed in 1932 and 1934, with strong price fluctuations which produced alarm and protest, alternately from the public and the agricultural producers. Once the Franco regime took power, it decided to demonstrate the superiority of its own methods and carried intervention to extremes, very much in line with its interventionist ideology. The SNT, within the Ministry of Agriculture, would work out the prices at which it would buy the whole of the grain harvest, which it would later sell, as a monopolist, to the flour manufacturers. Foreign trade in grains was also in the hands of the SNT. Fearing overproduction but at the same time wishing to provide the Spanish population with cheap bread, the SNT fixed the buying prices very low. The consequences were what should have been expected, and harvests were lower than anticipated. The agricultural producers preferred to produce crops that were not controlled. Faced with this situation, the SNT turned its attention and intervention to more and more agricultural products, until all the cereals and legumes were included; they even went as far as to include birdseed! The harvests of all these controlled crops declined, leading to an alarming situation of shortage. History remembers the 1940s as "the hungry years" in Spain.

Figures 11.2 and 11.3 show the impact of the SNT on cereal production. The harvests of wheat and corn were below prewar levels until well into the 1950s. In the decade following the Civil War, wheat production per capita was reduced to two-thirds of what it had been before the war. The Franco government blamed the situation on the "persistent drought" and instituted the sadly infamous ration books, *cartillas de racionamiento*. The scarcities were palliated by some imports and the "black market." Importing food turned out to be both expensive and difficult in the midst of the world war in which the Franco regime was allied with the Axis powers. The blockade after the war presented the regime with a particularly difficult food problem, a situation that was salvaged in 1947–48 by the agreement with Argentina, the great provider of those years, whose dictator Juan Perón was an ideological sympathizer of Franco.[4] As far as the black market was concerned, it was well known and even tolerated; according to what people said at that time in Spain, it was corruption that made the dictatorship tolerable. So a large part of the harvest was sold illegally, and turned up clandestinely on the fringe of the retail bread market. In those years, tobacco and loaves of bread were sold in the street, illegal but ubiquitous.

It is difficult to understand the obstinacy with which the Franco regime clung, for more than a decade, to a policy that was so utterly out of line, and even more difficult when we learn that some of the scheme's directors were themselves aware of the causes of the disaster. One underlying cause was the political inertia of a regime that was profoundly conservative in nature, compounded by the arrogant resistance of those who enjoyed flaunting their power against any suggestion that they might admit their errors—a tendency Guillén de Castro had satirized in *Las mocedades del Cid*:[5]

> The first and proper thing [for the powerful],
> Strive always to be right;
> But if you guess it wrong
> Defend, don't budge, sit tight.

This is all the more applicable when the victims of bad decisions are without political representation. In addition, there was fear afoot, a fear of aggravating a serious inflationary situation, a fear of provoking even greater discontent while the price of bread was rising.[6] And finally, the policy was supported by the satisfied landowners who benefited most from the situation by supplying the black market, thanks to their political influence and economies of scale in clandestine transportation and distribution.

Even so, the guidelines were shifting a little during the 1950s; the situation was improving; there was a slow but broad change afoot on questions of economic policy. Minister of Agriculture Rafael Cavestany, "a man of broad technical knowledge and energetic in character [with] experience as an agri-

cultural entrepreneur and . . . fully conscious of the inefficiency of the intervention system," was the chief agent of change (Barciela, 1987, p. 265). The
work Cavestany did was not exactly revolutionary; he simply freed various
products from the iron hand of the SNT and established a more realistic price
system for the products that remained controlled, especially wheat. The
slow and partial normalization of Spain's world political situation also
helped, in particular its entry into several international organizations and its
agreements with the United States, which improved access to imports in
years of scarcity. Such years, however, were now rare, because prices that
had been fixed below the equilibrium level were transformed into prices
above the norm, and this turned the problem on its head. Already by the
end of the 1950s surpluses began to appear, and in the 1960s they turned
into a serious embarrassment. From a policy that claimed to defend the consumers (and starved them), the government switched to a policy that subsidized wheat production. One error had been replaced by another, and
further aggravated by a decline in bread consumption, inevitably brought
about by rising incomes and standards of living. The political power of the
wheat lobby kept the buying price high for a product whose demand was
falling and whose cultivation competed with animal feed, a product that was
in increasing demand as the consumption of meat and milk products rose.
The cost of storing unsold grain added to the ruinous policy of subsidized
prices that were far higher than the world market. And foreign sales, of
course, were still in the hands of the SNT. Caught in a lamentable paradox,
Spain was forced to export wheat at a loss and import cereals and stock feed,
also at a loss.

The cost of subsidizing wheat prices has been calculated by Barciela
(1981b). It was an enormous cost. The purchase, at excessive prices, of a
product that was then either stored or sold at a loss was a wasteful extrav-
agance that put the SNT into chronic deficit. The deficit was absorbed
through loans from the private banking system, chiefly from the Bank of
Spain, which was the final destination of promissory notes issued by the
SNT. The organization also found itself obliged to finance the construction of
a network of silos, since the excess grain had to be stored somewhere. It also
made subsidized loans to agricultural producers and sold fertilizers and seed
at low prices. All this was paid by loans from the Bank of Spain, loans which
the bank was obligated to grant and in such quantity as to seriously affect
the bank's discretion and independence in the field of monetary policies.
Thus in the 1960s nearly 20% of the increase in banknotes issued by the

Bank of Spain resulted from the debt-ridden position of the SNT. Credits to the SNT represented about 10% of the total amount of bills in circulation, and the debt the SNT owed to the Bank of Spain at the end of 1968 represented nothing less than 1.8% of the national income for that year (income figures from Alcaide). The economic cost of this policy was enormous, by any measure exorbitant. In 1967 the SNT had become the SNC (C for "cereals"), and in 1971, after 34 years in business, it was further transformed into the Servicio Nacional de Productos Agrarios (SENPA), with less well-defined functions and powers. After more than three decades, the tenure of a state agency whose errors were absolutely monumental was drawing to a close. These errors—essentially a policy of low prices in years of scarcity and high prices in times of abundance—were paid for by the immense majority of Spaniards, while just a few benefited tremendously from the system.

Nor did state intervention in agricultural markets end there. The SENPA continued to buy up wheat under a monopoly regime. Later, from 1984 onwards, in conjunction with the FORPPA (Fund for the Ordering and Control of Agricultural Products and Prices) created in 1968, the group continued to subsidize the production of wheat and fix minimum buying prices, although it was no longer a monopoly buyer. At this point agricultural producers were no longer obligated to sell to the SENPA though they might choose to continue to do so. Undoubtedly they would do so if the market price fell below the SENPA price, which thus became a minimum or "support price."

The Politics of Water, Settlement, and the Consolidation of Fragmented Land Holdings (Concentración Parcelaria)

The Republican agricultural reform, which had been moderately radical insofar as it envisaged modifications in the property regime through expropriations and confiscations, did not get a chance to be implemented: we shall never know whether those changes would have been viable in the long run in a climate of peace. Another kind of agricultural reform, the so-called "technical" reform, which aimed to improve the rural situation without changing the ownership structure, was put into motion in different versions, with greater or lesser success, during the whole of the twentieth century. The water policy was perhaps the most successful and spectacular. The reasons for success are obvious: in a country as harsh and dry as Spain, a conversion to irrigation obviously represents a remarkable step ahead.

To the outsider it might seem obvious that some kind of water policy would be utterly necessary, but such a policy was slow to evolve and even slower to put into practice. Although some nineteenth-century thinkers and politicians argued that it was necessary to increase the amount of land under irrigation (Jovellanos had said so as early as the end of the eighteenth century), the great leaders who were finally, in the early twentieth century, able to forge a public consensus on the need for a national program for reservoirs and irrigation were Joaquín Costa and Ricardo Macías Picavea (Ortega Cantero, 1984). The development of hydroelectricity during that period, in Spain as in many other countries, undoubtedly helped to sway public opinion. Expensive construction of dams and reservoirs could be justified on two counts, the production of electricity and the extension of irrigable land, with a happy complementarity that both processes would help modernize the countryside and improve peasant life. But in addition to favorable public opinion, the necessary capital would have to be found for tasks of such great scope, along with a coordinated plan of action which would avoid duplications and waste. All these factors point to the need for state action, but before the Civil War the issue was frustrated by the slow pace at which the ideas of the hydraulic interventionists were able to gain ground, and by continuous political instability. The first attempt to carry out an integrated plan of action was the creation of the Hydraulic Confederation in 1926, with the object of tackling problems by focusing on each complete river basin. The realization of a project of this breadth had achieved success and notoriety in the United States in the 1930s; the Tennessee Valley Authority, which carried out an integrated program in the Tennessee River basin, set in motion a scheme to control flooding, to extend irrigation, to facilitate new settlements, and to produce electricity. In Spain, however, the achievements of the Hydraulic Confederations in these matters were few and far between.

Planners soon came to realize that extending the amount of irrigated land would affect the regime of exploitation (Torres, 1956, chap. II, and Benelbas, 1989, pp. 200 ff.). Irrigated lands allowed greater subdivisions of properties and there was a popular saying that "irrigation dissolves *latifundia*";[7] it is no surprise, therefore, that the irrigation policy met with resistance from many large landowners. Perhaps the first law that attempted to combine the extension of irrigation with new settlements was the *Ley de Obras de Puesta en Riego* (OPER, 1932, the Law on Extension of Irrigation), whose short life limited what it could achieve, although its ideas survived. The same can be said of the Manuel Lorenzo Pardo's *Plan de Obras Hidráulicas*, drafted with a national focus, whose major innovation, later to become so polemical, was the drawing off of water from surplus areas to the benefit of zones that were chronically in deficit. Progress was slow, and in the end most of the reservoirs were not built until the second half of the twentieth century. This was, however, a very important public works program, probably the best economic success of the Franco regime. Working with ideas about water economics that had been developed in an earlier period, the plan could draw upon the resources and construction capacity of an authoritarian state and could also benefit from the greater investment possibilities that derived from a rising national income. Between 1940 and 1970 Spain's reservoir capacity increased tenfold, from 3.6 to 36.9 million cubic meters. By 1987 capacity had increased further to 42 million cubic meters. The amount of irrigation did not increase to the same extent. Land under irrigation went from 1.4 million hectares to about 2.2 million hectares in 1970 and 3.1 million in 1987, which is to say that it doubled and a little more, in 47 years. Of course, in a mountainous country such as Spain it is easier to dam up water than to convey it to suitable thirsty land. Even so, the increase in land under irrigation represents very important progress. The irrigated area went from 7.4% to the total in 1970 to 15.3% in 1987. This doubling in the proportion of irrigated land is one of the keys to understanding the agricultural growth of these years.

The water policy had a logical complement, a settlement policy that was based on the premise of giving land to peasants without taking it from anyone. That task should of course be part of a radical land reform, because it is ultimately a question of settling farmhands on the land and making them into small proprietors. But if land reform often seems to amount to robbing Peter to pay Paul, the attempt to create brand new settlements tries to pay Paul without taking from anybody. Where, then, might these lands come from? The normal way would be land improvement: characteristically, land that was formerly barren or not used would be brought into production by means of an irrigation point (which is what the OPER, cited earlier, had proposed), or rehabilitated by a highway, by new settlements, or by reclamation of former swamps, for example. It could be public land or lands that were bought from their owners, not expropriated. The politics of colonization was thus a conservative agricultural reform, but whatever one's political credo may be, no one should object to something if it works well (as Chinese Communist leader Deng Xiao Ping said, "it doesn't matter what color the cat is, so long as it catches mice"). However, to be truly effective, the policy of colonization in Spain ought to have gone hand in hand with the extension of irrigation; otherwise, the newly settled peasants would get only marginal land and skimpy allotments. This is what had happened during the successive colonization legislations of the first half of the twentieth century, beginning with the law introduced by González Besada in 1907. But with the rapid growth of irrigation in the 1950s, developing the *colonias* acquired certain importance. However, to put it bluntly, the ambitious plans of the National Colonization Institute (created in 1939) simply failed to come to fruition in the 1940s; the number of peasants settled was very small, and even more modest were the size and quality of the lands that were made over to these settlements (Barciela, 1986b, p. 408). In contrast, because of the newly irrigated territories, the settlement of peasants in the 1950s and 1960s was much more extensive.

Another aspect of the conservative "technical agricultural reform" was the rearrangements of small plots (*concentración parcelaria*). While the issue of large and small landholdings had attracted more political attention, the fragmentation of properties, which is politically neutral, could be more important economically and constitute a major obstacle to growth. In the Castile-León region, for example, the smallest agricultural property that could make a medium-size tractor profitable was about 45 hectares, and the average size of property in this region was 35 hectares, although two-thirds of the land belonged to properties of about 60 hectares. This may seem to be more or less adequate, but it turns out that the average size of an individual parcel of land in this zone in the 1950s was a mere .6 hectares. That means that the average proprietor with 35 hectares of land, had about 60 diminutive, scattered plots, which made cultivation itself, never mind mechanization, almost unfeasible. In Spain as a whole, in 1960, the average number of plots per owner was 14, the highest in Europe (Simpson, 1993, p. 397).

The cooperative is one remedy for this kind of situation, but Iberian individualism and lack of state support has made Spanish agricultural cooperation into a pallid reflection of what it is in other European countries.[8] The concentration of plots began in the 1950s (the first law dates from 1952); it is a complicated procedure through which a state agency manages, at the request of interested parties, the grouping together of plots by means of exchanges and agreements, a lengthy administrative process in all. The drawback of the process as it has been carried out in Spain is that the result, however positive, has been insufficient. The plots, although larger, still remain small. In the case cited earlier, of Castile-León, the average size of plot went from .6 hectares to 4.6, still far below the required minimum size for mechanization. So although from the outset of the program until the end of 1986 the impressive figure of 5.6 million hectares has been "concentrated," and that is more than one-quarter of the cultivated land in the whole of Spain, the problem of excessive fragmentation continues to present a serious obstacle to agricultural modernization.

Evolution and Growth

Over the long period, of course, substantial changes are evident. The data on agricultural production[9] (see Table 11.2 and Figure 11.1) show vigorous growth during the twentieth century. In real terms, agricultural production increased by 2.07% per year between 1901 and 1983 (see Table 11.3), becoming 5.4 times larger; in terms of production per capita the increase was

Table 11.2.   Agricultural output, productivity, and yields, 1900–1980 (at 1910 prices)

Year	(1) Output[a]	(2) Productivity[b]	(3) Yield[c]	(4) Agricultural output as % of GDP
1900	4,408	846	247	35
1910	5,392	1,050	281	35
1920	6,688	1,446	314	39
1930	7,540	1,843	359	29
1950	7,880	1,472	404	31
1960	15,754	3,354	723	21
1970	18,984	6,416	916	11
1980	24,503	14,532	1,256	7

a. Entries are in millions of pesetas at 1910 prices; except those for 1900 and 1950, they are nine-year averages

b. In 1910 pesetas per worker

c. In 1910 pesetas per cultivated hectare; the 1920 figure quoted is actually for 1922; that for 1930 is actually for 1931

Sources: cols. 1–3 calculated from *Grupo de Estudios Rurales* (1987) and *Estadísticas Históricas,* (ed.) Carreras (1989); col. 4 from Prados (1993) and Baiges, Molinas, and Sebastián (1987)

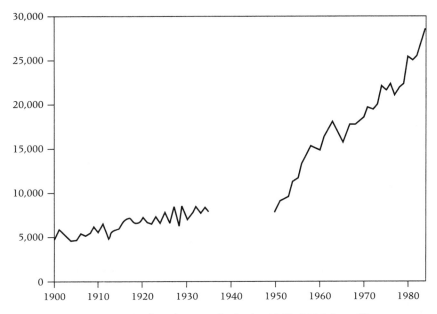

Figure 11.1. Gross agricultural output in Spain, 1900–1985 (in million pesetas at 1910 values)

Table 11.3. Rates of growth of agricultural production, 1901–1983 (calculated on three-year averages)

Period	Absolute growth	Per head
1901–1983	2.07	1.18
1901–1934	1.34	0.53
1934–1951	0.63	−0.22
1951–1983	3.61	2.62
1934–1983	2.56	1.63

Source: calculated from Table 11.2

1.18% per year, which is 2.6 times larger than in 1901. The growth was much more rapid, both in absolute and per capita terms, in the second half of the century than in the first, as can be appreciated from a brief glance at Figure 11.1. Concretely, the rate of growth per capita was almost five times higher in the period 1950–1983 than from 1900 to 1934. Nevertheless, agricultural production grew much slower than national income, which happens in almost all countries during industrialization. This produces the phenomenon which is reflected in column 4 of Table 11.2, and which we can identify as the progressive relative shrinkage of the agrarian sector, a shrinkage which is evident not only in the proportion of national income produced by agriculture, but also in the proportion of economically active population so employed. This reflects changes in both supply and demand. In the first place, the demand for food grows less than proportionally to the growth of income (Engel's Law), and secondly, as productivity rises and given that the market is limited, the demand for agricultural labor grows slowly; indeed, it may decline.

We can also calculate measures of productivity. One very simple measure can be formed by dividing agricultural income by the number of agricultural workers, although unfortunately we are not able to separate out and exclude the manpower occupied in fishing (col. 2, Table 11.2). However coarse the measure may be, the trend is very clear: the period 1900 to 1930 saw increases that we can term modest: productivity doubled in those years, which is the equivalent of an annual growth rate of 2.26%. From 1930 to 1950 labor productivity fell, as a result of the Civil War and the first phase of the Franco regime policies. Between 1950 and 1980 the changes were spectacular. In thirty years productivity increased tenfold, which is the equivalent of an annual rate of 8.11%. Growth in the 1970s was particularly notable: productivity increased almost 2.5 times, an annual rate of 9.17%. This growth spurt is all the more extraordinary since it came on the heels of earlier decades of strong growth, and at a time of crisis in the industrial and service sectors. (On this growth see Pérez Blanco in PEE 16 and comparative calculations by P. Fraile, 1991.)

All these results, of course, go *pari passu* with heavy capitalization in agriculture and a tremendous rural exodus (Table 11.4, col. 1). This exodus began rather timidly in the first third of the century; the agricultural working population fell from 5.2 million in 1900 to 4.1 million in 1930. The trend was reversed between the Civil War and 1950, and by then the working rural population stood at 5.4 million, surely the highest figure in the history of

Spain. The enormous decline in manpower sets in the second half of the century; according to Roser Nicolau in *Estadísticas Históricas,* by 1980 agriculture was employing only 1.7 million workers. Parallel to the capitalization of agriculture, a process of "dehumanization" was also going on.

The growing capitalization of Spanish agriculture is described in every recent work,[10] and shown in Table 11.4. The number of tractors increased from 4,000 to 611,000 between 1932 and 1984 (over 150 times more in 52 years). In this same period harvesting machinery in use also multiplied by a similar figure. The use of artificial fertilizers per hectare increased sixfold. In the case of fertilizers the measure is very crude, simply the sum of nitrogen, phosphates, and potassium, but it is a very eloquent indicator (Gallego's figures for 1980 are a little higher than those given by Barciela). And correlatively, as shown by García Delgado and Muñoz Cidad (1990), the consumption of energy per hectare also grew a great deal, almost quadrupling between 1964 and 1984, a growth rate equal to that already reported in the number of irrigable hectares and those with sprinkling capacity. Naredo (1986) has shown that the agricultural sector changed from being a strong exporter of capital during the first twenty years of the Franco regime, to being a net importer of capital after 1970.

Table 11.4.   Indicators of capitalization in Spanish agriculture: manpower, machinery, and fertilizers, 1907/8 through 1984

Year	(1) Numbers of workers in thousands	(2) Harvesting machines	(3) Tractors	(4) Fertilizers[a]
1907/1908	5,158.4	—	—	5.5
1932	4,090.0	335	4,048	17.1
1945	5,070.3	—	59	7.9
1950	5,353.5	—	12,798	17.3
1955	5,025.0	942	27,671	29.4
1960	4,696.4	5,025	56,845	36.9
1970	2,958.7	31,596	259,819	72.1
1980	1,686.1	41,568	523,907	102.7
1984	—	44,686	611,433	90.7

a. Kilograms per hectare of phosphate, nitrogen, and potassium fertilizers

Sources: Estadísticas Históricas, (ed.) Carreras (1989), and Gallego (1986b); some figures are averages and others are arrived at by linear interpolation

Although the data available will not allow us to estimate a production function for the period before 1964, it is clear that the growth of agricultural income was possible because of an increase in capital inputs and a reduction in manpower. This last assertion, however has to be qualified on two points. Whether measured in terms of active workers or in hours worked, labor inputs were certainly reduced by more than two-thirds between 1950 and 1980; if we were to measure labor inputs in constant pesetas, this reduction would be much less, because real agricultural wages increased as the number of workers declined. Something rather similar would occur if we were to weight worker contribution by some kind of index of quality. In distinction to his predecessors, the agricultural worker of the most recent decades is not only fully able to read, but also competent to use those new agricultural and business techniques that are implied in Table 11.4: complex machinery, new irrigation systems, agricultural chemistry, adaptation to market conditions, and above all the decision-making capacity to choose well within this new universe of technical strategies. This real increase in the human capital component in agriculture has been achieved despite the other major phenomenon indicated by investigators: the aging of the peasant population.

What has been the motive force behind this rapid agricultural growth? I know of no rigorous study on this very important topic but it seems clear that the process has occurred following the lines described in the well-known Arthur Lewis model. According to this bisectoral model, in a semi-developed economy two sectors coexist side by side: one modern and the other a subsistence sector. In both sectors salary levels are determined by the respective marginal product of labor. In the subsistence sector, where there are large pockets of disguised unemployment, the marginal product of labor is zero, and the salary will be the minimum living wage. Traditional agriculture is the most typical case of a subsistence sector. According to Lewis (1955), as the modern sector grows, its demand for labor increases and salary levels rise; productivity in this sector is high and rising, and this draws off labor from the subsistence sector to the modern one, a transfer that will depend upon the rate of growth in the latter. These transfers, or rural exoduses, will go on raising the cost of labor in the subsistence sector, where productivity will continue to rise as disguised unemployment is reduced. When it finally disappears, salary increases will be more rapid and it will then become advantageous to replace labor by substituting machinery and by other innovations that increase productivity, for example irrigation and fertilizers. In this manner, stimulated by growth in the modern sector, the subsistence sector as such will in the end disappear, blending into the other sector. This is what seems to have happened to Spanish agriculture in the twentieth century. The process was already under way in the first decades; the Civil War and the first period of Franco's control caused an interruption and some retrenchment, but, as we have seen, growth was renewed and took off at a powerful pace in the second half of the century.[11]

To be sure, this growth has been achieved through important structural modifications. Neither the structure of output nor the pattern of consumption remained constant during this evolution. These structural changes came as much from supply factors as from demand factors. On the supply side, as agriculture became commercialized and technologically more sophisticated, the peasants grew more produce for the market and less for home consumption. In producing for the commercial sector, the peasant stopped growing subsistence items; his production became more flexible and he adapted himself to market conditions and to his own natural comparative advantages of production. Typically in a country like Spain the peasant will produce less cereals and will turn towards horticultural products, fruit growing, and stock farming. This trend will be reinforced by demand factors: as the standard of living of consumers rises, their demand, under the effect of Engel's Law, will be directed towards foodstuffs that are highly income-elastic, items such as meat, fish, milk products, fresh vegetables; relatively speaking, traditional subsistence goods like cereals and legumes will be abandoned. The consumption of bread cereals has been reduced by one-half between the prewar period and today, from more than 150 kgs. per person per year to about 75 kgs. And it is a happy circumstance that Spain's comparative agricultural advantage has tended to coincide with rising demand for items that are highly income-elastic.

Figure 11.2 shows this change in productive structure very clearly. After the tremendous depression of the 1940s, wheat production has remained at about the prewar level in absolute terms, some 4.5 million tons annually, although in fact production per capita fits better to a bell curve, increasing in the 1950s and 1960s as a consequence of the subsidy policy through the SNT, and diminishing in the 1970s and 1980s in response to falling demand and a policy that was a little less irrational. Without persistent protection on the part of Spain and the European Community alike, the wheat harvest would be much smaller, bread would be cheaper, and most food items would doubtless be cheaper as well.

In contrast to the static trend for wheat, production of food items with

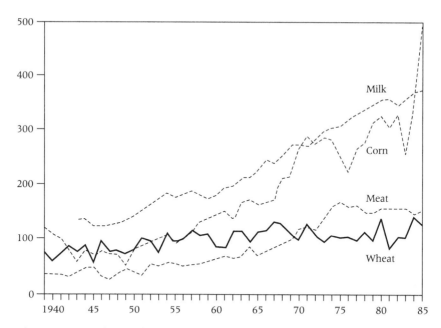

Figure 11.2. Indices of key agricultural outputs, 1939–1985 (1931/1935=100)

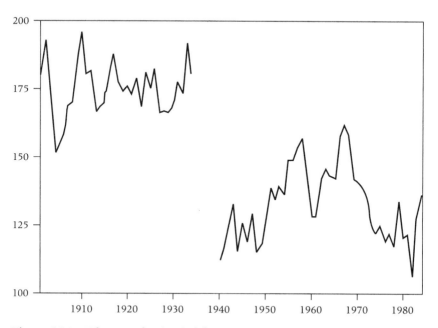

Figure 11.3. Wheat production in kilograms per capita, 1901–1984 (three-year moving averages).

Table 11.5. Livestock censuses, 1891–1984 (in thousands)

	(1) Cattle	(2) Sheep	(3) Pigs
1891	2,218	13,359	1,921
1910	2,369	15,970	2,424
1920	3,397	19,237	4,229
1931	3,654	19,401	4,811
1940	3,899	24,237	5,613
1950	3,112	16,344	2,688
1960	3,640	22,622	6,032
1970	4,282	17,005	7,621
1980	4,495	14,180	11,263
1984	4,942	17,053	11,962

Sources: *Estadísticas Históricas,* (ed.) Carreras (1989), *Anuarios Estadísticos de España,* and *Estadísticas Históricas de la Producción Agraria Española*

high income elasticity has grown a lot more, including corn, a cereal that has been little known in Spain until recently. The large increase in corn production is not for human consumption directly but for use as animal fodder, hence it is related to beef and milk production. The large increase in milk consumption is remarkable; it seems to have been one of the few agricultural products whose output did not decline during the Civil War.[12] The figures for meat show a continuous increase in production from the 1950s to the 1970s, though we must bear in mind that these figures refer only to beef production. The relative figures for poultry and pork show a much more spectacular rise, and the same goes for fish, the other important source of animal protein. It is well known that Spain's fish consumption is one of the highest in Europe; it is less well known that Spain's beef consumption is just a little above half of the norm for the European Union, while the consumption of poultry is double the European average.[13]

The Sea and the Meseta

Fishing has long been a traditional activity in Spain, which is not surprising given the extent of its coastline and its seafaring history; consequently fish figures prominently on the Spaniard's dinner table. This tradition has become consolidated in the twentieth century, since the introduction of refrigeration and rapid transport systems have facilitated massive consumption of fresh fish inland, in Madrid but also elsewhere. The amount of fish unloaded

Table 11.6. Main products of the livestock industry, 1923–1984

Year	(1) Beef and veal[a]	(2) Poultry	(3) Pork	(4) Lamb and mutton	(5) Milk	(6) Eggs
1923[b]	203	93	258	25	765	131
1930	267	–	274	171	1,330	140
1940	83	–	–	–	2,363[c]	–
1950	91	–	–	–	2,489	216
1960	160	13	258	110	3,185	312
1970	308	499	492	127	4,895	683
1980	418	885	986	127	6,394	980
1984	389	789	1,192	127	6,835	927

a. Cols. 1–4, in thousand tons; col. 5, in million liters; col. 6, in million dozens

b. Figures for 1923 are for consumption, except for eggs

c. Figure is for 1943

Sources: as for Table 11.5

from vessels in Spain increased from the end of the nineteenth century, at a time when there is evidence that meat consumption was falling.[14] This allows us to suppose that to a certain extent fresh fish exerted a "substitution influence . . . to the detriment of livestock production," in the words of Giráldez, during the first third of the twentieth century.

As a consequence of the increased fish consumption, the volume of fish off-loaded in Spanish ports increased rapidly during the first half of the twentieth century, a growth that outstripped most other economic measures. Thus fishing went from representing .5% of Gross Domestic Product around 1910 to 1% on the eve of the Civil War and to more than 1.5% during the 1940s, a proportion that later was to decline little by little, though in 1980 fishing still produced about 1% of GDP. This relative decline has recently accelerated to an absolute falling off, because the traditional fishing banks are becoming exhausted, because of increasingly exclusionary policies of countries owning fishing areas, and because of quotas imposed by the European Union. The reduction in volume of fish landed is reflected in a diminished fishing fleet, a considerable reduction in fishing manpower, and a changing position in the trade balance. From being an exporter, Spain has recently become a net importer of fresh fish.

The open hill lands, *los montes*, contribute only a very small fraction of the total agricultural income: in 1980 about 2.5%, which is only about .68% of the GDP, and the figure is similar for those earlier and later years for which we have comparable data. Keeping in mind that the open hill lands occupy 55% of the total surface area of Spain, this seems to indicate very low productivity. Confirming one aspect of this, Spain has long suffered a deficit in wood production and is an importer of this raw material. In compensation, cork, another forestry product, has traditionally been an important export item.

Before entering a final judgment of condemnation on the Spanish forestry industry, we ought to reflect on certain unusual elements of the issue. In Spain, much more than half of the land that is defined as *monte* is, properly speaking, barren; of the wooded parts of the open country, less than half is, properly speaking, forest; and in any case the most significant economic contribution made by the wooded open hillside is not included in any calculation of national income, its value being incalculable, based on what we call indivisible externalities. The two main externalities or external economies of woodland are its function as an antierosion agent, and its effects upon climate. But there are further externalities, and their importance overall is so massive that the material product of forests and open hills within the GDP, that part which figures in the accounts, is the least element of their very real economic significance.

It is well known that woody ground cover retains the soil and prevents heavy rainfall from carrying it away under washout conditions. Where this ground cover is missing, the action of wind and water erodes the top soil and leaves the underlying rock barren, a problem of the utmost importance in a dry and rocky country like Spain. The antierosion function of the wooded open countryside was already known by the specialists at the beginning of the century. Ricardo Codorniú's words in 1902 are very eloquent: "It shocks one to see the erosion, . . . as though a huge monster had thrust his gigantic talons wherever it saw the hill slopes denuded of bushy vegetation, rooting up, so to speak, shreds of the flesh of the fatherland, for where the rock was left bare, what is left behind is only the skeleton of the fatherland."[15]

Another benefit of woodland had been long known intuitively, and already Lucas Mallada had written in 1882 that deforestation "accentuates in the extreme the dryness of the land." Nowadays it is known for certain that the forest cover encourages rainfall and humidity. Other externalities of the open countryside are the prevention or moderation of heavy run-off and floods, and this in turn limits the amount of soil that enters the reservoirs. And above and beyond all this, the forests offer irreplaceable opportunities for education, scientific investigation, relaxation, and ecological renewal, since the trees clean the air, using up carbon dioxide and giving back oxygen.

Throughout its history Spain has been subject to serious deforestation. References to abundant and leafy Spanish woodlands are legion in the medieval and Renaissance periods.[16] From that time forward a process of forest destruction was set in motion which has accelerated in the modern period. At the beginning of the twentieth century, Joaquín Costa denounced the "hatchet of disentail," blaming the privatization of land under *desamortización* for deforestation and its effects. And Costa's much respected opinion had many supporters. However, the roles of the protagonists of the forestry drama are not entirely clear; neither is privatization the unmistakable villain, nor is the administration of the public domain the blameless handsome hero of the story.

In the first place, deforestation has not been uniquely a Spanish phenomenon but a European one as well, the lamentable and unavoidable consequence of demographic growth. And in almost all the other countries it has been more extensive than in Spain, for the simple reason that Spanish population density is among the lowest in Europe. In the whole of Europe deforestation has been more an economic problem than a juridical one. But this does not mean that there is no cause for alarm and no "forestry" problem in Spain; far from it. First, although there is a higher proportion of shrub wasteland in Spain than in the other European countries, the consequences of deforestation are far graver because of the dry climate. The external effects of woodland are more necessary than in other countries that are less threatened by desertification. In addition, Spain's forests are of poorer quality, less dense and slower-growing than those of almost all of the other European countries (Tamames, 1990, p. 181).

As we saw in Chapter 3, disentail was a necessary process, again the consequence of inexorable population growth. Without it land reclamation and the extension of grain-sown land would have gone ahead anyway, perhaps in a manner that was even more disorganized and damaging. The looting and plundering of public property is an ancient and established tradition in Spain. "That which is held in common belongs to no one," goes an Asturian adage in very common usage. And to add a further point, the present-day management of the national parks at Doñana and Damiel shows very clearly that the Spanish state is far from being a model manager, in terms of conserving the national natural heritage. Thanks to *desamortización*, at least the public land became clearly marked off from the private, and the process of defining responsibilities and competencies could thereby be set in motion. On the other hand, the Madoz Law established the nontransferable, inalienable nature of a large part of the wastelands and open mountain country, yet in spite of this extensive sections of woodland were privatized and put under the plow. In the absence of an authentic agrarian revolution that would have multiplied yields, stimulated large migratory movements of population, permitted free import of grains, and fostered an educational and scientific program of the sort that seems unthinkable in nineteenth-century Spain, it is difficult to see any other way that is would have been possible to feed a growing population.

When considering the ethics of property management, it is frequently assumed that the individual proprietor is a thoughtless speculator. But it can equally be the case that the owner of a forest might embrace conservation and improvement in his management strategy. It is also true, of course, that market forces may induce the proprietor to plant species that are profitable rather than ecologically appropriate, or to put new ground under the plow when demographic pressure made agriculture more profitable than forestry. This is not the case in Spain today, rather the reverse; rural depopulation, so much lamented in some quarters, provides a magnificent opportunity to rehabilitate the bulk of the nation's forestry resources. In any case it would be worthwhile to carry out comparative studies on the results of different forms of management, state, local, and private, before advancing *a priori* judgments. However, since the major contributions of the forests to the quality of public life are best described as indivisible externalities, it would make sense that they should be under public administration.[17]

During the twentieth century the state adopted two major policy positions, both of them correct when properly pursued: the protection and consolidation of the state forestry resources, whether public or private, and reforestation. The task of protecting the forests and open wastelands has been entrusted to the forestry engineers and to ICONA, the Institute for Nature Conservation. The first of the Special Schools for Forestry Engineers was founded in Villaviciosa de Odón, near Madrid, in 1848, and the graduates from those schools have been responsible for many of the studies about Spain's forestry problems. Forestry engineers dominated the Dirección General de Montes (State Office for Management of Open Forest and Shrubland) in the old Ministry of Public Works *(Fomento)*, the predecessor of both the Ministry of Agriculture and the Forestry Administration. ICONA, created in 1971, has been charged with a number of responsibilities and undertakings previously within the Ministry of Agriculture, principally by the Dirección General de Montes. Largely as a consequence of a body of opinion created by the Forestry engineers and the "regenerationists," most particularly Costa, Mallada, and Macías Picavea, the Hydrographic Confederations began a process of reforestation which had been going on during the Republic and was taken up again on much broader scale after the Civil War. Although reforestation is utterly necessary, not all of it has been successful; the excessive planting of conifers has been widely criticized, and also that of the eucalyptus and poplar, species that are profitable and fast growing but problematical (eucalyptus is highly combustible, and both species are thirsty, absorbing water resources that might otherwise replenish the water table).

The struggle against forest fires, a growing menace with pernicious results, is also a responsibility of ICONA and seems to be one of the areas where its performance could produce happier results.

The European Challenge

In *Through the Looking Glass,* the Red Queen, in conversation with Alice, makes a statement that has much impressed the development economists and the occasional economic historian: "Now, here, you see, it takes all the running you can do, to keep in the same place." And this is the case with Spanish agriculture in the twentieth century. At the end of the accelerated growth that we have described, Spanish agriculture remains as much behind the European norm as it was at the beginning of the century. Table 11.7 shows us the situation in 1980: Spain's sectoral productivity (calculated by dividing the percentage of Gross Domestic Product contributed by agriculture by the percentage of human resources that it uses) was lower than the productivity of each and every one of the ten countries that then formed the European Community. Now in general, the agricultural sector normally has a productivity below the average for the whole of the economy. For the Community as a whole every 1% of workers in agriculture produced .73% of the GDP; the average productivity in agriculture thus came out to be a little less than three-quarters of total average productivity. There were variations of course; in Denmark, Belgium, Holland, and the United Kingdom agricultural productivity was above their respective national average productivities, and this was particularly marked in the last three. The Mediter-

Table 11.7.   The share of agriculture in the GNP and its productivity among members of the European Economic Community, 1980

	(1) Agricultural production as a % of Gross National Product	(2) Agricultural workers as a % of total working population	(3) Relative agricultural productivity, col. 1/col. 2
Belgium	4.7	2.9	1.62
Denmark	9.2	8.2	1.12
Germany	3.8	5.9	0.64
Greece	18.0	30.3	0.59
France	6.7	8.8	0.76
Ireland	19.3	18.9	1.02
Italy	8.6	13.9	0.62
Luxembourg	3.6	5.7	0.63
Holland	7.7	4.5	1.71
United Kingdom	3.8	2.6	1.46
EEC(10)	5.8	8.0	0.73
Spain	7.1	18.5	0.38

Source: Camilleri (1984) and own calculations

ranean economies offer the opposite picture with productivity about 60% of the national average in the cases of Italy and Greece. But the Spanish case is much worse than even the other Mediterranean agricultures, given that its sectoral productivity at .38 is not much more than one-third of the national average productivity.

We need not ask if it was always thus, for we already know that the answer is in the affirmative; productivity per worker in Spanish agriculture has varied little in terms relative to Europe throughout the twentieth century. It improved somewhat in the first third of the century, but the Civil War and the first period of Franco's rule threw everything so far behind that in the 1960s and 1970s increased productivity did little more than recover lost ground. And what is troubling is not just low productivity, but that yields (production per hectare) are also low. According to calculations by O'Brien and Prados (1992), Spain's productivity in 1980 was somewhat below that for Italy, though not as far below as in Table 11.7, which is calculated from other data and by other methods. Now the yields per hectare from Spanish agriculture at that date, according to these authors, were well below half of the figures for Italy, and Italy itself is in the lower part of the table for the whole of Europe, both for yields and for productivity.

The causes have been palliated but they have not disappeared: the inevitable dryness of climate, the persistence of small landholdings, the misguided concentration on cereals in areas where they are not suitable (Spanish wheat yields in 1980 were 38% of the average for the EEC, whereas in stock raising or fruit production Spain was at the median or above), the low degree of capitalization, which in spite of spectacular increases continues to be below the European norm, the low level of fertilization, insufficient technical knowledge, and "the almost total retreat from agricultural research" (Barciela, 1986b, p. 445).

Spain entered the European Community in 1986, and in general the consequences for agriculture have been as anticipated. On the one hand, the commercial agricultural deficit increased, which is natural since a broad section of Spanish agriculture is not competitive. On the other hand, there has been a welcome reallocation of resources towards the more competitive sectors (fruit, vegetables, some sub-sectors of animal husbandry) and a reduction in resources allocated to the less competitive sectors, such as wheat. These trends ought to be enhanced by the structure of food demand, which is also different from the European norm. Spain tends to consume precisely those food items in which its competitive advantage is greatest, not only the traditional Mediterranean products such as olive oil, fresh fruits and fresh vegetables, but also milk, eggs, and poultry, in addition to fresh fish. But this healthy trend, restructuring production in alignment with Spain's natural agricultural advantages, is being hobbled by an interventionist policy pursued by the European Community, which is now taking a leaf out of the book that was written by Spain, copying the venerable intervention mechanisms that Spain has known so long, pre-Franco, in the Franco years, and even after!

In effect, the so-called Common Agricultural Policy looks very like Spain's own interventionist policy. The Common Agricultural Policy works through the control of agricultural prices; in Spain it is known by its unfortunate acronym FEOGA (which in Spanish is close enough to the word "ugly" to be associated that way). The functions of FEOGA are very similar to those that were previously in the hands of FORPPA and SENPA. Thanks to FEOGA most Spanish agricultural products are subsidized, generally through price guarantees, much as they had been under SENPA since 1984. There would be little to object to in this policy if these guaranteed prices were destined to protect the agricultural producers and consumers from the kind of wide-ranging price fluctuations that in agricultural markets are largely caused by variations in supply. However, this is not the case; subjected to strong pressures from the agricultural sector (including physical violence, as the Spanish truck drivers, frequently subjected to violent attacks by French farmers, know very well), FEOGA has systematically fixed agricultural prices above the equilibrium level. At these prices, agriculture produces much more than the market can absorb and the surplus is sold to FEOGA.

It is well documented that this policy clearly favors the large agricultural producers, with much better capacity both in production and in adaptation, rather than the small producers it is supposedly designed to help. As a result, FEOGA now accumulates the famous wheat and butter mountains and the no less celebrated lakes of wine and milk whose conservation and management entails additional expenditure above and beyond the enormous cost of buying those products at higher than market prices. This storage cost is so large that to remedy it a third kind of expenditure is incurred, that of exporting at a loss to Third World countries.[18] It is not surprising therefore that the Common Agricultural Policy alone costs no less than three quarters of the European Union budget. And this is precisely Europe's Achilles heel. The costs are so enormous that surely in the end a certain degree of rationality will be forced into play, the chief and simple proof of which will be embodied in the reduction or modification of price guarantees. In reality, this is the logical policy, to agree on some sensibly defined food stocks and to adjust prices to meet those objectives. The prices will go down when the mountains and lakes begin to form and will go up when they threaten to disappear.

And why is this rational policy not followed? The answer is simple: although the number of farmers goes steadily down, so that the copious bonuses that producers receive as subsidy seems affordable, they continue nonetheless to constitute a powerful group with closely allied interests, a real lobby capable of applying pressure, giving bribes, threatening, resorting to rioting and violence. Here, as in so many other cases, society prefers to pay the blackmail rather than face up to a social problem that distresses the man in the street, although he does not really understand it.

CHAPTER 12

Industrial Takeoff

Industry and Politics

If economic historians agree that the nineteenth was a century of failure in the industrialization of Spain, they will also agree that the twentieth was the century of success. But beyond that generality disagreements begin to creep in, because the profession is very far from unanimous on questions of the rhythms and causes of the process. Traditional opinion held that industrialization was a phenomenon of the twentieth century largely because of the policy of tariff protection and the state intervention which so characterized this period. One prestigious author who has most clearly maintained that opinion is Ramón Tamames, who in a recent edition of his textbook continues to assert the following: "The new industry destined to meet the interior market demand could not begin to emerge . . . without tariff protection. . . . [I]n 1892 protectionism was definitively established for Spanish industry and from that date onwards industrialization has not looked back."

Many other analysts, such as Pugés and Paris Eguilaz, had maintained this thesis in earlier publications, and others have repeated the theme of a turning point about 1900 (thanks to tariff protection) as a generally accepted fact. One well-regarded economist, Jürgen Donges (1976, pp. 25–26), offers perhaps the best reasoned version of this theory:

> The protection system acted as a catalyst to set the industrialization process in motion because of its inherent tendency to improve the manufacturing sector's domestic terms of trade, consequently drawing primary factors of production from other branches of the economy. To this effect it is necessary to add the fact that protection of the interior market offers attractive investment opportunities and thus tends to encourage the import of capital,

which is precisely the factor most keenly lacking in the Spanish economy at the beginning of the twentieth century.

Recent research, however, leads us to doubt the traditional explanation. The work of Prados de la Escosura, for example, has shown that external trade was one of the most dynamic sectors of the Spanish economy in the nineteenth century. In addition, Pedro Fraile's work on one of the most protected sectors, the iron and steel industry, suggests that the tariff merely led to the formation of a metallurgical oligopoly in the 1920s and 1930s, which "impeded the metal industry from growth, from diversification and from the task of converting itself into the leading sector, as it did within other European economies" (Fraile, 1985, p. 100). In general, for Fraile, "the effect of prohibitive protection of Spanish industry during the first half of the twentieth century was a delay [in development] relative to the rest of Europe" (Fraile, 1991, p. 216).

But perhaps the most definitive argument against the traditional line of thinking can be found in the Index of Industrial Production created by Carreras, which claims that "There exists no discontinuity at all in the rhythm of industrial growth around 1900, nor around 1890, nor around 1906 . . . What there is in the 90 years before the Civil War is a long period of growth, sometimes more rapid, sometimes more leisurely, which leads us to understand that the industrialization trend in Spain is of long standing" (Carreras, 1987, p. 284).

The impression given by these latest works is that Spanish industrialization was a fairly autonomous process, less dependent upon economic policy than had been thought. On the supply side and in terms of demand as well, industrial production seems to have evolved in the long run independently of political changes.

The process of industrialization requires an expanding market, or an important technological innovation, or preferably both. In permitting a broadening in the scale of production, an expanding market will stimulate innovation and mass production, which is the essence of the industrial revolution. But technological innovation on its own can produce the same effect in a static market by replacing an old product with a new one that is better or cheaper. In the nineteenth century, slow growth both in agriculture and in population condemned Spanish industry to languish in the absence of export and innovation opportunities. Only a few industries were able to develop—those that exported (mining products late in the century) or innovated (the cotton industry at mid-century). By making inputs expensive, stifling competition, and contributing to the closure of foreign markets, tariff protection did nothing but slow down industrialization. But in the twentieth century things were different. Greater demographic growth, technological innovation stimulated by imported foreign technology (both experts and processes), and the incorporation of new generations of workers, managers, and capitalists (itself the result of a long, cumulative process)[1] were the main features that favored diversification and industrial growth. It is very doubtful that any particular policy aimed at enhancing industrial potential would have played an important role in this process. The parallels between Spain's economic evolution and that of its European neighbors lead one to think that the growing integration of Spain into the European economy had more influence on its economic development than policies that tended to isolate the country and stand in the way of that integration.

In the nineteenth century, the sole policy aimed at stimulating industrialization that was actually put into practice was the tariff, the famous protectionism that we have discussed so much. In contrast, twentieth-century Spain saw the initiation of a policy of active state intervention to develop industry. This intervention started with the 1907 *Ley de Fomento de la Industria Nacional* (Law Promoting National Industry), which stipulated that the state should preferentially purchase goods of national origin (in this Spain was imitating earlier practices, especially from France and Hungary)[2] and created a commission to protect national production. Many more such attempts were to follow, among them the important law of 1917 (May 2), which was to lead, three years later, to the creation of the Banco de Crédito Industrial (Tortella and Jiménez, 1986, chap. I). This policy was redoubled after the Civil War, especially with the Laws of October 24 and November 24, 1939, whose objectives were the development of a Spanish industrial base that would be self-sufficient. This decidedly interventionist legislation, which anticipated subsidies, special credits, tax exemptions, direct state purchasing, and the prohibition of competition went hand in hand, of course, with commercial legislation and a tariff policy that went beyond the merely protectionist to all-out autarky. The crowning glory of the Franco industrialization policy was the creation of the Instituto Nacional de Industria (Law of September 25, 1941). To all this one should also add a plethora of complex sectoral credit policies, which established special conditions for certain branches of industry and intervened in the credit market to that end, operating directly through the official banking organs and also legislating conditions for the private banking sector.

Did all this institutional superstructure contribute to the growth of industry? It is very debatable. Rather, the result was a development that was focused inwards, limited by the extent of the national market, and above all enormously dependent upon imports of capital and technology.

Diversification

Figure 12.1 eloquently reflects one of the characteristics of Spanish economic development in the twentieth century: the stagnation of the traditional light industries and the growth of basic or heavy industries. In this Spain did no more than follow Hoffmann's Law, according to which industrialization starts first in the consumer industries and, as the process moves forward, embraces the capital goods industries, that is, the industries whose principal client is industry itself. This evolution is reflected in Table 12.1,

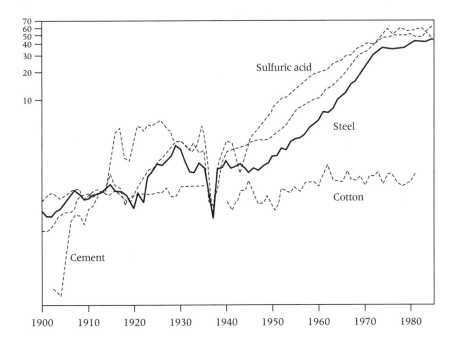

Table 12.1. Spanish industry by sectors, 1900–1980 (in percentages)

Year	(1) Energy	(2) Mining	(3) Heavy industry	(4) Machinery	(5) Consumer industries	(6) Hoffmann index[a]
1900	9	20	11	11	49	0.44
1910	12	20	12	8	48	0.41
1920	14	11	9	11	55	0.36
1930	15	10	12	18	46	0.66
1940	24	5	12	19	40	0.77
1950	27	6	12	19	36	0.86
1960	27	5	17	19	33	1.09
1970	20	2	20	35	23	2.39
1980	24	2	24	29	21	2.53

a. (Col. 3 + Col. 4)/Col. 5
Source: calculated from Carreras (1987), Table 11.8

where a Hoffmann index has been constructed. The importance of the basic industries, columns 3 and 4, is related to the importance of the consumer industries (column 5). It helps us to appreciate the growing importance of the consumer industries until the end of World War I, a strong push from the basic industries in the 1920s, and from then onwards a continuous increase in the basic sectors, which overtook the consumer industries for the first time around 1960 (a date coinciding with the 1959 stabilization plan). By 1980 the basic sector was two and a half times larger than the consumer sector, and the consumer sector had declined from representing 50% of total industrial output in 1920 to only one-fifth today. The situation is almost exactly inverted when we look at the basic industries (cols. 3 and 4), which represented 21.5% of industrial output in 1920 and 53% by 1980.

The most important consumer industry, and indeed the most important sector overall until well into the twentieth century, was textiles, and within that, cotton. Its most pronounced characteristic during the first third of the twentieth century was stagnation (see Figure 12.1). But the sector did manage to achieve a series of transformations. Renouncing any attempt at international competition right at its outset in the nineteenth century, the industry had laid claim to the principle of the protected national market, demanding and generally obtaining high tariffs. After the middle of the century, the cotton producers discovered that the home market was not growing as much as they had hoped, and they then managed to obtain a monopoly of the colonial trade too. The loss of the colonies at the end of the nineteenth century set before them two dreaded alternatives, to stagnate or to export. "After 1898, for the first time the Spanish cotton industry seriously confronted the possibilities of competing openly in the world market" (Sudrià, 1983, p. 376). The interesting thing is that it did so. Although exports to Cuba fell somewhat after independence, this was more than compensated by penetration into other markets such as Argentina and Uruguay, so that on the eve of the Great War Spain was exporting more cotton textiles to the Americas than in 1898, and something similar can be said of exports to the rest of the world. In total, the cotton industry went from exporting insignificant fractions of its production in the nineteenth century to exporting about 10% in the first third of the twentieth century. All this, however, did not bring about any substantial technological improvements; in part the industry managed its exports through bounties and subsidies, that is to say, by resorting to dumping. The industry continued to be predominantly small-scale and antiquated in production techniques; the market was protected and there was little competition.

The food industry also experienced considerable growth. The sugar industry, whose production tripled in this period, offers an interesting, characteristic picture. During the greater part of the nineteenth century Spain had consumed cane sugar, largely imported from Cuba and Puerto Rico, and the rest was produced in Spain, above all in Motril, on the Mediterranean, south of Granada. From mid-century onwards peninsular sugar was favored by a taxation system that discriminated against the Cuban product. This discrimination became more pronounced in the 1880s, when the sugar-beet industry was introduced into Spain, first in Granada. Powerful state protection stimulated inordinate growth in home production. After the loss of Cuba, tariff protection increased, and a heavy tax was levied on sugar consumption. Spanish sugar was in fact very expensive and consumption relatively low, a situation provoking a threat of imminent overproduction. Instead of lowering prices, the industry formed the Sociedad General Azucarera in 1903, a cartel for sugar producers. The relative failure of this arrangement, whose profits initially attracted more competition, motivated the producers to seek state intervention to achieve what they themselves could not have managed, the prevention of competition and the creation of an oligopoly. The state's collapse under pressure from the sugar manufacturers proved to be of lasting influence; with greater or lesser success the last governments of the Restoration and those of the First Dictatorship and of the Republic all intervened in the sugar market, prohibiting the entry of new companies, fixing prices, and establishing quotas. The result was a relatively high price for sugar and a level of consumption far below the European norm, although comparable to other Mediterranean countries.[3]

It now becomes clear why protection of the home-based consumer industries, concretely the cotton and sugar industries, in the long run contributed to the Disaster of 1898 through the economic hardship inflicted on the Spanish colonies. The Laws of Commercial Relations with the West Indies (1882) and the taxation and tariff measures that were part of that legislation were devices to force the West Indies to consume Spanish textiles and flour, at the same time that their principal export commodity was excluded from the Spanish market. The knowledge that they were being implacably exploited by Spain helped develop a spirit of rebellion among the Cubans. It makes sense to assume that independence would have occurred eventually in any case, but the armed conflict might have been avoided if economic inequality had not brought the parties to their positions of intransigence (Tortella, 1964).

Although the textile industry stagnated, the food industry in general expanded considerably during the first third of the twentieth century: it seems clear that the diet of the average Spaniard improved.[4] But not everything the food industry produced was destined for the home market: some branches such as the canning industry, wine, and oil production were strong exporters.[5] Other enterprises that were not export-oriented also flourished: the flour and baking industries, beer brewers, and chocolate manufacturers increased their production considerably. And not only was there strong growth, but also visible modernization of production methods in these industries.

It is also worth indicating here how the mechanism of industrial protection operated to the detriment of competitive industries, as Perpiñá (1972) has shown.[6] One example is vegetable canning, in which Spain enjoys, as is well known, a clear, absolute advantage, let alone a comparative one. Yet the Spanish canning industry could not sell the finished product abroad (canned fruit, jams, and preserves), but almost exclusively exported pulps that the importing countries then turned into preserves. The reason was that the high price of two protected products, sugar and coal (possibly tinplate as well), rendered the finished product too expensive (Martínez Carrión, 1989). As Flores de Lemus had already made clear in a famous parliamen-

tary address, the "protection" system turns out to be nothing more than robbing Peter to pay Paul.

As we saw earlier, in the economic history of modern Spain, as in that of
many other countries, the Hoffmann Law seems to apply. After all, this
"law" does no more than draw attention to the natural sequence of economic development: consumer industries develop first because their market
is already at hand, from the beginning. As these industries mechanize, they
need capital goods—machines and equipment that are produced by what
we call the basic or heavy industries (this is why demand in this latter sector
is known as "derived demand"). Only through extensive international trade
have some nations been able to escape Hoffmann's Law. By exporting, some
capital goods industries have been able to grow faster than if they had been
limited to the domestic market. In Spain, growing protectionism saw to it
that the "law" operated with no holds barred. Heavy industry, which had
had no opportunity to develop by providing agricultural equipment or supplying the railroads in the earlier parts of the nineteenth century, took off at
the end of the century in the heat of a protectionism that was almost suffocating. What would have happened without that protection? There is no
reason to doubt that the Hoffmann Law would have operated in Spain as in
most other countries, and probably faster than it actually did. The iron and
steel industries are a good example.

At the end of the nineteenth century Spain was producing some 300,000
tons of pig iron per year, and less than 200,000 tons of wrought iron. Steel
production grew to reach a million tons in 1929 (the five-year average for
1925–1929 was 742,000 tons and that for 1930–1934, 654,000 tons). This
growth has been seen as a triumph of industrial protectionism (Tamames,
1900, p. 323; Velarde, 1968, pp. 84–85). Such an opinion is debatable.

Most of the steel was produced in Vizcaya by a single company, Altos
Hornos de Vizcaya, the result of the merger in 1902 of three large iron and
steel companies: Altos Hornos de Bilbao, the Vizcaya, and the Iberia. In 1933
the paid-up capital of Altos Hornos (Blast Furnaces) was 36% of the total
capital in the Spanish iron and steel industry. The next largest companies
were the Duro-Felguera (Asturian, although with head offices in Madrid),
the Siderúrgica del Mediterráneo (Mediterranean Iron and Steel Company,
later on called Altos Hornos de Sagunto, with Basque capital registered in
Bilbao), the Fábrica de Mieres, the Santa Barbara Company (both Asturian),
and one other Basque company, the Basconia. The Basque companies were

producing two-thirds of Spain's output, and among them Altos Hornos de Vizcaya enjoyed primacy.

The Spanish iron and steel industry was showing clear signs of its oligopolistic structure, which state protection helped to promote. It seems clear that this protection in the end turned out to be more of an obstacle than a stimulant to growth. For one thing, although tariff protection directly benefited the iron and steel producers, the protection of national coal certainly harmed them, and from this stems "the paradox that [the Basques] sought tariff protection for their own products, in iron and steel, while simultaneously trying to arrange that protection for Asturian coal be denied" (Tamames, 1990, p. 322). Furthermore, since it was sheltered from external competition by the tariff and from internal competition by its oligopolistic structure, the industry chose to operate under inflexible supply conditions, what an economist would call a rigid supply curve, which means that it responded to increasing demand by increasing prices rather than by increasing production. Although this oligopolistic structure could be found "in almost all countries," Spain's supply rigidity was exceptional. Thus "almost from the beginning of the century, the shortage of steel and its high prices had been recognized as an obstacle to Spanish industrial development" (Fraile, 1985). The Spanish ironmasters complained insistently of the small capacity of the Spanish market, but the reality is, as Fraile has shown, that the greater responsibility for the scant growth in steel production fell to the producers themselves. In spite of the symbolic figure of the million tons of steel produced in 1929, the truth is that Spanish steel production remained very modest, especially bearing in mind the country's abundant ore deposits. By contrast, in Italy, which was almost completely without coal and iron, steel production in the first decades of the twentieth century grew much more rapidly, and in 1929 Italy's production was more than twice that of Spain (Table 12.2).

Cement production is another very important basic industry, with the principal demand for this product coming from the construction industry. Many aspects of economic modernization create powerful growth impacts in the construction industry, a many-faceted and protean industry, and the output of cement, a homogeneous and easily quantified product, is a good indicator of this growth. An important part of modernization is urbanization, with a resultant increase in residential construction. And industrialization itself requires the construction of factories and housing for plant and equipment; agricultural modernization also requires the construction of

Table 12.2.   Steel production in various countries in 1930

	Steel production (in thousand tons)	Population (in thousands)	Production (in tons) per 1,000 population
Belgium	3,359	8,092	415
United States	41,351	123,077	336
France	9,444	41,228	229
Germany	12,536	64,962	193
United Kingdom	7,444	44,795	166
Czechoslovakia	1,817	14,730	123
Sweden	611	6,142	99
Austria	468	6,678	70
Italy	1,743	41,177	42
Hungary	369	8,688	42
Poland	1,237	32,107	39
SPAIN	929	23,564	39
Rumania	157	18,057	9

Sources: calculated from Mitchell (1976) and *U.S. Historical Statistics*

buildings such as silos, sheds, and warehouses. At the same time the need for public works projects expands: roads, railroads, ports, and reservoirs. The cement that was traditionally used, called natural cement, was a clay or limestone soil that was quarried. Artificial or Portland cement is an English invention from the beginning of the nineteenth century, which is made by mixing, burning, and crushing a mixture of clay and limestone soils to produce a homogenized product that gives better results, with better hardening qualities. In Spain the production of artificial cement began in the first years of the twentieth century; the first factory dates from 1899. Gómez Mendoza (1987, p. 327) conjectures that the dating of this event "could make one think of a possible connection with the colonial disaster, [both in] the repatriation of capital, and [in] the search for new investment opportunities in sectors other than consumer goods, which had been hardest hit by the loss of the last colonies."

Gómez Mendoza's own works, however (1987, 1991), offer a very important additional explanation: a growing demand for this new type of cement. Because it was more homogeneous and thus of better quality, and in more elastic supply, artificial cement would be sought in periods of particularly keen growth in the building industry, and especially when the size and complexity of the work demanded the quality and reliability that Portland cement offered. In fact most of these demand factors emerged in Spain around the turn of the century, as Table 12.3 shows. At about that time larger and taller buildings became more popular, and this called for more cement and of better quality. The rhythm of residential construction also picked up (in terms of apartments, not of the number of buildings), with the exception of the troubled second decade of the century. Investment in public works, another large consumer of cement, also grew (although with ups and downs) from the middle of the nineteenth century. In the twentieth, a falling off occurred in the first decade, doubtless because of the budgetary restrictions introduced by Villaverde's Stabilization Plan, but a large increase in reservoir construction also occurred at the beginning of the new century (Gómez Mendoza, 1991, pp. 199–202).

This growing demand gave rise to new construction companies (FOCSA, Cubiertas y Tejados, Agromán, Huarte, and Entrecanales y Tavora), as well as several cement manufacturing companies (Tudela-Veguín, Rezola, Asland, and Portland). These were formed in the first years of the new century, and they were soon able to devise agreements to restrict competition. The cement industry has a natural proclivity towards oligopoly, and the Spanish branch was not going to fall short in that respect. Little is known about international cement pricing, but we know enough about prices within Spain (Coll, 1986; Gómez Mendoza, 1987a, 1987b; Paris Eguilaz, 1943, esp. p. 122) to be able to say that despite certain almost unavoidable problems of coordination, the cement industry's oligopolistic strategy turned out to be highly successful; and despite increased production between 1900 and 1930, prices also rose, with increases far above the general price index. The evidence suggests, then, that in the absence of oligopoly and official protection production would have increased more. In terms of production per head of population (see Table 12.4) the Spanish cement industry, around 1933, was still operating at only a modest level.

The chemical industry includes a very wide range of seemingly unrelated activities, from perfumes and photography to the production of sulfuric and nitric acids, by way of plastics, artificial fibers, fertilizers, pharmaceutics, and a great many other products. Here we can only comment upon the evolution of some of the more important parts. First and foremost, in Spain this sector is also almost exclusively a product of the twentieth century. As Nadal has emphasized, Spain's chemical industry was virtually nonexistent in the nineteenth century, in large part because of low demand, a consequence of the general backwardness of the country. But there must have been supply

Table 12.3. Aspects of the construction industry in Spain, 1860–1935

Period	RESIDENTIAL CONSTRUCTION: Stock of Buildings in Spain				
	Total buildings (in thousands)	Increase	Total number of stories (in thousands)	Increase	Ratio of stories to buildings
1860	3,630.4	—	6,486.5	—	1.7867
1888	4,206.3	575.9	7,464.0	977.5	1.7745
1900	4,602.9	396.6	8,158.5	694.5	1.7725
1910	4,887.6	284.7	8,830.4	671.9	1.8067
1920	5,116.2	228.6	9,256.6	426.6	1.8093
1930	5,555.4	439.2	10,231.3	974.7	1.8417

Average Annual Increase (rate of construction)

Period	Buildings	%	Stories	%
1860–1888	32.0	8.8	54.3	8.4
1888–1900	33.1	7.9	57.9	7.8
1900–1910	28.5	6.2	67.2	8.2
1910–1920	22.9	4.7	42.6	4.8
1920–1930	43.9	8.6	97.5	10.5

Period	PUBLIC WORKS: Investment in million pesetas			
	Roads	Railroads	Ports[a]	Total
1850–1854	89.6	—	—	89.6
1855–1859	97.7	206.5	10.9	315.1
1860–1869	227.6	1,043.6	37.4	1,308.6
1870–1879	258.7	468.2	45.4	772.3
1880–1889	462.7	888.4	45.4	1,396.5
1890–1899	403.4	858.0	165.4	1,426.8
1900–1909	334.5	517.0	118.8	970.3
1910–1919	386.5	443.3	243.8	1,073.6
1920–1929	1,020.2	1,324.6	368.8	2,713.6
1920–1924	266.2	—	—	—
1925–1929	754.0	—	—	—
1930–1935	612.2	1,740.2	157.5	2,509.9

a. The figures for "Ports" for 1890 through 1929 are estimated
Sources: calculated from Gómez Mendoza (1987) and (1991)

Table 12.4. Cement production in various countries, ca. 1933

	(1) Cement (in thousand tons)	(2) Population (in thousands, ca. 1930)	(3) Production per thousand population
Belgium	1,985	8,092	241.0
Denmark	554	3,551	156.0
France	5,221	41,228	126.6
United Kingdom	4,470	44,795	99.8
United States	10,905	123,077	88.6
Italy	3,553	41,177	86.3
Holland	360	7,936	45.4
SPAIN	1,046	23,564	44.4
Greece	200	6,395	31.3
Poland	411	32,107	12.8

Sources: calculated from *Anuario Estadístico* (1943–44), *U.S. Historical Statistics,* and Mitchell (1976)

factors that limited supply, since the first modern companies to appear were largely foreign in terms of both capital and management. This was the case with the first large company, the Sociedad Española de la Dinamita, created in Bilbao in 1872 to supply this important explosive to the growing Spanish mineral extraction industry, which was then entering its heyday. The company was a subsidiary of the Nobel group, created with capital and directors that were principally French and Belgian, with some German and British participation (Tortella, 1983, and above, Chapter 4). Later on, the Sociedad Electroquímica de Flix was established in Tarragona (1897) to produce caustic soda by electrolysis, this time with German capital and technicians; in addition, a Spanish branch of the Belgian company, Solvay, was opened in Torrelavega, Santander, in 1908, to produce caustic soda by the Solvay process. However, two of the first chemical companies founded in Barcelona seem to have been domestic, although one of them has its origin in a family business that was initially French, the Cros Company. The Sociedad Anónima Cros was established in 1904 to make artificial fertilizers, in particular superphosphates. Seven years earlier, the Sociedad Española de Carburos Metálicos (Metallic Carbides) had been established to produce gases such as calcium carbide, oxygen, and acetylene. About the same time the Unión Resinera Española was founded in Bilbao, a company that owned extensive areas of woodland and set out to develop derived forestry products, in particular resins. The first large perfume company that we have information about is the Perfumería Gal, founded in Madrid in 1901. Also in Madrid in 1919 one of the first Spanish pharmaceutical companies was established, the Instituto de Biología y Sueroterapia (Serum Therapy) (Robert, 1959; Tamames, 1960; AFYDSADE).

The artificial fertilizer industry is particularly interesting. Superphosphates are produced by combining calcium phosphate and sulfuric acid, and they are much more easily absorbed into the soil than simple phosphates. The phosphates are extracted from the earth or from the slag left over by the basic (Thomas) process for making steel. For the Dynamite Company, it was natural to use the sulfuric acid that they themselves produced, and was then left over from the manufacture of nitroglycerine, to make superphosphates. However, in the first years sales of superphosphates were very slow, for their use did not become widespread until well into the twentieth century. Then the field started to attract competitors such as the Cros Company. Nitrogen-based fertilizers began to be produced commercially at the beginning of this century, thanks to various processes for fixing nitrogen from the air by means of electricity (the best known of which is the Haber-Bosch process). The great virtue of these fertilizers is that they substantially improved the yield of cereal crops, so basic to Spain's food supply in these years. Two factories to produce nitrates were created after the First World War, one called Energía e Industrias Aragonesas, 1918, and the other the Sociedad Ibérica del Nitrógeno, in 1922; for both these enterprises the technology was French, as was part of the capital. In this industry, however, the basic problem was frankly one of supply; in 1935 Spain hardly produced 5% of its national consumption (Bustelo, 1957). Only under the protection afforded by Franco's self-sufficiency regime was the Spanish nitrate fertilizers industry able to prosper, and it was to collapse again with the liberalization of trade that followed the end of the dictatorship. The third major mineral nutrient for plants is potassium. The potassium salts that are used as fertilizers (carnallite and sylvite) are minerals that are subject only to the minimal processing prior to application; for this reason their production is more a matter of mining than of industry proper. In Europe there are three major sources of potassium; one in Germany at Stassfurt, between Leipzig and Magdeburg, one in Alsace, and one in the basin of the Ebro, in Spain. This one, the last to be discovered, began to be exploited about 1925 in its richest section, the Catalán zone, a triangle between Cardona, Suria, and Sallent in the valleys of the rivers Cardener and Llobregat, near Manresa. The Compañía Minas de Potasa de Suria, a subsidiary of Solvay founded in 1902, was the first to go into operation. About the same time the Unión Española de Explosivos bought the potash deposits in Cardona, going into production ten years later. In 1917 the company's legal monopoly on explosives had expired, and the Unión was looking for areas where it could benefit from horizontal and vertical integration (Tortella, 1983, 1987, and 1992). Founded in 1929, Potasas Ibéricas, a subsidiary of the French company Kali-Sainte-Thérèse, acquired the deposits at Sallent. In fact, potassium fertilizers need humid soils; for that reason Spanish consumption was limited, and the companies thought more in terms of exports. Spanish production increased very rapidly, by a factor of ten between 1925 and 1935, but confronted with Spanish agriculture's limited absorption capacity, low demand because of the Great Depression, and competition from the *Kalisyndikat* (the Franco-German potassium cartel), the Spanish combine was forced into integration with the rival Franco-German cartel a few months before the beginning of the Civil War.

Once the Civil War was over, production and export expanded considerably. European competitors were involved in their own war, the Depression had ended, Spanish consumption increased with expanded irrigation, the *Kalisyndikat* was dissolved, Stassfurt was now in the newly formed Eastern Germany, and new, non–European producers emerged. However, today there is a *de facto* European cartel all over again, and the Spanish producers are once more part of it.

Sulfuric acid, perhaps the most basic and characteristic component of the chemical industry, experienced strong growth from very low initial levels of production at the beginning of the century. In broad strokes, its evolution was very similar to the other major indicators of growth in the basic industries.

Figure 12.1 allows us to appreciate several of the features we have been discussing. Observe the contrast between a consumer industry that was almost static (cotton) and some basic industries patently in expansion (cement, steel, and sulfuric acid). The chart also allows us to verify the contrast that is characteristic of basic industries in comparison with consumer industries, the greater sensitivity of these to economic fluctuations which stem from the recognized mechanisms of the multiplier and the accelerator. Cement, sulfuric acid, and steel production fell enormously during the Great War, recovered vigorously during the 1920s, and declined slightly again with the Great Depression; it is well known, and the graph confirms the fact, that the Spanish textile industry did not suffer during the Republic, rather the contrary. Also notable is the partial recovery in the basic industries around 1934–35, perhaps the effect of the multiplier and accelerator effects from sustained consumer expenditures and the good harvests in 1932 and 1934, a recovery that the Civil War seems to have curtailed.

As a symbol of the industrial diversification that was taking place in the first third of the twentieth century, more than for its quantitative importance, it is worth mentioning that Spain launched its own small automobile industry, the Hispano-Suiza Company, in Barcelona in 1904, when there were hardly any motor vehicles at all in Spain. Manufacturing chassis, engines, and a small quantity of luxury automobiles, the Hispano-Suiza developed very successfully until it was hit by the Great Depression and disappeared during the Civil War. The company also constructed engines for boats and airplanes. In prewar Spain a nascent aeronautic industry also existed, called Construcciones Aeronáuticas (CASA), in Getafe, Madrid, a semi-artisanal producer of small military airplanes (Sanz, 1926; AFYDSADE).

To conclude this section it is perhaps timely to quote the following synthesis from Donges (1976, p. 32): "During the first third of the twentieth century Spain recovered a good part of the ground previously lost, and at the end of that period it appeared to be a country whose economy, although producing a national income well below that of many European countries, industrially speaking was already relatively advanced."

Autarky and Monopoly

The period between 1930 and 1950 approximately can perhaps be best described (paraphrasing the title of a film about the Civil War[7]) as "The Long Vacation of Spanish Industrialization"; as can be seen from Figure 12.2, according to Carreras' index, the level of industrialization achieved in 1930, measured per head of population, was not achieved again until 1952. This abrupt interruption in a phase of industrialization that despite its problems had been picking up in rhythm, volume, and diversity since the middle of the nineteenth century, is a singular phenomenon within the economic history of Europe, particular to Spain. The causes are complex and although some are common to the whole of Europe, others are exclusively Spanish.

The most important feature Spain had in common with other countries was the Great Depression of the 1930s and the concomitant restrictions on trade. Yet it is well known that the Depression affected other countries more seriously than Spain, and although Spain's basic industries were hit badly in 1931 and 1932, starting in 1933 it seemed that a recovery had set in. All in all, in comparative terms, Spanish industry did not come out too badly.[8]

Of far greater and more serious importance are the events that were exclusive to Spain. In first place, of course, was the Civil War, which obviously damaged industrial production very gravely. The problem was not so much physical destruction, which seems to have been of little importance, but rather general disorganization, fragmentation of markets, interruption of communications, shortage of raw materials, energy supplies, and lack of workers at all levels, in the fields and factories as well as in top and middle management. Although the global indicators do not give figures for the war years, partial information from the production of iron and steel, cement, and sulfuric acid shows serious declines in output for the years 1936 and 1937, with partial recoveries in 1938 and 1939. Thus the total and partial indices for 1940 reveal production well below prewar levels.

What now seems more difficult to explain is the slow speed of recovery af-

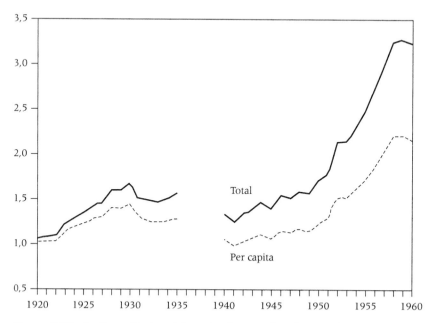

Figure 12.2. Indices of industrial production, total and per capita, 1920–1960 (1913=1)

ter 1940, and it is here that indigenous causes seem to predominate. Without any doubt, the Second World War must have affected Spanish industry, just as it affected the other neutral countries. For Spain, however, the impact of the war contained elements that worked both ways, some favorable and others unfavorable. On the one hand the interruption of normal communications and the demands and restrictions that the war imposed upon the warring nations obviously had to affect both the supply of raw materials and access to markets. But on the other hand, the economic dislocations suffered by the parties to the war temporarily eliminated a group of serious competitors and increased the demand for certain goods in those same countries. In synthesis, if the war hurt industry in the neutral and noncombatant countries on the supply side, on the demand side it certainly conferred benefits. It is here that the Spanish peculiarities begin to resurface. With industrial capacity that had survived the Civil War almost intact (Hombravella et al., 1971, I, pp. 166–170), and with a remarkable endowment of mineral and energy resources (coal and hydroelectricity), Spain ought to have been able to exact some benefit from a situation that was sad but inevitable, to stimulate exports and help industrial recovery. But this was not to be: for ideological reasons, or compelled by circumstances, or both, the Franco authorities instituted a policy that did very little to foster industrial production. Their ignorance in these matters was so profound that even they were surprised by the scant response of private industry to measures that they believed would act as stimulants to trade (Martín Aceña and Comín, 1991, pp. 44–52). Although the government blamed the destruction of the Civil War and world conditions, the truth is that the stagnation owed much more to ill-formulated policy than to circumstances; indeed they could have profited from them but just did not know how.

Let us look at some of the mistakes. In the first place, although there is little that economic policy could have done to avoid it, Franco's alignment with the Axis powers placed the country firmly in the group that had little access to raw materials and energy, particularly petroleum. In relation to this, the Civil War was paid for dearly in terms of indebtedness. The Franco authorities repeatedly blamed the Republican government for having sent gold from the Bank of Spain to Russia, but they were careful not to reveal the massive export consignments to Germany and Italy during World War II that were not purchases but payments for debts incurred earlier (Viñas et al., 1979, pp. 374–412).

In the second place, the ideology of nationalism and autarky did nothing at all to favor exchanges abroad; loans from the Allies were distrusted and the Axis powers were in no way disposed to be generous. This made it very difficult to import raw materials, although their importance was clearly recognized.

In the third place, regardless of repeated proclamations that "national reconstruction" was one of the aims and objectives of the Franco regime, the fact is that "the state dedicated proportionately less resources to the maintenance, repair and construction of infrastructure . . . after the war than before it. . . . Put in other words, net fixed capital formation was much less than in the immediate pre-war [period]" (Carreras, 1989, p. 21). Apart from other considerations, this was clearly a lost opportunity to stimulate the growth of basic industry.

In the fourth place, doubtless for reasons of prestige that were ill-informed, the authorities maintained an exchange rate that was overvalued. This hurt exports to the Allied and neutral countries because the goods were overpriced, yet these exports were critically needed to earn foreign exchange to pay for imports.

In the fifth place, and related to the above, the government established import controls and rationed foreign exchange (a system already practiced widely by European governments during the Depression but strengthened and extended to unusual lengths by the Franco regime). This simply produced further obstacles that hobbled the system, controlling the import of primary materials and investment goods through mechanisms in which economic criteria for allocating resources were replaced by criteria that were political or military, or based purely on personal influence.

In the sixth place, during the 1940s wages were maintained far below pre-war levels; leaving aside considerations of ethics, this fall in wages, although it might benefit management (and thus in the long run might stimulate investment), in the medium and short run caused downward pressure on the demand for industrial products, especially textiles. This explains the stagnation in the production index for textiles for those years (see Figure 12.1).[9] In short, the demand factors that might have stimulated production (both for basic industry and for the consumer sector) were missing.

In the seventh place, the government froze the price of electricity during the whole of the 1940s, in the erroneous belief that this would stimulate industry. Now the prices were frozen in nominal terms, and since this was a period of increasing inflation, electricity was being sold at decreasing real prices. In consequence the electricity industry stopped investing, demand outran supply, and the tiresome, dreaded service restrictions appeared; daily cuts in electricity supply did not end until the next decade, when electricity tariffs were more in line with the general evolution of prices.

And in the eighth place, the regime established a system of extreme interventionism in industrial matters, formulated through two laws of 1939 (October 24 and November 24) which discouraged and restricted investment. The first, the *Ley de Protección y Fomento de las Nuevas Industrias* (Protection and Development of New Industries) opened with a long expository preamble on the intention to secure self-sufficiency, proclaiming the need to "redeem Spain from importation of those exotic goods that could be produced or manufactured in the area of our own Nation." The law envisaged declaring certain industries to be "of national interest," a declaration that conferred tremendous advantages but also a high degree of state intervention. The second law, the *Ley de Ordinación y Defensa de la Industria* (Rationalization and Defense of Industry), classified industries according to their military significance, exercised state control over the establishment of new companies, restricted foreign participation (both in terms of capital and management), established the obligatory use of Spanish products, and limited the import of manufacturing techniques. These laws were hedged with numerous decrees which completed the government's tightly woven interventionist fabric. Combined with an iron control of external trade, this legislation left very little legal margin for private industrial initiative. From today's perspective it seems utterly inevitable that this "death embrace" paralyzed an industrial sector that the regime continuously insisted it wanted to succor.

The Franco authorities, however, laid the blame for industrial stagnation on private initiative and decided, in consequence, to strengthen the public presence and public participation in industry, with the creation of the Instituto Nacional de Industria (INI) in September 1941. The driving force behind INI and its president until 1963 was José Antonio Suanzes, a naval engineer who was a personal friend of Franco's and a strong supporter of industrialization and self-sufficiency at all costs; it is interesting to note that originally INI was to be called the National Institute for Autarky (Martín Aceña and Comín, 1991, p. 52). Suanzes is of considerable importance in Spain's economic history because his personal political influence might suffice to explain the strong pro-industrial bias of the Franco regime, which when all is said and done was a military dictatorship with major support from the Church and landowners, groups that are normally little interested in industrialization, and perhaps even hostile to it. The model that inspired the INI was the Italian Istituto per la Ricostruzione Industriale (IRI), founded in 1933 to take over a great deal of Italy's basic industry in a financial rescue operation during the Great Depression, and which later was converted into the giant holding company for Italy's public industrial sector.

The basic idea behind the creation of INI was that Spanish industrialization was an utmost priority and had to be achieved whatever the price. The private sector had proved incapable of achieving industrialization because of a lack of a "spirit of initiative," and perhaps because of a mean delight in profit combined with poor capacity to achieve it. Imported capital or technology could lead to "being captive to the will of others, what amounted to foreign interventionism . . . And hence the necessity for firm state action, embodied in this case in the National Institute of Industry."[10]

The INI (like the IRI) was conceived as a huge holding company; its main job was to promote or participate in those companies which, to the directors of INI, seemed worthy of support and development. From the mid-1940s onwards, therefore, one can speak of an "INI group" of industrial companies in which the institute's role was either partial or total. The institute specialized in basic industries and prioritized energy (petroleum and electricity, under large companies like the Calvo Sotelo, REPESA, ENDESA, and ENHER) and iron and steel, through ENSIDESA. It also paid serious attention to the construction of transportation equipment: in automobile manufacture, Pegaso-ENASA and SEAT, which acquired the old factories that had belonged to the Hispano-Suiza; in aviation, CASA (acquired in 1943) and HASA, which took over the aeronautical part of the Hispano-Suiza. The institute was also involved in shipbuilding (the Bazán Company and Astilleros de Cádiz); mining (Adaro and Fosfatos de Bucra); transportation (Iberia, Aviaco, Elcano); and chemicals, metallurgy, and mechanical engineering.

The amount of effort that went into the INI was nothing less than titanic, but it is appropriate to ask, as have Schwartz and González (1978), whether it was not arbitrary and wasteful. Suanzes, who was so long INI's president, had what these authors have called an engineering mentality, seeking production for its own sake without reference to comparative costs, in particular the opportunity cost, and without finding out whether these resources could not have been more profitably used in other ventures. Although, as Martín Aceña and Comín tell us, the INI was the "outstanding supporter of import substitution during the 1950s," these authors agree with Schwartz and González that this "development strategy that was interventionist and aimed at self-sufficiency led to an inefficient allocation of resources." Curi-

ously, however successful INI might have been in the realm of import substitution, and regardless of the xenophobia of its president, its own hunger for
imports was very large in these years. There can be no doubt that the INI of
the heroic period, that is to say during the Suanzes presidency, managed to
forge an extensive industrial base for Spain, but left it with a fundamental
weakness, its lack of ability to compete. This, as we shall see, caused serious
problems in the 1950s, the INI's period of most rapid growth. As Donges explains (1976, pp. 42–43),

> the costs and prices of products have tended to be high (if one compares
> with international levels). Thus the state companies, in supplying other in-
> dustries with basic inputs, imposed a higher level of costs on the economic
> system. . . . This redounded . . . to the detriment of Spanish industry's ability
> to compete internationally . . . Adding up the accounts, it does not seem
> that the INI contributed during that period [the 1940s and 1950s] to the
> efficient operation of private industry; or that it had effectively combated
> the existence of monopolies.

The magnitude of Spain's industrial stagnation during the 1940s can be appreciated by comparison with Italy, as shown in Figure 12.3. The Italian case
shows us that the destruction of war explains very little: after six years of a
world war far longer and more destructive than the Spanish Civil War, during which output was reduced to little more than one-fifth, Italy's industrial
production took only four years to recover to the 1940 level. Ten years after
the end of World War II, the Italian index of production was almost twice
what it had been in 1940; ten years after the Civil War the Spanish index
was still below that for 1935. Spain's lag was exceptional; although not as
rapidly as in Italy, production indices in France and the United Kingdom also
recovered at a good pace during the ten years after World War II (Mitchell,
1976, table EI).

   From 1950 the situation in Spain changed. The next decade was a period
of various serious tensions, but clearly a time of economic growth and a
surge in industrialization. It is sufficient to glance at Figures 12.1 or 12..2 to
confirm this. Even the cotton industry grew during this decade. This growth
period suffered an interruption with the 1959 stabilization plan, which provoked a fall in the index in 1960 as it ushered in a profound change in the
framework of economic policy, a change that was to permit another period
of rapid growth from 1961 to 1973. Now the following question arises: if the
policy of intervention and self-sufficiency was not substantially modified

until 1959, how can we explain the rapid growth of the 1950s? If the stagnation of the 1940s was due to this policy, the stagnation ought to have persisted so long as that policy remained in place. We cannot give a totally satisfactory answer to this question with the level of information we have at this stage, but we can point out that from 1950 onwards various small modifications in economic policy were introduced, changes that permitted greater levels of growth.

Around 1950 a series of administrative changes occurred, which. while leaving the old autarky laws standing, managed to modify the way they were applied. Perhaps the most important, from the point of view of economic policy, was that Suanzes left the presidency of INI, a post which since 1945 had been combined with that of Minister of Industry and Commerce. Government changes introduced in 1951 divided his old ministry into two. Industry became the responsibility of Joaquín Planell, a friend who shared Suanzes' military background, but a person more open to argument. Commerce was to be the responsibility of Manuel Arburúa, a bank official more familiar with economic matters than his predecessor. While little changed in the letter of the law, the new leadership was much more amenable to opening up international trade, a trend that was reflected in the growing impor-

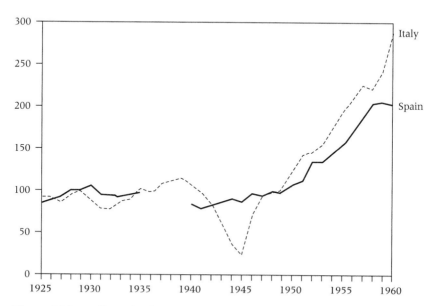

Figure 12.3. Indices of industrial production in Spain and Italy, 1925–1960 (1929=100)

tance (though still at very modest levels) of the external sector in national income, and in the changing composition of foreign trade. Whereas in the earlier decade foreign trade, on average, contributed 6.8% of the national income, in the 1950s this proportion rose slightly to 8.7%. Nothing spectacular here, in any event rather modest, less than one might have hoped for; but combined with certain qualitative changes this modest development explains a good part of the industrial growth that was emerging.

In the first place, the structure of imports changed. There was a remarkable increase in the import of capital investment goods, which more than tripled in constant peseta terms between 1949 and 1957; at the same time, food imports declined. As Manuel de Torres and his collaborators (1960) demonstrated (in a benchmark article which today we might characterize as cliometric), the correlation between the import of capital goods and growth in national income was very high between 1930 and 1960.[11] This presented serious problems, however, because Spain's foreign trade balance tended to produce a deficit, so that foreign exchange revenue was in very short supply. The balance of payments problem was therefore a limitation on imports and hence on national income growth. This explains the stagnation of the 1940s and the major interruptions in growth in the 1950s. In this respect two additional factors are influential: the agreement between Spain and the United States, and Spain's growing success in import substitution.

The first negative factor I enumerated in reviewing Spain's stagnation in the 1940s was its alignment with the Axis powers. This prejudiced its position not only during World War II, but also in the postwar period, since Spain remained diplomatically isolated and was deprived of the benefit of participation in the Marshall Plan. After 1951, however, Spain began to receive help from the United States, and in 1953 both sides signed an agreement through which Spain would lease to the United States military bases in Rota, Torrejón, and Zaragoza; in return the United States would give economic, military, and technical aid to Spain. Although not as ample as the Marshall aid to other countries, the support from the United States removed the logjam in Spain's international trade account, permitting increased imports of both foodstuffs and investment materials. Table 12.5 shows very clearly how imports of capital goods increased immediately after 1950.

At the same time, the process of import substitution took off in Spain, in agriculture as well as in industry, and especially in consumer goods.[12] This also helped to alleviate the balance of payments problem and to allow increased imports of capital goods and fuels that industry needed. Thus, while

Table 12.5. Imports of capital goods and the terms of trade between agriculture and industry, 1931–1959

Year	Capital goods[a]	Terms of trade[b]
1931	17.5	—
1932	14.0	—
1933	15.4	—
1934	19.6	—
1935	20.8	—
1940	5.4	1.0000
1941	4.7	1.0972
1942	6.3	1.1583
1943	6.2	1.2356
1944	4.1	1.1408
1945	4.2	1.0101
1946	5.9	1.1337
1947	6.9	1.3777
1948	8.5	1.4272
1949	9.8	1.5018
1950	8.4	1.4623
1951	10.4	1.9318
1952	16.3	2.0650
1953	22.9	2.0960
1954	25.9	2.2396
1955	26.1	2.2971
1956	32.3	1.9964
1957	31.1	2.0641
1958	—	1.7945
1959	—	1.8179

a. In million pesetas at 1935 values
b. Quotient of price indices
Sources: col. 1, Torres (1960); col. 2, calculated from González (1979), p. 118

foodstuffs represented 25% of imports in 1949, ten years later they were only 11%. In the same interval, capital goods destined for industry had increased from 13% to 20% of total imports.

Another factor to take into account was the improvement in the terms of trade between agriculture and industry, as González pointed out (1979, pp. 113–130). Between 1945 and 1955 the terms of trade between the two sectors, as measured by the ratio of the respective price indices, more than doubled in favor of industry.[13] Combined with low wage levels in the 1940s (although there was a certain recovery from 1953 onwards which perhaps explains the growth in the cotton industry), this development leads us to suppose that the industrial sector was highly profitable, which in turn explains the rise in investment in two stages, the first starting in 1848 and the second in 1953. Thus between 1949 and 1959 investment rose from 11% to 18% of national income. This rise in capital formation was above all the response of the private sector. Attracted by high industrial profits and confident in the iron discipline the state imposed on the labor market, business entrepreneurs in 1948 and later were investing as they had not done since 1930 (Carreras, 1985). If to this we add a more tolerant attitude towards prices, especially electricity rates, which produced a strong expansive spurt in electricity production, we get an economic picture very similar to that of the previous decade, but with a character completely altered by just a few simple touches here and there.

Yet despite the spectacular growth that these simple modifications had permitted, the picture remained basically the same. The system was full of "internal contradictions" which in the long run would bring it to the "limits of economic growth," in the phrase of Manuel Román (1971). The most obvious of these limits and contradictions were: (1) the method of financing this growth, which was inflationary; (2) the stranglehold regulation of the external sector; (3) tensions in the labor market; and (4) the supply rigidities that the system generated. The order of this listing is somewhat arbitrary; as is characteristic in economics we again find ourselves confronted with a network of circular causation.

INFLATIONARY FINANCING. The state played a key role in industrial development, deploying a tangled thicket of laws and directives that included direct intervention through the INI, the Bank of Industrial Credit, an endless chain of autonomous bodies, and budgetary measures. During the 1950s the state embarked upon an ambitious entrepreneurial program and public works. The years of INI's strongest expansion saw the development of Spain's basic industries, the construction of ENSIDESA (for iron and steel production), SEAT (for automobiles), and the large petroleum and metallurgical refineries. During this period every public company—and in good measure the private ones too—put into practice José Antonio Suanzes' maxim "to produce at whatever price." This program was financed basically through bank credit, which in the end was monetized through the expan-

sion of bank deposits and paper currency. In the course of expansion the total liabilities of INI reached inordinate levels, arriving in 1960 at a historical
maximum of 8% of the national income (calculated from Martín Aceña and
Comín, 1989, table 1). As we shall see in Chapter 14, the amount of money
in circulation expanded very considerably in these years, fed in great part by
the public deficit. The national level of saving was simply insufficient to
cover the amount of ongoing investment, and the government resorted,
more or less knowingly, to financing the shortfall through inflation.

EXTERNAL BOTTLENECKS. This growth by forced march, so to speak,
depended on importing capital goods which had to be paid for by foreign reserves that could only come through exports, given that the state's own
thicket of legal regulations put serious difficulties in the way of importing
capital and exporting services. The greater part of Spanish exports were agricultural products, and during these years the export of oranges surged. But
internal inflation, the overvalued exchange rate, and the protection afforded to national producers made Spanish products tremendously expensive on the export market, and they lost their competitiveness; the country
was continually threatened by a deficit on the commercial balance of trade,
and tight import controls were enforced. (The other components of the balance of payments in such a closed economy were of little importance.) In
these circumstances, difficulties came to a head in the spring of 1956, when
late frosts severely damaged the orange crop; the repercussions of this mete-
orological incident on the commercial balance of trade and on the whole national economy were very important, and served to accelerate the reform of
the system embodied in the 1959 stabilization plan.

THE LABOR MARKET. After the Civil War, the Franco regime controlled
the labor market very tightly; salaries were fixed by decree. As we saw, this
allowed real wages to fall during the 1940s. The growth and inflation in the
1950s caused strong pressure to adjust the salary schedule, a theme that became highly politicized as confrontation between Franco and the workers
developed, with the employers at the margin. In the face of growing labor
militancy, the government began to use salary revisions as a means of controlling public order. The steep salary increases of 1955, measures of social
appeasement and self-aggrandizement introduced by Minister of Labor José
Antonio Girón, only served to heighten inflation, and it turned out that at
the end of two years real wages were so eroded that the workers had made

no real gains. On the other hand, the counterpart of low salary levels was security of employment, and this condition certainly hampered any chance of rising productivity. In an inflationary market this was not very important, but for exports it was quite disastrous.

The Franco system also generated *supply rigidity.* In many sectors of the economy, and especially industry, one can detect indicators of monopoly tendencies, in some cases as far back as the end of the nineteenth century.[14] Monopolistic conditions evolve in particular industries for various reasons. One is the desire on the part of the business owners to raise profits by clubbing together with other owners to agree to raise prices, as Adam Smith had denounced in a celebrated passage in *The Wealth of Nations* (p. 128). But this form of collusion is not always possible, since in the usual competitive regime high profits generated by high prices will normally attract new competitors, which will push down prices. In order for monopolistic conditions to exist, two basic conditions must be met: certain social or technical conditions that permit the monopoly, and a policy of state intervention that favors it.

The technical bases are many and diverse. In the case of certain public services, like electricity or running water, a system of free competition is not easy to maintain. In general, goods in inelastic demand, those for which substitutes are not readily available, tend to be offered under monopoly conditions. The same happens with those goods whose production methods benefit from large economies of scale; in these conditions the large companies are advantaged since they can saturate the market almost at a moment's notice. Among industries of this type are automobiles, iron and steel, cement and petroleum, for example. In the case of electricity all the aforementioned conditions apply; public service, rigid demand, and economies of scale. The examples could be multiplied.

Now in conditions like this the role played by the state is crucial, because its intervention can modify, for better or worse, the extent to which pro-monopoly technical conditions prevail. Historically speaking, the Spanish state has shown considerable partiality for monopolistic situations. (See the useful summary in Tamames, 1961, pp. 177–200.) To begin with, there is a rich tradition of legal or state monopolies, from the Casa de Contratación which controlled commerce with Spanish America in the early sixteenth century right through to the now finally abolished, the long-lived and very durable Petroleum Monopoly (CAMPSA), without counting products as diverse as stamped paper (for collecting taxes), salt, tobacco, matches and explosives.

In addition, the deep-seated interventionism of the Spanish state has favored the formation of private monopolies, as in the case of sugar, banking (see Chapter 14), and various others. Perhaps the strongest form of state interventionism is to be found in tariff protection. Tariff barriers impeded competition from foreign competitors, thus permitting a few Spanish firms to take control of the national market. The state had been notoriously remiss in attempting to combat monopoly practices and had notably failed to emulate other countries that have utilized a series of measures which Spain could also have adopted. Some of these measures are of a legal nature and others are more connected business practices. The legal instruments can forbid monopolistic conduct such as cartels, market sharing, and general agreements against competition. The business-based solution consists of the state creating companies that compete in sectors that are controlled by private monopolies. In this latter aspect the INI could have played an important role,[15] and indeed at certain points in time, concretely in the creation of ENSIDESA (the iron and steel works), this very argument was put forward as justification. In the long run, however, the INI not only failed to act as a competitor but in many cases became a participant in monopoly situations, even to the point of becoming a life-preserver for industries and companies unable to sustain themselves in the face of outside competition.

One cannot say that the Spanish state acted out of ignorance, since among the serious studies in applied economics published in the 1950s and 1960s one can find a number of works about monopolistic factors in Spanish industry[16] which show beyond a doubt the existence of industrial sectors that were powerfully monopolistic, such as the iron and steel industry, electricity, cement, various important subsectors of the chemicals industry such as fertilizers and sulfuric acid, glass, paper, sugar, and coal. This is without counting the banking industry, discussed in a later chapter, which to a great extent acted as a bonding mechanism, the glue that held the monopolistic industries together.

It is well known in economic theory that the monopolist sells smaller quantities at higher prices than the competitive producer. The monopoly buyer, for his part, buys goods at low prices and in smaller quantity than the buyer in a competitive situation. It is easy to see that all of us contribute to the extraordinary profits that fall to the monopolist through higher prices and lower salaries than those that would apply if there were no monopoly. This is the economic cost of such an institution. The 1950s were probably the culminating period for monopolies in Spain, because the conditions were perfect: the highest degree of protection, strong state intervention, defense of the producer at all costs, economic growth, industrialization, and inflation. This last was both cause and consequence of the monopoly situation; consequence because monopoly generates high prices, and cause because the inflation heightened demand rigidity. With the relative liberalization that followed the 1959 stabilization plan one would expect the power of the monopolists to diminish. This, at least, is what seems to have happened in banking. Yet despite the political democratization that has been happening since 1975, and the entry into the European Community ten years later, the Spanish state continues to treat monopolies with great caution and is totally lacking in any specific policy to foster competition, except for a rather tame Court for the Promotion of Competition.

After a decade of accelerated growth, at the end of the 1950s the Spanish economy found itself in a cul-de-sac. Growth and industrialization had taken place within a framework of controls and interventions which in reality constituted just as many other obstacles to growth, and only with the help of another series of regulations and exceptions had companies managed to shake off the suffocating embrace of state bureaucracy. But all this tangle of dispositions, orders, and counterorders in the long run constituted a Gordian knot which had tied up the economy and could not be untied patiently, bit by bit. Partial measures would not suffice: things would have to be settled once and for all; the country had to cut its losses, and that is what the stabilization plan did.

Liberalization and Modernization

The effects of the stabilization plan on the Spanish economy were profound, indeed they were probably more profound than the plan's creators anticipated. The immediate effect was a powerful recession which lasted a whole year, from the middle of 1959 until the middle of 1960, although as González indicates (1979, p. 269), in some ways this recession had already begun in 1957. From the middle of 1960 until the international crisis that began in 1973, however, the economy enjoyed a period of growth completely without precedent in Spain. Already the first third of the century, especially the 1920s, were years of undoubted expansion; then, after a long parenthesis, the 1950s again saw a return to economic growth. But the

1960s were a period of development that was much more rapid and comprehensive. If there is one decade that can be identified as that of the Spanish Industrial Revolution, it is certainly the 1960s.

The leader in this boom was the industrial sector, and within it, following the pattern already noted, it was the new subsectors which set the norm, so that in addition to growing very rapidly the Spanish economy also experienced a massive and profound transformation. It industrialized radically, and at the same time industry became technologically sophisticated. The Hoffmann index (Table 12.1) in this decade increased from 1.1 to 2.4, its greatest jump during the twentieth century, and certainly in the whole history of Spain. Such growth implies that in ten years the economy evolved from a situation where basic industry and the consumer sector were almost equally important to another in which basic industry was almost two and a half times as important as the consumer sector. Only in the 1920s did the Hoffmann index increase in a comparable manner, when it almost doubled; but of course the gain was less impressive because it started at a much lower level.

During this decade industry grew far faster than the economy as a whole. The contribution of industry to the Gross Domestic Product went from 26% in 1964 to 34% in 1974, with a much smaller increase in labor participation. The population active in this sector went from 25% to just 26% in the same period, so we can see that industrial labor productivity improved substantially faster than overall productivity. In fact, Table 12.7 shows that average industrial productivity, based on a labor force that hovered around 3 million workers until 1970, had increased by 100% between 1964 and 1973, which implies an annual rate of 8%, way above the increase in general productivity.

The industrial sector was also outstanding in terms of the absolute growth achieved. Whereas in the period 1958–1972 the GDP grew at an average annual rate of 6.2%, total industrial production grew at 10.4%,[17] a figure that conceals some remarkable variations. The principal industrial sectors can be divided into three groups according to their rate of growth during the period, as in Table 12.6. In general, the traditional consumer industries predominate in the slower growth sector; there is nothing unusual here, given that the Hoffmann index leads us to expect this. In fact there is only one traditional industry in the fast growth group, shoe manufacture. The consumer industries that performed better are the ones with higher income elasticity, that is, those where demand grows as income grows, but at a

Table 12.6. Main industrial sectors and their growth rates, 1958–1972

Slow Growth (less than 9.4%)
  Railroad equipment (0.2)
  Motorcycles, bicycles (2.4)
  Textiles (3.6)
  Wood and cork (4.3)
  Tobacco (4.5)
  Drinks (7.1)
  Food stuffs (7.2)
  Leather (9.0)
  Printing and publishing (9.1)

Average Growth (9.4% to 11.4%)
  Nonelectrical machinery (9.4)
  Furniture (9.4)
  Ready-made clothing(10.2)
  Nonferrous mining (10.9)

Fast Growth (more than 11.4%)
  Footwear (11.5)
  Refining and petrochemicals (11.9)
  Nonferrous metals (12.0)
  Paper (12.8)
  Iron and steel (13.1)
  Electrical machinery (13.4)
  Naval construction (14.0)
  Heavy machinery (14.0)
  Other industries (14.4)
  Chemicals (14.4)
  Rubber (15.3)
  Automobiles (21.7)

Source: Donges (1976), p. 158

higher rate. The clothing industry grew three times faster than its parent, textiles, and furniture (though not included in the table) responded well, reflecting strong growth in the construction industry.

Among the high growth industries, the ones that we have considered basic predominate: chemicals, iron and steel, and various aspects of mechanical engineering. The brightest star of the period was the automobile industry, and here again we run into income elasticity; motorcycles and bicycles stagnate while the motor vehicle takes off, in the economic sense. And

Table 12.7.   Industrial production and productivity, 1964–1985, in 1970 pesetas

	(1) Production[a]	(2) Working Population[b]	(3) Productivity[c]
1964	435.4	2.915	149.38
1965	486.0	2.857	170.10
1966	536.0	2.906	184.48
1967	565.4	3.003	188.26
1968	610.4	2.999	203.52
1969	693.3	3.094	224.11
1970	749.5	3.096	242.09
1971	795.7	3.153	252.34
1972	912.7	3.251	280.76
1973	1,010.1	3.364	300.23
1974	1,072.7	3.476	308.58
1975	1,066.4	3.494	305.25
1976	1,103.1	3.517	313.67
1977	1,154.6	3.568	323.63
1978	1,177.6	3.520	334.59
1979	1,176.4	3.251	361.86
1980	1,180.9	3.098	381.13
1981	1,186.8	2.978	398.52
1982	1,180.4	2.816	419.18
1983	1,209.9	2.750	439.96
1984	1,228.4	2.681	458.19
1985	1,255.4	2.589	484.90

a. In million pesetas
b. In millions
c. Col. 1/Col. 2
Source: Baiges, Molinas, and Sebastián (1987), and own calculations

closely allied to the automobile industry, we find exceptional growth in rubber, whose main product was motor tires. Growth in some industries will later present problems; these are the industries of intermediate technology with relatively heavy labor inputs, such as naval construction, iron and steel, mining (especially coal mining), and some branches of the chemicals industry.

The growth of the automobile industry is paradigmatic of the development of the 1960s. At the time of the stabilization plan little attention was paid to this sector. It was small (about 38,000 private cars were produced in 1959) and dominated by the state-owned SEAT (Sociedad Española de Automóviles de Turismo, of which INI was the major shareholder), which in turn was a subsidiary of the Italian enterprise FIAT. Essentially, the models were manufactured in Italy and assembled in Spain, where they were sold at astronomical prices. I find it symptomatic of the early disregard for this sector that Tamames shows such lack of confidence in the automobile industry in the first edition of his text book (1960)[18] and that furthermore the First Development Plan, published in 1963, didn't even mention[19] it when it dedicated a whole chapter to handicraft industries. As happened with tourism (but in greater measure, because that sector did in fact receive some attention in the plan and a more confident prediction from Tamames), the impressive growth of the Spanish automobile industry was a surprise for one and all. Many believed, and not without reason, that the production of automobiles in Spain was no more than a prestige operation, very much along the lines of Suanzes' INI, and with little economic future.

The tremendous growth of the automobile industry, whose production grew annually by 22% between 1958 and 1973, is paradigmatic in its unexpectedness and in various other features. First, it showed the relative maturity and potential of Spanish industry, in particular of the labor force, which handled a newly introduced series of operations that were relatively complex with such success. In the second place, it showed off the rising standard of living and the acquisitive power that were characteristic of this kind of growth process; during the 1960s the Spanish automobile industry (with prices way above international levels) sold practically all its output to the home market. And thirdly, motor vehicles were, literally, the motive power of industrialization in those years; their derived demand explains the development of at least three additional sectors: rubber production, iron and steel, and petroleum refining. It is also worth mentioning that although Tamames was not happy that the industry should be born "so fragmented," the proliferation of companies (after SEAT came Renault, Citroen, Morris-Leyland, Chrysler-Talbot, Ford, and later on General Motors) was beneficial because it encouraged competition, contributing to increased productivity and lower prices. Although SEAT maintained its leading position in the sector during the whole of the period, its market share was declining.

Figure 12.4 shows the impressive growth of the automobile industry and its progress in leaps and bounds, as well as its obvious sensitivity to short-term fluctuations in the economy at large. It also shows considerable growth in steel production, whose major client was clearly the automobile industry itself. The iron and steel industry in general had been stagnating since the 1920s. In 1956 steel per capita production was less than it had been in 1929. Protected by the tariff, the industry remained oligopolistic, and this resulted in high prices, with production way below demand. When the ENSIDESA factory at Avilés came into production, things began to change; within a few years the automobile, mechanical engineering, and shipbuilding industries began to grow, helped also by a degree of decontrol of iron and steel imports. Although in the long run ENSIDESA too would demand state protection for this sector, its entry into the market contributed at the beginning to breaking the monopoly, as did the arrival of foreign competition. Just as happened in the automobile industry, iron and steel, which had been a traditional import sector, began to export production in the 1970s.

Growth in basic chemicals is reflected in the production of sulfuric acid, but the chemical industry is very diverse, with principal branches that grew a great deal. The production of nitrogen fertilizers, which before the war had not been able to compete with imports, after the war developed briskly, thanks to protection, growing capitalization, and technical improvements in agriculture. The pharmaceutical industry also grew, each year more dependent upon Spain's social medicine system as a chief client. Petrochemicals and

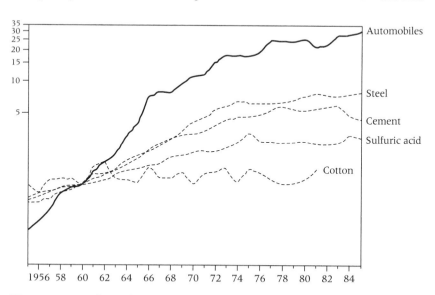

Figure 12.4. Indices of key industrial outputs, 1955–1985 (semi-logarithmic scale, 1960=1)

plastics were, to all intents and purposes, born in the 1960s, and in spite of the justifiable criticism that misuse of plastic containers has provoked, we should recognize in that growth a further measure of rising living standards.

There is no point here in commenting on the industrial sectors separately, because in fact they all grew notably, almost without exception. Even the large traditional sectors, textiles and foods, experienced appreciable growth, although in expanding below the average they were losing ground in relative terms.

Many factors have been mentioned in attempting to explain this "industrial revolution," but they can all be reduced to one essential element, the liberalization of trade and industry. This liberalization had domestic and foreign aspects.. Both were very significant, but the exterior element was of greater importance. Opening Spain up to the outside world destroyed the restrictions that had suffocated the Spanish economy during the last years of the 1950s. The proof is that after a decade in which industrial exports as a whole stagnated, in the 1960s they grew at a rate of 14.2% per annum. But it was not only direct exports that benefited industry. For some important industrial sectors (automobiles, iron and steel, manufactured goods, petrochemicals, petroleum refining, and chemicals in general) the only important market was the home market. For these, opening up Spain's trade connections was crucial: first, industries benefited from general growth and rising living standards that the new trading pattern engendered, and in addition, freer trading permitted an increase in capital goods imports, thanks to which technology could advance and productivity could rise.

For numerous sectors, however, exporting was vital, and among these one traditional industry stands out. True, it was hobbled by all the ancestral defects that Spanish industry was heir to (atomization, artesanal production methods, shortages of raw materials), but it possessed in its human capital (the organization and commercial instincts of its managers, the skills of its workers) the resources that enabled that industry to take advantage of an excellent world situation: this was the footwear industry. The key to the overwhelming success of the liberalization of Spain's economy lay, in fact, in the worldwide boom of those years. With this liberalization Spain could participate in one of the most rapid growth spurts that the world economy has ever experienced.[20] This growth engendered a rising standard of living and rising demand for consumer goods that notably benefited Spain's light industry. Footwear exports increased during the 1960s at an average rate of 41.5% per year—a rate that was almost incredible even for an industry that already had enjoyed a history of export sales—until this became the leading export sector. Other consumer industries that exported in great quantities were leather manufactures, the timber industry, cork, furniture, paper, and publishing. Among the heavy and basic industries, rubber (for tires), machinery, nonferrous mining (in particular mercury and potash) and shipbuilding also contributed to exports.

We have been talking about liberalization and opening up the Spanish economy, but the reader should remember, with Auguste Comte, that "tout est rélatif," and nothing was more relative than Spain's liberalism while Franco was in power. The stabilization plan and the measures that followed it marked a clear change in the guidelines for Spain's economic policy; but, to pay heed to another well-known French adage, "plus ça change, plus c'est la même chose": when the politics of dictatorship was changing most, the core elements were more stubborn than ever. Economic reality had been asserting itself, and the regime was making the right moves in adapting itself, but the changes came very slowly, with resistance and with many backward steps. Thus, if the fiercest and most visible controls disappeared, many survived and other new ones were created, more subtle, but equally real and operative. In terms of industrial policy, which was one of the dictator's favorite interests, protectionism and many monopoly features survived, although in different forms, more complex, more refined. One symbol of the industrial self-sufficiency power group was toppled with the angry resignation of Suanzes from the presidency of the INI at the end of 1963; yet the INI itself survived, and in modified form continued to play a powerful role in the industrial politics of the regime. The quantitative restrictions on external trade were much reduced, but were replaced by the highly protectionist 1960 tariff and additional new direct controls on international trade. In 1963 the Law on Practices Restrictive to Competition was proclaimed, but the policy continued to favor monopoly behavior, and above all monopolistic structures (González, 1979, p. 317). And so on and so forth; one could mention many other similar details.

In reality, it was as though the politicians of the 1960s, frightened by the 1959 reforms, had been putting patches here and there to try to reconstruct the old autarky "bunker" and had stopped half way through the task. The introduction of French-style "flexible planning" in the early 1960s (*Planes de Desarrollo*) was already chipping away at the "process of introducing the market economy, whose political implications were not acceptable to the regime; the development plans seem to be some odd kind of interventionist contraption, a little more suitable, a little more refined than the obsolete autarkic system," in the words of Martín Aceña and Comín (1991, p. 219).

The stringent industrial laws of 1939 were partially replaced. In 1959 the conditions under which capital could be imported were relaxed; the 1963 Law on Top Priority Industries *(Ley de Industrias de Interés Preferente)* modified the harshest elements of the earlier rules for "industries of national interest"; the decision was made to operate in terms of credit support rather than rigid controls; and development policy was focused towards regions or sectors, rather than individual companies. In addition, the state conceded certain benefits (tax credits or credit facilities) through joint agreements with certain companies, in return for their commitment to specific functions, typically to maintain a certain level of investment. But this system did not produce good results. In the first place, the state was not really able to ensure that the company would actually fulfill the agreement that had been reached, and also the "joint agreements" created "an enormous apparatus for subsidies and discounts of a different type, which gave rise to considerable discrimination between those companies within the agreement and those outside" (Maravall, 1987, p. 176). The administrative system for establishing and expanding companies was liberalized, but in 1963, under the pretext of avoiding the creation of too many small firms, the government reinstated a system of licenses and requirements for setting up new companies. According to González (1979, p. 322), "[although] it was not enforced with much rigor it certainly constituted a source of privilege for the old established industries, which in no way were obliged to meet the minimum size requirements imposed on newcomers."

Many more interventionist devices were created, such as "development poles," special export credits, export permits of first, second, or third category, and price controls. "Spanish Industry was conceived by López Bravo and López Rodó as one huge company, of which they were directors. The result of this return to state controls was, as any economist would have imagined, the rebirth of privileged positions for companies with friends in the government, and an unsatisfactory distribution of investment" (González, 1979, pp. 321 and 323).

The system went into crisis in 1969, when the "MATESA case"—a typical product of the state's development-oriented interventionism—became a public issue. Preoccupied with the trade deficit that was essentially structural, the policy "directors" decided to promote industrial exports through incentives such as preferential credit. For reasons that remain unclear (it would have been more logical to assign the task to the Banco Exterior), they entrusted the management of these export credits to the Bank of Industrial Credit, and the credits were given to companies in proportion to volumes exported, which the company seeking support was required to substantiate with documentation. A series of bureaucratic safeguards against fraud were created, but naturally they did not work. The MATESA company, a manufacturer of textile looms, discovered that by exporting its goods fraudulently, that is, by selling the looms to branches abroad that the company had set up for this specific purpose, they could obtain astronomical credit figures, on very favorable terms. With this system in place they could actually finance their own exports, perhaps at a profit. The actual sale of the looms in the countries abroad soon became a secondary consideration. When the truth was finally established, the political scandal was tremendous, because the Falangist faction in the government managed to use the case to inflict serious political damage upon Opus Dei, a religious group with which various economic ministers and the president of MATESA were closely related. The question was repeatedly aired in the press for months, a highly unusual occurrence in Franco's Spain, where control of information was very strict. This public discussion was possible because the Falange still wielded considerable power, and because at that moment they could count on the connivance of Minister of Information Manuel Fraga. This is not the place to go into details.[21] As it happened, instead of Opus Dei it was the paternalistic pro-development policy that suffered the most acute damage. The comedy of errors that lead to the MATESA scandal showed that the state could not play at being the managing director of a whole market economy. More than the corruption involved (there were much murkier deals in the shadowy history of the Franco regime economy), what MATESA brought to light was the scandalous incompetence of the system of bureaucratic controls which "the directors" had thought up. In a system that was so hierarchical, the businessman who earned the support of the authorities could do almost as he wished, because the bureaucrats charged with applying the law did not dare to treat a "friend of the minister" like any other John Citizen. The distribution of resources, therefore, was not made according to the logic of the economic market, but according to political favor. Pro-development paternalism replaced "market competition with competition among the industrial cliques, who competed not on price, not on quality nor costs, but rather in the acquisition of official favors: the politicians in control of the development process managed the business like quasi-enlightened despots" (González, 1979, p. 300).

In the final years of the Franco dictatorship, a gradual weakening of this kind of industrial policy was certainly evident. The problem, however, lay in the slow pace of this second transition towards liberalization, and that was because of the tremendous lack of appropriate ideas among the leading power brokers, Franco and his trusted friends. They wanted a freer economy but feared the political consequences of economic freedom. In consequence, lacking any program, the leading figures in economic policy during the last Franco years found themselves completely without a sense of direction when the world fuel crisis of 1973 set in. Meanwhile, the market distortions of the pro-development stage had favored the growth of industries that had little future, such as shipbuilding, iron and steel, and coal. The industrial inheritance of this pro-development phase was to become a very heavy burden indeed for Spaniards in the post-Franco era.

Reconversion

From the mid-1960s to the mid-1980s Spain lived through a period of profound economic crisis which was characterized, as in other Western nations, by very low growth in national income, including some years of negative growth, by high rates of inflation and unemployment, and by negative investment, that is to say a running down of its stock of capital. The industrial sector, construction, and the service sector, especially banking, experienced steep declines in their growth rates from 1973 onwards, with the construction industry frequently displaying negative figures; in some months the index of total industrial production declined. People had begun to speak of "de-industrialization" both for Spain and for some other countries; in the Spanish case this was justified by a decline in manpower employed in industry and the slight fall in the share that this sector contributed to total national income.

Let us disaggregate so we can better grasp the measure of this industrial deceleration. If we separate the energy industry from manufacturing activities, for example, we see that the crisis affected the latter far more heavily, which is not surprising. The energy sector, in spite of several contractions related to sudden price increases, rode out the storm without too many problems. Manufacturing industry, in contrast, was very severely affected by the crisis, to the point that its growth rate was negative (-2.2% per annum between 1978 and 1984 (Segura, 1989, p. 31).

Within manufacturing, it was the traditional sectors that suffered most. They are those customarily referred to as "sectors of weak demand" (included here are nonferrous and nonmetallic mining, textiles, clothing, and footwear), along with other sectors generally considered to be of "medium demand" (for example, machinery manufacture and rolling stock). In any case it is interesting to point out that only two sectors grew during these six years, the food industry (doubtless stimulated by the salary increases that dominated the period), and office machinery, probably benefiting from the introduction of computers in the 1980s.

The causes of this grave crisis, probably the most serious to hit the Spanish economy in the twentieth century, included some international components, since it occurred more or less simultaneously in other countries, though a little later in Spain. But for Spain there were internal elements too, which help to explain this time lag.

The International Context

Two phenomena unleashed the international crisis. On the one side was the breakdown of the Bretton Woods international system of payments, described in Chapter 14; on the other side was the energy crisis.

The rise in fuel prices was, without any doubt, the immediate detonator, the cause of the crisis in industry. The situation, already unstable at the beginning of the decade, was suddenly aggravated by an event that was of political origin, but which had vast economic repercussions. The so-called Yom Kippur War in the Middle East, between Israel and various Arab countries, produced a sudden surge of solidarity between the Arab oil-producing nations. This in turn revitalized an institution created many years earlier and until then inoperative: the Organization of Petroleum Exporting Countries, the cartel that is today famously known by its acronym, OPEC.

Acting in concert, OPEC drastically increased petroleum prices, and given the market sector that these producers controlled and the demand structure, these new prices simply and inescapably forced themselves upon the market. At the time, various strange, alarmist, and outlandish stories circulated about the economic significance of the price increase. OPEC itself went to great lengths to present the measure as one of conservation, justified by a supposedly imminent shortage of the product. In reality, this was far from the truth. In simple terms this power play was generated by a temporary co-incidence of interests among OPEC's heterogeneous members, between a group that for a long time had been requesting a price rise that would im-prove the terms of trade for the oil-producing nations, and another group of nations which, traditionally fearful of endangering the *status quo* of interna-tional trade, felt suddenly compelled to support the rise out of political soli-darity.

The rise in petroleum prices had an enormous impact on economies in general and the developed economies in particular, since they were very de-pendent upon the fuel supplied from these countries. Petroleum is the most utilized source of fossil energy in the world; most productive processes and transportation, plus direct consumption for heating, are geared to petroleum and its derivatives. For this reason the demand for petroleum is extremely rigid, and especially so in the short run. Once the new system of interna-tional prices was in place, the large petroleum consumers, which is tanta-mount to saying the industrialized countries, had no other remedy than to absorb the new costs at their own expense. The inflationary impact of the new fuel prices was of course very strong, and the consuming nations were obliged to mitigate the situation with political restrictions. All in all, in the short run the new price structure implied a powerful redistribution of re-sources in favor of the petroleum exporting nations at the expense of the consumers.

The effects of this radical upheaval in the price structure were reflected dramatically in the industrialized economies. Given the already mentioned inelasticity of demand, imports of petroleum products had to be maintained in the same volume but for much more money, which of course disturbed the balance of payments. And the rise in energy prices had to have repercus-sions for the public. Since gasoline is so widely used, the higher prices had considerable inflationary impact, which among other things would also af-fect the balance of payments. Under the circumstances a rational policy ought to have led to a weaker demand for petroleum, through measures de-signed to stimulate conservation and the development of alternative energy sources, thus moderating the inflationary pressure. This policy ought to have produced a deceleration of economic growth in general, affecting par-ticularly those activities most dependent upon petroleum, that is to say, manufacturing, transportation, and related activities such as tourism.

Thus insofar as the petroleum crisis forced the governments of the indus-trialized nations to introduce restrictive measures to moderate demand and palliate balance of payments problems, and insofar as policy decisions were made that modified the world price structure at the expense of certain industries and other activities like tourism and construction, it was inevitable that these activities would be affected, and that the resulting depression would be transmitted internationally.

Features Particular to Spain

Of course, the forces that shaped the contraction of foreign economies also affected the Spanish economy. But it is not surprising that the case of Spain should have some of its own special features. Although the majority of the economic circumstances were about the same for Spain as for its neighbors, other features were exclusive to Spain, like the exceptional situation of the political transition, with its own undoubted economic repercussions, and the peculiar inheritance of Franco's economic policies.

POLITICAL FACTORS—THE TRANSITION TO DEMOCRACY. Economists have tended to pay little attention to the political factor when studying the origin of the ten-year crisis in 1975–1985. However, as Martínez Méndez affirms, "it is almost impossible to explain long-term Spanish economic evolution over recent years without paying some attention to political events [to which, however, it is] extremely difficult . . . to apportion appropriate weight." And that, as the author himself explains, is principally for two reasons: the scant attention that the government paid to economic policy during the period of institutional transition, and the element of uncertainty due to the political transition itself, which particularly affected business leaders in their decision-making (Martínez Méndez, 1982, p. 35).

This element of uncertainty, the difficulty of weighing alternatives, is the factor of greater importance because it explains the radical fall in investment. The business community's lack of confidence in the new system, although doubtless justified in part by the circumstances, contained an element that was purely political. The business sector had been accustomed to the rules of the game as defined by the Franco regime (although debilitated enough by the way those rules were applied during the later years). Hence participation in a new institutional framework that was uncertain and still evolving provoked a strong sense of "anxiety in the face of the new situation." Quoting again from Martínez Méndez (1982, p. 39), the final months of the Franco dictatorship and the initial ones of the Monarchy were enveloped in the greatest political uncertainty. [Later on] there would be a large number of clear and important changes in the political and economic environment in which businesses were to make their decisions. It could be argued, with some justification, that there was nothing in the new framework to alarm any businessman from a western developed country, as can be proved by the high level of foreign direct investment in Spain in recent years, but that would mean overlooking the most relevant fact, which is that the new circumstances were very different from those of the past, much more comfortable for businessmen.

More concrete uncertainties accompanied this political apprehension: for one thing, about how the labor market would be organized and what roles the employers' organizations, the unions, and the state would have to play. Likewise, it was not clear how the new democratic political system would function, not only on paper (that is to say how the legal framework would be shaped from the Constitution downwards) but in terms of how it would really operate; in concrete terms, what would the parties of the left do when they were in power, given that they had been excluded from it since 1939, and above all what kind of economic policy would they pursue? This state of uncertainty, this incognito, was cleared up starting in 1982 and contributed more than a little to the upturn in investment that is seen from 1985 onwards.[22] And in addition, the business community was concerned about how political and economic relations would be handled between Spain and the rest of Europe, and concretely with the European Community. This unknown also was clarified in the mid-1980s, with Spain's entry into the European Community and NATO, and this outcome further contributed to the rebirth of confidence.

THE ECONOMIC TRANSITION. If the industrial crisis in its totality was much more severe in Spain than in other countries, this was because its particular problems of economic and political transition coincided with the normal and more foreseeable elements of the international crisis. The repercussions of the international depression were obviously going to show up in Spain through the balance of payments. And here again we face the mixture of political and economic factors that are so difficult to disentangle. In the politically uncertain years between the death of Carrero Blanco and the proclamation of the Constitution, it was difficult for the treasury to take decisions that could have unpopular consequences. Thus, as has been told many, many times, Barrera de Irimo and his successors opted for what has been called a "compensatory policy," which consisted of sheltering the consumer from the high price of crude oil. That meant, of course, that it was the state that would absorb this cost, with a considerable reduction in its income. Given that Spain's demand for petroleum was more rigid than that of other European countries, the consequence of this "compensatory policy" was that in Spain consumption continued to rise, and with it, of course, petroleum imports.[23] The result of this policy on the balance of payments could hardly have been unforeseen; the deficits on the current account reached previously unknown amounts,[24] and with the exception of 1978, the deficits continued until 1984.

The principal justification for the compensatory policy in relation to energy prices was the belief that the increases in petroleum prices were going to be short-lived. When this turned out to be incorrect, measures were taken to rectify the deteriorating balance of payments. Although with some delay, the practice of sheltering the consumer was abandoned, and because of justified fear of the resulting inflation, the government introduced a restrictive monetary policy which was obviously going to raise interest rates. To palliate the deteriorating balance of payments, the government resorted to two devaluations in February 1976 and in July 1977, one of whose immediate effects was, of course, to make imports more expensive and to contribute further to inflation. All these economic policy measures, although doubtless justifiable in the circumstances (and some of them had long been expected), added to and intensified the uncertainty of economic decision-makers, for the sociopolitical reasons that Martínez Méndez expressed so well.

The consequence of all these changes was bound to be a fall in investment, a stagnation of home consumption and national income, and an increase in unemployment, all these being characteristic of the Spanish economy during the decade 1975 to 1984.

THE LEGACY OF THE FRANCO REGIME.   In spite of the real industrial growth that we have described above, the industry that had developed under Franco's interventionist regime was suffering from patent defects which the crisis exposed. These included excessive specialization in products that were high in labor content and technologically backward, basically the traditional industries, textiles, iron and steel, shipbuilding and mining; not enough competition because of traditional protection through tariffs and regulated credit; poor labor mobility; and endemic monopoly. Moreover, industry was heavily dependent upon imported technology and in general had little technical autonomy, to a large extent because there was little state and private investment in research. And the economy was also heavily energy dependent; concretely, Spain consumed a high proportion of energy per unit of output, about the average in the European Community, which was particularly serious in the circumstances. On another front, the financial structure was poorly balanced, and companies were excessively dependent on credit, which made them particularly vulnerable under a restrictive monetary policy. All these structural defects were, at least in part, the consequence of the Franco regime's economic policy, which showed a lack of confidence in market forces and competition, was interventionistic and distrustful in the face of scientific endeavor, defensive of special interests, and, as we shall see, was utterly chaotic in its energy policy.

Crises produce traumas that are painful but inevitable. In the Spanish case, as in Europe as a whole, it was clear that the industrial sector would have to remedy these serious defects and modify its structure to meet the new circumstances. This implied abandoning unprofitable activities, closing companies, and transferring resources to competitive activities: this is the process that Schumpeter called "creative destruction." Constant adaptation to changes in the market is the essence of growth and the market economy's secret of success. But it involves painful and distressing transitions for people who are not able to adapt: workers who lose their employment and do not find another and capitalists who have to write off amounts of capital equipment and fail to find alternative profitable investment opportunities are the victims of change and progress. It is a frequent political error to try to maintain employment and investments without economic justification. The role of the state in these cases ought to be to reduce the trauma as far as possible, and accelerate the transition by means of unemployment insurance on the one hand, and on the other, by reeducating workers and promoting investment in activities with a future. It is not a case of working against the market, but rather of facilitating and hastening the changes that the market imposes. This is what a policy of "industrial reconversion" should do; the concept once provoked open hostility, but well carried out, it is the only justifiable state action in a situation of crisis.

For the reasons we have seen, the reconversion policy was long delayed in

Spain. Until 1980 the only existing industrial policy amounted to subsidizing companies or sectors in difficulties, that is, stop-gap measures. In 1981 and 1982 the legislature passed a decree and a law on industrial rehabilitation which, in conjunction with other decrees, focused on various sectors and industries. For Martín Aceña and Comín (1991, p. 315), the "planning and general objectives of the reconversion initiated in 1981 were correct and the economic necessity was beyond any doubt [although] serious obstacles arose when the proposals came to be applied." For Segura and his collaborators (1989, pp. 411–412), the reconversion policy adopted by the UCD, the Union of Centrist Democrats, which governed from 1977 to 1982, deserves harsher judgment:

> It was structured around the short-term interests of the industrial groups that were best able to apply political pressure . . . the situation in those sectors embraced by the reconversion did not improve and the investments that were utterly essential to modernization were not carried out . . . in spite of the considerable cost in terms of public money [the reconversion] was inadequate [because] it did not lead to a definitive improvement in the economic health of the various sectors, an error which in the case of the iron and steel sector was to necessitate new and copious subsidies in 1984—and later.
>
> The 1981–1982 "reconversion" reminds one, in many aspects, of the Special Agreements under the Economic and Social Development plans begun in 1964, which signaled the end of that brief period of liberalization for the Spanish economy that had begun in 1959.

The bold undeniable fact is that the industrial crisis did not go away: in 1982 and 1983 production continued to fall and unemployment continued to rise.

The electoral success of the Socialists at the end of 1982, with a clear parliamentary majority and a clear reformist mandate, implied the formulation of a more structured and more coherent economic policy. On the matter of industrial reconversion, the government did not abandon the issue but had the good judgment to recognize that such a policy was essential and had to be applied more rigorously than had been done by its predecessor. The essential element of the 1984 Law on Reconversion and Reindustrialization was not so much to compensate the companies for losses suffered, but rather to develop new investments which would facilitate the creation of new industries and move manpower into more viable areas. To this end the law envisaged credits and subsidies to new investments and the creation of "zones of urgent reindustrialization," in an attempt to make good use of external economies in the regions where old industries were dying out, and to minimize the displacement of workers. Plans were also drawn up for anticipated retirement, and the INI was also forced to adopt the principles and the logic of reconversion, reducing labor force, accelerating the amortization of outdated capital, and rationalizing investments.

There can be no question about the success of the reconversion plan. It was carried out with courage: on more than one occasion the changes lead to confrontations and threats of physical violence against some high-ranking officials in the Ministry of Industry. From 1985 onwards, industrial investment and production picked up remarkably; in fact, a period of strong growth was evident until 1990. To be sure, it is difficult to know how far this success was due to the program itself, and how far it was the product of external factors such as Spain's entry into the European Community, the improvement in the world economy, or the fall in the price of petroleum, all of which occurred in the middle of the 1980s.

Another serious problem left over from the Franco years was that of state industries. INI posed a difficult dilemma: although it was a typical Francoist institution (of well-known Mussolinian inspiration) and a heavy drag on the budget, the labor unions had always been against its abolition since it provided thousands of cushy public-sector jobs. On this point, and for these reasons, Socialist as well as conservative governments had been indecisive about what to do with INI ever since the restoration of democracy. In 1981 a government of the right-of-center UCD (Unión de Centro Democrático, Adolfo Suárez's party) took petroleum out of the INI and created the INH (Instituto Nacional de Hidrocarburos, National Petroleum Institute). In 1992, in a new split, the Socialist government took the profitable firms out of INI, grouping them within a new body, called TENEO. Then, in 1995, another Socialist government finally abolished INI and created two new public holding companies: SEPI (Sociedad Estatal de Participaciones Industriales), comprising TENEO and INH, and AIE (Agencia Industrial del Estado), which included the firms that were losing money and thus were still a load on the budget. In 1996 a Popular (conservative) government abolished TENEO, which was subsumed into SEPI, and in 1997 it did away with the separation between profit-making and money-losing firms. AIE was reunited with SEPI so that, after all these maneuvers, all that had been achieved was to change the old name of INI for the less reminiscent and more friendly-sounding SEPI. The only real difference was the state's firm purpose of carrying out privatization, already manifest in the last Socialist governments, and which the Popular party pursued enthusiastically. This caused the old clumsy giant to shrink somewhat, although many problems still persist in the form of unsaleable white (or rather black) elephants such as HUNOSA or the steel mills.

The Energy Problem

"If the Agricultural Revolution is the process whereby man came to control and increase the supply of biological converters (plants and animals), the Industrial Revolution can be regarded as the process whereby the large scale exploitation of new sources of energy by means of inanimate converters was set on foot" (Cipolla, 1970, p. 51).

This statement is, of course, just as applicable to Spain as to the rest of the world. The process of replacing animate energy with inanimate sources of power happened in Spain in the twentieth century, which is when the industrial transition occurred. While Spain in 1900 consumed about 5 million tons of coal-equivalent in inanimate energy, in 1980 it consumed about 107 million tons. As might be expected, the rise in fossil fuel consumption had begun in the second half of the nineteenth century, with the slow industrial growth that was then emerging. In 1860 the total coal consumption was less than 1 million tons (see Table 12.8) but it grew progressively throughout the final decades of the century. Now, while in the nineteenth century practically all the fossil fuel in use was coal, in the twentieth century alternative sources and forms of production and consumption begin to appear. At the beginning of the twentieth century Spain was using 225 kgs. of coal per capita per annum, which was characteristic of the Mediterranean countries at the dawn of industrialization; the more advanced countries all consumed more than 1,000 kgs. per capita, while the figure for the most industrialized was more than 2,000 (Sudrià, 1987, p. 317). Of course, these figures do not include certain other forms of energy typical of preindustrial structures: human and animal power, vegetable fuels, straw and wood, and power sources based on windmills and water wheels. In Catalonia, for example, direct water power was very important in the second half of the nineteenth century (Carreras, 1983a).

It has been said that "insufficiency of energy was one of the explanatory elements in the lateness of Spain's industrialization" (Tamames, 1990, p. 255). This is, of course, a widely held opinion, but it is highly debatable

Table 12.8.   Consumption of primary energy in Spain, 1860–1980
(equivalents of million tons of coal, figures rounded)

	(1)	(2)	(3)	(4)	(5)	(6)
				Hydro-		
	Total	Coal	Petroleum	electricity	Gas	Nuclear
1860	0.8	0.8	—	—	—	—
1870	1.3	1.3	—	—	—	—
1880	1.8	1.8	—	—	—	—
1890	3.0	2.9	0.1	—	—	—
1900	4.7	4.6	0.1	0.1	—	—
1910	6.5	6.3	—	0.2	—	—
1920	7.1	6.1	0.1	1.0	—	—
1930	12.4	9.7	0.6	2.1	—	—
1940	13.9	9.1	1.4	3.4	—	—
1950	18.6	12.5	2.6	3.6	—	—
1960	31.2	14.7	8.6	8.0	—	—
1970	63.4	15.9	37.0	10.0	0.2	0.4
1980	106.5	25.0	66.3	10.7	3.0	1.6

— = Zero or insignificant

Sources: Carreras in *Estadísticas Históricas,* (ed.) Carreras (1989), Sudrià (1987), and own calculations

because countries endowed with much poorer energy resources, like Sweden, Holland, Switzerland, and Japan, achieved high levels of development and industrialization earlier than Spain. Both coal and petroleum are easily transportable, so that imports can remedy the shortage in deficit countries. In fact, in Spain itself, the regions that industrialized early, Catalonia and the Basque Country, were coal-poor regions, while the coal-rich regions, Asturias, León and western Andalucía, industrialized much later and incompletely, a fact that poses some questions about what we might call energy determinism. As has been implied earlier, if the energy sector was an obstacle to industrial growth, it was the energy policy that was problematic, not the resource endowment itself. In short, as so many authors following Perpiñá have pointed out, the protection of Spanish coal amounted to an indiscriminate charge upon the whole of Spanish industry. The most interesting work on this topic has been done by Coll (1985; and Coll and Sudrià, 1987).

Government policy on coal during the twentieth century has been characterized by intense commercial protectionism and other political aids to production. Tariff protection was relatively moderate at 10%, and until the Great War imports accounted for about half of Spanish consumption. The situation changed radically after that. During the war the dearth of imports stimulated a large increase in national production, but also brought about a steep rise in prices; in the postwar period demand and production fell. It was at this moment that fiercely interventionist legislation was introduced, culminating in the decree of February 27, 1926, which not only mandated the consumption of Spanish coal for the fleet (it had been so obligated since 1896) but also that a high proportion of fuel used for private industry (railroads, iron and steel, smelting, gas, cement, electricity, textiles, and sugar) should also be domestic. The consequence was, of course, a progressive decline in coal imports, which became merely a residual in Spanish consumption. After the Civil War, because of the controls on external trade, coal imports continued to play only a marginal role until the 1960s. From then onwards, with the liberalization subsequent to the stabilization plan, Spanish coal, unable to compete with foreign coal (which itself was suffering serious competition from petroleum), simply threw in the towel. With this metaphor borrowed from boxing I mean to say that the private companies abandoned all pretense at competition and did all they possibly could to become nationalized, which they achieved in 1967. In that year HUNOSA was founded (an acronym for Collieries of the North) when the INI bought out the Asturian coal companies. From that date forward HUNOSA became the heaviest burden within the INI, even when the petroleum crisis of the 1970s produced a certain improvement in coal consumption. Table 12.8 clearly indicates the progressive decline in the relative importance of coal in the Spanish economy, starting about 1920.

Sebastián Coll has tried to measure the effect of protecting coal within the Spanish economy at large during the first third of the twentieth century (Coll, 1985; Coll and Sudrià, 1987, chap. VII). The results show that the cost was very small in relation to national income. It would be hasty, however, to deduce from this that protection was irrelevant. To a great extent, the cost of protection was small because coal production represented only a small fraction of the national economy (.59% of GDP and 2.2% of industrial value added around 1925, Coll's terminal date, calculated on the basis of figures from Alcaide, 1976). In relation to the coal industry itself, however, the cost of protection was quite another matter; it actually represented 25% of the sectoral value added. Coll's excellent study also shows that even for the heaviest industrial consumers of coal, such as cement and gas, the cost of fuel was less than one-third of total costs in the 1920s and 1930s. Perhaps the question we ought to ask is why the coal sector was of so little importance when coal represented 80% of Spain's energy consumption. The answer is, of course, that on the eve of the Civil War, Spain was still a country with very low per capita fuel consumption, 457 kgs. of coal equivalent per year compared with a world average of 729, with the industrialized countries consuming over 2,000. Coll's study uses a neoclassical, static approach that measures the cost of protection at a certain moment with the parameters of that moment. It is possible that the true answer to the question might rest in the parameters themselves; perhaps energy consumption was so low because of the protection that had been afforded to the coal industry. But the answer to this question would require the construction of a counterfactual model that would estimate what the level of industrialization would have been if the price of coal had been lower than it was. With the level of information we have at the moment, the construction of such a model is virtually impossible.

Nor was the government's policy on petroleum handled well during the greater part of the twentieth century. Gasoline did not begin to be important in Spain until after World War I, when its consumption began to grow rapidly. Even so, it continued to be only a minor component of total energy consumption until the middle of the century. From 1918 onwards the use of the internal combustion engine was coming into general use in transportation and in industry, and these were the large consumers of petroleum products, with gasoline the single most important component of that demand (Tortella, 1990). In 1927, with demand for hydrocarbon products fully on the rise, a Spanish petroleum monopoly was created (excluding the Canary Islands) and put under the control of CAMPSA. Since Spain at that time was not producing a single drop of petroleum oil, the monopoly referred to the distribution and sale of products, but it included also what was termed "industrial handling," that is, refining, and production if there were to be any. The new creation was utterly emblematic of Primo de Rivera and his Treasury Minister, José Calvo Sotelo, for whom the Petroleum Monopoly represented an institution that had "an exalted nation- and state-building design" (Calvo Sotelo, 1974, p. 155), though with scant justification in economic terms, as its history proves.

The legal framework of the monopoly was full of contradictions: on the one hand the hope was that CAMPSA would not only increase tax revenues but also create an oil-refining industry, intensify prospecting, develop the production of alternative fuels, and a long list of other things. At the same time, however, the degree of state control over the company (the enterprise was a private undertaking whose major stockholders were the large banks) was so pervasive, and the property rights so poorly defined, that CAMPSA refused to take on the additional responsibilities the law assigned to it, limiting itself exclusively to importing and distributing the designated products, religiously collecting moneys, and keeping account of prices and corresponding taxes. CAMPSA understood, not without reason, that the copious investment necessary for the creation of a refinery industry and an exploration program were very risky in that the law could be interpreted (and in fact it was later so interpreted) to mean that every fixed investment related to the monopoly would become property of the state. On the other hand, the profitability of the CAMPSA shares during the first twenty years of its operation was not very high, so it was difficult to raise the capital that would have been required to put such projects into operation.

CAMPSA disappointed its creator, and limited itself "to the condition of a retail shopkeeper, buying and selling without competitors and without responsibilities" (Calvo Sotelo, 1974, p. 155). This condition was sealed into the Law of 1947, which permitted the state to carry out for itself, or to delegate, the operations initially assigned to CAMPSA. The INI, through the Calvo Sotelo National Company (founded in 1942 in memory of the creator of CAMPSA) and REPESA installed the first refineries on the Spanish mainland (CEPSA had been founded in 1930 to exploit a refinery in Tenerife). From then until 1981 the state petroleum operation was in complete disarray (and by virtue of the monopoly there was none other), because CAMPSA was controlled by the Treasury, and the INI companies were operated under the Minister of Industry. So regardless of the monopoly there was a complete lack of coherent policy; for the Treasury and CAMPSA the important thing was to collect revenue, to sell, which is to say, to import. Prospecting, the only means of achieving real petroleum independence, was carried out only at a slow pace, delayed by the peculiar domestic circumstances and the scant opportunity that was afforded to foreign capital. The sector that was developed successfully, thanks to the INI, was petroleum refining, which in the end was to make Spain a net exporter of refined products.

It has been argued, in favor of CAMPSA, that at least the amount of revenue grew as petroleum imports also increased. Even that is debatable. There are reasons to suppose that the ordinary fiscal system (tariffs and indirect taxes) could have functioned as well or better than the monopoly system, because lack of competition, as is well known, is a disincentive to productivity (Tortella, 1990, pp. 104 ff.; Sudrià, 1987, p. 327).

From the 1950s onwards Spain's consumption of petroleum took off, as it did in the rest of the world. But in Spain the change was very striking, since petroleum shot up from being a relatively unimportant energy source, 14% of total energy consumption in 1950, to 58% of consumption 20 years later in 1970, and this over a period when total energy consumption increased more than threefold (see Table 12.8, col. 1). The severe lack of political coordination came to a head in the crisis of the 1970s. The rise in petroleum prices surprised the Spanish authorities, which, as we have seen, took years to adopt measures that were logical in the face of the new situation: to pass the new gasoline prices on to the home market, to try to develop an energy plan, and to combine the state petroleum companies (including CAMPSA) within one organization, the National Hydrocarbon Institute (INH), which was split off from the INI but (like that body) was dependent upon the Ministry of Industry. Later on, when entry into the Common Market made it necessary to legally abolish the petroleum monopoly, Spain was finally ready to carry out this transformation in an orderly fashion.

Electricity is, strictly speaking, an intermediate form of energy which is obtained from primary sources such as coal, petroleum, waterfalls, atomic power, the wind, or the sun. It has many advantages, which is why we resort to using energy in that form, rather than using the primary sources directly. Among these advantages are cleanliness, ease in transport and distribution, and divisibility; in comparison, energy derived from water, wind, and the sun may not be easy to consume directly *in situ*. The first uses of electricity were for illumination, and this was also so in Spain, where the first power station was that of Dalmáu and Xifra, founded in 1875 in Barcelona. It was only at the beginning of the twentieth century that transmission of power over large distances by means of high tension cables became possible, so earlier power plants were small and set in urban centers, with power used largely for electric lighting and generated by motors fueled with gas, petroleum, or coal. When it became possible to transport current over long distances, the industry changed radically. Since it was now possible to produce power far away from where it was to be consumed, power stations could be much larger and water power could be utilized. Within Europe, Spain enjoys good conditions for producing hydroelectricity because of its mountainous terrain and steep gradients, although irregularity of rainfall and river currents is a problem.

Thus at the beginning of the century the large hydroelectric companies began to appear and a process of radical concentration was set in motion. The first large company in the sector, the Sevillana de Electricidad, was founded in 1884. In 1901 came Hidroeléctrica Ibérica, later Iberduero, and in 1907 the Hidroeléctrica Española. All these companies were developed by Basque engineers and with Basque capital. Their spheres of operation were centered first in western Andalucía, in the north for the second phase, and later in the east. In 1911 two companies were formed, Eléctricas Reunidas de Zaragoza (Germán et al., 1990) and the Barcelona Traction, Light, and Power. The Zaragoza company amalgamated a series of smaller Aragonese companies. The other, with head offices in Toronto, Canada, and under multinational capital, was in charge of generating electricity and operating a tramway system in Barcelona. Popularly known as the Canadiense, after the Civil War it was the object of a sensational lawsuit which enabled the financier Juan March to appropriate it, whereupon he changed its name to FECSA (Fuerzas Eléctricas de Cataluña) (Dixon, 1985, chap. XIX). With the incorporation of some smaller companies into the Union Eléctrica Madrileña in 1912 (today the Union FENOSA), the picture of how the large companies or electrical groups were formed is complete. The largest Spanish company in the electricity industry of the day, however, was the multinational CHADE (Compañía Hispano-Americana de Electricidad), which after the First World War acquired the installations in Argentina, Uruguay, and Chile of a subsidiary of the German company AEG (Allgemeine Elektrizitaets Gesellschaft). The CHADE was created at the initiative of the Banco Urquijo, with participation of other banks and entities, Spanish and foreign alike. Its long-time President was the lawyer and politician Francisco Cambó; it was finally nationalized by the Argentinian government after World War II.

Electricity consumption rose very considerably after the Great War,[25] responding (as in the case of petroleum) to the enormous rise in coal prices, and also to the rapid industrialization and growth of transport capacity. As Sudrià says so expressively (1987, p. 323): "The industrial consumer, urged on by growing demand and well paid, rapidly replaced the steam engine that consumed coal with electricity which was offered him cheaply and without restrictions."

In this period hydroelectricity was predominant; coal production served for little more than to regularize production in periods of drought. Another characteristic of this period is the relative absence of state intervention; rates and contracts remained at the discretion of the parties involved.

After the Civil War, considerable changes in this sector took place. Two parallel phenomena emerged, both of them inevitable: state intervention and growing integration. In the first place consumption continued to increase at a steep rate, and the outdated phenomenon of restrictions appeared again. It was natural to expect increasing integration in an industry with such strong seasonality in both production and consumption, particularly since there was very little competition. (There cannot be much competition in an industry where the product is delivered through a single distribution network.) Under these conditions increasing interchanges between companies made sense, following their own tendency to cooperate in making more rational and economical use of the national grid as a whole. With this notion in mind, UNESA was created (Unidad Eléctrica), with the participation of the principal companies, to organize the distribution of electric current throughout the network as a whole. This sort of integration had already been put into practice in other countries (UNIE in France, UGBE in Belgium).

In the face of the industry's growing integration it was also logical that the state should become interested in matters such as electrical tariffs. On this point the government made one wise move, towards developing a nationally unified rate schedule (the Unified Maximum Rate), and one unwise move, to freeze that rate for more than a decade. Since the cost structures of the various generating companies were different, a compensatory mechanism was formed in 1953 (OFILE; Oficina Liquidadora de Energía), which paid compensation to the companies for whom the unified tariff was prejudicial. Another form of state intervention came from the INI, which entered the sector with a series of companies that produced electricity like ENDESA (Empresa Nacional de Electricidad), ENCASO, and others. The role played by the INI in the energy sector was very important until the creation of the Instituto Nacional de Hidrocarburos, and still continues to be of some importance.

The increase in demand for electrical energy, in large part because of low tariffs, was not met with anything approaching an equivalent increase in supply, which produced the surprising phenomenon of power rationing. Restrictions were first introduced in 1944, during the Franco regime's long postwar period, when the power supply was interrupted during some hours of the day depending on demand and the weather, specifically rainfall. According to Sudrià, these restrictions were not lifted until 1955. They had serious consequences for industrial production, whose output was reduced, according to his estimate, by an average of 7% annually during those years (Sudrià, 1987), and this without taking into account consumer hardship and inconvenience. The immediate cause of these power cuts was the very limited construction program undertaken by the electric companies: generating capacity grew very slowly during these years and production simply could not keep pace with a demand that was growing very rapidly. Blame for this limited growth in generating capacity must be attributed to the very same fixed price policy, which meant that in real terms the price of a kilowatt of power in 1950 was only 17% of what it had cost in 1936. This drastic fall in the selling price certainly dissuaded the companies from carrying out much-needed investments, and of course it also deprived them of the very means to do so. As Sudrià pointed out (1987, p. 334), the reason for this absurd policy lay in the government's wish "to maintain the fallacy of an equilibrium of prices and salaries at 1936 levels, which could only be accomplished in those sectors which operated under controlled prices, and where there was no possibility of resorting to the black market."

The difficulties of importing capital equipment and the general malfunctioning of the Franco regime's controlled economy also contributed to a slump in the construction industry. In the 1950s, when prices were unfrozen and imports became less difficult, generating capacity increased considerably, at a rate twice that of the previous decade. At last a certain amount of liberalization and acceptance of market economy rules had managed to put an end to the dreaded power cuts.

The increase in generating capacity was principally achieved through the construction of reservoirs and hydroelectric plants in the 1950s and 1960s. But it was plain to see that the country's hydroelectric capacity was reaching its limit, since demand continued to grow at an exponential rate. In the face of a fixed supply of hydroelectricity, energy producers increasingly turned to other fuel sources; new thermal generators used coal in the first place, then diesel oil, nuclear power, and more recently, natural gas. In 1983 hydroelectric power represented 9% of Spain's energy consumption, a proportion similar to that for France and Italy, countries with comparable conditions of water supply; in 1987 hydroelectricity contributed 21% of total electricity generated, compared with 48% from conventional power stations and 31% from nuclear power.

Although its use dates back to the middle of the nineteenth century, the role of gas in Spain's energy budget has remained marginal until very recently, which is regrettable because it is a clean energy source, priced well below petroleum in terms of calorific value, and more abundant in the immediate environment. In this area too it is necessary to indicate some serious political errors which, combined with other factors, explain Spain's low level of consumption of this particular energy source. In the nineteenth century, when all gas consumed was obtained from coal, the small quantity can be attributed to the high price of Spanish coal at a time of limited industrialization and urbanization. And this, in turn, explains the absence of a distribution network.

After World War II new types of gas became more widespread. Petroleum-based propane and butane gases came into production, and natural gas began to be available. Now natural gas is much more abundant in Europe than petroleum, and consequently its production and consumption have flourished. Spain does not appear to have large reserves of natural gas (although they are larger than its petroleum reserves) but its neighbors are better endowed, especially Algeria, and it would seem logical to develop the consumption of a fuel that is a clean energy source, and relatively cheap. However, the consumption of natural gas demands a distribution network of gas mains, and so far Spain has lacked this network, and until very recently nothing has been done to address the problem. Gas consumption began to grow in the 1960s because of increased urbanization and higher standards of living, but the Franco regime preferred, doubtless for lack of a long-term vision, to stay with the system that distributed petroleum gas from home to home, in kitchen-sized carboys. Given the inertia with which CAMPSA approached every potential innovation, it was decided to entrust the production and distribution of the petroleum gases to a new company whose capital was divided between CAMPSA and the INI; Butano SA was created in 1957. The ubiquitous cylinders have become so identified by their special tone of orange that this particular color has now entered the vernacular vocabulary; the term *bombona* (carboy) refers to the portable gas container and is also used as an adjective to denote the newly appreciated color. The sale of bottled gas obviated the necessity of the fixed investment that a mains gas supply network would have entailed, but this put a heavy charge on the variable costs of distribution (Sudrià, 1984), to say nothing of urban congestion caused by the delivery trucks. Later on the increase in petroleum prices underlined the double error committed.

One private company in this area showed much better judgment than the Franco government. In 1960 the Catalana de Gas joined a European consortium to import liquid gas from Algeria, to be piped through Spain, which in this matter clearly has a locational advantage. It met with immediate opposition from the state, concretely from the petroleum monopoly, which over twelve long years obstructed the Catalán company in its efforts to bring North African gas into the Spanish market.[26] After the failure of the attempt with Algeria, the Catalana signed an agreement with Libya and began to import natural liquid gas, which it re-gasified in its plant in Barcelona. When in 1972 the government finally decided to change its policy in favor of imported natural gas, it did so by acquiring, through forced purchase, the factory owned by Catalana de Gas. At that time ENAGAS was created, and substituted for the Catalana in the contracts with Algeria and Libya. Yet until very recently the construction of a network of gas pipelines connecting the principal cities has not been initiated. In 1990 an agreement was signed between REPSOL (a fuel company that is part of the INH) and the Caixa de Barcelona (representing the Catalana), which will permit the joint operation of both companies, the private and the public, in the distribution of natural gas in Spain; it is hoped that consumption will grow rapidly as network construction advances.

Table 12.9.   Industrial production in four key sectors, 1900 to 1985
(in thousand metric tons)

	Cotton	Steel	Cement	Sulfuric Acid
1900	66	199	186	—
	78	168	189	—
	85	166	202	6
	80	193	245	5
	71	201	287	4
1905	76	247	297	12
	87	280	299	25
	92	325	330	33
	95	297	487	34
	71	254	472	26
1910	73	261	484	37
	90	286	486	40
	93	297	525	54
	88	316	512	60
	84	356	474	70

Table 12.9   *(continued)*

	Cotton	Steel	Cement	Sulfuric Acid
1915	143	387	476	100
	102	323	536	270
	97	315	462	307
	60	301	401	136
	74	240	369	122
1920	81	205	480	203
	82	306	590	326
	83	231	729	264
	83	476	863	320
	80	529	917	320
1925	87	630	1,106	350
	84	614	1,183	368
	98	676	1,453	289
	76	782	1,542	282
	79	1,007	1,820	168
1930	101	934	1,839	224
	98	649	1,630	185
	107	532	1,465	161
	99	507	1,762	173
	104	649	1,362	216
1935	103	595	1,463	338
	—	373	400	104
	—	167	347	45
	—	574	563	112
	—	584	1,081	151
1940	76	695	1,402	215
	54	574	1,463	203
	69	601	1,507	164
	92	654	1,516	95
	88	579	1,579	160
1945	122	512	1,704	218
	72	575	1,847	262
	62	548	1,921	298
	68	624	1,858	353
	79	652	1,848	403
1950	60	779	2,065	456
	56	791	2,325	565
	97	980	2,508	640
	89	900	2,789	650
	81	1,102	3,404	721

Table 12.9   *(continued)*

	Cotton	Steel	Cement	Sulfuric Acid
1955	100	1,211	3,930	799
	83	1,202	4,313	859
	111	1,345	4,489	979
	113	1,560	4,817	1,072
	115	1,699	5,164	1,131
1960	99	1,791	5,235	1,132
	142	2,340	6,068	1,236
	176	2,311	6,738	1,249
	117	2,492	7,153	1,462
	114	3,150	8,117	1,528
1965	109	3,516	9,361	1,616
	154	3,847	11,252	1,781
	117	4,512	12,764	1,796
	117	4,971	14,676	2,067
	133	5,981	16,013	2,152
1970	102	7,394	16,536	2,309
	128	8,025	16,993	2,454
	132	9,536	19,442	2,325
	148	10,484	22,239	2,595
	104	11,473	23,660	2,919
1975	144	11,137	23,970	3,624
	133	11,002	25,202	2,957
	111	11,102	27,995	2,997
	102	11,269	30,230	2,965
	105	11,795	28,051	2,950
1980	115	12,841	28,010	3,052
	142	13,514	28,752	2,873
	—	—	29,604	2,805
	—	—	30,637	2,861
	—	—	—	3,517
1985	—	—	—	3,238

Sources: col. 1, presumed consumption of raw cotton (production plus imports), Carreras in *Estadísticas Históricas,* (ed.) Carreras (1989); col. 2, Carreras in *Estadísticas Historicas* (1989); col. 3, natural cement plus artificial cement; Carreras in *Estadísticas Históricas* (1989) and Coll (1986); col. 4, 1902–1935: Figures from Carreras in *Estadísticas Históricas* (1989) adjusted upwards from Kreps, cited in Mitchell (1976), p. 463, assuming a linear relationship between figures from Carreras and Kreps. Carreras admits there is some underestimation in his figures (which are drawn from the series *Estadísticas Mineras*). We know that in 1892 the *Sociedad Española de Dinamita* alone produced 5,400 tons of sulfuric acid (Tortella, unpublished). For 1902, *Estadísticas Históricas* estimates production at 658 tons. For the 1936–1985 period, Carreras in *Estadísticas Históricas* (1989)

CHAPTER **13**

The Foreign Sector

The Balance of Payments

The economic relationships that any one country has with the rest of the world are encapsulated in its Balance of International Payments. This is simply an accounting document that reports the economic transactions, both incomes and expenditures, which a country, through its residents, has carried out with the rest of the world, generally within the period of a year.[1] Access to an accounting document of this complex nature permits its users a fuller grasp and a more confident analysis and understanding of the international economic relationships than would be available from materials based upon less systematic sources. For this reason historians, economists, and politicians often turn to these figures to improve their grasp of economic reality; such is their value that scholars have even tried to reconstruct these documents for periods for which they are lacking.

For the Spanish case, we have a series of complete balances from 1931 onwards, except for the gap caused by the Civil War, 1935–1939. From 1959 onwards the work of preparing the balance of payments has been the responsibility of the official statistical publications office of the Economics Ministry. For the years before this we rely on the work of the team led by Santiago Chamorro, which published a cleaned-up version of the accounts during the years of the Second Republic that were coordinated by the Research Office of the Bank of Spain under the direction of Francisco Jáinaga; Chamorro also constructed balance of payments figures for the period 1940 to 1958, based on official documents, in particular the account books of the Instituto Español de Moneda Extranjera (IEME, or Spanish Institute of Foreign Money). This fairly long series allows us to detect structural changes in Spain's economy during the twentieth century through these international relationships.[2]

For the years before these, our knowledge and understanding are very fragmentary. The part that is usually most important in the balance of payments (and generally the better documented one) is the balance of trade, the series of payments that are the result of exports and imports of merchandise. As we already saw in Chapter 5, the trade balance for Spain, calculated on the basis of figures from Customs statistics, has been known and available annually since 1850, and for occasional years since the end of the eighteenth century. There are even figures available that allow us partial reconstructions from the beginning of that century, but for other components, capital movements for example, our understanding is very incomplete.

Figure 13.1 offers us various measures of how Spain's economy was connected to the rest of the world, measured by the weight of the exterior sector as a percentage of national income. Three measures are presented, (A) total international payments, (B) current account transactions, and (C) foreign trade, and they show very similar growth patterns, which is of course very much to be expected. Total international payments, as the term indicates, is the sum of foreign incomes and expenditures generated and incurred by the

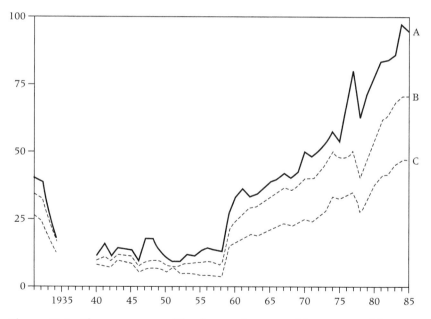

Figure 13.1. Three measures of the degree of commercial openness of the Spanish economy, 1930–1985 (A, international payments; B, current account balances; and C, international trade, as a percentage of national income)

Spanish economy on both sides of the account, credits plus debits. Now the balance of payments, like every accounting instrument, is always formally in equilibrium, so this measure exaggerates to some extent the part of national income generated by external transactions; the figure is exaggerated in that the entry for total payments includes the ups and downs of foreign reserves and short-term capital movements, which are not strictly speaking part of the national income, as well as errors and omissions. However, this variable describes, in a very expressive fashion, the orientation of an economy, whether towards self-sufficiency or towards open trade relations. In the Spanish case it tells us what we already knew indirectly: the enormous contraction in international payments in the 1930s, an effect of the Great Depression, the tremendous isolation of the Spanish economy during the greater part of the Franco era, and the gradual opening up to trade after the 1959 stabilization plan. One should bear in mind, however, what the chart so clearly indicates: the ratio of international payments to national income for 1931 (a year when the international crisis was already being felt) was not achieved again until 1967. From then onwards, yes, we do find strong growth, doubtless because of the progressive softening of tariffs and Spain's gradual entry into the Common Market.

Although traditionally the degree of openness of an economy is estimated from the total of imports and exports as a proportion of national income, it is more exact to measure it as the sum of current account transactions, because that includes trade not only in goods but also in services as part of the national income. This measure, curve B on the graph, tells us that while at the lowest point during the autarky period only 7% of national income came from foreign trade, by 1985 this proportion was ten times larger; goods and services involved in international trade then amounted to almost 70% of the national income. The problem is that this measure is only known from 1931 onwards. Figures on the commercial balance have much greater continuity. Fortunately, however, both measures evolve in a roughly parallel manner, as can be seen from the graph, so that we can extrapolate on the basis of the Commercial Balance without too much fear of making an error.

Figure 13.2 presents a longer-term picture of the degree of openness of the Spanish economy based upon Customs records, almost from the beginning of the century, the curve marked C in the previous chart. The evolution is almost identical to the curve obtained from the balance of payments from the Economic Ministry for the period where series from both sources are available. The graph shows us something we had already observed in studying agriculture and industry: the tendency towards autarky was already present before the Franco takeover, although that regime took the principle of self-sufficiency to ridiculous extremes. The severe and growing protectionism practiced during the first third of the century continued to isolate the economy from the rest of the world, and the degree of openness, something above 20% on this measure in the early years of the century (already very low), declined to an average level of about 18% in the 1920s decade, and this includes 1930, an exceptional year when exports increased a lot and imports too, to some extent. The fall in the 1930s was not so much due to Spanish protectionism, which was becoming more conspicuous (as it was elsewhere), as to the Great Depression. The truly exceptional element for Spain, however, is the very low and declining level of trade during the 1940s and the 1950s. For Spain the years of World War II could have provided an opportunity to export, as happened in the First World War for Spain and during the Second for Argentina. The oft-used pretext of the destruction wrought by the Civil War is no longer credible. Today we know that the damage was not so extensive, and in any case it could have been made good so much earlier.[3] A rational economic policy would have encouraged the production of exportable agricultural surpluses much earlier than the end of

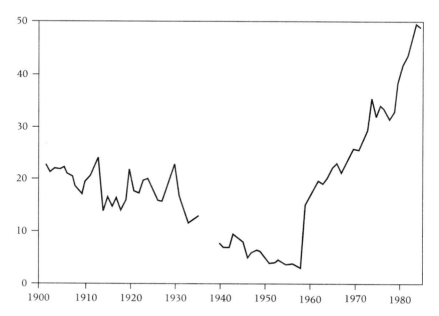

Figure 13.2. The degree of commercial openness of the Spanish economy: foreign trade as a percentage of national income, 1901–1984

the war. And after the war was over the obsession with self-sufficiency and the persecution mania of the Franco regime isolated Spain from the tremendous economic and commercial development which was already starting to blossom in Europe at the end of the 1940s.

The abrupt jump in foreign trade that followed upon the heels of the 1959 stabilization and liberalization plan is a good indicator of how artificial and contrived was the earlier policy. The change in trend is utterly remarkable. In five years the degree of openness shot up from a mere 3% of national income to more than 20%, a figure which returned the economy to prewar levels. In other words, the volume of foreign trade went from just 3% of national income in 1959 to more than 20% just five years later. The years of tremendous growth and industrialization, the 1960s and the beginning of the 1970s, are years of spectacular growth in external trade, which frankly contradicts those who argued that industrialization needed tariff protection. And lastly, both graphs register a major halt due to the crisis of the 1970s and a return to growth in external trade from 1978 onwards.

Figures 13.3 and 13.4 display a panorama of the structural changes occurring within the Spanish balance of payments from 1931 to 1990— changes that were indeed considerable. We can distinguish four periods. Let us look

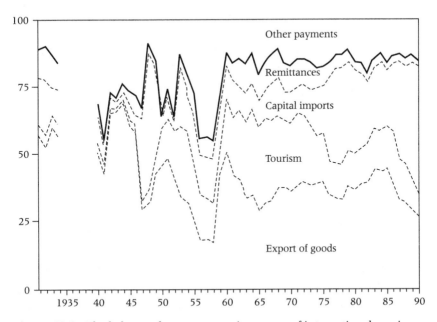

Figure 13.3. The balance of payments; main sources of international earnings (as percentages of total), 1930–1990

first at the exports side of the picture, Figure 13.3. In the first phase, the short period of the Second Republic, exports of goods represented about 60% of earnings, the import of capital about 15%, remittances from emigrants abroad were about 11%, and tourism was 4%. The remaining 10% included an entry for freightage earned and the import of dividends, doubtless from Spanish America where Spanish investment holdings were of some importance.

The second phase is the period of autarky, the years of the 1940s and 1950s, with the complete break in 1959. The first characteristic of these years is the fall in earnings from exported goods; although there were severe oscillations, export earnings declined from 65% in the first years of the 1940s to only 18% at the end of the 1950s. Even with the total trading account virtually stagnating, the importance of export earnings declined spectacularly. This was not simply the direct consequence of economic isolation but basically stemmed from a loss of competitiveness, which arose from various factors: the absurd overvaluation of the peseta (maintained out of some ill-advised sense of prestige) which made Spanish products expensive abroad; Spain's extremely low productivity, an indirect result of isolation which was obstructing the import of capital equipment, personnel, and

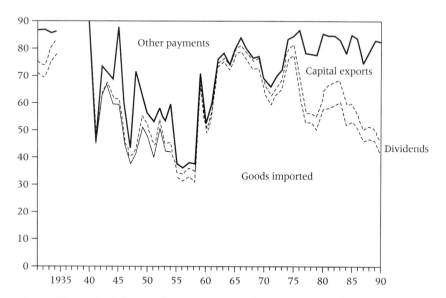

Figure 13.4. The balance of payments: main international outlays, 1930–1990 (as percentages of total)

technical advice; the generally low level of education; and finally the regulatory interventionism that was so dear to that regime, and so rooted in the Spanish mentality. The fall in earnings from goods exported was compensated by an increase in tourism in the 1950s, due to growing prosperity in Europe and North America and low costs in the service sector where low productivity is much less important. Sporadic capital movements show up in 1947 and 1948, which doubtless represent the state loans from Argentina in those years, and others that begin in 1953, related to the pact with the United States. There were also years when the residual category became important, and within that sector the errors and omissions sub-group. And since we find a similar pattern in the import accounts, Figure 13.4, the unavoidable conclusion must be that the tightly constructed controls over exterior trade were systematically outmaneuvered. There is no doubt at all that there were large and clandestine export consignments (transactions that, by some means or other, avoided inspection or registration), for which no earnings were recorded because they were used to buy goods that were imported (also clandestinely), thus bypassing not only the state's manipulation of exchange rates, but also the vexatious controls that almost inevitably impeded any opportunity to take advantage of favorable conditions in the international markets.

We can discern a certain structural change in the balance of payments in the 1950s. The role of exports continued to decline and other sectors which later were going to be very important began to matter—income from tourism, capital imports, and to a lesser extent remittances from Spaniards working abroad. This analysis lends support to the opinion of those who believe that the beginning of change in the Spanish economy was already visible in the 1950s. Thanks to the 1959 stabilization plan, the trends towards liberalization and modernization which had emerged several years earlier had scope to operate.

The third period, the years of Franco's so called pro-development policy, 1959 to 1975, presents very different characteristics. The whole picture became more stable; errors and omissions became much less important, an indication that contraband declined, among other reasons because of the greater freedom of trade with a newly realistic exchange rate. Exports of goods picked up a little but stabilized at a low level, about 35%. The important protagonist here, without doubt, was tourism,, which in the middle 1960s was a major contributor, becoming even more important than exports for a few years. The import of capital represented about 15% on average. After the crisis of 1973 things again begin to change: tourism declined and capital imports increased. Another important feature of the development years was emigrant remittances, which reached 10% and then began to decline after the crisis of 1973.

It is also worth noting that, in the years following the stabilization plan, the balance of payments account more resembled the years of the 1930s than the years of autarky, especially the 1940s. In spite of the Great Depression and commercial restrictions, the Spanish economy was more liberal in the Second Republic than in the first Franco years. Remittances from workers abroad, capital imports, and even tourism were of greater importance under the Republic than during the "ominous" first decade of Franco's dictatorship. This is something that we have also seen in relation to other sectors. The Civil War and the first Franco period produced a radical regression within the Spanish economy, a kind of sudden jump backwards into self-sufficiency and primary production, a regression that did not begin to correct itself until the 1950s. Figure 13.3 creates the impression of a basic continuity between the 1930s and the 1960s, with a large and anomalous interruption during the 1940s and the 1950s.

The fourth period began with the 1973 crisis and the end of the dictatorship in 1975 and extends to 1990. In these years both imports and exports gained renewed importance, although there was a downturn in 1985. Tourism picked up somewhat after 1981 but did not recover its relative vigor of twenty years earlier. The leading feature in this last period was clearly the import of capital, which towards 1990 was the most important entry in the balance of payments, reaching close to twice the value of exports.[4] This situation, which was allowing the peseta to remain overvalued, for several years created a deceptive sensation of economic euphoria, but in fact excessive inflation was making serious inroads into Spain's ability to compete internationally: the nose dive of declining exports after 1985 offers crowning proof of this deterioration. The return to hard reality, for the Spaniards and for foreign investors alike, took place within the framework of the quincentenary celebrations of the voyages of Columbus in September and October 1992. The peseta plummeted on the international markets, making it utterly necessary to make policy adjustments against inflation and to meet the minimum economic requirements derived from Spain's membership of the European Union.

In closing our discussion of Figure 13.3, we should note another phenomenon that is clearly manifest from the data on national income and the labor force, that is, the growing tertiarization of the Spanish economy. Exports of merchandise derived from the primary and industrial sectors declined drastically over these years, and were partially replaced by tourism and emigrant remittances, an export of services.

The evolution of the major debit categories on the account (meaning payments) appears in Figure 13.4, and here we find far more continuity than with incomes. During the greater part of the period under consideration, specifically until 1975, a very high proportion of payments was for goods imported in comparison with the export sector, where the sale of services made a substantial contribution. During the Republic and Franco's so-called pro-development period (the 1960s), about three-quarters of payments were for goods, with some fluctuations that are to be expected. In spite of what the chart indicates, this proportion cannot have declined much during the period of imposed self-sufficiency, since a portion of imports were certainly not recorded because of contraband activity. After 1975 the relative weight of imports began to decline gradually, and this was accompanied by growing capital exports, an unequivocal indication of a certain degree of maturity in the Spanish economy. And little by little the export of dividend payments increased, a consequence of the significant growth of foreign investment in Spain.

Figure 13.5 also offers a very cogent summary measure of Spain's international trade position from 1940 to 1990. Taking transactions under all categories into account, the chart indicates the net final balancing item each year, a debit or a credit on Spain's foreign exchange reserves, expressed as a percentage of the total payments. Prior to 1940 these balances were very small indeed and for this reason have been omitted. The chart is based on three-year moving averages to simplify interpretation. It suggests two major periods, separated by the 1959 stabilization plan. In the self-sufficiency period the balance of payments crisis becomes noticeable after World War II, when exceptional circumstances operated to Spain's profit. After the end of the war we find a chronic deficit, alleviated only by the import of capital after the Spain–United States Treaty was signed in 1953. From this perspective it is easier to appreciate the Copernican change of direction on political policy, and particularly on commercial policy, implicit in the 1959 stabilization plan. The repeated negative balances, which were probably even greater because of the clandestine exports of capital that I have earlier referred to, were simply exhausting the foreign trade reserves, so that by 1959 the country had to come face to face with a harsh reality: either to cut off imports or to suspend payments. In the words of one of the central actors in the drama (Fuentes Quintana, 1986, p. 141): "Of the gold reserves, worth 57 million dollars [that were remaining], 54 millions were in a special gold reserve in the Bank of Spain which could only be appropriated under special legislation, and this figure represented only one month of imports. Of course if one looked at the whole picture, in terms of net balances, Spain's debtor position was even worse." It was the desperate situation that autarky had produced in Spain, and not the omniscience of our dictator, that induced him to agree reluctantly to the reforms that were being proposed.

The graph charts the success of the plan, which radically changed the balance of payments picture. From the mid-1960s to the beginning of the 1980s, monetary outflows were not very large nor were the deficit periods very long; in contrast, additions to foreign currency reserves were larger and more frequent. From that time onwards the stock of foreign assets continued to grow, although the effect of the petroleum crises in 1973 and 1979 are clearly visible.

Since information prior to 1931 is quite incomplete, attempts to quantify the long-term picture of Spain's transactions with the rest of the world

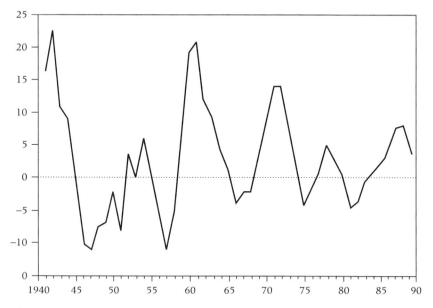

Figure 13.5. Net monetary movements in the Spanish balance of payments, 1940–1990 (as a percentage of total payments, three-year averages)

have been necessarily based upon some guesswork for almost all components, even the best-documented trade balance figures. Even so, certain conclusions seem to be beyond doubt. (1) The commercial trade deficit was chronic, a characteristic that seems to be one of the most permanent elements of the Spanish balance of payments account. (2) Emigrant remittances made a considerable contribution, obviously the result of outmigration from the second half of the nineteenth century and greatly accentuated at the beginning of the twentieth. (3) Tourism, although in its infancy, was already beginning to play a visible role in the 1920s. (4) Capital imports were already of considerable significance, another characteristic that also dates from the second half of the nineteenth century. In the last analysis, all the important categories present in the period 1931–1934 also reappear in the 1960s; as in so many other sectors then, there seems to be a basic historical continuity in Spain's balance of payments.

The Balance of Trade

Table 13.1 shows the structural changes in Spain's balance of trade throughout the twentieth century, in broad categories. It certainly confirms what we have been saying in earlier chapters about agriculture and industry. Until well into the second half of the century, foodstuffs represented the mainstay of Spanish external trade, more than half of exports and about 20% of imports. This is natural; as a predominantly agricultural country Spain exported this kind of product, but we should also bear in mind the increasing role played by the food manufacturing sector, which means that total value added from agricultural exports was also growing. The degree to which the economy was evolving is shown by increasing exports of machinery, from very small quantities before the Civil War to about 12% by value in the 1970s and 1980s. All in all, what we have been calling heavy industry or capital goods went from 12% of exports in 1929 to 53% in 1985, and within that, of course, machinery and motor vehicles show particularly strong growth.

Figures for 1922, for exports and imports alike, are not really typical of the period because of proximity to the First World War and the postwar depression; figures for 1921, not reproduced here, are even more atypical. It is perhaps the lingering effects of the war conditions that make capital goods, the heavy industry sector, relatively important in exports at 19%, and so unimportant in imports, only 10%. In these years imports of raw materials for the

Table 13.1. The components of Spain's foreign trade, 1922–1985 (in percentages)

	Exports								
	1922	1929	1939	1942	1951	1965	1973	1978	1985
Food and agriculture	57	61	67	51	53	48	30	20	15
Chems., plastics, rubber	8	4	7	9	6	9	8	10	11
Metal & metal manufacture	11	7	5	6	10	6	11	16	15
Machinery	0	0	1	1	2	5	10	12	12
Transport equipment	—	—	—	—	—	5	12	14	15
(Automobiles, trucks)	—	—	—	—	—	(2)	(6)	(10)	(13)
Other	24	28	20	33	29	27	29	28	32
Total exports	100	100	100	100	100	100	100	100	100
% Autos/trans. equip	—	—	—	—	—	41	47	77	86
Total heavy industry	19	12	13	16	18	25	40	51	53

	Imports								
	1922	1929	1939	1942	1951	1965	1973	1978	1985
Food and agriculture	22	23	17	36	21	21	18	17	11
Chems., plastics, rubber	4	12	16	15	15	11	12	11	10
Metal & metal manufacture	4	6	6	4	6	14	9	6	7
Machinery	2	18	18	13	17	23	21	15	15
Transport equipment	—	—	—	—	—	4	6	4	5
(Automobiles, trucks)	—	—	—	—	—	(2)	(3)	(3)	(5)
Oil & related products	2	5	5	5	12	10	13	28	36
Other	66	36	38	27	29	17	21	19	16
Total imports	100	100	100	100	100	100	100	100	100
% Autos/trans. equip.	—	—	—	—	—	66	54	81	85
Total heavy industry	10	36	40	32	37	52	48	36	37

— no data available. Figures have been rounded

Sources: calculated from *Anuarios Estadísticos,* INE (1958)

textile industries (included in "other") are high, surely because of accumulated demand from the war years. The year 1942 is also atypical, because of the impact of the Civil War; here we can see a fall in food exports, and since the total level of exports was also falling, this indicates the depth of crisis in Spanish agriculture in the postwar period that we saw in Chapter 11. We also find this confirmed in the high proportion of food imports for that year.

The role of Mediterranean agriculture in external trade during the first half of the century can be appreciated from Table 13.2, which shows exports under the most important headings for these products as a percentage of total exports, in five-year averages. Over the whole period from 1900 to 1955 Mediterranean exports (fresh fruit and olive oil, but excluding wine and fresh vegetables) amounted to no less than 23% by value, and this was achieved with only 3% of the total cultivated area, and of course it is understood that a certain proportion of output was devoted to home consumption.

The growth of the automobile industry can be seen very clearly in the external trade figures. Until 1960 transportation items cannot be distinguished from machinery in general, but from that date onwards there was rapid growth in that sector, which was increasingly composed of automobiles. This category also appears on the imports side of the table, but is of lesser importance in percentage terms. In 1965 total imports were three times as large as total exports, so that Spain imported three times as many automobiles as it exported, in transactions that appear as 2% of both export and im-

Table 13.2. Exports of fresh fruit and olive oil as percentages of the total value of all exports, 1905–1950 (five-year averages)

	Oranges	All citrus fruit	All fruit	Fruit + olive oil
1905	6.4	6.5	10.8	14.4
1910	6.1	6.2	11.2	15.3
1915	4.3	4.4	8.3	13.5
1920	4.8	5.0	10.6	17.0
1925	10.7	10.9	18.5	24.5
1930	14.2	14.6	22.9	33.0
1945	5.3	6.2	13.1	16.3
1950	5.9	6.9	13.4	19.5

Source: calculated from *Instituto Nacional de Estadística* (1958)

port sections of the table. By 1973, with total imports twice as large as total exports, car exports and imports were about equal in number terms; from then onwards Spain was a net exporter of motor vehicles.

On the imports side one should first note the stable proportion of foodstuffs; apart from a significant rise during the hungry 1940s, foodstuffs show a notable regularity, about 20% of all imports, with a gently declining trend from the 1960s onwards (because other sectors, like capital goods and more recently petroleum, were growing). The heavy industry sector (chemicals, metal goods and machinery, and transportation equipment, largely capital equipment) also shows considerable regularity, at about 35% of all imports with the exception of the atypical 1922 and the years of rapid industrialization, the 1960s and early 1970s. In summary, what we find is exactly what we should expect to find, since the twentieth century is witness to the country's economic modernization, and the import of capital goods is the fundamental productive investment—generally speaking, the *sine qua non* of economic growth. Yet as the country undergoes technological transformation and begins to export its own capital goods, it is natural that the role of capital equipment imports should decline.[5]

And last, I wish to underline the rapid increase in imports of petroleum and byproducts, which coincides with the periods of expansion. After the rapid growth of the 1920s, the Great Depression, the Civil War, and the depression of the 1940s (complicated for Spain by difficulties with the Allies who controlled the greater part of petroleum production), the import and consumption of petroleum products maintained a downward trend, a constant proportion of what was basically a decline in total external trade. The recovery of growth in the second half of the century produced a spectacular increase in demand for petroleum products, and the 1973 crisis seems to have done nothing to mitigate this. Here, however, appearances are somewhat misleading; in the long run rising gasoline prices have helped to limit imports, but rather belatedly; the reduction has made itself felt only from 1985 onwards. The sequence is approximately the following: in the first years of the crisis, 1973–1977, the Spanish authorities did precious little to limit consumption, since very little of the price increase for crude oil was passed on to the consumer. The quantity of imports continued to rise, and with the meteoric rise in prices the value of imports also rose meteorically. And when interior prices were finally allowed to rise, beginning in 1977, the second rise in crude prices in 1979 meant that the petroleum bill still continued to increase, in spite of a progressive limitation in imports in physical terms. Starting in the mid-1980s the petroleum bill began to fall very rapidly, because the fall in crude prices at that time coincided with a fall in quantities imported, although this change is not reflected in Table 13.1.

Table 13.3 shows the geographic distribution of Spanish exports. From this we learn of the close relationship between Spain and its European trade partners, particularly its close neighbors. In addition to the traditional relationships with France and England, in the twentieth century trade with Germany and the United States became quite important, and Italy became the third European trading partner in terms of volume. The most important century-long trends are the declining role of trade with the United Kingdom, the rising importance of the United States (until the 1970s), and the growing geographic diversification evident in the moderately declining importance of the seven European countries in the table. Although since the 1950s it may seem that the United States and Europe have been substitute markets for Spanish exports, one rising when the other falls, in total the combined proportion also shows a moderate decline, confirming a trend towards diversification that has recently been somewhat subdued by Spain's entry into the European Union.

As far as fluctuations are concerned, it is interesting to point out the atypical nature of the first period reported in Table 13.3, when conditions of war suppressed exports to countries like Germany, Belgium, and Holland and increased the importance of the relationship with France instead. During World War II, in contrast, Germany (Spain's ally) received nearly 30% of Spanish exports. The occupied countries, France, Belgium, and Holland, imported very little directly from Spain, although they probably received some re-exports from Germany. Finally, part of the diversification apparent in the last period (measured by the combined exports to all eight countries in the table, which fell from 63.7% to 55.5%) can be explained by the petroleum crisis, which enriched the members of OPEC and converted those countries into greater markets for our exports.

The Terms of Trade

Just as the terms of trade improved for Spain during the greater part of the nineteenth century, they seem to have deteriorated in the twentieth, as Figure 13.6 shows (the reversal in fact dates from the last decades of the nineteenth). The assertion is somewhat tentative because the index constructed by Tena (Figure 13.6) indicates the "net barter terms of trade," a simple quo-

Table 13.3. Geographic distribution of Spain's exports, 1915/1918 through 1980/1984 (percentages of total exports)

Years	France	United Kingdom	Germany	Italy	Portugal	Belgium	Holland	Total of 7 countries	United States
1915–1918	38.9	18.6	0.0	5.3	2.1	0.0	0.6	65.5	6.2
1931–1935	17.1	23.6	10.1	4.5	1.1	4.6	4.7	65.7	8.1
1941–1944	2.5	18.5	29.8	6.9	2.0	0.6	0.6	60.9	8.2
1951–1955	9.1	16.6	11.1	2.1	0.7	3.9	4.4	47.9	12.1
1961–1963	9.9	15.5	13.6	7.4	1.4	2.8	3.9	54.5	10.8
1971–1972	11.6	8.4	12.0	5.7	2.8	2.4	5.0	47.9	15.8
1980–1984*	15.3	7.7	9.4	6.2	2.5	2.5	4.7	48.3	7.2

* no data for 1981

Source: Tena in *Estadísticas Históricas*, (ed.) Carreras (1989)

tient of price indices: export prices divided by import prices. Taking into account problematic statistics of external trade[6] and the serious problems that all countries encountered with monetary policy and exchange rates in the twentieth century, this index may contain some errors; it would be useful to see other comparable measures that would permit further refinements and comparisons. However, there can be no doubt that the trend was downwards. The cause of this decline can be found, at least in part, in the severe restriction of external trade; very specifically, restrictions on imports made the overall demand for imported goods extremely inelastic, because the items that were indeed imported were almost all indispensable. Where there are no restrictions, the importer and the merchant can choose and be more demanding in matters of price. This is perhaps what can fairly be deduced from the transitory improvement in the terms of trade after the 1959 liberalization, an improvement that was interrupted by the oil crisis in 1973. The almost uninterrupted fall in the terms of trade from then on is due to the inelastic demand for petroleum, a deterioration that has doubtless affected all the countries that import petroleum products.

For the first half of the century fluctuations in the terms of trade are con-

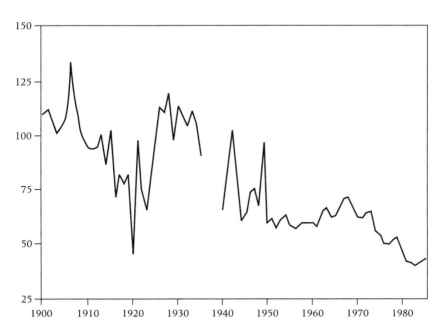

Figure 13.6. Net terms of trade between Spain and the rest of the world, 1900–1985

siderable, but the general downward trend can be explained in terms of century-long changes in world markets. In fact since the 1880s the trend has been towards lower raw material prices, first agricultural products and then mining materials a decade later. Spain, as an exporter of raw materials, could not avoid the effects of this worldwide trend, although there was improvement in the 1920s, due at least in part to the monetary stabilizations that moderated European prices for Spanish purchasers. The marked deterioration in the terms of trade during World War I was caused by quite the opposite effect; war-induced inflation made prices rise in other European countries more rapidly than in Spain.

The transitory improvement in Spain's terms of trade in the 1960s can also be attributed to changes in Spanish economic and commercial structure that we have seen above. In a world where raw material prices are tending to decline (this is a general trend with exceptions, as the petroleum market showed us in the 1970s and 1980s), the transition towards an economy based on industry and services ought to produce a tendency towards better terms of trade.

CHAPTER 14

The Evolution of Money and Banking

A Fiduciary Circulation

One of the peculiarities of the Spanish economy within the European context of the first third of the twentieth century is the unusual nature of its money. To put it simply, Spain was different from almost all the other European countries in that it never adopted the gold standard. This implies that after the demonetization of gold in 1883 (see Chapter 6), the monetary standard used in Spain was a fiduciary standard, and the value of Spanish currency was not determined by its intrinsic content. For countries on the gold standard the value of a coin was equivalent to the value of its metal content, but in Spain values were assigned by the issuing authority, a role which in fact was performed, and continues to be performed, by the Bank of Spain and the state, acting jointly. The gold standard system, which came into general use in Europe and other advanced countries during the last quarter of the nineteenth century, implied that the monetary sector (and consequently the credit sector) of subscribing countries should be subject to a set of specific rules whereby the supply of money would be limited to a certain proportion of the stock of gold each country possessed. This system has its advantages and disadvantages.

The essential advantage is that the gold standard guarantees monetary stability, since it imposes an automatic limit on the ability to issue paper money and coins, a limit that is defined by the stock of gold. Related to this is the advantage of easy convertibility with all the other currencies based upon the same system, and that brings with it, of course, easy commercial relations and capital movements with other countries within the system. These countries were already by the middle of the nineteenth century the most advanced countries of their day, and the advantages and disadvantages of the gold standard were very similar to those which today stem from Spain's membership of the European Monetary System.

The principal drawback of the system is the reverse of the advantage: the obverse of monetary stability is a rigidity that limits room for discretion. In submitting to an impersonal system of controls, the monetary authority may be forced to accept difficult, undesirable situations, such as a sudden loss of gold or an increase in unemployment, without being able to take corrective monetary measures. A country that is very jealous of its monetary sovereignty (and of its economy in general) would have had misgivings about the gold standard similar to contemporary objections to the European Monetary System. The same can be said about external relations. A country that fears opening up its economy to the forces of free trade will view the gold standard as something of a dangerous Trojan horse.

The gold standard has a further problematic aspect: the inelasticity of money supply inherent in the system can present problems both domestically and at the international level. As economic development evolves, in the long run the demand for money rises faster than national income, which is to say that the velocity with which money circulates tends to slow down. Thus to avoid both inflation and deflation, the supply of money (the amount of money in circulation) ought to grow *pari pasu* with the demand for money. The gold standard system, however, tends to slow down growth of the money supply by tying it to the existence of bullion reserves. This is, in fact, the great defect that Keynes recognized in the gold standard: it limited the supply of money and tended to produce deflation. "If money could be grown like a crop or manufactured like a motor-car, depressions would be avoided or mitigated," he asserted with a certain touch of optimism (Keynes, orig. ed. 1936; 1960 ed., pp. 230–231).

For Spain, it was doubtless the fear of the foreign trade deficit that prevailed in the minds of the economic decision-makers in 1833, when they decided to suspend fixed convertibility between gold and the peseta—a fear that certainly shaped the reluctance of later politicians to go back on that decision. With that decision taken, and more by omission than through conviction, Spain acquired the doubtful honor of being one of the few European countries where the gold standard was never adopted. Some observers might claim that in so doing Spain displayed a certain degree of laudable foresight, since eventually every nation ended up abandoning the gold standard in the 1930s, changing over to a fiduciary system as Spain had done half a century earlier and as Keynes, in the 1920s, had foreseen would be advisable. This impression of financial acuity is contradicted, however, by various attempts that Spain made to introduce the gold standard during the first third of the twentieth century. The best known one was tried under the leadership of José Calvo Sotelo in 1929, preceded by a number of others, all prior to World War I, sponsored by Raimundo Fernández Villaverde, Tirso Rodrigáñez, Juan Navarro Reverter, and Augusto González Besada (see Anes, 1974).

Note that the determining factor each time seems to have been the existence of gold. It was the sudden flight of gold that provoked the much discussed suspension in 1883, and without doubt it was the increases in gold stocks following the Villaverde stabilization, and later on the positive commercial balances during World War I, that encouraged these attempts to install the gold standard. In short, if Spain did not adopt the gold standard early on, it was not a matter of doctrinal principle, but rather that its politicians (above all the officials within the Bank of Spain) feared that chronic deficits in the balance of trade and in the national budget in the long run would cause massive losses of gold, making the project nonviable. This conviction and the reasons behind it were embodied in the most important document published on this matter, the famous *Dictámen de la Comisión del Patrón Oro*, the Report of the Commission on the Gold Standard, 1929, whose authors argued that "the collapse of the exchange rate" was the consequence of a monetary policy that was subordinated to the needs of a treasury chronically in deficit. That is to say, according to the Commission Report the quantity of money in circulation was largely determined by the loans that the Bank of Spain made to the government (this was certainly so in the nineteenth century, but not so much in the twentieth). The chronic deficit meant that these loans were excessive, and this surplus of pesetas provoked a tendency to depreciation. For that reason the Commission found it very doubtful that the gold standard could be maintained in Spain in the long run if the government did not balance the budget.

At this point it may be appropriate to introduce some further refinements in the terms we are using. The "supply of money" is the sum of all instruments of payments in an economy. As there is a series of goods or assets that are considered quasi-money, the definition of the "money supply" can vary according to whether these assets are included or not. For this reason we refer to M_1, a restrictive definition of the money supply that includes only coins (gold and silver), banknotes, and deposits on current account. A broader definition, called M_2 or the "liquid assets held by the public," additionally includes savings accounts in commercial banks and savings banks. A yet broader definition, M_3, includes other assets that are less liquid, such as term deposits, invested funds, and similar items. The most basic and most restrictive definition of the money supply, M_0 (high-powered money), is the sum of monetary assets (almost all of them issued by the Central Bank) that the private banking system uses as reserves; essentially, metallic money, gold and silver, banknotes from the Central Bank, and credit balances that the private banks hold with the Central Bank. We could say that this high-powered money, M_0, is the contribution of the Central Bank or monetary authority to the supply of money.[1]

Figure 14.1 shows, on a semi-logarithmic scale, the evolution of these monetary variables in Spain throughout the twentieth century, in trajectories that were obviously impacted by the Civil War. Before the war, growth was very moderate, except during World War I. This moderation is particularly clear in M_0 and M_1, which were the measures that the monetary authorities paid attention to during those years. The strict control the authorities exercised over these amounts is connected to their attempts to reintroduce the gold standard. In fact, over this period the Spanish govern-

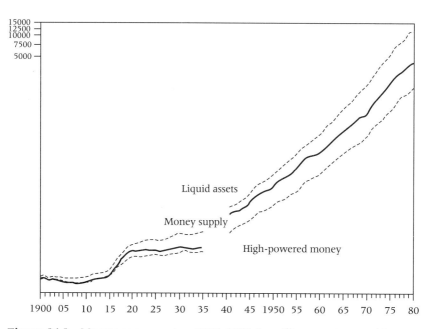

Figure 14.1. Monetary aggregates, 1900–1980 (in million pesetas, semi-logarithmic scale)

ment maintained an iron grip that was perhaps excessive over the amount of money in circulation. Proof that this control must have been too harsh is established in Figure 14.3, which for the period 1900 to 1980 shows the velocity of money circulation, which we define as the ratio of national income to the supply of money, using two definitions of the money supply, M_1 and M_2. Naturally the profile would vary according to the measure of national income used for the numerator (gross or net domestic product, gross or net national product), and according to the definition of money supply (M_1, M_2, or M_3) in the denominator. Essentially, however, there will be no large differences between the various versions, and this is what Figure 14.3 shows us. Although the chart does not go back to the nineteenth century, it seems that the velocity of Spanish money circulation began to increase from the moment that Spain demonetized gold in 1883, a phenomenon that lasted until the Great War. But since then the secular trend has been downwards, a trend that is general and confirms Spain's economic growth, as Milton Friedman has pointed out.[2] That implies that for almost 40 years national income must have grown more rapidly than the amount of money in circulation, a phenomenon unknown during periods of economic growth. In Italy, a country of similar characteristics, the velocity of money circulation actually declined during this period (Cohen, 1972). This slow growth of the money supply in a country not subject to the formal control of the gold standard reveals an ambivalent attitude among the monetary authorities of the period: a desire for "monetary respectability" on the one hand, and on the other hand a fear of the consequences of automatic controls under the gold standard.

The velocity of money circulation fell substantially during the Great War and the following years, from the combined effects of a large expansion in the supply of money and the postwar depression. Although later on the deflationist policy helped it to recover somewhat, it never again reached the high prewar levels. Something similar happened during the Civil War. Although we do not have data for the years of the conflict, it is clear that the velocity of money fell steeply because of a significant expansion in the amount of high-powered money, and that during the 1940s the nominal national income expanded more rapidly than the amount of money in circulation. This phenomenon is curious because we know, on the one hand, that national income per capita remained very low during this decade, and on the other hand that high-powered money supply grew faster than in any other earlier period of peace. What probably happened is that the composition of the high-powered money (M_0) changed, the use of banknotes increased, and that made the velocity of circulation speed up. After the Civil War, without the restrictive control of the gold standard and no preoccupation about "monetary respectability," the amount of money in circulation increased at the considerable annual rate of 13.7% (the prewar rate had been 3.1% per annum). After 1951, with fluctuations much less violent, the velocity again took up its normal secular downward trend. It is interesting, however, to observe certain contrasts between the two velocity measures presented in Figure 14.3. While V_2, based on the larger money supply, declined both immediately before and after the Civil War, V_1 is approximately constant in both periods, although at a lower level in the second period. This is a clear indication of the growing importance of the new types of monetary assets, less liquid but more profitable, like savings accounts in banks and savings institutions, which are included in M_2, but not in M_1.

Another interesting phenomenon is the change in the composition of the money supply, a change that was quite considerable, especially in the period 1900 to 1960, as can be seen in Figure 14.2. During the first third of the century we see the continuation of a process already begun in the second half of the nineteenth century; banknotes and checks drawn on deposits were be-

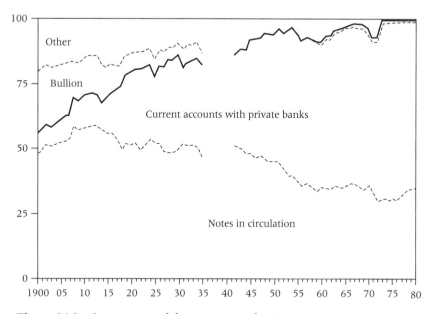

Figure 14.2. Components of the money supply, 1900–1980 (in percentages)

coming the usual means of payment and coins were gradually becoming less important, effectively reduced to the role of providing small change. (In this Spain was merely following the practice of other countries, for even where the gold standard was in force the usual medium of circulation was paper money, which in those countries was of course convertible to gold.) These changes in the money supply were quite substantial; while in 1900 silver coins had constituted 25% of high-powered money (M_0) and 23% of the money supply (M_1), by 1935 these figures had fallen to insignificant proportions, 6% and 3% respectively. At the start of the Civil War silver disappeared from circulation, so that the only metallic money circulating from that time onwards was small change in copper, nickel, aluminum, and that obviously was only a small proportion of the total circulation.

The banknote, the principal component of the money supply in the first decades of the century, gradually yielded its place to the enormous growth in deposits. At the same time private banking was becoming the principal financial subsector, the role the Bank of Spain had played as central bank during the whole of the nineteenth century and the first years of the twenti-

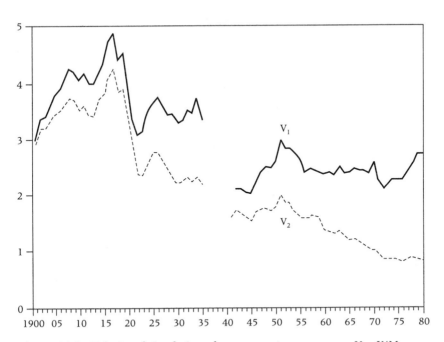

Figure 14.3. Velocity of circulation of money, on two measures, $V_1 = Y/M_1$, $V_2 = Y/M_2$, 1900–1980

eth. High-powered money reveals a similar trend, but the Civil War caused a massive discontinuity. In 1935 banknotes represented about 60% of M_0, but four years later, when the war ended, they were no less than 90% of M_0 (see Figure 14.4). This is surely because the precarious conditions in postwar Spain and the Second World War produced uncertainty and an extraordinary demand for banknotes, some of which were destined to be hoarded, creating a demand to which the authorities responded with a steep increase in supply. Now, within the total amount of money in circulation some components circulate much faster than others; coins go from hand to hand much faster than banknotes, and notes faster than bank deposits. The large increase in the relative weight of notes within the monetary supply would explain the increase in the velocity of money circulation in the 1940s, a decade when real income increased very little. In several aspects this was a decade of economic regression; the acceleration of the circulation of banknotes indicates that this was also a decade of monetary regression. The uppermost residual section labeled "other" in Figure 14.2 principally represents Bank of Spain deposits held by the public at large.

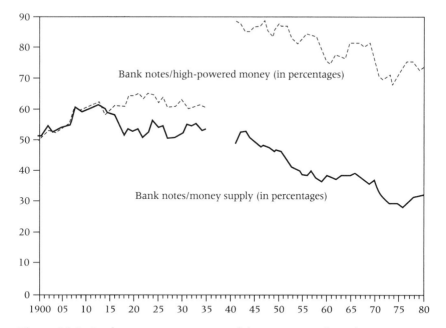

Figure 14.4. Banknotes as a percentage of the money supply and as a percentage of high-powered money, 1900–1980

Why did the various measures of money in circulation evolve in the way indicated in Figure 14.1? Fortunately, monetary analysis allows us to shed some light on that question.[3] Simplifying to a point of exaggeration, the supply of money increased because it responded to a growing demand for money, a demand that grew as an integral part of the process of economic development. Pushing the analysis a little further, however, scholars generally make a distinction between four major sectors that create the demand for money and credit, in response to which the monetary authority (essentially the Bank of Spain) creates primary or high-powered money, M_0. These four groups are: private banking, the public sector, the foreign sector, and private individuals. The importance of this last group is residual and declining, since as the central bank continues to consolidate its position as the bankers' bank, its relationship with private individuals increasingly takes place through the rest of the banking system. Quantitatively speaking, during the twentieth century the two most important components of the demand for money have been the private banks and the foreign sector. The *private banking sector* constitutes the strongest and most stable element: in reality its demand is for basic bank reserves which allow private banks to create secondary money as a response to the demands of the economy at large—demands from the public, individuals, but also the state; in a word, demands that represent the GDP. The *foreign sector* has been important in certain periods, but has generally been subject to large fluctuations. In periods when the balance of payments was in surplus, periods like the Great War and the 1960s, exporters earned gold and foreign exchange for conversion into pesetas, and the growth of reserves created a parallel growth in high-powered money. In periods of deficit such as the Great Depression, the 1950s, or after 1973, the foreign sector of course shrank. The *public sector* comes in third place. Before the Civil War it frequently acted as a brake, because of the purposely restrictive policy that we have already noted. After that war its role has been uniformly expansive. But the real importance of the public sector in creating a demand for money is greater than the figures indicate, since its demand for credit is often met through the private banking sector. And through monetary policy directives the public sector can regulate the rate of expansion of high-powered money. Proof of this fact is that, without recourse to any standard or automatic control, high-powered money grew only gradually before the Civil War and rapidly afterwards, simply obeying the particular orientations of different economic policies.

What were the consequences of Spain's peculiar monetary position in the period before the Civil War, when Spain was a fiduciary island in a gold standard sea? It is difficult to give a categorical answer to this question, because it would require a counterfactual exercise: how would the economy have evolved if Spain had been on the gold standard? But it is certainly possible to formulate a conjectural response. One of the consequences of Spain's peculiar monetary policy was to isolate its economy from those of its neighbors and other countries. In making international monetary transactions difficult, the already considerable tariff barriers were reinforced while capital flows were impeded (Martín Aceña, 1994). Given that the Spanish economy benefited from being opened up to the exterior, monetary isolation could not have been anything other than prejudicial. On the positive side, fiduciary control conferred a great deal of discretion upon those in charge of economic policy. Freedom from the discipline of the gold standard ought to have permitted a monetary policy that was more decidedly oriented towards economic development, for example, by adapting the growth of the money supply to development needs. But this discretion was rarely used to good purpose. Obviously eager to ensure their own "monetary respectability," the Spanish politicians maintained a restrictive policy that impeded greater growth of high-powered money except during the Great War, when a tremendous surge in external trade caused a sudden jump in the amount of money in circulation; and not even that period of decontrol was used to beneficial effect. During the 1920s and 1930s, however, it does indeed seem that the discretionary monetary policy may have been adapted to the economy's needs, thanks in part to an increase in the amount of money in circulation that was beyond the control of the monetary authorities, that is to say, liquid assets held by the public, M_2. Moderate expansion of M_2 in the 1920s permitted the growth of national income with stable prices, and a flexible monetary policy during the Second Republic managed to palliate the worst consequences of the Great Depression.[4]

The Private Banking Sector

As in so many facets of Spanish life, the turn of the century also marked a watershed in matters of banking. It is reasonable to conjecture that this must bear some relationship to the change in economic policy and important movements of private capital that followed 1898. The repatriation of capital following the loss of the colonies, the increase in economic activity after the Cuban War, and the stimulus to exports that the Villaverde plan produced through price stabilization doubtless facilitated the supply and stimulated the demand for new credit institutions. Many of the banks founded about the beginning of the century figure prominently in Spain's economic history: the Hispano-Americano in 1900, the Vizcaya in 1901, and the Banco Español de Crédito in 1900; somewhat later came the Banco Urquijo in 1918, the Banco Central in 1919, the Banco Popular in 1926, and the Banco Exterior in 1929. Indeed, all the larger elements in Spain's banking system date from before the Civil War and the largest institutions, except for the Banco Central, were founded at the dawn of twentieth century if not earlier. Table 14.1 shows the growth in the number of Spanish banks from the end of the nineteenth century until 1983.

Another way of viewing the evolving maturity of the Spanish banking industry after the turn of the century is by confirming the declining position of the Bank of Spain in its role of *primus inter pares* in the banking world. For example, in the first decades of the century, when deposits in private banks were growing (with the exception of the Catalán Bank), deposits in the Bank of Spain itself stayed at the same level or even declined. While at the end of the nineteenth century deposits held in the Bank of Spain represented 75% of total deposits within the whole banking industry, in 1913 this proportion had fallen to 60%, and in 1934 to 20%. In many aspects one can consider the first third of the twentieth century as the formative period for Spanish banking. During these years the essential characteristics that have lasted through to today were set in place. Of these certainly the most relevant is the dominance of a small number of banks involved in what we term "mixed" banking, very much in the manner of the great German banks. It was the practice for commercial banks to involve themselves in the promo-

Table 14.1.   Number of banks in Spain, 1900–1983

Year	Number of banks	Year	Number of banks	Year	Number of banks
1900	36	1929	94	1966	126
1905	50	1934	86	1970	111
1910	60	1942	108	1973	109
1914	61	1950	142	1980	125
1920	91	1960	109	1983	133

Sources: Tedde (1974); Muñoz (1969); Tortella and Palafox (1983); Fanjul and Maravall (1985); *Anuarios Estadísticos; Anuarios Estadísticos de la Banca Privada*

tion and support of companies while holding a high proportion of those companies' shares in their investment portfolios. The second characteristic was, and continues to be, a notable concentration in the industry. For example, in 1923 the six large banks (the Hispano-Americano, Bilbao, Urquijo, Central, Vizcaya, and Español de Crédito), which numerically speaking represented 6.6% of all existing banks, held more than 40% of the paid-up capital in the whole of the private banking sector, and more than 50% of deposits. And as a third characteristic, these banks shared many features of holding companies: through portfolio operations, long-term loans, and a network of interlocking directorships, each one managed to set itself up as the financial hub of a group of diversified companies, mostly industrial enterprises in mining, transportation, or the energy sector. A fourth characteristic is a strong geographic concentration; Madrid and Bilbao between them were the central headquarters of the "six." Barcelona, long ago the main center of private banking, was relegated to third place and increasingly to the periphery; this became particularly obvious when the venerable Banco de Barcelona closed its doors in 1920. The last characteristic that stands out is the growth of networks of branches which effectively converted the major banks into businesses of national compass.

Of the three major banking regions, Madrid and the Basque Country tended to adopt a form of mixed banking, while in Catalonia this model failed to catch on (see Chapter 6). It was perhaps in the Basque Country that this kind of banking evolved in its most notable and genuine form, since for Madrid the role of capital city clearly introduced very particular factors. In addition to the Banco de Vizcaya, a large number of new banks appeared in the Basque Country, beginning with the Banco de Comercio in 1891 and then the Guipuzcoano (1900), the Banco de Vitoria (1900) and the Crédito de la Unión Minera (1901). In the long run the Banco de Bilbao and the Banco de Vizcaya emerged as leaders; the former absorbed the Banco del Comercio in 1901 (although some formal independence was maintained), while the Vizcaya absorbed other small entities. The once active and powerful Crédito de la Unión Minera, after a stumble in 1914 that seemed to have no serious consequences, went bankrupt in 1925.

In Madrid two large banks were formed at the beginning of the century. The Banco Hispano-Americano was created, as its name suggests, for "the development of Hispano-American trade"; its founders were Spanish businessmen living in Mexico and other parts of Spanish America. Antonio Basagoiti headed this group of entrepreneurs, who repatriated capital to

Spain after the independence of Cuba, Puerto Rico, and the Philippines. It was the first private bank to set up a network of branches throughout the whole of Spain. The origin of the Banco Español de Crédito is very different, since it was really a continuation of the old Crédito Mobiliario Español (see Chapter 6) strengthened by new French and Spanish capital. The "Banesto" (as it later came to be known) inherited the stock portfolio of the Crédito Mobiliario, and at first its progress was quite slow. Although it was said at the beginning that it was neither a bank (but rather a holding company) nor Spanish (the majority of the capital was French) nor concerned with credit (supposedly it was not a bank at all), in the end it vindicated its name; in addition to operating widely as a bank, by the end of the 1920s its capital has passed almost entirely into Spanish hands.

Later on, two other important institutions appeared in Madrid, the Banco Urquijo and the Banco Central. The first grew out of a banking house with a long history, dating back to an alliance of the founder of the dynasty, Estanislao de Urquijo, with the House of Rothschild in Madrid during the reign of Fernando VII (Otazu, 1987); it was already very powerful at the time of the Restoration. In contrast the Banco Central had nothing old about it other than the idea. It was the Marqués de Campo who came up with it, name and all, also at the time of the Restoration: the idea was to form a bank that would join together various provincial banking houses in the capital city. And this was exactly what transpired. The Banco Central counted among its principal partners the Banco de la Unión Minera, the Madrid house of Aldama, the Banco de Santander, the Guipuzcoano, and a number of provincial banks and banking houses.

The emergence of this strong banking group in the first years of the century brought changes to the Spanish financial market that were qualitative as well as quantitative. Perhaps the most important in this respect was that in becoming more complex, the credit structure was also modernized. As it began to shrink in relative size, the Bank of Spain could go about taking responsibility for the normal functions of a central bank in greater measure: instead of dealing directly with the public and the Treasury, the bank acted, on the one hand, as the "bankers bank," and on the other as the co-formulator and executor of Spain's monetary policy. During the nineteenth century the Bank of Spain had been acting more as the bank for the government, and had been competing with the private banks in its relations with the public, both in attracting resources and in making credit available. During the first decades of the twentieth century, the bank forged a new role that was to become very important. With help from the Villaverde stabilization and the powerful, newly formed private banks, and taking advantage of the freedom that the fiduciary system offered, the Bank of Spain began to forge a new relationship with the private banking industry which brought about the indirect monetization of the national debt.

The mechanism was the following. Thus far the Bank of Spain had been acquiring the debt that the government issued to cover the budget deficit. As a counterpart of this debt the bank issued bearer notes which it delivered to the state, and which the state then used to pay its debts. This was what we term a direct monetization of the debt. The Villaverde stabilization made it possible to balance the budgets, so for some years the government did not need to issue further debt nor the bank to issue further notes. The debt portfolio of the Bank of Spain stabilized, and the government even made efforts to eliminate the deficit. When budget deficits reappeared (at the time of the Moroccan War and later during the Great War), the existence of a strong private banking sector allowed a conversion to the system of "indirect monetization" of the debt. From 1917 onwards, the bank officially offered favorable lending conditions that made it very attractive for the private banking sector to borrow from the bank, using government bonds as collateral. Thus it was the private banks that bought debt bonds, knowing that they could be used to underwrite cheap credit with the Bank of Spain. In this way, the Bank of Spain became a "bankers' bank, and lender of last resort." The private banks financed the budget deficit and legally used the debt as backing for their deposits, knowing that in an emergency it could be used to obtain credit from the Bank of Spain. All in all, the system was less inflationary than the "direct monetization" had been, because the private banks acted to a certain degree as a shock absorber and the central bank did not have to issue notes in compensation for the debt to the extent that it had done under the former system.

This new state of affairs was reflected in the 1921 *Ley de Ordenación Bancaria* (Law on Banking Regulations), whose principal author was Finance Minister Francisco Cambó. This was the first law that regulated the Bank of Spain as the central bank and private banks just as private entities, establishing a division of functions and indicating various channels of relationships that until that date had been left almost totally to the initiative of the interested parties. Among other details, the new law introduced two innovations that were important in making the Bank of Spain an effective instrument of the government's monetary policy: (1) it was empowered to concede loans on preferential interest rates to private banks that were affiliated with the Central Banking Council, the Consejo Superior Bancario that this same law created; and (2) the law gave guidelines for joint intervention of the government and the bank on matters relating to the international value of the peseta. As far as private banking was concerned, in addition to the creation of the CSB for purposes of control and information, the law established a series of classifications and defined geographic zones of operation.

In spite of the success of the new law, the ability of the Bank of Spain to control the creation of money remained severely limited, because while the automatic collateral loan mechanism for the public debt might still be alive and well, the interest rate that governed credit relations between the bank and the banking industry was in the hands of the Treasury, and that institution always kept the collateral loan rate below the discount rate, which the bank itself was free to define. This being the case, the capacity of the central bank to control credit through the rediscounting of bills of exchange was almost nonexistent, since the private banks could always avoid the rediscount mechanism, obtaining credit instead from the Bank of Spain through the debt support mechanism.

Ten years later, in November 1931, a new banking law, dictated more by political than by economic motives, tightened the government's control over the Bank of Spain; among other items the government would appoint three members of the bank's board of directors and would play a greater part in interest rate policy. This initiated a process of growing state intervention in the bank, which was to culminate in its nationalization in 1962. The quantitative and qualitative growth in Spain's banking industry is indicated in Figure 14.5, which shows the growth of total banking assets in relation to national income. For Goldsmith,[5] a financial interrelations ratio of 1 represents the threshold of financial maturity, and Spain, which had just about reached that degree of maturity in the early 1930s, did not reach it again until 35 years later.

In contrast to so many facets of the Spanish experience, the Civil War did not really constitute a watershed in the history of Spanish banking, although Figure 14.5 shows a considerable reduction in the importance of the banking deposits within the economy. The postwar period gave rise to a number of short-term problems, the most acute of which was how to get back to normal conditions after a highly abnormal period of three years. Concretely, the problem was to rejoin the monetary and credit systems, split asunder by the war, while absorbing and accommodating the losses inflicted by the war itself. During the early postwar years the government enacted a series of measures culminating with the Banking Law of 1946 which emphasized strong state intervention in the banking industry. They were (1) the so-called banking *status quo*, whereby the state exercised strict control of the creation, fusion, and absorption of banks (this was supposed to keep the number of banks stable and restrict competition); (2) the Bank of Spain was subjected to state control even more rigorous than that imposed in 1931; (3) the Spanish Institute for Foreign Currency (Instituto Español de Moneda Extranjera) was created as a dependency of the Ministry of Commerce and put in charge of all aspects of international monetary relations; (4) the Office of Banking and Stock Exchange Control (Dirección General de Banca y Bolsa) was created with responsibility for inspecting the banking sector; and (5) the Treasury's grip over monetary policy, in particular interest rates, was further tightened. As can be deduced from all of this, the Bank of Spain found itself relegated almost exclusively to the role of issuing banknotes, and the government took charge of monetary policy, although with a certain lack of coordination, since domestic policy was in the hands of the Treasury while foreign matters were handled by the Ministry of Commerce.

In this situation of *numerus clausus*, the characteristic polarization of Span-

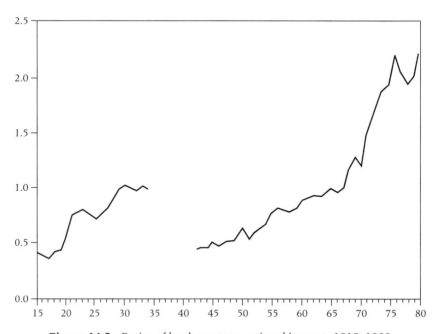

Figure 14.5. Ratios of bank assets to national income, 1915–1980

ish private banks became even more acute, and a small number of large banks increased their already large holdings. One feature of the new situation was that the government fixed extremely low interest rates for the whole banking industry; it seems that the government feared that if banks paid better rates on deposits, the public would not take up the national debt. As a consequence, outside of paying some illegal "topping off" rates, the banks were only able to compete for deposits by constructing networks of branches, and also through mergers. Because interest rates on deposits were fixed at a low rate, any funds that could be captured were obviously going to be remunerative, and thus we find that large banks were buying up smaller banks simply to absorb their deposits. Both mergers and branch networks grew spectacularly in these years. Between 1940 and 1956 the five largest banks absorbed 61 others and their combined network of branch offices grew from 959 to 1,619. In spite of these mergers, the number of banks did not actually decline during these years (see Table 14.4), which indicates that the famous *status quo* was more elastic than it appeared to be (Martín Aceña, 1990, 1990a, and 1991).

We have repeatedly noted the mixed nature of the Spanish banking industry. This means that alongside their commercial activities (short-term loans, typically discounting bills of exchange and loans of less than a year), the large banks have also engaged in business activities and the promotion of companies (long-term loans, the acquisition and sale of shares, bonds, debentures, and the national debt). In contrast, the Anglo-Saxon world considers this admixture unorthodox and dangerous, since the commercial banks, whose deposits are short-term (typically current account deposits), incur serious risks if they make long-term loans. In these countries the task of providing long-term financial support for industry and public works has been left to the market, and specifically to the stock market. However, the cases of Germany, Japan, and Italy show that it is possible for the banking industry to combine both types of activities if the proper precautions are taken, precautions that consist basically of not making long-term loans in excess of long-term liabilities, including capital reserves and long-term deposits. It was Gerschenkron (1965, ch. I) who used evidence from these countries to argue that the more backward the country, the more appropriate was the development of a mixed banking system (plus state intervention) to catch up on lost time, and indeed, already Schumpeter (1961, originally in 1911) had attributed this role to the banking industry in his famous model of economic growth. Almost at the same time that Gerschenkron was

writing his celebrated book, a Spanish banker, Villalonga (1961), was justifying the role of mixed banking in Spain:

> In Spain . . . there exists no rich bourgeoisie, nor a powerful middle class . . .
> sufficient capacity for savings and for capital is [simply] lacking. In this situ-
> ation there was no other recourse, in mobilizing the state, than to utilize a
> part of the commercial and deposit funds entrusted to the banking industry
> . . . and thus in the economic and banking resurgence that came with
> the new century, the Spanish banking industry, driven by necessity rather
> than any technical, scientific or deliberate plan, adopted the character of a
> "mixed" banking sector.

Thus, from the second decade of the century, the banking industry developed in close symbiosis with industry, and above all heavy industry: the major banks promoted and were major shareholders in companies involved
in mining, metal refining, electrical generation, heavy chemicals, and construction, and they participated in state companies such as the Banco de
Crédito Industrial and CAMPSA. Beyond their commercial business, the
major banks adopted the role of holding companies or portfolio managers,
forming groups or conglomerates of companies which they controlled totally or in part. It is perfectly possible that Gerschenkron in the general case,
and Villalonga for Spain's case in particular, were correct, and that if the
banks had not assumed this role the capitalization of industry would have
been much slower. Other authors have argued to the contrary (as much for
Spain as for Germany[6]), that the monopolistic factors implicit in this symbiosis between the banks and industry were an obstacle to the proper allocation of resources, and thus an obstacle to growth. It is very difficult to choose
between these two hypotheses, since each may have been correct for some
periods yet incorrect for others.

It is appropriate to ask whether the behavior of mixed banking in countries enjoying fast growth might not disprove the Anglo-Saxon claim about
the advantages of the separation of commercial banking from business
banking. To answer in the affirmative is probably a little hasty. Suffice it to
recall the tremendous repercussions of the Great Depression on the mixed
banking industries in Germany, Italy, and Austria in the 1930s,[7] although
similar serious repercussions also took place in the United States, a country
with specialized banking in the Anglo-Saxon tradition. The Spanish case is
different because, free from the gold standard, Spain had a monetary system
that offered much more flexibility. In reality, it was the fiduciary system that

has permitted the development of mixed banking in Spain, since the risks inherent in the system were compensated by the role played by the Bank of Spain as lender of last resort, a role it could fulfill more easily because it did not have to maintain the discipline of the gold standard system. Furthermore, the automatic collateral loan system allowed the banks to combine their long-term assets in such a way that they could turn to the Bank of Spain for collateral loans in moments of distress.

With the Bank of Spain relegated to the role of issuing money and the state and the banking industry engaged in the task of financing an industrialization moving at full speed, inflation took off in Spain in the 1950s. In the euphoric atmosphere of self-sufficiency that was prevalent in those years, this rise in prices would have been happily accepted if its consequences had not brought into focus the tremendous contradictions of such a policy: inflation produced a deficit in the balance of payments and exhausted the foreign exchange reserves, without which no country can keep on importing in order to keep on growing (see Chapter 13). Starting in 1957 serious readjustments in economic policy were initiated, culminating in the stabilization plan of 1959. This included a banking reform, whose centerpiece was the Ley de Bases de Ordenación del Crédito y la Banca (Law on Banking Principles for the Regulation of Credit and Banking) of April 14, 1962. Perhaps the most positive and permanent component of this reform was the definitive nationalization of the Bank of Spain, and the transfer to that body of most of the inspection functions that had formerly been the responsibility of the Office of Banking and the stock market. In addition, the bank would receive funding to take up the executive role on monetary policy that the new law assigned to it. In contrast, the attempt to separate commercial banking from industrial banking fell short, surely because the economic reasons why mixed banking was working well in Spain continued to persist: namely, outside of the banks there was no market for capital in sufficient amount to meet the real needs of the economy.

This law ushered in a period of intense restructuring of the banking industry. The old principle of the *status quo* was at last partially abandoned. About twenty new small or medium-sized banks came into being. To be sure, most of them, inexpert and speculative as they were, proved to be incapable of dealing with competition and the crisis that arrived ten years later. The bank law also suffered from a further shortcoming; while the final word on decisions remained with the government, monetary policy management was still divided between the surviving Instituto Español de Moneda Extranjera and the recently created Instituto de Crédito a Medio y Largo Plazo, (later rebaptized the Instituto de Crédito Oficial). And finally, the system of privileged access to credit channels, one of the principal instruments of the "economic planning" which in those years was very much in vogue, in the end became a weapon that turned upon its creators.

The system's defects became patently obvious when the famous MATESA scandal erupted, an economic episode that gave rise to one of the biggest political crises of the Franco regime. Its ultimate cause lay in a system of special credits designed to stimulate the export of capital goods, a favorite project of the economic ministers of the day. For mysterious reasons the administration of these export credits was made the responsibility of the Banco de Crédito Industrial, which had no experience in this type of operation. The BCI granted a disproportionately large amount of credit to a textile machinery company which was submitting documentation that was fraudulent, though formally correct. The textile company, MATESA, was making looms of a new design which it "exported" to its own foreign subsidiaries. Thanks to these false exports it was obtaining enormous amounts of official credit that permitted it to continue in operation. Despite the bank's suspicions, the legal and administrative system itself obliged it to keep on fulfilling MATESA's credit requests. Perhaps in the end MATESA would have really sold some of its machines abroad. We shall never know, because when the fraud was discovered in 1969, the scandal became enormously politicized; the Falangist press aired the matter in banner headlines in an attempt to bring shame and disrepute to Opus Dei, a religious group well represented within Franco's cabinet that had become very powerful, and particularly dominant in the economic ministries. This was one of very few of the regime's financial scandals that actually reached the newspapers, and it marked the beginning of the breakup of Franco's political system. For MATESA, the affair brought ruin, and its losses (and through it the losses of the official credit system) reached figures that were astronomical at that time. As a consequence, a revision of the banking legislation was set in motion, along with a gradual liberalization beginning in 1971. Later on these changes were coupled with the deregulation that was a requirement for Spain's entry into the European Community.

This process took place under difficult circumstances. The deregulation of banking was carried out within the general framework of liberalizing the Spanish economy, which in turn was part of the transition from dictatorship to democracy following Franco's death. These difficulties were aggravated

by the international crisis of the 1970s, which affected Spain with some delay, but forcefully. The crisis had been triggered by two events: the rise in petroleum prices motivated by Arab hostility towards Israel and the Western
countries, and the breakdown of the Bretton Woods agreement on international payments, precipitated by the incapacity of the United States to face
up to its commitments as the centerpiece of that system. This failure, due to
a structural deficit in the North American balance of payments and accentuated by the Vietnam War, forced the United States to abandon external gold
convertibility of the dollar, and with this, international trade entered a period of *de facto* floating exchange rates. The uncertainty of this situation provoked a major disturbance of the world economic equilibrium.

Although the international crisis began in 1973, it was not felt in Spain
until several years later, because the last governments of the Franco era, preoccupied with the regime's increasing fragility and believing that the rise in
petroleum prices would be transitory, decided that the state should absorb
the costs of the rising energy prices instead of passing increases on to the
consumer. This increased the budget deficit and limited the room for maneuver available to the transitional governments. When the crisis hit, the
most affected sectors were tourism, property investment, construction, and
heavy industry. The banking industry, and above all the new banks, had invested heavily in these areas because they had been very profitable in the
earlier period. In consequence, the banking system itself was seriously affected by a depression, which in the beginning seemed to be reaching only
the more marginal components, but in the end shook the whole system at
its foundations.

From the sum total of about 110 banks that were in operation in 1977,
more than half, almost 60, found themselves in difficulties between that
date and 1985. It is true that the most heavily affected banks were small
ones; their total capital or deposits represented less than 30% of the whole
banking sector in 1980, when they employed 27% of the industry's workforce. But although the majority of these banks in trouble were small and
new, some of the ones that disappeared were old and large, most notably
the Banco Urquijo, which suspended payments in 1981. The crisis reached
its most spectacular moment in 1982–83, when the holding company
RUMASA, a company that controlled eighteen banks, was nationalized by
the newly elected Socialist government. Although it was to affect many
banks, the crisis did not cause the disappearance of any, and for this reason
no loss shows up in Table 14.1. Thanks to the salvage operation mounted by

the monetary authorities, even the most heavily damaged units managed to survive. The crisis, however, is clearly registered in Figure 14.5, where we can see, at the end of the 1970s, a marked decline in the amount of banking assets in relation to national income.

The Bank of Spain had foreseen the sector's difficulties and tried to draw up an institutional framework that would absorb the shocks. It was soon decided that everything possible had to be done to avoid panic situations by preventing suspensions of payment and bankruptcies. The guiding principle for the monetary authority was the protection of deposit holders and the assignment of responsibility to managers and shareholders, in different degrees of course, for decisions for which they should properly be held responsible. The main policy instrument was to be the Deposit Guarantee Fund, Fondo de Garantía de Depósitos (FGD), an organism inspired by the analogous body created in the United States during the Depression years of the 1930s and the New Deal, the Federal Deposit Insurance Corporation (FDIC). The FGD was legally created at the end of 1977, but a series of legal problems impaired its effectiveness, and in the interim a second institution was set up. This was the Banking Corporation (Corporación Bancaria), a private entity that was to carry out, provisionally, the role that had been entrusted to the FGD. The Banking Corporation was financed in equal parts by private banks and the Bank of Spain, and its mission was to help banks in difficulties, or to buy them out. In certain cases a loan and restructuring were sufficient to get the affected business back on its feet. Most frequently, the bank would need some broader form of intervention; in many cases it was a question of replacing managers and directors and acquiring part or all of the bank's capital. The buying price would then be decided on the basis of asset valuation. Once the Banking Corporation was in charge of the bank, the most problematic and least liquid assets were sold; once the company had been cleaned up and freed of its most acute problems, it was a question of seeking a new buyer, preferably another bank. In 1981 a series of decrees improved the legal operating capacity of the FGD, and later on the Banking Corporation was dissolved. From then onwards the work of straightening up the banking system was in the hands of the FGD, which operated according to the same guidelines as its predecessor.

While the crisis was working its way through the banking system, the liberalization continued all the same: interest rates were gradually loosened, beginning with the longer-term rates (to stimulate capital formation), the principle of *status quo* was put aside, and the legal distinction between commercial and investing banks was again abandoned. Perhaps the most important feature was that the legal restraints on establishing foreign banks were gradually relaxed. The responsible authorities, the Banking Corporation, the FGD, and the Bank of Spain, seeking to sell banks that had been "cleaned up" or "were convalescent," saw the opportunity to kill two birds with one stone. In advancing such sales they had two ends in mind: to strengthen competition, and to overcome the reluctance of the national banking sector to take part in operations necessary to clean up the industry.

Looking to a future role in the European Community capital market, Spanish banks have recently carried out a series of mergers whose primordial aim has been to reach a size adequate for competition in that arena. The Spanish state has looked favorably on these mergers and supported them with fiscal measures. The two major Basque banks joined together in 1988 to form the Banco Bilbao Vizcaya, the two largest saving banks in Catalonia merged in 1990 to form the Caja de Barcelona (la Caixa) and the two largest banks in Madrid, the Central and the Hispano Americano merged in 1991 to form the Banco Central Hispano.

The Savings Banks and the Official Banking Sector

During the twentieth century, the savings banks gradually set aside their initial charitable role and became more like other financial institutions. The process was gradual, and the transition by no means indicates that the savings banks have become exactly like the private banks, principally because they continue to be nonprofit organizations in the sense that they have no owners nor shareholders.

The transition, both quantitative and legislative, evolved on a roughly parallel track. As the savings banks' share of the market increased, the appropriate public bodies extended to them greater and greater recognition as financial establishments. At the end of the nineteenth century, their market share (the fraction that their deposits represented within the whole financial system) had been about 10%, after having hovered around 15% during the 1880s and 1890s. Figure 14.6 shows the evolution of that quota throughout the present century. In general, the wars reduced their market share; during the years 1894–1898 (not represented in the graph), in 1914–1918, and 1936–1939 their holdings fell markedly. This is obviously because liquidity preference changes in times of uncertainty, and the public chooses to keep money in current account deposits where it is more readily available. In the long run, however, the savings banks have grown more than the financial system as a whole, and their market share has risen from a little more than 10% in 1900 to almost 40% in 1990.

As the savings banks grew and expanded their role as repositories of a growing share of total national savings, the legal treatment and social consideration that were afforded them also changed, as Manuel Titos (1991) has shown very clearly. Originally they had been set up as benevolent institutions whose principal aim was to develop the savings habit among the lower classes; in this purpose they were often considered to be subsidiary to other organisms such as the Monte de Piedad, the official pawnshop in Madrid, or the Sociedad Económica, an educational body in Valencia. Their remarkable growth, both in the number of establishments and the quantity of deposits accumulated at the end of the nineteenth century and the beginning of the twentieth made it necessary to start looking at them in a different light. A series of decrees in the 1920s and 1930s embody this change: they created an institute to oversee the savings banks, the Instituto de Crédito de las Cajas de Ahorros (ICCA, Institute for Savings Banks Credit); imposed investment coefficients (see below); regulated and expanded the range of activities open to the savings banks (most importantly, permitted operations with public

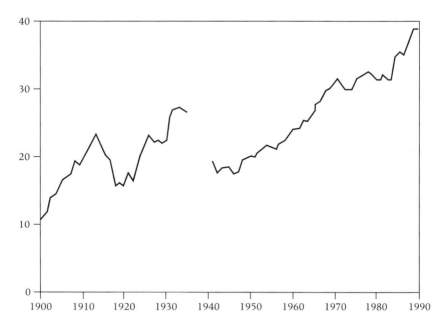

Figure 14.6. The market share of savings banks, 1900–1990 (in percentages)

funds and mortgage loans); and officially recognized the trend towards cooperation and partnership between member banks. This trend was, in fact, creating a counterweight to the banks' own innate localism. The savings banks were compensating for their parochial character through a growing tendency to form associations with other savings banks, and proof is to be found in the creation of the Spanish Confederation of Savings Banks in 1926.

Under Franco the savings banks were primarily viewed as a source of funds to be employed to the government's ends. The state controlled these funds by means of obligatory investment coefficients, which reduced to a minimum the freedom of the banks' governing bodies to handle their resources as they saw fit. A series of legal measures defined this situation, through which the savings banks in effect financed many of the favorite projects of the Franco regime, from the *universidades laborales* (workingman's universities, a sort of glorified vocational school) to ENSIDESA, the iron and steel giant. Recognition that the savings banks were financially important was made patent when in 1957 they were put under the control of the Finance Ministry; previously they had been controlled by the Labor Ministry and before that by the Department of the Interior. This new position was confirmed in the Banking Law of 1962, which included regulating the savings banks, treating them more or less as regular banks, although the regular banks continued to be supervised by the Bank of Spain and the Institute for Long and Medium Term Credit, whereas the savings banks were still under the ICCA. With the end of the Franco regime and the simultaneous process of bank liberalization, the notion that the savings banks were effectively normal financial organizations was completely established. In 1971 the ICCA was eliminated, and the savings banks were put directly under the control of the Bank of Spain; in 1977 the distinctions that had existed between them and the ordinary banks became even more blurred when they were allowed to carry out just the same operations as the banks, in particular to discount bills (thus meeting an ancient complaint of the savings banks), and the old obligatory investment coefficients were further reduced, continuing a trend dating from the 1962 legislation. In two aspects, however, the savings banks are still irreducibly different from the banks, each derived from their nonprofit character, their governing bodies, and the distribution of profits. Since they have no owners, the savings banks do not have stockholder committees, and their administrative bodies represent a wide spectrum of interests. Traditionally, the founding members and the deposit holders had held a leading role in management. In 1985 a new law essentially municipalized them, giving the town halls almost as much weight as the deposit holders in the administrative councils—in fact giving them more than equal weight, because the deposit holders had very diverse opinions and did not function as a cohesive group. The other distinct aspect of the savings banks relates to the distribution of profits. In not having owners, they do not pay dividends and their profits are allocated to reserves and to investments that are considered "socially necessary and appropriate," companies in the health field, for example, and cultural and other nonprofit activities that have also been subject to state regulation.

The "official" banking sector is also, in large part, a twentieth-century phenomenon. Only the Bank of Spain and the Banco Hipotecario, already discussed in Chapter 6, were founded in the nineteenth century. Spain's official banking sector was born during the decade following World War I, doubtless because of the powerful surge of economic nationalism at that time. Strictly speaking, this new subsector did not belong to the state. Although created by a state that retained a powerful role in policy issues, the new official banks were legally speaking private corporations (like their predecessors, the Bank of Spain and the Banco Hipotecario)—private not only in the formal sense, but also in the broader sense that most of their capital was contributed by private shareholders.

The first "official bank" of this new wave was the Bank of Industrial Credit (BCI), born after a long gestation period following the 1917 *Ley de Protección a la Industria Nacional* (Law on the Protection of National Industry), a direct consequence of the jittery economic climate caused by World War I. The law envisaged the creation of an official bank which would guarantee the supply of long-term credit that industry needed, needs which the Bank of Spain neither could nor should fill, which the Banco Hipotecario was not equipped to perform, and which, in the opinion of many business leaders, the private banks were not offering under satisfactory terms. Curiously, when the bank was finally commissioned in 1920, it was the private banking sector that constituted the majority of shareholders. In the long run, the BCI did not compete with the private banking sector but rather complemented it; several of its directors came from private banks and had considerable influence on BCI policy, in such a way that many of the BCI loans, made under favorable conditions, complemented credit arrangements and relationships between the private banks and particular companies. Private influence grew to such an extent that at the end of the 1950s there was a good deal of tension between the president of the BCI and the board of directors because the latter considered that the president, acting on governmental instructions, was restricting the prerogative of the board in the matter of making loans;[8] in other words, there was a conflict between the state and the representatives of the private banks on the BCI's board about to how to allocate credit.

The Banco de Crédito Local (BCL) was founded in 1925. Its principal aim was to lend to urban and rural municipalities, which had been granted the authority under the Municipal Statute of 1924 to borrow money. The creative initiative of the BCL came from the Recasens brothers, bankers and businessmen who were very keen supporters of the Primo de Rivera dictatorship. In fact the Banco de Catalonia of which the brothers were directors became the principal shareholder in this new "official bank." Another such bank, Banco Exterior, was founded in 1928 at the initiative of José Calvo Sotelo, despite some opposition from the Bank of Spain and considerable part of the private banking industry. Its aim was to provide banking services to international trade, to support companies dedicated to that activity, and to participate, in general, in foreign operations. The Recasens brothers were also very important in the early years of the Banco Exterior (Tedde, 1993). In addition, two other credit institutions were created in this period which were not strictly speaking banks, but more like official credit agencies. One of these, the Servicio Nacional de Crédito Agrícola, was founded in 1925 to help agriculture (see Chapter 11). In 1920 a similar agency to provide help to the seafaring and shipping industries had been founded under the Ministry of the Navy. After the Civil War, in 1939, the Instituto para la Reconstrucción was founded to help with the war damage, and the 1962 Banking Law converted this group into the Banco de Crédito de la Construcción.

The feature that distinguished these "service agencies" and "institutes" from the official banks is that they were simply and directly controlled by the relevant ministry, whereas the banks were structured as corporations and thus had a degree of discretion in determining their own policy. These official corporations, however, were far from comparable to the private sector companies; not only were they subject to rigid statutory norms that regulated the conditions of loans and the scope of economic activity, but also their resources came largely from the state (but in different proportions, of course), through bonds which the state guaranteed.

The "official" banking sector was nationalized through the Banking Law of 1962 *(Ley de Bases de Ordenación del Crédito y de la Banca)*. Through this legislation the state acquired the whole of its capital, thus becoming the sole shareholder, except that the Banco Exterior, in which the state was merely the major shareholder, continued to be considered a private bank. The legal position of the banks was changed from public companies to "bodies under public law" subject completely to the will of the state, without the obstacle of a board of private shareholders, which had presented such problems in the case of the BCI. Coordination remained entrusted to the Institute of Long and Medium Term Credit (Instituto de Crédito a Largo y Medio Plazo). Thus was created what the government of the day hoped would be an effective policy instrument for the economic planning of the 1960s. The MATESA scandal was eventually to prove that the strategy had failed miserably. Since then this official banking sector survives without any clear idea of aims or objectives. In 1971 the Law on the Organization and Regulation of Official Credit tried without success to modernize this subsector. Apart from changing the complicated name to the more reasonable Institute of Official Credit (ICO) and turning these banks back into corporations, it did little else that was effective. In fact these official banks were being financed, through the mechanism of the mandatory coefficients, at the expense of the savings banks and the private banks that were obliged to acquire the bonds through which the official banks obtained their resources.

In truth the existence of an official credit sector has no other justification than the assumption that the market and the private sector are not fulfilling their function in an adequate manner. This is distinctly likely on certain occasions: for example, the same shortage of capital that would justify mixed banking could also justify, as Gerschenkron asserted, state intervention in the economy, and this might be one of the most logical forms of such state intervention. The state would contribute to capital formation, creating banking units parallel to the private sector. When all is said and done, history shows that the first modern credit institutions were in fact official banks. Another situation in which an official credit subsector might be justified can be found where private banking was operating under monopoly conditions: the role of the official bank in this case would be to compete in the market in order to reestablish conditions of free competition. These seem to me the only assumptions which justify the existence of an official banking sector. Frequently, however, the point of such institutions has not been sufficiently clear to legislators and managers, and the results of this lack of clarity has been counterproductive. Often, and this has happened in Spain, the state itself establishes an institutional framework that favors monopolistic practices within the banking industry; then, seeking to remedy the situation, instead of liberalizing or eliminating the institutional framework, it creates or reinforces an "official" banking sector. The remedy flounders when, instead of trying to compete, the official sector is merely "captured" by the private banks, this clearly leading to further strengthening of the monopolistic elements, as happened with the BCI.

At the present time, wishing to give the official banking sector a more "private" appearance, the Instituto de Crédito Oficial has been re-baptized as the Argentaria Corporation; private capital has been admitted, and the official banking entities have been fused into a single unit. All this took place in 1991; it is still very early to know whether this is simply a question of window dressing, or whether it is going to have more permanent effects.

Oligopolistic Competition

Banking in general has a bad reputation, and Spanish banking is particularly bad in this respect. It is a historical fact, dating back at least to the unpopularity of money lenders, particularly Jews, in the Middle Ages. But it is also true that bankers were frequently Liberals (and this was particularly true in the nineteenth century), in some cases visionary reformers with a touch of socialism, as is especially the case of the famous Pereire brothers in France. In Spain the equivalent outstanding case would be that of Juan Alvarez Mendizábal, who was a banker before becoming a politician, but generally speaking the image of bankers as people who are conservative and self-serving somehow lingers over the profession. It is true that bankers are poor friends of disorder, since credit (the word itself underlines this quality) is based upon confidence, which uncertainty destroys. In Spain the twentieth-century development of the industry, its penchant for mixing banking with commercial ventures, its economic and geographical concentration, were all elements that reinforced the image of wealth and power concentrated in few hands. And it was understood that the banking sector supported the Franco regime; the notion that it was "one of its pillars" was frequently repeated. These ideas were not lacking in substance, as we know, although they call for some careful interpretation: the image of a banking oligopoly might make one forget that small and medium-sized banks also existed, although they were much less powerful. The image of undivided support for the Francoist political regime would fail to recognize the diversity of opinions even among the key major banks, and the many confrontations they had with the politicians in power, who in turn were far from holding a single consistent opinion where banking matters were concerned.

However, it is a fact that banking is a very special kind of business that moves in that murky, indeterminate terrain between the public and the private spheres. And private banking is not even completely private, in that it creates money under a privilege granted by the state. Of course the money that a private bank creates is not legal tender, but it is universally accepted with official approval, just as the banknote is no longer bank money—although it was originally—but government money. In exchange for this privilege of being able to create money, the private banks are subject to stronger state interference than the majority of economic agencies have to accommodate. After the Great Depression in the 1930s, bank regulation increased enormously worldwide; in Franco's Spain this intervention reached extremes, and we have seen many sides of this. To compensate for this powerful state intervention, the Spanish banks were almost completely sheltered from competition, and this allowed them to make large profits with little risk. And I should repeat that this situation was not very different from other countries, except that in Spain state intervention went much further.

But public opinion was clearly wrong in thinking that this situation was beyond remedy. Even though it did not get rid of restrictions, the Banking Law of 1962 changed the rules of the game substantially; among other things the concept of *numerus clausus* disappeared, which as we know from elsewhere never implied total closure anyway. Later on came the liberalization and the crises of the 1970s and 1980s, all of which changed some features of the banking sector in a radical manner. First, the degree of monopoly in the banking industry declined continuously after the Banking Law of 1962, which is indicated by the share of the market held by the six big banks, or by other more refined indices of concentration.[9] Second, competition became keener because of the following factors: (a) the deregulation of savings banks increasingly allowed them to compete in the same markets as the traditional banks; (b) decontrol of interest rates introduced that most characteristic element of the marketplace, price competition; and (c) relaxation of obstructive legislation permitted foreign banks to enter the Spanish market.

The consequence of all these factors has been that the banking sector has lost most of the special characteristics which distinguished it not only from other business sectors, but also from banking systems in other countries. Profitability rates within Spanish banking as a whole do not seem to be much different from the average in other European countries, although the large Spanish banks continue to earn profits that are higher than those of their European counterparts. At the same time, the banking structure that had seemed virtually set in stone since the 1920s was forced to undergo profound modifications as the result of the crisis that began in the 1970s, and this dynamism has been maintained since the crisis, especially through the recent series of mergers and takeovers.

CHAPTER 15

The Changing Role
of the State

The Mercantilist Tradition

State intervention in the economy has had a long and powerful tradition in Spain. Even at the height of the Liberal era, in the second half of the nineteenth century, the Spanish state continued to wield considerable power. Now in the twentieth century a number of factors, in the world at large as well as in Spain, have influenced attitudes towards state intervention. In the international sphere we can point to the end of laissez-faire, to use Keynes' famous expression, and the growing influence of totalitarian political systems (Communist or fascist). On the domestic front, the triumph of the military dictatorships of Primo de Rivera and Franco, both ideologically aligned with fascism, made it almost inevitable that state intervention would grow so much as to be almost stifling at times. The classic example is the decade of the 1940s, when the state, in its keen desire to intervene, enveloped the Spanish economy in an embrace that almost amounted to the kiss of death. Although state intervention has been moderating slowly in the second half of the twentieth century, here again, following the international trend, Spain continues to be a country where the state maintain a strong economic presence: the mercantilist tradition continues to enjoy substantial influence, as much in the workings of the state itself as in its inertia; and like most national bureaucracies, the state considers itself providential, and so does the public at large. In the words of Fuentes Quintana (1986, p. 150):

> of all the European countries, Spain is the country where corporate capitalism can boast the oldest and most powerful roots. Arbitrary interventionism and the economy of privilege constitute the dominant features of this cor-

porate capitalism which has always refused to make the expensive adjustments that a competitive system would call for, and has sought, in state support, the help that it needed to avoid adapting its behavior to the demands of market competition.

The Spanish public is remarkably reluctant when it comes to assimilating the premises and basic methods of economic reasoning. Decades, even centuries perhaps, of alienation between government and the governed, among many other factors, have made the average Spaniard fearful of the state, while at the same time harboring unreal expectations of that semi-divine institution that seems to be above the laws of society and political economy and to have inexhaustible coffers and powers that extend in every direction. Spaniards show no signs of having yet assimilated the basic fiscal idea that budget expenditure is either generated from ordinary incomes or from extraordinary incomes, and that the former are almost always taxes, and that the latter normally produce debt and inflation. Or, in the famous expression attributed to Milton Friedman, "there is no such thing as a free lunch" for the simple reason that production costs effort. Most Spaniards seem utterly impervious to the elementary principles of economics, and this is a symptom of educational failure on the part of Spanish economists. It seems unbelievable that so many thousands of students each year pass through the classrooms of the Economics faculties, since their experience there obviously has little impact upon public opinion. The economists have not been good professors, or else they have not been good popularizers; or else—and why not say so?—they have been bad economists, since more than one among them distrusts the very science that he teaches. Only a very few years ago some people used the term "bourgeois" to describe our science with innuendoes that were not only pejorative, but also suggested that there were other kinds of economics that were closer to the truth and ethically more correct.

It is a mistake to believe, however, that the size of the government corresponds to the degree of interventionism. On the contrary, the correlation, if there is one, seems to be inverse, yielding the fiscal paradox of state interventionism. In effect, the reader who compares the relative importance of public expenditure in national income from country to country (see Table 15.1) would be surprised to find that a state as interventionist as twentieth-century Spain played such a small role in the whole economy, and, moreover, that the difference between Spain and its neighboring countries in this

Table 15.1.   The share of public expenditure in national income in various countries, 1900–1902 through 1970–1972 (in percentages)

Country	1900–1902	1935–1938	1956–1960	1970–1972
United States	6.8	21.3	31.1	34.1
France	14.4	30.5	51.7	49.0
United Kingdom	14.4	23.4	36.3	50.3
Germany	16.2	42.2	44.4	35.6
Canada	9.5	29.4	35.2	35.7
Italy	7.1	13.6	28.1	37.8
Spain[a]	9.4	13.5	11.2	17.3
Spain[b]	—	—	14.8	21.3

a. Central government expenditure as a fraction of national income (Alcaide series, 1976)

b. All public expenditures (including those of regional governments) as a fraction of national income

Source: Comín (1990)

respect has been increasing almost invariably throughout the century. If the Spanish state was so interventionist (which seems to imply omnipresent), why was state participation so relatively small in monetary terms? Comín shows us that these two features represent two faces of the same coin: "in the Spanish case there is an inverse evolution in state intervention through regulation and through the mechanisms of the budget" (Comín, 1990a, p. 438). The case seems to have a certain generality to it; the growth of state participation that occurred universally during the twentieth century tended to take one of two alternative forms, either regulation or direct state action. Regulation costs almost nothing. A certain activity is regulated, and the state bears only the responsibility of applying the appropriate sanctions. In contrast, direct state action does involve a cost; the state has to create an agency or office to carry out its mandate and has to shoulder the necessary investment and operating costs.

Although the situation changed after Franco's death in 1975, during the greater part of the twentieth century the Spanish state has preferred regulation to direct action, perhaps rightly so, given its notorious inefficiency. To give an example, it has preferred to develop national industry by imposing protective tariffs rather than through subsidizing or creating companies.[1] Of course the tariff is a form of subsidy, but it is a special kind of subsidy paid for by the private sector; as far as the state is concerned, it produces an income by way of tariff revenues (whether or not tariff income would actually rise when the tariff was increased would depend upon the elasticity of demand for the item or items in question).

Is there an explanation for this behavior? Indeed, there is, and it is rooted in the archaic nature of the old taxation system. Until very recently the Spanish fiscal system has been very antiquated and rudimentary, and indeed in many respects it still remains so: consequently, in addition to being unfair it is also inefficient and rigid; in other words, it does not collect much tax (see Chapter 7). As for the system's inefficiency—it benefits the powerful classes, and they fiercely resist any reform. As we saw in Chapter 7, it turned out to be impossible for Spanish legislators "to get through the tough outer skin of the privileged classes," to use Comín's expression (1990b, p. 866). This has been one of the Spanish facts of life since the eighteenth century, and the exceptions have been extremely rare and incomplete; one, the Mon-Santillán reform of 1845, and the other the Fuentes-Ordóñez reform in 1977. Between these two events lie 132 years of legislative petrifaction so far as taxation is concerned, and this has been one of the great millstones that have choked Spanish economic development.

Scholars who have studied taxation systems have arrived at some concepts that can help us here. Taxation should be sufficient, that is to say it should be capable of defraying the costs of its own operation without entailing debt in the long run; the tax should be flexible, with the tax collected increasing in proportion to the contributors' capacity to pay, in other words revenue should increase with income; and a tax should be fair, which means it should operate to palliate the inequalities produced by the economic system; in essence, contributors ought to pay in relation to their economic capacity. If the rich not only pay more, but also pay a greater proportion of their income in taxes than do the poor, then the system is termed progressive.[2] Now then, to be generous we can say that the Spanish taxation system has rarely enjoyed any of these qualities, and this way we can avoid using the word "never"! Let us look first at the issue of sufficiency. Because the taxation system was less than sufficient (in the technical sense used here), an increase in expenditures produced an increase in the deficit. Already in Chapter 7 we saw the inauspicious consequences that accumulated deficits produced in the nineteenth century. This instilled, with some justification, the "holy fear of the deficit" in the Treasury ministers and the presidents of the government themselves, all of whom in the end preferred a state that was small and very interventionist, rather than one that was large and very deeply in debt.

The Problems of the Treasury

The twentieth century opened with the so-called Villaverde reform, which in reality was not a true reform but rather a series of timely modifications to the Mon-Santillán system. This reform, however, constituted the most important fiscal benchmark between the first modernization of the Treasury and the second one carried out by Fuentes and Ordóñez. The Villaverde reform is just one more proof that, in Spain at least, serious taxation modifications could only be introduced under extraordinary circumstances. While the Mon-Santillán reform was enacted under the aegis of the Moderados to stabilize the political situation at the end of the Carlist War and the Espartero Regency, and the Fuentes-Ordóñez reform took place within the framework of establishing democracy after the Franco dictatorship, the Villaverde reform was implemented when peaceful conditions returned after the massive upheavals of the war with Cuba. In all three cases it was a matter of putting the Treasury's house in order after a period that one can reasonably describe as anomalous.

Raimundo Fernández Villaverde's most crucial problem in 1900 was to put an end to the inflationary situation stemming from the public debt raised to finance the Cuban War. In fact, the most important part of his stabilization plan, implemented when he was Treasury Minister in the conservative government of Francisco Silvela, was the debt conversion of 1899. By means of that conversion Villaverde was able to achieve the objective of his taxation reform, which was to arrive at budgetary equilibrium, or more exactly to achieve a surplus. The surplus was needed so that the government could buy back some of the debt bonds held by the Bank of Spain, which inturn would limit or even reduce the amount of banknotes in circulation, since the bank was authorized to use the debt bonds as high-powered money. As a good quantifier, Villaverde was convinced, and with justification, that reducing the number of banknotes in circulation would stabilize prices.

To achieve a budgetary surplus Villaverde modified a series of taxes that were already on the books and, to the great indignation of the debt holders, introduced a tax on debt interest. In addition to the major innovation, the so-called *contribución de utilidades* (utilities tax), which established three rates assessing tax on income from work, from capital, and from company profits, the reform also streamlined a series of other taxes already in place, as Villaverde himself explained (Fuentes, 1990, p. 57). However, the utilities tax constituted an important innovation because it adapted the taxation system to the realities of capitalist development, even though the experts of the day uniformly agreed that the tax imposed on business profits was obscure and confused.[3] On its own terms, however, the Villaverde reform was a big success, because what ensued was probably the largest series of budgetary surpluses that Spain has ever seen. The consequences were as Villaverde had hoped: prices were stabilized, and the peseta appreciated on the international money markets.

The next three-quarters of a century are witness to the most abject fiscal paralysis. The many reform projects, frequent adjustments, and various attempts to substantially improve the taxation system all failed, and long decades passed with no attempt at fiscal reform whatsoever. The basic problem in the Spanish taxation system stemmed from its inflexibility. This was as much due to the Treasury's own outdated bureaucracy (Cambó called it "a rudimentary taxation administration") as it was the fault of its direct tax system, an antiquated model based on "quota and output". Instead of being assessed on total income, which is the basis of Spain's contemporary income tax system, producers were assessed on the basis of volume produced. This system, rough and ready and rigid as it was, did have some advantages. It was convenient for the wealthy, who could reduce their tax obligation by diversifying output and by concealing sources of wealth, and its simplicity meant that tax collection could be carried out by relatively unskilled personnel. Furthermore, by applying the quota system these two advantages could be further enhanced. But the tremendous disadvantages lay in rigidity and injustice, most notoriously in rural areas, where without proper information on the sources of income the authorities tended to collect the same amount year in and year out, regardless of harvest failures or real incomes. Referring to this long period of stagnation during the twentieth century (which came on the heels of an earlier long half-century of immobility in the nineteenth), one of the great specialists on this theme has coined the term "the silent tax reform" (Fuentes Quintana, 1990, chap. 3). Why "silent" and not "nonexistent"? Because although it proved impossible to crack open the armorplated, conservative attitude towards taxation, there was a group of more far-sighted specialists (among whom Antonio Flores de Lemus stands out) right there in the offices of the Treasury itself, a group well aware that open reform was politically not viable. These experts managed, however, to design a series of minor adjustments, conforming to a general plan but also within a strategy "where political know-how and the established norms of tax collection were combined, in variable proportions, as conditions dictated." If the armor plate could not be perforated, they did manage to dent it here and there. Furthermore, the silent reform, however frustrating and parsimonious, made way for the real reform later on in a very important way. These successive small changes and research studies molded public opinion little by little, so that radical reform could be proposed directly at the appropriate political moment. The silent work carried out by Flores was continued decades later by Fuentes himself, who found, in the transition to democracy that followed Franco's dictatorship, just the right moment to propose the fiscal reform that had been so long awaited, and found in Francisco Fernández Ordóñez a Treasury Minister prepared to seek and secure approval for it in the Cortes.

Some of the stages in this silent reform are worth examining. As Comín suggests (1990b, p. 865, and 1988, p. 601), Villaverde's reform was little more than a well-placed Band-Aid. The proof is that after 1909, when expenditure rose, the deficit returned; the system remained rigid and thus in the long run insufficient. And attempts at reform failed one after another, as they came up against the armored, conservative anti-tax lobby. A typical example is that of José Calvo Sotelo in 1926. Here the occasion seemed to be just exactly right to carry the reform through. Calvo Sotelo, Treasury Minister in the Primo de Rivera government, had been invited by the dictator himself to take on the problem of tax reform. Since the regime was a dictatorship, there were no parliamentary obstacles to its proclamation; moreover, the character and energy of the minister, who at all costs wanted to be known to history as the Treasury reformer, seemed to guarantee the success of the project. And although the project included taxes on incomes and profits (it contained the germ of the modern Spanish income tax), coming as it did from a highly conservative regime, it was far from hard on the moneyed classes. But not even with all these factors in its favor did the project succeed. The dictator, under personal pressure from friends or close political allies, went back on his original proposal and left Calvo Sotelo high and dry. In the words of Comín, "The Spanish privileged classes carried more weight than Primo de Rivera's Minister of the Treasury" (1990b, p. 865). In the end it was "the quiet obstinacy of the majority of the conservative classes . . .

the egotistical inflexibility of the powerful citizens" that triumphed, in the words of Calvo Sotelo himself. But he did not resign; he found compensation in effecting certain moderate changes to the tax system, and by way of self-consolation committed one of the greatest errors of his lifetime in establishing the Petroleum Monopoly as a source of income for the Treasury.[4]

Another type of failure was that of the income tax plan devised by Jaume Carner, Treasury Minister in the Azaña government in 1932. Here again, the occasion seemed to present a great opportunity: the Republican Cortes with a left-leaning majority was in favor of change (almost in favor of revolution) following the accession of the Republic the year before. Because of this, Carner managed the approval of his proposal with relative ease; it was called "the complementary income tax" because of its modest and gradualist aims. Carner, taking advice from Flores de Lemus, the author of this project of such long gestation, did not hope to introduce the new schedule immediately but simply advocated a complementary assessment to the tax on production, with many exemptions and extremely low rates. It was a question of gently shaping a new view of the taxation question, creating new social attitudes on the part of the public and Treasury personnel both, so that later on, it was hoped, attitudes would change to a point where the old taxes could be replaced. In this case the failure was not legislative but rather political and administrative. Although the new tax was approved in the Cortes, the conservatives arrived back in power little more than a year later, and with the hasty rashness of political events in the years that culminated in the Civil War, the gradualist plans that had been so carefully crafted by Carner and Flores de Lemus were ruined. The income tax would stay in its complementary form for another 45 years.

Now it would have been not just surprising but almost against nature if any real Treasury reform had been enacted under the long Franco regime. As Tamames says (1990, p. 685), "At the end of a Civil War, with the triumph of the most conservative group, it would have been a historical inconsistency for that group to have encumbered itself with a greater taxation burden than before." In a word, the party with the armor-plated anti-taxation system won the war. And so frequent adjustments were made to shore up the archaic structure, always trying to squeeze more revenue out of the old outdated machinery; changes were made, but always based on the principle of leaving the core system unchanged. An eloquent example of these changes that achieved nothing is Navarro's reform in 1957, which reverted to the old system of direct taxation by quotas, in a version that called for "global agreements and evaluations." Now the nineteenth-century quota system was one of the antiquated practices that had been disappearing bit by bit during the relative modernization of the twentieth century. But the Navarro reform went right back to it, this time proposing agreements with corporations and groups of interested parties in industry and commerce; in this quota system the Treasury made a global assessment of what a sector or subsector could pay and negotiated the agreed valuation with the corresponding professional group, which in turn undertook to raise the agreed amount for the state.[5] However surprising it may seem, this sudden retrograde step proved to be a very effective tax collection mechanism, although only for a few years. And thus in spite of new modifications and redefinitions of the income tax, which even in 1964 was still termed "general" although in fact it continued to be "complementary," the regressive indirect taxes were even more important on the income side of the budget during the last years of the Franco regime than they had been in the nineteenth century (see Table 15.2). "It was difficult to find any other Treasury in Europe that had managed to remain as technically backward as the Spanish."[6]

The real reform arrived at last with democracy. Following what is almost the Spanish tradition, the reform took place at a favorable political moment through the collaboration of a specialist (Fuentes Quintana) and a Minister of the Treasury (Fernández Ordóñez) who was firmly committed to bringing the project home to port.[7] The major outlines of the reform had been known for many years, from two reports produced under Fuentes Quintana at a government think-tank, the *Instituto de Estudios Fiscales.* These reports were well known and understood among financial experts and by 1977 had the assent of the principal political groups. This agreement was expressed in the famous Pact of Moncloa (the name of the Spanish government headquarters), and it was an important political document whose reach went far beyond fiscal reform pure and simple. Its major elements were a simplification of the tax structure and, above all, the introduction of the personal income tax as the major direct tax, which would be complemented by another direct tax on company profits, the *impuesto sobre la renta de las sociedades.* Under the heading of indirect taxes, the principal innovation was the introduction of the value-added tax (VAT) as a substitute for the traditional consumer taxes, lately called "taxes on business turnover" *(tráfico de empresas).* The reform was not approved in its totality (the VAT was left for later on), but the most important section—the income tax—did pass. Although it was incomplete and retained serious defects that left Fuentes Quintana him-

Table 15.2.   Comparison of the central government budgets of Spain, 1850–90, 1971, and 1980 (in percentages)

	1850–90	1971	1980
A. EXPENDITURES			
A1. Interest on the national debt	27.3	2.4	1.8
A2. Pensions, compensations	6.6	9.7	7.8
A3. Ministry of Justice	7.6	2.2	1.6
A4. Ministry of Defense, Army, Navy, etc.	25.3	12.9	12.5
A5. Ministry of the Interior (Government)	3.1	10.2	6.0
A6. Ministry of the Treasury (Economy and Commerce)	18.0	1.5	1.8
A7. Ministry of Development *(Fomento)* (Education, Public Works, Industry, Agriculture, Labor, Health, Transportation, Culture)	9.0	46.4	56.1
A8. Other	3.1	14.8	12.4
A9. Total expenditures	100.0	100.0	100.0
B. INCOMES			
B1. Direct taxes	27.9	28.9	44.9
B2. Indirect taxes	47.5	54.1	38.1
B2.1. Property transfers	(2.6)	(7.5)	(6.3)
B2.2. Consumer taxes, monopolies	(26.1)	(13.7)	(11.1)
B2.3. Stamp tax, company taxes	(5.0)	(12.8)	(5.3)
B2.4. Customs	(13.3)	(7.0)	(7.8)
B2.5. Document taxes	(0.5)	—	—
B2.6. Luxury tax	—	(12.8)	(7.6)
B2.7. Others	(0.0)	(0.3)	(0.0)
B3. Rates and transfers	9.6	12.0	8.9
B3.1. Games and lotteries	(8.3)	(2.3)	(4.5)
B3.2. Payment in lieu of military service	(1.3)	—	—
B3.3. Post office, etc	—	(2.4)	(4.4)
B3.4. Others	(0.0)	(7.3)	(0.0)
B4. National heritage incomes	8.4	4.5	4.0
B4.1. National property sales	(5.6)	—	—
B4.2. Other	(2.8)	(4.5)	(4.0)
B5. Other income	6.6	0.5	4.0
B6. Total incomes	100.0	100.0	100.0

Source: Tortella (1991), p. 121, *Anuarios Estadísticos,* and own calculations.

self dissatisfied (1990, chaps. 5 and 6), the 1977–78 reform achieved the long-awaited modernization of the Spanish taxation system. The simplest demonstration of its impact can be seen in the change that occurred in the distribution of tax receipts (see Table 15.2). In 1971 more than half of government revenue had come from indirect taxes (line B2), of which consumer taxes carried the most weight (lines B2.2 to B2.4 and B2.6); this situation was similar but even worse than it had been a century earlier. The Fuentes-Ordóñez reform turned everything upside down; in 1980 direct taxes (line B1) were, at last, larger than indirect taxes. And among the direct taxes, the income tax, the most modern and egalitarian tax, generated almost the whole amount. The archaic taxes on production had disappeared, and the Spanish taxation system had overcome almost a hundred years of backwardness.

But serious problems remain. Although the VAT was eventually adopted as part of the economic package that accompanied Spain's entry into the European Community, the reform was never completely carried through, mainly for political reasons. Furthermore, the income tax itself presents increasingly serious problems: perhaps the main problem lies in faulty inspection routines. Serious income concealment and tax evasion still exist so that the poor still pay most (rather as happened under the old quota systems), since income from employment, in the form of wages, is the easiest to detect. Because of this the system is again tending to show signs of rigidity and insufficiency, a situation that the government has tried to rectify by allowing a huge rise in the national debt in the 1980s and by increasing income tax rates. These measures have sharpened both unfairness and income concealment. Furthermore, the income tax is excessively progressive (something that inflation only makes worse), and this is a great disincentive to orthodox, legal employment and an additional invitation to fraud. In response to this problem, Fuentes Quintana himself, the father of the reform, has expressed his support for a simplification of the tariffs and a reduction of the highest rates (1990, chap. 6). In general, as the specialists know, the most important aspect of any fiscal reform is the existence of an administrative machinery that can make it work, and in Spain, according to Comín (1990b, p. 878), "the levels of tax evasion are explained by weakness in the fiscal administration and the poverty of available statistical information: shortages of staff and limited means of carrying out inspections favor the continued existence of widespread fraud."

Will this situation be remedied? Can the achievement of the 1977–78 reform be crowned? History makes pessimists of us all; only in extremely un-usual circumstances have real reforms been enacted. Perhaps the economy permits a degree of optimism; after all, only modifications and administra-tive improvements are needed at this point, not serious reform, and these may be achieved under a democratic government and with the standard of living that Spain today enjoys.

On matters of public expenditure, the most important changes that have occurred in the twentieth century can be seen in Table 15.2, especially lines A1, A4 and A7. If in the last century the interest on the debt consumed more than a quarter of the budget, a century later this burden had become much more bearable, although the tremendous growth of debt in the 1980s has turned that trend around; from 1980 to 1985 the relative cost of servicing the debt increased tenfold (not in the table). Military expenditure, similar to the debt burden in the nineteenth century, also declined in the twentieth. Although armaments were much cheaper then than they are today, the enormous cost of military personnel meant that a quarter of the whole bud-get was spent on defense; a century later this proportion had been cut in half. The reductions under these two headings have been offset by enor-mous growth in expenditures by the Ministry of Development (*Fomento*). What happened is that this ministry has been divided and subdivided time and again since the beginning of the century; a large number of sectoral ministries (the economic ministries) that used to be divisions of the "mother" ministry have been separated off, and the original, like a truly self-sacrificing mother, has in the end disappeared. The growth and prolifer-ation of the Ministry of Development is the best indicator of the economi-cally proactive policies that characterize all nation states in the twentieth century. These new ministries (in Madrid there is still a large building so named—the *Nuevos Ministerios*—that was planned in the 1930s, destined originally to house them all and today capable of accommodating only three) have been the executors of these proactive policies, and this explains the large increase in the corresponding budgetary allocations (line A7). (Not to confuse the past with the present: in 1996 the Ministry of Public Works was rebaptized Fomento, an incongruous throwback.)

The escalation of expenses under the economic ministries took place in four big steps, three of which coincide with as many periods of crisis, which can be identified in Figure 15.1. The first surge came after World War I, part of the wave of economic activism of the postwar crisis. Above all, it was pub-lic works outlays that expanded; in those years expenditures under the eco-

nomic ministries went from something above 10% to 20% of the total. The
second increase occurred during the Republic: here the crisis corresponds
with the ideology of state intervention and the social policy of the Republicans. The largest increases were in education; although in relative terms expenditures for transport and agriculture grew more, they remained low in
absolute terms. In this short period, expenditures by the economic ministries grew from 20% to 30%. After the Civil War, the interventionist state
was born anew; we can almost say it reached its apogee, but while it intervened through regulation, the early Francoist state undertook little by itself.
So the third expansion did not occur until the first years of the pro-development period, concretely 1963 and 1964, when there were large increases in
expenditures for agriculture and public works, and smaller increases for
transport and education. In fact, the explosion in demand for university-
level education dates from this point, but the big increase in expenditure for
higher education begins somewhat later, driven by demographic as well as
political factors. The expenditure of these economic ministries increased
from a little below 30% to more than 40% of the total in a matter of two or
three years. The last great leap forward happens in the 1970s, in the transi-

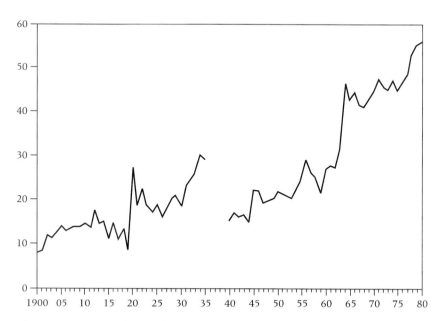

Figure 15.1. Expenditure of the economic ministries *(Fomento)* as a percentage
of total government expenditure, 1900–1980

tion and the first years of democracy. This is the jump that shows up in Table 15.2, line A7, from 46% in 1971 to 56% in 1980. Here the major increases occur in transport and education, in that order, followed by housing and industry. One should bear in mind, however, that the enormous increase in another aspect of the activist economic policy, that of Social Security (basically free medical care and unemployment pay), is not included in the state budget.

This expansion of "Development and Sons" implies an important change in the nature of state intervention in Spain, from an interventionist state to a proactive, protagonist state, an evolution that we already learned had taken place in the rest of Europe a couple of decades earlier. Under Franco the state promulgated exhausting and labyrinthine rules of the game, and maintained them with a justice system that was frequently arbitrary. Since then the state has been changing its tune, has gradually moved towards accepting the market rules of play, and has joined the other partners in the game, although its size and political power make it seem a giant among pygmies, a giant furthermore that sometimes acts as both prosecutor and defendant. But this is not the place to discuss the philosophy that ought to control the norms of state behavior. The facts are as follows. On the one hand, the state (in the broadest sense of the word, that is to say, the public sector) that is increasingly activist and behaving according to market rules turns into an entrepreneur: the INI is the classical example of this type of activity, wherein the state behaves as a public company, subject, at least in principle, to the same norms as any private competitor. Yet on the other hand, the state (at least until the 1980s) is the provider of a host of welfare services to which the citizens feel entitled: Social Security (which encompasses public health, unemployment subsidies, and pensions), education, public works, housing, agricultural subsidies, public transport, and cultural activities. As a consequence of all this, public sector services, which in 1958 amounted to 1.4% of national income, in 1986 represented 14.6%. If to this concept we now add current transfers, which are similar in nature but more specifically aimed at particular needs, we find that the heading we might call "welfare state," which represented 3.4% of national income in 1958, by 1986 accounted for 37.4% of national income. If we now further add to this that the government's employment bill has doubled in the same period, from 4.9% to 10.5% of national income, and that capital costs have doubled, from 3.2% to 5.8%, we have some idea of how this growth in the role of the state has been produced.[8]

If one long-standing and hard-wearing characteristic of the Spanish budget has been a resistance to changes on the income side, the other face of the coin is obviously the persistent deficit. As Comín points out, "The most notorious characteristic of the Spanish taxation system has been its insufficiency. Between 1850 and 1981 there were only 29 years when the budget was in surplus; this means that only one in five budgets yielded a positive balance" (Comín in EH, p. 402).

If those budgetary surpluses were rare events in the nineteenth century, they were almost as rare in the twentieth, although two periods of surplus were registered: the first decade of the century and the period 1952 through 1965, of which nine years produced a surplus. The consequence of this persistent deficit could not be any different in the twentieth century from what it had been in the nineteenth: the inevitable, unavoidable presence of the national debt. However, while in the nineteenth century the debt reached positively threatening proportions, as we saw in Chapter 7, in the twentieth century its relative size has been smaller, as one can see in Table 15.3.

The table might lead to an optimistic conclusion were it not for the recent growth in the debt, as indicated for the level in 1985, the last figure in the series from Comín. While not approaching the extremely high levels of the past century, the rapid rise in the volume of debt during the 1980s does present serious budgetary problems, because the state has had to meet very considerable interest payments in a period of rapid growth in public expenditures at large.

In contrast to the past, however, within the context of the whole twentieth century the debt has been only a minor problem, largely because, al-

Table 15.3.   The national debt as a percentage of national income, 1880–1885 through 1985

Period	%
1880–1885	167.67
1900–1905	116.63
1920–1925	56.36
1940–1945	76.62
1960–1965	21.82
1980–1985	20.51
1985	36.91

Source: Calculated from Comín (1987)

though it has grown persistently, it has grown more slowly than national income, so that the newly issued debt necessary to cover the deficit has been of declining relative weight. But this does not mean that one should discount its importance, even outside of this recent new resurgence. Certainly the placement of the debt in financial markets has been as constant a preoccupation of the governments of this century as it was for those of the last, and as a consequence there has been frequent state interference in monetary policy, as we saw in Chapter 14. It is well known, to give an anecdotal example, that the principal reason why the Franco authorities kept the bank interest rates so low was the fear that higher rates would have competed with the national debt.

Economic growth has made the burden of debt lighter; also its treatment has been modernized. As income grew and the debt became relatively smaller, the problem of finding savings sources able and willing to purchase bonds has become much easier to resolve. In the nineteenth century this was not so, and the government had to resort to all kinds of expediencies, many of them reprehensible not only technically but also ethically (see Chapter 7). To recapitulate this history, the most orthodox method was to draw on foreign credit: the external debt was very important in the nineteenth century and less important in the twentieth. Less orthodox was the direct monetization of the debt, through direct recourse to the Bank of Spain: the public debt was considered as high-powered money, whereby the bank could issue notes in proportion to the amount of debt it was holding. This was, in fact, its incentive for lending; indeed, in certain cases it was utterly necessary, simply because the Bank of Spain would otherwise have been short of the resources needed to meet the state's expenses. This policy implied a relaxation of the gold standard discipline, and was in fact the major reason why this type of monetary standard was not in operation in Spain. And here is another serious monetary consequence of the fiscal problems. The inflationary effects of this easy money policy made themselves particularly felt in the 1890s and were eventually solved through the Villaverde stabilization plan. In the twentieth century, with the growth of private banking (itself a result of economic growth) and an expansion in the volume of savings, it was possible to turn to private banking to finance the debt: this was done through the system of indirect monetization (see Chapter 14) which restrained inflationary tendencies. This system, much criticized by the economists of the 1950s, was abolished in 1957 but replaced by something rather similar, the mandatory quotas through which banks and savings institutions were obliged to invest a part of their holdings in debt bonds. The inflationary tendencies were in fact mitigated, but the state continued to rely on the banks to finance its deficit. This solution, which is frequent in underdeveloped countries where savings are in short supply, was also criticized by contemporary economists, among other reasons because of the distortion this introduces into the financial system.

As the volume of savings grows and capital markets develop, it gets easier for the state to turn to these sources for financing, along with the private companies and in competition with them. The principal advantage of this practice, which has been increasingly adopted since 1975, is that it is not coercive. Furthermore, it is more orthodox and rational, economically speaking, because this way the state is obliged to pay for the resources it uses at the market rate, which limits the extent of possible abuse of credit and reflects the true cost of the deficit. One disadvantage has been pointed out: this method tends to produce a certain crowding out in financial markets, because the state's enormous appetite for borrowed money causes interest rates to rise and makes credit more expensive for the private sector. And furthermore, rising interest rates aggravate the budget by making debt servicing even more expensive. But we should question these so called disadvantages. After all, it is supposed that, like any other economic agent, the state will be sensitive to the rising cost of credit and that an increase in these financial costs would encourage the government to reduce the deficit. The disadvantage is not the method of financing *per se*, which is the preferred method, but the state's tendency to be guided (more often than not) by political rather than economic considerations.

A last practice to recall is one that is today fortunately discarded, the nineteenth-century method of conversions and arrangements, which more often than not implied concealed repudiations of the debt. As we saw in Chapter 7, this system, in addition to being immoral (contractual changes introduced unilaterally were invariably harmful to the lender), was ruinous for the country because once the reputation of the Spanish government had been lost, it was forced to pay extremely high rates of interest for successive loans. Perhaps if the state had repudiated the debt just once and had not needed to seek further credit, one might argue that this was good business, although ethically reproachable. But to defraud its creditors and then immediately run to them for more credit was to put the country at the mercy of some very angry investors, who felt they had been victimized and were disposed to claim reparations with a vengeance in the next transaction for the losses they had suffered in the last one.

Money and Inflation

In the nineteenth century monetary policy was subordinated to fiscal policy, and we have already seen that this also occurred during most of the twentieth century. The principal features of twentieth-century monetary policy have already been outlined in the first and second sections of Chapter 14. Here we add just a few comments about these practices and their effects. The principal objective of monetary policy is to control the amount of money available, so that supply is approximately equal to demand. Maladjustment in these variables produces economic disequilibria: inflation in the case that money supply outstrips demand, deflation in the opposite case. Both situations are undesirable, though there seems to be a generalized opinion in favor of inflation. Deflation, or falling prices, can count on few supporters, which may seem curious, since we are all consumers; its drawback is that it tends to paralyze economic activity. If prices fall, one should buy as little as possible today since tomorrow prices will be even lower. As demand falls, companies reduce their production levels, and employment and income decline. In short order the depression we have all learned to fear so much is, figuratively, at the doorstep. Conversely, inflation, which is sometimes compared to a drug, has many partisans, since (like many drugs) it produces euphoria in the initial stages; if prices increase it makes sense to buy as soon as possible; this keeps the production system busy and leads to activity and prosperity. Now, if there is so much in its favor, why do we struggle so much against inflation? Because, like so many drugs, it damages the body social seriously even if society is not aware of it. In the first place, the euphoric effects of inflation tend to dissipate in time, so that larger price increases are necessary to produce the same effect; this gives rise to the situation now known as "stagflation," stagnation with inflation, which the world economy experienced most markedly in the 1970s and 1980s. When this point has been reached the policy makers can go two ways. They can continue to inject money into the economy and to keep activity rates buoyant, but this leads to galloping inflation whose devastating results were seen in Germany in the 1920s, in Argentina in the 1970s and 1980s, and in Brazil until recently, to cite a few well-known examples. Or the authorities can try to put a brake on inflation by means of stabilizing measures which, to be effective, ought to produce the much-feared deflation all over again. We can see, then, that inflation is a transitory solution which by its very nature creates more problems than it resolves. But its pernicious effects do not end there, because inflation is the culture medium, the breeding ground wherein great social injustices and serious economic distortions are nurtured. The distortions occur because inflation, in stimulating consumption, is by definition a disincentive to saving. In order to be able to invest without saving, society has to create artificial methods of payment, using "forced savings" which in turn further feed the inflationary tendencies. At the same time, an inflationary perspective creates a speculative atmosphere; any serviceable asset turns out to be attractive since it will always turn a profit so long as the inflation holds. Unless interest rates go up astronomically, going into debt is good business. Often the rate of inflation is higher than nominal interest rates, which implies that the real cost of borrowing money in these circumstances is negative. All of this seriously affects the rationality behind the allocation of resources. The social injustice of inflation can be summarized very simply: it helps the strong and ruins the weak. In effect, the social groups in power can increase their incomes in line with price increases or even do better; typically businessmen, professionals, and unionized workers are able at least to withstand the impact of inflation or may even benefit from it. On the other hand groups with little power, typically the retired, the unemployed, or nonunionized workers, see their purchasing power eroded as prices rise; although they may get some minor rise in income, they are almost always losing ground without realizing it. The "monetary illusion" conceals that inflation is a tax, the so-called inflation tax.

A comparison of Figures 15.1 and 15.2 shows that Spanish monetary policy in the twentieth century has had two distinct periods, before and after the Civil War. During the first third of the century, monetary policy controlled the supply of money as strictly as if Spain had been on the gold standard—perhaps even more strictly.[9] The period of the First World War is different, of course, but inflation in those years was universal. Iron-fisted control of the money supply in the 1920s and 1930s managed to produce a mild deflation which neither caused alarming rates of unemployment nor obstructed several years of considerable economic growth. After the Civil War the panorama changed drastically; here the norm was an inflation rate that hovered around 10% (the average rate between 1940 and 1984 was

9.9%) and on occasions was in excess of 20% (specifically in 1946, 1951, and 1977). We note three sub-periods: 1939–1951, 1952–1970, and 1971–1984. In the first and last periods inflation was clearly higher than in the central period; the rates were 14.5%, 4.7%, and 14.9% respectively, and it is clear that faster economic growth occurred precisely in the period of lower inflation. In this the Spanish panorama is not very different from the international scene. The collapse of the gold standard in the 1930s, the inflation induced by the Second World War, and the policies aimed at growth and full employment in the postwar period in Western Europe, North America, and Japan led to long-term price trajectories that were all rather similar. But in Spain inflation was more marked than elsewhere, and the government was obliged to introduce a series of devaluations after the first major devaluation that occurred within the context of the 1959 stabilization plan.

With the liberalization of the banking system begun during the last years of the Franco era, Spain's monetary policy entered what we might call an age of maturity. The major intellectual leaders of this transition were Luis Angel Rojo of the Research Department of the Bank of Spain (following the tradition of Joan Sardá, who in that same post had been one of the creators

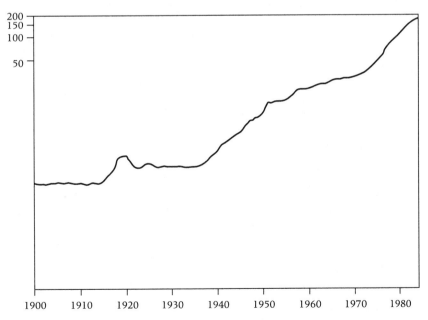

Figure 15.2. The Spanish price index, 1900–1985 (semi-logarithmic scale, 1913=1)

of the political liberalization begun in 1957 and embodied in the 1959 stabilization plan), and Mariano Rubio, vice-governor of the same bank. These men favored the acceptance of "monetarist" or "Friedmanist" ideas in drawing up the bank's operation plan. The fundamental idea was that the bank, as an autonomous body, should design and carry out monetary policy in accordance with particular chosen aims, essentially to control the supply of money with the criteria we have discussed. This plan, already accepted by the last ministers in Franco's Treasury, would require for its successful development a precise estimate of the money supply and an effective strategy for its control. We have already seen in Chapter 14 that the definition adopted for the money supply can vary: in general, the more developed a country, the more complex will be its credit system, and the wider the definition that should be adopted for means of control (M_3 instead of M_1). As far as the instruments of monetary control are concerned, the bank's intervention in the credit market as buyer or seller of Treasury bonds (what is called open market policy), the issuance of bonds especially designed for these ends, the variation in the bank's interest rates, and the establishment of mandatory coefficients for the banking sector are all methods, in inverse order of effectiveness, that can be called upon to achieve the desired regulation.

All this panoply of techniques was gradually brought into play between 1973 and 1979. It may seem paradoxical that these were the years that saw the banking crisis and the turn of the inflationary tide, but the paradox can be explained. We already know that the banking crisis was due to a combination of factors, the most important of which were the world industrial crisis brought on by rising oil prices after 1973, the weakness of a sector of the Spanish banking system that arose after the relative liberalization in 1962, and the powerless position this sector found itself in after the more radical liberalization of the 1970s. In the words of an expert from the Bank of Spain,

in the central years of the 1970s the political willingness to do battle with inflation was not very strong. The general problems of the political transition were considered more important than short-term economic considerations. Consequently the monetary target proposed . . . was not very ambitious; growth rates in the money supply as high as 20% or 21% were accepted, which would by no means combat the existing inflation, although it was hoped that they would not add more fuel to the fire of [rising] prices

. . . The first energetic tug at the monetary reins was applied in 1977, within the framework of the Moncloa Pacts.[10]

Indeed, starting in 1977 inflation began to ease very slowly, although it remained above 10% annually until well into the 1980s (Ojeda Eiseley, 1988, p. 62).

The effects of inflation, along with a very regressive taxation policy that was not changed until 1977, contributed to a polarization in the distribution of income. In view of the realities and policies of that regime, it should come as no surprise that during the Franco era the personal and geographic distribution of income became increasingly skewed, and here too Spain differed from its European neighbors. In contrast, the tax policy introduced in 1977–78 by the Fuentes-Ordóñez reform had an immediate effect in improving the distribution of income, which by 1980 was already considerably closer to that of the other European countries.[11]

From Autarky to the European Market

Trade policy has been very important in Spain's economic history; it has, in fact, been the main instrument of economic policy until well into the twentieth century. Only the recent growth of the Development Ministry (*Fomento*) has produced any real decline in the importance of this venerable policy instrument, whose key component, almost until the Civil War, was the customs tariff.

As an economic weapon, the tariff was at its most powerful at the beginning of the century; after the protectionist turn in 1892 came the Law of Tariff Bases in 1906, which repealed the 1869 law and provided for tariff revisions every five years, a law that stayed on the books for more than half a century. The tariff levels embodied in this new law were, generally speaking, more protectionist than those of 1892, as the 1906 law aimed at "comprehensiveness" in the sense that it planned to protect "everything"—a goal that is literally impossible, since, for example, protecting a capital goods industry will damage that industry's customers (see the case of the food canning industry, Chapter 12). The tariff was revised in 1911, but with no major modifications. Because of inflation and other war-related distortions, the revisions due in 1916 were postponed until 1921; in that year very substantial modifications were introduced, a necessary response to the major price increases and structural changes caused by the war. These revisions were embodied in the so-called Cambó tariff of 1922, the brain-child of Francisco Cambó, at that time Minister of the Treasury. Although this plan represented a more rational approach than earlier legislation (it was more technically complete and favored importing raw materials, for example), the Cambó tariff still constituted a powerful barrier to international trade. At about that time the League of Nations classified Spain as the most protectionist country in Europe after the Soviet Union, which banned international trade completely. But a laboriously negotiated series of commercial treaties did permit exports to grow during the 1920s, especially for Mediterranean agricultural produce, so the degree to which Spain's economy was open to international exchange, while admittedly restricted, remained stable and did not actually decline.[12]

As the Depression set in, the tariff became less effective and the government turned to a drastic repertory of rough-and-ready measures to achieve its ends, the most important of which were quantitative restrictions and foreign exchange controls. Quantitative restrictions had been the favorite commercial weapons of the mercantilist era; the tariff introduced at the end of the eighteenth century, however protectionist it might have seemed, in fact represented a measure of commercial liberalization. But in the 1930s mercantilist methods again found favor, not only in Spain but throughout the world. The tariff, after all, is no more than a tax on foreign trade, whereas quantitative restrictions represent a prohibition, either outright or partial. The most simple are absolute prohibitions, but there are also more complex measures, like quota systems that permit the import or export of a certain annual quantity of a determined product. To this end import licenses are issued (occasionally for exports, but typically the quota controls are on imports), which are granted to a certain dealer for a quantity, a price, and a period of time. To develop this kind of licensing system it is necessary to draw up a register of importers (or exporters) among whom the licenses will be distributed. And this path leads us to a veritable paradise of interventionism, or some might say the gates of hell. But this is not the end of it: there is the additional complication of exchange controls. Through this system the state determines the value of its money on the world market and monopolizes trade in foreign currencies, that is, it forbids private individuals to hold foreign balances. Thus when a dealer wishes to import a product he has to request the corresponding license not only for the right to import the goods, but also for the right to ask another government office (in the Franco period it was the IEME) for permission to buy the currency necessary to pay the foreign supplier. Conversely, any Spanish dealer who exports goods is obligated to sell the currency he earns to the state. And even that is not the whole story; the state invented a system of multiple exchanges whereby, as monopoly owner of foreign exchange currencies, it sold them at varying prices depending upon the operations for which they were requested. Thus the state would sell foreign exchange at less advantageous rates for those products whose importation it did not view favorably, or at times when it was particularly short of that specific currency, or for whatever other reason.

These labyrinthine controls were instituted during the Depression of the 1930s, but the Franco regime adopted them with enthusiastic pleasure and perfected and refined them to unbelievable lengths, above all in the 1940s. After all, the official objective of the economic policy of Franco's regime until 1959 was to achieve self-sufficiency, economic autarky. Something similar occurred earlier in the Soviet Union, in Mussolini's Italy, and in Hitler's Germany, where governments refined the use of quotas and bilateral agreements. Bilateral agreements applied quotas that were different from country to country, and foreign trade intervention arrived at the absolute apogee of control with barter arrangements to exchange physical quantities of goods that avoided the question of price entirely. In brief, taking a massive leap backwards, the Francoist authorities managed to recreate something close to Stone Age economics. One can imagine, in addition to the contraction of trade and the economic irrationality which these systems introduced, the great opportunity for corruption that the system provided; the civil servant who distributed the import licenses, for example, had the means at his fingertips to enrich a certain trader simply by showing generosity in the concession of import licenses; the temptation of bribery was enormous on both sides.

We already know that starting in the 1950s the tight web of controls began to loosen, even if at a very slow pace. A very important step in this direction was the 1959 stabilization plan, which did not remove any of the obstacles completely but nonetheless expanded quotas, reduced prohibitions, and devalued the peseta to a reasonable rate—a move that put an end to the multiple exchange system. When these quantitative restrictions on external trade had been reduced, the tariff again became important, after thirty years of being practically discarded but not repealed (in fact tariffs had been continuously enforced and revenues collected). However, the old Cambó tariff had become very outmoded and in 1960 a new tariff was legislated, which we shall call the Ullastres tariff since it was drawn up and enacted under the aegis of Alberto Ullastres, Minister of Commerce at that time.

The Ullastres tariff was also highly protectionist. According to Fuentes Quintana (1986, p. 144), "it burdened the Spanish economy with the ballast of some customs duties that were so excessive as to admit no comparison whatever with any of the economies within the OECD." But that was not the most important aspect. The major problem was that the tariff remained entangled in a thicket of complementary and interventionist provisions, so that the situation at the end of the 1960s, although more liberal, was as complex (if not more so) as before the stabilization plan. From the mid-1950s, and especially after 1957, when the Treaty of Rome (precursor of the Common Market and antecedent of the present-day European Union) was signed, it became clear that the Franco government was being forced to recognize the failure of its policy of economic autarky and was deciding, albeit reluctantly, to seek cooperation with the international organizations. And of course this was a world trend, and particularly a European trend, at that time. After recovering from the devastation of World War II, Western Europe sought to eliminate the restraints to trade that had been inherited from the war and followed instead a path toward integration for which the Treaty of Rome marked a very important advance.[13] Spain was trying to become part of this alliance and to this end needed to adapt its institutions to the norms of the wider community. In those years the effort was quite futile, since the key institution within the European community was the democratic system, and it seemed unthinkable that Spain might adopt such a system while General Franco was still in power. True, commercial norms could be adapted and negotiated, but even this was not easy because company owners, civil servants, and politicians, including Franco himself, reacted with fierce resistance to liberalization.

This bedrock resistance was the reason behind the tangle of interventionist controls that accompanied the new Ullastres tariff. Among the improvements that were introduced was the adoption of Brussels Tariff System, which facilitated relations with the Common Market, and the abolition of the famous "second" column. Now, as Viñas has shown (1979, p. 1202), the tariff did not have just two columns but many: to the normal single column or "definitive" tariff another column was added, with "transition" duties that were higher and intended to buffer, for certain industries, the impact of the transition to liberalization. Although these extra duties were to be eliminated gradually, the state anticipated further duties that were termed "circumstantial and flexible" and were basically conceived for discretionary use if any producer complained of unfair international competition. It is true that some reduction in tariffs was carried out in 1962 and 1964, but the fear of external competition was still very strong and led the government to add certain so-called "fiscal" duties, which were in reality simple surcharges on top of the usual tariffs. These were increased and rebaptized in 1964 with the complex title of Interior Compensating Taxes for Domestic Charges (ICGI). And not even that was the end of the story; it continued with compensating duties, anti-dumping duties, and regulating duties as well as other forms of assistance conceded to national producers to console them for the distasteful job of having to compete. These included production subsidies, subsidized loans, and the notorious *acciones concertadas* (coordinated activities). The last-mentioned items were agreements between the government and a company (or group of companies) which committed companies to produce quantities of goods in particular locations and circumstances, in return for special support conditions such as surcharges or exemptions on tariffs, favorable credit terms, or subsidies. The different types of tariff rates reflected a complicated casuistry but they amounted to basically the same thing: particular surcharges where the producer felt that competition was harmful. To top it all off, there were quantitative restrictions; though some were phased out during the early 1960s, others remained until the end of the Franco regime. The result of all this protective red tape was that the amount of liberalization that was actually achieved during the so-called pro-development years under Franco, while difficult to measure, must have been very small. Essentially what happened is that various small tariff reductions were matched by increases in the compensatory taxes (the ICGI), so that things remained almost as they had been. And furthermore, this thicket of controls was constructed in an entirely discretionary and arbitrary manner, yielding, as Fuentes Quintana put it, to "the interests of certain groups and sectors, an exact picture of our corporate capitalism . . . [the] sectors that were the most visible and enjoyed the greatest influence with those in power." According to a rigorous empirical study of the question, in the Spain of the 1960s "protection tended to be highest in those sectors controlled by the 'ruling classes.'"[14]

The single really important modification came with the Preferential Tariff Agreement with the European Economic Community, or the Common Market. At the end of eight years of humiliating indifference on the part of the European Commission, in 1970 Spain managed to obtain signature to an agreement that was really just a simple commercial treaty, because (although the Franco regime never wanted to recognize the hard truth) incorporation into the Community was impossible while the dictatorship persisted. The preferential agreement involved mutual tariff reductions and the progressive abolition of quantitative controls by Spain. Finally, in 1977, in full flush of the transition to democracy, Spain sought full membership of the Community and this time the proposal was welcomed, not just with attention but with genuine interest. That did not reduce the difficulty of negotiations, which were long and hard. In the first place, Spain's entry was negotiated simultaneously with that of Portugal; in the second place, Spain was right in the middle of a banking crisis—a crisis also felt throughout Europe in general, although with lesser intensity—and was struggling to restructure its industrial base. Because of these special circumstances Spain sought a long period of transition to dismantle the interventionist structures and to adapt to competition, and this further complicated negotiations. The entry of Spain into the Common Market took effect in 1986, and the transition period was completed in 1993. With this step Spain renounced many of its discretionary powers in relation to commercial policy, and since the European Union, however much we may regret it, continues to be primarily a customs union, it is now in Brussels that these policies are hammered out.

Communities and Regions

Spain is a country of strong regional contrasts, based upon historical, linguistic, and geographical differences. This diversity is a common characteristic in countries that have been settled for a long time, and for this reason diversity is also to be found in many other European nations, including notably Switzerland, Belgium, and Great Britain. Spain is one of the oldest European nations, and its diverse historical and linguistic identities have remained well defined—even to a certain degree have been accentuated by the problems and tensions of economic development in the nineteenth and twentieth centuries. The great mountain barriers, the lack of navigable rivers, the massive form of the Iberian peninsula have made transportation and communications difficult between regions, and this helps to explain disparities in economic growth. Even though the overall tenor of life in nineteenth-century Spain was one of slow economic growth, the regional dynamic was far from uniform.

After a long eclipse that lasted through almost the whole of the early mod-

ern period, Catalonia entered a long period of sustained growth at the beginning of the eighteenth century that put it at the head of Spanish economic
development. This progress was evident in all economic sectors: in demography, in agriculture, in commerce, and in industry. Among the factors which
explain this differential growth are the following: good agricultural conditions, both physical and institutional; the relative abundance of water and
hydraulic power thanks to the Ebro Valley and the slope of the Pyrenees;
and a good commercial location, especially favored by the conditions and
traditions of the port of Barcelona, which may have played an economic role
similar to that which Wrigley attributes to London in respect of English economic development. Furthermore, the region was rich in human resources,
this dating from a tradition of independence among the peasantry as early as
the settlement of Guadalupe (a royal writ which in 1486 brought closure to
a long peasant war and granted farmers stable rights to the land they tilled,
even if they were not outright owners); it also enjoyed a long commercial
tradition and political autonomy, in Catalonia in general and Barcelona in
particular.[15] In the second half of the nineteenth century two new phenomena intervened to reshape the economic order. The first was the ascendancy
of the Basque region, which industrialized at a great pace, taking advantage
of an increase in iron ore exports. The Basques too enjoyed an accumulation
of financial and human capital, thanks to commercial developments which
had also begun (as in Catalonia) in the eighteenth century, again with the
geographic advantages of a coastal location and close connections with England. The second phenomenon was the relative slowing down of Andalucía,
in spite of its mineral wealth, the fertility of some of its agricultural districts, and the commercial vocation of its Mediterranean and Atlantic coasts.
Scholars have presented several arguments to explain Andalucía's loss of
economic position: the structure of land holding, with *latifundia* especially
powerful in the western areas (Bernal, 1974); the limited educational level
of the population, much of it explained by the asymmetric social structure
which the property structure gave rise to (Núñez, 1992, chap. 7); the shortage of energy sources; and tariff protectionism, which noticeably damaged
Andalucía simply because it was an exporting region.[16]

During the first half of the twentieth century, approximately until 1960
(the stabilization plan probably represents a moment of change here too),
regional economic development was shaped according to the well-known
model formulated by Román Perpiñá, in which state intervention aimed at
insulating the Spanish economy, and thereby benefited those sectors and re-

gions that produced for the home market to the detriment of those oriented towards exports. Under this policy, the most favored regions were obviously the two that were most industrially advanced, Catalonia and the Basque Country, which could sell to a captive market at prices well above international levels; at the same time the backward agricultural regions, concretely Old Castile (now Castile-León), also benefited. We already saw the effects of protection in agriculture and industry in Chapters 10 and 12. For the exporting industries—Mediterranean agriculture, mining, certain light industries such as food canning and footwear, mostly localized on the Mediterranean and south Atlantic coast, in Valencia and particularly in Andalucía— protection was a burden, since it made labor and raw materials more expensive and brought them no countervailing benefit to help them compete in the international market. Yet these exports, however hobbled by the costs of protection for the noncompetitive industrial sectors and small in quantitative terms, were vital to finance the imports of raw materials, energy, and equipment that these same noncompetitive industries needed. The Perpiñá model has continued in operation until very recently, because we have already seen that if the Spanish state has reluctantly renounced protectionism at any cost, this was done primarily in exchange for our entry into Europe. And it still seems that things are not going to change too much, because Europe is showing signs of attitudes very much like the traditional Spanish posture, but on a continental scale. International competition "intra-Europe" is becoming sharper, but Europe, under the captaincy of France in this matter, seems disposed to protect its noncompetitive sectors, and especially agriculture, from "exterior" international competition.

But returning to the Spanish regions, according to Jeffrey Williamson's (1965) well-known thesis on the evolution of regional disparities during economic growth, such differences are heightened in the first stages of growth and diminish later on. The Spanish experience in the contemporary period appears to confirm this idea, although there are subtle nuances of difference. According to the estimates we have at hand, which are much more reliable for the twentieth century than for the nineteenth, and particularly reliable after 1957, the deviations in income per capita in each region, related to an average for the whole of Spain, indexed at 1, have evolved as shown in Table 15.4.

The figures come originally from Alvarez Llano (1986) and have been recalculated by Martín Rodríguez and Carreras, who obtained virtually the same results. The last two lines of Table 15.4 show standard deviations; the upper figure is an unweighted deviation while the bottom line shows this statistic weighted by the population for each region, the work of Carreras.[17] The results show interesting parallels and discrepancies. In the first place it seems that the 1860 data contain serious errors, concretely an exaggerated value for income in Madrid, with probable under-valuation in Asturias, Canarias, and Cantabria, which would explain why both disparity measures are so high for this year. In any case, both standard deviation series measures show an increase in regional disparity throughout the nineteenth century, confirming the Williamson hypothesis. In the twentieth century, however, the two series diverge. The weighted measure shows an increase in disparity until 1960, which is, as Carreras points out (p. 15), the moment when "modern data on the regional distribution of income in Spain begin," but also the moment when economic policy changed radically. After that, the measure indicates clear and rapid convergence. The unweighted measure, on the contrary, shows a continuous decline in disparity through the

Table 15.4. Disparities in income per capita in the Spanish regions, 1800–1983

	1800	1860	1901	1930	1960	1973	1979	1983
Andalucía	1.43	1.14	0.89	0.77	0.719	0.717	0.718	0.715
Aragón	0.92	1.02	1.04	1.02	1.030	0.998	1.057	1.024
Asturias	0.69	0.62	0.94	0.79	1.142	0.928	0.962	0.966
Baleares	1.44	0.88	0.80	0.97	1.105	1.329	1.215	1.373
Canarias	0.65	0.53	0.67	0.61	0.735	0.861	0.851	0.879
Cantabria	1.24	1.07	1.27	0.86	1.274	1.025	1.043	1.082
Castilla/La Mancha	0.88	0.94	0.88	0.83	0.647	0.745	0.758	0.710
Castilla/León	1.05	0.84	0.91	0.88	0.801	0.807	0.840	0.870
Catalonia	1.02	1.24	1.53	1.87	1.404	1.305	1.276	1.244
Extremadura	1.26	0.80	0.71	0.77	0.626	0.592	0.596	0.581
Galicia	0.51	0.51	0.65	0.58	0.707	0.714	0.798	0.788
Madrid	1.13	3.10	2.22	1.29	1.478	1.391	1.389	1.391
Murcia	0.64	0.76	0.73	0.71	0.744	0.790	0.805	0.763
Navarra	1.71	1.00	1.01	1.14	1.176	1.116	1.069	1.097
País Vasco	0.74	1.11	1.25	1.46	1.751	1.387	1.121	1.139
La Rioja	0.92	1.00	0.96	0.90	1.169	1.044	1.096	1.129
Valencia	0.71	0.95	0.90	1.21	1.157	1.023	1.028	1.025
St. deviation	0.324	0.555	0.373	0.320	0.319	0.245	0.207	0.227
Carreras	0.205	0.241	0.236	0.295	0.317	0.233	n.d.	0.186

Sources: calculated from Martín Rodríguez (1990); the last line from Carreras (1990)

whole of the century, with just a minor turn in the other direction between 1979 and 1983, the result of the economic crisis.[18]

Although they may seem surprising, these discrepancies can be easily explained. The explanation lies in migratory movements during the twentieth century, and elementary economic theory would lead us to expect that this migratory behavior would be economically rational, with migration from regions with lower incomes to the more prosperous ones. We already saw in Chapter 10 that the redistribution of Spanish population in the modern period has been perfectly logical from the economic point of view, and these migrations have tended to diminish the regional inequalities in income per capita. For this reason the unweighted measure of average disparity registers a sustained decline: when migrants turn up in the richer regions, the growth of income per capita is dampened there, and correlatively where the population in the poorer areas declines, or shows only restricted growth, income per capita will rise to approach the average. The weighted index is based on two kinds of changes, changes in earnings and *de facto* changes in the population distribution from census to census. So although the unweighted index shows us how regional income disparities have declined, the weighted index, in taking into account that more people now reside in the higher-income areas (and fewer in the lower-income areas), is telling us that the real convergence is less than the simple measure would indicate, and actually shows an increase in disparity during the better part of the twentieth century. But finally the almost inevitable trend towards equality predominates (caused above all by tremendous increases in agricultural productivity), and the differences in regional income are reduced. The crisis of the 1970s and 1980s turned the trend around because it affected the nonindustrial regions seriously, and because the migrations had ceased by that time. The unweighted index shows this very clearly; the weighted one would perhaps show this trend as well, but since we do not have the data for 1979 we cannot tell.

Until very recently, therefore, the state has contributed to sharpening the differences between regions, favoring those which had greater political power and economic weight. Conversely, the spontaneous behavior of economic forces has tended to counterbalance the state's actions, and migrations tended to equalize regional per capita incomes. Beginning in the 1960s, the state began to adopt a policy avowedly in favor of regional equality; the post-Franco governments recognized regional autonomy and created a Territorial Compensation Fund to correct economic disequilibria. In addition, entry into the European Union has given the Spanish regions access to the European Regional Development Fund. Now then, because of the inherently protective policy of the European Union, the danger exists of a recurrence of something that already happened in Spain and was described by Perpiñá: that the most powerful and less competitive sectors might again be favored, this time by economically misguided policies of the regional autonomous councils in their allocation of funds coming from the European Union—misguided, since paying people from the poorer regions to stay put is self-defeating in the long run.

As we have seen, convergence is produced spontaneously and the state should intervene as little as possible, because its intervention in the long run favors the powerful, whether that means regions, companies, or individuals. Furthermore, it should not put obstacles in the way of migrations, which are the escape valve when all else fails. The appropriate and crucial state role in promoting regional equilibrium is investment in human capital, that is, in education, through preferential allocations from the Territorial Compensation Fund, because the role of technical skills in economic development increases daily, and it is this type of capital which differentiates one region from another. Moreover, education is an investment that can rarely be squandered. Even such basic investments as those carried out on transport systems, canals, and other kinds of social-overhead capital run the risk of being wasted in regions that depopulate, as has happened with so many railroad lines. But human capital is another story: although a region may lose population, the emigrants take the investment that their own education represents with them, so it is not wasted, and although the capital invested in any human being is lost at death, the enormous expansion in life expectancy means that such investments are even more profitable today than they have been in earlier periods. And finally, we should not forget that educated individuals transmit their education to their children: not just facts but also attitudes towards learning. Clearly, it should be in education that those international compensation funds should be invested, almost exclusively.

CHAPTER 16

Conclusions

Spain, Europe, and the World

One of the missions of economic history is to contribute to a better understanding of political reality, both in the past and the present. In the Spanish case the mission has been fulfilled beyond any doubt. The advances that have been made in the last decades in economic history allow us better to understand and interpret the problems of Spain's recent history.

The impressive economic growth that the world, and especially the Western world, has experienced in the last two centuries has been accompanied by powerful political upheavals which in too many cases have erupted into armed conflict. This is not the time or place to rewrite world history in the light of economic evolution, however exciting that task might be. But it is appropriate to make quite clear that the convulsions of Spain's recent history, although presenting characteristics that are particular and original to this country, plainly fall within the framework of the social transformations that capitalist economic development has introduced into Western Europe.

The massive international conflicts—from the War of North American Independence, the Napoleonic wars, and the wars of Spanish-American Independence up to the two world wars in the twentieth century, along with important revolutions and civil wars, from the French Revolution to the Russian Revolution, including the German wars, 1860 to 1870, and the Japanese expansionist wars against China and Russia—all are conflicts that find their origin in the processes of economic growth.

Economic growth provokes changes in the social equilibrium; economic progress causes the power of some groups to increase at the expense of others. Characteristically, this occurs also with nations, the most cohesive and articulate of social groups. The wars of independence signify the decision of an economically emergent group (or one that for whatever reason considers itself to be in the emergent category) to shake itself loose from the protection or control of some national group in order to acquire for itself the same privileged organization and recognition. This is what happened in America, but also in Europe, notably in the cases of Italy and Germany in the nineteenth century and the Balkan nations and the Slavic fringe in the twentieth; and this is the case, worldwide, in what we recognize as the "national and anti-colonial revolutions" of the twentieth century. Other types of conflict also result from these redistributions of power—these rearrangements of the social equilibrium. The great revolutions, for instance, are the consequence of the rebellion of an emergent group—whose emergence is due precisely to economic development—against an established order, which is the juridical and political framework of the earlier social equilibrium, the *status quo ante.*

The French Revolution—and before it the English Revolution of the seventeenth century—was the struggle for political power on the part of a new social agglomeration that we can collectively designate as the "bourgeoisie," a group that characteristically derived the greater part of its income from mercantile activities, commerce, industry, and capitalist agriculture. Rather than wresting the power of the old aristocracy (the nobility, the Church, and the absolutist bureaucracy whose incomes were derived from land and from political power in the form of taxation and feudal levies), the triumphant bourgeoisie began to share power with the aristocracy, over a long period of accommodation which followed the violent explosion from 1789 to 1815. This readjustment took place, with greater or lesser intensity, throughout the whole of Europe at a pace that for the most part was shaped by the speed of economic development. It evolved through a process of flows and counterflows, which were sometimes resolved through political and military struggles such as the revolutions of 1830 and 1848; it developed from the end of the Napoleonic wars to the outbreak of World War I. This was a period of economic growth without precedent, a growth that was greatly facilitated by a political stability that permitted collaboration between the groups in power: these, much simplified, were the aristocracy, the land owners, and the bourgeoisie, that is, the owners of industrial and mercantile capital.

The political equilibrium of the nineteenth century was broken in 1914. Subsequently, the Russian Revolution precipitated another power shift and process of realignment, with the "proletariat" now taking the leading part—a social group whose major source of income was generated by wages from employment. This group had also been growing in numbers and in complexity as a consequence of the expansion of industry and the tertiary sector. The "proletarian revolution," like the bourgeois revolution a century earlier, spread throughout the world in tandem with economic development that provoked the process of industrialization and tertiarization, again not without strong resistance from other political forces, of which the fascist movements are the best example. Once the combatants of the Second World War had beaten back the obstacle that fascism represented, the proletarian revolution consolidated access to power for salaried workers through their political organizations, trades unions, and socialist parties. And again like the bourgeoisie a century earlier, the proletariat did not displace the political groups of the former status quo but rather began to share power with them, forming a majority block established thanks to a democratic political system. Since 1945, the economic policies based upon a collaboration of the majority of social groups have produced, sustained, and accelerated economic growth without precedent, accompanied by an inflation that is also sustained and without precedent.

In contrast, in Soviet Russia proper after 1917 (and in the other Communist bloc countries after World War II) the "proletarian dictatorship" prevailed; that is, this social group had monopolized power and displaced other groups (the aristocrats and the bourgeois, to abbreviate), to form an omnipotent and all-present state bureaucracy that ended up strangling economic growth. This frustration of economic progress froze the social structure in these countries, in the end alienating the population at large and bringing it to a growing desire to imitate the capitalistic and democratic system. The ongoing friction between economic and social stagnation on the one hand and the alienation of the majority on the other was resolved in 1990 by the speedy and more or less pacific dissolution of the Communist bureaucracy, with the consequent adoption of the democratic political system in the hope of moving towards a standard of living comparable with that of the Western countries. In the Soviet Union itself, where the Communist bureaucracy had been in power for more than three generations, the abolition of the proletarian dictatorship set in motion in 1985 under the so-called *perestroika* turned out to be slower and more difficult than in Eastern Europe.

Spain's history fits well within the historical and conceptual framework outlined here, given its determining characteristics as a country on Europe's southern periphery, shaped by its own past and its particular geographic-environmental endowment. Spain belongs to the group of the earliest European nations with political, linguistic, and cultural characteristics that were shaped in the Middle Ages, reshaped since the fifteenth century, and continually reinforced, one could almost say "reforged," during that long early modern period in which imperial expansion and the Golden Century, the *Siglo de Oro*, gave way to an Iron Century of depression and progressive retreat from contact with the centers of economic progress and political power.

It is a commonplace observation that the economic modernization known as the Industrial Revolution had it origins in northeastern Europe and spread out from there in a more or less concentric pattern. The western and southern fringes of Europe were more backward, and economic modernization arrived there later. Throughout this book we have discussed the causes of this backwardness in southern Europe, and more concretely in Spain. Very broadly, they are of two sorts: geographic and cultural. Spain's geographical location and endowment did not permit the successful diffusion of the "agricultural revolution"; and its southern culture—authoritarian, Catholic, and little disposed to philosophical speculation, to scientific reasoning, to universal education, and to technological innovation—for a long time resisted the social change that economic progress required.

Eastern Europe was largely forced in the postwar period to take the Communist shortcut to economic development, and this shortcut turned out to be a dead end. The return of these countries to the royal road of economic modernization is too recent for history to make any reasoned assessment of this new day's march. But historians can take stock of the countries of southern Europe, whose inclination was toward the dead end of fascism rather than communism. These countries have seen vigorous recovery during the twentieth century, and although they are still somewhat behind their neighbors to the north, they have regained some of the time wasted in the nineteenth century.

Various factors explain this change. Of first and primordial importance is the role that the early developed European countries have played as the motor of economic growth in "peripheral Europe": their markets for consumer goods, capital goods, and labor, and their exports of capital and technological know-how have contributed powerfully to economic growth in the south. But the internal engines of growth have also been important. For one thing, agricultural backwardness has been palliated by new conditions. European demand for food and the development of new production techniques have brought about a "Mediterranean agricultural revolution" very different from that of the nineteenth century, no longer based on cereals but rather on a wide range of crops, some traditional, like the vine and the olive, some newer crops such as citrus and other fresh fruits, crops from irrigated market gardening like tomatoes and flowers, and also some industrial crops, sugar beet, cotton, and sunflowers. And in addition, the whole of Europe has been experiencing the development of a dual growth pattern first identified by W. Arthur Lewis. According to the Lewis model, Spain would represent the *subsistence sector* and Western Europe the *capitalist sector.* Development within the capitalist sector caused a labor shortage which prompted a transfer of workers from Spain to Europe. This transfer, the massive out-migration of the 1960s, in turn dried up labor reserves in Spain, causing salaries to rise; this in turn stimulated mechanization in agriculture and a substantial increase in living standards, with consequent rising demand for industrial products. All these phenomena caused irreversible economic development in all its dimensions (industrialization, urbanization, and tertiarization), which even the return of emigrants and other repercussions of the 1973 crisis could not reverse, although the growth rate did in fact slow down.

There can be no doubt, therefore, that the economic history of Spain, regardless of its special circumstances, is best understood within the framework of Western Europe, and that being a neighbor of Europe's more developed countries has been a stimulus to growth. Two conclusions seem to be suggested by this analysis. In the first place, contrary to the arguments of many authors, Vicens Vives and Tamames among the most respectable, Spain has benefited from interchange with its neighbors. The persistent efforts of protectionists and autarkists to isolate the Spanish economy, although benefiting certain specific sectors in the short run, in the long run caused only damage to economic development in general. And for the same reasons, the pessimistic proposition that latecomers suffer damage at the hands of their more developed neighbors seems unjustified. The countries of the European periphery, underdeveloped in the nineteenth century, have largely overcome their backwardness thanks to their proximity and close economic relationships with the developed "core" countries. As far as we can generalize from the Spanish case, it is in the interests of the world's "peripheral" countries to open their economies to trade rather than to isolate themselves.

Economic Growth and Political Development

At the same time, we must not underestimate the internal growth factors. In particular, the unquestionable social and political changes that have taken place (albeit with the same kind of delay that we observed in the economic sector) have contributed to a general modernization. This is manifest in improvement in education, in the public health system, and in the state's fiscal and administrative apparatus.

The interrelationships between economics and politics are almost always complex and tortuous, and especially so in the Spanish case. A superficial analysis might lead to the oft-stated conclusion that Spain is different from the rest of Europe, that Spain was politically democratic when it was economically backward, and that the Spanish temperament does not adapt well to the democratic system. This interpretation does not seem to be correct. In Europe generally the nineteenth century was an era of struggle for democracy, and for the participation, within the democratic process, of increasing numbers of ordinary people. The principle of universal suffrage was not established with any degree of generality until well into the twentieth century. Now in fact the consolidation of the democratic system went hand in hand with economic development. The distressingly difficult and incomplete introduction of liberal democracy in Spain in the nineteenth century, and its breakdown in the twentieth, were a consequence or function of the slow and incomplete nature of Spain's economic growth. Faced with the tensions produced by this growth in the twentieth century, and aggravated by world instability after World War I and by fear of the Bolshevik Revolution, the Spanish people, along with the Italians and the Portuguese, opted in favor of conservative or fascist dictatorships. This same solution attracted other countries of the European periphery during these same years.

The Spanish nineteenth century seems to me to provide irrefutable proof that political development has no stability without parallel economic development. In Chapter 2 I presented a general interpretation of this thesis, so a brief reminder will suffice at this point. Spain was one of the cradles of liberalism—the very word is Spanish, coined at the Cortes of Cádiz which promulgated Europe's first Liberal constitution. Moreover, a part of Spanish society, inheriting the political mantle of that parliamentary body, persevered throughout the whole century to procure the conclusive establishment of a liberal system, even though that same liberal system would collapse time and time again. A highly indicative symptom of this breakdown is the proclamation of four other constitutions, in 1837, 1845, 1869, and 1876, without counting several abortive attempts throughout the century. Although eventually the liberal regime apparently managed to establish itself at the time of the Restoration, this was precisely because of systematic falsification of the system. The Restoration in reality was no more than enlightened despotism disguised as liberalism, and this distortion was the result of shortcomings within Spanish society as a whole. Meager economic growth kept the majority of the Spanish population in poverty and ignorance, incapable of assuming the responsibilities of democracy, not even in the form of the restricted suffrage that prevailed in most European nations during the nineteenth century.

The huge mass of illiterate peasants that constituted the majority of the Spanish people had many of the characteristics which Díaz de Moral (1967) attributed to the working class in Andalucía, and that are typical of underdeveloped peoples: general indifference to the daily political debate and periodic violent explosions into riots and commotions, if not outright civil wars. In this situation, which the slow pace of economic progress perpetuated throughout the nineteenth century, the differences between the informed political minorities—the two branches of liberalism, the Carlist absolutists, and the groups to their left, republicans, socialists, and anarchists—could not be resolved by recourse to elections because no coherent political majority existed to play the role of arbitrator. Politics was, by definition, an occupation for minorities, with force the ultimate weapon: the military coup, the revolt, or the civil war. The only way to escape this impasse, which engulfed Spain from the uprising at Aranjuez in 1808 to the Sagunto insurrection in 1876, was an agreement between the political minorities to take turns in holding power, through a series of simulated elections. This was the inspired vision, the brain child of Antonio Cánovas, crystallized in the Pardo Pact. But the Restoration equilibrium, which much resembled Giolitti's *trasformismo* in Italy and the Portuguese *rotativismo,* was based on a society that was backward and static, yet at the same time breaking apart under the strains of economic development. The new urban classes were soon to burst upon the scene, calling into question the validity of the already outdated agreement between Cánovas and Sagasta.

In twentieth-century Spain, the impetus of economic growth created a situation of mounting pressure, with repeated revolutionary attempts between 1916 and 1936. The pseudo-democratic system of the Restoration found it increasingly difficult to accommodate the diverse tensions that were developing within a rapidly changing society. The political scene became progressively polarized between a proletariat with clear sympathies towards a socialist or anarchist revolution, and the middle and upper classes which tended to favor a military or authoritarian solution. As in the rest of Europe and especially at the periphery, Mussolini's example provoked imitations. While the economy was growing, the political scene veered alarmingly from one extreme to another. The Restoration solution broke apart in 1923 with General Miguel Primo de Rivera's coup, and (as in Italy) the King sanctioned the new regime. The dictatorship lasted six years, and upon its demise, after a year of doubts, trials, and errors, the King abdicated and the Second Republic was proclaimed, a radically democratic regime which, in addition to the political challenge, had to confront the grave difficulties resulting from the Great Depression. Even though the international economic crisis did not devastate Spain as much as other European countries, it certainly caused a great collapse of economic and political confidence. Social polarization continued to increase, and while the democratic forces vacillated, the extreme right and left were planning, with little dissimulation, the conquest of power by violence. And just as in Italy and Portugal, the dissolution of the artificial political equilibrium at the end of the nineteenth century produced such tension and insecurity among the middle and upper social classes that in the end these groups threw their support to a dictatorial solution. But in Spain there was such popular resistance to dictatorship that a genuinely democratic Republic was established in 1931; against this regime various insurrections were attempted, and the last of these resulted in civil war.

The Spanish Civil War, then, was a bloody episode in the transition of a country towards modernity, an episode that was enormously charged with consequence, because its outcome defined the nature of the political channels through which the next and crucial phase of political and economic growth would have to evolve. The victory went to the extreme right, and thus the revolutionary and democratic options were discarded. It was the Franco dictatorship that was going to preside over the era of transformation to an industrial, technified economy. In all of this, the unusual and original elements are, first, that Spain was one of the few countries which remained on the margin of both world wars; second, that the internal social struggle broke out into the Civil War; and third, that the dictatorship that won the war managed such extraordinary longevity, comparable only to that of Salazar in neighboring Portugal.

The role that Franco played in Spanish history has parallels in other countries: Cromwell's protectorate in seventeenth-century England, the Bonaparte eras in France, the parliamentary despotism of Bismarck in newly unified Germany, Mussolini's fascism in Italy, and Stalin's dictatorship in the USSR. All of those personal regimes share the common thread of being authoritarian solutions to the problem of how to discipline the turbulence inherent in the transition to modernity. Of course, the personal distinction, reputation, and influence of the respective autocrats are very different, and in this parceling out Spain was one of the less favored nations, perhaps for its own good, since Franco elicited so little sympathy among the Spanish people that the possibility that the regime might continue after his death (continuismo) was soon dispelled.

Now the surprising fact about the Franco dictatorship is how long it lasted. Apart from the personal longevity of the dictator, who remained in power until his death at 82 years of age, the explanation lies in two factors combined: the harsh and bloody origins of the regime and the fear of communism. Born out of a Civil War that was conducted with the Caudillo's proverbial implacability and locked into power by a repression that was deadly in its ferocity, the Franco regime was left with no opposition. The regime's own semi-totalitarian nature was certainly enough to impede the reshaping of any political force that might in time have created a viable alternative. The only possibility of dispatching Franco and his regime would have depended upon disaffection on the part of the right-wing groups that supported him. But despite the physical liquidation of the left, the conservatives evidently felt that, like the legendary Cid, it could still win battles from beyond the grave. Furthermore, with unquestionable skill in manipulating the fear of revolution among his followers, invoking supposed conspiracies from within and from without, and managing events so that the wounds of the Civil War remained raw and in public view, the dictator managed to prevent the obvious fissures within the rightist block from eroding the edifice itself.

Without the fear of communism that was so powerful not only among Spanish conservatives but also among Western governments in general, it is most unlikely that the Franco dictatorship could have survived the demise of its Axis allies. It was not the semi-constitutional window-dressing with which Franco camouflaged his system that saved his regime after World War II, for those were trappings that deceived no one except those who wanted to be deceived. It was, rather, the fierce determination of the dictator to stay in power at whatever cost that dissuaded those of moderate views, both at home and abroad, from attempting to force a change, for fear that a new armed confrontation would give the victory to the revolutionary faction, the Communists.

It was during this long period of Franco's dictatorship that Spain experienced its transformation into an industrial and relatively modern country.

Should we therefore attribute that change to the regime itself? Clearly not. We know that the growth process had already been set in motion prior to 1936, and the evolution of the Spanish economy was very much affected by what was happening to its European neighbors. There might be better grounds for saying that the Franco regime was more an obstacle to growth than an agent of development. At any rate, there is no doubt that Franco's economic policy left its imprint on the economy that developed under his control.

The history of Franco's economy can be divided into two long periods, the first until 1959, an economy tailored by the fascist autarky, and the second from 1959 to its end in 1975, an economy with some liberal tendency towards opening up trade. It was the dismal failure of the first phase that determined the reluctant transition to the second, with an ideological incongruence that political propaganda tried to represent, after the fact, as a planned sequence of events. In reality and in retrospect, the evolution of Franco's economic policy displays an unquestionable thread of logic if we admit that its first and most important purpose was to keep the dictator in power at whatever cost. In reality this policy tells us as much about the Caudillo's strategic methods as it does about the changes that were taking place within Spanish society. There are some interesting parallels between the way that Franco carried out operations during the Civil War and the way he drew up the master plan for his economic policy over the years of his long dictatorship. During the war it was his own failures and the Republican attacks that defined the principal stages of the struggle. Rather than following a preconceived plan, the various operations and phases of the Francoist strategy looked more like reactive tactics, the defense of positions already taken. The major victories, Brunete, Teruel, and the Ebro, were achieved by repelling enemy attacks, thus converting initial defeats into triumphs. The grand strategic design of the Franco offensive—a war of attrition in which he counted upon superiority in supplies and equipment—emerged because of the failure of the lightning attack on Madrid, which in turn was a consequence of the failure of the attempted coup on July 18.

Something similar seems to have happened with the major guidelines on economic policy. The broad masterstrokes of the pro-development, liberalist policy of the 1960s and 1970s—a plan that was loudly touted as the shining glory of the regime—in fact was drawn up and presented in the aftermath of the total failure of the fascist-autarkist policy of the previous twenty years. And in both these fundamental phases, the minor modifications in policy were generally responses to emergencies caused by serious failures in the system.

The two decades prior to the 1959 stabilization plan, which we have called the autarky or self-sufficiency period, were different one from the other. The first decade, still much influenced by the old Axis allies, was much more interventionist and autarkist in nature and experienced some very serious economic and political setbacks. Spain remained virtually isolated from the international scene, both politically and economically, the promised economic recovery was not consummated, income per capita remained below the 1935 level, and the population at large suffered serious hardships. The second decade was characterized by a softening of political, economic, and diplomatic positions, changes that the circumstances required and the international situation (the Korean War and the Cold War) to a certain extent facilitated. The treaties between Spain and the United States not only gave Spain a breathing space with its balance of payments problem, thus permitting an increase in trade relations with the rest of the world, but they also facilitated a change of political atmosphere and rhetoric: the market economy and economic liberalism ceased to be unacceptable, heretical, or "anti-Spanish," and in contrast began to represent real options within the government's economic policy. This softening of positions was accompanied by some real economic growth, not exempt, however, from serious problems. By 1954 income per capita was approaching prewar levels, and growth continued uninterrupted. But an economy as backward and capital-hungry as was the Spanish had an inordinately strong propensity to import; in addition, market pressures for both capital and consumer goods, combined with an archaic fiscal structure and a policy of state investment virtually free of orthodox financial norms, provoked price increases that were very soon evident in the labor market. The result was a rapid and powerful inflationary spiral. The Spanish economy soon became noncompetitive, even though the labor component of Spain's exports was relatively inexpensive. The consequent deficit in the commercial balance of trade was not being offset, neither by income from services nor by capital imports, which remained tightly restricted by legislation seeking to enforce self-sufficiency. Transfers (in the form of U.S. aid) were not sufficient to make good the deficit, and in the end gold reserves and foreign balances came very close to exhaustion. By the middle of 1958 a suspension of imports was imminent because the means of payment was simply no longer available.

It was this crisis rather than any premeditated design that determined the radical change in economic policy embodied in the 1959 stabilization plan. For many months Franco resisted this Copernican about-face in managing the economy that his ministers were advising, although he was to boast about it in later years. The success of the plan surprised even its supporters. After a year of recession in 1960, economic growth in that decade was spectacular, in spite of serious problems. The explanation lies in the smooth working of simple market mechanisms: the peseta was devalued, a unified exchange rate was established (abolishing the multiple exchange rates that were still operative), and the budget was reduced. These two features sharpened the competitive edge of the Spanish economy and reduced inflation. The relaxation of frontier controls, for finances and personnel both, made way for the emergence of two phenomena that were unexpected and of fundamental importance, namely, the development of tourism and the massive outflow of workers to foreign countries. This exportation of services of one kind or another (in effect income from tourism and foreign salary remittances both represent an export of services) allowed Spain to resolve the balance of payments problem, which otherwise would have been as bad as in the earlier decade, because the Spanish propensity to import continued to be much higher than the country's ability to pay with exported goods.

The liberalization begun in 1959 was only partial, however, and during the 1960s there were perhaps as many steps backwards as there were forwards. The dictator had an instinctual distrust of everything that signified freedom, and he made no exception where the economy was concerned. Within the group of his collaborators there was a long and fierce battle which brought the partisans of the market economy, members of Opus Dei (a religious order with strong political ambitions) face to face with the old guard, the Falangists who were nostalgic for the earlier era of autarky; between the two groups Franco managed to sustain a carefully crafted equilibrium.

The last change of course, Franco's last economic reorientation towards a more liberal position, resulted from yet another failure. After the 1959 stabilization plan, in the face of a rising commercial deficit and with predictable mistrust towards the capacity of automatic market mechanisms to produce an equilibrium, the policy-makers adopted a system to stimulate exports. This policy provided a complicated system of credits to companies that could prove, with documentation, a determined volume of exports. It gave rise to a gigantic fraud in which the official Bank of Industrial Credit and various ministers were implicated, although more through incompetence than through direct wrongdoing. The scandal that burst out into the open in the summer of 1969 seemed initially to involve a serious loss of prestige for Opus Dei, to which almost all the economic ministers belonged, but in the end it actually paved the way for a renewal of the liberalization process, particularly in the banking and credit sectors. This process continued into the transition phase after Franco's death, and into the subsequent democratic regime. Clearly, in the last years of the Franco regime the dictator's advanced age and state of health prevented his anti-liberal instincts from prevailing over the social pressures for closer relations with the European and Western economies.

Post-Franco Spain is a good example that supports the case for a moderate form of economic determinism. A country which can be called the cradle of liberalism, which during almost two centuries had waged a struggle worthy of Sisyphus in pursuit of parliamentary and democratic stability and had failed in the undertaking, nonetheless made the transition to democracy with success at the end of forty years of a dictatorship that was programmatically anti-democratic. It is surprising how easily the problems and the solutions which the Civil War had curtailed turned up again for reconsideration in 1976. Spain after Franco was obviously very different from what it had been in 1936, for even if the regime had constructed a pressure cooker that had kept the lid on the boiling energy of the transition to modernity, profound economic and social changes had occurred during those four decades. Yet the seaming together of modern with pre-Civil War Spain was done with astonishing ease: perhaps the clearest symbol of this continuity is that Josep Tarradellas, a council member of the former Catalán Republican government, was appointed to the presidency of that same body during the transitional stage of the return to democracy. This painless merger without the former political instability stems from the remarkable economic growth which had taken place between the two dates. The Spain of 1976 was industrialized, urbanized, and, miracle of miracles, was a country capable of adopting a democratic system after forty years of a political regime whose fundamental justifying axiom was that Spaniards, by nature, were incapable of living in a democracy—forty years of authoritarianism which had prevented the formation of a political class able to handle the workings of an apparatus as complicated as a parliamentary system. Nevertheless, from 1976 to 1979 the prodigious feat of creating a democracy without democrats, or at least without practiced democrats, was successfully carried out. But the "Spanish democratic miracle" is no more difficult to explain than the economic miracle; in reality they are the two faces of the same coin. For a modern, economically developed country, democracy is the natural form of political organization. And for this reason democracy emerged out of Franco's Spain, in the same way that a century earlier in Cuba, free sons and daughters were born to parents who had been born in slavery.

And just as had happened in 1868 and 1931, the transition to democracy in 1976 took place right in the midst of an economic crisis. The problems of political transition were much complicated by an economic transition that could be postponed no longer, notwithstanding the serious world crisis. Economic transition required a further liberalization of trade restrictions, an approach that had been so reluctantly initiated in the second phase of Franco's modernization. Ideological questions aside, economic reform was indispensable for various reasons. It was needed because a political reform that set up the traditional democratic division of powers and recognized the autonomy of the regional communities was obviously going to fragment and decentralize the organs of economic decision-making. In addition, there was a broad consensus among the specialists and the politicians alike that liberalization of economic policy had shown itself to be the most efficient mechanism for economic growth. And finally, a large majority had repeatedly expressed the desire that Spain should become a member of the European Community, something that the Franco regime, for obvious reasons, had not been able to achieve. Entry into the European Community would require a harmonization of structures that in the Spanish case was almost synonymous with the relaxation of state intervention.

To these three reasons we must add two others, one ideological, perhaps the most important, and the other more immediate and pressing. Ideologically, although Spain has a long tradition of state intervention and although the usual market mechanisms were not really well rooted in the popular conscience, the interventionist economy had lost much prestige under the previous regime. By the second half of the 1970s the dismantling of state intervention in the economy was almost as much a topic of general conversation as was the demolition of the political dictatorial apparatus. And of immediate importance, Franco's economic legacy was seriously compromised because the interventionist measures had long been used to cover up serious deficiencies in the country's productive capacity. These deficiencies had become more acute because of the world crisis, but were really structural in nature. Spain's heavy industry, one of the spoiled daughters of the Franco regime, was in no way competitive and only survived thanks to state protection. This was also the case in many other European countries with the same branches of industry, especially naval construction and iron and steel, but in Spain the situation was more serious because the relative cost of labor had increased more than in other countries, and because stronger state protection had cradled these industries until they were way out of line with international costs and prices. What was required was a reduction in state aid to many companies, the closing of many plants, and a restructuring of production that would substitute activities with better future prospects and provide employment to redundant workers, what came to be known as industrial reconversion.

For all these reasons, economic reform simply could not be postponed any longer; but that does not mean that it could be carried out without difficulties—much to the contrary. The essential purpose of reform was to make Spain's industrial capacity more competitive, and that would require a reduction in costs and also serious reductions in personnel. The timing could not have been worse, because the world crisis of the 1970s was already producing layoffs and rising unemployment throughout the industrialized world. Emigration stopped being the escape valve for unemployment at home; in fact, starting in 1973 the number of repatriations was higher than the number leaving Spain. Unemployment began to rise, and the situation was further aggravated when the international crisis depressed the demand for Spanish goods and slowed down tourism. Thus the two pillars that had supported the balance of payments since 1959 collapsed, and in addition private investment plunged during these years of uncertainty, to the extreme point of reaching negative balances in some years: the country was disinvesting, reducing its capital stock. The effects on employment were devastating.

In the face of this mountain of difficulties the governments of the transition and the first democratic phase, under Adolfo Suárez and Leopoldo Calvo Sotelo, sidestepped the question of basic reform, particularly the much feared industrial rationalization. Absorbed as they were with political problems, they gave priority to stop-gap economic measures, and some of them were highly successful. Of major importance were the 1977 Moncloa Pacts, which—thanks to government agreements with the trades unions and employers' organizations—secured a degree of moderation for increases in prices and salaries and thus slowed down inflation. The interesting point here is that the whole array of circumstances militated against a successful outcome in this transitional stage. The one and only, but decisive, factor in favor was structural, perhaps better described as a phenomenon of the twentieth century: the per capita income, with all that this implies in terms of culture and capacity for peaceful coexistence, was simply much higher than it had been in former transitions. The democratic regime, therefore, was so much more robust than in those other occasions, and the upheavals that would have impeded the transition in 1931, or even more so in 1868, could not prevent these changes from going ahead successfully, in spite of all the prognostications to the contrary.

This rapid and successful transition to modernity did carry its own price tag and peculiarities, however. The progression from Franco's dictatorship to a social democracy in a matter of seven years represented a revolution that involved major costs and brought serious problems in its wake. On the one hand, the height of the transition coincided with serious disturbances caused by the crises of the 1970s and the 1980s. On the other hand, all levels of the public had to accommodate to the stress of a veritable leap from a society that had been archaic and dictatorial to one that had pretensions to being at the vanguard of European society at the threshold of the twenty-first century—and all this in little more than five years. The transformation was radical enough; at the same time it took place in an atmosphere of such dizzying change that few really understood what was happening. The change consisted of the recognition of a series of very natural and reasonable citizens' rights that were designed to bring all Spaniards into line with citizens of countries in the European Community—to "homologize" Spain with Europe, to use the phrase of the day—but in fact it also implied an accelerated growth in public expenditure, as Table 16.1 indicates.

According to the data, Spain's public expenditure expressed as a percentage of the Gross Domestic Product grew much faster from 1975 to 1986 than in other countries, including Sweden and Italy, which were famous in those years for the amount of their public outlays. In 1975 Spanish public spending as a fraction of GDP was notably smaller than in adjoining countries, including Portugal, where the proportion was 28.7%. Unfortunately, the World Bank gives no parallel figure for Portugal in 1986, but in that year Spain's public spending, although among the lowest in the group, was higher than Germany's, and its growth had been nothing short of spectacular, an average growth rate of 4.78% per annum. Sweden had the next highest growth rate, at 4.09% per annum. If we include the spending of all public administrations (of which the most important are those of the Autonomous Regions *(Comunidades)*, Spanish public expenditure as a percentage of

Table 16.1.   Public expenditure as a percentage of GNP for various countries, 1975 and 1986 (in current values of own currencies, in billions)

	Spain	France	Italy	United Kingdom	Sweden	West Germany
1. Gross National Product in 1975	6,023.0	1,467.9	144,509	105.8	300.8	1,026.9
2. Public expenditure in 1975	1,096.6	502.7	41,838	38.6	32.0	283.6
3. Gross National Product in 1986	31,979.0	5,013.0	891,216	379.5	933.7	1,931.2
4. Public expenditure in 1986	9,730.2	2,144.8	392,320	141.27	395.73	553.19
5. Row 1/row 2 as a %	18.2	34.2	29.0	36.5	27.3	27.6
6. Row 3/row 4 as a %	30.4	42.8	44.0	37.2	42.4	28.6
7. Row 6/row 5 as a %	1.67	1.25	1.52	1.02	1.55	1.04
Annual Average Increase	4.78	2.37	3.88	0.19	4.09	0.33

Sources: World Bank and my own calculations

GDP had grown from 25% to 42% in this period of eleven years, a growth rate of 5% per year.

More than anything else, this tremendous growth in public expenditure derived from the recognition of certain civil rights which can be lumped together under the category of Welfare State, which includes education, health, pensions, and unemployment insurance. One cannot really object to these increases in the abstract, since they were absolutely essential for catching up with Europe; but there is no doubt that the speed with which these measures were adopted caused serious economic distortions, provoking an explosion of expectations above and beyond what could be justified in terms of what the economy could bear. Faced with a sudden jump in the opportunity cost of labor, the labor market became severely distorted and fragmented, and this of necessity was reflected in strong increases in real salaries. The introduction of a warmly welcomed unemployment insurance failed to produce what would have been the logical *quid pro quo,* greater flexibility in the labor market. In this situation companies were reluctant to expand their labor force, and the market became unbalanced: some workers were either employed or had rights to unemployment insurance, while others had never been employed, and their number continued to grow. In the expansive atmosphere of the 1980s this segmentation and rigidity did not present too many problems, particularly since unemployment (which continued high) was on a declining trend. But the loss of competitive edge that this implied for Spanish economy as it continued integrating into Europe had to lead to devaluation and cutbacks in welfare policy. All this took place in 1992 and 1993, with consequent tension and social confrontation.

As Table 16.1 shows, similar phenomena have taken place throughout Europe. The difference with Spain is one of degree. All this does not mean that one should make an unduly pessimistic prognosis: the transition to democracy and modernity has taken place and is irreversible. But that does not solve all the problems, for as always happens in history, just as we benefit from successful moves, we must also pay for past errors; the bill for the optimistic excesses of the transition is still outstanding, in the form of high unemployment in the late 1990s.

The Future as History

History helps us to understand society, and this understanding helps us to puzzle out what options the future is likely to hold. This has been the pole star that guided the creators of the world's great historical theories from Ibn Khaldun and Vico to Marx and Toynbee. The fact that these grand paradigms continue to be superseded does not invalidate history's predictive mission, just as the renovation of scientific paradigms does not invalidate, but to the contrary sharpens, the predictive power of science.

Of all the branches of history, economic history has been one of the most fruitful in producing normative paradigms, perhaps because economics is the most solid and predictive of the social sciences. The typical paradigms in economic history are those that address development in stages, from Roscher through Gerschenkron to Rostow, and the inevitable Marx, who coined the famous phrase that the history of the developed nations is the future of the backward ones. And there are other approaches that do not have the sequential rigidity of the multiphasic models, but still contain categorical predictions. Examples of these are the pessimistic models of David Ricardo and Thomas Malthus, basically very similar to each other, according to which the demographic growth that economic growth brings in its wake will annul the benefits of growth and condemn humanity to live at the subsistence level. Under the Malthus scheme this could be avoided if humankind could moderate the reproductive impulse. According to Ricardo, it could be postponed by technological progress; even so, in his view society was moving towards a social polarization between landowners, who benefit from the inexorable rise in food prices, and the rest who are condemned to live at the subsistence level. In contrast to the pessimism of Ricardo and Malthus, the prediction of the neoclassical model (already implicit in Adam Smith, the grand classicist and mentor of these two pessimists) is optimistic, as is shown, for example, by John Hicks (1969) or Richard Easterlin (1981). The neoclassical model is diffusionist: it predicts that the gains stemming from technological progress are diffused and spread out to all participants in the market system. If the whole world were a single market, economic development would embrace the whole world and would be determined by the rate of technological progress. Unequal development would be the fault of the obstacles that prevent worldwide economic unification.

Yet the obstacles to growth are so great that the neoclassical model is constantly being modified to include them, in attempts to explain increasing disparities in levels of economic development and living standards. In this book we have insisted on the importance of physical factors and human resources in explaining the peculiarities of Spanish economic development. Broadly speaking, Spain's economic history displays great similarities with other countries of similar physical and cultural characteristics, beginning with its neighbors Italy and Portugal. This resemblance increases our confidence in the explanations I have been proposing. In brief, the economies of Mediterranean Europe had fallen behind and become disconnected from what we might call the Western European norm in the nineteenth century, and then regained some of the lost ground in the twentieth century (all of it, in the case of Italy). A process of "convergence" has therefore taken place through which Spain has become economically and politically European, if still below the European norm. It is this process that I have been trying to explain throughout this book.

All these historical considerations simplify an attempt at prognosis. Since Spain is now a "European" country, it seems improbable that it might suffer in the future the kinds of massive political or economic convulsions it has suffered in the past, despite the relative (but manifest) inexperience of its economic and political leaders. Its economic evolution is now advanced enough to sustain that center that was lacking in the nineteenth century—a sociocultural middle class that will probably serve us well as keel, ballast, and rudder for whatever stormy passages may lie ahead in the oceans of the twenty-first century. This stability has been characteristic of the other European countries (except for Germany and Austria during the Great Depression) since the middle of the last century, but had eluded the Mediterranean countries until very recently. If economic history can be useful in making predictions, the destiny of Spain (and of the Mediterranean) is inextricably linked to the rest of Western Europe in the short and medium run. Moving on from this optimistic conclusion the unknowns seem to be two: what is the economic future of Europe? and what will be Spain's relative position in that Europe?

The first question, undoubtedly very interesting, lies outside the ambit of this book, although we do know that Europe is one of the most richly endowed and egalitarian regions in the world, an assessment which surely permits a moderate degree of optimism about the Continent's future. On the second question, that of Spain's position in Europe, we can and ought to venture some hypotheses. Put in other words, the question is whether Spain will be the laggard, in tow behind Europe for a long time, its per capita income clearly below the average and its status frankly that of a second class participant in the decision-making centers of Europe. To me the answer is a definite yes, despite all the wishful thinking and confidence in the theories of convergence. My relative pessimism derives from some well-founded impressions. In the first place, the key to economic growth at the end of the twentieth century, even more than in earlier epochs, lies in human capital, and Spain does not seem to be aware of the gravity of the problem, nor do I see any readiness on the part of the state to assume the obligations and responsibilities that the solution to this problem demands. Neither citizens nor politicians seem prepared to make the necessary sacrifices to improve the educational system at all levels, and this is a dead weight with serious medium- and long-range implications. The general level of education is among the lowest in Europe, and Spain's economic future within the Community is correspondingly equally unpromising. And the persistence of certain difficult traits, scars still present from the Franco period and much more firmly rooted in Spanish society than his critics believed, add to this sense of pessimism. These scars range from an inefficient public sector and an archaic administration to specific attitudes and conduct that are still interventionist in nature, distrustful of market mechanisms and of the logic of free competition. Curiously, these modes of thought and conduct exist not only among Franco's political descendants, but equally among his bitterest enemies. The behavior and policies that these views give rise to put serious obstacles in the way of economic progress. They fragment and distort markets, particularly the labor market; they promote privilege and monopolistic situations; they penalize competitive behavior and put a premium on inefficiency, fomenting fraud, injustice, inequality, etc. The major consequence is a slow rate of economic growth, on occasions negative, that is far below the country's potential. So long as things stay the same, the much dreamed-of objective of reaching the European norm will remain an unattainable ideal.

It is true, of course, that many of these barriers to growth are present in other countries, including Spain's European neighbors. But they are not present to the same extent. Two obvious examples are inflation and unemployment. While both of these inherited conditions are present throughout the European Community, in Spain both inflation and unemployment are at levels well above the Community mean. So long as this continues, it will be very difficult for Spain to avoid being the squad bringing up the rear. Spain's economic history thus allows a measure of optimism, but only in moderation.

Could the example of Spain be useful to underdeveloped countries? Could the case of a country that falls behind in the nineteenth century and makes up the lost ground in the twentieth raise the hopes, for the coming century, of those countries which have been excluded from the world economic revolution in the last fifty years? The answer, again, must be cautious and conditional. The experience of the countries at the European periphery, including Spain, shows that there is nothing inevitable about underdevelopment, and that economic relations with the advanced countries enhance development in the backward ones. But it also shows that deviations from the normal pattern are paid for dearly, particularly low investment in human capital. In this respect, the rate of demographic growth is of tremendous importance, something that is often forgotten in discussions about capital formation. High rates of population growth are a major obstacle to the accumulation of human capital for the simple reason that they create a demand for education that is likely to exceed the supply available. In a rapidly growing population the proportion of children to adults, and thus the proportion of students to teachers, is far too high to achieve adequate levels of effective schooling. A high demographic growth rate causes other serious problems, but that of underinvestment in human capital tends to be neglected. It is characteristic of today's developed countries that throughout their history their demographic growth rates were very moderate; there are few exceptions to this, the most notable being that of the United States of America. The European case is particularly well known, and Spain has been fully European in this respect. Even during periods of European demographic explosion in the nineteenth century, rates of population growth rarely exceeded 1% per annum, and today they are rapidly approaching zero in several European countries; although this presents its own problems, it must be seen as a hopeful sign for the future of the planet.

Conversely, while European population levels are approaching stability, the poorest and most vulnerable countries in Africa, the Middle East, Latin America, and Southern Asia display inordinately high rates of population growth, almost invariably reaching 3% per annum. The consequences of this growth are alarming, and some of them make headlines in the press in their most tragic aspects as wars, famines, epidemics, deforestation. Because of this fundamental cause of backwardness, it is doubtful whether the case of Spain's economic development is applicable to many countries in the Third World; with such high rates of demographic growth, those countries have little chance to escape the subsistence trap. They are caught in the often cited "vicious circle of poverty," which implies a low investment in human and physical capital, or even negative investment if we take into account the destruction of natural resources, a situation that makes it impossible to raise the level of productivity and thereby the standard of living.

Another vicious demographic circle is related to sex discrimination and to sexual exploitation. Women suffer many forms of discrimination in the underdeveloped countries, among others, educational discrimination: in the Third World illiteracy is far higher among women than among men. Now it is known that there is an inverse relationship between women's educational levels and their fertility: on average, women with more education have fewer children. Greater investment in education in the poor countries, with special emphasis on women's access to instruction, would contribute to the solution of three major problems: the shortage of human capital, sexual discrimination, and overpopulation. It would constitute a crucial step towards the escape from poverty for the Third World.

Unfortunately, the outlook for any reduction in economic and social polarization in the world does not look very promising. On the one side are the countries of the temperate zones whose agrarian conditions permitted the agricultural revolution and then the industrial revolution, which have endowed them with reserves of physical and human capital that predict a continuation of today's high standards of living or even some further growth.

On the other side are the tropical and semi-tropical countries whose experience has clearly deviated from this norm, doubtless for historical reasons but primarily for reasons of geography. These countries have become trapped in the "vicious circle of poverty" from which it is going to be very difficult to escape. To its good fortune, Spain belongs to the first group.

CHRONOLOGY

NOTES

WORKS CITED

INDEX

Chronology

Economic Events (Spain)	Political Events (Spain)	International Events
		1694 Bank of England founded
		1709 Abraham Darby's coking furnace
	1700–1713 War of Succession	
	1713–1746 Reign of Felipe V	1710 Thomas Newcomen's steam engine
1715 Transfer of the Casa de Contratación from Seville to Cádiz		1723 John Kay's "flying shuttle"
	1746–1759 Reign of Fernando VI	
1749 Reforms and cadastre of the Marqués de la Ensenada		
	1759–1788 Reign of Carlos III	1764 John Roebuck manufactures sulfuric acid
1766 The Riot of Esquilache		1767 James Hargreaves invents the "spinning jenny"
		1769 Richard Arkwright patents the "water frame"
		1776 American Declaration of Independence
		1776 James Watt's steam engine
		1776 *The Wealth of Nations* (Adam Smith)
1778 Decree of free trade with America		
1780 First issue of *vales reales*		
1782 Bank of San Carlos founded		1784 Henry Cort's "puddling process" for iron
		1785 Cartwright's automatic loom
		1785 C. Berthollet's application of bleach in the industrial production of textiles
		1787 N. Leblanc's method for manufacture of caustic soda

Economic Events (Spain)	*Political Events (Spain)*	*International Events*
	1788–1808 Reign of Carlos IV	1789 French Revolution; abolition of feudalism in France
		1791 The Le Chapelier Law abolished trade guilds in France
1796 *Informe sobre la Ley Agraria* (Jovellanos)		1797 The Bank of England suspends gold convertibility
1798 Godoy's *desamortización* (disentail)		1800 Bank of France founded
		1800 Volta's electrical cell
		1804 Richard Trevithick's mining railroad
	1808–1813 War of Independence	
1811 Abolition of seigniorial jurisdictions by the Parliament of Cádiz	1812 The Constitution of Cádiz	
1813 Dissolution of trade guilds		
1814 *Informe sobre Instrucción Pública* (Quintana)	1814 Fernando VII's coup d'état, beginning six years of absolutist rule.	1815 The (protectionist) Corn Laws adopted in England
		1816 England legally adopts the gold standard
		1819 The Bank of England restores banknote convertibility
	1820–1823 Liberal Triennium	
1822 Central University of Madrid is founded	1823–1833 Fernando VII's "ominous" absolutist decade	
	1824 Conclusive loss of colonies on the American continent	1825 The Stevensons' first passenger train from Stockton to Darlington
		1825 Richard Roberts invents the "self-acting mule" (spinning machine)
1829 Commercial code adopted.		
1829 Bank of San Fernando founded		
1831 Madrid Stock Exchange		1832 Cyrus Vance's mechanical harvester
1832 Development Ministry (Fomento)	1833–1839 First Carlist War. The Liberals return to power and divide into two parties, Moderates and Progressives.	1834 German Customs Union (Zollverein)
1835 The Bonoplata brothers' factory, "El Vapor," is set on fire		
1836 Mendizábal's disentail of monastic properties (*clero regular*)		
1836 Abolition of the Mesta		
1839 Madrid Savings Bank	1840–1843 The Espartero Regency	1840 Justus von Liebig publishes his treatise on chemistry in agriculture
1841 Espartero's disentail of properties of the secular clergy		

Economic Events (Spain)	*Political Events (Spain)*	*International Events*
		1842–1854 The compound steam engine and the propeller make transoceanic steam navigation possible
	1843–1868 Reign of Isabel II	
1844 Bank of Isabel II	1844–1854 The Moderado decade	
1844 Bank of Barcelona		
1845 Mon-Santillán tax reform		1846 Abolition of the Corn Laws in England
1848 Subsistence crisis		1848 political and economic crises in Europe
1848 Law on joint stock companies		1848 *The Communist Manifesto* (Marx and Engels)
1848 Monetary reform		
1848 "La España Industrial" (textile company)		
1849 Banking law: New Bank of San Fernando		
1851 Bravo Murillo's debt renegotiation		1852 Crédit Mobilier Français founded (France)
1855 Law on railroads	1854–1856 The Progressive Biennium	
1855 General law on disentailment (Madoz)		
1856 Laws on note-issuing banks (Bank of Spain) and business banks (Crédito Mobiliario Español)	1856–1868 Liberals (under O'Donnell) and Moderates (Narváez) alternate in power	1856 Henry Bessemer's steel converter
1856 "La Maquinista Terrestre y Marítima"		
1857 Subsistence crisis		
1857 Law on public education (Moyano)		
1857 First official census		
1857 Bank of Santander		
1857 Bank of Bilbao		
1857 MZA Railroad		
1858 Ferrocarril del Norte		
1859 Law on mining		1859 First oil well in Oil Creek, Pennsylvania
1859 Submarine "Ictíneo" constructed by Narcís Monturiol		1860 Anglo-French Free Trade Treaty (Cobden-Chevalier)
		1861 Liberation of the serfs in Russia
		1861 Ernest Solvay patents his process for producing washing soda commercially
1864 Monetary reform: the escudo		1862 Abolition of slavery in the United States; Homestead Act and Morrill Act (which creates Land Grant Colleges)
1864 Beginning of bank crisis		1865 Latin Monetary Union

Economic Events (Spain)	Political Events (Spain)	International Events
		1866 International financial crisis
		1866 A. Nobel invents dynamite
		1866 Siemens-Martin steel furnace
		1867 *Das Kapital* (Karl Marx)
1868 Critical food shortages	1868 "Glorious Revolution"(September)	1868 Meiji Revolution in Japan
1868 Monetary reform: the peseta	1868–1874 The revolutionary six years	
	1868 Universal male suffrage	
1869 Company law		1869 J. D. Rockefeller founds Standard Oil
1869 The Figuerola tariff		1871 Karl Menger and W. S. Jeavons initiate the Marginalist Revolution in economics
1872 The Río Tinto Copper Company		
1872 Banco Hipotecario (mortgage bank)		1873 Germany adopts the gold standard
1874 Monopoly of banknote issue conceded to the Bank of Spain		
1875 Suspension of the *base quinta* of the 1869 tariff	1875 Bourbon monarchy restored; onset of the Restoration (1876–1922)	1875 Reichsbank, German Central Bank, founded
	1875–1884 Reign of Alfonso XII	
1876 Institución Libre de Enseñanza		1876 Alexander Graham Bell's telephone
1877 Ferrocarriles Andaluces		1877 Latin Monetary Union suspends the minting of silver coins
		1879 Thomas-Gilchrist steel converter
		1879 Bismark's protectionist tariff
1882 National Institute of Emigration		1882 Bank of Japan founded
1883 Gold-peseta convertibility suspended		1883 Swan and Edison's electric light company
1884 Commercial code	1884 Death of Alfonso XII. Beginning of the regency of the Hapsburg María Cristina.	1884 International crisis; falling prices for foods and raw materials
1884 Cholera epidemic		
1884 First Bessemer converters	1884 The Pact of the Pardo	1885 Karl Benz automobile
1888 Abolition of slavery in Cuba		
1888 Isaac Peral's submarine		
1891 Cánovas' protectionist tariff	1890 Universal male suffrage re-established	1892 Rudolf Diesel motor engine

Economic Events (Spain)	Political Events (Spain)	International Events
		1893 Bank of Italy founded
		1893 Westinghouse's alternating current generator
	1895–1898 Cuban War	
1897 Explosives monopoly		1897 Russia and Japan adopt the gold standard
1898 Loss of Cuba, Puerto Rico, and the Philippines		
1899 Villaverde's stabilization plan		1900 United States officially adopts the gold standard
1900 Ministry of Public Education and Fine Arts, which after 1902 assumes the cost of public education		
1901 Banco Hispano Americano		
1902 Banco Español de Crédito	1902–1931 Reign of Alfonso XIII	
1902 Altos Hornos de Vizcaya		
1902 Campaign for vaccination		
1903 Institute for Social Reform		1903 The Wright brothers' airplane
		1903 Henry Ford motor company founded (Model T is introduced in 1908)
		1905 The first tractors
1906 Protectionist tariff		
1907 Law on development of national industry		
1907 Committee to Sponsor Scientific Study Abroad		1907 Stolypin's Agrarian Reform in Russia
	1909 The "Tragic Week"	1913 "Cracking" method for refining petroleum
		1914–1918 First World War. General suspension of gold convertibility for banknotes
1917 Law on protection of national industry		1917 Russian Revolution. Birth of the USSR
1918 World influenza epidemic		
1918 Banco Urquijo		
1919 Banco Central		
1920 Ministry of Labor		
1920 Bankruptcy of the Bank of Barcelona		
1921 Cambó's banking law		1921 Lenin launches the New Economic Policy (NEP) in the USSR
1921 The Cambó Tariff		1922 Genoa Conference: establishes gold exchange standard
	1923–1929 Primo de Rivera's dictatorship	

Economic Events (Spain)	*Political Events (Spain)*	*International Events*
1924 Juan de la Cierva's *auto-giro* (early form of helicopter)		1925 Britain restores sterling convertibility at the prewar rate. Most Western countries restore convertibility at about this time, but with devaluations
1926 Banco Popular Español		1926 General strike in Britain
1927 Petroleum monopoly: CAMPSA founded		
		1929 First Five-Year Plan in the USSR
		1929 Stock market crash in the United States. Onset of the Great Depression
	1930–1931 Provisional governments of Berenguer and Aznar	
1931 The Ministry of Development is replaced by two separate ministries, one for Public Works, the other for Agriculture, Industry, and Commerce	1931–1936 Second Republic; Women get the vote	1931 Britain goes off the gold standard
1932 Law on agrarian reform		1932 Banking crises in Austria, Germany and the United States
		1933 Roosevelt's "New Deal"; United States goes off the gold standard
		1933 Creation of the Istituto de Reconstruzione Industriale in Italy
1934 Ministry of Agriculture is separated from the Ministry of Agriculture and Commerce	1936–1939 Civil War	1936 *General Theory of Employment, Interest and Money* (J. M. Keynes)
1939 National Wheat Service created	1939–1975 Franco's dictatorship	1939 Discovery of the possibilities of nuclear fission in Germany and the United States
1939–1951 Food rationing and ration books		
1942 State Railroad System [RENFE]		
1942 Creation of the Instituto Nacional de Industria [INI]		
1944–1954 Electricity restrictions		1944 Bretton Woods Agreement: World Bank and International Monetary Fund
		1948 Marshall Plan: creation of the Organization for European Economic Cooperation
		1950 European Payments Union
1951 Separation of ministries of Commerce and Industry		

Economic Events (Spain)	*Political Events (Spain)*	*International Events*
		1952 von Neumann's electronic computer
1953 Spain-United States agreement (economic, military and technical)		
1957 Fiscal reform		1957 Treaty of Rome creates the European Common Market (Italy, France, Germany, Benelux)
1959 Stabilization plan		
1960 Ullastres tariff (protectionist)		
1962 New banking baw (nationalizes Bank of Spain)		
1964 First development plan		
1969 MATESA scandal		
1970 Preferential trade agreement with the European Common Market		1971 United States abandons the Bretton Woods Agreement. A period of floating exchange rates begins
		1972 Britain, Ireland, and Denmark join the Common Market
	1975 Death of Franco	1973 First international petroleum crisis
	1976 Law on political reform	
1977 Fuentes-Ordóñez tax reform; modern personal income tax established	1977–1982 Governments of the Unified Central Democrats	
1977 Deposit Guarantee Fund		
1978–1985 Banking crisis	1979 Democratic Constitution	1979 Second international petroleum crisis
		1979 European Monetary System established
1981 Onset of industrial reconversion	1981 Tejero's failed coup d'état	1981 Greece joins the European Community
1983 Law on industrial reconversion		
1986 Spain and Portugal join the European Community	1982 Onset of the Socialist era	
1989 Spain joins the European Monetary System		
1992 Peseta devalued		1991 Treaty of Maastricht
		1992 Crisis of the European Monetary System. British pound and Italian lira abandon the EMS
	1996 Popular Party (conservative) government	

Notes

1. Introduction

1. With some modifications, this chapter is based on Tortella (1994).
2. Tortella (1973), p. 132. For a slightly different view see Carreras (1984), p. 146.
3. The series on income per capita in Portugal is derived from calculations by Leandro Prados de la Escosura that are based on Valério (1983) and Bairoch (1976), with the 1980 figure adapted from Summers and Heston (1988). In order to maintain the relative homogeneity of the series as reworked by Prados, I refrained from using the more recent series by Justino (1987), and also because the relatively small differences between the two series in no way affect the reasoning here, which is based on major trends. For the other series see Tortella (1994).
4. Cafagna (1973), p. 292.
5. Tortella (1970), p. 351; Nadal (1975), pp. 82–86.
6. Pereira (1983), p. 315.
7. Molinas and Prados de la Escosura (1989), p. 397.
8. See, for example, Cipolla (1976), esp. chaps. 2, 3, 6, and 7. For a microeconomic analysis of the geographic barriers to the diffusion of agricultural techniques in nineteenth-century Italy see Galassi (1986). Simpson (1987) relates technological backwardness in Spain to the abundance of work and the scarcity of human capital.
9. The same can be said of Portugal: Lains (1988).
10. Gómez Mendoza and Simpson (1988), pp. 57–91; Simpson, (1989).
11. See Tortella (1985a), table 3.5, p. 79, and Lains (1988).
12. Cafagna (1973), pp. 301–302. This is clearly an important component of the rise in real wages detected by Vera Zamagni (1984, 1986), although dietary levels remained very low in the cities. On commercialization and subsistence farming in Italian agriculture from the end of the nineteenth century, see Federico (1986).
13. See, for example, Tortella (1985a, 1978).
14. Reis (1982, 1987), Lains (1988), Pereira (1983).
15. Orlando (1969).

16. Livi-Bacci (1968).
17. This is Prados's interpretation of the Spanish case (1988, chap. 4).
18. Robledo (1988), Cazzola (1988), Leite (1987), and Reis (1988). While the first two emphasize the impact of the "crisis" on external migration, Reis lays greater emphasis on internal population movements; the Leite series shows a clear increase in Portuguese emigration in the last quarter of the nineteenth century. Toniolo (1988), chap. 10, stresses the high rate of concealed unemployment in Italian agriculture, at least until the outbreak of World War I.
19. Prados (1988), pp. 206–210. The conclusions for Portugal are very similar: Lains (1988).
20. Cafagna (1973), Toniolo (1988), chap. 10.
21. Pounds (1947), pp. 217–219. The words in Spanish are in the original.
22. Silva (1980).
23. Bergier (1983), pp. 106, 179.
24. Ibid., pp. 177–179.
25. On the effects of protectionism in Spain see Tortella (1985b) and Prados (1988), chap. 5. For Portugal, Reis (1982) and Lains (1987) and (1988); for a different opinion see Pereira (1983, 1984), and her debate with me in the *RHE* (1985, chap. 3, p. 3). For Italy, Toniolo (1988), chap. 10. Both Galassi (1986) and Simpson (1988) blame tariff protection for primitive technology and low agricultural productivity in Italy and Spain.
26. See Galassi and Cohen (1992).
27. Cipolla (1969).
28. Sandberg (1982), especially pp. 686–690.
29. See summaries in Núñez (1992), and Núñez and Tortella (1993), esp. pp. 15–38; for criticism of one of the most representative "skeptics" see Grubb (1988) and Núñez (1989b).
30. Two Italians, Carlo Cipolla (1969) and Vera Zamagni (1978), are among the forerunners in the new studies in this field. A Spaniard, Cerrolaza (1955), is also among the leaders. Some of Zamagni's important work is translated into Spanish and brought up to date in Núñez and Tortella (1993).
31. Reis (1987) cites many instances when industrial leaders expressed concern on this matter.
32. Although the story is merely anecdotal, I find the following phrase from a French Catholic priest very illuminating: "the purest, the most innocent, the most Christian, do not know how to read or write," quoted in Furet and Ozouf (1982), p. 65.
33. Stone (1969); Furet and Ozouf (1982), pp. 59–63.
34. Bergier (1983), p. 177.
35. On Spain in particular, the figures given in Mitchell (1976) certainly exaggerate the impression of stagnation.
36. The even more striking growth in school attendance in the United Kingdom may also come as a surprise. In reality, the greater part of this is a statistical aber-

ration. British levels of school attendance before 1880 were far higher than our figures show, but since a large number of schools were private, they were not included in the statistics. The information for Britain thus reflects, more than anything else, the substitution of public schools for private schools, a change which mostly occurred in the second half of the nineteenth century. One should also take note that the declines observed in data from Sweden, Great Britain, and France after 1900 reflect demographic rather than educational changes. As the relative importance of young persons declines within the total population, so does this measure of students per 1,000 population.

37. See, for example, references in Núñez (1992), chap VII.
38. See also Reis (1993) and Zamagni (1993). In the Spanish case at least there may have been some tacit agreement between Church and state to avoid competition.
39. The differential in demand for education in various regions of Spain has been studied by Núñez (1992); see chap. VII.
40. At least the span of a whole generation, according to Bowman and Anderson (1963), Núñez (1992), and Mironov (1993). Sandberg (1982) has suggested a century.
41. That this was a matter of *push* rather than of *pull* seems evident to me from the fact that the greater part of the migration was to other countries. For more on this see the works cited in note 25 above. The best and most rigorously assembled series on Spanish emigration is found in Sánchez Alonso (1990).
42. See Tortella (1985b) and above, esp. note 25.

2. The Nineteenth Century

1. Tedde (1988); Hamilton (1970); E. N. White (1987).
2. Bazant (1977), Lynch (1976); Quiroz (1993) for Peru.
3. An unweighted index, see Hamilton (1947), chap. 5.
4. Hamilton (1947), table 11 and figure V, pp. 172–73.
5. Herr (1958), Barbier and Klein (1985), Ringrose (1970), the Equipo Madrid (1988).
6. César Silió referred to this as the "unforgivable mortality," quoted in Pérez Moreda (1985).
7. See R. Nicolau in *Estadísticas Históricas*, ed. Carreras (1989).
8. Complutum was the Latin name of Alcalá; Alcalá is an Arabic word meaning "the fortress."

3. Agriculture

1. For a contrary opinion see Prados (1988), esp. chap. 3.
2. Simón Segura (1973), p. 60; Artola (1973), p. 149.
3. Herr (1974), p. 82, n.76; Herr (1989), chap. V.

4. Herr (1974), and above all his monumental (1989), see esp. chap. XX.
5. See the *Comisión para el Estudio* (1909); *Dirección General de Aduanas* (1986); Luis y Yagüe (1903); Membiela y Salgado (1885); Pérez Moreda (1980); Ringrose (1983); Saénz Díaz (1878); Sánchez-Albornoz (1977); Simpson (1985a) and (1989); and Tortella (1983c).
6. See later, ch. 4, and Sudrià (1983a).
7. *Comisión para el Estudio* (1909); Garrabou (1978); Maluquer de Motes (1983); *La Reforma Arancelaria* (1890); Simpson (1987).
8. There is no doubt, however, that this role was fulfilled in the twentieth century: see Chapter 11.
9. Fuentes Quintana (1990), pp. 18–20; Comín (1984).

4. Industry

1. Tortella (1973); Mateo del Peral (1974); Martín Niño (1972).
2. For France see Caron (1981), pp. 95, 130; for Belgium and Switzerland, Milward and Saul (1973), chap. 7, and Bergier (1983).
3. Prados (1983); Izard (1973); *Estadística de los Presupuestos Generales del Estado* (1891).
4. A rough woollen cloth, primarily used for cleaning.
5. Cameron (1961); Tortella (1973) and (1978); Sánchez-Albornoz (1977).
6. Gómez Mendoza (1982), (1989), pp. 91–102.
7. Carnero (1980), chap. 4; Puig Raposo (1993).
8. Flinn(1955); Nadal(1975), pp. 115–121.
9. Tortella (1974a), esp. the Tedde article.
10. Nadal (1975), pp. 102–103; Núñez Romero-Balmas (1985).
11. Nadal (1975), p. 100–102; Estevan Senís (1966).
12. Avery (1974); Harvey (1981); Coll (1983).
13. On the early stages of this relationship see Otazu (1987).
14. *Estadística de los Presupuestos Generales del Estado* (1891), p. 138; *Estadística de los Presupuestos Generales del Estado* (1909), p. 332.
15. For these kinds of impacts in the copper industry, see Coll (1983).
16. Nadal (1975), pp. 137–148; Anes and Ojeda (1983).

5. Transportation and Commerce

1. For a contrasting opinion see Valdaliso (1991), p. 63, n. 56.
2. Torres Villanueva (1989); Valdaliso (1991), p. 98; Montero (1990), esp. p. 403ff.
3. This decision was made in the belief that Spain's more mountainous terrain called for more powerful locomotives that would be larger and therefore would require a broader support base.
4. Tedde (1978, 1980, and 1981).

5. Tedde (1978a), pp. 38–46; Gómez Mendoza (1989), pp. 69–77.

6. Fenoaltea (1978, 1981) argues that in the Italian case maritime transport provided a good alternative to the railroad. But the figures on coastal traffic assembled in Frax (1981), p. 39, cast a doubt on this position.

7. However, this estimate may be an exaggeration. Table 5.1 indicates that the volume of maritime traffic was quite close to the volume of railroad traffic during the last quarter of the nineteenth century. Although passenger traffic may have been relatively more important for the railroad (this is not necessarily the case because much of the increasing flow of emigrants fell to the maritime transport sector), it seems fair to assume that these two transport sectors contributed in similar proportion to the national income. This would indicate that transportation (not including road and coastal trade) contributed about 20% of the national income. This proportion seems excessive if we bear in mind that in 1990, in an economy which is much more transport-dependent, this sector (including roads, air traffic, and oil pipelines) contributed only 3.6% of the national income.

8. Gómez Mendoza (1989), p. 116. The employment figures are calculated from *Estadísticas Históricas* and *Anuarios Estadísticos 1860–1861*. See also Anes (1978).

9. For a supporting opinion see Maluquer (1988). Zamagni (1990), p. 213, argues a somewhat similar case for the Italian railroads.

10. Sánchez-Albornoz (1975b, 1977); Sánchez-Albornoz and Carnero (1981); Grupo de Estudios de Historia Rural (1980, 1981).

11. This phenomenon has been noted by the Grupo de Estudios de Historia Rural (1981a), p. 78, which argues that "olive oil prices offer only a blurred and equivocal picture of market integration." Gómez Mendoza (1989), p. 139 gives a contrary explanation. It is true that the GEHR's formulation is ambiguous, but the figures certainly speak for themselves.

12. See especially Andrés Alvarez (1943, 1945); Tortella and others (1978); Prados (1981, 1982, 1986); Tena (1985, 1988).

13. See, in this respect, Prados (1982a), esp. chap. 4, and Tena in *Estadísticas Históricas*, Table 8.1. According to this author the degree of openness increased from 5.6% in 1830 to 25.5% in 1890, to fall slowly after that. Overall the Spanish economy remained more closed than the English or the French, although a little less closed than the Italian.

14. Prados (1982a), chap. 5; and (1988), pp. 210–219; Tena in *Estadísticas Históricas*.

15. The quantitative estimates are still very questionable: compare García López (1992).

16. R. Anes (1970), p. 202; Sardá (1948), p. 274.

17. The accumulated figure up to 1890 is taken from Table 5.6 (1,226.8 plus 2,144.9 equals 3,371.7), to which must be added the amount invested in the decade 1891–1900, which was 382.7 million francs (Table 5.4). Applying the average rate of depreciation for the decade from Table III in Tortella (1978), which is 1.24448, gives us some 476.3 million pesetas: then 3,371.7 + 476.3 = 3,848.0.

6. Money and Banking

1. The first Governor of the Bank of Spain, Ramón Santillán, was the guiding light of the fiscal reform known by his name, the author of the first history of the Bank of Spain (1865) and a distinguished economic historian.
2. Tortella (1973), chap. II; see also Artola (1978), I, pp. 20–21.
3. Tortella (1973), chaps. III, IV, VII and VIII.
4. The concession decree (March 19, 1874) was signed by José Echegaray, Treasury Minister of the Executive Council of the Republic (presided over by General Francisco Serrano). See Tortella (1973), pp. 314–317.
5. Casares (1984); Lacomba and Ruíz (1990).
6. Tortella (1973); Pascual and Sudrià (1993).
7. Tortella (1973), App. D; Tortella (1974), II, X.
8. For a later and slightly different estimate see Martín Aceña (1985), App. V. Although this estimate is more correct, the small difference involved and a desire to maintain comparability with Table 6.1 has led me to retain the former.

7. The Role of the State

1. *Estadística de los Presupuestos Generales del Estado* (Budget Statistics); Tortella (1981), pp. 132–133; Comín (1985, 1988), passim.
2. The officials responsible for compiling the annual *Estadística de los Presupuestos Generales del Estado* habitually introduced a small accounting anomaly which concealed the persistent and embarrassing deficit. The essential deceit lay in including the national debt within Treasury income under the rubric "extraordinary incomes." As is well known, the national debt was issued precisely to cover the deficit, which is the difference between ordinary incomes and expenditures, that is to say, ordinary incomes that do not bring the nation into a state of indebtedness. Thus to restore the accounts to reality, we have to reduce the income figure by at least the national debt portion of "extraordinary incomes." I have done this (see Tortella, 1981) and so has Comín in numerous works. But not every historian has known how to avoid this pitfall, even though this "accounting trick" within the EP was first pointed out by Martín Niño (1972, pp. 63–65), and fully exposed by the compiler of EP himself, González de la Peña (introduction, p. xix).
3. Cameron (1961), p. 406.
4. Adam Smith (1776; 1937 ed.), p 863.
5. This is only true above the highest tariff levels which produce maximum revenue. For lower tariffs, yields and protection are still positively correlated, but at these levels the protective effect of the tariff is insignificant.
6. Nadal and Tortella (1974), pp. 243–322; Vicens Vives (1961), pp. 520–521; Vilar (1962), III, pp. 469 ff.
7. On these questions see Serrano Sanz (1987).

8. On these points see R. Anes (1974); Anes and Fernández Pulgar (1970): Sardà (1948); Tortella (1973 and 1974); Martín Aceña (1985).
9. Not all cases of falling prices are either cause or effect of economic depression, no matter what one reads in some economic history textbooks.

8. The Entrepreneurial Factor

1. Report by S. P. Cockerell, Commercial Attaché of the British Embassy in Madrid, *Report of the Year 1906 on the Trade and Commerce of Spain,* in Parliamentary Papers, 1908, Vol. CXVI, p. 36.
2. Lester Thurow, interviewed in *El País,* January 20, 1993.
3. The chief administrative agency for the regulation and development of trade between Spain and its American empire; established by Royal Decree in Seville in 1503.
4. Tedde (1988), chaps. 2, 3 and 8, esp. pp. 196–201.
5. Cameron (1989), p. 313; and (1961), p. 92.
6. Broder (1981), pp. 793–797; Lacomba and Ruiz (1990), pp. 51–52.
7. Sánchez-Albornoz (1977); Tedde (1974); Broder (1981), pp. 798–808; *El País,* February 23, 1987.
8. Platt (1983); Tedde (1978); also Gómez Mendoza (1989).
9. Bernal (1992); Simpson (1987); Tortella (1985).
10. The author is referring here to special profits arising out of a monopoly situation, usually referred to as monopoly rents.

9. The Twentieth Century

1. The data we are working with in this chapter differ slightly from the more stylized figures used in Chapter 1, among other elements, for example, in the monetary unit used; the major trends are not affected by these differences.

11. Agricultural Transformation

1. Huguet de Vilar (1921), quoted in Gómez Mendoza (1992), p. 101.
2. The major authority on the SNT is Carlos Barciela. See esp. (1981a) and (1981b).
3. On this question see, for example, Tortella (1991a), pp. 44–52.
4. Franco took advantage of Perón's political sympathy to cheat him and did not pay for the wheat that had been purchased on credit; see Rein (1993), esp. chaps. 3 and 6.
5. Guillén de Castro, *Las mocedades del Cid* (Madrid: Espasa Calpe, colección Austral, 1971), p 34:
     procure siempre acertalla
     el honrado y principal

　　　pero si acertare mal

　　　defendella y no emendalla.

6. In the following chapter we shall see the identical error was committed with respect to electricity tariffs, again with parallel consequences.

7. The phrase comes from the agrarian specialist Severino Aznar; the exact expression seems to be "water dissolves the big estates." Monclús and Oyón (1986), p. 359.

8. In Spain in the 1970s only .1% of agricultural workers were *cooperativistas*. In France in the following decade the corresponding figure was 80%; Simpson (1995), p. 230.

9. The series on agricultural production in the twentieth century is calculated as follows: I have spliced together the annual series from GEHR (1987) for 1900–1935 with that from Barciela in the EH series. The figures from GEHR are in pesetas at 1910 values. To make the two series comparable I have deflated the Barciela series with: #1, the index of wholesale prices from INE, and #2, the same index up to 1963 and then with the agrarian deflator from 1964 onwards, a series taken from Baiges, Molinas and Sebastián (1987).

10. See, for example, García Delgado and Muñoz Cidad (1990), Colino (1993), Tamames (1990), Naredo (1986).

11. Although he does not mention Lewis specifically, this seems to be Barciela's interpretation (1987), pp. 270–272.

12. I use the term "seems to be" because the statistics for these year inspire little confidence; the estimate for cows fell in the 1940s and 1950s after a surprising rise during the Civil War.

13. Simpson (1995), table 12.3; Camilleri (1984), p. 471; EH.

14. Giráldez (1991); on the fall in meat consumption, see Gómez Mendoza and Simpson (1988).

15. Quoted in Gómez Mendoza (1992), p. 99.

16. On the development of scholarly interest in deforestation (the "*forestalista*" school), see Gómez Mendoza (1992); for a tirade against *desamortización,* Sanz (1986).

17. As Jiménez Blanco (1991) intelligently points out, public administration is a necessary condition, but not sufficient for its preservation.

18. The export of goods below domestic market prices is called dumping. And the European Union itself, which systematically dumps its own agricultural products, constantly denounces Japan for doing the same with its automobiles and electronic equipment.

12. Industrial Takeoff

1. On this see Cabrera (1983) and Gortázar (1986).

2. See Kemp (1989), pp. 732–733, and Eddie (1989), pp. 869–875.

3. Martín Rodríguez (1982, 1987); Biescas (1984); Jiménez Blanco (1986).

4. Gómez Mendoza and Simpson (1988) argue the contrary for Madrid; however,

the evidence on Barcelona seems to indicate an improvement: figures from the ACB indicate that meat consumption in the city of Barcelona increased from some 41 kgs. per person for the year 1903 and 49 kgs. for 1914; it fell somewhat during the World War. See also Gómez Mendoza and Martín Aceña (1984), esp. p. 17, which leads one to believe that there was an increase in meat consumption throughout the whole of Spain in this period; see also Tortella (1983c).

5. Martínez Carrión (1989), Gómez Mendoza and Martín Aceña (1983), Pujol (1986), Zambrana (1987).

6. Originally published in 1936.

7. "The Long Vacations of 36" (*"Las largas vacaciones del 36"*), film directed by Jaime Camino.

8. On this question see Palafox (1991), Hernández Andreu (1980), Comín and Martín Aceña (1984), and Comín (1987).

9. The peak that can be observed in the index for the cotton industry for 1945 coincides with a similar peak in the index of real wages in Ferner and Fina (1988, table A-2).

10. The sections in inverted commas are Suanzes' own words quoted by Martín Aceña and Comín (1991), pp. 52–66, who also make a critical assessment of these ideas.

11. Reworking his data I have calculated the equation

$$Y = 642 + 583M \qquad R^2 = 0.88 \qquad DW = 1.94$$
$$(23.8) \ (13.0)$$

for the period 1931–1957, where Y = Income and M = capital goods imports (both per head of population in constant pesetas). This equation shows the close association between both variables; from it one can deduce that each peseta invested in imported capital goods produced 583 pesetas in income.

12. González (1979), pp. 105–111, esp. table II-12; Donges (1976), pp. 150–157.

13. It increased by a factor of 2.3.

14. The term monopoly is used here in its broadest sense, to include oligopoly and monopsony.

15. As the earlier citation from Donges, already quoted, spells out.

16. De la Sierra (1953), Velarde (1955), Muñoz Linares (1955), Tamames (1961 and 1967).

17. The rate of growth of Gross Domestic Product has been calculated from figures by economists from the Bank of Spain reproduced in *Estadísticas Históricas*, (ed.) Carreras (1989), table 13.15; industrial growth is calculated from Donges (1976), p. 158.

18. Tamames said (1960), p. 355, that "from the macro-economic point of view automobile manufacture did not seem suitable . . . for the simple reason that the absorption capacity of [Spain's] market, estimated at 60,000 automobiles a year, is smaller than the optimum size of that kind of operation [. . . which] in the European countries varies between 200,000 and 300,000 units per year." I do not know who calculated that estimated market capacity but would not give much credit to those predictions; in 1962 national production was already much

ahead of that estimate and five years later the number of automobiles produced and sold in Spain exceeded that figure by a factor of five.

19. See Presidencia del Gobierno (1963), *Plan de desarrollo económico para el período 1964–67;* also Beltrán (1965) and Prados Arrarte (1965).

20. Argentina and the other countries that isolated themselves from the world economy, notably the Communist bloc countries, suffered a major slowdown, in relative terms, from which they are today struggling to recover.

21. The literature on this is abundant. For a recent summary see Tortella and Jiménez (1986), chap. VI.

22. See for example Myro (1990), p. 530 (table 1), and Segura and others (1989), table 3.1 and figure 3.1, where this recovery can be seen very clearly, starting in 1984.

23. Martínez Méndez (1982), p. 17 (figure 4F). See also below, Figure 13.5.

24. Baiges, Molinas and Sebastián (1987), pp. 182–183 (table VI.12).

25. It is not unequivocally correct, as Tamames says (1990), p. 280, following Redonet (1961), that this period was one of stagnant consumption. Between 1915 and 1935 the average annual increase was 9% according to figures from Carreras (1989). On the problems posed by this growth, see Antolín (1988, 1990) and Sudrià (1990b).

26. The hostility towards the Catalana de Gas reached the most colorful extremes; as a by-product of re-gasification, Catalana produced a nontrivial amount of propane, which the government-operated Butano company refused to buy from them. The government also denied an export permit for it, with the consequence that the company had no other option than to dispose of the gas by burning it (see Durán Farell in *El País,* 1990).

13. The Foreign Sector

1. The reader may consult Tortella (1991), chap. IX, and Requeijo (1985), *passim.*

2. These series have been spliced together and homogenized so that long-term comparisons can be made. For the autarky period (1940–1960) the figures on the balance of trade have been replaced by data from the Dirección General de Aduanas (Customs), which seem more reliable than those from the IEME, used by the Chamorro team. The differences between the two series are quite substantial, with the series from IEME creating a profile that is hardly credible. For the balances of payments for the period of the Republic, see Chamorro and Morales (1976); for those during the self-sufficiency period, Chamorro et al. (1975); for an interesting historical outline see Chamorro (1976).

3. The recovery of the German, Italian, and French economies, for example, after far greater destruction during World War II, was largely achieved within two or three years; Spain's recovery took much longer than a decade.

4. Spain in the 1980s constitutes a typical case of what is known as a "young debtor" country, with a deficit on current account and major capital imports.

5. On the key role played by capital goods imports, especially the difficulties during the 1950s, see Chapter 12.

6. See Tena (1985) and Prados (1981), with solutions that seem almost definitive to some problems of very long standing. See the index by Tena in EH.

14. The Evolution of Money and Banking

1. See Tortella (1991), chap. VII, and for more detail, Martín Aceña (1985).

2. Friedman and Schwartz (1971), esp. pp. 679–682; also Tortella (1983) and bibliography in both works.

3. Above all see Martín Aceña (1984 and 1985), Poveda (1972), and Rojo and Pérez (1977).

4. Martín Aceña (1984); Tortella and Palafox (1983).

5. See Goldsmith (1969) for his Financial Interrelations Ratio.

6. Muñoz (1969); Tamames (1961); Neuburger and Stokes (1974).

7. Hardach (1984); Ciocca and Toniolo (1984); Nötel (1984).

8. Tortella and Jiménez (1986).

9. Fanjul and Maravall (1985); Mañas (1992).

15. The Changing Role of the State

1. The major exception to this principle is the INI (see chap. 12).

2. For a more complete enumeration see Chapter 7.

3. Fuentes Quintana (1990), p. 58–59; Comín (1990b), p. 865.

4. See above, Chapter 12; and Tortella (1990). The quotation is from Calvo Sotelo in (1974), p. 92.

5. As both Fuentes Quintana (1990), p. 462, and Comín (1990b), p. 870 indicate, this system had already been used by the Fascist Italian Treasury.

6. Fuentes Quintana (1990), p. 454.

7. In this case the specialist was also a Minister and Vice-president of the government. But he also needed the support of the Minister of Finance, upon whom he could count quite unconditionally.

8. The figures from Comín (1990a), table 8; for a strong and well-reasoned defense of state intervention, see Segura (1990).

9. See Chapter 14, and Martín Aceña (1984).

10. Poveda (1986), p. 47; on these questions see also Poveda (1972), and Rojo and Pérez (1977).

11. Alcaide (1986).

12. Serrano Sanz (1986); Palafox (1986); Tena in EH. The tariffs of the day were especially designed with the negotiation of commercial treaties in mind. This gave rise to the concept of the double column (sometimes triple); the first column indicated the (higher) duties to be applied to goods coming from countries without special treaties; the second column represented duties to be applied to coun-

tries with treaties. The specific treaties negotiated the items of one or the other column that would be applicable. In principle the columns could not be modified, although on occasions they were in fact changed.

13. The original signatories in Rome were Italy, France, Germany and the Benelux countries; they were later joined by the United Kingdom, Ireland, and Denmark and later still by Greece. Spain and Portugal would finally become members in 1986. In 1995 Austria, Sweden, and Finland joined.

14. Fuentes Quintana (1986), pp. 144–145; the empirical study is the doctoral dissertation of Bataller (1983), see p. 276.

15. There may have been one further determinant: the fact that Catalonia had lost two wars (the War of Secession in 1652 and that of Succession in 1714) immediately before the beginning of this growth period seems to confirm the thesis of Mancur Olson (1982) that an institutional *tabula rasa* favors economic growth. Many of the other explanatory factors were already to be found in Vilar (1962) and Vicens (1961).

16. Tedde (1985) offers an excellent and innovative explanatory synthesis.

17. In reality, in weighting income per capita by the population, Carreras is dividing and multiplying by the same factor (the regional population) and obtaining the provincial income figures over again, or something very close in magnitude.

18. Martín Rodríguez (1990), pp. 734–738, and Cuadrado (1990).

Works Cited

AA.VV. (1983): *Historia de Andalucía.* Vol. V. *Los inicios del capitalismo. (1621–1778).* Barcelona: Cupsa-Planeta.

AA.VV. (1985): *Banque et investissements en Mediterranée a l'èpoque contemporaine.* Actes du Colloque de Marseille, 4–5, février 1982. Marseille: Chambre de Commerce et d'Industrie de Marseille.

Alcaide, Julio (1976): "Una revisión urgente de la serie de renta nacional española en el siglo XX," in Ministerio de Hacienda.

——— (1986): "Política de distribución de la renta," in Gámir (ed.), pp. 517–29.

Álvarez Llano, Roberto (1986): "Evolución de la estructura económica regional de España en la historia: una aproximación," *Situación.*

Andrés Álvarez, Valentín (1943): "Historia y crítica de los valores de nuestra balanza de comercio," *MC,* 4.

——— (1945): "Las balanzas estadísticas de nuestro comercio exterior," *REP,* 1, 1.

Anes Álvarez, Gonzalo (1970a): "La agricultura española desde comienzos del siglo XIX hasta 1868: algunos problemas," in Banco de España (1970a), pp. 235–63.

——— (1975): *El Antiguo Régimen: Los Borbones.* Madrid: Alianza/Alfaguara.

Anes Álvarez, R. and C. Fernández Pulgar (1970): "La creación de la peseta en la evolución del sistema monetario de 1847 a 1868," in Tortella et al., pp. 147–86.

Anes Álvarez, Rafael (1970): "Las inversiones extranjeras en España de 1855 a 1880," in Tortella et al., pp. 187–202.

——— (1974): "El Banco de España (1874–1914): un banco nacional," in Tortella (dir.), pp. 107–215.

——— (1978): "Relaciones entre el ferrocarril y la economía española (1865–1935)," in Anes and Tedde, pp. 355–512.

Anes Álvarez, Rafael and Germán Ojeda (1983): "La industria asturiana en la segunda mitad del siglo XIX: de la industrialización a la expansión hullera," *RHE,* I, 2, pp. 13–29.

Anes Álvarez, Rafael and Pedro Tedde (1978): *Los ferrocarriles en España, 1844–1943.* Vol. II. *Los ferrocarriles y la economía.* Madrid: Servicio de Estudios del Banco de España.

485

Anes, G., L. A. Rojo, and P. Tedde (eds.) (1983): *Historia económica y pensamiento social. Estudios en homenaje a Diego Mateo del Peral*. Madrid: Alianza/Banco de España.

Antolín, Francesca (1988): "Electricidad y crecimiento económico. Los inicios de la electricidad en España," *RHE*, IV, 3, pp. 635–55.

———— (1990): "Electricidad y crecimiento económico. Una hipótesis de investigación," *RHE*, VIII, 3, pp. 661–71.

Arango, Joaquín (1987): "La modernización demográfica de la sociedad española," in Nadal, Carreras, and Sudrià (eds.), pp. 201–36.

Armengaud, André (1973): "Population in Europe, 1700–1914," in Cipolla (ed.) (1973a), pp. 22–76.

Artola, Miguel (1973): *La burguesía revolucionaria (1808–1869)*. Madrid: Alianza/Alfaguara.

———— (1978): *Antiguo Régimen y Revolución Liberal*. Barcelona: Ariel.

———— (ed.) (1988): *Enciclopedia de Historia de España*. Vol. I. *Economía, Sociedad*. Madrid: Alianza.

Artola, Miguel and L. M. Bilbao (eds.) (1984): *Estudios de Hacienda: de Ensenada a Mon*. Madrid: Instituto de Estudios Fiscales.

Asociación de Historia Económica (1993): *V Congreso de la Asociación de Historia Económica [Ponencias]*. San Sebastián: Universidad del País Vasco.

Avery, David (1974): *Not on Queen Victoria's Birthday. The Story of the Rio Tinto Mines*. London: Collins.

Baiges, J., C. Molinas, and M. Sebastian (1987): *La economía española, 1964–1985: datos, fuentes y análisis*. Madrid: Instituto de Estudios Fiscales.

Bairoch, Paul (1965): "Niveaux de développement économique de 1810 à 1910," *AESC*, 20.

———— (1976): Commerce extérieur et développement économique de l'Europe au XIXe siècle. Paris: Ecole des Hautes Etudes en Sciences Sociales.

Banco de España (1970): *El Banco de España. Una historia económica*. Madrid: Banco de España.

———— (1970a): *Ensayos sobre la economía española a mediados del siglo XIX*. Madrid: Banco de España.

Barbier, Jacques A. and Herbert S. Klein (1985): "Las prioridades de un monarca ilustrado: el gasto público bajo el reinado de Carlos III," *RHE*, III, 3, pp. 473–95.

Barciela, Carlos (1981a): "La agricultura cerealista en la España contemporánea: el mercado triguero y el Servicio Nacional del Trigo." Ph.D. thesis, Universidad Complutense de Madrid.

———— (1981b): *La financiación del Servicio Nacional del Trigo, 1937–1971*. Madrid: Banco de España.

———— (1986a): "El mercado negro de productos agrarios en la posguerra, 1939–1953," in Fontana (ed.), pp. 192–205.

———— (1986b): "Introducción," in Garrabou, Barciela, and Jiménez Blanco (eds.), pp. 383–454.

———— (1987): "Crecimiento y cambio en la agricultura española desde la Guerra Civil," in Nadal, Carreras, and Sudrià (eds.), pp. 258–79.

Barros, Afonso de (ed.) (1980): "A agricultura latifundiária na Península Ibérica." Seminário realizado de 12 a 14 de Dezembro de 1979. Oeiras: Fundaçao Calouste Gulbenkian.

Bataller Martín, Francisco (1983): "The Determinants of Import Protection in a Developing Country: Spain in the 1960s." Ph.D. thesis, Ohio State University. Ann Arbor, Mich.: University Microfilms International.

Bazant, Jan (1977): *A Concise History of México, from Hidalgo to Cárdenas, 1805–1940.* Cambridge: Cambridge University Press.

Beltrán, Lucas (1965): *Explicación del Plan de Desarrollo.* Madrid: Sociedad de Estudios y Publicaciones.

Benelbas Tapinero, León (1989): "La revolució tecnològica, 1955–1984," in Benelbas et al., pp. 170–208.

Benelbas Tapinero, León et al. (1989): *Població, agricultura i energia.* Vol. 5, *Història econòmica de la Catalunya contemporània.* Barcelona: Enciclopèdia Catalana.

Bergier, Jean-François (1983): *Histoire économique de la Suisse.* Lausanne: Payot.

Bernal, Antonio Miguel (1992): "L'impresa agraria in Spagna (secoli XIX e XX)," *ASI,* 8, pp. 117–40.

Biescas Ferrer, José Antonio (1984): "Rasgos específicos en la evolución de la industria azucarera en España a lo largo del primer tercio del siglo XX," in García Delgado (ed.), 147–59.

Bilbao Bilbao, Luis M. (1983a): "La siderurgia vasca, 1720–1885. Atraso tecnológico, política arancelaria y eficiencia económica," in *Noveno congreso de estudios vascos.*

——— (1985): "Renovación tecnológica y estructura del sector siderúrgico en el País Vasco durante la primera etapa de la industrialización (1849–1880). Aproximación comparativa con la industria algodonera de Cataluña," in González Portilla et al. (eds.), pp. 211–28.

Bordo, Michael D. and Forrest Capie (1994): *Monetary Regimes in Transition.* Cambridge: Cambridge University Press.

Bowman, Mary Jean and C. Arnold Anderson (1963): "Concerning the Role of Education in Development," in Geertz (ed.).

Broder, Albert (1976): "Les investissements étrangers en Espagne au XIXe siècle: Méthodologie et quantification," *RHES,* pp. 29–62.

——— (1981): "Le rôle des interêts économiques étrangers dans la croissance de l'Espagne au XIXe siècle, 1767–1924." Ph.D. thesis, Université de Paris I.

——— (1985): "Le financement et le contrôle de l'industrie électrique dans les pays de la façade nord de la Mediterranée: 1890–1929," in AA.VV, pp. 85–102.

Buesa, Mikel (1992): "Patentes e innovación tecnológica en la industria española (1967–1986)," in García Delgado and Serrano Sanz, pp. 819–55.

Bustelo [Vázquez], F[rancisco] (1957): "Notas y comentarios sobre los orígenes de la industria española del nitrógeno," *MC,* 63, pp. 23–40.

Bustelo, Francisco and Gabriel Tortella (1976): "Monetary Inflation in Spain, 1800–1970," *JEEH,* 5, pp. 141–50.

Cabrera, Mercedes (1983): *La patronal ante la II República. Organizaciones y estrategia (1931–1936).* Madrid: Siglo XXI.

Cafagna, L. (1973): "The Industrial Revolution in Italy, 1830–1914," in Cipolla, ed. (1973b), pp. 279–328.

Calvo Sotelo, José (1974): *Mis servicios al Estado. Seis años de gestión. Apuntes para la Historia*, 2nd ed. Madrid: Instituto de Estudios de Administración Local.

Cameron, Rondo (1961): *France and the Economic Development of Europe, 1800–1914. Conquest of Peace and Seeds of War.* Princeton: Princeton University Press.

——— (1989): *A Concise Economic History of the World. From Paleolithic Times to the Present.* New York: Oxford University Press.

——— (ed.) (1972): *Banking and Economic Development. Some Lessons of History.* New York: Oxford University Press.

Camilleri Lapeyre, Arturo (dir.) (1984): *La agricultura española ante la CEE.* Madrid: Instituto de Estudios Económicos.

Carande, Ramón (1949): *Carlos V y sus banqueros. La Hacienda real de Castilla.* Madrid: Sociedad de Estudios y Publicaciones.

Carmona Badía, Joám (1990): *El atraso industrial de Galicia. Auge y liquidación de las manufacturas textiles (1750–1900).* Barcelona: Ariel.

Carnero, Teresa (1980): *Expansión vinícola y atraso agrario (1870–1900).* [Madrid]: Servicio de Publicaciones Agrarias.

Caron, François (1981): *Histoire économique de la France, XIXè-XXè siècles.* Paris: Armand Colin.

Carr, Raymond (1966): *Spain, 1808–1839.* Oxford: Clarendon Press.

Carreras, Albert (1983): "La producció industrial espanyola i italiana des de mitjan del segle XIX fins a l'actualitat." 3 vols. Ph.D. thesis, Universidad Autónoma de Barcelona.

——— (1983): "El aprovechamiento de la energía hidráulica en Cataluña. 1840–1920. Una aproximación a su estudio," *RHE,* I, 2, pp. 31–63.

——— (1984): "La producción industrial española, 1842–1981: construcción de un índice anual," *RHE,* II, 1, pp. 127–57.

——— (1985): "Gasto nacional bruto y formación de capital en España, 1849–1958: primer ensayo de estimación," in Martín Aceña and Prados (eds.), pp. 117–51.

——— (1987): "La industria: atraso y modernización," in Nadal, Carreras, and Sudrià (eds.), pp. 280–312.

——— (1987a): "An Annual Index of Spanish Industrial Output," in Sánchez-Albornoz (ed.), pp. 75–89.

——— (1989): "Depresión económica y cambio estructural durante el decenio bélico (1936–1945)," in García Delgado (ed.), pp. 3–33.

——— (1990): "Fuentes y datos para el análisis regional de la industrialización española," in Nadal and Carreras (eds.), pp. 3–20.

——— (ed.) (1989): *Estadísticas históricas de España, siglos XIX-XX.* Madrid: Fundación Banco Exterior.

Carreras, Albert and Xavier Tafunell (1993): "La gran empresa en España contemporánea: entre el mercado y el estado," in Comín and Martín Aceña, pp. 73–90.

Casares, María Teresa (1984): *El Banco Hipotecario de España a través de sus prestatarios.* Madrid: Banco Hipotecario.

Castañeda, Luis (1993): "Crédito y mercado monetario no bancario en Barcelona a mediados del siglo XIX. Algunas consideraciones sobre la pervivencia de instrumentos financieros tradicionales," Asociación de Historia Económica, pp. 297–306.

Cazzola, Franco (1988): "Aspectos y problemas de la crisis agraria en Italia," in Garrabou (ed.).

Cerrolaza, Alfredo (1955): "Analfabetismo y renta," in Guzmán Reina et al.

Chamorro, Santiago (1976): "Bosquejo histórico de la Balanza de Pagos de España," *ICE.*

Chamorro, Santiago et al. (1975): "Las Balanzas de Pagos de España en el período de la autarquía," *ICE,* 502, pp. 161–87.

Chamorro, Santiago and Remedios Morales (1976): "Las balanzas de pagos de Francisco Jáinaga," *ICE.*

Chastagnaret, Gérard (1972): "La législation de 1825 et l'évolution des activités minières," Papers of I Coloquio de Historia Económica de España, Barcelona.

——— (1973): "Contribution a l'étude de la production et des producteurs de Houille des Asturies de 1861 à 1914," *MCV.*

——— (1985): "Le secteur minier dans l'economie espagnole au XIXe siecle," Ph.D. thesis, Université de Provence.

Checkland, S. G. (1967): *The Mines of Tharsis. Roman, French and British Enterprise in Spain.* London: Allen and Unwin.

Chilcote, Ronald H. (19968): *Spain's Iron and Steel Industry.* Austin: University of Texas Press.

Ciocca, Pierluigi y Gianni Toniolo (1984): "Industry and Finance in Italy, 1918–1940," *JEEH,* 13, 2, pp. 113–36.

Cipolla, Carlo M. (1969): *Literacy and Economic Development in the West.* Baltimore: Penguin Books.

——— (1970): *The Economic History of World Population.* Middlesex, England: Penguin Books.

——— (ed.) (1973a): *The Industrial Revolution. The Fontana Economic History of Europe,* Vol. 3. London: Collins/Fontana Books.

——— (ed.) (1973b): *The Emergence of Industrial Societies.* Part One. *The Fontana Economic History of Europe,* Vol. 4. London: Collins/Fontana Books.

——— (1976): *Before the Industrial Revolution. European Society and Economy, 1000–1700.* London: Methuen.

Coatsworth, John H. (1976): *Crecimiento contra desarrollo: el impacto económico de los ferrocarriles en el porfiriato.* Vol. I. México: Sepsetentas.

Cohen, Jon S. (1972): "Italy, 1861–1914," in Cameron (ed.), pp. 58–90.

——— (1988): "Was Italian Fascism a Developmental Dictatorship? Some Evidence to the Contrary," *EHR,* 41, pp. 95–113.

Colino Sueiras, José (1993): "Sector agrario," in García Delgado (dir.), pp. 169–90.

Coll Martín, S. and C. Sudrià (1987): *El carbón en España, 1770–1961. Una historia económica*. Madrid: Turner.

Coll Martín, Sebastián (1983): "Las empresas mineras del Sudoeste español, 1850–1914," in Anes, Rojo, and Tedde (eds.), pp. 399–429.

——— (1985): "El coste social de la protección arancelaria a la minería del carbón en España, 1877–1925," in Martín Aceña and Prados (eds.).

——— (1986): "Producción y valor añadido del sector de los cementos," mimeo. Informe "Proyecto Europeo." Banco de España.

Colmeiro, Manuel (1965): *Historia de la economía política en España*. 2 vols. Madrid: Taurus.

Comín, Francisco (1984): "Algunos resultados de la Reforma Tributaria de Mon-Santillán," in Artola and Bilbao (eds.).

——— (1985): *Fuentes cuantitativas para el estudio del sector público en España, 1801–1980*. Madrid: Instituto de Estudios Fiscales.

——— (1987): "Perfil histórico de la Deuda pública española," *PEE,* 33, pp. 86–119.

——— (1987a): "La economía española en el período de entreguerras (1919–1935)," in Nadal, Carreras, and Sudrià (eds.), pp. 105–49.

——— (1988): *Hacienda y economía en la España contemporánea (1800–1936)*. 2 vols. Madrid: Instituto de Estudios Fiscales.

——— (1990): *Las cuentas de la Hacienda preliberal en España (1800–1855)*. Madrid: Banco de España, Servicio de Estudios.

——— (1990a): "Las Administraciones públicas," in García Delgado (dir.), pp. 431–69.

——— (1990b): "Reforma tributaria y política fiscal," in García Delgado (dir.), pp. 859–901.

——— (1996): *Historia de la Hacienda Pública*. Vol. II. *España (1800–1995)*. Barcelona: Crítica.

Comín, Francisco and Pablo Martín Aceña (1984): "La política monetaria y fiscal durante la dictadura y la segunda república," *PEE,* 20, pp. 236–61.

——— (1991): *Historia de la empresa pública en España*. Madrid: Espasa Calpe.

——— (eds.)(1996): *La empresa en la historia de España*. Madrid: Civitas.

Comisión para el Estudio . . . (1909): Comisión para el estudio de la producción y consumo de trigo. Su nombramiento. Actas de sus sesiones. Dictamen y apéndices. Madrid.

Cordero, Ramón and Fernando Menéndez (1978): "El sistema ferroviario español," in Artola (ed.), pp. 161–338.

Cuadrado Roura, Juan R. (1990): "La crisis económica y la redefinición del mapa económico regional," in García Delgado (dir), pp. 745–64.

De Ryck, Luc (s.f.): "Les entreprises Otlet, un example d'initiative belge dans les chemins de fer espagnols (1887–1914)," typescript.

Deane, Phyllis (1965): *The First Industrial Revolution*. Cambridge: Cambridge University Press.

Delgado y Orellana, José Antonio (1966): "La casa de Domecq D'Usquain. Ensayo genealógico nobiliario." Privately printed: Sevilla.

Díaz del Moral, Juan (1967): *Historia de las agitaciones campesinas andaluzas. Córdoba. Antecedentes para una reforma agraria.* Madrid: Alianza.

Díez, Fernando (1992): "La crisis gremial y los problemas de la sedería valenciana (ss. XVIII-XIX)," *RHE*, X, 1.

Dirección General de Aduanas (1896): *Informe acerca de la producción, comercio y consumo de trigo en España.* Madrid: Sucesores de Rivadeneira.

Dixon, Arturo (1985): *Señor monopolio. La asombrosa vida de Juan March.* Barcelona: Editorial Planeta.

Donges, Juergen B. (1976): *La industrialización en España. Políticas, logros, perspectivas.* Barcelona: Oikos-tau.

Dopico, Fausto (1982): "Productividade, rendementos e tecnoloxía na agricultura galega de fins do seculo XIX," *Grial. Anexo Historia,* 1.

Easterlin, Richard A (1981): "Why Isn't the Whole World Developed?," *JEH,* 41, pp. 1–19.

Eddie, Scott M. (1989): "Economic Policy and Economic Development in Austria-Hungary, 1867–1913," in Mathias and Pollard (eds.), pp. 814–86.

Equipo Madrid de Estudios Históricos (1988): *Carlos III, Madrid y la Ilustración. Contradicciones de un proyecto reformista.* Madrid: Siglo XXI.

Estapé, Fabián (ed.) (1973): *Textos olvidados.* Madrid: Instituto de Estudios Fiscales.

Estevan Senís, María Teresa (1966): "La minería cartagenera, 1840–1919. Aspectos económicos y sociales," *Hispania,* 101, pp. 61–95.

Fanjul, Oscar and Fernando Maravall (1985): *La eficiencia del sistema bancario español.* Madrid: Alianza.

Federico, G. (1986): "Mercantilizzazione e sviluppo economico in Italia (1860–1940)," *RSE,* 3, 2.

Fenoaltea, Stefano (1978): "Riflessioni sull'esperienza industriale italiana dal Risorgimento alla prima guerra mondiale," in Toniolo (ed.).

——— (1981): "Los ferrocarriles y la industrialización italiana: Análisis y reconsideración," in RENFE, pp. 81–101.

Fernández de Pinedo and Hernández Marco (eds.) (1988): *La industrialización del norte de España (Estado de la cuestión).* Barcelona: Crítica/Universidad del País Vasco.

Ferner, Anthony y Lluis Fina (1988): "La dinámica salarial durante el franquismo: el caso de RENFE," *RHE,* VI, 1, pp. 131–61.

Financiero, El (1926): Libro conmemorativo del XXV aniversario de su fundación, Madrid: El Financiero.

Flinn, M. W. (1955): "British Steel and Spanish Ore: 1871–1914," *EHR,* VIII, pp. 84–90.

Flora, Peter (1983): *State, Economy and Society in Western Europe.* Vol. I. *The Growth of Mass Democracies and Welfare States.* Frankfurt: Campus Verlag.

Fogel, Robert William (1964): *Railroads and American Economic Growth. Essays in Econometric History.* Baltimore: Johns Hopkins University Press.

Fontana, Josep (1971): *La quiebra de la monarquía absoluta, 1814–1820 (La crisis del Antiguo Régimen en España).* Barcelona: Ariel.

——— (1973a): *Hacienda y Estado en la crisis final del Antiguo Régimen español: 1823–1833.* Madrid: Instituto de Estudios Fiscales.

——— (1973b): *Cambio económico y actitudes políticas en la España del siglo XIX.* Barcelona: Ariel.

——— (1977): *La revolución liberal. Política y Hacienda en 1833–1845.* Madrid: Instituto de Estudios Fiscales.

——— (ed.) (1986): *España bajo el franquismo.* Barcelona: Crítica.

Fraile, Pedro (1985): "El fracaso de la revolución industrial en España: Un modelo cerrado de industrialización," *ICE,* 623, pp. 97–104.

——— (1985a): "El País Vasco y el mercado mundial, 1900–1930," in Sánchez-Albornoz (ed.), pp. 226–51.

——— (1991): *Industrialización y grupos de presión: la economía política de la protección en España, 1900–1950.* Madrid: Alianza.

Frax Rosales, E. and M. J. Matilla Quiza (1988): "Transporte, comercio y comunicaciones," in Artola (ed.), pp. 191–263.

Frax Rosales, Esperanza (1981): *Puertos y comercio de cabotaje en España, 1857–1934.* Madrid: Banco de España.

Fremdling, Rainer (1977): "Railroads and German Economic Growth: A Leading Sector Analysis with a Comparison to the United States and Great Britain," *JEH,* 3, pp. 583–604.

Fremdling, Rainer and Patrick K. O'Brien (eds.) (1983): *Productivity in the Economies of Europe.* Stuttgart: Klett-Cotta.

Friedman, Milton and A. J. Schwartz (1971): *A Monetary History of the United States, 1867–1960.* Princeton, N.J.: N.B.E.R./Princeton University Press.

Fua, G. (ed.) (1969): *Lo sviluppo economico in Italia,* 3 vols. Milán: F. Angeli.

Fuentes Quintana, Enrique (1986): "La economía española desde el Plan de Estabilización de 1959: el papel del sector exterior," in Martínez Vara (ed.), pp. 131–57.

——— (1987): "Introducción," in Sardá, pp. 17–6.

——— (1990): *Las reformas tributarias en España. Teoría, historia y propuestas.* Barcelona: Crítica.

Fundación Foessa (1976): *Estudios sociológicos sobre la situación social de España, 1975.* Madrid: Euramérica.

Furet, François and Jacques Ozouf (1982): *Reading and Writing. Literacy in France from Calvin to Jules Ferry.* Cambridge: Cambridge University Press.

Galassi, F. (1986): "Reassessing Mediterranean Agriculture: Retardation and Growth in Tuscany, 1870–1914," *RSE,* 3, 3, pp. 91–121.

Galassi, F. and J. S. Cohen (1992): "La agricultura italiana, 1860–1930: tendencias de la producción y diferencias en la productividad regional," in Prados y Zamagni (eds.), pp. 171–229.

Gallego Martínez, Domingo (1986a): "La producción agraria de Alava, Navarra y La Rioja desde mediados del siglo XIX a 1935," Ph.D. thesis. Madrid: Universidad Complutense.

————— (1986b): "Transformaciones técnicas de la agricultura española en el primer tercio del siglo XX," in Garrabou, Barciela and Jiménez Blanco (eds.).

Gámir, Luis (dir.) (1986): *Política económica de España*. Madrid: Alianza.

García Delgado, J. L. and J. Segura (eds.) (1978): *Ciencia social y análisis económico. Estudios en homenaje al Profesor Valentín Andrés Alvarez*. Madrid: Tecnos.

García Delgado, J. L. and C. Muñoz Cidad (1990): "La agricultura: cambios estructurales en los últimos decenios," in García Delgado (dir.), pp. 119–52.

García Delgado, José Luis (coor.) (1992): *Economía española, cultura y sociedad. Homenaje a Juan Velarde*. Madrid: Eudema.

————— (dir.) (1990): *España, economía,* 2nd ed. Madrid: Espasa Calpe.

————— (dir.) (1990a): *Electricidad y desarrollo económico: perspectiva histórica de un siglo*. Oviedo: Hidroeléctrica del Cantábrico.

————— (dir.) (1993): *Lecciones de economía española*. Madrid: Civitas.

————— (ed.) (1984): *España, 1898–1936: Estructuras y Cambio*. Coloquio de la Universidad Complutense sobre la España contemporánea. Madrid: Universidad Complutense.

————— (ed.) (1985): *La España de la Restauración: política, economía, legislación y cultura*. Madrid: Siglo XXI.

————— (ed.) (1986): *La crisis de la Restauración: España entre la primera guerra mundial y la II República*. Madrid: Siglo XXI.

————— (ed.) (1989): *El primer franquismo. España durante la segunda guerra mundial*. Madrid: Siglo XXI.

García López, José Ramón (1987): *Los comerciantes banqueros en el sistema bancario español. Estudio de casas de banca asturianas en el siglo XIX*. Oviedo: Universidad de Oviedo.

————— (1992): *Las remesas de los emigrantes españoles en América. Siglos XIX y XX*. Gijón: Ediciones Júcar.

García Ruiz, J. L. and G. Tortella (1993): "Trayectorias divergentes, paralelas y convergentes: la historia del Banco Hispano Americano y del Banco Central, 1901–1965," Asociación de Historia Económica, pp. 339–55.

García Sanz, A. and R. Garrabou (eds.) (1985): *Historia agraria de la España contemporánea*. Vol. I. *Cambio social y nuevas formas de propiedad (1800–1850)*. Barcelona: Crítica.

García Sanz, Angel (1991): "Desarrollo del capitalismo agrario en Castilla y León en el siglo XIX. Algunos testimonios, algunas reflexiones y un epílogo," in Yun Casalilla (ed.), pp. 19–46.

Garrabou, Ramón (1979): "Cultius, collites i rendiments a la Segarra i Alt Anoia: els comptes d'unes finques de Guissona, Sant Martí i Castellfollit de Riubregós," *EHA*, 1.

————— (ed.) (1988): *La crisis agraria de fines del siglo XIX*. Barcelona: Crítica.

Garrabou, R., C. Barciela, and J. I. Jiménez Blanco (eds.) (1986): *Historia agraria de la agricultura contemporánea*. Vol. 3. *El fin de la agricultura tradicional (1900–1960)*. Barcelona: Crítica.

Geertz, Clifford (ed.) (1963): *Old Societies and New States*. Glencoe, Ill.: The Free Press.

Germán Zubero, Luis (1990): "La industrialización de Aragón. Atraso y dualismo interno," in Nadal and Carreras, pp 185–218.

Germán Zubero, L., V. Pinilla, and H. Español (1990): *Eléctricas Reunidas de Zaragoza (1910–1986). El desarrollo del sector eléctrico en Aragón*. Zaragoza: IFC.

Gerschenkron, Alexander (1965): *Economic Backwardness in Historical Perspective. A Book of Essays*. New York: Praeger.

Giráldez Rivero, Jesús (1991): "Fuentes estadísticas y producción pesquera en España (1880–1936): una primera aproximación," *RHE*, IX, 3, pp. 513–32.

Goldsmith, Raymond W. (1969): *Financial Structure and Development*. New Haven: Yale University Press.

Gómez Mendoza, A. and P. Martín Aceña (1983): "El sector de la alimentación: series de producción, 1880–1935," mimeo. Informe "Proyecto Europeo." Banco de España.

Gómez Mendoza, A. and J. Simpson (1988): "El consumo de carne en Madrid durante el primer tercio del siglo XX," *MC*, 186, pp. 57–91.

Gómez Mendoza, Antonio (1982): *Ferrocarriles y cambio económico en España (1855–1913). Un enfoque de nueva historia económica*. Madrid: Alianza.

——— (1984): "La industria de construcciones navales, 1850–1935," typescript. Informe "Proyecto Europeo." Banco de España.

——— (1987a): "La formación de un cártel en el primer tercio del siglo XX: La industria del cemento portland," *RHE*, V, 2, pp. 325–26.

——— (1987b): "Oligopoly and Economic Efficiency: Portland Cement in Spain (1899–1935)," *RSE*, 4, pp. 76–95.

——— (1989): *Ferrocarril, industria y mercado en la industrialización de España*. Madrid: Espasa Calpe.

——— (1991): "Las obras públicas (1850–1935)," in Comín and Martín Aceña (eds.).

Gómez Mendoza, Josefina (1992): *Ciencia y política de los montes españoles (1848–1936)*. Madrid: ICONA.

González Portilla, M. et al. (eds.) (1985): *Industrialización y Nacionalismo. Análisis comparativos*. Actas del I Coloquio Vasco-Catalán de Historia, Sitges, 1982. Bellaterra: Universidad Autónoma de Barcelona.

González, Manuel-Jesús (1979): *La economía política del franquismo (1940–1970). Dirigismo, mercado y planificación*. Madrid: Tecnos.

Gortázar, Guillermo (1986): *Alfonso XIII, hombre de negocios. Persistencia del Antiguo Régimen, modernización económica y crisis política, 1902–1931*. Madrid: Alianza.

Grubb, Farley (1988): "Reseña de Harvey J. Graff, *The Labyrinths of Literacy. Reflections on Literacy Past and Present*," JEH, 48, pp. 798–99.

Grupo de Estudios de Historia Rural (1980): *Los precios del trigo y la cebada en España, 1891–1907*. Madrid: Banco de España.

——— (1981): *Los precios del aceite de oliva en España, 1891–1916*. Madrid: Banco de España.

—— (1983): "Notas sobre la producción agraria española, 1891–1931," *RHE*, I, 2, pp. 185–252.

—— (1987): "Un índice de la producción agraria española, 1891–1935," *HPE*, 108, pp. 411–22.

—— (1991): *Estadísticas históricas de la producción agraria española.* Madrid: Ministerio de Agricultura, Pesca, y Alimentación.

Guzmán Reina, Antonio et al. (1955): *Causas y remedios del analfabetismo en España.* Madrid: Ministerio de Educación Nacional.

Gwinner, Arturo (1973): "La política comercial de España en los últimos decenios," in Estapé (ed.), pp. 361–333.

Hamilton, Earl J. (1938): "The Decline of Spain," *EHR*, VIII, 2, pp. 168–79.

—— (1947): *War and Prices in Spain 1651–1800.* Cambridge, Mass.: Harvard University Press.

—— (1948): *El florecimiento del capitalismo y otros ensayos de Historia económica.* Madrid: Revista de Occidente.

—— (1970): "El Banco Nacional de San Carlos (1782–1829)," in Banco de España (1970).

Hardach, Gerd (1984): "Banking and Industry in Germany in the Interwar Period, 1919–1939," *JEEH*, 13, 2, pp. 203–34.

Harrison, Joseph (1974): "Catalan Business and the Loss of Cuba, 1878–1914," *EHR*, XXVII, 3, pp. 431–41.

Harvey, Charles E. (1981): *The Rio Tinto Company. An Economic History of a Leading International Mining Concern, 1873–1954.* Penzance, Cornwall: Alison Hodge.

Hawke, G. R. (1970): *Railways and Economic Growth in England and Wales, 1840–1870.* Oxford: Clarendon Press.

Hernández Andreu, Juan (1980): *Depresión económica en España 1925–1934. Crisis mundial antes de la Guerra Civil española.* Madrid: Instituto de Estudios Fiscales.

Hernández Andreu, Juan and José Luis García Ruiz (eds.) (1994): *Lecturas de historia empresarial.* Madrid: Civitas.

Herr, Richard (1958): *The Eighteenth-Century Revolution in Spain.* Princeton, N.J.: Princeton University Press.

—— (1974a): "El significado de la desamortización en España," *MC*, 131, pp. 55–94.

—— (1974b): "La vente des propriétés de mainmorte en Espagne, 1798–1808," *AESC*, 29, pp. 215–28.

—— (1989): *Rural Change and Royal Finances in Spain at the End of the Old Regime.* Berkeley: University of California Press.

Hicks, John (1969): *A Theory of Economic History.* Oxford: Oxford University Press.

Hoyo, Andrés (1993): "La evolución del mercado de valores en España. La Bolsa de Madrid, 1831–1874," in Asociación de Historia Económica, pp. 371–383.

Huguet del Villar, Emilio (1921): *El valor geográfico de España. Ensayo de ecética.* Madrid.

Instituto Nacional de Estadística (1958): *Comercio exterior de España. Números índices (1901–1956).* Madrid: Instituto Nacional de Estadística.

Izard, Miguel (1973): *Industrialización y obrerismo. Las tres clases del vapor, 1869–1913.* Barcelona: Ariel.

Jeffs, Julian (1970): *Sherry.* London: Faber & Faber.

Jiménez Blanco, José Ignacio (1986): "La remolacha y los problemas de la industria azucarera en España, 1880–1914," in Garrabou, Barciela, and Jiménez Blanco (eds.), pp. 280–316.

——— (1991): "Los montes de propiedad pública (1833–1936)," in Comín and Martín Aceña (eds.), pp. 241–81.

Justino, David (1987): "A evoluçao do produto nacional bruto em Portugal, 1850–1910—algumas estimativas provisórias," *AS,* 23, pp. 451–61.

Kagan, Richard L. (1974): *Students and Society in Early Modern Spain.* Baltimore: Johns Hopkins University Press.

Kearney, Hugh (1971): *Science and Change, 1500–1700.* New York: World University Library.

Kemp, Tom (1989a): "Economic and social policy in France," in Mathias and Pollard (eds.), pp. 691–751.

Keynes, John Maynard (1960; orig. 1936): *The General Theory of Employment, Interest, and Money.* London: Macmillan.

Lacomba, Juan Antonio and Gumensindo Ruiz (1990): *Una historia del Banco Hipotecario de España (1872–1986).* Madrid: Alianza.

Lains, Pedro (1987): "O proteccionismo em Portugal (1842–1913): Um caso mal sucedido de industrializaçao 'concorrencial'," *AS,* 23, pp. 4481–503.

——— (1988): "A Agricultura e a Indústria no crescimento económico portugues, 1850–1913," mimeo. Universidade de Lisboa, Instituto de Ciencias Sociais.

Leite, J. Costa (1987): "Emigraçao portuguesa: A lei e os números (1855–1914)," *AS,* 23, pp. 465–80.

Lewis, W. Arthur (1955): *The Theory of Economic Growth.* Homewood, Ill.: Irwin.

Livi-Bacci, Massimo (1968): "Fertility and Nuptiality Changes in Spain from the Late 18th to the Early 20th Century," *Population Studies,* 22.

Llopis Agelan, Enrique (1983): "Algunas consideraciones acerca de la producción agraria castellana en los veinticinco últimos años del Antiguo Régimen," *IE,* 21.

Lockwood, William W. (1968): *The Economic Development of Japan. Growth and Structural Change.* Expanded ed. Princeton, NJ: Princeton University Press.

Luis Y Yagüe, R. (1903): *Bromatología popular urbana.* Madrid.

Lynch, John (1976): *Las revoluciones hispanoamericanas, 1808–1826.* Barcelona: Ariel.

Madoz, Pascual (1848): *Madrid. Audiencia, provincia, intendencia, vicaría, partido y villa.* Madrid.

——— (1948–50): *Diccionario geográfico-estadístico-histórico de España y sus posesiones de Ultramar.* 16 vols. Madrid.

Madrazo, Santos (1991): *La edad de oro de las diligencias. Madrid y el tráfico de viajeros en España antes del ferrocarril.* Madrid: Nerea.

Malefakis, Edward (1971): *Reforma agraria y revolución campesina en la España del siglo XX.* Barcelona: Ariel.

Maluquer de Motes, Jordi (1983a): "Las relaciones entre agricultura i indústria en el desenvolupament capitalista catalá del vuit-cents. Algunes hipótesis." Valencia: Institució Alfóns el Magnànim.

_____(1987): "De la crisis colonial a la guerra europea: veinte años de economía española," in Nadal, Carreras, and Sudrià (eds.), pp. 62–104.

—————— (1988): "Factores y condicionamientos del proceso de industrialización en el siglo XIX: el caso español," in Fernández Pinedo and Hernández Marco (eds.), pp. 13–36.

Mañas Antón, Luis (1992): "El sector financiero español ante su integración en el Mercado Unico," in Viñals (ed.), pp. 463–548.

Maravall, Fernando (1987): *Economía y política industrial en España*. Madrid: Ediciones Pirámide.

Martín Aceña, P. and F. Comín (1989): "La financiación del INI, 1941–1986," *PEE,* 38, pp. 135–58.

—————— (1991): *INI. 50 años de industrialización de España*. Madrid: Espasa Calpe.

—————— (eds.) (1990): *Empresa pública e industrialización en España*. Madrid: Alianza.

Martín Aceña, P. and L. Prados (eds.) (1985): *La Nueva Historia Económica en España*. Madrid: Tecnos.

Martín Aceña, Pablo (1984): *La política monetaria en España, 1919–1935*. Madrid: Instituto de Estudios Fiscales.

—————— (1985): *La cantidad de dinero en España, 1900–1935*. Madrid: Banco de España.

—————— (1985a): "Desarrollo y modernización del sistema financiero, 1844–1935," in Sánchez-Albornoz, pp. 121–46.

—————— (1990): "La política monetaria en España, 1940–1962," mimeo.

—————— (1990a): "La banca pública antes de la Guerra Civil," typescript.

—————— (1991): "Los problemas monetarios al término de la Guerra Civil," typescript.

—————— (1994): "Spain During the Classical Gold Standard Years, 1880–1914," in Bordo and Capie (eds.).

Martín Niño, Jesús (1972): *La Hacienda española y la Revolución de 1968*. Madrid: Instituto de Estudios Fiscales.

Martín Rodríguez, Manuel (1982): *Azúcar y descolonización. Origen y desenlace de una crisis agraria en la Vega de Granada. El "Ingenio de San Juan," 1882–1904*. Granada: Caja General de Ahorros.

—————— (1987): "La industria azucarera española, 1914–1936," *REH,* V, 2, pp. 301–23.

—————— (1990): "Evolución de las disparidades regionales: una perspectiva histórica," in García Delgado (dir.), pp. 703–43.

Martínez Carrión, José Miguel (1989): "Formación y desarrollo de la industria de conservas vegetales en España, 1850–1935," *RHE,* VII, 3, pp. 619–49.

Martínez Méndez, Pedro (1982): *El proceso de ajuste de la economía española: 1973–1980*. Madrid: Banco de España.

Martínez Santos, Vicente (1981): *Cara y cruz de la sedería valenciana (siglos XVIII y XIX)*. Valencia: Ediciones Alfonso el Magnánimo.

Martínez Vara, Tomás (ed.) (1986): *Mercado y desarrollo económico en la España contemporánea*. Madrid: Siglo XXI.

Mateo del Peral, Diego (1974): "Economía y política durante el sexenio liberal. Catálogo de legislación (1868–1874)," in Tortella (dir.) (1974b), pp. 11–74.

Mathias, Peter and Sidney Pollard (eds.) (1989): *The Cambridge Economic History of Europe.* Vol. VIII. *The Industrial Economies: The Development of Economic and Social Policies.* Cambridge: Cambridge University Press.

Membiela y Salgado, Roque (1885): *Higiene popular. La cuestión obrera en España o estado de nuestras clases necesitadas y medios para mejorar su situación.* Santiago.

Miguel, Amando de (1977): *La pirámide social española.* Barcelona: Fundación Juan March.

Milward, A. S. and S. B. Saul (1973): *The Economic Development of Continental Europe, 1780–1870.* London: Allen & Unwin.

Ministerio de Hacienda (1976): *Datos básicos para la historia financiera de España (1850–1975).* Madrid: Instituto de Estudios Fiscales.

Ministerio de Industria y Energía (1988): *España: 200 años de tecnología.* Madrid: INI y RENFE.

Mironov, Boris N. (1993): "Educación y desarrollo económico en Rusia, siglos XIX y XX," in Núñez and Tortella (eds.), pp. 271–306.

Mitchell, B. R. (1976): *European Historical Statistics, 1750–1970.* New York: Columbia University Press.

Molinas, C. and L. Prados de la Escosura (1989): "Was Spain Different? Spanish Historical Backwardness Revisited," *EEH,* 26, 4, pp. 385–402.

Monclús, F. J. y J. L. Oyón (1986): "De la colonización interior a la colonización integral (1900–1936)," in Garrabou, Barciela, and Jiménez Blanco (eds.), pp. 347–80.

Montero, Manu (1990): *Mineros, banqueros y navieros.* Leioa: Universidad de País Vasco.

Muñoz Linares, Carlos (1955): "El pliopolio en algunos sectores del sistema económico español," *REP,* 6, 1.

Muñoz, Juan (1969): *El poder de la banca en España.* Vizcaya: Zero.

Myro Sánchez, Rafael (1990): "La evolución de las principales magnitudes: una presentación de conjunto," in García Delgado (dir.), pp. 527–58.

Nadal, Jordi (1972): "Industrialización y desindustrialización del sureste español," *MC,* 120, pp. 3–80.

——— (1975): *El fracaso de la revolución industrial en España, 1814–1913.* Barcelona: Ariel.

——— (1983): "Los Bonaplata: tres generaciones de industriales catalanes en la España del siglo XIX," *RHE,* I, 1, pp. 79–95.

——— (1985): "Un siglo de industrialización en España, 1833–1930," in Sánchez-Albornoz (ed.), pp. 89–101.

——— (1986): "La debilidad de la industria química española en el siglo XIX. Un problema de demanda," *MC,* 176, pp. 33–70.

——— (1987): "La industria fabril española en 1900. Una aproximación," in Nadal, Carreras, and Sudrià (eds.), pp. 23–61.

Nadal, J., A. Carreras, and C. Sudrià (eds.) (1987): *La economía española en el siglo XX. Una perspectiva histórica*. Barcelona: Ariel.

Nadal, Jordi and Albert Carreras (eds.) (1990): *Pautas regionales de la industrialización española (siglos XIX y XX)*. Barcelona: Ariel.

Nadal, Jordi and Gabriel Tortella (eds.) (1974): *Agricultura, comercio colonial y crecimiento económico en la España contemporánea*. Barcelona: Ariel.

Naredo, José Manuel (1986): "La agricultura española en el desarrollo económico," in Garrabou, Barciela, and Jiménez Blanco (eds.), pp. 454–98.

Neuburger, Hugh and Houston H. Stokes (1974): "German Banks and German Growth, 1883–1913: An Empirical View," *JEH,* 34, pp. 710–31.

Nötel, Rudolf (1984): "Money, Banking, and Industry in Interwar Austria and Hungary," *JEEH,* 13, 2, pp. 137–202.

Núñez Romero-Balmas, Gregorio (1985): "Crecimiento sin desarrollo: la minería del distrito de Berja en la etapa de apogeo (1820–1850)," *RHE,* III, 2, pp. 265–96.

——— (1991): "Fuentes belgas sobre la electrificación de los tranvías españoles. Le Recueil Financier de Bruselas," *RHE,* IX, 3, pp. 561–73.

——— (1993): *La Sevillana de Electricidad (1894/1930) y la promoción multinacional en el sector electrotécnico*. Granada: Ediciones Némesis.

Núñez, C. E. and G. Tortella (1993): *La maldición divina. Ignorancia y atraso económico en perspectiva histórica*. Madrid: Alianza.

Núñez, Clara Eugenia (1991): "El gasto público en educación entre 1860 y 1935," *HPE,* special issue, pp. 121–46.

——— (1992): *La fuente de la riqueza. Educación y desarrollo económico en la España contemporánea*. Madrid: Alianza

O'Brien, P. K. and L. Prados de la Escosura (1992): "Agricultural Productivity and European Industrialization, 1890–1980," *EHR,* 45, 3, pp. 514–36.

Ojeda Eiseley, Alonso (1988): *Indices de precios en España en el período 1913–1987*. Madrid: Banco de España.

Olson, Mancur (1982): *The Rise and Decline of Nations. Economic Growth, Stagflation, and Social Rigidities*. New Haven: Yale University Press.

Orlando, G. (1969): "Progressi e difficolta dell'agricoltura," in Fuà (ed.).

Ortega Cantero, Nicolás (1984): "Las propuestas hidráulicas del reformismo republicano: del fomento del regadío a la articulación del Plan Nacional de Obras Hidráulicas," *AyS,* 32, pp. 109–97.

Ortíz-Villajos, José María (1994): "Patentes, ingenieros superiores y crecimiento económico en España, 1850–1930," in *Cambio tecnológico y desarrollo económico, II.* VII Simposio de historia económica, Universidad Autónoma de Barcelona, pp. 156–72.

——— (1997): "Tecnología y desarrollo económico en la España contemporánea. Estudio de las patentes registradas en España entre 1882 y 1935." 2 vols. Ph.D. thesis, Universidad de Alcalá.

Otazu, Alfonso (1987): *Los Rothschild y sus socios españoles (1820–1850)*. Madrid: O. Hs. Ediciones.

Palafox, Jordi (1986): "Comercio exterior y vía nacionalista. Algunas consideraciones," in García Delgado (ed.).

———— (1987): "Exportaciones, demanda interna y crecimiento económico en el País Valenciano," in Sánchez-Albornoz (ed.).

———— (1991): *Atraso económico y democracia. La Segunda República y la economía española, 1892–1936.* Barcelona: Editorial Crítica.

Parejo Barranco, Antonio (1989): *La industria lanera española en la segunda mitad del siglo XIX.* Málaga: Universidad de Málaga.

Paris Eguilaz, Higinio (1943): *El movimiento de precios en España. Su importancia para una política de intervención.* Madrid: CSIC.

Pascual, Pere and Carles Sudrià (1993): "Bancos y moneda en Cataluña, 1844–1859: del monopolio bancario al 'free banking.'" Asociación de Historia Económica, pp. 395–405.

Payne, Peter L. (1987): "Industrial Entrepreneurship and Management in Great Britain," in Mathias and Postan (eds.), part I, pp. 180–230.

Pereira, Miriam Halpern (1983): *Livre Cambio e Desenvolvimento Economico. Portugal na segunda metade do século XIX.* 2nd ed. Lisbon: Sá da Costa Editora.

———— (1984): *Política y economía. Portugal en los siglos XIX y XX.* Barcelona: Ariel.

Pérez Blanco, José María (n.d.): "Rasgos macroeconómicos básicos de la evolución de la agricultura española, 1964–1982: crisis actual," *PEE,* 16.

Pérez Moreda, Vicente (1980): *Las crisis de mortalidad en la España interior (siglos XVI-XIX).* Madrid: Siglo XXI.

———— (1983): "En defensa del Censo de Godoy: observaciones previas al estudio de la población activa española de finales del siglo XVIII," in Anes, Rojo, and Tedde (eds.), pp. 283–99.

———— (1985): "La modernización demográfica, 1800–1930," in Sánchez-Albornoz (ed.), pp. 25–62.

Perpiñá y Grau, Román (1972): *De economía hispana, infraestructura, historia.* Barcelona: Ariel.

Pike, Ruth (1966): *Enterprise and Adventure. The Genoese in Seville and the Opening of the New World.* Ithaca, N.Y.: Cornell University Press.

Platt, D. C. M. (1983): "Finanzas extranjeras en España, 1820–1870," *RHE,* I, 1, pp. 121–50.

Pollard, Sidney (1973): "Industrialization and the European Economy," *EHR,* XXIV, 4.

———— (1982): *Peaceful Conquest: The Industrialization of Europe 1760–1970.* Oxford: Oxford University Press

Pounds, N. G. (1947): *An Historical and Political Geography of Europe,* London: George G. Harrap.

Poveda Anadón, Raimundo (1972): *La creación de dinero en España, 1956–1970. Análisis y política.* Madrid: Instituto de Estudios Fiscales.

———— (1986): "Política monetaria y financiera," in Gámir, pp. 29–48.

Prados Arrarte, Jesús (1965): *El plan de desarrollo de España 1964–67. Exposición y crítica.* Madrid: Tecnos.

Prados de la Escosura, Leandro (1981): "Las estadísticas españolas de comercio exterior 1850–1913: el problema de las 'valoraciones'," *MC,* 156, pp. 43–60.

——— (1982): Comercio exterior y crecimiento económico en España, 1826–1913: tendencias a largo plazo, Madrid: Banco de España.

——— (1982b): "Comercio exterior y cambio económico en España (1792–1849)," in Fontana (ed.), pp. 171–249.

——— (1983): "Producción y consumo de tejidos en España, 1800–1913," in Anes, Rojo, and Tedde (eds.), pp. 455-71.

——— (1985): "Las relaciones reales de intercambio entre España y Gran Bretaña durante los siglos XVIII y XIX," in Martín Aceña and Prados (eds.), pp. 119–65.

——— (1986): "Una serie anual del comercio exterior español (1821–1913)," *RHE,* IV, 1, pp. 103–50.

——— (1988): *De imperio a nación. Crecimiento y atraso económico en España (1780–1930).* Madrid: Alianza.

——— (1993a): "Long-run Economic Growth in Spain Since 1800: An International Perspective," in Szirmai, Van Ark, and Pilat (eds.).

——— (1993b): "Spain's Gross Domestic Product, 1850–1990. A New Series," *MEH.*

Prados de la Escosura, Leandro and Vera Zamagni (eds.) (1992): *El desarrollo económico en la Europa del Sur. España e Italia en perspectiva histórica.* Madrid: Alianza.

Presidencia del Gobierno (1963): *Plan de desarrollo económico para el período 1964–67.* Madrid: Comisaría del Plan de Desarrollo Económico.

Puig Raposo, Nuria (1993): "La modernización de la industria del alcohol en Tarragona, Ciudad Real, Navarra y Granada (1888–1953)," in Asociación de Historia Económica, pp. 645–62.

Pujol Andreu, Josep (1986): "Las crisis de sobreproducción en el sector vitivinícola catalán, 1892–1935," in Garrabou, Barciela, and Jiménez Blanco (eds.), pp. 317–46.

Quiroz, Alfonso W. (1993): *Deudas olvidadas. Instrumentos de crédito en la economía colonial peruana, 1750–1820.* Lima: Pontificia Universidad Católica de Perú.

Redonet Maura, José Luis (1961): "La industria de energía eléctrica en España," *Arbor,* pp. 59–91.

Reforma Arancelaria . . ., La (1890): *La Reforma arancelaria y los tratados de comercio.* Información escrita de la Comisión creada por R. D. de 10 de Octubre de 1889. 6 vols. Madrid: Sucesores de Rivadeneira.

Reher, David, N. Pombo, and B. Nogueras (1990): *España a la luz del censo de 1887.* Madrid: INE.

Reher, David-Sven (1986): "Desarrollo urbano y evolución de la población: España, 1787–1930," *RHE,* IV, 1, pp. 39–66.

Reig, Ernest (1990): "La adhesión española al Mercado Común Agrícola," in García Delgado (dir.), pp. 153–76.

Rein, Raanan (1993): *The Franco-Perón Alliance. Relations between Spain and Argentina, 1946–1955,* Pittsburgh: University of Pittsburgh Press.

Reis, Jaime (1982): "Latifúndio e progresso técnico: a difusao da debulha mecânica no Alentejo, 1860–1930," *AS*, 18, 2, pp. 371–433.

———— (1987): "A industrializaçao num país de desenvolvimento lento e tardio: Portugal, 1870–1913," *AS*, 23, pp. 207–27.

———— (1988): "Pan y vino: la crisis agrícola en Portugal a finales del siglo XIX," in Garrabou (ed.).

———— (1993): "El analfabetismo en Portugal en el siglo XIX: una interpretación," in Núñez and Tortella (eds.), pp. 237–69.

RENFE (1981): *Los ferrocarriles y el desarrollo económico de Europa Occidental durante el siglo XIX.* Madrid: Publicaciones de RENFE.

Requeijo, Jaime (1985): *Introducción a la balanza de pagos de España,* 2d. ed. Madrid: Tecnos.

Reseña geográfica y estadística de España (1888). Madrid: Imprenta de la Dirección General del Instituto Geográfico y Estadístico.

Ringrose, David (1970): *Transportation and Economic Stagnation in Spain, 1750–1850.* Durham, N.C.: Duke University Press.

———— (1983): *Madrid and the Spanish Economy, 1560–1850.* Berkeley: University of California Press.

Robert Robert, Antonio (1959): "Industria Química" (fragmento), in *Estudios sobre la unidad económica europea,* VIII, part 2a. Madrid: Estudios Económicos Españoles y Europeos.

Robledo, Ricardo (1988): "Crisis agraria y éxodo rural: emigración española a Ultramar, 1880–1920," in Garrabou (ed.), pp. 212–44.

Rogers, James E. Thorold (1891): *The Economic Interpretation of History.* Londres: T. Fisher Unwin.

Rojo, Luis Angel and José Pérez (1977): *La política monetaria en España: objetivos e instrumentos.* Madrid: Banco de España.

Román, Manuel (1971): *The Limits of Economic Growth in Spain.* New York: Praeger.

Ros Hombravella, J. et al. (1973): *Capitalismo español: de la autarquía a la estabilización.* I *(1939–1950);* II *(1950–1959).* Madrid: Edicusa.

Rosés i Vendoiro, Joan Ramón (1993): "Primeras hipótesis sobre la función de los bancos en la industrialización catalana (1829–1883)," Asociación de Historia Económica, pp. 447–60.

Ruiz Martín, Felipe (1990): *Las finanzas de la Monarquía hispánica en tiempos de Felipe IV (1621–1665).* Madrid: Academia de la Historia.

Sáenz Díaz, Manuel (1878): "Estudio de los alimentos que consume la clase labradora y los braceros de algunas provincias de España," in *Memorias de la Real Academia de Ciencias Exactas, Físicas y Naturales,* vol. 8. Madrid.

Sánchez Alonso, Blanca (1990): "Una nueva serie anual de la emigración española: 1882–1930," *RHE*, VIII, 1, pp. 133–70.

———— (1993): "Los determinantes de la emigración española, 1880–1930." Ph.D. thesis, Instituto Universitario Europeo.

Sánchez-Albornoz, N. and T. Carnero (1981): *Los precios agrícolas durante la segunda mitad del siglo XIX.* Vol. II. *Vino y aceite.* Madrid: Tecnos/Servicio de Estudios de Banco de España.

Sánchez-Albornoz, Nicolás (1963): *Las crisis de subsistencia de España en el siglo XIX.* Rosario, Argentina: Instituto de Investigaciones Históricas .

———— (1964): "Crisis de subsistencias y recesión demográfica: España en 1868," *A,* pp. 27–40.

———— (1968): *España hace un siglo: una economía dual.* Barcelona: Ediciones Península.

———— (1975a): *Jalones en la modernización de España.* Barcelona: Ariel.

———— (1975b): *Los precios agrícolas durante la segunda mitad del siglo XIX.* Vol. I. *Trigo y cebada.* Madrid: Servicio de Estudios del Banco de España.

———— (1977): *España hace un siglo: una economía dual.* Rev. and enl. ed. Madrid: Alianza.

———— (ed.) (1985): *La modernización económica de España.* Madrid: Alianza. (In English, 1987, New York: New York University Press)

Sandberg, Lars G. (1982): "Ignorance, Poverty and Economic Backwardness in the Early Stages of European Industrialization: Variations on Alexander Gerschenkron's Grand Theme," *JEEH,* 11, 3, pp. 675–97. (In Spanish, 1993, in Núñez and Tortella (eds.), pp. 142–70)

Santillán, Ramón (1865): *Memoria histórica sobre los bancos.* Madrid: Fortanet (rept. 1982, Banco de España).

Sanz Ayán, Carmen (1988): *Los banqueros de Carlos II.* Valladolid: Universidad de Valladolid.

Sanz, Angel B. (1926): "Automovilismo, aviación y radiotelefonía," in *El Financiero,* pp. 387–96.

Sanz, Jesús (1986): "La historia contemporánea de los montes públicos españoles, 1812–1930. Notas y reflexiones (II)," in Garrabou, Barciela, and Jiménez Blanco (eds.), pp. 142–70.

Sardá, Juan (1948): *La política monetaria y las fluctuaciones de la economía española en el siglo XIX.* Madrid: CSIC.

———— (1987): *Escritos (1948–1980).* Madrid: Banco de España.

Sarrailh, Jean (1957): *La España Ilustrada de la segunda mitad del siglo XVIII* (trad. Antonio Alatorre). México: Fondo de Cultura Económica.

Schultz, Theodore W. (ed.) (1971): *Investment in Human Capital.* New York: Free Press.

———— (1974): *Economics of the Family, Marriage, Children, and Human Capital.* Chicago: The University of Chicago Press.

Schumpeter, Joseph A. (1961): *The Theory of Economic Development. An Enquiry into Profits, Capital, Credit, Interest, and the Business Cycle.* New York: Oxford University Press.

Schwartz, Pedro and Manuel Jesús González (1978): *Una historia del Instituto Nacional de Industria (1941–1976).* Madrid: Tecnos.

Segura, Julio (1990): "Intervención pública y política de bienestar: el papel del Estado," in García Delgado (dir.), pp. 831–57.

——— et al. (1989): *La industria española en la crisis (1978–1984)*. Madrid: Alianza.

Serrano Sanz, José María (1986): "La política arancelaria española al término de la primera guerra mundial: proteccionismo, Arancel Cambó y tratados comerciales," in García Delgado (ed.), pp. 199–223.

——— (1987): *El viraje proteccionista en la Restauración. La política comercial española, 1875–1895*. Madrid: Siglo XXI.

Shaw, Valerie J. (1977): "Exportaciones y despegue económico: el mineral de hierro de Vizcaya, la región de la ría de Bilbao y algunas de sus aplicaciones para España," *MC*, 142, pp. 87ff.

Sierra, Fermín de la (1953): *La concentración económica en las industrias básicas españolas*. Madrid: Instituto de Estudios Políticos.

Silva, C. da (1980): "Acerca da génese das relaçoes de produçao características do latifúndio em Portugal," in Barros (ed.), pp. 47–96.

Simon Segura, Francisco (1973): *La desamortización española del siglo XIX*. Madrid: Instituto de Estudios Fiscales.

Simpson, James (1985): "La producción de vinos en Jerez de la Frontera, 1850–1900," in Martín Aceña and Prados (eds.), pp. 166–91.

——— (1985a): "El consumo y producción de cereales panificables," mimeo. Informe "Proyecto Europeo," Banco de España.

——— (1987): "La elección de técnica en el cultivo triguero y el atraso de la agricultura española a finales del siglo XIX," *RHE*, V, 2, pp. 271–99.

——— (1988): "Technical Change, Labour Absorption and Living Standards in Andalucía 1886–1936," work paper #8810, Universidad Complutense.

——— (1989): "La producción agraria y el consumo español en el siglo XIX," *RHE*, VII, 2, pp. 355–88.

——— (1989b): "New Estimates for Agricultural Production 1890–1936," mimeo.

——— (1992): "Los límites del crecimiento agrario: España, 1860–1936," in Prados and Zamagni (eds.), pp. 103–38.

——— (1995): *Spanish Agriculture: The Long Siesta, 1765–1965*. Cambridge, Eng.: Cambridge University Press. (In Spanish, 1997, Madrid: Alianza Editorial.)

Smith, Adam (1776): *An Inquiry into the Nature and Causes of the Wealth of Nations*. New York: The Modern Library [1937].

Solow, Robert M. (1957): "Technical Change and the Aggregate Production Function," *Review of Economics and Statistics*, 34, pp. 312–20.

Stone, Lawrence (1969): "Literacy and Education in England, 1640–1900," *PP*, 42.

Sudrià, Carles (1983): "Notas sobre la implantación y el desarrollo de la industria de gas en España, 1840–1901," *RHE*, I, 2, pp. 97–118.

——— (1983a): "La exportación en el desarrollo de la industria algodonera española, 1875–1920," *RHE*, I, 2, pp. 369–86.

——— (1984): "Atraso económico y resistencia a la innovación: el caso del gas natural en España," *DAG*, 5.

——— (1987): "Un factor determinante: la energía," in Nadal, Carreras, and Sudrià (eds.), pp. 313–63.

——— (1990): "La industria eléctrica y el desarrollo económico de España," in García Delgado (ed.), pp. 149–84.

————— (1990b): "La electricidad en España antes de la guerra civil: una réplica," *RHE*, VIII, 3, pp. 651–60.

Summers, Robert y Alan Heston (1988): "A New Set of International Comparisons of Real Product and Price Levels Estimates for 130 Countries, 1950–1985," *RIW*, 34, 1.

Svennilson, I. (1954): *Growth and Stagnation in the European Economy.* Geneva.

Szirmai, A., B. Van Ark, and D. Pilat, eds. (1993): *Explaining Economic Growth. Essays in Honor of Angus Maddison,* Amsterdam: North Holland.

Tallada Pauli, José Ma. (1946): *Historia de las finanzas españolas en el siglo XIX.* Madrid: Espasa-Calpe.

Tamames, Ramón (1960): *Estructura económica de España.* Madrid: Sociedad de Estudios y Publicaciones.

————— (1961): *La lucha contra los monopolios.* Madrid: Tecnos.

————— (1967): *Los monopolios en España,* Madrid: ZYX.

————— (1974): *Estructura económica de España.* 3 vols. Madrid: Guadiana.

————— (1990): *Estructura económica de España,* 19th ed. Madrid: Alianza.

Tedde de Lorca, Pedro (1974): "La banca privada española durante la Restauración (1974–1914)," in Tortella (dir.), pp. 217–455.

————— (1978): "Las compañías ferroviarias en España, 1855–1935," in Artola (ed.), II, pp. 11–356.

————— (1980): "La Compañía de los Ferrocarriles Andaluces (1878–1920): una empresa de transportes en la España de la Restauración," *IE*.

————— (1981): "Capital y ferrocarriles: la estrategia de la Compañía de Ferrocarriles Andaluces en el conjunto ferroviario español (1874–1900)," in RENFE, pp. 165–84.

————— (1983): "Comerciantes y banqueros madrileños al final del Antiguo Régimen," in Anes, Rojo, and Tedde (eds.), pp. 301–31.

————— (1985): "Sobre los orígenes históricos del subdesarrollo andaluz: algunas hipótesis," in Sánchez-Albornoz (ed.), pp. 299–318.

————— (1985b): "El gasto público en España, 1875–1906: un análisis comparativo con las economías europeas," in Martín Aceña and Prados (eds.), pp. 233–61.

————— (1987): "Los negocios de Cabarrús con la Real Hacienda (1780–1783)," *RHE*, V, 3, pp. 527–51.

————— (1988): *El Banco de San Carlos (1782–1829).* Madrid: Banco de España/ Alianza.

————— (1991): "La naturaleza de las Cajas de Ahorros: sus raíces históricas," *PEE*, 46.

————— (1993): "El Banco Exterior de España, una aproximación histórica," typescript.

Tena Junguito, Antonio (1985): "Una reconstrucción del comercio exterior español, 1914–1935: la rectificación de las estadísticas oficiales," *RHE*, III, 1, pp. 77–119.

————— (1988): "Importación, niveles de protección y producción de material eléctrico en España (1890–1935)," *RHE*, VI, 2, pp. 341–71.

————— (1989): "Comercio exterior," in *EH*.

Titos Martínez, Manuel (1979): "La Caja General de Depósitos (1852–1874)," *MC*.

——— (1989): "La Caja de Madrid en el siglo XIX: ¿Actividad asistencial o financiera?" *RHE,* VII, 3, pp. 557–87.

——— (1991): "La respuesta histórica de las Cajas de Ahorros a las demandas de la sociedad española," *PEE.*

Tomás y Valiente, Francisco (1971): *El marco político de la desamortización en España.* Barcelona: Ariel.

Toniolo, Gianni (1988): *Storia economica dell'Italia liberale 1850–1918.* Bologna: Il Mulino.

——— (ed.) (1978): *L'economia italiana 1861–1940.* Rome: Laterza.

Torres Martínez, Manuel de (1956): *Juicio de la actual política española.* Madrid: Aguilar.

——— et al. (1960): "El comercio exterior y el desarrollo económico español," *ICE* (Dec.), pp. 18–56.

Torres Villanueva, Eugenio (1989): *Ramón de la Sota: historia económica de un empresario (1857–1936),* 2 vols. Madrid: Editorial de la Universidad Complutense.

Tortella, Gabriel (1964): "El desarrollo de la industria azucarera y la guerra de Cuba," *MC,* 91, pp. 131–163.

——— (1973): *Los orígenes del capitalismo en España. Banca, industria y ferrocarriles en el siglo XIX.* Madrid: Tecnos.

——— (1974): "Las magnitudes monetarias y sus determinantes," in Tortella (dir.) (1974a), pp. 457–534.

——— (1978): "La formación de capital en España, 1874–1914: reflexiones para un planteamiento de la cuestión," *HPE,* 55, pp. 399–415.

——— (1981): "La economía española, 1830–1900," in Tuñón de Lara (ed.), pp. 133–40.

——— (1983a): "National Income Estimation by Means of Monetary Variables, the Case of Spain, 1772–1972. Some Preliminary Results," in Fremdling and O'Brien (eds.)

——— (1983b): "La primera gran empresa química española: la Sociedad Española de la Dinamita (1872–1896)," in Anes, Rojo and Tedde (eds.), pp. 431–53.

——— (1985a): "Producción y productividad agraria, 1830–1930," in Sánchez-Albornoz (ed.), pp. 63–88.

——— (1985b): "La economía española a finales del siglo XIX y principios del siglo XX," in García Delgado (ed.), pp. 81–116.

——— (1987): "Agriculture: A Slow Moving Sector, 1830–1935," in Sánchez-Albornoz (ed.).

——— (1987b): "La implantación del monopolio de los explosivos en España," *HPE,* 108/9, pp. 393–409.

——— (1990): "CAMPSA y el monopolio de petróleos, 1927–1947," in Martín Aceña and Comín (eds.).

——— (1991): "El monopolio de petróleos y CAMPSA, 1927–1947," *HPE,* special issue, pp. 171–89.

——— (1991a): *Introducción a la economía para historiadores.* 2d ed. Madrid: Tecnos.

——— (1992a): "La integración vertical de una gran empresa durante la dictadura de Primo de Rivera. La Unión Española de Explosivos, 1917–1929," in García Delgado (coor.), pp. 359–93.

——— (1992b): "La historia económica de España en el siglo XIX: ensayo comparativo con los casos de Italia y Portugal," in Prados and Zamagni (eds.), pp. 56–80.

——— (1994): "Patterns of Economic Retardation and Recovery in Southwestern Europe in the Nineteenth and Twentieth Centuries," *EHR*, 47, 1, pp. 1–24.

——— (s.f.): "Historia de la Unión Española de Explosivos," typescript.

——— (dir.) (1974a): *La Banca española en la Restauración*. I. *Política y finanzas*. Madrid: Banco de España.

——— (dir.) (1974b): *La Banca española en la Restauración*. II. *Datos para una historia económica*. Madrid: Banco de España.

——— et al. (1970): *Ensayos sobre la economía española a mediados del siglo XIX, realizados en el Servicio de Estudios del Banco de España*. Madrid: Raycar Impresores.

——— et al. (1978): "La balanza del comercio exterior español: un experimento histórico-estadístico, 1875–1913," in García Delgado and Segura (eds.), pp. 487–513.

——— et al. (1981): *Historia de España* (Tuñón de Lara, dir.). Barcelona: Labor.

Tortella, Gabriel and J. C. Jiménez (1986): *Historia del Banco de Crédito Industrial*. Madrid: Alianza/Banco de Crédito Industrial.

Tortella, Gabriel and Jordi Palafox (1983): "Banca e industria en España, 1918–1936," *IE*, 20, pp. 33–64.

Tortella, Teresa (forthcoming). "Guide to Sources of Information on Foreign Investment in Spain (1780–1914)," International Council of Archives.

Tuñón de Lara, Manuel (ed.) (1981): *Revolución burguesa, oligarquía y constitucionalismo (1834–1923)* (Vol. VIII, *Historia de España)*, Barcelona: Labor.

U.S. Bureau of the Census (1960): *Historical Statistics of the United States: Colonial Times to 1957*. Washington: U.S. Government Printing Office.

Valdaliso, Jesús M. (1991): *Los navieros vascos y la marina mercante en España, 1860–1935. Una historia económica*. Bilbao: Instituto Vasco de Administración Pública.

Valério, Nuno (1983) "O produto nacional de Portugal entre 1913 e 1947: Uma primeira aproximaçao," *RHEeS*.

Vandellós, Josep A. (1985): *Catalunya, poble decadent*. Barcelona: Edicons 62.

Velarde Fuertes, Juan (1955): "Consideraciones sobre alguna actividades monopolísticas en el mercado papelero español," *REP*, 6, 3.

——— (1967): *Sobre la decadencia económica de España*. Madrid: Tecnos.

——— (1968): *Política económica de la dictadura*. Madrid: Guadiana.

——— (ed.) (1969): *Lecturas de economía española*. Madrid: Gredos.

Vicens i Vives, J. and M. Llorens (1961): *Industrials i polítics del segle XIX*. Barcelona: Editorial Vicens Vives.

Vicens Vives, Jaime (1959): *Manual de Historia Económica de España*. Barcelona: Teide.

Vilar, Pierre (1962): *La Catalogne dans l'Espagne moderne. Recherches sur les fondements économiques des structures nationales*. 3 vols. Paris: SEVPEN.

Villalonga Villalba, Ignacio (1961): "La banca española en lo que va de siglo," *Arbor,* pp. 93–111.

Viñals, José (ed.) (1992): *La economía española ante el Mercado Unico europeo. Las claves del proceso de integración.* Madrid: Alianza.

Viñas, Angel et al. (1979): *Política comercial exterior en España (1931–1975).* 2 vols. Madrid: Banco Exterior de España.

Vincent, Bernard (1983): "Economía y sociedad en el Reino de Granada (Siglo XVIII)," in AA.VV., pp. 377–405.

White, Eugene N. (1987): "¿Fueron inflacionarias las finanzas estatales en el siglo XVIII? Una nueva interpretación de los vales reales," *RHE,* V, 3, pp. 509–26.

Williamson, Jeffrey G. (1965): "Regional Inequality and the Process of Regional Development: A Description of the Patterns," *Economic Development and Cultural Change,* 42, 1, pp. 3–45.

Willis, Robert J. (1974): "Economic Theory of Fertility Behavior," in Schultz (ed.), pp. 25–75.

Woodruff, William (1966): *The Impact of Western Man. A Study of Europe's Role in the World Economy, 1750–1960.* New York: St. Martin's Press.

Yun Casalilla, Bartolomé (ed.) (1991): *Estudios sobre capitalismo agrario, crédito e industria en Castilla (siglos XIX y XX).* Salamanca: Junta de Castilla y León.

Zamagni, Vera (1978): "Istruzione e sviluppo economico. Il caso italiano 1861–1913," in Toniolo (ed.), pp. 137–78.

———— (1984): "The Daily Wages of Industrial Workers in the Giolittian Period (1898–1913)," *RSE,* 1, pp. 59–93.

———— (1986): "A Comparison of Real Industrial Wages in Belgium, France, Germany, Italy, Sweden and the U.K. in the First Decade of the XXth Century . . ." Paper given at the Bellaggio Conference on "Productivity: International Comparisons . . ."

———— (1993): "Instrucción y desarrollo económico en Italia, 1861–1913," in Núñez and Tortella (eds.), pp. 181–222.

Zambrana Pineda, Juan Francisco (1987): *Crisis y modernización del olivar español.* Madrid: Ministerio de Agricultura, Pesca y Alimentación.

Abbreviations for Journals

A	*Anuario del Instituto de Investigaciones Históricas*
AESC	*Annales E. S. C.*
AS	*Análise Social*
ASI	*Annali di Storia d'Impresa*
AyS	*Agricultura y Sociedad*
DAG	*Documents d'Anàlisi Geogràfica*
EEH	*Explorations in Economic History*
EHA	*Estudis d'Historia Agraria*
EHR	*Economic History Review, 2nd ser.*
HPE	*Hacienda Pública Española*

ICE	*Información Comercial Española*
IE	*Investigaciones Económicas*
JEEH	*Journal of European Economic History*
JEH	*Journal of Economic History*
MC	*Moneda y Crédito*
MCV	*Mélanges de la Casa de Velázquez*
MEH	*Ministerio de Economía y Hacienda, Dirección General de Planificación, Documentos de Trabajo*
PEE	*Papeles de Economía Española*
PP	*Past and Present*
REP	*Revista de Economía Política*
RHE	*Revista de Historia Económica*
RHES	*Revue d'Histoire Economique et Sociale*
RHEeS	*Revista de História Económica e Social*
RIW	*Review of Income and Wealth*
RSE	*Rivista di Storia Economica*

Index

Absentee ownership, 12
Acciones concertadas, see Production agreements
AEG. *See* Allegmeine Elektrizitaets Gesellschaft
Aeronautic industry (CASA), 313, 318
Agencia Industrial del Estado (AIE), 345
Agrarian reform. *See* Land reform
Agricultura Española, La (journal), 181
Agricultural Reform Law, 269, 271–272
Agriculture: economic development and, 7–11, 20, 67–68; foreign competition and, 20; modernization in, 20; eighteenth-century trends, 23–27; nineteenth-century trends, 31, 50, 59–67, 68–69; protectionism and, 41, 66–67, 200, 267–269; land distribution and, 51; disentailment and, 58–59; production and productivity trends, 59–67, 68–69, 282–284, 294–296; fallow land, 63–64; Mediterranean, 65–66, 71–72, 443–444; contributions to economic development, 68–72; tax burden of, 70; exports, 71–72, 324, 369, 371; chemical industry and, 93; budget deficits and, 178; land tax and, 178–182; innovation and foreign entrepreneurs in, 210–212; credit, 273–274; state intervention, 274–278; water policy, 278–280; land under irrigation, 280; plot fragmentation and, 281–282; twentieth-century trends, 282–284, 286–287, 294–296; workforce trends, 284–285; capitalization of, 285; human capital and, 286; growth in, 286–287; productive structure changes, 287–289; fishing industry, 289–290; woodlands and open hill lands, 290–294; compared to European Community agriculture, 294–296; European Community agricultural policy and, 296–297; industry and, 322–323; revolution in, 443
Agustín de Heredia, Manuel, 86

AIE. *See* Agencia Industrial del Estado
Alcalá de los Gazules, 181
Alcalá University, 48
Alcohol production, 94
Alcoy, 83
Aldama family, 389
Alfonso XII, 29–30, 184, 198
Algeria, 355, 356
Allegmeine Elektrizitaets Gesellschaft (AEG), 217, 218, 352
Almadén, 107, 108, 189
Almanac Mercantil, 208
Altos Hornos de Bilbao/Vizcaya, 89, 305
Altos Hornos y Fábricas de Hierro y Acero, 88, 89
Alvarez Llano, Roberto, 436
American Civil War, 79, 140
American Iron and Steel Association, 101
Anarchists, 237
Andalucía, 435, 436; iron and steel industry, 86–87; wine industry, 92; population growth, 258
Anes, Rafael, 165
Antequera, 83
Anti-colonial revolutions, 441
Arburúa, Manuel, 320
Ardanaz, Constantino, 185
Argentaria Corporation, 405
Argentina, 276, 365; migration to, 40; foreign trade with Spain, 144; capital export to, 148; cotton textile exports to, 303
Aribau, Benaventura Carlos, 197
Association for Tariff Reform, 197
Astilleros del Nervión, 95
Asturiana de Minas, 94
Asturias, 87
Autarkist policy/period: economic practices and policies of, 315–317; role of the Instituto Nacional de Industria, 317–319; economic growth under, 319–320; modifications encouraging growth, 320–

Autarkist policy/period (continued)
323; inflationary financing, 323–324;
foreign trade bottlenecks, 324; labor
market and, 324–325; supply rigidity
and, 325; monopolies and, 325–327; liberalization, 327–337; MATESA scandal,
335–337; transition to democracy, 340–
341; legacy of, 342–343; early tendencies toward, 362; balance of payments
and, 364; private banking and, 391–393;
protectionist trade policy, 431–432; history of, 449, 450
Automobile industry, 313; effects of liberalization on, 329–332; foreign trade and,
371–372
Axis powers, 315, 321
Ayacucho, battle of, 28
Azaña regime, 271, 415
Azcárate, Gumersindo, 197

Balance of payments: nineteenth-century
trends, 147–155; energy crisis and, 342;
work of preparing, 359; current account
transactions in, 360, 361; international
payments in, 360–361; twentieth-cen-
tury trends, 360–369
Balance of trade, 360; nineteenth-century
trends, 135–147; under Franco, 324;
twentieth-century trends, 369–373
Banco Alemán Transatlántico, 210
Banco Bilbao Vizcaya, 399
Banco Central, 387, 389
Banco Central Hispano, 399
Banco de Barcelona, 162, 163, 166, 167,
168, 170, 220, 388
Banco de Bilbao, 166, 167, 168, 388
Banco de Catalonia, 403
Banco de Comercio, 168, 388
Banco de Crédito Agrícola, 273
Banco de Crédito de la Construcción, 403
Banco de Crédito Industrial, 300, 366, 394,
396, 402–403
Banco de Crédito Local, 403
Banco de Isabel II, 162
Banco de la Unión Minera, 389
Banco de San Fernando, 161–162, 163,
202
Banco de Santander, 167, 168, 389
Banco de Vitoria, 388
Banco de Vizcaya, 387, 388
Banco di Roma, 210
Banco Español Comercial, 210

Banco Español de Crédito, 209, 387, 389
Banco Español de San Fernando, 162
Banco Exterior, 387, 403, 404
Banco Franco-Español, 209
Banco General de Madrid, 209
Banco Guipuzcoano, 388, 389
Banco Hipotecario, 166–167, 189, 191,
192, 273, 402
Banco Hispano, 134
Banco Hispano-Alemán, 210
Banco Hispano-Americano, 221, 387, 388–
389
Banco Nacional de San Carlos, 23, 162,
202, 208
Banco Popular de España, 209, 387
Banco Urquijo, 134, 387, 389
Banking, 23, 337; agricultural savings and,
71; railroads and, 121; export activities
and, 146; nineteenth-century history,
161–170; issuing banks, 164, 165–166,
167; credit societies, 164–165, 167–168,
171; mixed banking, 167–169, 171–172,
387–388, 393–395; joint-stock banks,
168–169; savings banks, 169, 399–402;
presence of foreigners in, 208–210;
Spanish entrepreneurs, 220–221; agricultural credit and, 273–274; money
supply and, 383, 385; crisis in, 397–399;
foreign banks, 399; "official" sector,
402–405; reputation of, 405; Franco regime and, 405–406; twentieth-century
trends, 405–407; monopoly and, 406;
national debt and, 423–424. See also Private banking
Banking Corporation (Corporación
Bancaria), 398, 399
Banking laws, 121, 163, 202, 203, 390–
391; of 1856, 164; of 1946, 392; of 1962,
395, 401, 403–404, 406
"Bank money," 204
Banknotes, 160, 202, 204; issuing banks
and, 164, 165–166; in money supply
growth and composition, 382–384
Bank of Spain, 170, 171–172, 383; current
account balances, 161; number of
branches, 162, 166; creation of, 163;
monopoly of note issue, 165–166; absorption of issuing banks, 167; short-
term state loans, 167; concessions given
to, 191, 192; monopoly of banknote issue, 191; agricultural credit and, 274;
costs of wheat subsidization and, 277–

278; private banking and, 387, 388–389; evolution as a central bank, 389–391; Banking Law of 1946 and, 392; nationalization of, 395; banking crisis and, 398, 399; savings banks and, 401; twentieth-century monetary policy and, 427–428
Banque de Paris et des Pays Bas (Paribas), 191, 209
Baracaldo, 88
Barcelona: urbanization, 44; industrialization, 74; cotton industry, 76; woolen industry, 82; shipping industry, 95, 119–120; gas companies, 112; railroad connections, 122, 123; banking, 168, 388; electric industry, 217, 218, 351; tramway companies, 218; twentieth century social unrest, 236, 237; city planning, 261
Barcelona de Electricidad, 218
Barcelona-Tarragona-Francia railroad, 123
Barcelona Traction, Light, and Power Company, 218, 352
Barcelona-Zaragoza-Pamplona railroad, 122
Barrera de Irimo, Antonio, 342
Basagoiti, Antonio, 220–221, 388–389
Basconia Company, 305
Base quinta (customs tariff), 199
Basque Country: iron and steel industry, 87–89, 305–306; ore export industry, 100, 103, 104; shipping industry, 120; regional tariffs and, 131; banking, 168, 170, 388, 399; hydroelectricity, 352; economic history of, 435; state interventionism and, 436
Bauer, Ignacio, 209
Begoña, 87
Béjar, 83
Belgium: literacy in, 12, 13, 17; Spanish ore industry and, 98, 100; Spanish zinc mining and, 107, 215; Spanish streetcar companies and, 218; Spanish explosives industry and, 310
Bessemer, Henry, 98; Bessemer converters, 85, 89, 98, 102, 213
Bicycles, 329
Bilbaína de Navegación, 120
Bilbao, 87; ore export industry, 100, 103, 104; banking, 388
Bimetallism, 158, 159–160
Birth rates, 37–38; declining, 242–243, 245, 246, 252–256; birth control, 254
Bisectoral model of growth, 286–287

Black market, 276
Bonaparte, Joseph, 53, 54
Bonaplata brothers, 76
Borrego, Andrés, 197
Bosch y Labrús, Pedro, 197
Bossism *(caciquismo)*, 27, 31, 180
Bravo Murillo reform, 187, 188
Bretton Woods agreement, 338, 397
Broder, Albert, 151, 152, 153, 217
Brussels Tariff System, 432
Budget: history of, 156; nineteenth-century trends, 176–184; revenue sources, 178–183; expenditures, 183–184
Budget deficits: economic development and, 5, 12; nineteenth-century trends, 176–178, 184; wheat subsidization and, 277–278; twentieth-century trends, 422
Budget Statistics, 179, 183
Building industry, 307–309
Business: entrepreneurship and, 206–227; entrepreneurial attitudes, 219–227; Spanish entrepreneurs, 220–221. See also Banking, Industry
Butano SA, 355

Cabarrus, François, 208
Cabotaje, see Coastal trade
Caciquismo, see Bossism
Caixa (Caja) de Barcelona, 356, 399
Caja de Depósitos, 169
Calvo Sotelo, José, 349, 379, 403, 414–415
Calvo Sotelo, Leopoldo, 454
Calvo Sotelo National Company, 350
Camacho reform *(arreglo)*, 176, 187, 189
Cambó, Francisco, 352, 390, 430; tariff, 268, 430, 431
Cameron, Rondo, 187, 208
Campo, José, 112, 217, 220
CAMPSA, 325, 349–351, 355, 394
Canary Islands, 258
Canga Argüelles, José, 53
Canning industry, 304–305
Cánovas del Castillo, Antonio, 29–30, 446; tariff, 41
Capital goods, 70; exports, 148; imports, 148, 321, 324, 366, 369. See also Foreign investment
Capital markets: effect of government finances on, 156; crowding-out effect in, 157; budget deficits and, 178
Carande, Ramón, 107
Carlists/Carlist Party, 28, 30, 31, 175

Carlist wars, 35, 99, 116, 131, 186

Carlos III, 26, 27, 52, 194, 224

Carlos IV, 23, 27, 53, 58, 186

Carner, Jaume, 415

Carr, Raymond, 31

Carreras, Albert, 73, 111, 113–114, 218, 234, 299, 436, 437

Cartillas de evaluación, see Valuation books

Cartillas de racionamiento, see Ration books

Casa de Contratación de las Indias, 207

Castelar, Emilio, 197

Castile-León, 207–208, 281–282, 436

Cast iron, 85, 89

Catalana de Gas, 216, 356

Catalonia: demographic trends, 45; population occupational structure, 45–46; industrialization, 73, 74; cotton industry, 76–80; woolen industry, 82–83; silk industry, 83–84; grain-milling industry, 92; wine industry, 92; metallurgical and mechanical businesses, 94–95; soft coal deposits, 111; shipping industry, 119–120; banking, 168, 169–170, 399; studies of, 232–233; population growth, 257–258; land problem, 271; economic history of, 435; state interventionism and, 436

Catholic Church: literacy and, 17; education and, 48; disentailment of lands, 51–56, 58; state expenditures on, 183; anticapitalist views, 225

Catholic countries: birth rates and, 253

Caustic soda, 93, 216, 310

Cavestany, Rafael, 276–277

Cazalla de la Sierra, 86–87

Cédula personal, see Poll tax

Celibacy rates, 38

Cement industry, 220, 307–309, 312–313

Central Banking Council, 391

Central University of Madrid, 48

Cerdá, Ildefonso, 261

Cereals, 8, 9, 10, 20; eighteenth-century price trends, 23–26; nineteenth-century productivity levels, 60–64, 65; nineteenth-century export levels, 69; state intervention and, 275–276. *See also* Wheat

Chamorro, Santiago, 359

Checks, 381–382

Chemical industry, 93–94; mining and, 109; British, 214; foreign entrepreneurs, 216; growth and diversification in, 308,

310–312; foreign investment, 310; effects of liberalization on, 329, 332–333

Childbirth, 249

Child labor, 251

Cholera, 35, 247

Church, *see* Catholic Church

City planning, 261–262

Civil War, 236, 237, 239, 446; demographic consequences, 244, 248; impact on industrial growth, 314–315; industrial recovery and, 319; money supply and, 380, 381, 383, 384; Franco's actions in, 449

Climate: agriculture and, 10; famine and, 34–35

Clipper ships, 119–120

Clothing industry, 329

Coal: coal-gas industry, 112; imports, 143, 348; consumption levels, 346, 349

Coal industry: textile industry and, 75; iron and steel industry and, 84, 85–86; impact on industrialization, 110–112; railroads and, 128; protectionism and, 347–349

Coastal trade *(cabotaje)*, 116–118

Código Comercial, see Commercial Code

Codorniú, Ricardo, 291

Coinage, 157–158, 383

Coke (coal), 84, 86

Coll, Sebastián, 347, 348–349

Colmeiro, Manuel, 197, 224

Colonies: foreign trade and, 136; loss of, 235

Comín, F., 318, 335, 344, 410

Commerce: Catalonian labor force and, 45–46; internal trade, 130–134; tax on, 182; nineteenth century policies, 192–202. *See also* Foreign trade

Commercial Code *(Código comercial)* (1829), 130, 131

Commercial Trade Statistics, 147

Commercial treaties, 199, 222

Committee of Paris, 209

Common Agricultural Policy (EEC), 296–297

Common Market, 432, 433–434. *See also* European Economic Community

Communication, 133–134

Communism, 442, 448; Communist Party, 238

Compagnie des Mines de Cuivre d'Huelva, 97, 106, 214

Compagnie Minière des Asturies, 87
Compañía de Fundición y Construcción de Máquinas, 95
Compañía General de Crédito en España, 209, 217
Compañía Hispano-Americana de Electricidad, 352
Compañía Madrileña de Electricidad, 112, 217
Compañía Minas de Potasa de Suria, 312
Compañía Telefónica Nacional de España, 134
Compañía Transatlántica, 119
Compañía Ybarra, 88, 98
Compensatory taxes, 433
Comuneros, 207–208
La Concepción, 86
Consejo Superior Bancario, 391
Conservative Party, 29–30; disentailment and, 53; national debt and, 186
La Constancia, 86
Construcciones Aeronáuticas, 313
Construction industry, 307–309, 337, 354
Consumer goods: agricultural sector as consumer, 69; import levels, 143
Consumer industries: Hoffmann's law and, 301–302, 305; twentieth-century trends, 302–305; effects of liberalization on, 328–329, 333–334
Consumption. See Tuberculosis
Contribución de utilidades, 413. See also Taxes
Contribución industrial y de comercio, 182. See also Taxes
Contribución territorial, 178. See also Taxes
Conversions, 187–188, 189–190, 424–425
Copper mining: location of deposits, 105–106; Río Tinto Company, 106–107; foreign entrepreneurs, 214–215
Córdoba, 104, 105
Cork industry, 93
Corn Laws (England), 195, 196
Corporación Bancaria, 398, 399
Cortes: of Cádiz, 28, 29, 130, 445; disentailment and, 53–54
Costa, Joaquín, 279, 292
Cotton industry: Industrial Revolution and, 74; in England, 75, 76; growth and development of, 75–80; technology and, 76–77; raw cotton imports, 77–78; markets and, 78–80; contributions to Spanish economy, 80–81; protectionism and, 80–82, 196–197, 200, 302–303; impact

on other textile industries, 82, 84; energy sources and, 111; twentieth-century trends, 302–303
Credit: societies, 164–165, 167–168, 171; preferential, 335–336; Bank of Spain and, 391; institutions, 403, 404–405
Crédit Foncier et Agricole du Sud d'Espagne, 209
Crédit Lyonnais, 209
Crédit Mobilier, 164, 165, 171
Crédito de la Unión Minera, 388
Crédito Mobiliario Español, 165, 167, 208, 209, 217, 389
Crimean War, 35, 140, 163, 201
Cros, François, 216; Cros Company, 93, 310, 311
Cuba: Spanish cotton industry, 79–80; capital export to, 148; cotton textile exports to, 303
Cuban War, 41, 141, 190, 412
Currency: depreciation, 41, 171; units, 158
Current accounts: balances, 160–161; deposits, 204; transactions, balance of payments and, 360, 361
Customs revenues, 183
Customs tariffs: migration and, 41; impact on agricultural productivity, 66–67; wheat and, 66–67, 267–269; impact on exports, 67; cotton industry and, 80–82; "infant industry protection" and, 81–82, 144, 194; impact on foreign trade, 141, 201–202; assigned valuations of imports and exports, 146–147; function of, 192–193; nineteenth-century trends, 193–202; impact on economic development, 200; revenues from, 200–201; lobbying efforts for, 220; coal and, 348; twentieth-century trends, 429–430, 431–434; extra duties and, 432–433. See also Protectionism

Dalmau-Xifra Company, 112, 217
Debt: railroad companies and, 129. See also National debt
Deflation, 425, 426
Deforestation, 128, 291, 292
Delfín (steamship), 95
Democracy, 234–235, 240; transition period, 340–341, 452–455
Demographic trends: eighteenth century trends, 25; economic modernization

Demographic trends *(continued)*
and, 32; mortality rates, 32–36, 242–
243, 245, 246–248; nineteenth-century
trends, 32–38; birth rates, 37–38, 242–
243, 245, 246, 252–256; marriage patterns, 38–39; migration, 39–46; internal
population distribution, 41–44, 256–259;
urbanization, 44, 259–262; in Catalonia,
45–46; twentieth-century trends, 233–
234, 241–256; life expectancy, 248–252;
age at marriage, 254–255. *See also* Population
Deposit Guarantee Fund, 398
Derecho diferencial de bandera, see Flag tax
Derechos reales, see Real estate tax
Desamortización (disentail), 12, 26–27; marriage rates and, 39; overview of, 51–56;
Manuals, 54; impact on land ownership,
56–58; victims of, 58; agricultural pro-
ductivity and, 58–59; revenues from,
183; national debt and, 185, 186–187;
impact on woodlands and open hill
lands, 292–293
Deutsche Bank, 210, 217
Díaz de Moral, Juan, 446
Dictámen de la Comisión del Patrón Oro, see
Report of the Commission on the Gold
Standard
Dictatorships, 11, 236, 237–240. *See also*
Franco, Francisco; Franco regime
Diet, 69
Diezmos, see Tithes
Dirección General de Banca y Bolsa,
392
Dirección General de Estadística de la
Riqueza, 179
Dirección General de Montes, 293
Direct taxes, 178–182
Discount rates, 203
Diseases: epidemics, 35–36; endemic, 36;
reduced incidence, 247
Disentailment, Disentail, *see*
Desamortización
Doetsch, Heinrich, 215
Domecq family, 92, 212
Domestic markets: agricultural sector as,
69–70; cotton industry, 78–79; integra-
tion, 130–134
Donges, Jürgen B., 298–299, 319
Duro-Felguera company, 305
Duties, *see* Customs tariffs
Dynamite, 94, 109

Easterlin, Richard, 457
Eastern Europe, 443
Echegaray, José, 197
Economic determinism, 452
Economic development: historical pattern
of, 1–7, 228–231; agriculture and, 7–11,
20, 50; sociopolitical factors and, 11;
budget deficits and, 12; literacy and, 12–
17, 49; education and, 17–19; key factors in, 19–21; impact on seasonal life
patterns, 39; human capital and technology in, 46–47; transportation and, 115;
railroads and, 124–125, 128; foreign
trade and, 134–135; twentieth-century
trends, 228–231, 232, 233–234, 236–
340; mortality rates and, 246–247; declining birth rates and, 253–254; energy
and, 346
Economic history: nineteenth and twentieth centuries compared, 1–7; historical
periodization and, 231–234; twentieth-
century political history and, 234–240;
economic development and social transformations, 440–444; future trends,
457–462
Economic isolationism, 234
Economic ministries: expenditures, 419–
421
Education: school attendance, 17–19; poverty and, 19; human capital and, 46–47;
nineteenth-century trends, 47–49; backwardness in, 225–226; twentieth-century trends, 263–266; public expenditures on, 420; regional investment in,
439; in underdeveloped countries, 460
Election-rigging *(pucherazo)*, 27
Electric companies, 112, 217–218, 311,
352, 353
Electric industry, 112–113, 323; autarkic
policies and, 316–317; twentieth century
trends, 351–354
Electrochemical company (Flix), 217
Emigrant remittances, 147–148, 365, 366,
369
Emphyteutic leasing, 271
Empresa Nacional de Electricidad, 353
ENAGAS, 356
ENCASO, 353
Energy: nineteenth-century trends, 110–
113; agricultural consumption, 285; re-
conversion period and, 337; petroleum
crisis, 338–340; consumption levels, 346,

349, 351; industrialization and, 346–347; twentieth-century trends, 346–356

Energy crisis, 338–340; "compensatory policy" and, 342

Engel's Law, 287

Engineering, 94, 125; companies, 95. *See also* Mechanical engineering

English Revolution, 441

ENSIDESA, 318, 323, 326, 332

Entrepreneurism: weakness in, 206–208, 218–219; in iron and steel industries, 213–214; attitudes toward, 219–227; as lobbying for tariff protection, 220; in banking, 220–221. *See also* Foreign entrepreneurs

Epidemics, 35–36

Erosion, 291

Espartero, Baldomero, 55

Esquilache Riots, 26

Estadística de los Presupuestos, 179, 183

Estevan Senís, María Teresa, 214

Eucalyptus trees, 294

EuroLatin countries: historical pattern of economic development in, 4–7, 228–231; agriculture in, 7–11; literacy and, 12–17; education in, 18, 19; keys factors in economic development, 19–21

European Economic Community/European Union (EEC/EU), 341, 373, 396, 399, 432, 433–434, 439, 453; agricultural productivity, 294–296; agricultural policy of, 296–297

European Monetary System, 378

European Regional Development Fund, 439

Euskalduna company, 95

Exchange rate, 316

Excise taxes, 183

Explosives, 70, 94, 109, 216; monopoly on, 312

Exports: agricultural, 9, 69; impact of agricultural tariffs on, 67; wines, 92; pig iron, 100; loss of colonies and, 136; nineteenth century trends, 136–143; levels of, 137–142; structure, 142–143; impact on economic growth, 145–146; official valuations and, 146–147; capital, 148; cotton textiles, 303; under Franco, 324; preferential credit and, 335–336; twentieth century trends, 364–365, 369–371, 373. *See also* Foreign trade; Ore export industry

Fábrica del Desierto, 88

Fábrica de Mieres, 305

Fábrica de San Francisco, 88

Failure of the Industrial Revolution in Spain, The (Nadal), 233

Falange Party, 336, 396, 451

Fallow land, 63–64

Famines, 33–35, 69; epidemics and, 35–36

Fascism, 443. *See also* Franco regime

Federal Deposit Insurance Company, 398

La Felguera factory, 87

Female literacy, 15–16, 49

FEOGA, 296–297

Fernández Ordóñez, Francisco, 414, 416

Fernández Villaverde, Raimundo. *See* Villaverde, Raimundo Fernández

Fernando VII, 28, 29, 156, 175, 186, 195, 389

Ferrocarril del Norte, 122, 123, 124

Ferrocarriles Andaluces, 123, 124

Fertility. *See* Birth rates

Fertilizers, 216, 285, 310, 311–312, 332

FIAT, 331

Fiduciary standard/system, 160, 171, 202, 203, 204–205, 377, 378, 386, 394–395

Figuerola, Laureano, 158, 176, 197; tariff, 79, 197–199, 201

Fiscal duties, 433

Fiscal policy, 21; economic development and, 5; disentailment as, 54. *See also* Budget; National debt

Fiscal tariffs, 193

Fishing industry, 289–290

Flag tax *(derecho diferencial de bandera),* 195

"Flexible planning," 334

Flinn, M. W., 103

Flores de Lemus, Antonio, 194, 304–305, 413, 415

Flour-milling industry, 91–92

Fogel, Robert, 124–125

Fomento del Trabajo Nacional, 196–197

Fondo de Garantía de Depósitos, 398

Food industry, 92; entrepreneurship in, 220; twentieth-century trends, 303–305, 333, 338; imports and exports, 369

Food shortages. *See* Famines

Foreign entrepreneurs: in banking, 208–210; in railroads, 210; in agriculture, 211, 212; in mining and metallurgical industries, 212–216. *See also* Entrepreneurism; Foreign investment

Foreign exchange: autarkic policies and, 316; controls, 430–431

Foreign investment: in iron ore mining, 101–104; in railroads, 122, 124, 154–155, 210; overview of, 148–149; national debt levels and, 149, 150–151; nineteenth-century trends, 149–155; levels of, 150–152, 150–154; trade deficit and, 152–153; effects of, 153–155; in banks, 208–210; in chemical industry, 310. *See also* Foreign entrepreneurs

Foreign markets: cotton industry and, 79–80

Foreign sector: balance of trade, 135–147, 369–373; balance of payments, 147–155, 359–369; terms of trade, 373, 375–376; demand for money and, 385

Foreign trade: agricultural exports and, 9; economic development and, 134–135, 144–146; statistics of, 135–136; loss of colonies and, 136; nineteenth-century trends, 136–155; levels of, 137–142, 144; structure, 142–144; partners, 144, 373; terms of, 146, 373, 375–376; impact of tariffs on, 201–202; under Franco, 320–322, 324; import substitution and, 321–322; effects of liberalization on, 333; twentieth-century trends, 362–363, 369–373; quotas and bilateral agreements, 431. *See also* Exports; Imports; Customs tariffs

Forestry industry, 291, 293–294; products, 311

Fraga, Manuel, 336

Fraile, Pedro, 223, 234, 299

France: income per capita, 3, 228–231; literacy in, 12, 13, 17, 263; wine industry, 92, 93; Spanish ore export industry and, 98, 100, 213; Spanish lead mining and, 105, 214; Spanish railroads and, 122, 124, 155, 210; foreign trade with Spain, 144, 373; Spanish banking and, 208–209, 210; Spanish olive oil and, 211; Spanish gas companies and, 216, 217; Spanish explosives industry and, 310

Franco, Francisco, 236, 237–240, 447–448, 449. *See also* Franco regime

Franco-Belge des Mines de Somorrostro, 98

Franco regime: isolationism and, 234; demographic consequences, 244–245; education and, 264, 265; land reform revo-cation, 272; agriculture during, 274–278; reservoir construction, 280; industrial policy, 300–301; economic practices and policies of, 315–317; stabilization plan, 327–337, 365, 431, 451; transition to democracy, 340–341; electric power supply during, 353–354; balance of payments during, 364–366, 367; MATESA scandal and, 396; savings banks under, 401; banking and, 405–406; tax reform and, 415–416; protectionist trade policy, 431–433; European Economic Community and, 434; nature of, 447–448; fear of Communism and, 448; economic history of, 449–452; legacy of, 459–460. *See also* Autarkist policy/period

Free trade, 201; cotton industry, debates on, 80–82; era, 142; free trade v. protectionist debate, 193–194, 196, 197–199; history of, 195–196; principal defenders, 197; business opinion on, 222, 223

French Revolution, 441

Friedman, Milton, 381, 409

Fruits and vegetables, 61, 63, 65–66. *See also* Mediterranean agriculture

Fuentes-Ordóñez reform, 411, 412, 418, 429

Fuentes Quintana, Enrique, 368, 408–409, 414, 416, 418, 432, 433

Fund for the Ordering and Control of Agricultural Products and Prices (FORPPA), 278

Galicia, 83, 258, 271

Garay, Martín de, 175

García Delgado, José Luis, 285

García Sanz, Angel, 226

Gas industry, 112; foreign entrepreneurs in, 216–217; twentieth-century trends, 355–356

Gender: literacy levels and, 15–16, 49

General Office of Statistics on National Resources, 179

Generation of '98, 235

Genoa, 207

Geographic and Statistical Yearbook, 181

Germanías, 207–208

Germany: birth rate/mortality rate differential, 37; Spanish ore exports and, 100; railroads and, 125; foreign trade with Spain, 144, 373; Spanish banking and, 209–210; Spanish electric companies and, 217; Spanish explosives industry and, 310

Gerschenkron hypothesis, 172, 393, 394

Gil, Pedro, 112, 216

Giráldez Rivero, Jesús, 290

Girón, José Antonio, 324

Girona, Manuel, 163, 220; family, 95

Glorious Revolution, 29, 74, 96, 97, 123

Godoy, Manuel, 53, 186

Gold: bimetallist system and, 158, 159; national debt payments and, 189–190, 191; monetary system and, 202–203, 204; Bretton Woods and, 397

Gold standard, 160, 171, 204, 205, 377–379

Gómez Mendoza, Antonio, 125, 307

González, Manuel-Jesús, 318, 335

González Angel, Manuel, 212

González Besada, Augusto, 281, 379

Granada, 83; silk of, 175

Great Britain, 373; literacy in, 12, 13; birth rate/mortality rate differential, 37; cotton industry, 75, 76; Spanish ore export industry and, 98, 100, 213; Spanish lead mining and, 105, 214; Spanish copper mining and, 106; foreign trade with Spain, 144; terms of trade with Spain, 146; Free Trade movement and, 195, 196; Spanish banking and, 210; Spanish sherry industry and, 212; Spanish gas companies and, 216–217; population growth, 255

Great Depression, 314, 394, 406, 446

Gresham's Law, 159

Gross Domestic Product, 328

Grupo de Estudios de Historia Rural, 132, 268

Güell y Ferrer, Juan, 197

Guilds, 130–131

Guilhou brothers, 87, 191, 209

Haber-Bosch process, 311

Hajnal, John, 38

Hamilton, Earl J., 224, 225

Health, 35–36, 247; declining mortality rates, 246–247

Herr, Richard, 57–58

Hicks, John, 457

Higher education, 21; nineteenth-century trends, 48–49; backwardness in, 225–226; twentieth-century trends, 265–266

High-powered money, 380, 381–382, 383, 384, 385, 386

Hispano-Suiza Company, 313

Hoffmann's Law, 301–302, 305, 328

Human capital: interrelationship of education and technology, 46–47; nineteenth-century trends in education, 47–49; concepts of, 262; twentieth-century trends in education, 263–266; in agriculture, 286; regional investment in, 439; future development of, 459; in underdeveloped countries, 459–462

Hydraulic power, 74–75, 111, 346

Hydrochloric acid, 216

Hydroelectricity, 217–218, 279, 351–352, 354

Ibarra y Compañía, 120

Iberia company, 305

Idria mine, 107

Illiteracy. *See* Literacy/illiteracy

Import licensing, 430–431

Imports: raw cotton, 77–78; nineteenth-century trends, 140, 142, 143–144; official valuations and, 146–147; capital and capital goods, 148, 321, 324, 366, 369; autarkic policies and, 316; coal, 348; twentieth-century trends, 366, 369–373; petroleum, 372–373

Import substitution, 321–322

Income distribution, 429

Income per capita: historical patterns in, 3–4, 228–231; regional patterns in, 436–438

Income taxes, 416, 418

Industrialization: agriculture and, 20, 50; nineteenth-century trends, 73–75, 113–114; water resources and, 74–75; protectionism and, 81, 144, 194, 298–299, 305; energy sources and, 110–113; impact of foreign trade on, 144–146; limited capital and, 157; population growth rates and, 241–246; declining birth rates and, 253–254; impact of economic policy on, 298–301; state intervention and, 300–301; twentieth-century trends in growth, 301–315, 319–320, 327–333, 337–338; autarkic policies and, 315–327; U.S. assistance and, 321; liberalization period, 327–337; reconversion period, 337–346, 454; energy sources and policies, 346–356. *See also* Industry

Industrial Revolution, 346, 442; in Spain, 73–75; cotton and iron industries in, 74; energy sources and, 110

Industry: Catalonian labor force and, 45, 46; movement of labor from agriculture, 71; protectionism and, 81, 144, 194; budget deficits and, 178; tax on, 182; entrepreneurship, weakness of, 206–207, 218–219; foreign entrepreneurs and, 208–219; entrepreneurial attitudes, 219–227; state intervention and, 300–301; Hoffmann's Law and, 301–302, 305, 328; diversification in the twentieth century, 301–313; Great Depression and, 314; Civil War and, 314–315; World War II and, 315; autarkic policies and, 315–327; agriculture and, 322–323; investment in, 323; inflationary financing, 323–324; liberalization and, 327–337; oil crisis and, 338–340; Franco regime legacy and, 342–343; mixed banking and, 394. *See also* Industrialization

Infant mortality, 247, 251

Inflation, 365, 395; eighteenth century trends, 23–26; causes and nature of, 425–426; twentieth-century trends, 426–427, 428–429, 450, 460

Influenza, 248

Institución Libre de Enseñanza, 47, 48–49

Instituto de Biología y Sueroterapia, 311, 334

Instituto de Crédito a Largo y Medio Plazo, 396, 404

Instituto de Crédito de las Cajas de Ahorros, 400, 401

Instituto de Crédito Oficial (Argentaria), 396, 404, 405

Instituto de Estudios Fiscales, 416

Instituto Español de Moneda Extranjera, 359, 392, 395–396

Instituto Nacional de Emigración, 40

Instituto Nacional de Hidrocarburos (INH), 345, 351

Instituto Nacional de Industria (INI), 300, 317–319, 320, 323, 324, 326, 345–346, 348, 350, 353, 355, 421

Instituto para la Conservación de la Naturaleza (ICONA), 293, 294

Instituto para la Reconstrucción, 403

Instituto per la Ricostruzione Industriale (Italy), 318

Intellectual culture, 225

Interest rates, 203

Interior Compensating Taxes for Domestic Charges, 433

Internal trade: nineteenth-century trends, 130–134. *See also* Commerce

International payments, 360–361

Iron and steel industry: Industrial Revolution and, 74; coal and, 84, 85–86; development of, 84; smelting and refining processes, 85–86; regional centers, 86–89; nineteenth-century production levels, 89; railroad construction and, 89–90, 125; ore, exports and, 98, 103; import levels, 143; lack of entrepreneurism in, 213; twentieth-century trends, 305–306, 312–313; oligopolistic structure, 306; protectionism and, 306; liberalization and, 329; automobile manufacturing and, 332

Irrigation, 278–281

Isabel II, 28, 29, 107

Issuing banks, 164, 165–166, 167

Italy: income per capita, 3–4, 228–231; historical pattern of economic development in, 4–7; agriculture, 8, 9, 10, 11; literacy, 12, 13, 16, 263; education, 18, 19; liberalism and, 32; twentieth-century history, 238–239; Instituto per la Ricostruzione Industriale, 318; post-war industrial recovery, 319. *See also* EuroLatin countries

Jaén, 57, 104, 105

Jáinaga, Francisco, 359

Jaumandreu, Eudaldo, 197

Jerez de la Frontera, 181

Jews, 207

Joint-stock banks, 168–169

Jovellanos, Gaspar Melchor, 58, 269, 279

Kagan, Richard, 225

Kali-Sainte-Thérése (Kalisyndikat), 312

Keynes, John Maynard, 378

Krausistas, 48

Labor: in agriculture, 8, 68; transfer from agriculture to industry, 71; railroads and, 128, 133; autarkic policies and, 324–325; modern economic transitions and, 456–457. *See also* Workforce

Land: tenure, 12; taxes, 178–182; distribution, 269–272, 281–282; leasing, 271

Landowners: land tax and, 178, 180–182; water policy and, 279

Land ownership: marriage rates and, 38–39; effects of disentailment on, 56–58; agricultural productivity and, 58–59

Land reform: eighteenth century efforts, 26–27; *desamortización,* 51–58; under the Republic, 269–272; combined with irrigation policy, 280–281; consolidation of fragmented plots, 281–282

Latifundia, 12, 269

Latin Monetary Union, 158, 159

Law of Commercial Relations with the Antilles, 79, 304

Law of Credit Unions *(Ley de Sociedades de Crédito),* 121

Law of general disentail. *See* Madoz Law

Law of Protection and Development of New Industries, (1939) *(Ley de Protección y Fomento de las Nuevas Industrias),* 317

Law of Tariff Bases *(Ley de Bases Arancelarias),* 197–199, 429. *See also* Figuerola tariff.

Law of the Protection of the Fleet *(Ley de Protección a la Escuadra),* 95

Law on Banking Regulations (1921) *(Ley de Ordenación Bancaria),* 390–391

Law on Extension of Irrigation *(Ley de Obras de Puesta en Riego),* 279, 280

Law on Issuing Banks *(Ley de Bancos de Emisión),* 121, 163, 202, 203

Law on Mining Rights (1825), 121, 163, 202, 203

Law on Practices Restrictive to Competition, 334, 335, 402

Law on Principles for the Regulation of Credit and Banking (1962) *(Ley de Bases de Ordenación del Crédito y la Banca),* 395, 401, 403–404, 406

Law on Promoting National Industry *(Ley de Fomento de la Industria Nacional),* 300

Law on Railroads (1855; *Ley General de Ferrocarriles),* 89, 90, 120, 121

Law on Reconversion and Reindustrialization, 344–345

Law on the Protection of National Industry *(Ley de Protección a la Industria Nacional),* 402

Law on Top Priority Industries *(Ley de Industrias de Interés Preferente),* 335

Lead, 104–105, 214

League of Nations, 430

Lebon, Charles, 112, 216, 217; Lebon Company, 112

Lewis, W. Arthur, 286, 444; model, 286–287, 444

Liberalism, 27–32, 445–446

Liberals/Liberal Party, 29–30; educational reform and, 47–48; disentailment and, 58; reform of public finance and, 173, 175–176; national debt and, 186; free trade and, 199

Life expectancy, 248–252

Linear City, 261

Linen industry, 83

List, Friedrich, 194

Literacy/illiteracy: rates of, 12–14, 21; economic consequences of, 14–15, 16; gender gap in, 15–16, 49; religious factors in, 16–17, 49; school attendance and, 17–19; functional illiteracy, 21; nineteenth-century trends, 49; twentieth-century trends, 263

Livestock, 64–65

Livi-Bacci, Massimo, 37; hypothesis, 253

London Stock Exchange, 188

López, Antonio, 220

López Ballesteros, Luis, 175

López de Mollinedo, Gregorio, 217

López López, Antonio, 119

López Puigcerver "affidavit," 190

Lorenzo Pardo, Manuel, 279–280

Lotteries, 183, 184

Luchana Mining Company, 98

Luddites, 76

Machinery: imports, 143; exports, 369

Macías Picavea, Ricardo, 279

Madoz, Pascual, 55, 58

Madoz Law, 55–56, 293

Madrid: urbanization and, 44; rail network and, 130; stock market, 157; banking, 168, 169, 208, 388–389, 399; gas companies, 216–217; population growth, 257; city planning, 261

Madrid-Zaragoza-Alicante Railroad Company, 122, 123, 124, 191

Mail system, 133

Málaga, 86, 87

Mallada, Lucas, 291

Malthus, Thomas, 457

Manby and Partington Company, 216–217

Manual labor, 224

Manufacturing industries: reconversion period and, 337–338
Marbella Iron Company, 98
March, Juan, 352
María Cristina of Hapsburg-Lorena, 30, 184
María Cristina of Naples, 28
Maritime transport. *See* Shipping industry
Marriage patterns, 38–39; in Catalonia, 45; age at marriage, 254–255
Marshall Plan, 321
Martín Aceña, Pablo, 318, 335, 344
Martínez Carrión, José Miguel, 211
Martínez Méndez, Pedro, 340–341
Martín Rodríguez, Manuel, 220, 436
Marx, Karl, 237, 457
MATESA scandal, 396, 404, 452
Matheson, Hugh, 106, 215
Mayorazgo (indivisible property), 38, 52
Mechanical engineering, 95, 329. *See also* Engineering
Mediterranean agriculture, 65–66, 71–72, 443–444
Mediterranean Iron and Steel Company, 305
Memorial de Greuges, 79
Mendizábal, Juan Alvarez, 54, 58, 186, 405
Mercantilism, 408–412
Mercury mining, 107–108, 215
Mesta privileges, 26
Metallurgical industry, 95, 220
Mexico, 125, 192
Middle class, 458–459
Mieres, 87
Migration: nineteenth century trends, 39–46; agricultural protectionism and, 41; internal population distribution, 41–44, 256–259; regional income distribution and, 438
Miguel, Amando de, 252–253
Military coups, 28–29
Military expenditures, 419–421
Mill, John Stuart, 81, 145
Minifundia, 12
Mining: chemical industry and, 93–94, 109; location of deposits, 96; legislation affecting, 96–97; nineteenth-century trends, 96–110; causes of stagnation in, 97; engineering in, 109; foreign companies and entrepreneurs in, 109, 213–216; price of mineral exports and, 109–110; railroads and, 124; development of

production, 212–213. *See also individual industries*
Mixed banking, 167–169, 171–172, 387–388, 393–395
Moderates/Moderate Party, 28, 29, 48, 55
Mon, Alejandro, 175
Monarchy: state expenditures on, 184; confiscatory powers over mines, 212
Moncloa Pacts, 416, 454
Monetary policy: nineteenth-century trends, 202–205; energy crisis and, 342; Bank of Spain and, 390–391, 427–428; inflation and, 425–426; twentieth-century trends, 426–429. *See also* Monetary system; Money supply
Monetary system: nineteenth-century trends and policies, 157–161, 202–205; bimetallism and, 158, 159–160, 204; *peseta,* 158–159, 171; banknotes, 160, 204; fiduciary standard and, 160, 171, 202, 203, 204–205, 377, 378, 386; silver standard, 160, 204; current account balances, 160–161, 204; gold standard and, 377–379. *See also* Monetary policy; Money supply
Money markets: effect of government finances on, 156
Money supply: nineteenth-century characteristics and trends, 165, 166, 169, 203, 204, 205; gold standard and, 378; definition of, 379–380; high-powered money, 380, 381–382, 383, 384, 385, 386; growth in, 380–382; velocity of circulation, 381–382, 384; changing composition of, 382–384; demand and, 385; fiduciary standard and, 386. *See also* Monetary policy; Monetary system
Monopolies, 325–327, 406
Mon-Santillán reform, 156, 175–176, 411, 412
Monte de Piedad (Official Pawn Shop), 169, 400
Moret, Segismundo, 197
Moroccan War, 236
Mortality: levels of, 32–33, 36; famine and, 33–35; epidemics and, 35–36; endemic disease and, 36; birth rates and, 37; declining, 242–243, 245, 246–248; age and gender differences, 247–252
Mortgage Bank, *see* Banco Hipotecario
Mortmain, 52
Moyano Law, 47, 48

Nadal, Jordi, 105, 214, 215, 233
Napoleonic Wars, 116, 441
Naredo, José Manuel, 285
National Agricultural Credit Service, 269, 273
National Colonization Institute, 281
National debt: eighteenth-century trends, 22–23; nineteenth-century trends, 149, 150–151, 184–192; effects on money and capital, 156; official banks and, 162; causes of, 185–186, 190–191; American remittances and, 186; conversions and, 187–188, 189–190, 424–425; levels of, 188–189; concessions and, 189, 191–192; beneficiaries of, 192; victims of, 192; under Franco, 315; monetization of, 390, 423; twentieth-century trends, 422–425; financing of, 423–424
Nationalism, 315–316
National Wheat Service (SNT), 269, 274–278
NATO. *See* North Atlantic Treaty Organization
Natural gas, 355–356
Navarro Reverter, Juan, 379
Navarro Rubio, Mariano, 415–416
Navigation Acts (England), 195
Niño, Martín, 180
Nitrates, 311; nitric acid, 93, 94
Nobel, Alfred, 216
North Atlantic Treaty Organization (NATO), 341
Note-issuing banks. *See* Issuing banks, individual banks
Núñez, Clara Eugenia, 15, 49, 157, 226, 265

O'Donnell uprising, 35, 121
Office machinery, 338
Office of Banking and Stock Exchange, 392
Oil crisis, 338–340
Olive oil, 92, 132, 211
OPEC. *See* Organization of Petroleum Exporting Countries
Open hill lands, 290–291, 293
Opus Dei, 336, 396, 451, 452
Orange industry, 211, 324
Orconera Iron Ore Company, 94, 98, 99
Ore industry, 142; companies in, 80, 87, 88, 98; foreign steel industry and, 97–98; foreigners in, 98, 213; outputs, 98–100; foreign investment and, 101–104;

Basque economy and, 103, 104, 120; stimulation of other industries, 145
Organization of Petroleum Exporting Countries (OPEC), 338–340, 373
Ortiz-Villajos, José María, 219
O'Shea, Henry, 210

Palafox, Jordi, 268
Palasí, Villar, 264
Palencia, 83
Parcocha Iron Ore and Railway Company, 98
Pardo Pact, 30, 446
Paris Eguilaz, Higinio, 298
Pastor, Luis María, 187, 197
Patents, 219
Paternalism, 336–337
Peajes, 131
Peasants, 446; abandonment of agriculture, 20; seasonal life patterns and, 39; disentailment and, 58; consumer goods and, 69; land reform and, 271, 272; agricultural growth and, 287
Pegaso-ENASA, 318
Pereire brothers, 191, 208, 209, 217, 405
Perestroika, 442
Pérez Moreda, Vicente, 36
Perfume industry, 311
Perón, Juan, 276
Perpiñá y Grau, Román, 347, 435, 436
Peseta, 41, 158, 171, 365
Petrochemicals, 332–333
Petroleum, 347, 349–351; monopoly, 325, 349; energy crisis, 338–340; consumption levels, 351; import trends, 372–373
Pharmaceuticals, 311, 332
Phylloxera, 93, 140, 143, 211, 271
Pig iron, 85, 89, 98, 100
Pike, Ruth, 207
Pinelo, Francisco, 207
Plan Cerdá, 261
Plan de Obras Hidráulicas (Pardo), 279–280
Planell, Joaquín, 320
Platt, Christopher, 210
Poll tax *(cédula personal)*, 182
Popular Party, 345, 346
Population: distribution, 41–44, 256–259; density, 241, 258; growth, 241–246, 460–461. *See also* Demographic trends
Portland cement, 308–309
Portugal: historical pattern of economic development, 4–7; agriculture, 8, 9, 10, 11;

Portugal *(continued)*
  literacy, 12, 13, 16; education, 18, 19;
  liberalism and, 32. *See also* EuroLatin
  countries
Potash, 70, 93, 311–312
Pounds, N. G., 9–10
Po Valley (Italy), 8
Poverty: impact on education, 19; birth
  rates and, 37–38; land distribution and,
  51
Prados de la Escosura, Leandro, 73, 113–
  114, 147, 153, 234, 299
Preferential credit, 335–336
Preferential Tariff Agreement, 433
Price guarantees: European Community
  agricultural policy and, 296–297. *See also*
  Subsidization
Prices: eighteenth-century trends, 23–26;
  nineteenth-century trends, 204
Primary education, 47, 48, 49, 263–265
Primo de Rivera, Miguel, 236, 237, 349,
  414, 447
Primogeniture, 38
Private banking, 406; nineteenth-century
  trends, 168–169, 172; agricultural credit
  and, 274; money supply and, 383, 385;
  growth in, 386–389, 391; twentieth-century trends, 386–399; mixed banking
  and, 387–388, 393–395; evolution of the
  Bank of Spain and, 389–391; *status quo*
  principle, 392, 398; state intervention in,
  392–393; mergers and branch networks,
  393; reform and restructuring in, 395–
  396; MATESA scandal, 396; liberalization period, 396–399; national debt and,
  423. *See also* Banking
Production agreements *(acciones
  concertadas)*, 433
Progressives/Progressive Party, 28, 29, 79;
  educational reform and, 48;
  disentailment and, 53; industrialization
  and, 73–74; railroads and, 121, 128;
  banking system and, 163–164; national
  debt and, 186
Proletarian revolution, 441–442
Promotion of National Work, 196–197
Property rights, 96
Prost, Adolphe, 191, 208, 209
Protectionism: agriculture and, 41, 66–67,
  200, 267–269; wheat and, 66–67, 267–
  269; cotton industry and, 80–82, 196–
  197, 200, 302–303; infant industry hypothesis, 81–82, 144, 194; free trade v.
  protectionist debate, 193–194, 196, 197–
  199; history of, 194–195; Fomento del
  Trabajo Nacional, 196–197; principal defenders, 197; impact on economic development, 200; industrialization and, 298–
  299, 305; vegetable canning industry
  and, 304–305; iron and steel industry
  and, 306; coal industry and, 347–349;
  impact on Spain's economic openness,
  362; twentieth-century trends, 429–434;
  quantitative restrictions, 430, 433; foreign exchange controls, 430–431; quotas
  and bilateral agreements, 431. *See also*
  Customs tariffs
Provisional Republican Government, 166
Public expenditures, 419–421, 455–456
Public finance: effects on money and capi-
  tal markets, 156; evolution of, 173–176.
  See also Taxes; Treasury
Public granary *(pósito)*, 273
Public health. *See* Health
Public works expenditures, 419–420
Pucherazo, see Election rigging
Puddling furnace, 85
Puerto Rico, 79–80

Quintana, Manuel José, 47; report of, 47,
  49

Rabassa morta, 271
Railroads: iron and steel industry and, 89–
  90; mining industries and, 99, 124; compared with maritime transport, 117–118,
  119; legislation affecting, 120, 121;
  broad gauge, 120–121, 129; development of, 120–124; foreign investment
  and, 122, 124, 154–155, 210; major
  lines, 124, 126, 127; economic development and, 124–125, 128; sales of rolling
  stock, 125; construction and financing
  deficiencies, 128–129; unprofitability of,
  129; radial network of, 129–130; items
  carried, 132–133; labor mobility and,
  133; impact on import levels, 140; credit
  societies and, 164; concessions and, 191
Ramos, Rui, 16
Ration books *(cartillas de racionamiento)*, 276
Real Compañía Asturiana de Minas, 107,
  215
Recasens brothers, 403
Recession, 327

Reconversion period, 454; economic deceleration during, 337–338; oil crisis and, 338–340; transition to democracy and, 340–341; Franco regime legacy and, 342–343; industrial policy in, 343–346
Reforestation, 294
Regional tariffs, 131
Register of Lands for Expropriation, 272
Reis, Jaime, 16
Religion: literacy and, 16–17. *See also* Catholic Church
Remisa, Gaspar, 105
RENFE, 219
REPESA, 350
Report in Defense of the Moral and Material Interests of Catalonia, 79
Report of the Commission on the Gold Standard, 379
REPSOL, 356
Reseña Geográfica y Estadística, 181
Reservoirs, 279, 280, 354
Residential construction, 307, 309
Restoration, 29–30, 31, 446–447
Ricardo, David, 145, 457
Riego, Rafael del, 29
Río Tinto Company, 94, 106–107, 215
Risorgimento, 12
Riu, Emilio, 218
Rivas, Francisco de las, 88
Roads, 116, 119; tolls *(peajes, pontazgos),* 131
Rodrigáñez, Tirso, 379
Rodríguez, Gabriel, 197
Rogers, Thorold, 81
Rojo, Luis Angel, 427
Román, Manuel, 323
Romania, 37
Rothschild family, 168, 389; mercury and, 107, 108, 215; concessions and, 189, 191; Spanish banking and, 208, 209
Rubber industry, 330
Rubio, Mariano, 428
RUMASA, 397
Russian Revolution, 441–442

Sabadell, 82
Sail ships, 119–120
Salamanca, 57
Salamanca, José, 162, 261
Sánchez-Albornoz, Nicolás, 39, 80, 103, 110, 131, 134
Sánchez Alonso, Blanca, 40, 41

Sandberg, Lars, 14
Santa Barbara Company, 305
Santillán, Ramón, 175–176
Sardá, Juan, 151, 427–428
Sarrailh, Jean, 224, 226
Savings: from the agricultural sector, 70–71; inflation and, 426
Savings banks, 169, 274, 399–402, 406
School attendance, 263–264
Schuckert Company, 217
Schultz, Theodore, 262
Schumpeter, Joseph A., 46, 343
Schwartz, Pedro, 318
SEAT. *See* Sociedad Española de Automóviles de Turismo
Second Republic, 446: education and, 263–264, 266; land reform and, 269–272; balance of payments during, 359, 364, 366, 367
Segura, Julio, 344
Servicio Nacional de Crédito Agrícola, 403
Servicio Nacional de Productos Agrarios, 278
Servicio Nacional de Trigo (SNT), *see* National Wheat Service
Sevillana de Electricidad, 112, 217, 352
Seville, 86–87
Seville-Jerez-Cádiz Company, 122
Sexual exploitation, 461
Sharecropping, 12
Shaw, Valerie, 104
Sherry, 92, 181, 212
Shipping industry, 95; steamships, 95, 116, 119, 120; coastal trade, 116–118; international trade, 117, 118–119; compared with railroad transport, 117–118, 119; under sail, 119–120; Basque, 120
Shoe industry, 328–329, 333–334
Siderúrgica del Mediterráneo company, 305
Siemens Company, 218
Siemens-Martin furnaces, 85, 89, 103
Silk industry, 83–84
Silvela, Francisco, 412
Silver, 383: bimetallist system and, 158, 159, 160; monetary system and, 202–203, 204
Smallpox, 36, 247
Smelting, 85
Smith, Adam, 145, 165–166, 191–192, 262, 325, 457

Socialists, 344
Social unrest, 236–237
Sociedad Anónima Echeverría, 95
Sociedad Anónima Iberia, 89
Sociedad de Navegación e Industria, 95
Sociedad Económica, 400
Sociedad Electroquímica de Flix, 310
Sociedades Económicas de Amigos del País, 47
Sociedad Española de Automóviles de Turismo (SEAT), 318, 323, 331
Sociedad Española de Carburos Metálicos, 310
Sociedad Española de la Dinamita, 70, 94, 216, 310, 311
Sociedad Español Mercantil, 208, 209
Sociedad Estatal de Participaciones Industriales, 345
Sociedad General Azucarera, 303
Sociedad Ibérica del Nitrógeno, 311
Sociedad Pedro Duro y Compañía, 87
Sociedad Valencia de Crédito y Fomento, 220
Society: attitudes toward entrepreneurism, 224–227; social unrest, 236–237
Solow, Robert, 46, 262
Solvay company, 310
Soria, Arturo, 261
Sota y Aznar, 120
Soviet Union, 442
Spain: income per capita, 3–4, 228–231; historical pattern of economic development in, 4–7; eighteenth-century political history, 22–23; nineteenth-century political history, 27–32; twentieth-century political history, 234–240, 444–457; regional economic diversity and development, 434–439; European economic history and, 442–443, 442–444; economic and political development in, 444–457
Spanish-American War. See Cuban War
Stagflation, 425
Stamp tax, 182
State: administration of woodland and open wastelands, 293–294; industrial policy and, 300–301; public expenditures, 419–421, 455–456. See also State interventionism; Treasury
State companies, 394. See also Instituto Nacional de Industria
State interventionism: in wheat and cereal production, 274–278; sugar pricing and quotas, 303–304; under Franco, 317; tariffs and, 326, 410–411 (see also Protectionism); electric industry and, 353; private banking and, 392–393; history and nature of, 408–412; fiscal paradox of, 409–410; role of regulation in, 410; tax system failure and, 411–412; transformation of, 421; in foreign trade policy, 430–432; regional economic development and, 435–436, 438–439; democratic transition and, 453–455. See also Autarkist policy/period; Protectionism
Steamships, 95, 116, 119, 120
Steel, 85. See also Iron and steel; Iron and steel industry
Stock markets, 393
Stone, Lawrence, 17
Streetcar (tramway) companies, 218
Strikes, 236
Suanzes, José Antonio, 317, 319, 320, 323, 334
Suárez, Adolfo, 345, 454
Subsidization, 274–278
Sudrià, Carles, 217, 354
Sugar industry, 220, 303–304
Sulfur, 214
Sulfuric acid, 70, 93, 94, 216, 311, 312–313, 332
Sundheim, Wilhelm, 215
Superphosphates, 94, 216, 310, 311
Swank, James M., 101
Sweden, 85, 98, 101
Switzerland, 10, 11

Tafunell, Xavier, 218
Tamames, Ramón, 198, 200, 298, 331
Tariffs: regional, 131; operation of, 193; on electricity, 353; as a subsidy, 410–411. See also Customs tariffs; Protectionism
Tarradellas, Josep, 452
Tarragona, 211
Tarragona-Valencia-Almansa railroad, 123
Taxes/tax system: agricultural sector and, 70; modernization, 174–176, 416, 418–419; budget deficits and, 178; direct taxes, 178–182, 413; indirect, 182, 183; real estate, 182; liquor, 183; failure of, 411–412; Villaverde reform and, 412–413, 414; silent reform of, 413–416; tax evasion, 418